EXPLANATORY NOTES

CORPORATION TAX ACT 2010

GRANGIS UK Publishing

Adapted and published by GRANGIS (Grand Register Library).
Online: www.grangis.com
E-mail: contact@grangis.com

In this version:
ISBN: 979-8-88559-047-1

Note: This is the original version (as it was originally enacted). Title, sub-title and the generated date is as marked on the pages.

These notes refer to the Corporation Tax Act 2010 (c.4)

EXPLANATORY NOTES

CORPORATION TAX ACT 2010

PART 3: COMPANIES WITH SMALL PROFITS

Overview

Section 53: Leasing contracts and company reconstructions

Section 54: Non-UK resident company: receipts of interest, dividends or royalties

Chapter 3: Limited partners and members of limited liability partnerships

Section 55: Introduction to Chapter

Section 56: Restriction on reliefs for limited partners

Section 57: Meaning of "contribution to the firm"

Section 58: Meaning of "limited partner"

Section 59: Restriction on relief for members of LLPs

Section 60: Meaning of "contribution to the LLP"

Section 61: Unrelieved losses brought forward

Chapter 4: Property losses

Overview

Section 62: Relief for losses made in UK property business

Section 63: Company with investment business ceasing to carry on UK property business

Section 64: UK property business to be commercial or carried on for statutory functions

Section 65: UK furnished holiday lettings business treated as trade

Section 66: Relief for losses made in overseas property business

Section 67: Overseas property business to be commercial or carried on for statutory functions

Chapter 5: Losses on disposal of shares

Overview

Section 68: Share loss relief

Section 69: Eligibility conditions

Section 70: Entitlement to claim

Section 71: How relief works

Section 72: Limit on deduction if accounting period falls partly within 12 month period

Section 73: Subscription for shares

Section 74: Disposals of new shares

Section 162: Meaning of "normal commercial loan"

Section 163: Normal commercial loans: company's results or value of assets

Section 164: Sections 160 and 162: supplementary

Section 165: Proportion of profits available for distribution to which company is entitled

Section 166: Proportion of assets available for distribution to which company is entitled

Section 167: Profits or assets available for distribution and entitlement: supplementary

Section 168: Meaning of "the relevant accounting period"

Section 169: Application and interpretation of sections 170 to 182

Section 170: Shares or securities with limited rights

Section 171: Shares or securities with temporary rights

Section 172: Company A's proportion if shares etc have temporary rights

Section 173: Cases in which option arrangements are in place

Section 174: Company A's proportion if option arrangements in place

Sections 175 to 178

Overview

Section 175: Cases in which both sections 170 and 172 apply

Section 176: Cases in which both sections 170 and 174 apply

Section 177: Cases in which both sections 172 and 174 apply

Section 178: Cases in which sections 170, 172 and 174 all apply

Section 179: Cases in which surrendering or claimant company is non-UK resident

Section 180: Company A's proportion if non-UK resident involved

Section 181: Assumptions to be applied if non-UK resident company involved

Section 182: Assets etc referable to UK trade

Chapter 7: Miscellaneous provisions and interpretation of Part

Overview

Section 183: Payments for group relief

Section 184: References to "allowance" in CAA 2001

Section 229: Tax relief certificates

Section 230: No pre-arranged protection against risks

Chapter 3: General conditions

Overview

Section 231: No control of CDFI by investor

Section 232: Investor must have beneficial ownership

Section 233: Investor must not be accredited

Section 234: No acquisition of share in partnership

Section 235: No tax avoidance purpose

Chapter 4: Limitations on claims and attribution

Overview

Section 236: Loans: no claim after disposal or excessive repayments or receipts of value

Section 237: Securities or shares: no claim after disposal or excessive receipts of value

Section 238: No claim after loss of accreditation by the CDFI

Section 239: Accreditation of investor

Section 240: Attribution: general

Section 241: Attribution: bonus shares

Chapter 5: Withdrawal or reduction of CITR

Overview

Section 242: Introduction to Chapter

Section 243: Disposal of loan during 5 year period

Section 244: Disposal of securities or shares during 5 year period

Section 245: Repayment of loan capital during 5 year period

Section 246: Value received by investor during 6 year period: loans

Section 247: Value received by investor during 6 year period: securities or shares

Section 248: Receipts of insignificant value to be added together

Section 249: When value is received

Section 250: The amount of value received

Section 274: "Oil-related activities"

Section 275: "Ring fence income"

Section 276: "Ring fence profits"

Section 277: "Ring fence trade"

Section 278: Other definitions

Chapter 3: Deemed separate trade

Section 279: Oil–related activities treated as separate trade

Chapter 4: Calculation of profits

Overview

Section 280: Disposal to be valued by reference to section 2(5A) of OTA 1975

Section 281: Valuation where market value taken into account under section 2 of OTA 1975

Section 282: Valuation where disposal not sale at arm's length

Section 283: Valuation where excess of nominated proceeds

Section 284: Valuation where relevant appropriation but no disposal

Section 285: Valuation where appropriation to refining etc

Section 286: Restriction on debits to be brought into account

Section 287: Restriction on credits to be brought into account

Section 288: Sale and lease-back

Section 289: Reduction of expenditure by reference to regional development grant

Section 290: Adjustment as a result of regional development grant

Section 291: Tariff receipts etc

Section 292: Expenditure on and under abandonment guarantees

Section 293: Relief for reimbursement expenditure under abandonment guarantees

Section 294: Payment under abandonment guarantee not immediately applied

Section 295: Amounts excluded from section 293(1)

Section 296: Introduction to sections 297 and 298

Section 297: Relief for expenditure incurred by a participator in meeting defaulter's abandonment expenditure

Section 298: Reimbursement by defaulter in respect of certain abandonment expenditure

Section 299: Deduction of PRT in calculating income for corporation tax purposes

Section 300: Effect of repayment of PRT: general rule

Section 301: Effect of repayment of PRT: special rule

Section 302: Interest on repayment of PRT or APRT

Section 303: Management expenses

Section 304: Losses

Section 305: Group relief

Section 306: Capital allowances

Chapter 5: Ring fence expenditure supplement

Overview

Section 307: Overview of Chapter

Section 308: Qualifying companies

Section 309: Accounting periods

Section 310: The relevant percentage

Section 311: Limit on number of accounting periods for which supplement may be claimed

Section 312: Qualifying pre-commencement expenditure

Section 313: Unrelieved group ring fence profits for accounting periods

Section 314: Taxable ring fence profits for an accounting period

Section 315: Supplement in respect of a pre-commencement accounting period

Section 316: The mixed pool of qualifying pre-commencement expenditure and supplement previously allowed

Section 317: Reduction in respect of disposal receipts under CAA 2001

Section 318: Reduction in respect of unrelieved group ring fence profits

Section 319: The reference amount for a pre-commencement period

Section 320: Claims for pre-commencement supplement

Section 321: Supplement in respect of a post-commencement period

Section 322: Amount of post-commencement supplement for a post-commencement period.

Section 323: Ring fence losses

Section 324: Special rule for straddling periods

Section 325: The pool of ring fence losses and the pool of non-qualifying Schedule 19B losses

Section 326: The ring fence pool

Section 327: Reductions in respect of utilised ring fence losses

Section 328: Reductions in respect of unrelieved group ring fence profits

Section 329: The reference amount for a post-commencement period

Chapter 6: Supplementary charge in respect of ring fence trades

Section 330: Supplementary charge in respect of ring fence trades

Section 331: Meaning of "financing costs" etc

Section 332: Assessment, recovery and postponement of supplementary charge

Chapter 7: Reduction of supplementary charge for certain new oil fields

Overview

Section 333: Reduction of adjusted ring fence profits

Section 334: Company's pool of field allowances

Section 335: Carrying part of pool of field allowances into following period

Section 336: Carrying whole of pool of field allowances into following period

Section 337: Initial licensee to hold a field allowance

Section 338: Holding a field allowance on acquisition of equity share

Section 339: Unactivated amount of field allowance

Section 340: Introduction to section 341

Section 341: Activation of field allowance

Section 342: Introduction to sections 343 and 344

Section 343: Reference periods

Section 344: Activation of field allowance

Section 345: Introduction to sections 346 and 347

Section 346: Reduction of field allowance if equity disposed of

Section 347: Acquisition of field allowance if equity acquired

Section 348: Adjustments

Section 349: Orders

Section 350: "New oil field"

Section 351: "Authorisation of development of an oil field"

Section 352: "Qualifying oil field"

Section 353: "Small oil field"

Section 354: "Ultra heavy oil field"

Section 355: "Ultra high pressure/high temperature oil field"

Section 356: "Total field allowance for a new oil field"

Section 357: Other definitions

PART 9: LEASING PLANT OR MACHINERY

Overview

Chapter 1: Introduction

Section 358: Introduction to Part

Chapter 2: Long funding leases of plant or machinery

Overview

Section 359: Overview of Chapter

Section 360: Lessor under long funding finance lease: rental earnings

Section 361: Lessor under long funding finance lease: exceptional items

Section 362: Lessor under long funding finance lease making termination payment

Section 363: Lessor under long funding operating lease: periodic deduction

Section 364: "Starting value": general

Section 365: "Starting value" where plantor machinery originally unqualifying

Section 366: Long funding operating lease: lessor's additional expenditure

Section 367: Determination of remaining residual value resulting from lessor's first additional expenditure

Section 368: Determination of remaining residual value resulting from lessor's further additional expenditure

Section 369: Lessor under long funding operating lease: termination of lease

Section 370: Plant or machinery held as trading stock

Section 371: Adjustments where sections 360 to 369 subsequently disapplied by section 370

Section 372: Lessor also lessee under non–long funding lease

Section 373: Other avoidance

Section 374: Provision supplementing section 373

Section 375: Adjustments where sections 360 to 369 subsequently disapplied by section 373

Section 376: Films

Section 377: Lessee under long funding finance lease: limit on deductions

Section 378: Lessee under long funding finance lease: termination

Section 379: Lessee under long funding operating lease

Section 380: "Starting value" in section 379

Section 381: Interpretation of Chapter

Chapters 3 to 6: The sales of lessors Chapters

Overview

Chapter 3: Sales of lessors: leasing business carried on by a company alone

Overview

Section 382: Introduction to Chapter

Section 383: Income and matching expense in different accounting periods

Section 384: Amount of income and expense

Section 385: No carry back of the expense

Section 386: Relief for expense otherwise giving rise to carried forward loss

Section 387: "Business of leasing plant or machinery"

Section 388: "Relevant plant or machinery value" for condition A in section 387

Section 389: Provision supplementing section 388

Section 390: Relevant plant or machinery value where relevant company lessee under long funding lease etc

Overview

Chapter 1: Overview of Part

Section 438: Overview of Part

Chapter 2: Basic definitions

Overview

Section 439: "Close company"

Section 440: Basis of winding up under section 439(3)

Section 441: Treatment of some persons as participators or directors for the purposes of section 439(3)

Section 442: Particular types of company

Section 443: Companies controlled by or on behalf of Crown

Section 444: Companies involved with non-close companies

Section 445: Section 444: registered pension schemes

Section 446: Particular types of quoted company

Section 447: Section 446: meaning of "shares beneficially held by the public" etc

Sections 448 and 449: "Associate"; "associated company"

Section 450: "Control"

Section 451: Section 450: rights to be attributed etc

Section 452: "Director"

Sections 453 and 454 "Loan creditor"; "participator"

Chapter 3: Charge to tax in case of loan to participator

Section 455: Charge to tax in case of loan to participator

Section 456: Exceptions to the charge under section 455

Section 457: Section 456: meaning of "material interest in a company"

Section 458: Relief in case of repayment or release of loan

Section 459: Loan treated as made to participator

Section 460: Loan treated as made by close company

Section 461: Exception to section 460

Section 462: Determination of particular questions as a result of section 460

Section 481: Exemption from charges under provisions to which section 1173 applies

Section 482: Condition as to trading and miscellaneous incoming resources

Section 483: Exemption for profits from fund-raising events

Section 484: Exemption for profits from lotteries

Section 485: Exemption for property income etc

Section 486: Exemption for investment income and non-trading profits from loan relationships

Section 487: Exemption for public revenue dividends

Section 488: Exemption for certain miscellaneous income

Section 489: Exemption for income from estates in administration

Section 490: Eligible bodies

Section 491: Scientific research associations

Chapter 4: Restrictions on exemptions

Overview

Section 492: Restrictions on exemptions

Section 493: The non-exempt amount

Section 494: Attributing income to the non-exempt amount

Section 495: How income is attributed to the non-exempt amount

Section 496: Meaning of "non-charitable expenditure"

Section 497: Section 496: supplementary

Section 498: Section 496(1)(d): meaning of expenditure

Section 499: Section 496(1)(d): accounting period in which certain expenditure treated as incurred

Section 500: Section 496(1)(d): payment to body outside the UK

Section 501: Section 496(1)(g) and (h): investments and loans

Section 502: Transactions with substantial donors

Section 503: Meaning of "relievable gift"

Section 504: Non-charitable expenditure in substantial donor transactions

Section 505: Adjustment if section 504(1) and (2) applied to single transaction

Section 506: Section 504: certain payments and benefits to be ignored

Section 507: Transactions: exceptions

Section 508: Donors: exceptions

Section 509: Connected charities

Section 510: Substantial donor transactions: supplementary

Section 511: Approved charitable investments

Section 512: Securities which are approved charitable investments

Section 513: Conditions to be met for some securities

Section 514: Approved charitable loans

Section 515: Excess expenditure treated as non-charitable expenditure of earlier periods

Section 516: Rules for attributing excess expenditure to earlier periods

Section 517: Adjustments in consequence of section 515

PART 12: REAL ESTATE INVESTMENT TRUSTS

Overview

Chapter 1: Introduction

Section 518: Introduction to Part

Section 519: "Property rental business"

Section 520: "UK property rental business" of non-UK companies

Section 521: "UK company" and "non-UK company"

Section 522: "Residual business"

Chapter 2: Requirements for being a UK REIT

Section 523: Notice for a group of companies to become a UK REIT

Section 524: Notice for a company to become a UK REIT

Section 525: Notice under section 523 or 524: supplementary

Section 526: Duration of status as UK REIT

Section 527: Being a UK REIT in relation to an accounting period

Section 528: Conditions for company

Section 529: Conditions as to property rental business

Section 530: Condition as to distribution of profits

Section 531: Conditions as to balance of business

Section 532:Financial statements for group UK REITs

Section 533: Financial statements: supplementary

Chapter 3: Tax treatment of profits and gains of UK REITs

Section 534: Profits

Section 535: Gains

Chapter 4: Entering the UK REIT regime

Section 536: Effects of entry: corporation tax

Section 537: Effects of entry: CAA 2001

Section 538: Entry charge

Section 539: Calculation of the notional amount

Section 540: Election to treat notional income as arising in instalments

Chapter 5: Assets etc

Section 541: Ring-fencing of property rental business

Section 542: Disapplication of certain provisions

Section 543: Profit: financing-cost ratio

Section 544: Meaning of "property profits" and "property financing costs"

Section 545: Cancellation of tax advantage

Section 546: Appeal against notice under section 545

Section 547: Funds awaiting reinvestment

Chapter 6:Distributions

Section 548: Distributions: liability to tax

Section 549: Distributions: supplementary

Section 550: Attribution of distributions

Section 551: Tax consequences of distribution to holder of excessive rights

Section 552: "The section 552 amount"

Section 553: Meaning of "holder of excessive rights"

Section 554: Regulations: distributions to holders of excessive rights

Chapter 7: Gains etc

Section 555: Assets: change of use

Section 556: Disposal of assets

Section 557: Movement of assets into ring fence

Section 558: Demergers: disposal of asset

Section 559: Demergers: company leaving group UK REIT

Section 560: Interpretation of Chapter

Chapter 8: Breach of conditions in Chapter 2

Section 561: Notice of breach of relevant Chapter 2 condition

Section 562: Breach of conditions C and D in section 528 (conditions for company)

Section 563: Breach of conditions as to property rental business

Section 564: Breach of condition as to distribution of profits

Section 565: "The section 565 amount"

Section 566: Breach of condition B in section 531 in accounting period 1

Section 567: Meaning of "the notional amount"

Section 568: Breach of balance of business conditions after accounting period 1

Section 569: Chapter subject to section 572

Chapter 9: Leaving the UK REIT regime

Section 570: Overview of Chapter

Section 571: Termination by notice: group or company

Section 572: Termination by notice: officer of Revenue and Customs

Section 573: Notice under section 572: tax advantage

Section 574: Notice under section 572: serious breach

Section 575: Notice under section 572: breach of conditions as to property rental business

Section 576: Notice under section 572: breach of conditions as to balance of business

Section 577: Notice under section 572: multiple breaches of conditions in Chapter 2

Section 605: Property rental business: exclusion of business producing listed income

Section 606: Groups

Section 607: Meaning of "entry" and "cessation" etc

Section 608: References to assets

Section 609: Definitions

PART 13: OTHER SPECIAL TYPES OF COMPANY ETC

Overview

Chapter 1: Corporate beneficiaries under trusts

Overview

Section 610: Discretionary payments by trustees to companies

Section 611: Income tax provisions to apply in relation to trustees' expenses

Chapter 2: Authorised investment funds

Overview

Section 612: Overview of Chapter

Section 613: Meaning of "open-ended investment company"

Section 614: Applicable corporation tax rate

Section 615: Umbrella companies

Section 616: Meaning of "authorised unit trust" and "unit holder"

Section 617: Authorised unit trust treated as UK resident company

Section 618: Applicable corporation tax rate

Section 619: Umbrella schemes

Section 620: Court investment funds

Chapter 3: Unauthorised unit trusts

Overview

Section 621: Treatment of income

Section 622: Treatment of capital expenditure

Chapter 4: Securitisation companies

Overview

Section 623: Meaning of "securitisation company"

Section 624: Power to make regulations about the taxation of securitisation companies

Section 625: Regulations: supplementary

Chapter 5: Companies in liquidation or administration

Overview

Section 626: Meaning of "final year", "penultimate year" etc

Section 627: Meaning of "rate of corporation tax" in case of companies with small profits

Section 628: Company in liquidation: corporation tax rates

Section 629: Company in liquidation: making of assessment to tax

Section 630: Company in administration: corporation tax rates

Section 631: Company in administration: making of assessment to tax

Section 632: Meaning of rate being "fixed" or "proposed"

Section 633: Exemption for interest on overpaid tax in final accounting period

Chapter 6: Banks etc in compulsory liquidation

Overview

Section 634: Overview of Chapter

Section 635: Application of Chapter

Section 636: Charge to corporation tax on winding up receipts

Section 637: Transfer of rights to payment

Section 638: Allowable deductions

Section 639: Election to carry back

Section 640: Relationship of Chapter with other corporation tax provisions

Section 641: Interpretation of Chapter

Chapter 7: Co-operative housing associations

Overview of Chapter

Section 642: Disregard of rent from members and of interest payable

Section 643: Exemption for gains on a sale of property

Section 644: Approval of housing associations

Section 645: Tests to be satisfied by the association

Section 646: Delegation of powers to the Regulator of Social Housing

Section 647: Claims under section 642 or 643

Section 648: Adjustments of liability

Section 649: Power to make further provision

Chapter 8: Self-build societies

Overview of Chapter

Section 650: Meaning of "self-build society"

Section 651: Disregard of rent from members

Section 652: Exemption for gains on disposals of land to members

Section 653: Approval of self-build societies

Section 654: Delegation of powers to the Regulator of Social Housing

Section 655: Claims under section 651 or 652

Section 656: Adjustments of liability

Section 657: Power to make further provision

Chapter 9: Community amateur sports clubs

Overview

Section 658: Meaning of "community amateur sports club" and "registered club"

Section 659: Meaning of "open to the whole community"

Section 660: Meaning of "organised on an amateur basis"

Section 661: Meaning of "eligible sport", "qualifying purposes" etc

Section 662: Exemption for UK trading income

Section 663: Exemption for UK property income

Section 664: Exemption for interest and gift aid income

Section 665: Exemption for chargeable gains

Section 666: Exemptions reduced if non-qualifying expenditure incurred

Section 667: Rules for attributing surplus amount to earlier periods etc

Section 668: How income and gains are attributed

Section 669: Asset ceasing to be held for qualifying purposes etc

Section 670: Notification of HMRC decision

Section 671: Appeals

PART 14: CHANGE IN COMPANY OWNERSHIP

Overview

Chapter 1: Introduction

Section 672: Overview of Part

Chapter 2: Disallowance of trading losses

Overview

Section 673: Introduction to Chapter

Section 674: Disallowance of trading losses

Section 675: Disallowance of trading losses: calculation of balancing charges

Section 676: Disallowance of trading losses where company reconstruction without change in ownership

Chapter 3: Company with investment business: restrictions on relief: general provision

Overview

Section 677: Introduction to Chapter

Section 678: Notional split of accounting period in which change in ownership occurs

Section 679: Restriction on debits to be brought into account

Section 680: Restriction on the carry forward of non-trading deficit from loan relationships

Section 681: Restriction on relief for non-trading loss on intangible fixed assets

Section 682: Restriction on the deduction of expenses of management

Section 683: Disallowance of UK property business losses

Section 684: Disallowance of overseas property business losses

Section 685: Apportionment of amounts

Section 686: Meaning of certain expressions in section 685

Section 687: Adjustment to balancing charges if relief is restricted

Section 688: Meaning of "significant increase in the amount of a company's capital"

Sections 689 and 690: Amount A; amount B

Section 691: Meaning of "amount of capital"

Chapter 4: Company with investment business: restrictions on relief: asset transferred within group

Overview

Section 692: Introduction to Chapter

Section 693: Meaning of "amount of profits which represents a relevant gain"

Section 694: Meaning of "the relevant provisions"

Section 695: Notional split of accounting period in which change in ownership occurs

Section 696: Restriction on debits to be brought into account

Section 697: Restriction on the carry forward of non-trading deficit from loan relationships

Section 698: Restriction on relief for non-trading loss on intangible fixed assets

Section 699: Restrictions on the deduction of expenses of management

Section 700: Disallowance of UK property business losses

Section 701: Disallowance of overseas property business losses

Section 702: Apportionment of amounts

Section 703: Meaning of certain expressions in section 702

Chapter 5: Company without investment business: disallowance of property losses

Overview

Section 704: Company carrying on UK property business

Section 705: Company carrying on overseas property business

Chapter 6: Recovery of unpaid corporation tax

Overview

Section 706: Meaning of "linked" person

Section 707: Meaning of "control"

Section 708: Rights to be attributed for the purposes of section 707

Section 709: Meaning of "the relevant period"

Section 710: Recovery of unpaid corporation tax for accounting period beginning before change

Section 711: Conditions relating to company's trade or business

Section 712: Meaning of "a major change in the nature or conduct of a trade or business"

Section 713: Recovery of unpaid corporation tax for accounting period ending on or after change

Section 714: The expectation condition

Section 715: Meaning of "transaction entered into in connection with change in ownership"

Section 716: Interest

Section 717: Effect of payment in pursuance of assessment under section 710 or713

Section 718: Meaning of "associated company"

Chapter 7: Meaning of "change in the ownership of a company"

Overview

Section 719: Meaning of "change in the ownership of a company"

Section 720: Section 719: supplementary

Section 721: When things other than ordinary share capital may be taken into account: Chapters 2 to 5

Section 722: When things other than ordinary share capital may be taken into account: Chapter 6

Section 723: Changes in indirect ownership

Section 724: Disregard of change in company ownership

Section 725: Provision applying for the purposes of Chapters 2 to 5

Section 726: Interpretation of Chapter

Chapter 8: Supplementary provision

Sections 727 to 730: Extended time limit for assessment; provision of information about ownership of shares etc; meaning of "company with investment business"; meaning of "relevant non-trading debit"

PART 15: TRANSACTIONS IN SECURITIES

Overview

Sections 731 to 734: Overview of Part; meaning of "corporation tax advantage"; company liable to counteraction of corporation tax advantages; exception where no tax avoidance object shown

Section 735: Abnormal dividends used for exemptions or reliefs (circumstance A)

Sections 736 to 738: Receipt of consideration representing company's assets, future receipts or trading stock (circumstance C); receipt of consideration in connection with relevant company distribution (circumstance D); receipt of assets of relevant company (circumstance E)

Section 739: Meaning of "relevant company" in sections 737 and 738

Section 740: Abnormal dividends: general

Sections 741 and 742: Abnormal dividends: the excessive return condition and the excessive accrual condition

Sections 743 to 746: Preliminary notification that section 733 may apply, opposed notifications and counteraction notices

Sections 747 to 751: Timing of assessments in section 738 cases; application for clearance of transactions; effect of clearance notification under section 748; appeals against counteraction notices; interpretation of Part

PART 16: FACTORING OF INCOME ETC

Overview

Chapter 1: Transfers of income streams

Overview

Sections 752 to 757: Application of Chapter; value of transferred income treated as income; exception: amount otherwise taxed; exception: transfer by way of security; partnership shares; interpretation

Chapter 2: Finance arrangements

Overview

Section 758: Type 1 finance arrangement defined

Section 759: Certain tax consequences not to have effect

Section 760: Payments treated as borrower's income

Section 761: Deemed loan relationship if borrower is a company

Section 762: Deemed loan relationship if borrower is partnership with corporate member

Section 763: Type 2 finance arrangement defined

Section 764: Relevant change in relation to partnership

Section 765: Certain tax consequences not to have effect

Section 766: Deemed loan relationship

Section 767: Type 3 finance arrangement defined

Section 768: Certain tax consequences not to have effect

Section 792: Company receiving manufactured overseas dividend from UK resident etc

Section 793: Section 792: amount treated as withheld

Section 794: Company receiving manufactured overseas dividend from foreign payer

Section 795: Exemption of manufactured overseas dividends

Chapter 4: Further provision about manufactured payments

Overview

Sections 796 and 797: Manufactured dividends and manufactured overseas dividends: amounts exceeding underlying payments

Section 798: Manufactured overseas dividends less than underlying payments

Section 799: Manufactured payments under arrangements with unallowable purpose

Section 800: Arrangements with an unallowable purpose

Section 801: Sections 799 and 800: supplementary

Section 802: Powers about amounts representative of overseas dividends

Section 803: Power to deal with special cases

Section 804: Regulation-making powers: general

Chapter 5: Stock lending arrangements and repos

Overview

Sections 805 to 807: "Stock lending arrangement"; section 805: supplementary; "creditor repo", "creditor quasi-repo", "debtor repo" and "debtor quasi-repo"

Section 808: No tax credits for borrower under stock lending arrangement

Section 809: No tax credits for lender under creditor repo or creditor quasi-repo

Section 810: No tax credits for borrower under debtor repo or debtor quasi-repo

Section 811: Arrangements between companies to make distributions

Section 812: Deemed manufactured payments: stock lending arrangements

Chapter 6: Interpretation of Part

Sections 813 and 814: The gross amount of a manufactured overseas dividend etc; other interpretation

PART 18: TRANSACTIONS IN LAND

Overview

Sections 815 and 816: Introduction to Part; meaning of disposing of land

Section 817: Priority of other tax provisions

Section 818: Charge to tax on gains from transactions in land

Sections 819 and 820: Gains obtained from land disposals in some circumstances; person obtaining gain

Section 821: Company chargeable

Sections 822 to 826: Method of calculating gain; transactions, arrangements, sales and realisations relevant for Part; tracing value; meaning of "another person"; valuations and apportionments

Section 827 and 828: Gain attributable to period before intention to develop formed and disposals of shares in companies holding land as trading stock

Sections 829 and 830: Cases where consideration receivable by person not assessed; certificates of tax paid etc

Section 831: Clearance procedure

Section 832: Power to obtain information

Section 833: Interpretation of Part

PART 19: SALE AND LEASE-BACK ETC

Overview

Chapter 1: Payments connected with transferred land

Overview

Section 834: Overview

Section 835: Transferor or associate becomes liable for payment of rent

Section 836: Transferor or associate becomes liable for payment other than rent

Section 837: Relevant corporation tax relief

Section 838: Relevant corporation tax relief: deduction not to exceed commercial rent

Section 839: Deduction under section 76 of ICTA not to exceed commercial rent

Section 840: Carrying forward parts of payments

Section 841: Aggregation and apportionment of payments

Section 842: Payments made for later periods

Section 843: Exclusion of service charges etc

Section 844: Commercial rent: comparison with rent under a lease

Section 845: Commercial rent: comparison with payments other than rent

Section 846: Lease and rent

Section 847: Associated persons

Section 848: Land outside the UK

Chapter 2: New lease of land after assignment or surrender

Overview

Section 849: Overview

Section 850: New lease after assignment or surrender

Section 851: Taxation of consideration

Section 852: Position where new lease does not include all original property

Section 853: Relief for rent under new lease

Section 854: New lease treated as ending

Section 855: Position where rent reduces

Section 856: Position where lease may be ended

Section 857: Position where lease may be varied

Section 858: Lease treated as ending: rentcharge

Section 859: Lease varied to provide for increased rent

Section 860: Relevant corporation tax relief

Section 861: Linked persons

Section 862: Lease, lessee, lessor and rent

Chapter 3: Leased trading assets

Overview

Section 863: Overview of Chapter

Section 864: Leased trading assets

Section 865: Tax deduction not to exceed commercial rent

Section 866: Long funding finance leases

Sections 867 and 868: Commercial rent; lease

Chapter 2: Capital payments in respect of leases treated as income

Overview

Section 890: Capital payments in respect of leases treated as income

Section 891: Apportionments for leases of plant or machinery and other property

Section 892: Deduction where failure to make relevant capital payment expected

Section 893: Meaning in Chapter of "Capital payment", "relevant capital payment" etc

Section 894: Other interpretation of Chapter

PART 21: LEASING ARRANGEMENTS: FINANCE LEASES AND LOANS

Overview

Chapter 1: Introduction

Overview

Section 895: Overview of Part

Section 896: Normal rent

Section 897: Accountancy rental earnings

Section 898: Rental earnings

Chapter 2: Finance leases with return in capital form

Overview

Section 899: Arrangements to which this Chapter applies

Section 900: Purposes of this Chapter

Section 901: Application of this Chapter

Section 902: The conditions referred to in section 901(1)

Section 903: Provisions supplementing section 902

Section 904: The arrangements and circumstances referred to in section 902(8)

Section 905: Current lessor taxed by reference to accountancy rental earnings

Sections 906 to 910: Reduction of taxable rent by cumulative rental excesses

Overview

Section 906: Reduction of taxable rent by cumulative rental excesses: introduction

Section 907: Meaning of "accountancy rental excess" and "cumulative accountancy rental excess"

Section 908: Reduction of taxable rent by the cumulative accountancy rental excess

Section 909: Meaning of "normal rental excess" and "cumulative normal rental excess"

Section 910: Reduction of taxable rent by the cumulative normal rental excess

Sections 911 to 914: Relief for bad debts by reduction of cumulative rental excesses

Overview

Section 911: Relief for bad debts: reduction of cumulative accountancy rental excess

Section 912: Recovery of bad debts following reduction under section 911

Section 913: Relief for bad debts: reduction of cumulative normal rental excess

Section 914: Recovery of bad debts following reduction under section 913

Section 915: Effect of disposals of leases: general

Section 916: Assignments on which neither a gain nor a loss accrues

Sections 917 to 922: Capital allowances: clawback of major lump sums

Overview

Section 917: Effect of capital allowances: introduction

Section 918: Cases where expenditure taken into account under Part 2, 5 or 8 of CAA 2001

Section 919: Cases where expenditure taken into account under other provisions of CAA 2001

Section 920: Capital allowances deductions: waste disposal and cemeteries

Section 921: Capital allowances deductions: films

Section 922: Contributors to capital expenditure

Section 923: Pre-26 November 1996 schemes where this Chapter does not at first apply

Section 924: Post-25 November 1996 schemes to which Chapter 3 applied first

Chapter 3: Other finance leases

Overview

Section 925: Introduction to Chapter

Section 926: Purpose of this Chapter

Section 927: Leases to which this Chapter applies

Section 928: Current lessor taxed by reference to accountancy rental earnings

Section 929: Application of provisions of Chapter 2 for purposes of this Chapter

Chapter 4: Supplementary provisions

Overview

Section 930: Pre-26 November 1996 schemes and post-25 November 1996 schemes

Section 931: Time apportionment where periods of account do not coincide

Section 932: Periods of account and related periods of account and accounting periods

Section 933: Connected persons

Section 934: Assets which represent the leased asset

Section 935: Parent undertakings and consolidated group accounts

Section 936: Assessments and adjustments

Section 937: Interpretation of Part

PART 22: MISCELLANEOUS PROVISIONS

Overview

Chapter 1: Transfers of trade without a change of ownership

Overview

Section 938: Overview of Chapter

Section 939: Meaning of "transfer of a trade" and related expressions

Section 940: Transfers to which Chapter applies

Section 941: The ownership condition

Section 942: Options that may be applied for the purposes of the ownership condition

Section 943: The tax condition

Section 944: Modified application of Chapter 2 of Part 4

Section 945: Cases in which predecessor retains more liabilities than assets

Section 946: Rules for determining "L"

Section 947: Rules for determining "A"

Section 948: Modified application of CAA 2001

Section 949: Dual resident investing companies

Section 950: Transfers of trades involving business of leasing plant or machinery

Section 951: Part of trade treated as separate trade

Section 952: Apportionment if part of trade treated as separate trade

Section 953: Application of Chapter to further transfers of a trade

Chapter 2: Transfers of trade to obtain balancing allowances

Overview

Section 954: Transfer of activities on complete cessation of trade

Section 955: Transfer of activities on part cessation of trade

Section 956: Apportionment if part of trade treated as separate trade

Section 957: Supplementary and interpretative provisions

Chapter 3: Transfer of relief within partnerships

Overview

Section 958: Application

Section 959: Arrangements for transfer of relief

Section 960: Restrictions on use of reliefs

Section 961: Non-trading profits and losses

Section 962: Interpretation of Chapter

Chapter 4: Surrender of tax refund within group

Overview

Section 963: Power to surrender tax refund

Section 964: Effects of surrender of tax refund

Section 965: Interest on tax overpaid or underpaid

Section 966: Payments for surrendered tax refunds

Chapter 5: Set off of income tax deductions against corporation tax

Section 967: Deductions from payments received by UK resident companies

Section 968: Deductions from payments received by non-UK resident companies

Chapter 6: Collection etc of tax from UK representatives of non–UK resident companies

Overview

Section 969: Introduction to Chapter

Section 970: Obligations and liabilities in relation to corporation tax

Section 971: Exceptions

Section 972: Interpretation of Chapter

Chapter 7: Recovery of unpaid corporation tax due from non–UK resident company

Overview

Section 973: Introduction to Chapter

Section 974: Case in which this Chapter applies

Sections 975 and 976: Meaning of "the relevant period"; meaning of "related company"

Section 977: Notice requiring payment of unpaid tax

Section 978: Time limit for giving notice

Section 979: Amount payable in consortium case

Section 980: Chapter 7: supplementary

Chapter 8: Exemptions

Overview

Section 981: Exemption for trade unions and eligible employers' associations

Section 982: Qualifying income or gains

Section 983: Meaning of "trade union" and "eligible employers' association"

Section 984: Local authorities and local authority associations

Section 985: Health service bodies

Section 986: Meaning of "health service body"

Section 987: NHS foundation trusts

Section 988: Issue departments of the Reserve Bank of India and the State Bank of Pakistan

Section 989: Agricultural societies

Chapter 9: Other miscellaneous provisions

Overview

Section 990: European Economic Interest Groupings

Section 991: Harbour reorganisation schemes: corporation tax

Section 992: Harbour reorganisation schemes: capital allowances etc

Section 993: Harbour reorganisation schemes: chargeable gains

Section 994: Transfer of part of trade

Section 995: Interpretation of sections 991 to 994

Section 996: Use of different accounting practices within a group of companies

PART 23: COMPANY DISTRIBUTIONS

Overview

Chapter 1: Introduction

Section 997: Overview of Part

Chapter 2: Matters which are distributions

Section 998: Overview of Chapter

Section 999: Priority of negative rules

Section 1000: Meaning of "distribution"

Section 1001: Provisions related to paragraphs A to H in section 1000(1)

Section 1002: Exceptions for certain transfers of assets or liabilities between a company and its members

Section 1003: Redeemable share capital

Section 1004: Securities issued otherwise than for new consideration

Section 1005: Meaning of "non-commercial securities"

Section 1006: Distributions exceeding consideration received for issue of security

Section 1007: Securities issued at premium representing new consideration

Section 1008: Consideration for issue of security exceeding amount of principal

Section 1009: Securities reflecting dividends on certain shares etc: exclusion of section 1008

Section 1010: Meaning of "qualifying index" in section 1009

Section 1011: Meaning of "associated company" in section 1009

Section 1012: Hedging arrangements

Section 1013: Exception to section 1012

Section 1014: Meaning of "hedging arrangements"

Section 1015: Meaning of "special securities"

Section 1016: Meaning of "equity note" in section 1015

Section 1017: Section 1015: other interpretation

Section 1018: The principal secured: special securities

Section 1019: Relevant alternative finance return

Section 1020: Transfers of assets or liabilities treated as distributions

Section 1021: Section 1020 exceptions

Section 1022: Bonus issue following repayment of share capital treated as distribution

Section 1023: Exceptions to section 1022

Section 1024: Premiums paid on redemption of share capital

Section 1025: Share capital issued at a premium representing new consideration

Section 1026: Distributions following a bonus issue

Section 1027: Cap on amount of distributions affected by section 1026

Section 1028: Certain payments connected with exempt distributions

Chapter 3: Matters which are not distributions

Section 1029: Overview of Chapter

Section 1030: Distribution in respect of share capital in a winding up

Section 1031: Distribution as part of a cross-border merger

Section 1032: Interest etc paid in respect of certain securities

Section 1033: Purchase by unquoted trading company of own shares

Section 1034: Requirements as to residence

Section 1035: Requirement as to period of ownership

Section 1036: Determining the period of ownership

Section 1037: Requirement as to reduction of seller's interest as shareholder

Section 1038: Section 1037: effect of entitlement to profits

Section 1039: Requirements where purchasing company is a member of a group

Section 1040: Determining whether interests as shareholders in a group are substantially reduced

Section 1041: Section 1040: effect of entitlement to profits

Section 1042: Other requirements

Section 1043: Relaxation of requirements in certain cases

Section 1044: Advance clearance of payments by Commissioners

Section 1045: Advance clearance: supplementary

Section 1046: Information and returns

Section 1047: Meaning of "group" and "51% subsidiary" in sections 1033 to 1047

Section 1048: Sections 1033 to 1047: other interpretation

Section 1049: Stock dividends

Section 1050: Application of section 1049 where bonus share capital is converted etc

Section 1051: "Bonus share capital" and "in lieu of a cash dividend"

Section 1052: Share capital to which section 1049 applies: returns

Section 1053: Return periods

Section 1054: Building society payments

Section 1055: Industrial and provident societies: interest and share dividends

Section 1056: Dividend or bonus relating to transactions

Section 1057: UK agricultural or fishing co-operatives: interest and share dividends

Section 1058: Meaning of "UK agricultural or fishing co-operative"

Section 1059: Associated persons

Section 1060: Associated persons: trustees

Section 1061: Associated persons: personal representatives

Section 1062: Connected persons

Section 1088: Meaning of "chargeable payment"

Section 1089: Meaning of "chargeable payment": unquoted companies

Section 1090: Meaning of "company concerned in an exempt distribution"

Section 1091: Advance clearance of distributions

Section 1092: Advance clearance of payments

Section 1093: Requirements relating to applications for clearance

Section 1094: Decision of the Commissioners or tribunal

Section 1095: Exempt distributions: returns

Section 1096: Chargeable payments etc: returns

Section 1097: Information about person for whom a payment is received

Section 1098: "Unquoted company"

Section 1099: Other definitions etc

Chapter 6: Information and returns: further provisions

Overview

Section 1100: Qualifying distributions: right to request a statement

Section 1101: Non-qualifying distributions etc: returns and information

Section 1102: Non-qualifying distributions etc: additional information

Section 1103: Power to modify or replace sections 1101 and 1102

Section 1104: Company distributing dividend or interest: duty to provide tax certificates

Section 1105: Duties of nominees

Section 1106: Meaning of "tax certificate" etc

Section 1107: Penalties

Section 1108: Alternative means of compliance with sections 1104 and 1105

Chapter 7: Tax credits

Section 1109: Tax credits for certain recipients of exempt qualifying distributions

Section 1110: Recovery of overpaid tax credit etc

Section 1111: Section 1110: supplementary

Section 1137: "Recognised stock exchange"

Section 1138: "Research and development"

Section 1139: "Tax advantage"

Section 1140: "Unauthorised unit trust"

Chapter 2: Permanent establishments

Overview

Section 1141: Permanent establishments of companies

Section 1142: Agent of independent status

Section 1143: Preparatory or auxiliary activities

Section 1144: Alternative finance arrangements

Section 1145: The independent broker conditions

Section 1146: The independent investment manager conditions

Section 1147: Investment managers: the 20% rule

Section 1148: Section 1147: interpretation

Section 1149: Application of 20% rule to collective investment schemes

Section 1150: Meaning of "investment manager" and "investment transaction"

Section 1151: Lloyd's agents

Section 1152: Investment managers: disregard of certain chargeable profits

Section 1153: Miscellaneous

Chapter 3: Subsidiaries

Overview

Section 1154: Meaning of "51% subsidiary", "75% subsidiary" and "90% subsidiary"

Section 1155: Indirect ownership of ordinary share capital

Section 1156: Calculation of amounts owned indirectly: main rules

Section 1157: Adding fractions together

Chapter 4: Investment trusts

Overview

Section 1158: Meaning of "investment trust"

Section 1159: Conditions for approval

Section 1160: Calculation of income

Section 1161: The income retention condition: exceptions

Section 1162: The 15% holding limit: exceptions

Section 1163: Basic meaning of "holding in a company"

Section 1164: More about the meaning of "holding in a company"

Section 1165: Other interpretation

Chapter 5: Other Corporation Tax Acts provisions

Section 1166: Scotland

Section 1167: Sources of income within the charge to corporation tax or income tax

Section 1168: Payment of dividends

Section 1169: Settlements and trustees

Section 1170: Territorial sea of the United Kingdom

Section 1171: Orders and regulations

Section 1172: Apportionment to different periods

Section 1173: Miscellaneous charges

PART 25: DEFINITIONS FOR PURPOSES OF ACT AND FINAL PROVISIONS

Overview

Section 1174: Abbreviated references to Acts

Section 1175: Claims and elections

Section 1176: Meaning of "connected" persons and "control"

Section 1177: Minor and consequential amendments

Section 1178: Power to make consequential provision

Section 1179: Power to undo changes

Section 1180: Transitional provisions and savings

Section 1181: Repeals and revocations

Section 1182: Index of defined expressions

Section 1183: Extent

Section 1184: Commencement

Sections 256, 256A, 256B, 256C, 256D: Charities and gifts of non-business assets etc

Section 257: Gifts to charities etc

Charities Act 1993

Section 10: Disclosure of information to Commission

Section 25A: Meaning of "Scottish recognised body" and "Northern Ireland charity"

Finance Act 2000

Schedule 15: The corporate venturing scheme

Paragraph 21A

Paragraph 46(2)

Capital Allowances Act 2001

Section 63: Cases in which disposal value is nil

Section 99: The monetary limit

Section 253: Companies with investment business

Schedule A1: First-year tax credits

Finance Act 2002

Schedules 34 and 35: Stamp duty: withdrawal of group relief and withdrawal of relief for company acquisitions: supplementary provisions

Income Tax (Earnings and Pensions) Act 2003

Section 68: Meaning of "material interest" in a company

Schedule 2: Approved share incentive plans

Schedule 5: Enterprise management incentives

Companies (Audit, Investigations and Community Enterprise) Act 2004

Section 54: Becoming a charity or a Scottish charity: requirements

Income Tax (Trading and Other Income) Act 2005

Section 148D: Lessor under long funding operating lease: periodic deduction

Section 148E: long funding operating lease: lessor's additional expenditure

Section 148F: Lessor under long funding operating lease: termination of lease

Chapter 3 of Part 4: Dividends etc. from UK resident companies and tax credits etc. in respect of certain distributions

Section 415: Charge to tax under Chapter 6

Finance Act 2005

Section 84: Taxation of securitisation companies

Income Tax Act 2007

Section 151: Losses on disposal of shares: interpretation of Chapter

Sections 346, 348(7), 356, 361, 363, 365, 368, 369 and 373: Community investment tax relief

Sections 340 and 341: Application and criteria for accreditation and terms and conditions of accreditation

Section 355: Securities or shares: no claim after disposal or excessive receipts of value

Section 364: Value received by investor during 6 year period: securities or shares

Chapter 6 of Part 13: Avoidance involving leases of plant and machinery

Section 991: Meaning of "bank"

Section 999: Meaning of "local authority"

Section 1000: Meaning of "local authority association"

Schedule 2 Part 6: Transitionals and savings: losses on disposal of shares

Finance Act 2008

Schedule 19: Reduction of basic rate of income tax: transitional relief for gift aid charities

Charities Act (Northern Ireland) 2008

Section 45: Meaning of "Scottish recognised body" and "England and Wales charity" in sections 43 and 44

Company Tax Act 2009

Section 221A: Sums to which sections 217 to 221 do not apply

Section 520: Provision not at arm's length: non-deductibility of relevant return

Section 1219: Expenses of management of a company's investment business

Schedule 2: Transitionals and savings etc

PART 1: GENERAL PROVISIONS

PART 3: CURRENCY

PART 5: LOSSES ON DISPOSAL OF SHARES

Disposals of new shares

Relief after an exchange of shares for shares in another company

Interpretation of Chapter

Application in relation to corresponding bonus shares

PART 11: CLOSE COMPANIES

PART 12: CHARITABLE COMPANIES ETC

Transactions in deposits

Exemption for investment income and exemption for certain miscellaneous income

Transactions with substantial donors and non-charitable expenditure

PART 14: CO-OPERATIVE HOUSING ASSOCIATIONS AND SELF-BUILD SOCIETIES

Concurrent exercise of functions

Delegation of functions to the Regulator of Social Housing

PART 15: TRANSACTIONS IN SECURITIES

Transactions in securities: general

PART 16: FACTORING OF INCOME ETC

Application of section 771 (finance arrangements: exceptions)

Application of section 779 (income-transfer under loan or credit transaction)

PART 17: MANUFACTURED PAYMENTS AND REPOS

Manufactured dividends and manufactured overseas dividends: distributions paid before 1 July 2009

Manufactured overseas dividends: overseas dividends paid before 22 April 2009

PART 21: TRANSFERS OF TRADE WITHOUT A CHANGE IN OWNERSHIP

These notes refer to the Corporation Tax Act 2010
(c.4) which received Royal Assent on 3 March 2010

CORPORATION TAX ACT 2010

EXPLANATORY NOTES

INTRODUCTION

1. These explanatory notes relate to the Corporation Tax Act 2010 which received Royal Assent on 3 March 2010. They have been prepared by the Tax Law Rewrite project at HMRC to assist readers in understanding the Act. They do not form part of the Act and have not been endorsed by Parliament.

2. The notes need to be read in conjunction with the Act. They are not, and are not meant to be, a comprehensive description of its contents. So if a section or part of a section does not seem to require explanation or comment, none is given.

3. The commentary on each section indicates the main origin or origins of the section. A full statement of the origins of each section is contained in the Act's Table of Origins.

4. At the end of the commentary, there is supporting material in two annexes:

   - *Annex 1* contains details of the minor changes in the law made by the Act;
   - *Annex 2* contains lists of:
     - — the Extra-Statutory Concessions to which the Act gives effect,
     - — the minor changes made by the Act which involve giving statutory effect to principles derived from case law, and
     - — provisions not included in the Act on the grounds of redundancy.

Summary

5. The main purpose of the Corporation Tax Act is to rewrite primary corporation tax legislation so that it is clearer and easier to use but without changing its general effect.

6. This Act contains provisions which affect the calculation of liability such as losses and group relief. It also contains provisions dealing with distributions, avoidance and particular types of companies and activities.

7. The Act reproduces the law on which it is based. It does not generally change the meaning of the law. The minor changes which it does make are within the remit of the Tax Law Rewrite project and the Parliamentary process for the Act. In the main, such minor changes are intended to clarify existing provisions, make them consistent or bring the law into line with well established practice.

Background

The Tax Law Rewrite project

8. In December 1995 the Inland Revenue presented a report to Parliament on the scope for simplifying the UK tax system (*The Path to Tax Simplification*). The main

recommendation was that UK direct tax legislation should be rewritten in clearer, simpler language.

9. This recommendation was warmly welcomed, both in Parliament and in the tax community. In his November 1996 Budget speech the then Chancellor of the Exchequer (the Rt Hon Kenneth Clarke QC MP) announced that the Inland Revenue would propose detailed arrangements for a major project to rewrite direct tax legislation in plainer language.

10. The project team has been carrying out this work. The aim is that the rewritten legislation should use simpler language and structure than previous tax legislation. The members of the project are drawn from different backgrounds. They include HMRC employees, private sector tax professionals and parliamentary counsel including (as head of the drafting team) a senior member of the Parliamentary Counsel Office.

Steering Committee

11. The work of the project is overseen by a Steering Committee, chaired by the Rt Hon the Lord Newton of Braintree OBE DL. The membership of the Steering Committee as at 31 October 2009 was:

The Rt Hon the Lord Newton of Braintree OBE DL (Chairman)

Dr John Avery Jones CBE

Adam Broke

Nicholas Dee

Dave Hartnett CB

The Rt Hon Michael Jack MP

Eric Joyce MP

District Judge Rachel Karp

Professor John Tiley CBE

John Whiting OBE

Consultative Committee

12. The work is also reviewed by a Consultative Committee, representing the accountancy and legal professions and the interests of taxpayers. The membership of the Consultative Committee as at 31 October 2009 was:

Robina Dyall	*Chairman*
Adam Broke	*Special Committee of Tax Law Consultative Bodies*
Colin Campbell	*Formerly Confederation of British Industry*
Russell Chaplin	*London Chamber of Commerce & Industry*
Mary Fraser	*Association of Chartered Certified Accountants*
Malcolm Gammie CBE QC	*The Law Society*
Julian Ghosh QC	*Revenue Bar Association*
Keith Gordon	*Chartered Institute of Taxation*
Terry Hopes	*Institute of Chartered Accountants in England and Wales*

Vic Peake	*Federation of Small Businesses*
Isobel d'Inverno	*Law Society of Scotland*
Simon McKie	*Institute of Chartered Accountants in England and Wales*
Lakshmi Narain	*Chartered Institute of Taxation*
Francis Sandison	*The Law Society*
Michael Templeman	*Institute of Directors*
Professor David Williams	*Office of the Social Security Commissioners*
Mervyn Woods	*Confederation of British Industry*

Consultation

13. The work produced by the project has been subject to public consultation. This has allowed all interested parties an opportunity to comment on draft clauses.

14. Consultation took the form of a series of papers presenting clauses in draft and documents containing responses to comments received. These were published between September 2007 and October 2009. A draft Bill was published for consultation in March 2009. All these documents are available on the Tax Law Rewrite website.

15. In addition to this consultation the project also presented its papers to the Consultative and Steering Committees to inform them and to seek their views on particular issues. The project also consulted on an informal basis with specialists in particular subject areas. These included Russell Chaplin, Paul Bloom of Beechams LLP, Hugh Faulkner (Dairycrest), Krishna Sooben (Radio Taxis Group) and Tony Spillett of BDO LLP who advised the project as corporation tax practitioners.

16. Those who responded in writing to one or more of the papers or to the draft Bill include:

BDO LLP

Bircham Dyson Bell LLP

The British Property Federation

CASCS Development Forum

The Charity Law Association

Chartered Institute of Taxation

Colin Campbell

Confederation of British Industry

Ernst & Young LLP

Francis Sandison

Freshfields Bruckhaus Deringer LLP

Horwath Clark Whitehill

Institute of Chartered Accountants in England and Wales

KPMG LLP

Pinsent Masons LLP

PricewaterhouseCoopers LLP

Professor David Williams

Slaughter and May

The Law Society

The UK Oil Industry Taxation Committee

17. As there was some movement of material between this Act and the Taxation (International and Other Provisions) Act during the course of the work on the Bills, this list includes respondents to both Bills. The list excludes any individuals who requested that their responses be treated in confidence.

Corporation Tax Act

18. The Act contains provisions relating to:

- losses, gifts to charities and various reliefs available to companies such as group relief;
- distributions;
- particular types of companies and activities;
- avoidance; and
- definitions;

and completes the rewrite of most of the corporation tax provisions. The Corporation Tax Act 2009 and this Act take the place of ICTA as the main corporation tax Acts.

19. The Act has 1185 sections and four Schedules. The sections are arranged as follows:

Part 1: Overview

Part 2: Calculation of liability in respect of profits

Part 3: Companies with small profits

Part 4: Loss relief

Part 5: Group relief

Part 6: Charitable donations relief

Part 7: Community investment tax relief

Part 8: Oil activities

Part 9: Leasing plant or machinery

Part 10: Close companies

Part 11: Charitable companies etc

Part 12: Real Estate Investment Trusts

Part 13: Other special types of company etc

Part 14: Change in company ownership

Part 15: Transactions in securities

Part 16: Factoring of income etc

Part 17: Manufactured payments and repos

Part 18: Transactions in land

Part 19: Sale and lease–back etc

Part 20: Tax avoidance involving leasing plant or machinery

Part 21: Leasing arrangements: finance leases and loans

Part 22: Miscellaneous provisions

Part 23: Company distributions

Part 24: Corporation Tax Acts definitions etc

Part 25: Definitions for purposes of Act and final provisions

20. The Schedules are:

Schedule 1: Minor and consequential amendments

Schedule 2: Transitionals and savings etc

Schedule 3: Repeals and revocations

Schedule 4: Index of defined expressions

Glossary

21. The commentary uses a number of abbreviations. They are listed below.

AUT	*authorised unit trust*
CAA	*the Capital Allowances Act 2001*
CASC	*community amateur sports club*
CDFI	*community development finance institution*
CITR	*community investment tax relief*
CRCA	*the Commissioners for Revenue and Customs Act 2005*
CTA 2009	*the Corporation Tax Act 2009*
CVS	*corporate venturing scheme*
DTA	*double taxation arrangement*
EEA	*European Economic Area*
ESC	*Extra-statutory concession*
FA 1986	*Finance Act 1986 (and similarly for other Finance Acts)*
F(No 2)A	*Finance (No 2) Act*
FISMA	*the Financial Services and Markets Act 2000*
GAAP	*generally accepted accounting practice*
HMRC	*Her Majesty's Revenue and Customs*
ICTA	*the Income and Corporation Taxes Act 1988*
IHTA	*the Inheritance Tax Act 1984*
ITA	*the Income Tax Act 2007*
ITEPA	*the Income Tax (Earnings and Pensions) Act 2003*

ITTOIA	*the Income Tax (Trading and Other Income) Act 2005*
LLP	*limited liability partnership*
MOD	*manufactured overseas dividend*
OEIC	*open-ended investment company*
OTA 1975	*the Oil Taxation Act 1975*
PRT	*petroleum revenue tax*
SAYE	*Save As You Earn*
SP	*Statement of Practice*
TCGA	*the Taxation of Chargeable Gains Act 1992*
TIOPA	*the Taxation (International and Other Provisions) Act 2010*
TMA	*the Taxes Management Act 1970*
UK GAAP	*UK generally accepted accounting practice*
UK REIT	*Real Estate Investment Trust*
VAT	*value added tax*

Part 1: Introduction

Section 1: Overview of Act

22. This section describes the content of the Act. It is new.

Part 2: Calculation of liability in respect of profits

Overview

23. This Part is about the calculation of liability. Chapter 1 provides an introduction to the Part.

24. Chapter 2 is about the rates at which corporation tax is charged.

25. Chapter 3 is about the calculation of the amount of profits to which rates of corporation tax are applied.

26. Chapter 4 is about currency.

Chapter 1: Introduction

Section 2: Overview of Part

27. This section is new.

28. *Subsection (5)* explains that the final stages of the calculation of the corporation tax payable by a company are found in paragraph 8 of Schedule 18 to FA 1998.

Chapter 2: Rates at which corporation tax on profits charged

Section 3: Corporation tax rates

29. This section introduces the rates of corporation tax. It is based on section 2 of CTA 2009.

30. The main rate has to be set annually. But the small profits rate may, in principle, be set at any time. In practice the annual Finance Act sets the small profits rate (and the associated limits and fractions, if they change) for the financial year immediately

preceding the year for which it sets the main rate. So, for instance, section 7 of FA 2009 set the main rate for financial year 2010; and section 8 of the Act set the small companies' rate (renamed small profits rate in this Act) and fractions for the financial year 2009.

Chapter 3: Calculation of amount to which rates applied

Overview

31. This Chapter explains how to calculate the company's profits on which corporation tax is chargeable for an accounting period. These are the profits referred to in the first step in paragraph 8(1) of Schedule 18 to FA 1998. The applicable rates of corporation tax set out in the preceding Chapter of this Act are applied to the amount of these profits.

32. In this Act these profits are known as "taxable total profits".

33. The main corporation tax self-assessment provisions in Schedule 18 to FA 1998 have not been rewritten.

Section 4: Amount of profits to which corporation tax rates applied

34. This section sets out the stages by which the profits of a company on which corporation tax is chargeable are calculated. Subsections (1) and (2) are new and subsections (3) and (4) are based on section 834C of ICTA.

35. The starting point is to find a company's total profits. *Subsections (3)* and *(4)* rewrite the definition of total profits in section 834C of ICTA. Section 834C was inserted by CTA 2009 into ICTA: it is based on section 9(3) of ICTA which was repealed by CTA 2009.

36. Step 1 in subsection (3) refers to the amount in respect of which the company is chargeable under the charge to corporation tax on income after any reduction required to give effect to relief from tax. This covers reliefs that reduce one or more of the components of income subject to the charge. Relief for trade losses brought forward against trade profits of the subsequent accounting period is an example of a relief that operates against a single component of income. Reliefs that potentially operate against more than one component of income include relief under section 68 of the Act for losses on disposals of certain shares (see section 71(1)) and relief under section 457 of CTA 2009 for non-trading deficits from loan relationships.

37. Similarly Step 2 refers to the amount to be included in respect of chargeable gains (under section 8 of TCGA) after any reduction required to give effect to relief from tax. This caters for reliefs that operate to reduce the amount of chargeable gains that feeds into the total profits calculation:again relief under section 457 of CTA 2009 for non-trading deficits from loan relationships is an example of a relief that potentially operates in this way.

38. Under *subsection (4)* the calculation of total profits is subject to the provisions of the Corporation Tax Acts. One example of the kind of qualification covered by this subsection is provision of the kind to be found in Chapter 3 of Part 11 of the Act, under which certain income of charitable companies is not taken into account in calculating total profits (see, for example, section 478(1)).

39. "Total profits" is defined for the purposes of the Corporation Tax Acts by reference to section 4(3) and (4): see sections 1118(5) and 1119.

40. *Subsection (2)* completes the calculation of the profits of a company on which corporation tax is chargeable for an accounting period, in this Act the company's "taxable total profits". Step 1 starts with the total profits of the period. Step 2 provides for the deduction of any amounts which can be relieved against the total profits of the period.

41. The reference to amounts which *can* be relieved allows for particular rules about deductions from total profits such as those that apply to the calculation of ring fence profits from oil activities.

42. The qualification in subsection (4) for subsection (2) takes into account non-standard provision for relief such as the relief under section 459(1)(b) of CTA 2009 for non-trading deficits from loan relationships. Under section 462, relief is given by way of set off against components of total profits, but only *after* certain reliefs listed in section 463(5) of CTA which operate against total profits.

43. In Schedule 1 there is an amendment to section 1219(1) of CTA 2009 which deals with relief for expenses of management. In section 1219(1), which is based on section 75(1) of ICTA, the reference is to the deduction being made in calculating total profits. The amended subsection refers to the deduction being made from total profits.

44. Under the new section 1219(1A), the deduction for management expenses is given priority over all other deductions made in the calculation of taxable total profits.The effect of the law is not changed by this amendment and the revised wording accords with both current interpretation and practice.

Chapter 4: Currency

Overview

45. This Chapter contains a basic rule about the currency in which companies calculate and express their income and chargeable gains (see section 5) followed by four special rules (sections 6 to 9) which apply in certain cases, and rules dealing with how to convert losses carried backwards or forwards. It is based on sections 92 to 92E of FA 1993.

46. References in this Chapter to a company's "functional currency" are to the currency that is most commonly used in the general economic and business environment in which the company operates – so for a company operating primarily in the UK the "functional currency" is sterling.

47. Schedule 2 contains rules that cover circumstances where a company elects that changes made by FA 2009 should only apply to accounting periods beginning on or after the date on which FA 2009 received Royal Assent, instead of on or after 29 December 2007.

Section 5: Basic rule: sterling to be used

48. This section states the basic rule for the preparation of company tax returns. It also provides signposts to the four special rules, which detail how a company is to comply with the basic rule in certain cases. It is based on section 92 of FA 1993.

Section 6: UK resident company operating in sterling and preparing accounts in another currency

49. This section sets out the first special rule. It is based on section 92A of FA 1993.

50. This special rule applies to a UK resident company that prepares its accounts in a currency other than sterling and whose functional currency is sterling (see *subsection (1)*), and which has prepared its accounts in accordance with GAAP.

51. When this special rule applies, profits or losses (adjusted to comply with corporation tax rules) must be calculated in sterling.

Section 7: UK resident company operating in currency other than sterling and preparing accounts in another currency

52. This section sets out the second special rule. It is based on section 92B of FA 1993.

53. This special rule applies to a UK resident company whose functional currency is not sterling (see *subsection (1)(b)* and *(c)*), that prepares its accounts in a currency that is different from its functional currency and which has prepared its accounts in accordance with GAAP. It is immaterial whether the currency used to prepare the accounts is sterling or another currency.

54. When this special rule applies, the company's profits or losses (adjusted to comply with corporation tax rules) must be calculated in the functional currency. The resulting amount of those profits or losses must then be translated from the functional currency into sterling (see *subsection (2)*).

*Section 8: **UK resident company preparing accounts in currency other than sterling***

55. This section sets out the third special rule. It is based on section 92C of FA 1993.

56. This special rule applies to a UK resident company whose accounts currency is not sterling, but which is not subject to the special rule in either section 6 or section 7. This rule applies, for example, if the company's functional currency is the same as the currency used to prepare the accounts.

57. When this special rule applies, profits or losses (adjusted to comply with corporation tax rules) must be translated from the accounts currency into sterling.

*Section 9: **Non-UK resident company preparing return of accounts in currency other than sterling***

58. This section sets out the fourth special rule. It is based on sections 92C and 92E of FA 1993.

59. This special rule applies to a non-UK resident company which trades in the United Kingdom through a permanent establishment, and which in the preparation of its return of accounts for the permanent establishment has prepared its accounts in a currency which is not sterling.

60. When this special rule applies, profits or losses (adjusted to comply with corporation tax rules) must be translated from the accounts currency into sterling.

*Section 10: **The equivalent in another currency of a sterling amount***

61. This section provides the method of determining the "appropriate exchange rate" to be used for conversion of sterling amounts into another currency where required by section 7, 8 or 9. It is based on sections 92B, 92C and 92E of FA 1993.

*Section 11: **Sterling equivalents: basic rule***

62. This section sets out the method for translating an amount from a non-sterling currency into sterling where required by section 7, 8 or 9. It is based on sections 92D and 92E of FA 1993.

63. This section is subject to special rules dealing with losses carried forwards or backwards.

*Section 12: **Sterling equivalents: carried-back amounts***

64. This section sets out how a loss is to be converted into sterling from another currency in order to establish the sterling amount of a carried-back loss. It is based on section 92DA of FA 1993.

Section 13: Sterling equivalents: carried-forward amounts

65. This section sets out how a loss is to be converted into sterling from another currency in order to establish the sterling value of a loss carried forward to a later period. It is based on section 92DB of FA 1993.

Section 14: Carried-back amounts

66. This section applies where a company accounts in sterling or identifies sterling as its functional currency, but carries back a loss to an accounting period where it computed its profits and losses for tax purposes in a currency other than sterling. It is based on section 92DC of FA 1993.

Section 15: Carried-forward amounts

67. This section applies where a company accounts in sterling or identifies sterling as its functional currency, but carries forward a loss to an accounting period where it computes its profits and losses for tax purposes in a currency other than sterling. It is based on section 92DD of FA 1993.

Section 16: Sections 13(2) and 15(5): profit against which carried-forward amount to be set

68. This section provides interpretation of what is meant by the profit in a later period against which a loss is to be set off. It is based on section 92DE(3) and (4) of FA 1993.

Section 17: Interpretation of Chapter

69. This section provides interpretation of a number of terms used in the Chapter. It is based on sections 92DE and 92E of FA 1993.

Part 3: Companies with small profits

Overview

70. The profits of a company are charged to tax at a lower rate than the main corporation tax rate if the profits of the company are within certain limits.

71. A lower rate is used if the company's profits (for a full year) are no more than the "lower limit". In making this comparison, there may be two adjustments.

72. First, some franked investment income is added to the profits of the company.

73. Second, the amount of the "lower limit" is split between companies that are under common control.

Section 18: Profits charged at the small profits rate

74. This section sets out the three conditions for the small profits rate to apply. It is based on section 13 of ICTA.

75. The first condition is that the company is resident in the United Kingdom*in* the accounting period. If a company becomes, or ceases to be, resident in the United Kingdom an accounting period ends (see the rules about accounting periods in section 10 of CTA 2009). So the effect of this condition is that the company must be resident in the United Kingdom*throughout* the accounting period.

76. Some non-resident companies trading in the United Kingdom through a permanent establishment may be entitled to the small profits rate as a result of a provision of a DTA.

77. The second condition is that the company is not a "close investment-holding company". That expression is defined in section 34.

78. The third condition is that the "augmented profits" (defined in section 32) of the company do not exceed the lower limit. If the profits fall between that limit and the upper limit, marginal relief may be due in accordance with section 19.

79. This section does not include a requirement that the company should make a claim for the relief. See *Change 1* in Annex 1.

*Section 19: **Marginal relief***

80. This section is the first of five that set out the rules for marginal relief. It is based on section 13 of ICTA.

81. Two conditions for the reliefare the same as the first two conditions for entitlement to the small profits rate (see the commentary on section 18). But for the purposes of this relief there are two further conditions. The "augmented profits" (defined in section 32) of the company need to fall between:

- the "lower limit" (in ICTA, the "lower relevant maximum amount"); and
- the "upper limit" (in ICTA, the "upper relevant maximum amount").

82. The limits are set out in section 24.

83. Finally, if this section is to apply, the company must have no ring fence profits.

84. This section does not include a requirement that the company should make a claim for the relief. See *Change 1* in Annex 1.

*Section 20: **Company with only ring fence profits***

85. This section is the second of five that set out the rules for marginal relief. It is based on section 13 of ICTA, section 3 of FA 2007 and section 7 of FA 2008.

86. Three conditions for the reliefare the same as those for entitlement to marginal relief (see the commentary on section 19). But for the purposes of this section the augmented profits must include only ring fence profits.

87. *Subsection (2)* applies the "ring fence fraction" instead of the standard fraction (see section 19(2)).

*Section 21: **Company with ring fence profits and other profits***

88. This section is the third of five that set out the rules for marginal relief. It is based on section 3 of FA 2007 and section 7 of FA 2008.

89. Three conditions for the reliefare the same as those for entitlement to marginal relief (see the commentary on section 19). But for the purposes of this section the augmented profits include both ring fence and other profits.

90. *Subsection (2)* gives a deduction in two parts: one relating to the ring fence amount (see section 22); the other relating to the remaining amount (see section 23).

*Section 22: **The ring fence amount***

91. This section is the fourth of five that set out the rules for marginal relief. It is based on section 3 of FA 2007 and section 7 of FA 2008.

92. The section calculates the marginal relief available on the ring fence amount. It uses the appropriate part ("UR") of the upper limit.

*Section 23: **The remaining amount***

93. This section is the fifth of five that set out the rules for marginal relief. It is based on section 3 of FA 2007 and section 7 of FA 2008.

94. The section calculates the marginal relief available on the remaining (non-ring fence) amount. It uses the appropriate part ("UZ") of the upper limit.

*Section 24: **The lower limit and the upper limit***

95. This section sets the limits for small profits rate and marginal relief. It is based on section 13 of ICTA.

96. *Subsection (2)* deals with the straightforward case where there are no associated companies.

97. *Subsection (3)* deals with the case where there are associated companies. The limits are divided equally between the companies.

98. *Subsection (4)* reduces the limits if the company's accounting period is less than 12 months long.

*Section 25: **Associated companies***

99. This section defines "associated company" for the purpose of section 24. It is based on section 13 of ICTA.

100. *Subsection (1)* sets out the position if a company is an associated company for any part of an accounting period. It counts as an associated company for the whole of the accounting period.

101. *Subsection (2)* clarifies the position if more than one company is an associated company for different parts of an accounting period.

Example

> Company A claims small profits rate for its accounting period from 1 January2009 to 31 December 2009.
>
> A is associated with B in the period 1 January 2009 to 31 March 2009.
>
> A is associated with C in the period 1 October 2009 to 31 December 2009.

A has two associated companies in its accounting period ending on 31 December2009, even though it never has more than one at any time.

102. *Subsection (3)* is the rule that associated companies that carry on no business are ignored. The rule is modified by subsection (6).

103. *Subsection (4)* is the main rule for determining whether or not companies are "associated", based on "control".The rule is modified by subsection (6).

104. *Subsection (5)* defines "control" for the purpose of subsection (4). The definition is based on section 450 but is modified by subsection (6).

105. *Subsection (6)* introduces the special rules for associated companies in the next five sections.

*Section 26: **Section 25(3): treatment of certain non-trading companies***

106. This section is the rule that passive non-trading companies are ignored as associated companies. It is new. See *Change 2* in Annex 1.

107. *Subsection (1)* sets out the three conditions for the treatment in the section. The first two conditions reproduce the main words of SP5/94. The third condition introduces the concept of a "passive company", defined in subsection (3).

108. *Subsection (2)* is the result if the conditions are met: the company is treated as being within section 25(3) and is ignored for the purposes of claims for small profits rate by any company with which it is associated.

109. *Subsection (3)* reproduces the conditions in SP5/94 for a company to qualify as a passive company.See *Change 2* in Annex 1 for a fuller discussion of the conditions.

110. *Subsection (4)* sets out the condition that any dividends received from subsidiaries are distributed in full by the holding company.

111. *Subsection (5)* makes clear that a company that receives, or is due to receive, a dividend is not treated on that ground alone as having assets.

*Section 27: **Attribution to persons of rights and powers of their partners***

112. This section modifies the rule in section 25(4) and (5) about "control". It is based on section 13(4), (4A), (4B) and (4C) of ICTA.

113. Section 451 attributes to a person rights that belong to any associate of that person. In accordance with section 448, "associate" includes a (business) partner.

114. This section relaxes the rule about attributing a partner's rights unless tax planning arrangements are in place.

*Section 28: **Associated companies: fixed-rate preference shares***

115. This section is the rule that some fixed-rate preference shares are ignored in determining whether one company controls another. It is new. See *Change 3* in Annex1.

116. *Subsection (1)* sets out the three conditions for the special treatment. The second condition includes a reference to the company which holds the shares taking part in the management or conduct of the issuing company's business. It is unlikely that a company (rather than an individual) would do this but the section retains this part of the condition for the relaxation to apply.

117. *Subsection (2)* sets out a definition of "fixed-rate preference shares". ESC C9 refers to the definition in Schedule 28B to ICTA, which deals with venture capital trusts. The definition here reproduces the rewritten version in section 313(7) of ITA.

*Section 29: **Association through a loan creditor***

118. This section is the rule that some loan creditors are ignored in determining whether one company controls another. It is new. See *Change 3* in Annex 1.

119. *Subsection (1)* deals with the simple case of a loan creditor which would otherwise be associated with the company to which it has lent money. The subsection sets out the three conditions that have to be met if the loan creditor is to be ignored. The second condition ("no connection") is amplified in subsection (5).

120. *Subsections (2)* and *(3)* deal with the more complex case of two companies which would otherwise be associated with each other because they are controlled by the same loan creditor. The condition in subsection (2)(b) is amplified in subsection(5).

121. *Subsection (4)* defines "control" for the purpose of subsection (2)(a). The definition is based on section 450 but is modified by subsection (1) of this section (to eliminate some loan creditors) and sections 27 (to prevent attribution of some partners' rights), 28 (to eliminate some fixed-rate preference shares) and 30 (to eliminate some trustee companies).

122. *Subsection (5)* sets out the condition in ESC C9 that there is "no past or present connection" between the company and the loan creditor. It reflects the strict interpretation that is used in practice in applying the concession.

123. *Subsection (6)* imports the definition of "loan creditor" from section 453. Section 453(4) prevents a bank from being treated as a loan creditor just because of an ordinary bank loan.

Section 30: ***Association through a trustee***

124. This section deals with some holdings by trustees. It is new. See *Change 3* in Annex 1.

125. *Subsections (1)* and *(2)* deal with the case of two companies which would otherwise be associated with each other because they are controlled by the same trustees. If the trustees controlling each companyare treated as different "distinct" persons by section 474(1) of ITA the companies are not controlled by the same person and this section does not apply.

126. If this section applies,the rights or powers of the trustees are to be ignored in determining whether the companies are associated with each other. This treatment applies only if there is no other connection between the companies (see subsection (1)(b)).

127. *Subsection (3)(b)* means that subsection (1)(b) restatesthe condition in ESC C9 that there is "no past or present connection" between the companies. It reflects the strict interpretation that is used in practice in applying the concession.

Section 31: ***Power to obtain information***

128. This section allows an officer of HMRC to require information for the purposes of this Part. It is based on Schedule 12 to FA 1989.

129. *Subsection (1)* is an information power about shareholders.

130. *Subsections (3) and (4)* are information powers about bearer securities.

Section 32: ***Meaning of "augmented profits"***

131. This section defines the augmented profits which are compared with the limits in sections 19 and 24 to determine whether or not small profits rate is due. It is based on section 13 of ICTA.

132. In section 13 of ICTA the word "profits" is used in a special sense to mean the total of what are usually referred to as profits and some franked investment income. This may lead to confusion. So this section uses "taxable total profits" (see section 4(2)) to mean the amount on which corporation tax is charged and introduces a new term "augmented profits" which is used only in this Part.

133. *Subsection (1)* is the basic definition of "augmented profits". In determining whether a company's profits are "small" for the purposes of this Part, dividends receivedare taken into account, even though those dividends are not charged to corporation tax.

134. *Subsection (2)* excludes what is usually known as "group income". This comprises:

- distributions from companies in the same group as the receiving company; and
- distributions from trading companies ("quasi-subsidiaries" – defined in subsection (3)) which are owned by a consortium of which the receiving company is a member.

135. The meanings of "trading company" and "relevant holding company" in subsection (2)(b) are set out in section 33(4).

Section 33: ***Interpretation of section 32(2) and (3)***

136. This section expands the meaning of "51% subsidiary". It is based on section 13ZA of ICTA.

137. *Subsection (1)* is similar to the group relief rule (see section 151). It ensures that the tax relationship between companies is not based simply on share-holding if the share-holding does not represent the true economic relationship. So the subsection looks also at the equity holders' entitlement to profits and assets. "Equity holders" are defined in subsection(7) by reference to the group relief rules (see Chapter 6 of Part 5 of this Act).

138. *Subsection (2)* makes clear that the basic test for being a 51% subsidiary in section 1154(2) of this Act still applies.

139. *Subsection (3)* is similar to the group relief rule (see section 151). Shares held by a share dealer are ignored.

140. *Subsection (4)* provides the meaning of "trading company" for the quasi-subsidiaries in section 32(2)(b).

141. *Subsections (5)* and *(6)* are similar to the group relief rule (see section 153). But subsection (5)(b) and (c) includes an economic test for the 5% ownership requirement in a consortium.

Section 34: ***Close investment-holding companies***

142. This section defines the close investment-holding companies which are excluded from small profits rate by sections 18(b) and 19(1)(b). It is based on sections 13A and 839(8) of ICTA.

143. The rule about close investment-holding companies is an anti-avoidance rule. Without it, a wealthy individual could transfer investments to a company where undistributed income would bear tax at a rate lower than the individual's marginal rate.

144. The section uses the expression "candidate company" to describe the company which is being considered to determine whether or not it is a close investment-holding company.

145. *Subsection (1)* defines close investment-holding companies by exclusion. All close companies are close investment-holding companies unless they exist for "permitted purposes".

146. *Subsection (2)* sets out the permitted purposes. The first two purposes (paragraphs (a) and (b)) are concerned with the activities (broadly, trades and property businesses) of the candidate company itself. The last four purposes (paragraphs (c) to (f)) allow a candidate company to qualify as having a permitted purpose by reference to "qualifying companies" (and some others) with which it is closely connected.

147. *Subsection (3)* excludes from the property businesses in subsection (2)(b) letting to individuals who have a close connection with the candidate company.

148. *Subsection (4)* extends the purpose in subsection (2)(c) so that it covers not only investment in a qualifying company but also investment in another company which itself invests in a qualifying company.

149. *Subsection (5)* ensures that a company which exists for a permitted purpose does not become a close investment-holding company simply because it is wound up. But this special treatment lasts for only one accounting period.

150. *Subsection (6)* defines "qualifying company" by reference to the same purposes of trades and property businesses as apply to the candidate company in subsection (2)(a) and (b).

151. *Subsection (7)* provides two definitions for the section. In this section some permitted purposes depend on control of the candidate company. ESC C9 would operate against taxpayer companies in this context and so does not apply. It follows that the relaxations in sections 28 to 30 do not apply here and the meaning of "control" is different from that in section 25(4).

Part 4: Loss relief

Overview

152. This Part contains rules relating to various reliefs available for losses.

153. The reliefs are set out in separate Chapters.

154. The source legislation dealt with the carry forward of trade losses (section 393 of ICTA) before set off against total profits of the same accounting period or carry back (section 393A of ICTA). In practice companies tend to prefer to set losses off against total profits or carry them back rather than carry them forward. The rewritten legislation reflects this practice by dealing first with the set-off against total profits and carry back, from section 37 onwards, and then turning to the carry forward of losses in section 45.

Chapter 1: Introduction

Section 35: Overview of Part

155. This section provides an overview of the Part. It is new.

156. *Subsection (3)* refers to section 47 of CTA 2009 which is reproduced here in order to avoid the need to cross-refer to that Act:

(1) "The same rules apply for corporation tax purposes in calculating losses of a trade as apply in calculating profits.

(2) This is subject to any express provision to the contrary.

Chapter 2: Trade losses

Overview

157. This Chapter deals with relief for trading losses.

Section 36: Introduction to Chapter

158. This section provides an overview of the Chapter and also includes provision about the meaning of references to "trade" and "carrying on a trade" . In particular it carries forward the effect of sections 6(4)(b) and 834(2) of ICTA in providing that a "trade" includes an office. It is based on sections 6(4), 393(10), 393A(9) and 834(2) of ICTA.

Section 37: Relief for trade losses against total profits

159. This section explains how a loss in a trade may be relieved against total profits of the same or earlier periods. It is based on sections 6(4), 393A(1), (2), (3), (10) and 834(2) of ICTA.

160. *Subsection (3)(b)* establishes that a loss in trade may be carried back to the twelve month period prior to the accounting period in which the loss arose. The exceptions to this rule, where the carry–back period is extended, are set out in sections 39 to 42. These exceptions affect companies either rarely or not at all.

161. *Subsection (4)* deals with the order of set-off of losses claimed under subsection(3). Such losses must first be set against total profits of the loss making period before, if the claim so requires, being carried back to earlier periods. Where it is possible to carry

a loss back for more than one period (see sections 39 to 42) then the loss must be set against total profits of the most recent period before the balance of the loss can be carried back to the period preceding that period and so on.

162. *Subsections (5) and (6)* prohibit the carry back of losses from what used to be Case V trades but what are now referred to as trades "carried on wholly outside the United Kingdom". The courts established that a Case V trade was one that was carried on wholly outside the United Kingdom.

163. Ogilvie v Kitton (Surveyor of Taxes) (1908), 5 TC 338,Court of Exchequer (Scotland) determined that where a trade is "carried on" depends not only on the location of the day-to-day transactions of the trade but also on where the management and control of the company takes place. In the case of a company where the directors are responsible for management and control and that management and control function is exercised in the United Kingdom it is very unlikely that the company has a trade "carried on wholly outside the United Kingdom".

164. There is, however, one situation where a company managed and controlled in the United Kingdom may have a trade carried on wholly outside the United Kingdom. That is where the company is a partner in a partnership and the business of the partnership is managed and controlled abroad. By using the words "carried on" in the section the link with existing case law has been maintained.

165. *Subsection (7)* sets out the time limits for making a claim. The time limit may be extended by an officer of Revenue and Customs. See *Change 5* in Annex 1.

166. *Subsection (9)* provides that relief is subject to restriction or modification in accordance with provisions of the Corporation Tax Acts. Examples of such restrictions or modifications are to be found in:

- the rest of the Chapter;
- Chapter 3 of this Part (relief for losses in cases involving limited partnerships and limited liability partnerships);
- Section 304(relief for losses in relation to oil activities);
- Section 944 (modified application of Chapter 2 of Part 4 in relation to transfers of trade without a change in ownership); and
- Chapter 3 of Part 22 (relief for losses if company is a member of a partnership and certain arrangements for transferring relief are in place).

167. Subsection (2D) of section 393A has not been rewritten. The subsection was a signpost to section 393B where certain provisions relating to losses arising in a ring fence trade applied. The structure of the rewritten section makes such a signpost unnecessary.

168. Subsections (7), (7A) and (8) of section 393A have not been rewritten. These subsections dealt with excess trade charges. It is no longer possible for trade charges to arise and these subsections were therefore redundant.

169. The definition of charges in section 338A of ICTA was limited to qualifying donations to charity. To be added to trade losses (section 393(9) of ICTA) the charges must have beenpayments made wholly and exclusively for the purposes of the trade. Section 338A(3) stipulated that no payment that was deductible in computing profits should be treated as a charge. If a payment was made wholly and exclusively for the purposes of the trade it would be allowable as a deduction in computing profits. Hence, it could not be a charge.

Section 38: Limit on deduction if accounting period falls partly within 12 month period

170. Where a loss is being relieved against the profits of an earlier accounting period this section limits the relief available if that period falls partly within the twelve month period prior to the loss-making period. It is based on section 393A(2) of ICTA.

171. The effect of this section can be illustrated as follows:

Example

Accounting period 3	12m	01/01/11 to 31/12/11	Loss in trade	£24,000
Accounting period 2	8m	01/05/10 to 31/12/10	Total profits	£12,000
Accounting period 1	12m	01/05/09 to 30/04/10	Total profits	£15,000

The twelve month period prior to the loss making period is 01/01/10 to 31/12/10. Accounting period 2 falls wholly within this period and the loss in trade is sufficient to cover all of the total profits of this period. £12,000 of the loss in trade remains to be relieved. The proportion of Accounting period 1 that falls within the relevant twelve month period is 4/12. 4/12 of the total profits of Accounting period 1 is £5,000. Accordingly the amount to be deducted under section 37(3) cannot exceed £5,000. This means that £7,000 of the loss in trade arising in Accounting period 3 cannot be relieved under section 37.

Section 39: Terminal losses: extension of periods for which relief may be given

172. This section extends the length of the period referred to in section 37(3)(b) when a company ceases to trade and makes a terminal loss. It is based on section 393A(2A) and (2B) of ICTA.

173. The entitlement to make a claim remains an entitlement under section 37. If a loss has already been fully utilised under that section there is no possibility of relieving that loss again by virtue of the fact that it is a terminal loss within section 39.

Section 40: Ring fence trades: extension of periods for which relief may be given

174. This section extends the length of the period referred to in section 37(3)(b) when a company makes a loss in a ring fence trade and certain conditions are met. It is based on section 393A(2A), (2C) and (12) of ICTA.

175. The definition of a "ring fence trade" is to be found in section 162 of CAA. Broadly, such a trade is one concerned with oil extraction activities.

176. *Subsection (1)(b)* provides that in the loss-making period the company must have received an allowance under section 164 of CAA. Such an allowance is given in relation to expenditure incurred on the decommissioning of plant or machinery used in a ring fence trade.

Section 41: Sections 39 and 40: transfers of trade to obtain relief

177. This section prevents the transfer of terminal losses in certain circumstances. It is an anti-avoidance provision. It is based on section 393A(2E) of ICTA.

Section 42: Ring fence trades: further extension of period for relief

178. This section extends the period of relief for ring fence trades in certain circumstances. It is based on section 393B of ICTA.

179. For the section to apply a claim must have been made under section 39 (terminal losses: extension of periods for which relief may be given) or section 40 (ring fence trades:

extension of periods for which relief may be given). The normal relief period is therefore already extended from twelve months to three years.

180. If there are insufficient profits in the three year relief period this section allows the unrelieved loss to be carried back to earlier periods.

181. The intention is to provide relief for losses arising as a consequence of incurring expenditure on decommissioning costs.

182. If decommissioning expenditure is incurred and a loss arises after the ring fence trade has ceased then no claim to relief would at first sight appear to be possible. A claim under section 39 would fail as the loss did not arise in an accounting period that commenced in the final twelve months of a company's trade. A claim under section 40 would fail as the loss did not arise in a ring fence trade (that trade having ceased). But that analysis of section 39 overlooks section 165 of CAA. This treats post-cessation decommissioning expenditure as having been incurred in the chargeable period in which the trader ceased to carry on the trade. As a result a claim under section 39 (terminal losses: extension of periods for which relief may be given) is possible.

*Section 43: **Claim period in case of ring fence or mineral extraction trades***

183. This section extends the time limit for making claims under section 37 where the company has carried on a ring fence trade or a mineral extraction trade and certain conditions are met. It is based on section 393A(11) to (12) of ICTA.

*Section 44: **Trade must be commercial or carried on for statutory functions***

184. This section denies relief in relation to losses arising from trades which are not commercial. It is based on section 393A(3) and (4) of ICTA.

185. *Subsection (1)* refers to the making of a profit in the trade. "Profit" in this instance, as the context suggests, has its ordinary commercial meaning.

186. *Subsection (2)* provides for the case where the trade is carried on as part of a larger undertaking. In such a case the larger undertaking (that is, the undertaking as a whole) may be carried on with a view to the realisation of profits even if the trade itself is not.

187. In *subsection (4)*the reference to an Act includes Acts of the Scottish Parliament. See *Change 6* in Annex 1.

*Section 45: **Carry forward of trade loss against subsequent trade profits***

188. This section provides for trade losses which have not been relieved in accordance with section 37 to be carried forward and relieved against future trade profits. It is based on section 393 of ICTA.

189. *Subsection (6)* provides that relief is subject to restriction or modification in accordance with provisions of the Corporation Tax Acts. Examples of such restrictions or modifications are to be found in:

- the rest of the Chapter;
- Chapter 7 of this Part (write-off of government investment in a company); and
- Chapter 3 of Part 22 (relief for losses if company is a member of a partnership and certain arrangements for transferring relief are in place).

190. Subsection (9) of section 393 has not been rewritten. The subsection dealt with excess trade charges. It is no longer possible for trade charges to arise and this subsection is therefore redundant.

191. The definition of charges in section 338A of ICTA was limited to qualifying donations to charity. To be added to trade losses (section 393(9) of ICTA) the charges must

have beenpayments made wholly and exclusively for the purposes of the trade. Section 338A(3) stipulated that no payment that was deductible in computing profits should be treated as a charge. If a payment was made wholly and exclusively for the purposes of the trade it would be allowable as a deduction in computing profits. Hence, it could not be a charge.

*Section 46: **Use of trade-related interest and dividends if insufficient trade profits***

192. This section provides that certain interest and dividends are treated as trade profits if the profits are otherwise insufficient to use some or all of a carry-forward trade loss. It is based on section 393(8) of ICTA.

193. It is only interest and dividends that would otherwise be treated as receipts of the trade that can attract this treatment.

*Section 47: **Registered industrial and provident societies***

194. This section extends the scope of section 45 for registered industrial and provident societies. It is based on ESCC5.

195. The classes of income to which the section applies differ slightly from those in the concession. See *Change 7*in Annex 1.

*Section 48: **Farming or market gardening***

196. This section restricts, in certain cases, loss relief in respect of losses arising from a trade of farming or market gardening. It is based on section 397(2) to (8) of ICTA.

197. It is the first of a group of sections (sections 48 to 51) which deal with the potential restriction of losses where the losses arise in respect of a trade of farming or market gardening. It establishes the basic rule. None of these sections applies to trades other than farming or market gardening.

198. *Subsection (2)* sets out the circumstances in which loss relief is restricted. Broadly, this happens once losses have arisen for six successive years.

199. *Subsection (3)* sets out the exceptions to the restriction. Subsection (3)(b) provides that if the trade meets the "reasonable expectation of profit" test then the loss restriction does not apply.

200. Definitions of the terms "farming" and "market gardening" are to be found in section 1125.

*Section 49: **Reasonable expectation of profit***

201. This section sets out the "reasonable expectation of profit" test which, if met, enables relief to be given that would otherwise be restricted under section 48. It is based on section 397(3) and (5) of ICTA.

202. "Profit" in section 49 refers to profit in its ordinary commercial sense.

*Section 50: **Cessation of trades***

203. This section sets out the circumstances under which a trade is treated as having ceased. This is necessary in order to determine the length of the period during which losses have arisen in that trade for the purposes of section 48. It is based on section 397(8), (9) and (10) of ICTA.

204. *Subsection (4)* sets out the rules for determining whether certain individuals or companies are to be treated as the same person for the purposes of determining if *subsection (1)* applies.

Section 51: Companies treated as same person as individual

205. This section explains how to calculate losses for the purposes of section 48 where a trade has been transferred from an individual to a company but that individual and that company are treated as the same person by virtue of section 50. It is based on section 397(10) of ICTA.

206. *Subsection (4)* adapts rules in section 70 of ITA and section 203 of ITTOIA to deal with cases where profits or losses have not actually been calculated by reference to tax years. In such cases, the calculation of profits or losses for tax years is an arithmetical exercise, involving apportioning (on a time basis) the profits or losses of periods falling partly within the tax year, and combining these with the profits or losses of any periods falling completely within the tax year.

Section 52: Dealings in commodity futures

207. This section denies relief where losses have been made in a trade of dealing in commodity futures and certain other conditions are met. It is an anti-avoidance provision. It is based on section 399(2), (3) and (5) of ICTA.

208. *Subsection (5)* refers to a "recognised futures exchange" as defined in section 288(6) of TCGA. That subsection is reproduced here to avoid the need to cross-refer to that Act.

"(6) In this Act "recognised futures exchange" means the London International Financial Futures Exchange and any other futures exchange which is for the time being designated for the purposes of this Act by order made by the Board.

Section 53: Leasing contracts and company reconstructions

209. This section restricts relief in respect of certain leasing arrangements. It is anti-avoidance legislation. It is based on section 395 of ICTA.

Section 54: Non-UK resident company: receipts of interest, dividends or royalties

210. This section prohibits the deduction of losses under section 37 or45 or under section 436A of ICTA to the extent that such losses arise to a non-UK resident company as a result of excluding certain kinds of tax exempt income from the company's profits. It is based on section 808 of ICTA.

211. The source legislation was in Part 18 of ICTA (double taxation relief). The rewritten section is with other sections which restrict or otherwise affect the use of losses.

212. A non-UK resident company may utilise any losses that arise under section 37 or 45 provided that those losses are calculated on the basis that receipts of tax-exempt interest, dividends or royalties are included in the company's profits.

Chapter 3: Limited partners and members of limited liability partnerships

Section 55: Introduction to Chapter

213. This section provides an overview of the Chapter. It is new.

214. The Chapter applies to companies that are either limited partners or member of limited liability partnerships. It limits the amount of relief that may be given under section 37(other than against profits of the trade) or in respect of group relief. Carry-forward losses under section 45 are not affected.

215. Broadly, relief given must not exceed the amount that the company stands to lose commercially.

216. The source legislation expressed the amount that a partner stands to lose commercially by reference to the partner's contribution to the *trade* that a partnership carries on (the "contribution to the trade"). But, in such cases, the amount that a partner stands to lose commercially is more likely to be reflected in the partner's contribution to the *partnership* that carries on the trade.

217. So this Chapter makes a change by expressing the amount that a partner stands to lose commercially in terms of the partner's contribution to the partnership (the "contribution to the firm"). The change to "contribution to the firm" requires that the possibility of there being partnerships with more than one trade is addressed; and, for consistency with other partnerships, the possibility of a limited liability partnership carrying on more than one trade is also addressed.

218. This change also makes a number of clarifications as to what is included in a partner's contribution. See *Change 8* in Annex 1.

Section 56: Restriction on reliefs for limited partners

219. This section restricts certain reliefs available to a company that is a limited partner to the amount of the company's contribution to the firm. It is based on section 118 of ICTA.

220. *Subsection (3)* refers to a "contribution to the firm" whereas the source legislation refers to a "contribution to the trade". See *Change 8* in Annex 1.

221. *Subsection (6)* sets out how to apply *subsection (4)* and so limit relief if the firm is carrying on more than one trade. See *Change 8* in Annex 1.

Section 57: Meaning of "contribution to the firm"

222. This section defines "contribution to the firm" for the purposes of section 56. It is based on section 118(3) of ICTA.

223. The subsections set out the steps necessary to calculate the "contribution to the firm". The source legislation refers to a "contribution to the trade". This change and some points of clarification are covered in the change note. See *Change 8* in Annex 1.

224. *Subsection (5)* explains how amounts that have been drawn out or received back by the company but have been taxed as profits of a trade are to be excluded from the calculation. See *Change 9* in Annex 1.

Section 58: Meaning of "limited partner"

225. This section defines "limited partner" for the purposes of sections 56 and 57. It is based on section 118(2) of ICTA.

226. A limited partner of a limited partnership registered under the Limited Partnership Act 1907 is someone who is not entitled to take part in the management of the firm's business and is not liable for the debts or obligations of the firm beyond a certain limit. A limited partner of any other firm is someone who is similarly not entitled to take part in management and not liable for debts or obligations in accordance with the rules applying to the firm in question.

227. *Subsection (4)* is introduced as part of drafting in terms of a company's "contribution to the firm" in place of "contribution to the trade". See *Change 8* in Annex 1.

Section 59: Restriction on relief for members of LLPs

228. This section restricts certain reliefs available to a company that is a member of a limited liability partnership (LLP) to the amount of the company's contribution to the LLP. It is based on sections 118 and 118ZB of ICTA.

229. *Subsection (6)* sets out how to apply *subsection (4)* and so limit relief if the firm is carrying on more than one trade. See *Change 8* in Annex 1.

Section 60: Meaning of "contribution to the LLP"

230. This section defines "contribution to the LLP" for the purposes of section 59. It is based on sections 118ZB and 118ZC of ICTA.

231. An LLP formed under the Limited Liability Partnership Act 2000 is an entity with separate legal personality. That Act defines what is meant by contribution to a limited liability partnership.

232. *Subsection (3)* makes explicit the fact that capitalised undrawn profits are to be included in a company's contribution. See *Change 8* in Annex 1.

233. *Subsection (6)* explains how amounts that have been drawn out or received back by the company but have been taxed as profits of a trade are to be excluded from the calculation. See *Change 9* in Annex 1.

Section 61: Unrelieved losses brought forward

234. This section provides that relief may be given in a later accounting period for losses restricted in accordance with section 59, if certain conditions are met. It is based on section 118ZD of ICTA.

Chapter 4: Property losses

Overview

235. This Chapter deals with property business losses both from UK property businesses and from overseas property businesses.

Section 62: Relief for losses made in UK property business

236. This section provides relief for losses arising from a UK property business. It is based on sections 6(4), 392A and 834(2) of ICTA.

237. "UK property business" is defined in section 205 of CTA 2009. This definition is reproduced here in order to avoid the need to cross-refer:

> "A company's UK property business consists of—
> (a) every business which the company carries on for generating income from land in the United Kingdom, and
> (b) every transaction which the company enters into for that purpose otherwise than in the course of such a business.

238. *Subsections (4) and (5)* provide that any unused losses are to be carried forward and treated as UK property business losses of later periods. In other words such unused losses may be set against total profits of later periods.

239. *Subsection (6)* provides that relief is subject to restriction or modification in accordance with provisions of the Corporation Tax Acts. Examples of such restrictions or modifications are to be found in:

- Sections 56 (restriction on relief for limited partners), 57 (meaning of "contribution to the firm") and 58 (meaning of "limited partner");
- Chapter 7 of this Part (write off of government investment in a company).

Section 63: Company with investment business ceasing to carry on UK property business

240. This section provides a relaxation of the loss carry-forward rules where a company ceases to carry on a UK property business but continues to carry on an investment business. It is based on section 392A(3) of ICTA.

241. A company with investment business is defined in section 1218 of CTA 2009. This definition is reproduced here to avoid the need to cross-refer:

"""company with investment business" means a company whose business consists wholly or partly of making investments.

242. *Subsection (3)* refers to an unrelieved UK property business loss being carried forward to periods beyond the accounting period subsequent to that in which the UK property business ceased. Once the loss has been carried forward to the accounting period following the cessation period it loses its character as an unrelieved loss and becomes an expense of management. Hence there is no difficulty in carrying the amount forward to later accounting periods providing the investment business continues.

Section 64: UK property business to be commercial or carried on for statutory functions

243. This section provides that sections 62 and 63 only apply when a UK property business is carried on on a commercial basis or in the exercise of functions conferred by or under an Act. It is based on section 392A(5) to (7) of ICTA.

244. The reference to an Act in *subsection (1)* includes an Act of the Scottish Parliament. See *Change 6* in Annex 1.

245. The reference to "profit" in *subsection (2)* is to profit in its ordinary commercial sense.

Section 65: UK furnished holiday lettings business treated as trade

246. This section provides that a UK furnished holiday lettings (UKFHL) business is treated as a trade for loss relief purposes. It is based on section 503 of ICTA.

247. If a company carries on a UKFHL business and is a member of a partnership that also carries on a UKFHL business then the two businesses must be accounted for separately as section 1270(2) of CTA 2009 provides that the firm's UK property business cannot include business or transactions undertaken by the firm's individual partners.

Section 66: Relief for losses made in overseas property business

248. This section sets out the rules for relieving losses made in an overseas property business. It is based on section 392B of ICTA.

249. "Overseas property business" is defined in section 206 of CTA 2009. This definition is reproduced in order to avoid the need to cross-refer:

"(a) every business which the company carries on for generating income from land outside the United Kingdom, and

(b) every transaction which the company enters into for that purpose otherwise than in the course of such a business.

250. *Subsection (3)* provides that a loss from an overseas property business may be carried forward and set against future profits of that business. Such profits do not include chargeable gains.

251. *Subsection (6)* provides that relief is subject to restriction or modification in accordance with provisions of the Corporation Tax Acts. Examples of such restrictions or modifications are to be found in:

- Section 60 (meaning of "contribution to the LLP"); and
- Chapter 7 of this Part (write off of government investment in a company).

Section 67: Overseas property business to be commercial or carried on for statutory functions

252. This section provides that section 66 only applies when an overseas property business is carried on on a commercial basis or in the exercise of functions conferred by or under an Act. It is based on sections 392A(5) to (7) and 392B(2) of ICTA.

253. The reference to an Act in *subsection (1)* includes an Act of the Scottish Parliament. See *Change 6* in Annex 1.

254. Subsection (1) also refers to functions conferred by the law of a territory outside the United Kingdom. See *Change 10* in Annex 1.

255. The reference to "profit" in *subsection (2)* is to profit in its ordinary commercial sense.

Chapter 5: Losses on disposal of shares

Overview

256. This Chapter provides that, if an investment company incurs an allowable loss for the purposes of corporation tax on chargeable gains on the disposal of ordinary shares in a qualifying trading company for which it has subscribed, it may claim to set off the loss against its income for corporation tax purposes. It is based on Chapter 5A of Part 13 of ICTA.

Section 68: Share loss relief

257. This section introduces share loss relief. It is based on sections 573(1) and 575(1) and (3) of ICTA.

258. *Subsection (1)* outlines the basic structure of the relief, namely that a company ("the investor company") is eligible for share loss relief if the following conditions are met:

- the investor company has "subscribed for" shares in another company ("the investee company") (see the commentary on section 73),
- the investee company is a "qualifying trading company" (see the commentary on section 78),
- the investor company incurs an allowable loss for the purposes of corporation tax on chargeable gains on the disposal, and
- the investor company meets the eligibility conditions (see the commentary on section 69).

259. *Subsection (2)* provides that relief is only available if the disposal is of one of the kinds specified in paragraphs (a) to (d).

260. Subsection (2)(a) is based on section 575(1)(a) of ICTA which specifies as one of the kinds of disposal:

"a disposal by way of a bargain made at arm's length for full consideration.

261. The words "for full consideration" have been omitted from subsection (2)(a) on the basis that they add nothing. See *Change 11* in Annex 1.

Section 69: *Eligibility conditions*

262. This section sets out the conditions in relation to the investor company which must be met in order for the investor company to be eligible for share loss relief. It is based on section 573(1) and (5) of ICTA.

263. This section provides that the investor company must be an investment company (as defined in section 90) on the date of the disposal and for a continuous period ending on that date and must not be associated with the investee company or any member of its group.

Section 70: *Entitlement to claim*

264. This section deals with the making of a claim for share loss relief. It is based on section 573(2) and (3) of ICTA.

265. Share loss relief is obtained by way of a deduction in calculating the investor company's income for corporation tax purposes.

266. *Subsection (3)* makes clear that the words "if the company was then an investment company"in section 573(2)(b) of ICTA require that the company is an investment company throughout the relevant accounting period.

Section 71: *How relief works*

267. This section explains how the loss is to be deducted from income. It is based on section 573(2), (3) and (4A) of ICTA.

268. Section 573(4) of ICTA provides that share loss relief must be claimed before any deduction for "charges on income, expenses of management or other amounts which can be deducted from or set against or treated as reducing profits of any description".It has not been rewritten in this Chapter, but instead the order of priority is achieved in CTA 2009 and this Act in the following way.

269. Because share loss relief operates against the company's income (see *subsection (1)*), it falls to be deducted at Step 1 in section 4(3), i.e. on the way to finding the amount of the company's total profits. Charges on income, rewritten as charitable donations relief in Part 6, and expenses of management are to be deducted from the company's total profits at Step 2 in section 4(2). See section 189(1) of this Act and section 1219(1) of CTA 2009 (as amended by Schedule 1 to this Act). For another example of a deduction from total profits, seesection 37(3) (relief for trade losses against total profits).

270. This section provides that the amount not deducted from income of the accounting period in which the loss is incurred may be deducted from the income of earlier accounting periods ending within the immediately preceding period of 12 months (see Step 2 in subsection (1)). The extent to which a deduction may be made at Step 2 from an accounting period which falls only partly within that period of 12 months is limited in accordance with section 72.

271. *Subsection (6)* is new. It has been included to make explicit that the balance of any allowable loss for which share loss relief is not obtained continues to be capable of being claimed as a deduction under TCGA.

Section 72: *Limit on deduction if accounting period falls partly within 12 month period*

272. This section applies where an accounting period ends within 12 months before the accounting period in which the loss is incurred but begins before the beginning of that 12 month period. It is based on section 573(3) of ICTA.

273. This section ensures that a deduction can only be made at Step 2 in section 71(1) from that part of the income of the accounting period that is proportionate to the part of the accounting period falling within the 12 month period.

Section 73: ***Subscription for shares***

274. This section sets out the requirements relating to the subscription for shares in a qualifying trading company. It is based on sections 573(6) and 576K(3) of ICTA and includes a new provision relating to bonus shares.

275. *Subsection (2)* provides that shares are subscribed for by the investor company if they have been issued to the investor company in consideration of money or money's worth.

276. The shares must form part of the ordinary share capital of the investee company. See the definition of "shares" in section 90 and the commentary on that section.

277. *Subsection (3)* is new and treats "corresponding bonus shares" issued in respect of shares which have been subscribed for as themselves having been subscribed for. See *Change 12* in Annex 1.

278. *Subsection (4)* is new and provides that corresponding bonus shares are treated as subscribed for at the same time as the original shares were subscribed for. See *Change 12* in Annex 1.

Section 74: ***Disposals of new shares***

279. This section denies or restricts share loss relief on the disposal of shares which are identified by virtue of section 127 of TCGA with other shares previously held by the investor company, unless certain conditions are met. It is based on section 575(2) and (4) of ICTA.

280. The reference to section 87(3) at the end of *subsection (2)* makes clear that this section does not apply to an exchange of shares to which section 87(1) applies. See the commentary on section 87 and *Change 19* in Annex 1.

Section 75: ***Limits on relief***

281. This section deals with the calculation of the amount of share loss relief. It is based on section 576(1) of ICTA.

282. Section 576(1) of ICTA provides that, if the investor company disposes of shares for which it has subscribed and which form part of a holding, the share loss relief in relation to those shares is not to exceed the sums which would have been allowable as deductions in computing the allowable loss for the purposes of corporation tax on chargeable gains if the shares had not formed part of the holding.

283. Section 75 refines the circumstances in which the provision applies in connection with the changes in section 76 described in *Change 16* in Annex 1. See *Change 13* in Annex 1.

284. *Subsection (8)* explains what is meant by shares "that are not capable of being qualifying shares" for the purposes not only of this section but also of section 76. *Change 14* in Annex 1 contains a detailed explanation of why a mixed holding is defined for the purposes of section 76 in terms of a holding which includes such shares.

285. *Subsection (9)* extends this meaning for the purposes only of *subsection (5)* to cover reorganisations involving the issue of shares of a different class.

Section 76: ***Disposal of shares forming part of mixed holding***

286. This section deals with the identification of shares disposed of where those shares form part of a "mixed holding". It is based on section 576 of ICTA, with a number of changes.

287. Section 576 of ICTA is concerned with a holding which comprises shares for which a person has subscribed and shares which the person has acquired otherwise than by subscription.

288. *Subsection (1)* provides that this section applies to a holding in which some only of the shares are shares "that are not capable of being qualifying shares" (as defined in section 75(8)). See *Change 14*in Annex 1 which contains a detailed explanation of why a mixed holding has been defined in terms of a holding which includes such shares.

289. *Subsection (2)* provides that the section applies for the purpose of determining the questions:

- whether the shares disposed of are qualifying shares (as defined in section 75); and
- which of any qualifying shares acquired at different times are disposed of.

290. This is a change from section 576(1) of ICTA, which is not expressed to apply for the purpose of determining which of any qualifying shares are disposed of. See *Change 15*in Annex 1.

291. *Subsection (3)* introduces the rules for determining the questions in subsection (2), including in *subsection (4)* the application of the identification rules in sections 105 and 107 of TCGA. See *Change 16*in Annex 1.

292. *Subsection (7)* is new and puts on a statutory basis the practice under which questions which cannot be determined by the specific provisions of this section are to be determined on a just and reasonable basis. This subsection is principally required in cases where qualifying shares and shares which are not qualifying shares were acquired, or are treated as having been acquired, on the same day. See *Change 16*in Annex 1.

293. *Subsection (8)* (defining "holding") omitssection 576(1D)(b) of ICTA, which applies subsection (4) of section 104 of TCGA. That subsection can apply only to employees and is, therefore, otiose in relation to an investment company.

Section 77: ***Section 76: supplementary***

294. This section supplements section 76. It is new.

295. *Subsection (1)* determines the time of acquisition for the purposes of section 76 of shares issued in a reorganisation within the meaning of section 126 of TCGA to which section 127 of that Act applies. See *Change 17*in Annex 1.

296. *Subsection (2)* clarifies that shares held or disposed of by a nominee or bare trustee for a company are part of the company's holding for the purposes of section 76. See *Change 18*in Annex 1.

Section 78: ***Qualifying trading companies***

297. This section defines what is a qualifying trading company and introduces sections 79 to 85, which set out six specific requirements to be met by a company if it is to be a qualifying trading company. It is based on section 576A of ICTA.

298. Four of the requirements are to be met on the date of the disposal or, subject to certain conditions, at a time which is not more than three years before that date (see *subsection (2)*) and for a continuous period ending on that date or, subject to those conditions, at that time (see *subsection (3)*).

299. Two of the requirements are to be met only at or around the time of issue of the shares in respect of which the share loss relief is claimed (see *subsection (4)*).

Section 79: The trading requirement

300. This section sets out the first of the four requirements to be met throughout the period mentioned in section 78(3). It is based on section 576B of ICTA.

Section 80: Ceasing to meet trading requirement because of administration etc

301. This section supplements section 79 and deals with the consequences for the trading requirement of administration, receivership or winding up. It is based on section 576C of ICTA.

Section 81: The control and independence requirement

302. This section sets out the second of the four requirements to be met throughout the period mentioned in section 78(3). It is based on section 576D of ICTA.

303. Section 576D(3A) of ICTA, which applies section 839 of ICTA (connected persons) for the purposes of that section, has not been rewritten. Section 839 of ICTA is rewritten in section 1122 for the purposes of the Corporation Tax Acts and section 1176(1) applies that definition generally for the purposes of this Act.

Section 82: The qualifying subsidiaries requirement

304. This section sets out the third of the four requirements to be met throughout the period mentioned in section 78(3). It is based on section 576E of ICTA.

Section 83: The property managing subsidiaries requirement

305. This section sets out the last of the four requirements to be met throughout the period mentioned in section 78(3). It is based on section 576F of ICTA.

Section 84: The gross assets requirement

306. This section sets out the requirement to be met only at the times mentioned in section 78(4)(a). It is based on section 576G of ICTA.

Section 85: The unquoted status requirement

307. This section sets out the requirement to be met only at the time mentioned in section 78(4)(b). It is based on section 576H of ICTA.

Section 86: Power to amend requirements by Treasury order

308. This section enables the requirements in sections 79 to 85 to be amended by secondary legislation. It is based on section 576I of ICTA.

Section 87: Relief after an exchange of shares for shares in another company

309. This section and section 88 provide for continuity of the application of the requirements in sections 79 to 85 in the case of certain reconstructions which result in the issue of shares in a new company in exchange for shares in another company but do not involve any change in ownership of the underlying business. This section is based on section 576J of ICTA.

310. *Subsection (3)(a)* is new and resolves the apparent conflict between section 74 and this section. See *Change 19* in Annex 1.

Section 88: Substitution of new shares for old shares

311. This section sets out the consequences for the application of the requirements in sections 79 to 85 of an exchange to which section 87 applies. It is based on section 576K of ICTA.

312. The words "in relation to any subsequent disposal or other event" in section 304A(4) of ICTA on which section 576K(2) of ICTA is based were inadvertently omitted from section 576K(2) by ITA. They have been included in *subsection (2)* in conformity with section 146(2) of ITA, also based on section 304A(4) of ICTA.

*Section 89: **Deemed time of issue for certain shares***

313. This section determines the time of issue of corresponding bonus shares for the purposes of the provisions listed in *subsection (1)*. It is new.

314. *Subsection (2)* mirrors section 73(4). See *Change 20*in Annex 1.

*Section 90: **Interpretation of Chapter***

315. This section explains the meaning of expressions used in this Chapter. It is based on sections 130 and 576L of ICTA.

316. *Subsection (1)* includes the definition of "corresponding bonus shares". *Subsection (2)* amplifies that definition. See *Change 12* in Annex 1.

317. The definition of "investment company" is set out in full in subsection (1) rather than by cross–referring to and modifying the definition in section 130 of ICTA. References to savings banks and banks for savings have been omitted. See *Change 21*in Annex 1.

318. *Subsection (7)* is new and clarifies that the date of disposal is the time when the disposal is made or treated as made for the purposes of corporation tax on chargeable gains. See *Change 22*in Annex 1.

*Chapter 6: **Losses from miscellaneous transactions***

Overview

319. This Chapter deals with loss relief in respect of miscellaneous transactions.

*Section 91: **Relief for losses from miscellaneous transactions***

320. This section provides relief for losses arising from transactions that, had they resulted in gains, would have been treated as miscellaneous income. It is based on section 396 of ICTA.

321. *Subsections (4), (5) and (6)* ensure that such losses may only be relieved against miscellaneous income.

*Chapter 7: **Write–off of government investment***

Overview

322. This Chapter restricts losses where there has been a write-off of an amount of government investment in a company.

*Section 92: **Loss relief to be reduced if government investment is written off***

323. This section provides that if an amount of government investment in a company is written off that company's carry-forward losses are restricted by the amount written off. It is based on section 400(1) and (10) of ICTA.

*Section 93: **Groups of companies***

324. This section sets out the further rules that apply if section 92 applies and the company is a member of a group of companies. It is based on section 400(5) and (10) of ICTA.

325. In these circumstances *subsection (2)* provides that the restriction may be to the carry-forward losses of any of the group companies provided that the restriction is on a just and reasonable basis. For example, if the government investment had been in a holding company and that company had lent the money to a subsidiary then it would be appropriate to restrict the carry-forward losses of the subsidiary.

Section 94: Cases in which government investment is written off

326. This section sets out the three circumstances which constitute a write-off of government investment. It is based on section 400(7), (8), (9) and (10) of ICTA.

Section 95: Meaning of "carry-forward losses"

327. This section defines the five types of "carry-forward losses". It is based on section 400(2) to (4) of ICTA.

328. *Subsection (2)* provides that certain amounts are not to be included in the calculation of "carry-forward losses". The effect of this is to limit the reduction of loss relief provided for by section 92.

329. *Subsection (4)* sets out the order in which losses are to be set off against the various "carry-forward losses" set out at subsection (1).

Section 96: Interaction with other tax provisions

330. This section ensures that a company is not prevented from deducting an amount in calculating its profits of a trade simply because an amount of government investment in the company has been written off. It is based on section 400(6) and (9A) of ICTA.

Part 5: Group relief

Overview

331. This Part sets out the rules for group relief.

332. In the diagrams to the right of the text of this commentary, surrendering companies are shown in black; claimant companies are shown in white; and other companies are shown in grey.

Groups

333. The basic idea of group relief is to allow an enterprise to be taxed as a single unit even if it is carried on by more than one company. So, in the simplest case, a loss made by a parent company (P) may be set off against the profits of a wholly-owned subsidiary (S). Similarly, a loss made by the subsidiary may be set off against the parent's profits.

334. If one company is to surrender its losses to another, the two companies must be in the same group. In the case of a simple parent/subsidiary relationship, the definition in section 152 specifies that one company must be a "75% subsidiary" of the other.

335. In a less simple case, more than two companies may be involved. The group comprises all the companies that are 75% subsidiaries of a parent company, and the parent itself. For this purpose Chapter 3 of Part 24 of this Act makes clear that the necessary degree of ownership may be indirect. So, for instance, if P owns 75% of the shares in S and S owns all the shares in T, T is a 75% subsidiary of P and all three companies are members of a group.

Consortiums

336. If the shares in a single company (C) are held by other companies (M1, M2 etc), C may be a "company owned by a consortium". In that case, losses of C may be set off against the profits of M1, M2 etc. And the losses of M1, M2 etc may be set off against the profits of C.

337. If C is also a member of a group (with its subsidiary S) it may be possible for losses to flow between members of the group and M1, M2 etc. And if M1 is a member of a group (with its parent P) it may be possible for losses to flow between members of that group and C.

International

338. In the simplest case, all the companies involved are resident in the United Kingdom and carry on their businesses wholly in the United Kingdom. But the relief is extended to includethe losses of:

- some companies not resident in the United Kingdom that carry on a trade through a permanent establishment in the United Kingdom; and
- some companies resident in the EEA (or carrying on a trade through a permanent establishment there).

339. And the relief is restricted in some cases if a UK resident company's business is not carried on wholly in the United Kingdom.

Other reliefs

340. In addition to trading losses, some other reliefs may be surrendered by one company to another. The other reliefs are listed in section 99(1).

Equity holders

341. In some cases a simple test of shareholding does not accurately reflect the economic reality of the relationship between companies. So there are rules in Chapter 6 of this Part to establish the true economic relationship.

*Chapter 1: **Introduction***

Overview

342. This Chapter introduces the Part.

*Section 97: **Introduction to Part***

343. This section sets out the structure of the Part and introduces the expression "group relief". It is based on section 402(1) of ICTA.

*Chapter 2: **Surrender of company's losses etc for an accounting period***

Overview

344. This Chapter sets out what relief is available and the main restrictions on relief.

*Section 98: **Overview of Chapter***

345. This section sets out the structure of the Chapter. It is new.

Section 99: Surrendering of losses and other amounts

346. This section lists the losses and other amounts that may be surrendered as group relief. It is based on sections 402, 403, 403ZC and 403ZD of ICTA.

347. In ICTA the amounts are referred to as "trading losses and other amounts eligible for relief". The trading losses are explained in section 403ZA of ICTA. The "other amounts" are explained in sections 403ZB (excess capital allowances), 403ZC (non-trading deficit on loan relationships) and 403ZD (charges, Schedule A losses, management expenses and non-trading loss on intangible fixed assets).

348. This section adopts a similar approach by specifying the losses and other amounts that may be subject to a group relief claim. There is a more detailed explanation of each of those losses and other amounts in sections 100 to 104.

349. *Subsection (2)* uses a test of whether the losses and other amounts are "eligible for corporation tax relief".

350. *Subsections (3)* and *(4)* contrast the treatments of:

- amounts within paragraphs (a) to (c) of subsection (1), which may be surrendered whatever the profits of the surrendering company; and
- amounts within paragraphs (d) to (g) of subsection (1), which may be surrendered only to the extent that they exceed the surrendering company's total profits (see section 105(3)).

351. *Subsection (5)* refers to the other restrictions on amounts that may be surrendered in sections 106 to 110. It also refers to the restrictions (mentioned in section 403(4) of ICTA) that operate by making amounts not available for set off.

352. *Subsection (6)* cross-refers the requirement (in Schedule 18 to FA 1998) that the surrendering company must consent to the surrender.Section 130(2) requires that there is also a claim.

353. *Subsection (7)* introduces the label "surrenderable amounts" to refer to the losses and other amounts that may be surrendered.

Section 100: Meaning of "trading loss"

354. This section explains which trading losses are available for relief. It is based on section 403ZA of ICTA.

355. *Subsection (1)* is the link to the basic rule in section 99(1)(a).

356. *Subsection (2)* excludes from the available losses:

- losses made in a trade carried on wholly outside the United Kingdom (the profits of which were historically charged to tax under Schedule D Case V); and
- non-commercial losses for which relief would not be available to the surrendering company under the loss relief rules (see Part 4).

357. This section does not rewrite the requirement in section 403ZA(1) of ICTA that a trading loss is calculated in the same way as a loss within section 393A of ICTA. This is because the requirement is already rewritten in section 47 of CTA 2009.

Section 101: Meaning of "capital allowance excess"

358. This section explains which capital allowances are available for relief. It is based on section 403ZB of ICTA.

359. *Subsection (1)* is the link to the basic rule in section 99(1)(b). It identifies the capital allowances as those to be given in a qualifying activity of "special leasing".

360. A company may surrender the allowances which would otherwise be available for relief against its total profits under section 260 of CAA.

361. *Subsections (3)* and *(4)* set out how to deal with "special leasing" allowances that are brought forward:

- the amount to be surrendered is limited to the allowances for the current period, without regard to any allowances brought forward; and
- in calculating the excess of allowances over the leasing income of the current period, the amount of the income is not reduced by allowances brought forward.

Section 102: Meaning of "UK property business loss"

362. This section explains which property income losses are available for relief. It is based on section 403ZD(3) of ICTA.

363. *Subsection (1)* is the link to the basic rule in section 99(1)(e).

364. *Subsection (2)* makes clear that a loss brought forward under the loss relief rules (see Part 4) is not available even though those rules treat the loss as made in the surrender period.

365. A non-commercial property loss is not eligible for relief under the loss relief rules (see Part 4). So it is not "eligible for corporation tax relief (apart from this Part)" – see section 99(2). It follows that such a loss may not be surrendered as group relief and there is no need to rewrite section 403ZD(3)(b) of ICTA.

Section 103: Meaning of "management expenses"

366. This section explains which management expenses are available for relief. It is based on section 403ZD(4) of ICTA.

367. *Subsection (1)* is the link to the basic rule in section 99(1)(f).

368. *Subsection (2)* excludes from the available management expenses amounts brought forward from an earlier period under:

- section 1223 of CTA 2009 (management expenses carried forward); or
- the property loss rules (see Chapter 4 of Part 4 of this Act).

Section 104: Meaning of "non-trading loss on intangible fixed assets"

369. This section explains that a non-trading loss that is available for relief is one calculated under Part 8 of CTA 2009. It is based on section 403ZD(6) of ICTA.

370. *Subsection (1)* is the link to the basic rule in section 99(1)(g).

371. *Subsection (2)* excludes from the available loss amounts brought forward from an earlier period.

Section 105: Restriction on surrender of losses etc within section 99(1)(d) to (g)

372. This section sets out a special rule which applies only to "relevant amounts". They are:

- qualifying charitable donations;
- a UK property business loss;
- management expenses; and
- a non-trading loss on intangible assets.

373. The section is based on sections 403 and 403ZE of ICTA.

374. *Subsection (1)* introduces the "relevant amounts" to which the section applies.The "relevant amounts" do not include the main reliefs (trading losses, excess capital allowances and non-trading loan relationships deficits), which may be surrendered even if the surrendering company has profits against which the main reliefs may be set.

375. *Subsections (2)* and *(3)* are the main rule: the relevant amounts are available only to the extent that they cannot be deducted from the surrendering company's own profits.

376. *Subsection (4)* deals with the case where the reliefs are restricted. In that case, the subsection determines the make-up of the relief that is surrendered.

377. The rule in this section compares the amounts within section 99(1)(d) to (g) with the "surrendering company's gross profits". *Subsection (5)* defines "gross profits" for the purposes of this section.

378. *Subsection (6)* refers to one of the restrictions mentioned in section 403(4) of ICTA. The other restrictions are in sections 99(5) and 137(3)(e).

*Section 106: **Restriction on losses etc surrenderable by UK resident***

379. This section eliminates from group relief some amounts that are attributable to a foreign permanent establishment. It is based on section 403E of ICTA.

380. In most cases the profits of a foreign permanent establishment are taxed in the country where the permanent establishment is. The profits remain chargeable to United Kingdom tax but credit is given for foreign tax on the profits. If the permanent establishment is not profitable relief may be available for the loss etc in the foreign country. This section prevents relief being given for the same loss etc both in the foreign country and in the United Kingdom.

381. *Subsection (1)* restricts the operation of the section to companies resident in the United Kingdom.

382. *Subsection (2)* sets out the basic rule: a loss or other amount attributable to a foreign permanent establishment is not available for group relief if it qualifies for relief from non-UK tax.

383. *Subsections (3)* and *(4)* set out how to calculate the loss etc of a foreign permanent establishment. The calculation is done on the same basis as that for the calculation of the losses etc of a United Kingdom permanent establishment.

384. *Subsection (5)* explains the sort of relief from non-UK tax with which the section is concerned: it is relief from tax in the country where the permanent establishment is; and the relief is against the non-UK profits (defined in section 108) of any person other than the surrendering company. In other words, the section is concerned with foreign group relief.

385. *Subsections (6)* and *(7)* resolve a potential circularity in the rules. Foreign tax rules may deny relief for an amount if it qualifies for relief from United Kingdom tax. In that case, it would not be clear how the rule in subsection (5) operates.

386. The circularity is resolved by giving relief where the company is resident (that is, in the United Kingdom). But there is an exception to this rule if the company is also resident in the country where the permanent establishment is. In that case, United Kingdom relief is denied.

*Section 107: **Restriction on losses etc surrenderable by non-UK resident***

387. This section eliminates from group relief amounts that arise from activities that are not within the United Kingdom tax net, or are relieved abroad. It is based on section 403D of ICTA.

388. *Subsection (1)* restricts the operation of the section to companies not resident in the United Kingdom that carry on a trade through a permanent establishment in the United Kingdom.

389. *Subsection (2)* introduces the three conditions (A, B and C) that have to be met if the non-UK resident company is to be able to surrender group relief.

390. *Subsection (3)* sets out condition A. The activities of the company must bring it within the charge to corporation tax. So its business must be a trade carried on through a permanent establishment in the United Kingdom (see section 19 of CTA 2009).

391. *Subsection (4)* sets out condition B. A company may be within the charge to corporation tax because it carries on its business through a permanent establishment in the United Kingdom but those activities (for instance, those of an airline) may be exempt from United Kingdom tax as a result of a DTA. In that case, any losses arising from the exempt activities may not be surrendered as group relief.

392. *Subsections (5)* and *(6)* set out condition C. A loss or other amount attributable to a United Kingdom permanent establishment is not available for group relief if it qualifies for relief from non-UK tax.

393. *Subsection (7)* explains how Condition C works if a foreign tax system (such as those of France and Australia) operates by exempting foreign (in this case, United Kingdom) profits from tax in the foreign country. Such a system may need to calculate the United Kingdom profits in order to exempt them. But that calculation does not mean that the profits in question are the subject of foreign tax *relief.*

394. *Subsections (8)* and *(9)* resolve a potential circularity in the rules. Foreign tax rules may deny relief for an amount if it qualifies for relief from United Kingdom tax. In that case, it would not be clear how condition C operates.

395. The section changes the approach of section 403D(6) of ICTA. Instead of ignoring the condition in foreign tax law the section sets out the result. That is that the loss etc is treated as allowable for foreign tax.

396. Section 403D(11) of ICTA serves only to clarify the interface between relief under that section and relief under the EEA rules in sections 403F and 403G of ICTA. In this Act it is clear that relief under Chapter 2 of this Part is separate from, and (potentially) in addition to, relief under Chapter 3 of this Part. So section 403D(11) is not rewritten.

*Section 108: **Meaning of "non-UK profits"***

397. This section defines "non-UK profits"for sections 106 and 107. It is based on sections 403D and 403E of ICTA.

398. *Subsections (1)* and *(2)* set out the basic rule. The profits are those that are charged to "non-UK tax" (see section 187). The definition includes amounts that are taken into account in calculating those profits. But it does not include any profits that are taken into account in calculating the profits of any person for United Kingdom tax purposes.

399. *Subsection (3)* deals with profits that are exempted from United Kingdom tax by a DTA. Such profits may be non-UK profits. Subsection (2) refers to the "total profits" of any person. Section 4(3) defines that expression to include only amounts charged to corporation tax. So there is no need to exclude non-chargeable profits and section 403D(2)(a) of ICTA is not rewritten in this section.

*Section 109: **Restriction on losses etc surrenderable by dual resident***

400. This section restricts the relief available to dual resident investing companies. It is based on section 404 of ICTA.

401. *Subsections (1)* and *(2)* are the basic rule. A company that is resident both in the United Kingdom and in another country may not surrender losses etc as group relief. But the rule applies only to investing companies, a concept that is defined in the following subsections.

402. *Subsection (3)* defines the first sort of company to which the section applies. It is a company that does not carry on a trade.

403. *Subsection (4)* defines the second sort of company to which the section applies. It is a trading company whose activities are of a sort more usually associated with an investment business.

404. *Subsection (5)* defines the third sort of company to which the section applies. The rule prevents an investing company being "dressed up" as a trading company.

*Section 110: **Restriction on surrender of losses etc from alternative finance arrangements***

405. This section denies group relief if a deduction is disallowed by section 520 of CTA 2009. It is based on section 411ZA of ICTA.

*Chapter 3: **Surrendersmade by non-UK resident company resident or trading in the EEA***

Overview

406. This Chapter makes the United Kingdom group relief rules compatible with European Community law following the judgment in Marks and Spencer plc v Halsey, C446/03[1]. That case decided that in some circumstances it is contrary to the provisions of the EC Treaty on freedom of establishment to deny group relief to a UK resident parent for the losses of a non-UK resident subsidiary.

407. So this Chapter allows relief for foreign losses. But there are two main restrictions:

- the surrendering company must be resident in (or otherwise "related" to) an EEA territory; and
- the losses must not qualify for relief in the EEA territory.

*Section 111: **Overview of Chapter***

408. This section sets out the structure of the Chapter. It is new.

*Section 112: **EEA related definitions***

409. This section defines the expressions that are used in the Chapter to describe the connection of companies and their profits to the EEA. It is based on section 402 of, and Schedule 18A to, ICTA. The EEA comprises:

Austria	Greece	Netherlands
Belgium	Hungary	Norway
Bulgaria	Iceland	Poland
Cyprus	Ireland	Portugal
Czech Republic	Italy	Romania
Denmark	Latvia	Slovak Republic

1 See also [2008] STC 526.

Estonia	Liechtenstein	Slovenia
Finland	Lithuania	Spain
France	Luxembourg	Sweden
Germany	Malta	United Kingdom

Section 113: Steps to determine extent to which loss etc can be surrendered

410. This section sets out how to calculate how much of an "EEA amount" may be surrendered. It is based on section 403F of, and paragraph 11 of Schedule 18A to, ICTA.

411. *Subsection (2)* is a method statement.

412. *Step 1* eliminates any amount that is within the United Kingdom tax net and available for surrender under the rules in Chapter 2.

413. *Step 2* sets out the conditions that the EEA amount has to meet. The detail of the conditions is set out in sections 114 to 121. To the extent that the EEA amount meets these conditions it is the "qualifying part of the EEA amount".

414. *Step 3* requires the EEA amount to be recalculated using United Kingdom tax rules and the assumptions set out in sections 123 to 126.

415. In paragraph 11(4) of Schedule 18A to ICTA the assumptions are made in relation to "the provisions of this Chapter" (that is, Chapter 4 of Part 10 of ICTA). In fact the assumptions are used only for the purpose of recalculating the EEA amount. So in this Act they apply only for that restricted purpose.

416. *Step 4* compares the qualifying part of the EEA amount with the same proportion of the EEA amount recalculated in Step 3. The lower amount is the amount that may be surrendered.

417. *Step 5* requires a restriction for any amount excluded from relief by section 127 (arrangements).

418. *Subsection (3)* deals with the possibility that the accounting period assumed by section 125 does not coincide with the accounting period of the surrendering company. The subsection makes clear that the total of the recalculated amounts is compared with the qualifying part of the EEA amount. See *Change 23* in Annex 1.

419. *Subsection (4)* cross-refers to the need for consent to the surrender. This rule corresponds to the rule in section 99(6) for UK related companies.

Section 114: The equivalence condition

420. This section requires the EEA amount to correspond to an amount that would qualify for United Kingdom group relief. It is based on paragraph 2 of Schedule 18A to ICTA.

Section 115: The EEA tax loss condition: companies resident in EEA territory

421. This section identifies the EEA amount as one calculated in accordance with the relevant foreign tax law. It is based on paragraph 3 of Schedule 18A to ICTA.

422. *Subsection (1)* applies the section to companies resident in the EEA. The other sort of EEA related companies (those with an EEA permanent establishment) are dealt with in section 116.

423. *Subsection (2)* sets out the main condition: it establishes that the Chapter is concerned with an amount that has arisen for tax purposes in an EEA territory.

424. *Subsection (3)* excludes an amount that is attributable to a permanent establishment in the United Kingdom. Such an amount may qualify for relief under the rules in Chapter 2.

Section 116: The EEA tax loss condition: companies not resident in EEA territory

425. This section identifies the EEA amount in the case of a company with a permanent establishment in the EEA. It is based on paragraph 4 of Schedule 18A to ICTA.

426. *Subsection (1)* applies the section to companies not resident in the EEA. The other sort of EEA related companies (thoseresident in the EEA) are dealt with in section 115.

427. *Subsection (2)* sets out the main condition: it establishes that the Chapter is concerned with an amount that has arisen for tax purposes in an EEA territory.

428. *Subsection (3)* excludes an amount that arises from activities the profits of which would be exempt under a DTA.

429. *Subsection (4)* introduces subsections (5) and (6), which explain the sort of arrangements with which subsection (3) is concerned.

430. *Subsection (5)* sets out the relevant arrangements. They are arrangements between the EEA territory where the permanent establishment is and:

- the United Kingdom (paragraph (b)); or
- any other territory (paragraph (a)).

431. *Subsection (6)* identifies the effect of the DTA: it is that any profits from the activities in question would be exempt from tax in the EEA territory.

Section 117: The qualifying loss condition: general

432. This section introduces the rules which exclude from the EEA amount any amount that qualifies for relief abroad. It is based on paragraphs 5 to 7 of Schedule 18A to ICTA.

433. *Subsection (1)* makes clear that the EEA amount must meet the conditions in all of sections 118 to 120. Those conditions are expressed in the negative. So the conditions are met if foreign relief is *not* available.

434. *Subsection (3)* identifies the "relevant non-UK tax" as any foreign tax charged in the relevant EEA territory or in any territory where the surrendering company is resident.

435. *Subsection (4)* identifies the "resident territory" as any territory in which the surrendering company is resident, apart from the EEA territory to which the EEA company is related.

Section 118: The qualifying loss condition: relief for current and previous periods

436. This section sets out the condition that relief is not available for the current period or for a previous period. It is based on paragraph 6 of Schedule 18A to ICTA.

437. *Subsection (1)* introduces the section.

438. *Subsection (2)* deals with any part of the EEA amount that is deductible in calculating profits. The profits are those of any person (not just the surrendering company). And, for the purpose of this section, one looks at the current period and any previous period.

439. *Subsection (3)* is similar to subsection (2) but is concerned with relief that is available in a way other than as a deduction in calculating profits.

440. *Subsection (4)* makes clear that the section is concerned with whether the relief is available, not with whether it is actually given: the condition cannot be met simply by failing to make any necessary claim for relief.

Section 119: The qualifying loss condition: relief for future periods

441. This section sets out the condition that relief is not available for subsequent periods. It is based on paragraph 7 of Schedule 18A to ICTA.

442. *Subsection (1)* introduces the section.

443. *Subsection (2)* deals with any part of the EEA amount that may be deductible in calculating profits in any future period. The profits are those of any person (not just the surrendering company).

444. *Subsection (3)* is similar to subsection (2) but is concerned with relief that is available in a way other than as a deduction in calculating profits.

445. *Subsection (4)* determines that the possibility of foreign tax relief is to be considered as at the end of the period in which the EEA amount arises.

Section 120: The qualifying loss condition: non-UK tax relief in another territory

446. This section sets out the condition that relief is not available in any territory. It is based on paragraph 8 of Schedule 18A to ICTA.

447. *Subsection (1)* introduces the section.

448. *Subsection (2)* deals with any part of the EEA amount that may be deductible in calculating profits. The profits are those of any person (not just the surrendering company). Unlike sections 118 and 119, this section deals with tax relief in a territory which is neither the EEA territory where the EEA amount arises nor the territory where the surrendering company is resident. And it is concerned only with relief that has been given, not with relief that may be given.

449. *Subsection (3)* is similar to subsection (2) but is concerned with relief that is available in a way other than as a deduction in calculating profits.

Section 121: The precedence condition

450. This section deals with the possibility that relief is available in more than one territory. It is based on paragraph 9 of Schedule 18A to ICTA.

451. Suppose there is a chain of companies with a "top" holding company, a "bottom" trading company and a series of other companies each of which is both a subsidiary and a holding company. If the companies are resident in a variety of territories, where there are rules equivalent to those in this Chapter of the Act, it is possible for the losses of the "bottom" trading company to be relievable in several territories.

452. The section resolves the problem by providing that relief is assumed to be given at the lowest possible level in the chain. If the company at that level is UK resident, group relief is available.

453. *Subsection (1)* introduces the idea that relief may be available in a territory that is neither the United Kingdom nor the territory where the EEA amount arises.

454. *Subsection (2)* describes the chain of companies. Paragraph (a) establishes that the company in question is in the chain. Paragraph (b) establishes that higher in the chain there is a UK resident company. Paragraph (c) establishes that the surrendering company is a 75% subsidiary of that UK resident company. Paragraph (d) establishes that there is no other UK resident company in the chain between the surrendering company and the company in question.

455. If relief is available to the company in question it is excluded from the EEA amount.

456. *Subsection (3)* sets out the sorts of relief with which the section is concerned: they are the same as those in section 118(2) (a direct deduction) and (3) (other relief).

Example

A UK resident company U1 owns all the share capital in N, a company resident in the Netherlands.

N owns all the share capital in U2, a UK resident company.

U2 owns all the share capital in G, a company resident in Germany.

G owns all the share capital in F, a company resident in France.

U1 claims group relief for F's losses.

Subsection (2) of the section applies to G because:

(a) it is resident in Germany (not the relevant EEA territory, which is France);

(b) U2 owns (directly) share capital in G;

(c) F is a 75% subsidiary of U2; and

(d) F is not a subsidiary of U2 as a result of its being a 75% subsidiary of another UK resident company.

So Germany is a territory within subsection (2). If relief for F's loss is available in Germany no United Kingdom group relief is available. G's potential claim takes precedence over U1's claim because G is lower in the chain.

But, in relation to N:

(a) it is resident in the Netherlands (not the relevant EEA territory, which is France);

(b) the only UK resident company that owns share capital in N is U1;

(c) F is a 75% subsidiary of U1; but

(d) F is a subsidiary of U1 only as a result of its being a 75% subsidiary of another UK resident company (U2).

So the Netherlands is not a territory within subsection (2). Even if relief for F's loss is available in the Netherlands, United Kingdom group relief may be available to U2. U2's potential claim takes precedence over N's because U2 is lower in the chain.

Section 122: ***Assumptions to be made in recalculating EEA amount***

457. This section introduces sections 123 to 126. It is new.

Section 123: ***Assumptions as to UK residence***

458. This section is the first of four sets of assumptions to be made in recalculating the EEA amount using United Kingdom tax rules. It is based on paragraph 12 of Schedule 18A to ICTA.

459. *Subsection (1)* requires the assumption that the surrendering company is resident in the United Kingdom.

460. *Subsection (2)* makes clear that the assumption in subsection (1) does not:

- affect where the company's activities are carried on (but section 124 may make an assumption about that); or
- treat the company as ceasing to be UK resident at the end of the EEA accounting period (but section 125 treats the company's accounting period as ending then).

461. *Subsection (3)* requires the assumption that the surrendering company becomes UK resident at the beginning of the EEA accounting period.

Section 124: Assumptions as to places in which activities carried on

462. This section is the second of four sets of assumptions to be made in recalculating the EEA amount using United Kingdom tax rules.It is based on paragraph 13 of Schedule 18A to ICTA.

463. *Subsection (1)* requires the assumption that the company's activities are carried on in the United Kingdom instead of in the EEA territory. So any special rules about foreign income do not apply.

464. *Subsection (2)* makes clear that the assumption in subsection (1) includes the assumption that any land held by the surrendering company is in the United Kingdom.

465. *Subsection (3)* explains how the United Kingdom concepts of law in subsection (2) ("estate", "interest" and "rights") are to be applied to land that is outside the United Kingdom.

Section 125: Assumptions as to accounting periods

466. This section is the third of four sets of assumptions to be made in recalculating the EEA amount using United Kingdom tax rules.It is based on paragraph 14 of Schedule 18A to ICTA.

467. *Subsection (1)* determines the start of the accounting period for recalculating the surrendering company's EEA amount.

468. *Subsections (2)* to *(4)* determine when the accounting period ends. As in section 10 of CTA 2009, the accounting period ends at the end of the EEA accounting period or, if earlier, after 12 months.

469. The section clarifies the position if, exceptionally, the EEA accounting period is longer than two years. Paragraph 14 of Schedule 18A to ICTA does not explicitly cater for this possibility butthe only logical interpretation involves treating the process in sub-paragraphs (2) to (4) as iterative. So this section does not change the law.

Section 126: Assumptions in relation to capital allowances

470. This section is the last of four sets of assumptions to be made in recalculating the EEA amount using United Kingdom tax rules. It is based in paragraph 15 of Schedule 18A to ICTA.

471. *Subsection (1)* sets out when the section applies.

472. *Subsection (2)* invokes section 13 of CAA. So the surrendering company is treated as having incurred expenditure on the plant or machinery on the first day of the EEA accounting period. The amount of the expenditure is the market value of the plant or machinery.

473. *Subsection (3)* ensures that all the relevant rules in the plant and machinery Part of CAA apply in the recalculation of the EEA amount.

Section 127: Amounts excluded because of certain arrangements

474. This section is a rule to deal with contrived situations. It is based on section 403G of ICTA.

475. *Subsection (1)* excludes from the EEA amount any amount that arises from an "arrangement". The exclusion is mentioned in Step 5 of section 113(2). Subsection (1) (a) of the section ensures that the rule does not apply to any part of the EEA amount that is attributable to a United Kingdom permanent establishment. That part is dealt with under section 107.

476. *Subsection (2)* identifies the excluded amount by reference to "arrangements".

477. *Subsection (3)* tests the purpose of the arrangements. They are within this section if their main purpose is to secure group relief.

Section 128: Rules for recalculating EEA amount

478. This section requires the EEA amount to be recalculated using United Kingdom tax rules. It is based on paragraph 16 of Schedule 18A to ICTA.

479. If the recalculation results in a lower amount, the recalculated amount (or the relevant proportion of it) is the amount that may be surrendered as group relief (see Step 4 in section 113(2)).

480. *Subsection (1)* is the basic rule. The EEA amount is recalculated. Furthermore, any rule that would disallow the amount for United Kingdom tax purposes (such as the rule about non-commercial losses) is applied.

481. *Subsections (2)* to *(4)* allow the Treasury to make regulations about the recalculation of the EEA amount.

Chapter 4: Claims for group relief

Overview

482. This Chapter sets out the conditions for relief involving UK related companies (under Chapter 2) and EEA related companies (under Chapter 3). It also sets out restrictions on relief that may be given on claims.

Section 129: Overview of Chapter

483. This section sets out the structure of the Chapter. It is new.

Section 130: Group relief claims on amounts surrenderable under Chapter 2

484. This section sets out the basic rules for claims for group relief surrendered by UK related companies. It is based on section 402 of ICTA and paragraph 70 of Schedule 18 to FA 1998.

485. The corresponding rules for EEA related companies are in section 135.

486. *Subsection (2)* requires a claim by the claimant company. The surrender is required by section 99(6). The subsection goes on to set out three conditions for a claim.

- There must be a consent (see section 99(6)).
- There must be an overlapping period (see section 142).
- The relief must be available as a result of the existence of:
  - — a group (see section 131);
  - — a consortium, not involving a "link" company (see section 132); or
  - — a consortium involving a "link" company (see section 133).

487. The detail of each part of the third condition includes a requirement that the companies concerned are "UK related" (defined in section 134). That requirement in the case of a group is based on section 402(2) of ICTA.

488. In the case of a consortium it is explicit in section 402(3A) and (3B) of ICTA that the claimant and surrendering companies must be UK related.

489. In the case of a claim for the losses of a company (C) owned by a consortium, section 406(2) of ICTA applies only if the link company (L) could make a claim. That is the case only if L is UK related.

490. In the case of a claim by a company (C) owned by a consortium there is no explicit rule in section 406(5) of ICTA that is equivalent to the rule in section 406(2). But it is implicit in the section: indeed, subsection (8) can work only if the link company (L) is UK related; otherwise section 402(3A) and (3B) of ICTA would prevent L from being the surrendering company.

491. So each of the conditions in sections 131 to 133 is explicit in requiring that all of the surrendering, claimant and link companies are UK related.

492. *Subsection (3)* makes clear that more than one company may claim the relief available in the surrendering company. But the total claimed cannot exceed the relief available (see section 137(7)).

Section 131: ***The group condition***

493. This section deals with straightforward claims for group relief (that is, claims not involving consortiums) surrendered by a UK related company. It is based on section 402 of ICTA.

494. The corresponding rule for EEA related companies is in section 136.

Section 132: ***Consortium condition 1***

495. This section allows claims involving companies owned by a consortium. It is based on section 402 of ICTA.

496. *Subsection (2)* allows group relief to go "upwards" from a company owned by a consortium to a member of the consortium.

497. *Subsection (3)* allows group relief to go "downwards" from a member of a consortium to a company owned by the consortium.

498. *Subsections (4)* and *(5)* deny relief if the consortium relationship depends on shares that are held by a share-dealing company as part of its circulating capital.

Section 133: ***Consortium conditions 2 and 3***

499. This section extends the relief that is available to consortiums. It is based on sections 402 and 406 of ICTA.

500. The extension involves a company ("the link company") that is a consortium member and is also a member of a group. There are special rules for companies in the same group as the company owned by a consortium in sections 148 and 149.

501. *Subsection (1)* allows relief to go "upwards" from a company (C) owned by a consortium to a company (P) that is in the same group as the link company (L).

502. *Subsection (2)* allows relief to go "downwards" from a company (P) that is in the same group as the link company (L) to a company (C) owned by the consortium.

503. *Subsections (3)* and *(4)* deny relief if the consortium relationship depends on shares that are held by a share-dealing company as circulating capital.

504. The rule in subsections (3) and (4) is not explicit in the source legislation. If shares in C are held by L as circulating capital, section 402(4) of ICTA prevents a consortium claim by L. Similarly, C may not claim L's losses etc. It follows that when P steps into

the shoes of L in accordance with section 406(2) or (5) of ICTA P may not claim C's losses etc and C may not claim P's losses etc.

*Section 134: **Meaning of "UK related" company***

505. This section defines "UK related". It is based on section 402 of ICTA.

*Section 135: **Group relief claims on amounts surrenderable under Chapter 3***

506. This section gives the rules for claims for group relief surrendered by EEA related companies. It is based on section 402 of ICTA and paragraph 70 of Schedule 18 to FA 1998.

507. The corresponding rules for UK related companies are in section 130.

508. *Subsection (2)* requires a claim by the claimant company. The surrender is required by section 99(6). The subsection goes on to set out three conditions for a claim.

- There must be a consent (see section 99(6)).
- There must be an overlapping period (see section 142).
- The relief must be available as a result of the existence of a group (see section 136).

509. *Subsection (3)* makes clear that more than one company may claim the relief available in the surrendering company. But the total claimed cannot exceed the relief available (see section 137(7)).

*Section 136: **The EEA group condition***

510. This section sets out the condition for group relief to be surrendered by an EEA related company. It is based on section 402 of ICTA.

511. *Subsections (2)* and *(3)* set out the condition, that either the claimant company or the company that owns both it and the surrendering company is UK resident.

*Section 137: **Deduction from total profits***

512. This section explains how group relief is given to the claimant company. It is based on sections 403, 407 and 411 of ICTA.

513. *Subsection (1)* is the link to section 4.

514. *Subsection (2)* makes clear that the claimant company may claim all or part of the surrendering company's surrenderable amounts.

515. *Subsection (3)* subjects subsection (2) to the restrictions later in the Chapter. Paragraph (e) refers to one of the restrictions mentioned in section 403(4) of ICTA. The other restrictions in that subsection are referred to in sections 99(5) and 105(5) or are rewritten in section 109.

516. *Subsection (4)* is the rule that group relief is the final deduction to be given in arriving at a company's taxable profits, subject only to the exceptions set out in subsection (5).

517. *Subsection (5)* sets out the reliefs that are to be given *after* group relief. So, for instance, group relief may reduce a company's profits for an accounting period to an extent that there is a restriction to relief for losses carried back to that accounting period.

518. *Subsection (6)* makes clear that each relief in subsection (4) that depends on the making of a claim is to be taken account of on the assumption that the relevant claim is made. But there is an exception in the case of relief for non-trading loan relationship deficits: that relief is taken account of only if the relevant claim is actually made.

519. *Subsection (7)* ensures that an amount of relief is not given twice.

*Section 138: **Limitation on amount of group relief applying to all claims***

520. This section restricts the amount of group relief to the profits available to absorb it. It is based on section 403A of ICTA.

521. It compares the "unused part of the surrenderable amounts" (defined in section 139) with the "unrelieved part of the claimant company's available total profits" (defined in section 140). The amount of group relief is restricted to the lower of the two compared amounts.

*Section 139: **Unused part of the surrenderable amounts***

522. This section defines "unused part of the surrenderable amounts" for the purpose of section 138. It is based onsections 403A and 403B of ICTA.

523. *Subsection (1)* introduces the rules for calculating the "unused part of the surrenderable amounts". In particular, the rules cater for the cases where:

- the surrendering company and the claimant company have different accounting periods; or
- there are multiple claims for the surrendering company's losses etc.

524. *Subsection (2)* sets out the restriction to be made if the surrendering company and claimant company have different accounting periods. In that case the "surrender period" (see section 99(7)) and "claim period" (see section 130(2)) are not the same. The loss etc is apportioned on a time basis to the "overlapping period" (see section 142).

525. *Subsection (3)* introduces the calculation that has to be made if there are multiple claims for the surrendering company's loss etc. It considers what "prior claims" have been made and what "prior surrenders" have been made as a result.

526. *Subsection (4)* defines a "prior claim".

527. *Subsection (5)* is a method statement for calculating the total amount of any "prior claims". The overlapping period for any prior claim is given by section 142.

528. If no part of that overlapping period falls within the claim period of the current claim, that prior claim is ignored. But if part of theoverlapping period does fall within the claim period of the current claim a time-apportioned amount of the prior claim is taken into account.

529. The total of the amounts to be taken into account for prior claims is deducted to arrive at the usable amount of the surrenderable amounts.

*Section 140: **Unrelieved part of claimant company's available total profits***

530. This section defines "unrelieved part of the claimant company's available total profits" for the purpose of section 138. It is based onsections 403A, 403B and 403D of ICTA.

531. *Subsection (1)* introduces the rules for calculating the "unrelieved part of the claimant company's available total profits". In particular, the rules cater for the cases where:

- the surrendering company and the claimant company have different accounting periods; or
- there are other claims by the claimant company for the claim period.

532. *Subsection (2)* sets out the restriction to be made if the surrendering company and claimant company have different accounting periods. In that case the "surrender period" (see section 99(7)) and "claim period" (see section 130(2)) are not the same. The claimant company's available total profits are apportioned on a time basis to the "overlapping period" (see section 142).

533. *Subsection (3)* introduces the calculation that has to be made if there are other claims by the claimant company for the claim period. It considers what "prior claims" have been made and what "previously claimed group relief" has been given as a result.

534. *Subsection (4)* defines a "prior claim".

535. *Subsection (5)* is a method statement for calculating the total amount of any "prior claims". The overlapping period for any relevant prior claim is given by section 142.

536. If no part of that overlapping period falls within the claim period of the current claim, that prior claim is ignored. But if part of theoverlapping period does fall within the claim period of the current claim a time-apportioned amount of the prior claim is taken into account.

537. The total of the amounts to be taken into account for relevant prior claims is deducted to arrive at the unrelieved amount of the claimant company's total profits.

538. *Subsection (6)* apportions the previously claimed group relief to the period of the current claim.

539. *Subsection (7)* explains what is meant by "available total profits" in subsection (1). "Total profits" are defined in section 4 to include only amounts charged to corporation tax. So there is no need to exclude non-chargeable profits and section 403D(2)(a) of ICTA is not rewritten in this section.

540. Section 403A(2)(b) of ICTA refers to "total profits … reduced by … previously claimed group relief". Such group relief can have been given only against profits "as reduced by any other relief" (section 407(1)(b) of ICTA). So subsection (7) of this section makes clear that the total profits must be reduced by such other relief before being further reduced by group relief.

541. *Subsection (8)* deals with the case of a claimant company that is not resident in the United Kingdom. Its available total profits do not include any profits that are "double taxation exempt" (see section 186).

Section 141: ***Sections 139 and 140:supplementary***

542. This section sets out three rules about relevant prior claims. It is based on section 403A of ICTA.

543. *Subsection (1)* explains what happens if two or more claims are made at the same time. They are treated as made in whatever order the company or companies choose, by making an election.

544. The section does not specify that the election is to be made "by notice to any officer of the Board" (section 403A(7)(a) of ICTA). The rules in Schedule 18 to FA 1998 apply for the purposes of this Act. Either the election is to be made in a company's return or it is to be made to "an officer of the Board" (paragraph 2(1) of Schedule 1A to TMA, applied by paragraph 59 of Schedule 18 to FA 1998).

545. If no such election is made, the choice is made by HMRC.

546. *Subsection (2)* introduces the second rule, about measuring a relevant prior claim. The amount of such a claim is determined when it is made. So it takes account of any earlier claims; and takes no account of any later claims.

547. The section does not rewrite the rule in section 403A(6) of ICTA about a claim becoming final. See *Change 24* in Annex 1.

548. *Subsection (3)* sets out the third rule. It substitutes a "just and reasonable" apportionment for any time-apportionment prescribed by section 139 or 140.

*Section 142: **Meaning of "the overlapping period"***

549. This section defines "the overlapping period" for Chapter 4 of this Part of the Act. It is based on section 403A of ICTA. The expression as defined in this section is used in sections 139, 140, 143 and 144.

550. *Subsection (1)* is the basic rule. The overlapping period is the period that is common to:

- the surrender period (of the surrendering company – defined in section 99(7)); and
- the claim period (of the claimant company – defined in section 130(2)).

551. *Subsection (2)* excludes from the overlapping period any part of it during which the conditions for relief are not satisfied.

552. *Subsection (3)* sets out the conditions for relief that have to be satisfied during the overlapping period. Only one of the conditions is relevant to any claim. They are the conditions set out in sections 131 to 133 (for UK related companies) and 136 (for EEA related companies).

*Section 143: **Condition 1: surrendering company owned by consortium***

553. This section is the basic rule about relief surrendered by a company to a member of the consortium that owns it. It is based on section 403C of ICTA.

554. *Subsection (1)* ties the section to consortium condition 1: that is, a case that does not involve a link company. Cases involving link companies are dealt with in sections 145 and 146.

555. *Subsection (2)* restricts the relief by reference to the consortium member's interest in the surrendering company.

556. *Subsection (3)* sets out what that interest is. Usually it is the proportion represented by the consortium member's shareholding in the surrendering company. But if that shareholding entitles the consortium member to a lower proportion of the surrendering company's profits or assets the lower proportion is used.

557. *Subsection (4)* deals with the case where the consortium member's interest in the surrendering company varies in the overlapping period (see section 142). In that case an average is taken.

558. *Subsection (5)* deals with the case where a trading company (T) is indirectly owned by a consortium through a holding company (H) (see section 185). In that case the various proportions referred to in the section are calculated by reference to the consortium member's (M1's) interest in H.

*Section 144: **Condition 1: claimant company owned by consortium***

559. This section is the basic rule about relief surrendered by a member of a consortium to a company that is owned by the consortium. It is based on section 403C of ICTA.

560. *Subsection (1)* ties the section to consortium condition 1: that is, a case that does not involve a link company. Cases involving link companies are dealt with in sections 145 and 146.

561. *Subsection (2)* restricts the relief by reference to the consortium member's interest in the claimant company.

562. *Subsection (3)* sets out what that interest is. Usually it is the proportion represented by the consortium member's shareholding in the claimant company. But if that

shareholding entitles the consortium member to a lower proportion of the surrendering company's profits or assets the lower proportion is used.

563. *Subsection (4)* deals with the case where the consortium member's interest in the claimant company varies in the overlapping period (see section 142). In that case an average is taken.

564. *Subsection (5)* deals with the case where a trading company (T) is indirectly owned by a consortium through a holding company (H) (see section 185). In that case the various proportions referred to in the section are calculated by reference to the consortium member's (M1's) interest in H.

Section 145: Conditions 2 and 3: limitations in sections 143 and 144

565. This section is the basic rule about relief involving a link company (see section 133). It is based on section 406 of ICTA.

566. *Subsection (2)* deals with a claim by a company that is a member of the same group as the link company for relief from a company owned by the consortium.

567. The overlapping period for the claim is still determined by reference to the accounting periods of the actual claimant company (P) and the surrendering company (C). But the subsection treats the link company (L) as if it were the claimant company for the purpose of section 143(3). So the "applicable proportion" of the surrenderable amounts is based on L's interest in Cin the overlapping period (if necessary, based on an average of that period – see section 143(4)(b)).

568. *Subsection (3)* deals with a claim by a company owned by a consortium for relief from a company that is a member of the same group as the link company.

569. The overlapping period for the claim is still determined by reference to the accounting periods of the claimant company (C) and the actual surrendering company (P). But the subsection treats the link company (L) as if it were the surrendering company for the purpose of section 144(3). So the "applicable proportion" of C's profits is based on L's interest in C in the overlapping period (if necessary, based on an average of that period – see section 144(4)(b)).

Section 146: Conditions 2 and 3: companies in link company's group

570. This section restricts the amount of relief that can be claimed in cases involving link companies. It is based on section 406 of ICTA.

571. *Subsections (1)* to *(3)* deal with the case of the surrender of relief by a company owned by a consortium. The link company's group, as a whole, cannot claim more relief than would have been available to the link company alone.

572. *Subsections (4)>* to *(6)* deal with the case of the surrender of relief by the link company and members of its group to a company owned by the consortium. The claimant company cannot claim relief in an amount greater than its profits that would be available to absorb relief surrendered by the link company alone.

573. *Subsection (7)* explains how to operate the restriction in subsection (6) if the link company and claimant company have different accounting periods. The tests in section 144 are applied in the claimant company's accounting period.

574. *Subsection (8)* supplies definitions for the section.

Section 147: ***Conditions 1 and 2: surrenderable amounts including trading loss***

575. This section restricts the amount of trading losses that can be surrendered by a company owned by a consortium. It is based on section 403ZA of ICTA.

576. *Subsection (1)* applies the section to consortium condition 1: that is, a case that does not involve a link company.

577. *Subsection (2)* extends the section to consortium condition 2: that is, cases involving a link company (L) where the surrendering company (C) is owned by a consortium.

578. *Subsection (3)* is the rule that a trading loss within section 37 ("sideways relief") is not available for group relief to the extent that relief could be given for it within the surrendering company.

579. *Subsection (4)* explains how the rule in this section interacts with the rule in section 148: this section applies first to reduce the surrenderable losses.

Section 148: ***Conditions 1 and 2: surrendering company in group of companies***

580. This section treats the company owned by a consortium and any companies in its group as a single company for the purposes of surrenders by companies in the group. It is based on sections 405 and 406 of ICTA. The rule about companies in the same group as the consortium member is in section 146.

581. *Subsection (1)* applies the section to consortium condition 1: that is, a case that does not involve a link company.

582. *Subsection (2)* extends the section to consortium condition 2: that is, cases involving a link company (L) where the surrendering company (S) is owned by a consortium (or is a member of the same group as the company owned by the consortium).

583. *Subsections (3)* and *(4)* restrict the relief available to any excess of the surrenderable amounts over the "group's potential relief".

584. *Subsection (5)* sets out how to calculate the "group's potential relief". This is the amount of profits that could be covered by all the available losses etc within the group. As section 147(3) makes clear, within the individual companies in the group, trading losses are treated as set off first against other profits.

585. If the consortium company C and its subsidiary S have different accounting dates, it may be necessary to apportion a loss to the surrender period in determining the "group's potential relief". See *Change 25* in Annex 1.

586. *Subsection (6)* clarifies the basis on which the group relief claims are assumed to be made within the group.

Section 149: ***Conditions 1 and 3: claimant company in group of companies***

587. This section treats the company (C) owned by a consortium and any companies (S etc) in its group as a single company for the purposes of claims by companies in the group. It is based on section 405 of ICTA. The rule about companies in the same group as the consortium member is in section 146.

588. *Subsection (1)* applies the section to consortium condition 1: that is, a case that does not involve a link company.

589. *Subsection (2)* extends the section to consortium condition 3: that is, cases involving a link company (L) where the claimant company (S) is owned by a consortium (or is a member of the same group as the company owned by the consortium).

590. *Subsections (3)* to *(5)* restrict the relief available to the amount that remains after relief is notionally given by way of group relief for all the available losses etc within the group. But those available losses etc may already have been reduced by actual claims within the group.

591. *Subsection (6)* clarifies the basis on which the group relief claims are treated as already made within the group.

Chapter 5: Subsidiaries, groups and consortiums

Overview

592. This Chapter sets out the rules for determining the relationships between companies for the purpose of group relief.

Section 150: Overview of Chapter

593. This section introduces the Chapter. It is new.

Section 151: Meaning of "75% subsidiary" and "90% subsidiary"

594. This section explains what is meant by "75% subsidiary" and "90% subsidiary". It is based on section 413 of ICTA.

595. *Subsection (1)* imports the definitions in Chapter 3 of Part 24 of this Act.

596. *Subsection (2)* includes the share capital of a registered industrial or provident society in "ordinary share capital".

597. *Subsection (3)* excludes shares held as circulating capital by a company that deals in shares.

598. The section simplifies the rule in section 413(5) of ICTA by not dealing separately with indirect share holdings. If any of the companies in the ownership chain holds the relevant shares as circulating capital the chain is broken for the purposes of this section.

599. *Subsection (4)* introduces the additional tests for a company to be treated as a 75% subsidiary of another. They are that "equity holders" in the subsidiary must be beneficially entitled to:

- at least 75% of the subsidiary's profits; and
- at least 75% of the subsidiary's assets in a winding up.

600. The test for a "90% subsidiary" is in similar terms.

601. The detail of the rules about equity holders is set out in Chapter 6 of this Part of the Act.

Section 152: Groups of companies

602. This section sets out the conditions for companies to be treated as members of the same group. It is based on section 413 of ICTA.

603. In regulation 17 of the Taxation of Securitisation Companies Regulations 2006 (SI 2006/3296) there is a rule that a securitisation company (defined in regulation 4) is not to be treated as a member of a group or consortium. And regulation 8 of the Taxation of Insurance Securitisation Companies Regulations 2007 (SI 2007/3402) has a similar rule about insurance securitisation companies (defined in regulation 4). The regulations

continue to apply for the purposes of this Part of this Act as they apply for the purposes of Chapter 4 of Part 10 of ICTA.

604. Similar regulations relating to property securitisation companies have been published in draft for consultation.

Section 153: ***Companies owned by consortiums and members of consortiums***

605. This section sets out the conditions for a company to be "owned by a consortium". It is based on sections 402 and 413 of ICTA.

606. *Subsection (1)* sets out the two basic conditions.

607. *Subsection (3)* extends the relief that is available to consortiums. The extension involves trading companies in the same group as a holding company owned by a consortium. The corresponding extension to companies in the same group as a consortium member is in section 133(1) and (2).

608. "Holding company" is defined in section 185(2).

Section 154: ***Arrangements for transfer of member of group of companies etc***

609. This section counteracts arrangements designed to obtain group relief. It is based on section 410 of ICTA.

610. It is possible to arrange for a loss-making company in a group to become temporarily a member of a second group while the economic reality is that it remains a member of the first group. The section operates as soon as arrangements are made for the ownership of the company to change.

611. *Subsection (1)* appliesthe section potentially to any case involving two companies in a group.

612. *Subsection (2)* denies group relief (by treating the companies as not members of the same group) if "arrangements" are in place.

613. *Subsection (3)* sets out the three "effects" which bring arrangements within the section. They all involve a change in the control of one of the companies or of a trade that it carries on.

Section 155: ***Arrangements for transfer of company owned by consortium etc***

614. This section counteracts arrangements designed to obtain consortium relief. It is based on section 410 of ICTA.

615. It is possible to arrange for a loss-making company to become temporarily:

- a member of a consortium; or
- owned by a consortium

while the economic reality is that it is neither of these things. The section operates as soon as arrangements are made for the ownership of the company to change.

616. *Subsection (1)* appliesthe section potentially to any case involving a trading company and a consortium.

617. *Subsection (2)* denies group relief (by treating the trading company as not owned by a consortium) if "arrangements" are in place.

618. *Subsection (3)* sets out the four "effects" which bring arrangements within the section. They all involve a change in the control of the trading company or of a trade that it carries on.

619. *Subsection (5)* extends the operation of the section to cases where the trading company is owned indirectly by a consortium.

Section 156: Sections 154 and 155: supplementary

620. This section explains some of the terms used in the two previous sections. It is based on section 410 of ICTA.

621. The reference to Scottish Ministers in subsection (2)(b) reflects section 117 of the Scotland Act 1998.

622. The definitions of "connected persons" and "control" applied by section 410(5) of ICTA are not rewritten in this section. There are Act-wide definitions in section 1176.

Chapter 6: Equity holders and profits or assets available for distribution

Overview

623. This Chapter sets out how the rights of equity holders are determined in this Part. These rights (to profits and assets of a company) are used as alternatives to simple shareholding for determining interests in a company:

- in determining the proportion of a company's loss etc that can be surrendered to a member of a consortium that owns the company (section 143(3));
- in determining the proportion of a company's profits that can used to absorb losses etc surrendered by a member of a consortium that owns the company (section 144(3)); and
- in the tests as to whether or not a company is a 75% subsidiary (or a 90% subsidiary) of another (section 151(4)).

Section 157: Introduction to Chapter

624. This section sets out the structure of the Chapter. It is based on Schedule 18 to ICTA.

625. *Subsection (2)* gives two rules of interpretation for the Chapter.

Section 158: Meaning of "equity holder"

626. This section defines "equity holder". It is based on paragraph 1 of Schedule 18 to ICTA.

627. *Subsection (1)* establishes that an equity holder may be:

- a shareholder (but only in relation to "ordinary shares" – see section 160); or
- a loan creditor (but only in relation to loans that are not "normal commercial loans" – see section 162).

628. *Subsection (2)* sets out the tests in section 417 of ICTA (also rewritten in section 453) to determine whether a person is a loan creditor of a company.

Section 159: Use of relevant company's assets

629. This section extends the meaning of "equity holder". It is based on paragraph 1 of Schedule 18 to ICTA.

630. The section treats as an equity holder a person who provides money to a company so that it can acquire an asset which is used in a trade by the person who provided the money. The company claims capital allowances on the asset.

631. In this case the person who provides the money has an economic stake in the company, whose results depend on the profits of the trade in which the asset is used. And this

is the case even if the money is provided by way of, say, restricted preference shares which would not otherwise count towards the investor's stake in the company (see section 160).

632. *Subsection (1)* sets the scene, specifying the conditions to be met for the section to apply.

633. *Subsection (2)* is the main rule: the person who provides the money is treated an equity holder.

634. *Subsection (3)* sets out the capital allowances to which the company must be entitled if the section is to apply.

635. *Subsection (4)* excludes from the application of the section a normal commercial loan made in the course of a banking business. The exclusion applies only to the extent that the amount of the commercial loan exceeds the cost of the assets.

Section 160: ***Meaning of "ordinary shares"***

636. This section defines "ordinary shares" by excluding restricted preference shares from the holdings that are to be considered for the purposes of this Chapter. It is based on paragraph 1 of Schedule 18 to ICTA.

637. *Subsection (2)* introduces the five conditions that have to be met if the shares are to be excluded as restricted preference shares.

638. *Subsection (3)* is the first condition. There must be new consideration. "New consideration" is defined in section 157(2) by reference to section 1115.

639. *Subsections (4)* to *(7)* set out the other conditions.

Section 161: ***Meaning of "restricted right to dividends"***

640. This section defines restricted right to dividends for use in condition D in section 160(6). It is based on paragraph 1A of Schedule 18 to ICTA.

641. *Subsection (1)* sets out the condition that dividends should not represent more than a reasonable commercial rate of return. This condition must be met whichever of the other conditions is relied on.

642. *Subsection (2)* rewrites condition A in paragraph 1A(2) of Schedule 18 to ICTA. It relates to fixed rate shares.

643. *Subsection (3)* rewrites condition B in paragraph 1A(3) of Schedule 18 to ICTA. It relates to shares that carry a dividend based on a published index (see subsection (5)).

644. *Subsection (4)* rewrites condition C in paragraph 1A(4) of Schedule 18 to ICTA. It relates to shares that carry a dividend that may be reduced or not paid in special circumstances (see subsection (6)).

645. *Subsections (5)* to *(8)* provide interpretative rules for the section, including a Treasury power in relation to "special circumstances" for the purpose of subsection (4).

Section 162: ***Meaning of "normal commercial loan"***

646. This section defines normal commercial loans so that they can be excluded from the loansthat are to be considered for the purposes of this Chapter. It is based on paragraph 1 of Schedule 18 to ICTA.

647. *Subsection (1)* requires that the loan includes new consideration. "New consideration" is defined in section 157(2) by reference to section 1115.

648. The subsection also introduces the four further conditions for a loan to be excluded. The details of the conditions are in *subsections (2)* to *(5)*.

Section 163: Normal commercial loans: company's results or value of assets

649. This section explains some of the concepts used in section 162. It is based on paragraph 1 of Schedule 18 to ICTA.

650. *Subsection (1)* allows a "fixed" rate of interest to include a rate that depends inversely on the company's results. Interest at a rate that increases when the company's results improve is like a dividend. But there is no need to treat interest as a dividend if its rate reduces when the company's results improve.

651. *Subsection (2)* allows a "fixed" rate of interest to include a rate that depends inversely on the value of the company's assets. Interest at a rate that increases when the company's assets increase in value is like a dividend. But there is no need to treat interest as a dividend if its rate reduces when the company's assets increase in value.

652. *Subsections (3)* to *(6)* make clear that a loan is not treated as depending on the value of any of the company's assets (see section 162(4)(b)) simply because it is secured by a charge over land acquired with the loan.

Section 164: Sections 160 and 162: supplementary

653. This section explains how the "quoted parent company" test is applied. It is based on paragraph 1 of Schedule 18 to ICTA.

654. In accordance with section 158 a holder of restricted preference shares does not count as an equity holder. Such shares may carry the right to conversion into shares or securities in the company's "quoted parent company" (see section 160(4)(c)). In order to establish whether the company (S) is a 75% subsidiary of the possible quoted parent company (P) it may be necessary to know whether P is an equity holder in S (see section 151(4)). So the process becomes circular.

655. A similar circularity can result from consideration of whether a loan is a normal commercial loan. The loan may carry the right to conversion into shares or securities in the company's "quoted parent company" (see section 162(2)(c)). Again, it is necessary to establish whether the company is a 75% subsidiary of the possible quoted parent company.

656. *Subsection (1)* deals with shares. It applies if all the conditions in section 160 are met, apart from the one (B) which may depend on conversion to shares or securities in a quoted parent company.

657. *Subsection (2)* deals with securities. It applies if all the conditions in section 162 are met, apart from the one (A) which may depend on conversion to shares or securities in a quoted parent company.

658. *Subsection (3)* sets out the main condition for a company having a quoted parent company: it must be a 75% subsidiary; and the parent's shares must be quoted on a stock exchange.

659. *Subsection (6)* sets the scope of the rule which breaks the circularity. It applies only for the purposes of sections 160 and 162 and this section.

660. *Subsection (7)* is the rulewhich breaks the circularity: the "candidate company" is assumed to be a quoted parent company.

Section 165: Proportion of profits available for distribution to which company is entitled

661. This section sets out how to apply the tests in this Part that are based on an entitlement to a distribution of profits. It is based on paragraph 2 of Schedule 18 to ICTA.

662. The tests in this Part, based on an entitlement to a distribution of profits, are in sections 143(3)(b), 144(3)(b) and 151(4)(a). The tests are also applied, by cross-reference, in, for example, the rules about small profits relief (see section 33(7)).

663. *Subsection (1)* sets the scope of the section and introduces company A (the parent) and company B (the subsidiary).

664. *Subsection (2)* is the basic rule: the proportion of the profits to which company A is entitled is based on what it would get if all company B's profits of an accounting period were distributed to its equity holders. If there are no profits in that accounting period a notional profit of £100 is assumed.

665. *Subsection (3)* clarifies the position in the case where some of company B's profits are in fact distributed. The section is still concerned with the whole of its profits.

666. *Subsection (4)* requires that company B's profits are calculated in accordance with United Kingdom tax rules, wherever it is resident.

667. *Subsection (5)* makes clear that the section is not concerned with any payments that are repayments of capital.

668. *Subsection (6)* includes in company A's entitlement any payment which it gets as an equity holder even if the payment would not otherwise count as a distribution.

Section 166: ***Proportion of assets available for distribution to which company is entitled***

669. This section sets out how to apply the tests in this Part that are based on an entitlement to a distribution of assets in a winding up. It is based on paragraph 3 of Schedule 18 to ICTA.

670. The tests in this Part, based on an entitlement to a distribution of assets in a winding up, are in sections 143(3)(c), 144(3)(c) and 151(4)(b). The tests are also applied, by cross-reference, in the rules about small profits relief (see section 33(7)).

671. *Subsection (1)* sets the scope of the section and introduces company A (the parent) and company B (the subsidiary).

672. *Subsection (2)* is the basic rule: the proportion of the assets to which company A is entitled is based on what it would get if company B's net assets at the end of an accounting period were distributed to its equity holders in a winding up. If there are no net assets (or if there is no balance sheet) at the end of that accounting period net assets of a notional amount of £100 are assumed.

673. *Subsection (3)* identifies the gross assets of company B, from which its liabilities are deducted to arrive at its net assets.

674. *Subsection (4)* identifies the liabilities of company B, which are deducted from its gross assets to arrive at its net assets.

675. *Subsection (5)* includes in company A's entitlement any payment which it would get as an equity holder even if the payment would not otherwise count as a distribution of assets.

676. *Subsections (6)* and *(7)* make clear that the section is not concerned with any payments that are repayments of capital. This exclusion affects the calculations of both company B's gross assets and the amount to which the equity holder is entitled.

*Section 167: **Profits or assets available for distribution and entitlement: supplementary***

677. This section includes three special rules for calculating an equity holder's entitlements for the purposes of sections 143(3), 144(3) and 151(4). It is based on paragraphs 1 and 6 of Schedule 18 to ICTA.

*Section 168: **Meaning of "the relevant accounting period"***

678. This section defines some expressions. It is based on paragraph 7 of Schedule 18 to ICTA.

679. The "relevant accounting period" is used for the calculation of a company's entitlement to profits or assets. Such a calculation is used to determine whether or nota company:

- is a member of a group; or
- is owned by a consortium.

680. *Subsections (2)* and *(3)* explain how to make the calculations in the cases of non-UK resident companies.

*Section 169: **Application and interpretation of sections 170 to 182***

681. This section introduces a group of sections that deal with shares and securities that have restricted or temporary rights. It is based on paragraphs 4, 5 and 5F of Schedule 18 to ICTA.

*Section 170: **Shares or securities with limited rights***

682. This section requires an alternative calculation if an equity holder's rights (either to profits or to assets in a winding up) are restricted. It is based on paragraph 4 of Schedule 18 to ICTA.

683. *Subsection (1)* introduces the section. The calculation is made at the "relevant time" (see section 169(2)).

684. *Subsection (2)* requires a calculation of the "alternative proportion" on the assumption that all the restricted rights are waived. So, if those rights belong to the company in question, its proportion is reduced. But if the rights belong to other equity holders its proportion is increased.

685. *Subsection (3)* substitutes the alternative proportion for the proportion worked out using the basic rules, but only if the alternative proportion is smaller.

686. *Subsection (5)* makes clear that any sort of restriction of the rights of an equity holder is to be taken into account for the purposes of the section.

687. *Subsection (6)* draws attention to the fact that restrictions based on profits or assets referable to a trade carried on in the United Kingdom by a non-UK resident company are dealt with in sections 179 to 182 and not in this section.

*Section 171: **Shares or securities with temporary rights***

688. This section and section 172 require an alternative calculation if an equity holder's rights (either to profits or to assets in a winding up) are capable of changing. Both sections are based on paragraph 5 of Schedule 18 to ICTA.

689. *Subsection (1)* sets the scope of the section. If it applies, the consequences are set out in section 172. The calculation is made at the "relevant time" (see section 169(2)).

Section 172: Company A's proportion if shares etc have temporary rights

690. This section and section 171 require an alternative calculation if an equity holder's rights (either to profits or to assets in a winding up) are capable of changing. Both sections are based on paragraph 5 of Schedule 18 to ICTA.

691. *Subsection (1)* takes up the story from the previous section, which determines whether or not this section applies. To arrive at the "alternative proportion" one must assume that the rights of the equity holders are now what they will be at a "future time" when the rights become different (see section 171(2) and (3)).

692. *Subsection (2)* explains "relevant future time".

693. *Subsection (3)* is the rule that the alternative proportion is used if it is smaller than the proportion that would otherwise be used.

Section 173: Cases in which option arrangements are in place

694. This section defines "option arrangement" for the purpose of section 174. It is based on paragraph 5B of Schedule 18 to ICTA.

695. *Subsection (1)* is a cross-reference to section 174, which sets out the consequences of option arrangements.

696. *Subsection (2)* introduces the two conditions that have to be satisfied if an arrangement is to be an option arrangement.

697. *Subsection (3)* is the condition that the arrangement changes the equity holder's entitlement. The subsection refers (twice) to beneficial entitlement but paragraph 5B(2) of Schedule 18 to ICTA refers only to entitlement. This is not a change in the law because the option arrangements are relevant only if they are used for a "determination" to be made under paragraph 5B(7) of the Schedule. The determination is made in accordance with paragraph 2(1) or 3(1) of the Schedule. Those sub-paragraphs make clear that the Schedule is concerned only with beneficial entitlements.

698. *Subsection (4)* is the condition that the option may lead to a person acquiring shares or securities. Shares must be ordinary shares (defined in section 160). The option may be a "call" option, which gives a person the right to acquire the shares or securities; or a "put" option, which gives a person the right to require another person to acquire shares or securities.

699. *Subsection (5)* excludes rights that arise from an SAYE option scheme or that are to acquire normal commercial loans.Rights to acquire restricted preference shares (see section 160) are excluded by the reference to "ordinary shares" in subsection (4).

700. *Subsections (6)* and *(7)*set out the excluded rights under an SAYE option scheme.

Section 174: Company A's proportion if option arrangements in place

701. This section requires an alternative calculation if an equity holder's rights (either to profits or to assets in a winding up) are affected by option arrangements. It is based on paragraph 5B of Schedule 18 to ICTA.

702. There is a distinction between:

- an option which affects the rights carried by shares or securities; and
- an option which leads to the acquisition of shares or securities.

703. In the first case, such an option would fall within section 171. This section deals with the second case, which was considered in J Sainsbury plc v O'Connor (1991), 64 TC 208 CA[2].

704. *Subsection (1)* provides a method statement. It requires a calculation for every permutation of rights that may exist if options are exercised so that shares or securities in the company are acquired. The permutation that gives the lowest proportion is the "alternative proportion".

705. *Subsection (2)* is the rule that the alternative proportion is used if it is lower than the proportion that would otherwise be used.

Sections 175 to 178

Overview

706. The first step in a calculation of an equity holder's proportion of profits available for distribution is based on the equity holder's share holding (see section 165). The equivalent first step in the calculation of an equity holder's proportion of assets available for distribution in a winding up is in section 166.

707. The next step is to check whether there is a (lower) alternative proportion in accordance with the three special rules in:

- section 170 (limited rights);
- section 172 (temporary rights); or
- section 174 (options).

708. If only one of the special rules applies the lower alternative proportion is used. But sections 175 to 178 explain what happens if two or three of the special rules apply in the same case.

709. If two rules apply, there are four possible proportions:

- calculated under the basic rule in section 165 or 166;
- calculated under one of the special rules;
- calculated under the other of the special rules; or
- calculated under both rules together.

710. If all three rules apply, there are eight possible proportions.

711. In all cases, the lowest proportion is used.

*Section 175: **Cases in which both sections 170 and 172 apply***

712. This section deals with the first and second special rules. It is based on paragraph 5A of Schedule 18 to ICTA.

*Section 176: **Cases in which both sections 170 and 174 apply***

713. This section deals with the first and third special rules. It is based on paragraph 5C of Schedule 18 to ICTA.

*Section 177: **Cases in which both sections 172 and 174 apply***

714. This section deals with the second and third special rules. It is based on paragraph 5D of Schedule 18 to ICTA.

2 [1991] STC 318

Section 178: Cases in which sections 170, 172 and 174 all apply

715. This section deals with the first, second and third special rules. It is based on paragraph 5E of Schedule 18 to ICTA.

Section 179: Cases in which surrendering or claimant company is non-UK resident

716. This section introduces special rules about equity holders in non-UK resident companies. It is based on paragraph 5F of Schedule 18 to ICTA.

717. *Subsection (1)* sets the scope of the section.

718. *Subsection (2)* applies the special rules in section 180 if the equity holder's rights are used to establish whether or not a non-UK resident company is owned by a consortium.

719. *Subsection (3)* applies the special rules in section 180 if the equity holder's rights are used to establish whether or not a non-UK resident company is a subsidiary of another company.

720. *Subsection (4)* applies the special rules if ("Case 1") the equity holder's rights are referable to the profits or assets of the non-resident company's "UK trade". It also operates in this way if ("Case 2") the equity holder has rights under an option arrangement which are referable to the profits or assets of the non-resident company's UK trade. The extent to which profits or assets are referable to the company's UK trade is determined in accordance with section 182.

Section 180: Company A's proportion if non-UK resident involved

721. This section is the main special rule aboutequity holders in non-UK resident companies. It is based on paragraph 5F of Schedule 18 to ICTA.

722. *Subsection (1)* introduces the section: subsection (2) applies in cases where there are no limited rights, temporary rights or option arrangements; subsection (3) applies in other cases.

723. *Subsection (2)* deals with the straightforward case in which none of sections 170 (limited rights), 172 (temporary rights) or 174 (options) applies. The alternative proportion calculated on the assumptions in section 181 is used if it is lower than the proportion that would otherwise be used.

724. *Subsection (3)* is a method statement which deals with the more complicated cases involving sections 170 (limited rights), 172 (temporary rights) and 174 (options), either singly or in the various possible combinations (see sections 175 to 178). The rule is that any calculations under those sections is done again using the assumptions in section 181 and the result of that calculation is used if it is lower than the proportion would otherwise be.

Section 181: Assumptions to be applied if non-UK resident company involved

725. This section sets out how to calculate the "alternative proportion" for section 180. It is based on paragraph 5F of Schedule 18 to ICTA.

726. All the calculations under section 180 are done by reference to amounts that are "referable to company B's UK trade" (defined in section 182).

727. Assumptions 2 and 3 do not include £100 as an alternative to the company's United Kingdom profits or assets (see paragraph 5F(7)(b) of Schedule 18 to ICTA, which applies if the profits are between £1 and £99). This is because the alternative has little or no practical effect. See *Change 26* in Annex 1. In a case where there are no profits, section 165(2) substitutes the amount of £100.

728. Assumption 4 refers (three times) to beneficial entitlement but paragraph 5F(7)(c) and (8) of Schedule 18 to ICTA refers only to entitlement. This is not a change in the law because the option arrangements are relevant only if they are used for a "determination" to be made under paragraph 5F(4) or (5) of the Schedule. The determination is made in accordance with paragraph 2(1) or 3(1) of the Schedule. Those sub-paragraphs make clear that the Schedule is concerned only with beneficial entitlements.

*Section 182: **Assets etc referable to UK trade***

729. This section determines the extent to which amounts are referable to a company's "UK trade". It is based on paragraph 5F of Schedule 18 to ICTA.

730. *Paragraph (b)* of the section excludes amounts attributable to activities that are "double taxation exempt". That expression is defined in section 186.

*Chapter 7: **Miscellaneous provisions and interpretation of Part***

Overview

731. This Chapter contains definitions and two minor rules.

*Section 183: **Payments for group relief***

732. This section takes outside the tax system any payments for group relief. It is based on section 402 of ICTA.

733. Originally (from 1953 to 1967) a form of group relief was available, based on "subvention" payments from one company to another. The payment was allowed as a deduction, reducing the profits of the paying company; and it was a taxable receipt of the company receiving the payment. Such payments are no longer required by United Kingdom tax law. But they may be made by agreement between group members. This section ensures that they are neither allowed as a deduction nor taxed.

*Section 184: **References to "allowance" in CAA 2001***

734. This section clarifies the position if capital allowances are surrendered as group relief. It is based on section 411 of ICTA.

735. Capital allowances surrendered as group relief still count as having been made to the surrendering company. This means that a balancing charge on the surrendering company takes into account those surrendered allowances.

*Section 185: **"Trading company" and "holding company"***

736. This section provides definitions. It is based on section 413(3) of ICTA.

*Section 186: **When activities of a company are double taxation exempt***

737. This section explains what is meant by activities that are double taxation exempt. It is based on section 403D of, and paragraph 5F of Schedule 18 to, ICTA.

738. The definition is used in sections 107(4), 108(3), 140(8), and 182(b).

739. *Subsection (1)* makes the link between the *activities* that are described in the Part as exempt and the *profits* from those activities which are the subject of exemption under a DTA.

740. *Subsection (2)* makes clear that activities are to be treated as exempt whether or not any necessary claim for exemption is actually made.

741. *Subsection (3)* defines "double taxation arrangements" by reference tosection 2 of TIOPA. They are "... arrangements ... made in relation to any territory outside the

United Kingdom with a view to affording relief from double taxation in relation to ..." the taxes within subsection (3) of that section.

Section 187: *Meaning of "non-UK tax"*

742. This section defines "non-UK tax" for this Part of the Act. It is based on sections 403D and 403E of, and paragraph 17 of Schedule 18A to, ICTA. The expression is used in sections 106 to 109, 115 to 121 and 949.

743. *Subsection (1)* is the basic rule that the non-UK tax must correspond to United Kingdom income tax or corporation tax.

744. *Subsection (2)* makes clear that the non-UK tax need not be a national tax: it may be a tax imposed by a province or state of a foreign country.

Section 188: *Other definitions*

745. This section sets out definitions of expressions used in the Part. It is based on sections 6(4) and 413 of ICTA.

746. *Subsection (2)* defines "trade" so that it includes an office but does not refer to a company having a vocation or employment.See *Change 4* in Annex 1.

Part 6: Charitable donations relief

Overview

747. This Part deals with qualifying charitable donations, known as "charges on income" in the source legislation.

748. Chapter 1 gives relief for qualifying charitable donations and defines the term as qualifying payments and amounts treated as qualifying charitable donations. Chapter 2 deals with qualifying payments and Chapter 3 is about disposals treated as qualifying charitable donations.

749. For corporation tax purposes charges on income are now reduced to charitable donations only (see section 338A(2) of ICTA). A more accurate description has therefore been substituted for "charges on income". The term "charges on income" was dispensed with for income tax purposes by ITA and this Act now follows that path.

750. It is not considered that by relabelling "charges on income" as "qualifying charitable donations" there is any danger of either depriving a company of a relief which is due or allowing relief that is not due for a payment.

Chapter 1: *Nature of relief*

Overview

751. This Chapter allows a deduction from a company's total profits for qualifying charitable donations and explains what constitutes qualifying charitable donations. It is based on sections 338, 338A, and 339(1) of ICTA.

Section 189: *Relief for qualifying charitable donations*

752. This section allows qualifying charitable donations as deductions from a company's total profits. It is based on section 338 of ICTA.

753. Allowable deductions are limited to an amount which reduces the taxable total profits for a period to nil.

Section 190: ***Qualifying charitable donations: meaning***

754. This section gives the meaning of qualifying charitable donations. It is based on sections 338A(1) to (3) and 339(1) of ICTA.

755. *Subsection (2)* rewrites both section 338A(3) and section 339(1)(b) of ICTA. These two subsections cover the same ground.

756. A similar rule is found in section 337A(1)(b) of ICTA which provides that a company's income from any source is to be computed without any deduction in respect of charges on income. This is rewritten and inserted into Chapter 1 of Part 20 of CTA 2009 (restriction of deductions) by Schedule 1 but expressed as a qualifying charitable donation rather than a charge on income.

Chapter 2: ***Certain payments to charity***

Overview

757. This Chapter gives relief for certain payments of money by companies to charities. It is based on section 339 of ICTA.

Section 191: ***Qualifying payments***

758. This section sets out the conditions which have to be met if a sum paid to a charity is to be a qualifying payment and hence a qualifying charitable donation. It is based on section 339(1), (3B), (3E), and (3G) of ICTA.

Section 192: ***Condition as to repayment***

759. This section provides that under certain conditions a charitable payment is not subject to a "condition as to repayment" (see section 191(3)). It is based on sections 339(3BA) and (3BB) of ICTA.

760. *Subsection (6)*, in referring to non-charitable expenditure, rewrites the cross-reference to "section 505(4)" of ICTA in section 339(3BB) of ICTA as section 493 and section 515. Section 515 rewrites section 505(4) of ICTA and section 493 section 505(5) of ICTA. Non-charitable expenditure referred to in section 505(5) is, by implication, the same non-charitable expenditure as is referred to in section 505(4). It was considered helpful however to clarify in the rewrite that non-charitable expenditure in both the accounting period (section 505(4)) and previous accounting period (section 505(5)) are referred to by subsection (6).

Section 193: ***Associated acquisition etc***

761. This section specifies circumstances in which a payment to a charity is prevented from being a qualifying payment because of association with an acquisition of property by the charity from the donor or an associated company. It is based on section 339(3E) of ICTA.

Section 194: ***Distributions***

762. This section prevents a distribution from being a qualifying payment other than in the case of a payment from a company which is whollyowned by a charity. It is based on section 339(1), (1A) and (1B) of ICTA.

Section 195: ***Associated benefits***

763. This section prevents one or more payments which result in benefits from being qualifying payments, unless the benefits are within the limits set out in section 197 (restrictions on associated benefits). It is based on section 339(3B) of ICTA.

*Section 196: **Associated benefits: meaning***

764. This section explains for the purposes of the Chapter when a benefit is associated with a payment to a charity. It is based on section 339(3B) of ICTA.

*Section 197: **Restrictions on associated benefits***

765. This section sets out two conditions which, if either is met, mean that the restrictions on benefits associated with a payment to a charity are breached. It is based on section 339(3B), (3C), (3D) and (3DA) of ICTA.

766. The two conditions are:

- a stepped scale, depending on the amount of each payment (Condition A) – the "benefit per payment" test; and
- an overall monetary limit on benefits associated with the total of any payments to a single charity in the course of an accounting period – the "benefit per accounting period" test (Condition B). This is unrelated to the size of any particular payment.

767. Both these restrictions apply to any benefit "associated with" a payment.

*Section 198: **Payments and benefits linked to periods of less than 12 months***

768. This section modifies the application of section 197 where payments or benefits are linked to periods of less than 12 months. It is based on section 339(3DB), (3DC) and (3DD) of ICTA.

769. The section provides, according to the case, for annualising:

- the actual amount of the payment; or
- both the amount of the payment and the value of the benefit(s) associated with the payment.

770. Only the annualised amount in each case is to be compared with the cash limits given in section 197. This prevents periods of less than 12 months being used to exploit the cash limits.

771. *Subsection (8)* states the formula for annualising in each case. In the source legislation some of the conditions could overlap, so that more than one condition could apply to the payment(s) and associated benefits concerned. This subsection removes doubt about which might take priority by providing a priority rule where payments are made at intervals of less than 12 months. See *Change 27* in Annex 1.

*Section 199: **Payment attributed to earlier accounting period***

772. This section allows an election to be made for a payment to be attributed to an earlier accounting period which falls within a period of nine months prior to the date of the payment instead of the accounting period in which the payment is made. It is based on section 339(7AA) of ICTA.

773. *Subsection (3)* sets out the time within which a claim must be made. The reference in the source legislation to claims being to the Board of Inland Revenue has been changed. Claims are simply to an officer of Revenue and Customs. See *Change 5* in Annex 1.

*Section 200: **Company wholly owned by a charity***

774. This section sets out what conditions are required to be met in order for a company to be wholly owned by a charity. It is based on section 339(7AB) and (7AC) of ICTA.

Section 201: Associated persons

775. This section defines an associated person as a person who is connected with the company or who is connected with such a person. It is based on section 339(7A) of ICTA.

Section 202: "Charity"

776. This section defines "charity" for the purposes of the Chapter and is based on section 339(9) of ICTA.

777. Section 339(9) of ICTA defines charity, in part, by reference to the bodies mentioned in section 507 of ICTA. That section includes the Trustees of the BritishMuseum and the Trustees of the Natural History Museum. The BritishMuseum and NaturalHistoryMuseum are established for charitable purposes and so there is no need to refer to them separately in this definition.

Chapter 3: Certain disposals to charity

Overview

778. This Chapter gives relief to companies making donations to charities not by payments of money but by way of certain disposals including disposals at an undervalue. It is based on sections 587B to 587C of ICTA.

Section 203: Certain disposals of investments

779. This section sets out the requirements for relief. It is based on section 587B(1) and (2) of ICTA.

780. *Subsection (3)* prevents relief under section 105(2) of CTA 2009 where relief is given under this section. Section 105 of CTA 2009 deals with gifts of "articles" manufactured, or of a class or description sold by, the donor in the course of the trade. It is considered that this may include certain shares or securities which fall within this section.

Section 204: Meaning of qualifying investment

781. This section lists the types of investment that can attract relief. It is based on section 587B(9) to (9ZB) of ICTA.

Section 205: Meaning of qualifying interest in land

782. This section defines "qualifying interest in land" (one of the qualifying investments listed in section 204). It is based on section 587B(9A) to (9E) of ICTA.

783. *Subsections (2)* and *(3)* clarify the position where a company with a beneficial interest in a freehold or leasehold interest in land in the United Kingdom gives that beneficial interest to a charity along with any easement, servitude or right that benefits the land. For example, company A's land may only be accessible by way of an easement over B's land. If company A gives the charity both the land and the right over B's land, the disposal of the right is treated as a separate disposal.

784. Under *subsection (4)*, if a company with a freehold or leasehold interest carves out of that interest a lease for the benefit of the charity, the retention of the freehold or leasehold reversion does not prevent the disposal from being "of the whole beneficial interest".

785. Under *subsection (5)*, an agreement to acquire a freehold, or an agreement for a lease, is not a qualifying interest in land. So disposing of such an agreement would not constitute a disposal of a qualifying investment.

*Section 206: **The relievable amount***

786. This section sets out how to calculate the relievable amount, first in cases where the qualifying investment is transferred to the charity by way of gift (*subsection (1)*), and then where there is some, but not full, consideration for the transfer (*subsection (2)*). It is based on section 587B(4) to (7) of ICTA.

787. In each case, the computation starts with the value of the net benefit to the charity (V), either directly (as in subsection (1)) or in arriving at E (the excessof V over the consideration for the disposal) in subsection (2).

788. The detail of how V is calculated is in sections 209 to 212. But it is emphasised in the definition of V in subsection (1) that V must be considered both at, and immediately after, the time of disposal. If there is a difference between V at these two times, the lesser amount is taken.

789. *Subsection (3)* makes it explicit that if the amount given by either formula is negative the relievable amount is nil.

790. The treatment of incidental costs of disposal depends on whether the transfer is by way of gift or at an undervalue. If it is a gift, all the incidental costs areadded in arriving at the relievable amount. But if there is consideration for the disposal, there is an interplay between the capital gains tax treatment and the incidental costs.

791. Under section 257(2)(a) of TCGA a gift of a qualifying investment to a charity is treated as being for such a consideration as results in neither a loss nor a gain to the donor. Incidental costs are added only if that deemed consideration is greater than the actual consideration. But the amount added must not be greater than that excess. C is defined in *subsection (4)* to achieve this result.

*Section 207: **Incidental costs of making disposal***

792. This section defines "the incidental costs of making the disposal to the company making it". It is based on section 587B(9) of ICTA.

793. The section reproduces the relevant material in section 38(2) of TCGA to which section 587B(9) of ICTA cross-refers, with the exception of the reference to stamp duty and stamp duty land tax, which do not apply to transactions within this Chapter.

*Section 208: **Consideration***

794. This section makes provision about the calculation of the relievable amount in the case of disposal at an undervalue. It is based on section 587B(7) of ICTA.

795. The section applies section 48 of TCGA (consideration due after time of disposal). The main thrust of section 48 of TCGA is that full value is to be introduced into the computation of the gain. Only on a subsequent claim is the consideration to be reduced, either because the right to receive any amount is contingent or because any part of the consideration proves to be irrecoverable.

*Section 209: **Value of net benefit to charity***

796. This section is the first of four sections concerned with defining the value of the net benefit to the charity. It is based on section 587B(8A) and (8B) and (9) of ICTA.

797. In the simple case, where there are no disposal-related obligations, the value of the net benefit to the charity is the market value of the qualifying investment. As indicated in section 206, this has to be considered both at, and immediately after, the disposal.

798. If the charity is, or becomes, subject to an obligation that is related to the disposal of the qualifying investment to the charity, the market value of the investment is reduced

by the amount of the disposal-related liabilities (see section 212) under the obligation. These obligations must also be considered both at, and immediately after, the disposal.

*Section 210: **Market value of qualifying investments***

799. This section sets out how the market value of qualifying investments is to be determined. It is based on section 587B(9) to (11) of ICTA.

800. The methods are those laid down in sections 272 to 274 of TCGA. If an offshore fund publishes buy and sell prices, an interest in it is in effect subject to the same treatment as a unit trust scheme as laid down by section 272(5) of TCGA. The provisions of that subsection are reproduced here.

*Section 211: **Meaning of "disposal-related obligation"***

801. This section defines "disposal-related obligation". It is based on section 587B(8B) to (8D) and (9) of ICTA.

*Section 212: **Meaning and amount of "disposal-related liability"***

802. This section defines "disposal–related liability". It is based on section 587B(8E) to (8G) and (9) of ICTA.

803. *Subsection (2)* deals with contingent disposal-related obligations.

804. It is in the nature of a contingency that it may occur after the time of disposal; hence the words "at any time". If a contingency occurs later than immediately after the disposal, but existed as a possibility at the time of disposal, the value of the net benefit to the charity at the time of, or immediately after, the disposal must be reduced. All necessary adjustments must be made to give effect to this. Conversely, if the contingency does not occur, to that extent there is no obligation and no liability.

*Section 213: **Certificate required from charity***

805. This section, which is the first of four that deal specifically with qualifying interests in land, requires any claim for relief in relation to a qualifying interest in land to be supported by a certificate from the charity. It is based on section 587C(1), (4) and (5) of ICTA.

*Section 214: **Qualifying interests in land held jointly***

806. This section deals with a disposal of land by all joint holders where at least one of the owners is a qualifying company. It is based on section 587BA(1) to (5) and (13) of ICTA.

*Section 215: **Calculation of relievable amount etc where joint disposal of interest in land***

807. This section provides details for calculating the "relievable amount" in cases where there is a joint disposal of an interest in land. It is based on section 587BA(6) to (11) of ICTA.

808. If the joint owners include an individual *subsection (3)* directs the reader to Chapter 3 of Part 8 of ITA for the purposes of the relievable amount where that situation is catered for.

*Section 216: **Disqualifying events***

809. This section provides for the recovery of relief if a "disqualifying event" occurs within the "provisional period". It is based on section 587C(1) and (6) to (10) of ICTA.

810. In the simplest case, such an event occurs if any of the persons who made the disposal are entitled to buy the land back from the charity at an undervalue.

Section 217: "Charity"

811. This section defines "charity" for the purposes of the Chapter. It is based on section 587B(9) of ICTA.

Part 7: Community investment tax relief

Overview

812. This Part provides for community investment tax relief (CITR), that is corporation tax reductions for companies which invest in community development finance institutions (CDFIs). It is based on Schedule 16 to FA 2002.

813. Schedule 16 to FA 2002 as enacted also provided for CITR for individuals who invested in CDFIs, by way of reduction of income tax. Relief for individuals has been rewritten in Part 7 of ITA. This Part of this Act largely mirrors Part 7 of ITA.

814. Schedule 1 to ITA has inserted sections 151BA, 151BB and 151BC in TCGA, replacing paragraphs 40 and 41 of Schedule 16 to FA 2002 and, so far as they apply for the purposes of capital gains tax or corporation tax on chargeable gains, paragraphs 47 and 48(2) of that Schedule. Those sections of TCGA accordingly apply in relation to CITR for both individuals and companies.

Chapter 1: Introduction

Overview

815. This Chapter quantifies the tax reduction potentially available to a company, labels certain concepts and provides signposts to material contained elsewhere.

Section 218: Meaning of "CITR"

816. This section sets out a general description of the nature of the relief, an entitlement to tax reductions, and defines it as "CITR". It is new.

Section 219: Eligibility for CITR

817. This section summarises the general conditions which need to be met for a company ("the investor") to be eligible for CITR. It is based on paragraphs 1 and 4(1) of Schedule 16 to FA 2002.

818. *Subsection (1)(a)* requires that, for an investment in a CDFI to qualify for CITR, the CDFI must be accredited under Chapter 2 of Part 7 of ITA.

819. Chapter 2 of Part 7 of ITA provides that accreditation is to be made by the Secretary of State, sets out the criteria for accreditation, contains powers to determine the manner of making applications and the terms and conditions of accreditation, and authorises delegation of the Secretary of State's functions. These functions have been assigned to the Secretary of State for Business, Innovation and Skills.

820. Sections 340 and 341 in Chapter 2 of Part 7 of ITA contain powers for the Treasury to make regulations. The regulations in force are the Community Investment Tax Relief (Accreditation of Community Development Finance Institutions) Regulations 2003 (SI 2003/96), made under the predecessor of those powers in paragraphs 4 and 5 of Schedule 16 to FA 2002, as amended by the Community Investment Tax Relief (Accreditation of Community Development Finance Institutions) (Amendment) Regulations 2008 (SI 2008/383).

821. Regulations may make different provision for bodies whose principal objective in providing finance is to invest in enterprises whose business does not consist of financing other enterprises or does so only to the extent permitted by the regulations. If such a body is accredited, it is designated as a retail community development finance institution (a "retail CDFI"). See the commentary on section 340 of ITA in the explanatory notes on that Act.

822. The distinction between a retail CDFI and an accredited CDFI which is not a retail CDFI (a "wholesale CDFI") is relevant to the limits on the total value of investments which a CDFI can make for an accreditation period and which are set out in section 348(4) of ITA and section 229(4) of this Act. SI 2003/96 provides different limits on the value of investments which a retail CDFI and a wholesale CDFI may make in any enterprise.

823. As a consequence of the direct references to Chapter 2 of Part 7 of ITA in subsection (1)(a) of this section and elsewhere in this Part, it is unnecessary to rewrite paragraph 4(2)of Schedule 16 to FA 2002, as substituted by ITA, which contains signposts to the provisions of that Chapter.

*Section 220: **Form and amount of CITR***

824. This section specifies the amount of the corporation tax reduction available and the accounting periods for which it may be claimed. It is based on paragraph 20 of Schedule 16 to FA 2002.

825. The combined effect of *subsections (2)* and *(3)* is that the maximum tax reduction is 25% of the amount invested and is available at the rate of not more than 5% of that amount in each of five accounting periods beginning with that in which the investment is made.

*Section 221: **Meaning of "making an investment"***

826. This section provides that an investment in a CDFI may take the form of a loan or an issue of securities or shares. It is based on paragraph 2 of Schedule 16 to FA 2002. See also section 256 which extends the meaning of "loan" to include certain alternative finance arrangements.

*Section 222: **Determination of "the invested amount"***

827. This section sets out rules for determining the amount invested for the purposes of section 220.It is based on paragraph 21 of Schedule 16 to FA 2002. In particular, it deals with the complications which arise where a loan may be drawn down in tranches, by requiring the average capital balance of the loan in relation to the accounting period to be calculated.

*Section 223: **Meaning of "the 5 year period" and "the investment date"***

828. This section provides the definitions of two significant terms. It is based on paragraph 3 of Schedule 16 to FA 2002. "The 5 year period", which begins with "the investment date", is the period during which conditions as to the repayment or redemption of the investment are imposed.

*Section 224: **Overview of other Chapters of Part***

829. This section indicates the subject matter of the Chapters of this Part not previously mentioned in Chapter 1. It is new.

*Chapter 2: **Qualifying investments***

Overview

830. This Chapter sets out the conditions which must be met if an investment is to be a qualifying investment.

*Section 225: **Qualifying investments: introduction***

831. This section introduces:

- the respective conditions which apply to loans (section 226), to securities (section 227) and to shares (section 228), and
- the provisions which apply to all kinds of investment (sections 229 and 230).

It is based on paragraph 8 of Schedule 16 to FA 2002.

*Section 226: **Conditions to be met in relation to loans***

832. This section sets out the three conditions applicable to loans. It is based on paragraph 9 of Schedule 16 to FA 2002.

*Section 227: **Conditions to be met in relation to securities***

833. This section sets out the two conditions applicable to securities. It is based on paragraph 10 of Schedule 16 to FA 2002.

834. Condition A (*subsection (1)*) requires that securities must be subscribed for wholly in cash and fully paid for on the investment date. It is in similar terms to section 228(1) which sets out identical requirements in relation to shares.

835. Section 228(3) (based on paragraph 11(1) of Schedule 16 to FA 2002) provides that shares are not fully paid up for the purposes of section 228(1) if there is any undertaking to pay cash to the CDFI at a future date in connection with the acquisition of the shares. The effect of this is to distinguish the meaning of "paid up" for that purpose from the meaning of those words for the purposes of the Companies Acts in section 583 of the Companies Act 2006 which provides that a share is deemed paid up in cash, or allotted for cash, if the consideration for the allotment or payment up is an undertaking to pay cash to the company at a future date.

836. There is no similar provision in the Companies Acts applicable to the issue of securities, but the position in relation to securities has been made explicit by the inclusion of *subsection (3)*, equivalent to section 228(3). This clarification is not a change in either law or practice.

*Section 228: **Conditions to be met in relation to shares***

837. This section sets out the two conditions applicable to shares. It is based on paragraph 11 of Schedule 16 to FA 2002.

*Section 229: **Tax relief certificates***

838. This section sets limits on the value of investments in respect of which a CDFI may issue tax relief certificates in an accreditation period. It is based on paragraph 4(3) and 12 of Schedule 16 to FA 2002. Without a tax relief certificate, an investor may not claim CITR (see section 220(5)(b)).

839. *Subsections (2)* and *(3)* provide that the limit applies to the total value of investments in the CDFI made in the accreditation period by companies under this Part and by individuals under Part 7 of ITA.

840. *Subsection (4)* provides different amounts for the limits for retail and wholesale CDFIs. See the commentary on section 219.

841. *Subsections (6)* and *(7)* provide for the substitution of different amounts by Treasury order for the amounts in subsection (4). Subsection (7) is based on paragraph 12(5) of Schedule 16 to FA 2002 which provides that:

"Any such substitution shall have effect in relation to such accreditation periods as may be specified in the order; and those periods may, if the substitution increases the amount for the time being specified in sub-paragraph (2), include periods beginning before the order takes effect.

842. Subsection (7) corrects two infelicities in the source legislation. For "the amount" it substitutes "an amount" to avoid any doubt that the power to apply an increase retrospectively can be exercised if one only of the amounts in subsection (4) is increased. For "the order takes effect" it substitutes "the order comes into force". The wording in the source legislation could be misconstrued as referring to the time when the order is itself made. The substituted wording clarifies that the intended meaning is the time when the provisions of the order come into force.

843. In *subsection (8)*, the words "wholly or partly", which appear before "in contravention" in paragraph 12(6) of Schedule 16 to FA 2002, have been omitted as being unnecessary.

Section 230: No pre-arranged protection against risks

844. This section is an anti-avoidance provision concerned with ensuring that the investor is subject to all usual investment risks and is not protected from their effect by insurance, indemnity, guarantee or other means. It is based on paragraph 13 of Schedule 16 to FA 2002.

Chapter 3: General conditions

Overview

845. This Chapter contains various general conditions to be met by the investor. It is based on Part 4 of Schedule 16 to FA 2002.

Section 231: No control of CDFI by investor

846. This section provides that the investor does not qualify for CITR in relation to an investment if the investor or a person connected with the investor controls the CDFI at any time in the 5 year period. It is based on paragraph 14 of Schedule 16 to FA 2002.

847. The legal structure of a CDFI may take a number of forms. It may be a company or some other form of body corporate or it may be a partnership or some other form of unincorporated association. The different meanings of control needed to deal with the possible different forms of a CDFI's constitution are set out in *subsections (3)* to *(6)*.

Section 232: Investor must have beneficial ownership

848. This section provides that the investor must be the sole beneficial owner of the investment. It is based on paragraph 15 of Schedule 16 to FA 2002. Trustees and joint investors are thus precluded from obtaining CITR. But see section 262 which enables investments to be made by a nominee or a bare trustee for a company.

Section 233: Investor must not be accredited

849. This section prevents a CDFI claiming CITR in respect of an investment in another CDFI. It is based on paragraph 16 of Schedule 16 to FA 2002.

Section 234: No acquisition of share in partnership

850. This section provides that an investor cannot obtain CITR for capital contributed to a CDFI which is a partnership, including loan capital accounted for as partners' capital. It is based on paragraph 17 of Schedule 16 to FA 2002.

Section 235: No tax avoidance purpose

851. This section denies CITR if the investment is part of a scheme or arrangement the main purpose or one of the main purposes of which is the avoidance of tax. It is based on paragraph 18 of Schedule 16 to FA 2002.

Chapter 4: Limitations on claims and attribution

Overview

852. This Chapter is based on Part 5 of Schedule 16 to FA 2002 other than paragraphs 20 and 21. Sections 220 and 222 in Chapter 1 are based on those two paragraphs.

Section 236: Loans: no claim after disposal or excessive repayments or receipts of value

853. This section prevents a claim being made for any accounting period in respect of an investment by way of loan in certain circumstances. It is based on paragraph 22 of Schedule 16 to FA 2002. This section links to the provisions in sections 243, 245 and 246 which provide for a tax reduction already given to be recaptured in similar circumstances.

Section 237: Securities or shares: no claim after disposal or excessive receipts of value

854. This section sets out two conditions to be met before a claim can be made for any accounting period in respect of a subscription for securities or shares. It is based on paragraph 23 of Schedule 16 to FA 2002.

855. The first condition (*subsection (1)*) is that the investor has not disposed of the securities or shares before the first anniversary of the investment date which occurs after the end of the accounting period.

856. The second condition (*subsection(2)*) is that the investor has not received or is not treated as having received value from the CDFI in excess of the limits allowed under section 247.

Section 238: No claim after loss of accreditation by the CDFI

857. This section provides that no claim may be made if the CDFI ceases to be accredited. It is based on paragraph 24 of Schedule 16 to FA 2002.

858. Depending on the investment date and the date upon which the CDFI ceased to be accredited, this section may prevent a claim being made for the accounting period before that in which the CDFI ceased to be accredited (see *subsections (2)* to *(4)*).

859. Subsections (2) to (4) unpack paragraph 24(2) of Schedule 16 to FA 2002 in order to make its various elements clearer.

Section 239: Accreditation of investor

860. This section provides that no claim may be made if the investor becomes accredited as a CDFI. It is based on paragraph 25 of Schedule 16 to FA 2002. This section has no equivalent in Part 7 of ITA as an individual cannot be a CDFI.

861. Depending on the investment date and the date upon which the investor becomes accredited, this section may prevent a claim being made for the accounting period before that in which it became accredited (see *subsections (2)* to *(4)*).

862. *Subsections (3) to (5)* unpack paragraph 25(2) of Schedule 16 to FA 2002 in the same way that section 238(2) to (4) unpack paragraph 24(2) of that Schedule.

*Section 240: **Attribution: general***

863. This section sets out the general rules dealing with the attribution to the loan, securities or shares of the reduction in the investor's corporation tax liability for any accounting period made as a result of the investor's entitlement to CITR. It is based on paragraph 26(1) to (4), (7) and (8) of Schedule 16 to FA 2002.

864. Attribution is required for the purpose of determining the amount of the tax reduction which must be withdrawn or reduced in accordance with Chapter 5 of this Part.

*Section 241: **Attribution: bonus shares***

865. This section sets out additional rules relating to attribution, to deal with the consequences of an issue of "corresponding bonus shares" (see *subsection (4)*) to the investor in respect of the original shares included in the investment. It is based on paragraph 26(5) and (6) of Schedule 16 to FA 2002.

*Chapter 5: **Withdrawal or reduction of CITR***

Overview

866. This Chapter sets out the circumstances in which CITR attributable to an investment for any accounting period must be reduced to nil (withdrawn) or reduced proportionately. It is based on Part 6 of Schedule 16 to FA 2002.

*Section 242: **Introduction to Chapter***

867. This section provides an overview of the Chapter and contains signposts to its principal provisions. Apart from *subsection (3)*, it is new.

868. Subsection (3) is based on paragraph 33 of Schedule 16 to FA 2002,with the substitution of the term "the 6 year period" for the term "the period of restriction" in that paragraph but without any change in the definition of the term. The 6 year period is relevant to sections 246 and 247 which deal with receipts of value. As an anti-avoidance measure, receipts of value in the year before the investment dateare taken into account, as well as those in the 5 year period, which begins with the investment date. See the commentary on section 223 for the meaning of "the 5 year period" and "the investment date".

*Section 243: **Disposal of loan during 5 year period***

869. This section provides that the CITR attributable to a loan must be withdrawn if, within the 5 year period, the investor disposes (otherwise than by receiving repayment) of part of the loan or, unless it is by way of a permitted disposal, of the whole of the loan. It is based on paragraph 28 of Schedule 16 to FA 2002.

870. A permitted disposal is defined in *subsection (2)*. If the disposal is a permitted disposal, any tax reduction already obtained is not withdrawn, but no further tax reduction may be claimed (see sections 220(6) and 236).

*Section 244: **Disposal of securities or shares during 5 year period***

871. This section provides for the withdrawal or reduction of CITR attributable to securities or shares, if the investor disposes of the whole or part of the investment in the securities or shares (except upon repayment, redemption or repurchase by the CDFI) within the 5 year period and the CDFI is accredited at the time of the disposal. It is based on paragraph 29 of Schedule 16 to FA 2002.

872. *Subsections (2)* and *(3)* provide for different consequences depending upon whether the disposal is a qualifying disposal.

873. *Subsection (4)* defines what is a qualifying disposal. It is based on paragraph 29(4) of Schedule 16 to FA 2002 with the omission of the words "for full consideration" in paragraph(a). See *Change 11*in Annex 1.

874. There is inconsistency of language between paragraph 29(3) and (5) of Schedule 16 to FA 2002 which refer to CITR being attributable *for*an or any accounting period and paragraph 26(1)(b) of that Schedule (rewritten in section 240(1)) which defines references in that Schedule to "CITR attributable ... *in respect of*an accounting period". This section removes this inconsistency by substituting "in respect of" in *subsections (3)* and *(5)*.

875. Subsection (5)provides for circumstances where 5% of the invested amount is greater than the corporation tax liability of the investor for the accounting period.

Section 245: Repayment of loan capital during 5 year period

876. This section provides for the circumstances in which the CITR attributable to a loan must be withdrawn as a consequence of a repayment other than a "non–standard" repayment (see *subsections (3)* to *(5)*). It is based on paragraph 30 of Schedule 16 to FA 2002.

Section 246: Value received by investor during 6 year period: loans

877. This section applies if the investment consists of a loan and the investor or a person connected with the investor receives any value, other than an amount of insignificant value (as defined in *subsection (5)*), from the CDFI or a person connected with the CDFI in the 6 year period. It is based on paragraph 31 of Schedule 16 to FA 2002.

878. *Subsection (2)* provides that, if value is so received, the invested amount (see section 222) is adjusted by the amount treated as repaid and the investor is treated as having received a repayment other than a non-standard repayment for the purposes of section 245(see *subsection (4)*).

879. In subsection (5) the words "of value" have been added after "means an amount". This conforms the language of this subsection with that of sections 247(4), 248(4) and 252(4).

Section 247: Value received by investor during 6 year period: securities or shares

880. This section applies if the investment consists of securities or shares and the investor or a person connected with the investor receives any value, other than an amount of insignificant value (as defined in *subsection (4)*), from the CDFI or a person connected with the CDFI in the 6 year period. It is based on paragraph 32 of Schedule 16 to FA 2002.

881. *Subsection (2)* provides that, if value is so received and its amount wholly or partly exceeds the permitted level (see *subsection (3)*) by more than an amount of insignificant value, the CITR attributable to the investment must be withdrawn.

Section 248: Receipts of insignificant value to be added together

882. This section applies at a time when the investor receives value, if the investor has also received value earlier in the 6 year period and the total amount of the value received earlier was of insignificant value. It is based on paragraph 34 of Schedule 16 to FA 2002.

883. The amount of the receipt in question is to be added to the amounts of value previously received. If the total value of the amounts received is not an amount of insignificant value, the total value is treated as received at that time for the purposes of this Part, including in particular sections 245, 246 and 247.

884. *Subsection (8)* is new. It provides that this section is subject to section 251 which modifies the effect of this section and of sections 246, 247 and 252.

885. Sections 246(7) and 247(5) already provide that those sections are subject to section 251. Subsection (8) of this section and new subsection (5) of section 252 (see the commentary on that section) have been added to ensure consistency.

*Section 249: **When value is received***

886. This section explains when value is received. It is based on paragraph 35 of Schedule 16 to FA 2002.

887. In *subsection (1)(d)(i)*, as in section 366(1)(d) of ITA, the singular "associate" is used in place of the plural "associates" in paragraph 35(1)(d)(i) of Schedule 16 to FA 2002. Similarly in *subsection (1)(d)(ii)* the singular "a director or employee" is used instead of the plural "directors or employees" in paragraph 35(1)(d)(ii) of that Schedule.

*Section 250: **The amount of value received***

888. This section determines the respective values received in relation to the respective transactions listed in paragraphs (a) to (g) of section 249(1). It is based on paragraph 36 of Schedule 16 to FA 2002.

889. To give clarity, *subsection (1)* sets out the values against the paragraphs of section 249(1) in tabular form.

890. In a case falling within section 249(1)(d)(ii), the table permits the deduction of consideration which is given by a director or employee or an associate of a director or employee, in addition to consideration given by the investor or any associate of the investor. See *subsection (2)* and *Change 28* in Annex 1.

*Section 251: **Value received if there is more than one investment***

891. This section provides that, if there is more than one investment, any value received is to be apportioned among the investments according to the respective amounts invested and sets out how those amounts are to be calculated. It is based on paragraph 37 of Schedule 16 to FA 2002.

*Section 252: **Effect of receipt of value on future claims***

892. This section applies if an investor holding securities or shares receives value (other than an amount of insignificant value) but, because that value is less than the permitted level, the CITR attributable to those securities or shares is not withdrawn under section 247. It is based on paragraph 38 of Schedule 16 to FA 2002.

893. *Subsection (2)* reduces the amount invested (see section 222) in respect of which CITR may be claimed for the accounting periods specified in *subsection (3)*.

894. *Subsection (5)* is new. It provides that this section is subject to section 251 which modifies the effect of this section and of sections 246, 247 and 248.

895. Sections 246(7) and 247(5) already provide that those sections are subject to section 251. Subsection (5) of this section and new subsection (8) of section 248 (see the commentary on that section) have been added to ensure consistency.

*Section 253: **Receipts of value by or from connected persons***

896. This section extends the meaning of "the investor" and "the CDFI" in sections 246 to 252. It is based on paragraph 39 of Schedule 16 to FA 2002.

897. The words "if the context permits" have been added in this section. These words, which do not appear in paragraph 39 of Schedule 16 to FA 2002, do not change the law. They

make sections 246 to 252 clearer, by stating explicitly what is implicit in the source legislation.

*Section 254: **CITR subsequently found not to have been due***

898. This section provides the basis for making an assessment under section 255 in cases where a claim for a tax reduction has been incorrectly allowed. It is based on paragraph 27 of Schedule 16 to FA 2002.

*Section 255: **Manner of withdrawal or reduction of CITR***

899. This section authorises the making of assessments to recapture CITR attributable to an investment which has been withdrawn or reduced. It is based on paragraph 27 of Schedule 16 to FA 2002.

900. *Subsections (3)* and *(4)* are based on paragraph 27(5) and (6) of Schedule 16 to FA 2002 prospectively inserted by section 118 of, and paragraph 48 of Schedule 39 to, FA 2008 (time limits for assessments, claims etc) with effect from 1 April 2010 by virtue of the FA2008, Schedule 39 (Appointed Day, Transitional Provision and Savings) Order 2009 (SI 2009/403). The effect of thesesubsections is to preserve the right to make an assessment under this section not more than six years after the end of the accounting period for which the relief was obtained, when the normal time limit for the making of assessments under paragraph 46 of Schedule 18 to FA 1998 is reduced to four years by virtue of that Order bringing paragraph 42 of Schedule 39 to FA 2008 into force on 1 April 2010.

*Chapter 6: **Supplementary and general***

Overview

901. This Chapter contains provisions relating to alternative finance arrangements, other miscellaneous provisions and definitions applicable to this Part.

902. Sections 256 to 259 modify this Part to enable the range of permitted investments in, and by, CDFIs to include various Sharia'a-compliant financial products that in substance, but not in form, are equivalent to interest-bearing loans. Such products are to be treated as loans for the purposes of this Part.

*Section 256: **Meaning of "loan" and "interest"***

903. This section extends the meaning of the term "loan" to include purchase and resale arrangements, deposit arrangements and profit share agency arrangements and the meaning of the term "interest" to include profit share return under those alternative finance arrangements. It is based on section 54A(1) and (2) of FA 2005.

*Section 257: **Purchase and resale arrangements***

904. This section sets out how this Part has effect in relation to purchase and resale arrangements. It is based on section 54A(3) and (4) of FA 2005.

*Section 258: **Deposit arrangements***

905. This section sets out how this Part has effect in relation to deposit arrangements. It is based on section 54A(5) of FA 2005.

*Section 259: **Profit share agency arrangements***

906. This section sets out how this Part has effect in relation to profit share agency arrangements. It is based on section 54A(6) of FA 2005.

*Section 260: **Information to be provided by the investor***

907. This section imposes obligations on the investor to notify an officer of Revenue and Customs of events giving rise to the withdrawal or reduction of any CITR attributable to a loan or any securities or shares. It is based on paragraph 42 of Schedule 16 to FA 2002.

908. There is inconsistency of language between paragraph 42(1)(b) of Schedule 16 to FA 2002 which refers to CITR being attributable *for* any accounting period and paragraph 26(1)(b) of that Schedule (rewritten in section 240(1)) which defines references in that Schedule to "CITR attributable ... *in respect of* an accounting period". This section removes this inconsistency by substituting "in respect of" in *subsection (1)(b)*.

*Section 261: **Disclosure***

909. This section authorises disclosure of information between HMRC and the Secretary of State for the purpose of discharging their respective functions under this Part. It is based on paragraph 43 of Schedule 16 to FA 2002.

*Section 262: **Nominees***

910. This section allows for loans, securities or shares to be acquired, held and disposed of by nominees or bare trustees. It is based on paragraph 44 of Schedule 16 to FA 2002.

*Section 263: **Application for postponement of tax pending appeal***

911. This section ensures that the investor cannot claim to postpone any payment of tax under section 55 of TMA on the grounds that the investor is eligible for CITR unless a claim has actually been made. It is based on paragraph 45 of Schedule 16 to FA 2002.

*Section 264: **Identification of securities or shares on a disposal***

912. This section provides rules for the identification of the securities or shares disposed of for the purposes of this Part. It is based on paragraph 47 of Schedule 16 to FA 2002.

*Section 265: **Meaning of "issue of securities or shares"***

913. This section provides definitions, in relation to a body, of an issue of securities or shares by that body and, in relation to a company, of an issue of securities or shares to that company. It is based on paragraph 46 of Schedule 16 to FA 2002.

*Section 266: **Meaning of "disposal"***

914. This section defines "disposal". It is based on paragraph 48 of Schedule 16 to FA 2002.

*Section 267: **Construction of references to being "held continuously"***

915. This section explains what is meant by "held continuously", for the purposes of those sections of this Part which require the investment to have been "held continuously" by the investor during a specified period (see for example sections 247 and 252). It is based on paragraph 49 of Schedule 16 to FA 2002.

*Section 268: **Meaning of "associate"***

916. This section provides a definition of "associate", which is relevant to sections 249 and 250. It is based on paragraph 50 of Schedule 16 to FA 2002.

*Section 269: **Minor definitions etc***

917. This section explains various terms used in this Part. It is based on paragraph 51 of Schedule 16 to FA 2002.

918. With the exception of "body", the terms defined in paragraph 51(1) of Schedule 16 to FA 2002 have been omitted, as they are either no longer required or are defined generally for the purposes of this Act.

919. A definition of "bonus shares" has been added in *subsection (1).*

920. In *subsection (2)*, which determines when shares are to be treated as being of the same class, for the words "if dealt with on the Stock Exchange" in paragraph 51(2) of Schedule 16 to FA 2002 there are substituted the words:

> "if they were—
> (a) included in the official UK list and
> (b) admitted to trading on the London Stock Exchange."

See section 1005 of ITA as applied for corporation tax purposes by section 841 of ICTA for the meaning of "included in the official UK list".

921. The words used in paragraph 51(2) of Schedule 16 to FA 2002 have been in wide use in tax legislation from a time when the London Stock Exchange only operated a single market. The reference to the Stock Exchange is accordingly to be taken as a reference to the requirements of the London Stock Exchange in relation to shares traded on the main market, rather than on AIM or any other platform. The substituted words are intended to preserve and clarify the meaning of the source legislation and do not change the law.

922. Paragraph 51(3) of Schedule 16 to FA 2002, which applies section 839 of ICTA (connected persons) for the purposes of that Schedule, has not been rewritten. Section 839 of ICTA is rewritten in section 1122 for the purposes of the Corporation Tax Acts and section 1176(1) applies that definition generally for the purposes of this Act.

Part 8: Oil activities

Overview

923. This Part contains rules relating to the corporation tax charge, including the supplementary charge, on profits from oil extraction and related activities. It rewrites Chapter 5 of Part 12 of, and Schedule 19C, to ICTA, sections 62 to 65 of FA 1991 and Schedule 44 to FA 2009. Section 496A of, and Schedule 19B to, ICTA (exploration expenditure supplement) are not rewritten. These particular rules apply only to expenditure incurred before 1 January 2006. They are therefore of limited future application.

924. Some of the source legislation relates to both income tax and corporation tax – the necessary rules for income tax are inserted into ITTOIA (after section 225) by TIOPA, which comes into effect at the same time as this Act.

925. A number of PRT definitions are used in the corporation tax and income tax rules, and some parts of the legislation depend on calculations made for PRT purposes. In particular the legislation uses the PRT term "participator" (see section 12(1) of OTA 1975). The legislation for PRT is not itself being rewritten.

926. The definitions of "exploration and exploitation activities", "exploration and exploitation rights" and "designated area" are in section 1313 of CTA 2009. The equivalent income tax definitions are in section 874 of ITTOIA.

927. The extension of the United Kingdom to its territorial sea for the purposes of the scope of corporation tax, in section 830(1) of ICTA, is rewritten in section 1170 of this Act. The corresponding rule for income tax is section 1013 of ITA.

928. Oil is used as a shorthand throughout the commentary on these sections, but unless specifically mentioned the same rules and considerations apply to gas and other associated products.

929. The material is organised as follows:

- Chapter 1: Introduction
- Chapter 2: Basic definitions
- Chapter 3: Deemed separate trade
- Chapter 4: Calculation of profits
- Chapter 5: Ring fence expenditure supplement
- Chapter 6: Supplementary charge in respect of ring fence trades
- Chapter 7: Reduction of supplementary charge for certain new oil fields

*Chapter 1: **Introduction***

*Section 270: **Overview of Part***

930. This section provides an overview of the legislation. It is new.

*Chapter 2: **Basic definitions***

*Section 271: **"Associated companies"***

931. This section sets out the definition of "associated companies" for the purposes of the Part. It is based on section 502(3), (3A) and (4) of ICTA.

932. *Subsection (2)* applies the consortium relief rules in Part 5 of this Act for the purposes of this Part with the following modification.

933. Section 153 provides the conditions by which a company is a member of a consortium. The additional circumstance in section 153(3) is not relevant for the purposes of the oil taxation provisions. Section 271 therefore operates by adopting a definition of "owned by a consortium" which encompasses the meaning of section 153(1) and (2) only.

*Section 272: **"Oil extraction activities"***

934. This section sets out the definition of "oil extraction activities" for the purposes of this Part. It is based on section 502(1) and (2) of ICTA.

935. Certain definitions are taken from the PRT legislation in section 12 of OTA 1975.

936. The corresponding rule for income tax is section 225A of ITTOIA (inserted by Schedule 1 to TIOPA).

*Section 273: **"Oil rights"***

937. This section sets out the meaning of "oil rights" for the purposes of this Part. It is based on section 502(1) of ICTA.

938. The corresponding rule for income tax is section 225B of ITTOIA (inserted by Schedule 1 to TIOPA).

*Section 274: **"Oil-related activities"***

939. This section sets out a definition of "oil-related activities". It is based on section 492(1) of ICTA.

940. This definition underpins the meaning of "ring fence trade" in section 277 and the deeming of a separate trade for corporation tax purposes in section 279. The corresponding rule for income tax is section 16 of ITTOIA.

Section 275: "Ring fence income"

941. This section sets out the meaning of "ring fence income" for the purposes of this Part. It is based on section 502(1) of ICTA and section 62 of FA 1991.

942. This term is then picked up in section 276 as part of the definition of a company's "ring fence profits".

943. The corresponding rule for income tax is section 225C of ITTOIA (inserted by Schedule 1 to TIOPA).

Section 276: "Ring fence profits"

944. This section sets out the meaning of "ring fence profits" for the purposes of this Part. It is based on section 502(1) and (1A) of ICTA.

945. Although the definition is not explicitly limited to corporation tax in the source legislation, the term is only used in the legislation in relation to corporation tax. This term is therefore not included in the rewritten rules for income tax.

Section 277: "Ring fence trade"

946. This section sets out the meaning of "ring fence trade" for the purposes of this Part. It is based on section 502(1) of ICTA.

947. The corresponding rule for income tax is section 225D of ITTOIA (inserted by Schedule 1 to TIOPA).

Section 278: Other definitions

948. This section sets out further definitions necessary for this Part. It is based on sections 493(1A), 500(10) and 502(1) and (2) of ICTA, and section 62(2) of FA 1991.

949. The corresponding rule for income tax is section 225E of ITTOIA (inserted by Schedule 1 to TIOPA).

Chapter 3: Deemed separate trade

Section 279: Oil–related activities treated as separate trade

950. This section deems a separate trade of oil-related activities to exist for corporation tax purposes where a company carries on those activities as part of its trade. It is based on section 492(1) of ICTA. The corresponding rule for income tax is section 16 of ITTOIA.

Chapter 4: Calculation of profits

Overview

951. This Chapter contains the rules that determine how income/profits from a ring fence trade are calculated, to the extent that they differ from the calculation for any other type of trade. The starting point is that all normal trading income rules apply unless they are modified by a provision of this Chapter. The calculation may also be affected by the ring fence expenditure supplement rules set out in Chapter 5.

952. The general rules for the calculation of trading income for corporation tax purposes are in Part 3 of CTA 2009.

Section 280: Disposal to be valued by reference to section 2(5A) of OTA 1975

953. This section modifies the calculation of profits for corporation tax purposes where certain expenses are incurred in connection with the transportation of oil. It is based on section 493(A1) to (A3) of ICTA. There is no equivalent for income tax.

954. The starting point is section 2(5A) of OTA 1975, which involves situations where the seller disposes of oil at arm's length and is required to meet certain transportation costs – *subsection (6).*

955. Section 2(5A) OTA 1975 replaces:

- actual sales proceeds from a sale at arm's length under a contract which requires the seller to meet the transport costs,

with

- deemed proceeds based on a hypothetical sale at arm's length under which the seller does not have to meet the transport costs and has to transport the oil to the nearest landing point (or, in the case of onshore fields, to the place of extraction itself).

956. *Subsection (9)* adopts the price given by section 2(5A) of OTA 1975, for the seller only – it has no impact on the purchaser. Section 3(1)(f) of OTA 1975 allows transport costs for transportation to that point. If a company does not claim transportation costs for corporation tax then for practical purposes the price at that point is the actual sale price minus the transport costs to that point.

957. In order to prevent double counting, *subsections (7)*and *(8)* require that the company does not otherwise get a deduction for the transportation cost or "transportation allowance" against either its ring fence or non ring fence profits, as that allowance is in effect netted off to reach the price in subsection (9).

Section 281: ***Valuation where market value taken into account under section 2 of OTA 1975***

958. This section specifies that where the market value of oil is included in the calculation of profits for PRT purposes by OTA 1975 in place of the actual sale price, the same price applies for corporation tax. It is based on section 493(1) of ICTA.

959. The market value applies to both the seller and the purchaser. The section therefore retains the term "person" rather than "company" as the other party may not necessarily be a company. The market value is derived by way of a comprehensive scheme put in place for PRT purposes – see in particular section 2 of and Schedule 3 to OTA 1975.

960. The corresponding rule for income tax is section 225F of ITTOIA (inserted by Schedule 1 to TIOPA).

Section 282: ***Valuation where disposal not sale at arm's length***

961. This section applies a market value price where oil is disposed of otherwise than at arm's length, but where the disposal is not covered by the PRT rules. It is based on section 493(3), (5) and (6) of ICTA.

962. A common application of this rule is where oil is extracted from an oil field that is not within the scope of PRT following the reforms in FA 1993, which took fields given development consent on or after 16 March 1993 out of the scope of PRT.

963. This section also retains the term "person" because the transactions may not necessarily involve only companies.

964. The corresponding rule for income tax is section 225G of ITTOIA (inserted by Schedule 1 to TIOPA).

Section 283: ***Valuation where excess of nominated proceeds***

965. This section ensures that where the "nomination scheme" adds an amount to the disposal value of oil for PRT purposes, that amount is also added for corporation tax purposes. It is based on section 493(1A) of ICTA.

966. The corresponding rule for income tax is section 225H of ITTOIA (inserted by Schedule 1 to TIOPA).

967. The "nomination scheme" is part of the mechanism to ensure that the full value of oil extracted from the UK sector is reflected in the profits calculated for PRT and for the ring fence trade. A full description of the scheme can be found in HMRC guidance at OTM 5199.

968. The addition to the price for corporation tax purposes is made even if the relevant oil field is not within the scope of PRT – see *subsection (1)(b)*.

969. *Subsection (3)* provides for a deduction in computing the profits of a non-ring fence trade. The wording has been changed to clarify its meaning as the source legislation in section 493(1A)(b) of ICTA was unclear. See *Change 29* in Annex 1.

*Section 284: **Valuation where relevant appropriation but no disposal***

970. This section imposes a market value in a case where an oil producer does not sell the oil to another party but takes it into use in another of its businesses, such as refining. It is based on section 493(2) of ICTA.

971. The corresponding rule for income tax is section 225I of ITTOIA (inserted by Schedule 1 to TIOPA).

972. Where a market value is applied for PRT purposes by OTA 1975, that market value is used in the calculation of profits for corporation tax purposes – see *subsections (4)* and *(5)*. The market value also applies to the non-ring fence trade.

*Section 285: **Valuation where appropriation to refining etc***

973. This section imposes a market value in a case where an oil producer does not sell the oil to another party but takes it into use in another of its businesses, such as refining, and where the PRT rules do not apply. It is based on section 493(4), (5) and (6) of ICTA.

974. The corresponding rule for income tax is section 225J of ITTOIA (inserted by Schedule 1 to TIOPA).

975. In such a case the same calculation of market value is made using the PRT rules as if the PRT rules had applied to the appropriation.

*Section 286: **Restriction on debits to be brought into account***

976. This section modifies the loan relationship rules in the case of a ring fence trade. It is based on section 494(2) and (2A) of ICTA.

977. The section ensures that non-trading debits from a company's loan relationships cannot be set against the company's ring fence profits, unless the loan relationship represents money borrowed to finance oil extraction activities or to acquire oil rights. The loan relationship rules are in Parts 5 and 6 of CTA 2009.

978. *Subsection (5)*provides that where a non-trading debit is restricted in this way the legislation allows the company to have relief for the debit against other profits.

*Section 287: **Restriction on credits to be brought into account***

979. This section ensures that exchange gains in respect of loan relationships are not treated as part of the ring fence profits where the exchange gains do not arise from money borrowed to finance ring fence activities. It is based on section 494(2), (2ZA) and (2A) of ICTA.

980. The section operates in a similar way to section 286. Where a credit is excluded from the computation of ring fence profits it is brought into account by *subsection (5)*.

*Section 288: **Sale and lease-back***

981. This section ensures that where financing has been obtained by way of a sale and lease-back of assets, a deduction for the expenditure may not be made against ring fence profits unless certain conditions are met. It is based on section 494AA of ICTA.

982. *Subsections (6)* and *(7)*ensure thata deduction is only permitted against ring fence profits if the disposal proceeds are used in the ring fence trade.

983. Where the deduction is prevented from being given in full or in part against the ring fence profits, *subsection (8)* allows a deduction from other profits of the companyforany amount that has not been allowed because of this section.

984. This section has no income tax equivalent.

*Section 289: **Reduction of expenditure by reference to regional development grant***

985. This section restricts a deduction for expenditure incurred to the extent that the expenditure has been met by a regional development grant. It is based on section 495(1), (2) and (7) of ICTA.

986. The corresponding rule for income tax is section 225K of ITTOIA (inserted by Schedule 1 to TIOPA).

987. The main restriction in respect of a grant is applied by section 534 of CAA. This section applies essentially the same restriction to the purchaser of an asset who buys the asset from a connected party, and where that connected party received a regional development grant on the original acquisition or construction of the asset.

988. The source legislation applies to expenditure taken into account under Parts 2, 3 or 6 of CAA. Section 84 of FA 2008 repeals Part 3 of CAA for corporation tax purposes with respect to expenditure incurred on or after 1 April 2011. The section therefore applies to Parts 2 and 6 of CAA and the reference to Part 3 of CAA has been retained for the interim period by way of a transitional provision in Schedule 2.

*Section 290: **Adjustment as a result of regional development grant***

989. This section supplements section 289 and section 534 of CAA where the amount of expenditure involved is re-determined at a later date. It is based on section 495(3) to (7) of ICTA.

990. The corresponding rule for income tax is section 225L of ITTOIA (inserted by Schedule 1 to TIOPA).

991. The most likely application of regional development grants in the oil context is for onshore assets such as initial treatment plants to stabilise the crude oil arriving by pipeline. The eligibility of such assets for PRT relief, or the proportion that is eligible, can take some time to agree. As a result, the PRT position (which determines the amount eligible for capital allowances) may not be finalised for some time.

992. Accordingly, capital allowances could be given on the full amount in the "initial period", disregarding the grant, as section 534(2) of CAA or its predecessors would not have applied at that stage. *Subsection (5)* ensures that the position can be adjusted in a later period if a change in circumstances occurs.

993. Section 137 of FA 1982, referred to in the source legislation, was rewritten in section 534 of CAA.

994. The source legislation applies to expenditure taken into account under Parts 2, 3 or 6 of CAA. Section 84 of FA 2008 repeals Part 3 of CAA for corporation tax purposes with respect to expenditure incurred on or after 1 April 2011. The section therefore applies

to Parts 2 and 6 of CAA and the reference to Part 3 of CAA has been retained for the interim period by way of a transitional provision in Schedule 2.

Section 291: Tariff receipts etc

995. This section brings certain tariff receipts into the calculation of ring fence profits if those receipts would not otherwise be included. It is based on section 496 of ICTA.

996. The corresponding rule for income tax is section 225M of ITTOIA (inserted by Schedule 1 to TIOPA).

997. Tariff receipts arise where assets used in the ring fence trade are not used wholly for oil extraction by the owner but are used by other businesses in return for payment of a fee or "tariff". Typical examples include the use of pipelines and treatment plants.

998. Tax-exempt tariffing receipts arise where the oil field to which the assets are attached for PRT purposes is not within the charge to PRT and therefore the tariffs are not chargeable to PRT.

999. Definitions of "tariff receipt" and "tax-exempt tariffing receipt" have been included to aid users of the legislation.

Section 292: Expenditure on and under abandonment guarantees

1000. This section provides relief against corporation tax where an oil field participator incurs expenditure in obtaining an abandonment guarantee. It is based on sections 62 and 63(8) of FA 1991.

1001. The corresponding rule for income tax is section 225N of ITTOIA (inserted by Schedule 1 to TIOPA).

1002. The cost of decommissioning oil fields is eligible for relief under the capital allowances code. But as the majority of oil fields are shared between two or more participators there is a risk that one or more of the participators may not meet their share of the cost when the time comes. As a result participators have taken out guarantees with financial institutions to cover their share. This section provides relief for the cost of obtaining the guarantee.

Section 293: Relief for reimbursement expenditure under abandonment guarantees

1003. This section provides relief for a participator against ring fence profits where some or all of a participator's share of decommissioning costs is met by a guarantee and the participator subsequently reimburses the guarantor. It is based on section 63 of FA 1991.

1004. The corresponding rule for income tax is section 225O of ITTOIA (inserted by Schedule 1 to TIOPA).

Section 294: Payment under abandonment guarantee not immediately applied

1005. This section applies where a guarantor makes payments into a fund and the assets of the fund are subsequently used to cover decommissioning costs. It is based on section 62(4) of FA 1991.

1006. The corresponding rule for income tax is section 225P of ITTOIA (inserted by Schedule 1 to TIOPA).

1007. In such a case the rules for relief under section 292 or 293 apply to the expenditure when it is eventually met out of the assets of the fund.

*Section 295: **Amounts excluded from section 293(1)***

1008. This section restricts relief where amounts are repaid to a guarantor instead of being applied to meet decommissioning costs. It is based on section 63(2) of FA 1991.

1009. The corresponding rule for income tax is section 225Q of ITTOIA (inserted by Schedule 1 to TIOPA).

*Section 296: **Introduction to sections 297 and 298***

1010. This section sets out the circumstances in which sections 297 and 298 apply, and provides some related definitions. It is based on sections 64(1), (2) and (3) and 65(1) of FA 1991.

1011. The corresponding rule for income tax is section 225R of ITTOIA (inserted by Schedule 1 to TIOPA).

*Section 297: **Relief for expenditure incurred by a participator in meeting defaulter's abandonment expenditure***

1012. This section provides for relief to a participator who meets the decommissioning expenditure that should have been met by another participator (the "defaulter"). It is based on section 64(4) and (5) of FA 1991.

1013. The corresponding rule for income tax is section 225S of ITTOIA (inserted by Schedule 1 to TIOPA).

*Section 298: **Reimbursement by defaulter in respect of certain abandonment expenditure***

1014. This section applies where a defaulting participator reimburses another participator who has met the defaulter's liability for decommissioning expenditure. It is based on section 65 of FA 1991.

1015. The corresponding rule for income tax is section 225T of ITTOIA (inserted by Schedule 1 to TIOPA).

1016. Relief against ring fence profits is given to the defaulter, and the other participator is treated as receiving additional ring fence income.

1017. The time limit in *subsection (5)* was amended from six years to four years by paragraph 27 of Schedule 39 to FA 2008. This change takes effect by Order from 1 April 2010 (see article 2(2) of the Finance Act 2008, Schedule 39 (Appointed Day, Transitional Provisions and Savings) Order 2009 (SI 2009/403)).

*Section 299: **Deduction of PRT in calculating income for corporation tax purposes***

1018. This section provides that a company may deduct PRT paid as an expense in calculating profits from the ring fence trade. It is based on section 500(1), (2), and (3) of ICTA.

1019. Sections 300 and 301 set out what happens when PRT is repaid and section 302 deals with interest on PRT repayments.

*Section 300: **Effect of repayment of PRT: general rule***

1020. This section provides that when an amount of PRT is repaid the deduction under section 299 is reduced by the amount repaid. It is based on section 500(4) of ICTA.

1021. *Subsection (2)* provides thatthe repayment reduces or extinguishes the deduction for the original period for which the deduction was given, not the period when the repayment was received.

1022. The time limit in *subsection (3)* was amended from six years to four years by paragraph 23 of Schedule 39 to FA 2008. This change takes effect by Order from 1 April 2010 (see article 2(2) of the Finance Act 2008, Schedule 39 (Appointed Day, Transitional Provisions and Savings) Order 2009 (SI 2009/403)).

Section 301: Effect of repayment of PRT: special rule

1023. This section supplements section 300 in cases where the repayment derives from a carried back loss. It is based on section 500(5) to (10) of ICTA.

1024. In such a case the PRT repayment is treated as received, and hence the reduced deduction for corporation tax is applied, for the period in which the loss arose.

1025. The time limit in *subsection (6)* was amended from six years to four years by paragraph 23 of Schedule 39 to FA 2008. This change takes effect by Order from 1 April 2010 (see article 2(2) of SI 2009/403).

Section 302: Interest on repayment of PRT or APRT

1026. This section provides that interest paid to a participator on a repayment of PRT or advance PRT is disregarded in calculating profits for corporation tax purposes. It is based on section 501 of ICTA and paragraph 10 of Schedule 19 to FA 1982.

Section 303: Management expenses

1027. This section prohibits a deduction for expenses of management of an investment business against profits from a ring fence trade. It is based on section 492(3A) of ICTA.

Section 304: Losses

1028. This section prevents losses that arise in trades outside the ring fence from being set off against ring fence profits. It is based on section 492(3) and (4) of ICTA.

1029. Where a set-off is prevented in this way, *subsection (5)*allowsthe loss to be carried forward and set against future profits from "related activities", that is activities which, taken together with the ring fence trade, would be regarded as a single trade but for the specific ring fence rule in section 279.

1030. The equivalent income tax rule, originally in section 492(2) of ICTA, is in section 80 of ITA.

1031. See section 40 for rules about the extension of the loss carry-back period in a ring fence trade where allowances for abandonment expenditure under section 164 of CAA are involved; and section 43, which extends the time limit for making a claim where allowances are made under section 165 (general decommissioning expenditure after ceasing ring fence trade) or 416 (site restoration expenditure) of CAA.

Section 305: Group relief

1032. This section prevents group relief arising from losses, allowances or expenditure outside the ring fence trade from being set against profits from the ring fence trade. It is based on sections 492(8) and 494A(1), (2) and (3) of ICTA.

1033. *Subsections (2)* and *(3)* provide that where a company cannot use certain amounts against its ring fence profits, those ring fence profits are disregarded in calculating how much the company can surrender as group relief.

Section 306: Capital allowances

1034. This section ensures that capital allowances arising from "special leasing" cannot be deducted from a company's ring fence profits. It is based on section 492(6) and (7) of ICTA.

1035. The restriction does not apply to the extent that the leased asset is used in oil extraction activities by an associated company.

1036. Section 492(5) of ICTA is not rewritten as it is considered to be unnecessary. It prohibits the deduction of capital allowances given under section 258 of CAA against general profits. However, the deduction under section 258 of CAA can only be given against income from special leasing and not against other profits. Special leasing is defined in section 19 of CAA as leasing that is not part of any other qualifying activity. It is therefore not necessary to have a rule to protect ring fence income from this type of deduction.

Chapter 5: Ring fence expenditure supplement

Overview

1037. This Chapter rewrites the rules in Schedule 19C to ICTA, which provide a supplement for certain expenditure incurred on or after 1 January 2006. These rules superseded the exploration expenditure supplement in Schedule 19B to ICTA, which applies to expenditure incurred before 1 January 2006. Schedule 19B is therefore of limited future application and is not rewritten. This also means that certain terms used in this Chapter such as "the carried forward qualifying Schedule 19B amount" do not need to be altered.

Section 307: Overview of Chapter

1038. This section sets out an overview of the Chapter. It is based on paragraph 1 of Schedule 19C to ICTA.

Section 308: Qualifying companies

1039. This section sets out the definition of a qualifying company for the purposes of this Chapter. It is based on paragraph 2 of Schedule 19C to ICTA.

Section 309: Accounting periods

1040. This section sets out defined terms for accounting periods that lie either side of, or straddle, 1 January 2006. It is based on paragraph 3 of Schedule 19C to ICTA.

Section 310: The relevant percentage

1041. This section sets out the relevant percentage for the supplement and provides a power for the Treasury to vary the percentage by order. It is based on paragraph 4 of Schedule 19C to ICTA.

Section 311: Limit on number of accounting periods for which supplement may be claimed

1042. This section limits to six the number of accounting periods for which supplement may be claimed. It is based on paragraph 5 of Schedule 19C to ICTA.

1043. *Subsection (3)* directs that a claim for an accounting period under Schedule 19B to ICTA counts as part of the overall total of six accounting periods.

Section 312: Qualifying pre-commencement expenditure

1044. This section defines "qualifying pre-commencement expenditure" for the purposes of the Chapter. It is based on paragraph 6 of Schedule 19C to ICTA.

Section 313: Unrelieved group ring fence profits for accounting periods

1045. This section defines the term "unrelieved group ring fence profits" for an accounting period. It is based on paragraph 7 of Schedule 19C to ICTA.

1046. The broad scheme of the supplement is to increase the amount of certain expenditure and losses that cannot be relieved immediately to reflect the time value of the delay in obtaining effective tax relief. But where there are unrelieved profits from a ring fence trade elsewhere in the same group, some or all of the losses could have been used against those other ring fence profits in the same accounting period. Where this is the case supplement is restricted by section 318 or 328 as appropriate. The pool of expenditure eligible for supplement in a given period is reduced by the amount of any unrelieved group ring fence profits.

1047. This term applies for both pre-commencement and post-commencement supplement.

*Section 314: **Taxable ring fence profits for an accounting period***

1048. This section defines the term "taxable ring fence profits" for the purposes of the Chapter. It is based on paragraph 8 of Schedule 19C to ICTA.

1049. This term is used in section 313 to determine the amount of unrelieved group ring fence profits.

*Section 315: **Supplement in respect of a pre-commencement accounting period***

1050. This section sets out when a company may qualify for pre-commencement supplement, and how the supplement is given effect. It is based on paragraph 9 of Schedule 19C to ICTA.

1051. Supplement is given as a percentage of the "reference amount", which is defined in section 319. "Pre-commencement period" is defined in section 309.

*Section 316: **The mixed pool of qualifying pre-commencement expenditure and supplement previously allowed***

1052. This section sets out how the pool of expenditure that qualifies for pre-commencement supplement is determined. It is based on paragraph 10 of Schedule 19C to ICTA.

1053. The pool can include amounts carried forward from the exploration expenditure supplement in Schedule 19B to ICTA.

*Section 317: **Reduction in respect of disposal receipts under CAA 2001***

1054. This section restricts the amount of expenditure eligible for supplement where there is a relevant disposal receipt taken into account under CAA. It is based on paragraph 11 of Schedule 19C to ICTA.

*Section 318: **Reduction in respect of unrelieved group ring fence profits***

1055. This section restricts the amount eligible for supplement where some or all of the expenditure could have been surrendered as group relief. It is based on paragraph 12 of Schedule 19C to ICTA.

1056. The term "unrelieved group ring fence profits" is defined in section 313.

*Section 319: **The reference amount for a pre-commencement period***

1057. This section defines the "reference amount" for the purposes of section 315. It is based on paragraph 13 of Schedule 19C to ICTA.

1058. The reference amount is the amount on which supplement can be claimed, that is the eligible expenditure reduced under either or both of sections 317 and 318 as appropriate.

*Section 320: **Claims for pre-commencement supplement***

1059. This section sets out how a claim for pre-commencement supplement must be made and applies the time limit in paragraph 74 of Schedule 18 to FA 1998 to the claim. It is based on paragraph 14 of Schedule 19C to ICTA.

*Section 321: **Supplement in respect of a post-commencement period***

1060. This section sets out when a company may qualify for post-commencement supplement, and how the claim is given effect. It is based on paragraph 15, 17 and 18 of Schedule 19C to ICTA.

1061. The calculation of post-commencement supplement is set out in sections 322 to 329. Under *subsection (2)* the supplement is treated as a loss carried forward to be set against future profits from the ring fence trade.

*Section 322: **Amount of post-commencement supplement for a post-commencement period.***

1062. This section sets out how to calculate the amount of the post-commencement supplement. It is based on paragraph 16 of Schedule 19C to ICTA.

1063. The supplement is a percentage of the "reference amount". The percentage is specified in section 310 and "reference amount" for post-commencement supplement is defined in section 329.

*Section 323: **Ring fence losses***

1064. This section sets out how much of a trading loss from the ring fence trade is eligible for inclusion in the calculation of post-commencement supplement. It is based on paragraph 17 of Schedule 19C to ICTA.

1065. *Subsection (3)* provides thatlosses are not eligible for supplement if they could have been claimed against profits from an earlier accounting period.

*Section 324: **Special rule for straddling periods***

1066. This section sets out the rules that apply where a company's accounting period straddles 1 January 2006. It is based on paragraph 18 of Schedule 19C to ICTA.

*Section 325: **The pool of ring fence losses and the pool of non-qualifying Schedule 19B losses***

1067. This section sets out how to determine the company's pool of expenditure (the "ring fence pool") for the purposes of post-commencement supplement. It is based on paragraph 19 of Schedule 19C to ICTA.

1068. The ring fence pool includes qualifying amounts carried forward from the pool determined under Schedule 19B to ICTA. The section also defines a non-qualifying pool which contains non-qualifying amounts carried forward under Schedule 19B to ICTA.

*Section 326: **The ring fence pool***

1069. This section sets out how and when additions to and reductions of the ring fence pool are made. It is based on paragraph 20 of Schedule 19C to ICTA.

*Section 327: **Reductions in respect of utilised ring fence losses***

1070. This section sets out how reductions in the two pools are to be made when a ring fence loss is utilised against profits. It is based on paragraph 21 of Schedule 19C to ICTA.

1071. The general rule is that when losses carried forward are set against profits in a later period, the non-qualifying pool is reduced first and the ring fence pool is then reduced by any balance of the loss after the non-qualifying pool has been reduced to nil.

Section 328: Reductions in respect of unrelieved group ring fence profits

1072. This section sets out how the expenditure eligible for supplement is to be reduced where there is an amount of unrelieved group ring fence profits. It is based on paragraph 22 of Schedule 19C to ICTA.

1073. The term "unrelieved group ring fence profits" is defined in section 313.

Section 329: The reference amount for a post-commencement period

1074. This section sets out how to determine the reference amount, the amount on which supplement is calculated, for the purposes of post-commencement supplement. It is based on paragraph 23 of Schedule 19C to ICTA.

Chapter 6: Supplementary charge in respect of ring fence trades

Section 330: Supplementary charge in respect of ring fence trades

1075. This section imposes an additional charge to tax on an adjusted measure of profits from the ring fence trade. It is based on section 501A(1), (2), (3) and (12) of ICTA.

1076. The adjustment to profits for this purpose is that financing costs, defined in section 331, are left out of account.

1077. *Subsection (5)* makes Chapter 6 subject to Chapter 7, which contains provisions that reduce the supplementary charge for certain new oil fields.

Section 331: Meaning of "financing costs" etc

1078. This section defines the term "financing costs" for the purposes of the supplementary charge. It is based on section 501A(4) to (11) of ICTA.

Section 332: Assessment, recovery and postponement of supplementary charge

1079. This section sets out the arrangements for the administration of the supplementary charge. It is based on section 501B of ICTA.

1080. The general rule is that the supplementary charge is treated for all administrative purposes as corporation tax, unless specific rules apply. In particular, this ensures that the relevant rules in TMA and in Schedule 18 to FA 1998 can apply.

Chapter 7: Reduction of supplementary charge for certain new oil fields

Overview

1081. This Chapter provides an allowance, a "field allowance", which can reduce a company's adjusted ring fence profits from oil and gas production in the UK and UKcontinental shelf (UKCS).

1082. The allowance is available to certain categories of new oil and gas fields in the UK/ UKCS – small fields, ultra heavy oil fields and ultra high pressure/high temperature fields. Allowances from a company's interests in all qualifying fields in an accounting period are then pooled and offset against adjusted ring fence profits. Any unused amounts in the pool are carried forward to the next accounting period.

Section 333: Reduction of adjusted ring fence profits

1083. This section provides that a company's ring fence profits are to be reduced by the company's pool of field allowances. It is based on paragraph 1 of Schedule 44 to FA 2009.

Section 334: Company's pool of field allowances

1084. This section provides that a company's pool of field allowances for an accounting period is the amount of the company's pool of field allowances that is carried forward from the previous accounting period plus the aggregate of field allowances activated in the accounting period. It is based on paragraph 2 of Schedule 44 to FA 2009.

Section 335: Carrying part of pool of field allowances into following period

1085. This section provides the rules for determining the amount of field allowances that are carried forward into a future accounting period. It is based on paragraph 3 of Schedule 44 to FA 2009.

Section 336: Carrying whole of pool of field allowances into following period

1086. This section provides the rules for determining when the whole of the company's pool of field allowances is carried forward into a future accounting period. It is based on paragraph 4 of Schedule 44 to FA 2009.

Section 337: Initial licensee to hold a field allowance

1087. This section provides that from the day a new oil field is licensed, a company that is an initial licensee holds a field allowance determined by the company's equity share in the field. It is based on paragraph 5 of Schedule 44 to FA 2009.

Section 338: Holding a field allowance on acquisition of equity share

1088. This section provides a signpost to section 347(2) (acquisition of field allowance). It is based on paragraph 6 of Schedule 44 to FA 2009.

Section 339: Unactivated amount of field allowance

1089. This section provides the rules for determining the unactivated amount of field allowance when a company acquires a field allowance by virtue of section 337 (initial licensee) or section 347(2) (acquisition of field allowance). It is based on paragraph 7 of Schedule 44 to FA 2009.

Section 340: Introduction to section 341

1090. This section provides that four conditions need to be met in respect of a new oil field for the activation of field allowance where there is no change in equity share during the accounting period. It is based on paragraph 8 of Schedule 44 to FA 2009.

Section 341: Activation of field allowance

1091. This section provides the rules for determining the amount of field allowance to be activated in an accounting period when all conditions in section 340 are met. It is based on paragraph 9 of Schedule 44 to FA 2009.

Section 342: Introduction to sections 343 and 344

1092. This section deals with the situation where a company's equity share in a new oil field changes during the accounting period and provides four conditions which need to be met for sections 343 and 344 to apply. It is based on paragraph 10 of Schedule 44 to FA 2009.

*Section 343: **Reference periods***

1093. This section provides a definition of reference period for the purposes of section 344 where a company is not a licensee for a whole accounting period or where the equity share changes. It is based on paragraph 11 of Schedule 44 to FA 2009.

*Section 344: **Activation of field allowance***

1094. This section provides the calculation of field allowance for each reference period. It is based on paragraph 12 of Schedule 44 to FA 2009.

*Section 345: **Introduction to sections 346 and 347***

1095. This section deals with the treatment of transfers of field allowance and provides the conditions which need to be met for sections 346 and 347 to apply. It is based on paragraph 13 of Schedule 44 to FA 2009.

*Section 346: **Reduction of field allowance if equity disposed of***

1096. This sectionprovides the calculation for the remaining field allowance which a company ("the transferor") has, after it has disposed of some of the equity interest in a new oil field. It is based on paragraph 14 of Schedule 44 to FA 2009.

*Section 347: **Acquisition of field allowance if equity acquired***

1097. This section provides the calculation of field allowance where a company ("the transferee") acquires an equity interest in a new oil field. It is based on paragraph 15 of Schedule 44 to FA 2009.

*Section 348: **Adjustments***

1098. This section provides that if there is any alteration in a company's adjusted ring fence profits, necessary adjustments are made for the purposes of this Chapter. It is based on paragraph 16 of Schedule 44 to FA 2009.

*Section 349: **Orders***

1099. This section provides that the Commissioners for HMRC can make provision about qualifying oil fields (section 352) and the amount of the total field allowance for a new oil field (section 356). It is based on paragraph 17 of Schedule 44 to FA 2009.

*Section 350: **"New oil field"***

1100. This section provides the definition of "new oil field" for the purposes of this Chapter. It is based on paragraph 18 of Schedule 44 to FA 2009.

*Section 351: **"Authorisation of development of an oil field"***

1101. This section provides the definition of "authorisation of development of an oil field" for the purposes of this Chapter. It is based on paragraph 19 of Schedule 44 to FA 2009.

*Section 352: **"Qualifying oil field"***

1102. This section provides the definition of "qualifying oil field" for the purposes of this Chapter. It is based on paragraph 20 of Schedule 44 to FA 2009.

*Section 353: **"Small oil field"***

1103. This section provides the definition of "small oil field" for the purposes of this Chapter. It is based on paragraph 21 of Schedule 44 to FA 2009.

Section 354: "Ultra heavy oil field"

1104. This section provides the definition of "ultra heavy oil field" for the purposes of this Chapter. It is based on paragraph 22 of Schedule 44 to FA 2009.

Section 355: "Ultra high pressure/high temperature oil field"

1105. This section provides the definition of "ultra high pressure/high temperature oil field" for the purposes of this Chapter. It is based on paragraph 23 of Schedule 44 to FA 2009.

Section 356: "Total field allowance for a new oil field"

1106. This section provides the definition of "total field allowance for a new oil field" for the purposes of this Chapter. It is based on paragraph 24 of Schedule 44 to FA 2009.

Section 357: Other definitions

1107. This section provides various other definitions for the purposes of this Chapter. It is based on paragraph 25 of Schedule 44 to FA 2009.

Part 9: Leasing plant or machinery

Overview

1108. This Part rewrites two sets of provisions relating to the leasing of plant or machinery:

- Chapter 5A of Part 12 of ICTA (special rules for long funding leases of plant or machinery); and
- Schedule 10 to FA 2006 (sale etc of lessor companies etc).

Chapter 1: Introduction

Section 358: Introduction to Part

1109. This section provides an overview of the Chapters of the Part and their subject matter. It is based on paragraph 1 of Schedule 10 to FA 2006.

1110. *Subsection (4)* defines the term "the sales of lessors Chapters" to mean Chapters 3 to 6 of this Part.

1111. *Subsections (5)* to *(7)* introduce, and provide signposts to the definitions of, a "qualifying change of ownership" and a "qualifying change in a company's interest in a business". These are the events which give rise to charges and reliefs under the sales of lessors Chapters.

Chapter 2: Long funding leases of plant or machinery

Overview

1112. This Chapter rewrites Chapter 5A (special rules for long funding leases of plant or machinery) inserted into Part 12 of ICTA by Part 2 of Schedule 8 to FA 2006.

1113. Schedule 8 to FA 2006 reformed the way in which certain finance leases of plant or machinery, and operating leases of plant or machinery akin to such finance leases, are taxed. In broad terms it does so by amending ICTA, CAA and ITTOIA:

- to move entitlement to capital allowances in relation to the plant or machinery under such a lease – a "long funding lease" – from lessor to lessee; and

- to tax the lessor and lessee in relation to the financing of the plant or machinery through such a lease in much the same way as lender and borrower would be taxed in relation to financing the plant or machinery through a loan.

Section 359: ***Overview of Chapter***

1114. This section sets out the structure of the Chapter and contains a signpost to section 381 for the meaning of terms used in the Chapter. It is new.

1115. The Chapter is arranged so that it deals first with the calculation of the taxable profits of the lessor and then with the calculation of the taxable profits of the lessee. In each case it deals with the lessor or lessee first as party to a long funding finance lease and then as party to a long funding operating lease.

1116. The terms "long funding lease" and "long funding finance lease" take their meaning from Chapter 6A of Part 2 of CAA and "long funding operating lease" is defined by reference to those terms. See section 381(2).

1117. It is an integral part of the definition of "long funding lease" in CAA that the subject matter of the lease is plant or machinery (see sections 70G, 70J and 70K of CAA).

Section 360: ***Lessor under long funding finance lease: rental earnings***

1118. This section determines the taxable income of the lessor from a long funding finance lease. It is based on section 502B of ICTA.

1119. The taxable income is the amount of rental earnings. The calculation of rental earnings follows GAAP. The rental earnings is the amount that in accordance with that practice is to be treated as gross return on investment or, in a case where in accordance with that practice the lease is to be treated as a loan, as interest.

1120. Section 502B(3) of ICTA includes in relation to the lease the words "where it meets the finance lease test". Those words are otiose and have been omitted from *subsection (3)*.

1121. Section 502B(4) of ICTA refers to the lease being "treated as a loan in the accounts in question". There is no other reference to "accounts" in section 502B and those words have been changed in *subsection (4)* to read "treated as a loan for the period of account" linking back to the "period of account" mentioned in *subsection (1)*.

Section 361: ***Lessor under long funding finance lease: exceptional items***

1122. This section treats as taxable income or a revenue expense certain profits or losses in connection with a long funding finance lease which would not apart from this section be brought into account for corporation tax purposes. It is based on section 502C of ICTA.

1123. The profits and losses to be brought into account are those (whether of an income or capital nature) which in accordance with GAAP fall to be recognised for accounting purposes.

Section 362: ***Lessor under long funding finance lease making termination payment***

1124. This section prohibits a deduction by a lessor for a payment made in respect of the termination of a long funding finance lease if the amount of the payment is calculated by reference to "termination value". It is based on section 502D of ICTA.

1125. On termination of a finance lease of an asset, the lessor often makes a payment to the lessee, commonly referred to as a rebate of rentals. This payment principally represents partial reimbursement of payments made by the lessee in respect of the capital value of the asset, unencumbered possession of which has reverted to the lessor as a result of the termination. This section prevents such a payment from being deducted by the lessor for corporation tax purposes. But the section does not prevent the deduction of a payment to the extent it is in respect of a sum included in computing rental earnings (see *subsection (3)*).

1126. *Subsection (4)* is new and provides a signpost to the definition of "termination value".

Section 363: Lessor under long funding operating lease: periodic deduction

1127. This section compensates a lessor under a long funding operating lease for the fact that capital allowances in relation to the leased plant or machinery are not available to it. It is based on section 502E(1) to (3) and (6) to (9) of ICTA.

1128. In the case of an operating lease, the gross rentals are to be brought into account for corporation tax purposes. This achieved the correct result prior to FA2006, as the lessor was entitled to capital allowances which over the term of the lease balanced the amount brought into charge that represented payment of the capital value of the leased plant or machinery.

1129. This section replaces the role of capital allowances. It allows deductions in calculating the profits of the lessor for corporation tax purposes, which over the term of the lease equate in total to the expected reduction in value of the plant or machinery over the term.

1130. The words "had that value been estimated at that time" have been added in *subsection (4)(b)* to explain the reasoning behind the use of the words "would have been expected" in section 502E(6)(b) of ICTA.

1131. This section, together with sections 364 and 365, presents the calculation required by section 502E of ICTA in a substantially different way. The provision has been restructured to improve the accessibility of the legislation for lessor companies and their advisers, in particular by splitting out the different basis of calculation required where the lessor incurred expenditure on the provision of the plant or machinery otherwise than for a qualifying purpose.

Section 364: "Starting value": general

1132. This section determines the "starting value" of the plant or machinery for the purposes of the calculation required by section 363 except in the circumstances where section 365 applies. It is based on section 502E(4) and (5) of ICTA.

Section 365: "Starting value" where plantor machinery originally unqualifying

1133. This section determines the "starting value" of the plant or machinery for the purposes of the calculation required by section 363 in a case where, before the long funding operating lease commenced, the lessor incurred expenditure on the plant or machinery otherwise than for the purposes of a qualifying activity within the meaning of Part 2 of CAA. It is based on section 502E(4) and (5) of ICTA.

Section 366: Long funding operating lease: lessor's additional expenditure

1134. This section provides for an additional deduction by a lessor under a long funding operating lease if the lessor incurs additional expenditure in relation to the leased plant or machinery. It is based on section 502F(1) to (4) and (7) to (11) of ICTA.

1135. This section, together with sections 367 and 368, presents the calculation required by section 502F of ICTA in a substantially different way. The provision has been restructured to improve the accessibility of the legislation for lessor companies and their advisers, in particular by splitting out the different basis of calculation required where the lessor has previously incurred additional expenditure.

Section 367: Determination of remaining residual value resulting from lessor's first additional expenditure

1136. This section determines the amount of the remaining residual value of the plant or machinery for the purposes of section 366 as a result of the first occasion on which the lessor incurs additional expenditure. It is based on section 502F(5) and (6) of ICTA.

1137. The words "(or, if section 365 applies, would have been expected to be that value had that value been estimated at that time)" in *subsection (2)(b)* reflect the wording of section 363(4)(b). See the commentary on section 363.

Section 368: Determination of remaining residual value resulting from lessor's further additional expenditure

1138. This section determines the amount of the remaining residual value of the plant or machinery for the purposes of section 366 as a result of the second and subsequent occasions on which the lessor incurs additional expenditure. It is based on section 502F(5) and (6) of ICTA.

1139. The words "(or, if section 365 applies, would have been expected to be that value had that value been estimated at that time)" in *subsection (3)(a)* reflect the wording of section 363(4)(b). See the commentary on section 363.

Section 369: Lessor under long funding operating lease: termination of lease

1140. This section provides for the lessor to be treated as receiving income or, depending on the circumstances, incurring a revenue expense for corporation tax purposes on the termination of a long funding operating lease. It is based on section 502G of ICTA.

1141. Whether or not income is treated as being received or a revenue expense as being incurred is determined by reference to "the termination amount" and the amounts mentioned in *subsection (3)(a)* to *(c)*, but the amounts mentioned in subsection (3)(a) (amounts paid to the lessee by reference to the termination value) may not themselves be deducted (see *subsection (5)*).

1142. The presentation of the calculation required by section 502G of ICTA has been substantially restructured to improve the accessibility of the legislation for lessor companies and their advisers.

Section 370: Plant or machinery held as trading stock

1143. This section disapplies sections 360 to 369 if, apart from those sections, any part of the lessor's expenditure on the acquisition of the plant or machinery is allowable as a deduction for corporation tax purposes as a result of the plant or machinery forming part of the lessor's trading stock. It is based on section 502GA(1) to (3) of ICTA.

Section 371: Adjustments where sections 360 to 369 subsequently disapplied by section 370

1144. This section applies if sections 360 to 369 previously applied, but the condition in section 370(2) is subsequently met. It is based on section 502GA(4) and (5) of ICTA.

1145. The section provides for just and reasonable assessments and adjustments to assessments to be made in relation both to the amounts taken into account in accordance with sections 360 to 369 and to those to be taken into account in accordance with section 370.

Section 372: Lessor also lessee under non–long funding lease

1146. This section disapplies sections 360 to 369 in the case of a company which as lessor grants a long funding lease (lease B) of plant or machinery in which its interest is that of a lessee under a lease (lease A) which is not a long funding lease. It is based on section 502GB of ICTA.

1147. Section 70H of CAA provides that a lease otherwise capable of being a long funding lease is not a long funding lease as regards the lessee unless the lessee has made a tax return treating the lessee as taxable in relation to the lease in accordance with Chapter 5A of Part 12 of ICTA. *Subsection (3)(a)* ensures that, if a tax return is made validly treating lease A as being a long funding lease after lease B has been entered into, this section is treated as never having applied to lease B. *Subsection (3)(b)* ensures that this section does apply to lease B, if a tax return which treated lease A as being a long funding lease is subsequently amended so as not to treat it as such a lease.

*Section 373: **Other avoidance***

1148. This section disapplies sections 360 to 369 where three conditions are met. It is based on section 502GC(1) to (3) and (5) of ICTA.

1149. The three conditions counter arrangements involving a long funding lease which are intended to create tax profits which are substantially less than, or tax losses which are substantially greater than, the profits or losses arising from the arrangements as shown in the lessor company's accounts. The section may also apply where there is a tax loss and an accounting profit.

*Section 374: **Provision supplementing section 373***

1150. This section provides definitions and interpretation for the purposes of section 373. It is based on section 502GC(2), (4) and (6) to (8) of ICTA.

*Section 375: **Adjustments where sections 360 to 369 subsequently disapplied by section 373***

1151. This section applies if sections 360 to 369 have previously applied, but the conditions in section 373 are subsequently met. It is based on section 502GC(9) and(10) of ICTA.

1152. The section provides for just and reasonable assessments and adjustments to assessments to be made in relation both to the amounts taken into account in accordance with sections 360 to 369 and to those to be taken into account in accordance with section 373.

*Section 376: **Films***

1153. This section disapplies sections 360 to 369 in the case of a long funding lease of a film. It is based on section 502GD of ICTA.

*Section 377: **Lessee under long funding finance lease: limit on deductions***

1154. This section, the first of those relating to lessees, limits the amount which a lessee of plant or machinery under a long funding finance lease may deduct in calculating its profits for corporation tax purposes. It is based on section 502I of ICTA.

1155. The amount which may be deducted is limited to the amounts which in accordance with GAAP fall to be shown in the lessee's accounts as finance charges in respect of the lease (see *subsections (2)* and*(3)*).

1156. In certain circumstances in accordance with GAAP a long funding finance lease is treated as a loan for accounting purposes. This section applies as if such a lease were treated as a finance lease (see *subsection (4)*).

Section 378: Lessee under long funding finance lease: termination

1157. This section avoids double taxation by excluding from the lessee's calculation of its profits for corporation tax purposes any sum received by the lessee in relation to a long funding finance lease which is calculated by reference to "termination value". It is based on section 502J of ICTA.

1158. Such sums must, however, be brought into account as part of the disposal value for the purpose of capital allowances (see *subsection (3)* and section 70E of CAA).

1159. *Subsection (4)* is new and provides a signpost to the definition of "termination value".

Section 379: Lessee under long funding operating lease

1160. This section reduces the deductions which a lessee under a long funding operating lease of plant or machinery may make in calculating its profits for corporation tax purposes. It is based on section 502K(1) to (3) and (6) to (9) of ICTA.

1161. The amount of the deduction is reduced by reference to the expected reduction in value of the plant or machinery over the term of the lease. As the lessee is entitled to capital allowances, it effectively obtains relief through the allowances for the amount of the lease payments which it cannot deduct in calculating its profits.

1162. The words "had that value been estimated at the commencement of the term" have been added in *subsection (6)(b)* to explain the reasoning behind the use of the words "would have been expected" in section 502K(6)(b) of ICTA.

Section 380: "Starting value" in section 379

1163. This section determines the "starting value" of the plant or machinery for the purposes of the calculation required by section 379. It is based on section 502K(4) and(5) of ICTA.

Section 381: Interpretation of Chapter

1164. This section defines or provides signposts to the provisions defining terms used in the Chapter. It is based on section 502L of ICTA.

1165. To assist the user, this section expands on section 502L(4) of ICTA, rewritten in *subsection (1)*, by including numerous signposts to specific sections of Part 6A of CAA in *subsections (2)* and *(3)*.

Chapters 3 to 6: The sales of lessors Chapters

Overview

1166. The sales of lessors Chapters, based on Schedule 10 to FA 2006, are designed to deter arrangements which have the effect of converting the corporation tax deferral arising from the availability of capital allowances to companies which carry on a business of leasing plant or machinery into a permanent deferral of tax.

1167. The sales of lessors Chapters counter these arrangements by imposing a charge to corporation tax on the leasing company on any day:

- if there is a qualifying change of ownership of the company on that day; or
- in a case where the leasing business is carried on by the company in partnership, if there is a qualifying change on that day in the company's interest in the business.

1168. The tax charge is broadly equivalent to the tax benefit enjoyed down to that day and the rules are designed to ensure that it is borne by the selling group.

1169. In the case of a qualifying change in the ownership of the leasing company, a relief equivalent to the charge is given to the company on the day after the qualifying change and the rules ensure that the relief can only be accessed by the buying group. In the case of a qualifying change in the company's interest in a business carried on in partnership, relief is given to the other partner companies whose interest in the business carried on in partnership has increased.

1170. The effect of this is that a tax-driven sale to a loss making group is unattractive as the charge recovers the tax benefits taken by the selling group and a loss making buying group has no interest in an additional relief which merely increases its tax losses.

1171. The intended tax effect on a commercially driven sale to another (profitable) group is that it should be broadly neutral, as the charge and the relief cancel each other out. The relief is valuable to the profit making buying group and so it can be expected that the price paid reflects this and compensates the selling group for the tax charge.

Chapter 3: Sales of lessors: leasing business carried on by a company alone

Overview

1172. This Chapter deals with cases where a leasing business is carried on by a company alone. Chapter 4 deals with cases where the business is carried on by one or more companies in partnership with others.

Section 382: Introduction to Chapter

1173. This section introduces Chapter 3. It is based on paragraph 1(1) and (2) of Schedule 10 to FA 2006.

Section 383: Income and matching expense in different accounting periods

1174. This section provides for an accounting period to end if there is a "qualifying change of ownership" in relation to a company within the charge to corporation tax carrying on a business of leasing plant or machinery otherwise than in partnership. It is based on paragraph 3 of Schedule 10 to FA 2006.

1175. On the day the accounting period ends the company is treated as receiving an amount of income which is brought into account for that accounting period for corporation tax purposes. See *subsections (2)* and *(3)*.

1176. On the following day the company is treated as incurring an expense which is brought into account for a new accounting period for corporation tax purposes. See *subsections (4)* and *(5)*.

Section 384: Amount of income and expense

1177. This section contains a signpost to the sections which contain the provisions for calculating the amount of the income to be brought into account in accordance with section 383(2) and (3) and provides that the amount of the expense to be brought into account in accordance with section 383(4) and (5) is the same as the amount of the income. It is based on paragraph 4 of Schedule 10 to FA 2006.

Section 385: No carry back of the expense

1178. This section prevents any loss which arises in the later accounting period which derives from the expense from being carried back against profits of any earlier accounting period under section 37(3)(b). It is based on paragraph 5 of Schedule 10 to FA 2006.

Section 386: ***Relief for expense otherwise giving rise to carried forward loss***

1179. This section provides for the carrying forward of the expense to later accounting periods. It is based on paragraph 39 of Schedule 10 to FA 2006.

1180. If the company makes a loss in the accounting period which, in accordance with section 383(4)(b), begins on the day after the qualifying change of ownership, the loss derived from the expense treated as incurred under section 383(4)(a), which could otherwise only be carried forward and applied against the profits of the company's leasing trade, is instead to be treated as an expense of the next accounting period and so available for group relief in that period.

1181. If the company continues to make losses, so much of the loss as derives from the expense can similarly be treated as an expense of subsequent accounting periods which start within five years of the qualifying change of ownership, unless there is a subsequent qualifying change of ownership.

1182. The amount of the loss derived from the expense is indexed to up-rate its value and preserve the symmetry between the value of the charge and the value of the relief. See *subsection (2)*.

1183. Paragraph 39 of Schedule 10 to FA 2006 applies for the purposes of:

- paragraph 3 of that Schedule, in a case where the company carries on the leasing business alone; and
- paragraphs 23(4A) and 33 of that Schedule, in a case where the company carries on the business in partnership.

1184. It has been rewritten here for the purposes only of section 383. It has also been rewritten in two places in Chapter 4: in section 419 for the purposes of section 417(5) and in section 428 for the purposes of section 425. It is considered that it is helpful to paint the complete picture in each Chapter.

Section 387: ***"Business of leasing plant or machinery"***

1185. This section, read with sections 388 to 391, sets out the conditions for determining whether on any day a companycarries on a "business of leasing plant or machinery" for the purposes of Chapter 3. It is based on paragraph 6 of Schedule 10 to FA 2006.

1186. Condition A in *subsection (3)* is that at least one half of "the relevant plant or machinery value" (see section 388) relates to "qualifying leased plant or machinery" (see *subsection (7)*).

Section 388: ***"Relevant plant or machinery value" for condition A in section 387***

1187. This section sets out the method of calculating the relevant plant or machinery value on any day for the purposes of condition A in section 387(3). It is based on paragraph 7(1) to (3A) of Schedule 10 to FA 2006.

Section 389: ***Provision supplementing section 388***

1188. This section contains further details of the basis of the calculation to be made in accordance with section 388. It is based on paragraph 7(4) to (9) of Schedule 10 to FA2006.

Section 390: ***Relevant plant or machinery value where relevant company lessee under long funding lease etc***

1189. This section provides for adjustments to be made to the calculation in section 388 in certain circumstances. It is based on paragraph 7A of Schedule 10 to FA 2006.

1190. The circumstances are if the relevant company (see section 387(1)) is the lessee of the plant or machinery under a long funding finance lease or a long funding operating lease or is treated under section 67 of CAA as the owner of the plant or machinery under a hire purchase or similar contract.

Section 391: ***Relevant company's income for condition B in section 387***

1191. This section provides for the way in which income is to be calculated for the purposes of condition B in section 387(5). It is based on paragraph 8 of Schedule 10 to FA 2006.

Section 392: ***"Qualifying change of ownership"***

1192. This section, read with sections 393 to 398, determines what constitutes a "qualifying change of ownership" for the purposes of the sales of lessors Chapters. It is based on paragraph 10 of Schedule 10 to FA 2006.

1193. A qualifying change of ownership is a "relevant change" in the relationship between the company carrying on a business of leasing plant or machinery ("A") and its principal company. Section 393 determines what constitutes a "relevant change" where the relationship between A and its principal company is that of subsidiary and parent and section 394 deals with the case where the relationship is that of A and a member (or the parent company of a member) of a consortium, directly or indirectly, owning A.

1194. A qualifying change of ownership triggers A being treated as receiving income and incurring a matching expense not only for the purposes of section 383 in Chapter 3 where it carries on the business alone but also for the purposes of section 425 in Chapter 4 where it carries on the business in partnership.

Section 393: ***Qualifying 75% subsidiaries***

1195. This section defines the relationship between a principal company and its subsidiary and determines what constitutes a "relevant change" in that relationship for the purposes of section 392. It is based on paragraph 11 of Schedule 10 to FA 2006.

1196. A company is only capable of being a principal company if it is not itself a75% subsidiary of another company (see *subsections (1)(b)*, *(3)(c)* and *(5)*).

1197. A company carrying on a business of leasing plant or machinery ("A") has another company ("B") as its principal company if A is a qualifying 75% subsidiary, as defined in section 398, of B unless B is a qualifying 75% subsidiary of another company (see *subsection (1)*).

1198. If B is a 75% subsidiary of another company ("C"), then C is the principal company of A. But if C is a 75% subsidiary of another company ("D"), then D is the principal company of A. And so on.

1199. There is a "relevant change" in the relationship of A and the principal company if the relationship of A to the principal company ceases to be that of a qualifying 75% subsidiary or the chain of 75% qualifying subsidiaries is broken (see *subsections (2)*, *(4)* and *(6)*).

Section 394: ***Consortium relationships***

1200. This section defines the relationship between a company carrying on a business of leasing plant or machinery ("A") and a principal company of A where A is owned, directly or indirectly, by a consortium and determines what constitutes a "relevant change" in that relationship for the purposes of section 392. It is based on paragraph 12 of Schedule 10 to FA 2006.

1201. This section applies if A is either owned by a consortium or is a qualifying 90% subsidiary of a company owned by the consortium (see *subsections (1)(b)* and *(5)(b)*).

1202. A company is only capable of being a principal company if it is not itself a75% subsidiary of another company (see *subsections (1)*, *(5)* and *(7)*).

1203. Each company which is a member of the consortium ("E") is a principal company of A unless it is a qualifying 75% subsidiary of another company (see subsection (1)).

1204. If E is a 75% subsidiary of another company ("F"), then F is the principal company of A. But if F is a 75% subsidiary of another company ("G"), then G is the principal company of A. And so on.

1205. There is a "relevant change" in the relationship of A and a principal company on any day if E's "ownership proportion" is less at the end of the day than it was at the start of the day (see *subsections (2)*, *(6)(a)* and *(8)*).

1206. E's ownership proportion is measured by reference to the lowest of E's interest in the share capital of A, A's profits available for distribution and A's assets available on a winding up (see *subsection (3)*), except where A is a qualifying 90% subsidiary of a company owned by the consortium. In that case it is E's interest in the company of which A is a qualifying 90% subsidiary which is measured (see *subsection (4)*).

1207. The term "ownership proportion" has been substituted for the term "relevant fraction" in paragraph 12 of Schedule 10 to FA 2006. Similarly "proportion" has been used in place of "percentage". This change in language follows the change in language used in rewriting section 403C of ICTA (amount of relief in consortium cases) in this Act (see sections 143 and 144).

1208. If a company other than E is the principal company of A in relation to E's membership of the consortium, there is also a "relevant change" in the relationship of A and the principal company if E ceases to be a qualifying 75% subsidiary of the other company or the chain of 75% qualifying subsidiaries between the other company and E is broken (see *subsections (6)(b)* and *(8)(b)*).

Section 395: ***No qualifying change of ownership in the case of certain intra–group reorganisations***

1209. This section ensures that there is no qualifying change of ownership of A in the case of certain group reorganisations. It is based on paragraph 13 of Schedule 10 to FA 2006.

1210. The group reorganisations in question are ones following which A and all other companies involved remain qualifying 75% subsidiaries of the same principal company as before the reorganisation.

Section 396: ***No qualifying change of ownership where principal company's interest in consortium company unchanged***

1211. This section ensures that there is no qualifying change in ownership in the case of a change in the composition of a consortium but there is no change in the interest of the principal company in the consortium company. It is based on paragraph 13A of Schedule 10 to FA 2006.

Section 397: ***Companies owned by consortiums and members of consortiums***

1212. This section defines, for the purposes of the sales of lessors Chapters, what a company owned by a consortium means and who are the members of the consortium in relation to that company. It is based on paragraph 14 of Schedule 10 to FA 2006.

Section 398: ***"Qualifying 75% or 90% subsidiary" etc***

1213. This section sets out the tests for determining whether, for the purposes of the sales of lessors Chapters, a company is a "qualifying 75% subsidiary" or a "qualifying90% subsidiary" of another company. It is based on paragraph 15 of Schedule 10 to FA 2006.

1214. It uses the same approach as is used for determining whether companies are in the same group for group relief purposes but with a modification. This is that companies without share capital, such as companies limited by guarantee, can be treated as subsidiaries if they fall to be treated as controlled by another company. Such companies are also accommodated by applying Chapter 6 of Part 5 of this Act to treat their members as if they were equity holders.

1215. The reference in paragraph 15(1)(b) of Schedule 10 to FA 2006 to the definition of control in section 840 of ICTA has not been rewritten.. The definition of control is rewritten in section 1124 and section 1176(2) applies that definition for the purposes of this Act unless otherwise indicated.

*Section 399: **The amount of the income: the basic amount***

1216. This section gives the formula for determining the basic amount of income which is then to be adjusted in accordance with sections 404 to 406 to determine the amount of income for the purposes of section 383 on any day ("the relevant day"). It is based on paragraph 16 of Schedule 10 to FA 2006.

*Section 400: **"PM" in section 399***

1217. This section, read together with sections 401 and 402, determines the amount which is "PM" in the formula in section 399 on the relevant day. It is based on paragraph 17(1) to (2B) of Schedule 10 to FA2006.

1218. *Subsection (2)(d)* is new. It provides a link to section 407 which requires plant or machinery to be ignored in certain circumstances.

*Section 401: **Provisions supplementing section 400***

1219. This section contains further details of the basis of the calculation to be made in accordance with section 400 and gives the meaning of "the amounts shown in the appropriate balance sheet" in relation to the leasing company or an associated company. It is based on paragraph 17(3) to (8) of Schedule 10 to FA 2006.

*Section 402: **"PM" where relevant company lessee under long funding lease etc***

1220. This section provides for adjustments to be made to the calculation in section 400 in certain circumstances. It is based on paragraph 17A of Schedule 10 to FA 2006.

1221. The circumstances are if the relevant company (see section 399(5)) is the lessee of the plant or machinery under a long funding finance lease or a long funding operating lease or is treated under section 67 of CAA as the owner of the plant or machinery under a hire purchase or similar contract.

*Section 403: **"TWDV" in section 399***

1222. This section determines the amount which is "TWDV" in the formula in section 399 on the relevant day. It is based on paragraph 18 of Schedule 10 to FA2006.

1223. The TWDV amount is made up of the unrelieved qualifying expenditure in all single asset pools, class pools and the main pool. This is the amount at the start of the new accounting period following the relevant day but excludes any expenditure on the acquisition of plant or machinery on the relevant day except for plant or machinery acquired from associated companies. This adjustment ensures that amounts in respect of plant or machinery acquired from associated companies on the relevant day are included in both the PM and the TWDV amounts.

*Section 404: **Amount to be nil if basic amount negative***

1224. This section ensures that, if the formula in section 399(3) produces a negative basic amount, the amount of the company's income for the purposes of section 383 is nil. It is based on paragraph 19 of Schedule 10 to FA 2006.

*Section 405: **Adjustment to the basic amount: qualifying 75% subsidiaries***

1225. This sectionprovides for an adjustment to the basic amount if the company ceases to be a 75% subsidiary and becomes instead a consortium company or a qualifying 90% subsidiary of a consortium company. It is based on paragraph 20 of Schedule 10 to FA 2006.

1226. In these circumstances the basic amount is reduced to reflect the change in the economic control of the lessor company. The amount of the income is limited to the "appropriate percentage" of the basic amount, that is the difference between 100 per cent and the "ownership percentage" after the qualifying change of ownership (see *subsections (4)* and *(5)*).

1227. The term "ownership percentage" has been substituted for the term "relevant fraction" in paragraph 20 of Schedule 10 to FA 2006 and corresponds to the use of the term "ownership proportion" in sections 394 and 406.

*Section 406: **Adjustment to the basic amount: consortium relationships***

1228. This sectionprovides for an adjustment to the basic amount if the trigger event is a change in a consortium relationship. It is based on paragraph 21 of Schedule 10 to FA 2006.

1229. *Subsections (2)* and *(3)* apply if the qualifying change of ownership arises only because the ownership proportion (as defined in section 394(3) and (4)) at the end of the day is less than the ownership proportion at the start of the day (see section 394(2)). They provide that the amount of the income is limited to the "appropriate proportion" of the basic amount. The "appropriate proportion" is found by deducting the ownership proportion at the end of the day from the ownership proportion at the start of the day.

1230. *Subsection (4)* applies if the qualifying change of ownership does not arise solely because the ownership proportion at the end of the day is less than the ownership proportion at the start of the day (see for example section 394(6)(b) and(8)). It provides that the amount of the income is limited to the ownership proportion of the basic amount at the start of the day.

*Section 407: **Migration***

1231. This section deals with situations where a company comes within the charge to corporation tax as a result of migration to the United Kingdom. It is based on paragraph 22 of Schedule 10 to FA 2006.

1232. The section prevents the migration of a company to the United Kingdom which is coupled with a qualifying change of ownership on the same day giving rise to an expense in its first accounting period in relation to plant or machinery which would be shown in a balance sheet of the company drawn up in accordance with GAAP immediately before the day of its migration.

*Section 408: **"Associated company"***

1233. This section gives the meaning of "associated company" for the purposes of Chapter 3 only. It is based on paragraphs 7(10) and 9 of Schedule 10 to FA 2006.

Chapter 4: Sales of lessors: leasing business carried on by a company in partnership

Overview

1234. This Chapter deals with cases where the company is carrying on a leasing business in partnership with others. It is necessary to provide not only for changes in the ownership of the company itself but also for changes in the partners' interests in the partnership business, including the introduction and retirement of partners and changes in profit sharing ratios.

1235. This Chapter is based on Part 3 of Schedule 10 to FA 2006. The opportunity has been taken to set out in full certain provisions which in the source legislation operate by applying provisions of Part 2 of that Schedule with modifications. See sections 410 to 414 which restate in full the provisions of paragraphs 6 to 8 of Schedule 10 to FA 2006 as modified by paragraph 25 of that Schedule.

1236. Sections 417 to 424 deal with changes in the partnership and sections 425 to 429 deal with changes in the ownership of a company carrying on business in partnership.

Section 409: Introduction to Chapter

1237. This section introduces the Chapter and contains signposts to its principal provisions. It is based on paragraphs 23(1), 25(1) and (2) and 33(1) of Schedule 10 to FA 2006.

1238. In particular, it highlights the two events which may give rise to a charge and relief where a company carries on a leasing business in partnership.

Section 410: "Business of leasing plant or machinery"

1239. This section, read with sections 411 to 414, sets out the conditions for determining whether on any day a partnership carries on a "business of leasing plant or machinery" for the purposes of this Chapter. It is based on paragraph 25 of Schedule 10 to FA 2006.

1240. This section restates in full the provisions of paragraph 6 of Schedule 10 to FA2006 as applied by paragraph 25(1) and modified by paragraph 25(2) of that Schedule.

1241. Condition A in *subsection (2)* is that at least half of "the relevant plant or machinery value" (see section 411) relates to "qualifying leased plant or machinery".

1242. Paragraph 25(2) of Schedule 10 to FA 2006 provides that:

"Any reference in [paragraphs 6 to 8] to the relevant company is to be read as a reference to the partnership.

1243. Paragraph 6(5) of Schedule 10 to FA 2006 refers to "any company" and "the company". Although paragraph 25(2) of Schedule 10 to FA 2006 does not explicitly modify those references, it is implicit that for the purposes of Part 3 of that Schedule those references must also be read as references to the partnership. This has been made explicit in *subsection (6)*.

Section 411: "Relevant plant or machinery value" for condition A in section 410

1244. This section sets out the method of calculating the relevant plant or machinery value on any day for the purposes of condition A in section 410(2). It is based on paragraph 25 of Schedule 10 to FA 2006.

1245. This section restates in full the provisions of paragraph 7(1) to (3A) of Schedule 10 to FA 2006 as applied by paragraph 25(1) and modified by paragraph 25(2) and (3) of that Schedule.

Section 412: ***Provision supplementing section 411***

1246. This section contains further details of the basis of the calculation to be made in accordance with section 411. It is based on paragraph 25 of Schedule 10 to FA 2006.

1247. This section restates in full the provisions of paragraph 7(4) to (9) of Schedule 10 to FA 2006 as applied by paragraph 25(1) and modified by paragraph 25(2) of that Schedule.

1248. In giving effect to the implicit modifications made by paragraph 25(2) of Schedule 10 to FA 2006 to paragraph 7(4) and (7) of that Schedule, references have been included in *subsections (1)* and *(4)*both to the partnership and to any company, a company or the company. This is necessary as the question whether any plant or machinery is "relevant transferred plant or machinery" as regards any company mentioned in section 411(5) is determined by reference to the amounts which would be shown in the appropriate balance sheet of that company (seesection 411(4)).

Section 413: ***Relevant plant or machinery value where partnership lessee under long funding lease etc***

1249. This section provides for adjustments to be made to the calculation in section 411 in certain circumstances. It is based on paragraph 25 of Schedule 10 to FA2006.

1250. This section restates in full the provisions of paragraph 7A of Schedule 10 to FA 2006 as applied by paragraph 25(1) and modified by paragraph 25(2) and (3) of that Schedule.

1251. The circumstances are if the partnership is the lessee of the plant or machinery under a long funding finance lease or a long funding operating lease or is treated under section 67 of CAA as the owner of the plant or machinery under a hire purchase or similar contract.

Section 414: ***Partnership's income for condition B in section 410***

1252. This section provides for the way in which the partnership's income is to be calculated for the purposes of condition B in section 410(4). It is based on paragraph 25 of Schedule 10 to FA 2006.

1253. This section restates in full the provisions of paragraph 8 of Schedule 10 to FA2006 as applied by paragraph 25(1) and modified by paragraph 25(2) of that Schedule.

Section 415: ***"Qualifying change" in company's interest in a business***

1254. This section defines a "qualifying change" in a company's interest in a business by reference to a reduction in its "percentage share" in the profits or loss of the business. It is based on paragraph 27 of Schedule 10 to FA 2006.

Section 416: ***Determining the percentage share in the profits or loss of business***

1255. This section provides that a company's "percentage share" in the profits or loss of the business is to be determined on a just and reasonable basis. It is based on paragraph 28 of Schedule 10 to FA 2006.

Section 417: ***Partner company's income and other companies' matching expense***

1256. This section provides for the consequences of a "qualifying change" on any day in a company's interest in a leasing business carried on by it in partnership. It is based on paragraph 23 of Schedule 10 to FA 2006.

1257. A "qualifying change" is defined in section 415 and occurs if there is a reduction in the company's interest in the business.

1258. On the day of the qualifying change, the company is treated as receiving an amount of income and the other companies carrying on the business are treated as incurring an expense. In this case, there is no ending of an accounting period such as in section 383. The income and expense are recognised in the accounting period of the company which relates to the day of the qualifying change.

1259. If a single company is carrying on the business alone after the qualifying change, *subsection (5)* provides that the expense is treated as incurred by it at a time when it is carrying the business alone and is allowed as a deduction in calculating the profits of the business for the accounting period in which it is treated as incurred.

*Section 418: **Amount of income and expense***

1260. This section contains a signpost to the sections which contain the provisions for calculating the amount of the income to be brought into account in accordance with section 417(2)(a) and (3) and to the section determining the amount of the expense to be brought into account in accordance with section 417(2)(b) and (4) or (5). It is based on paragraph 24 of Schedule 10 to FA 2006.

*Section 419: **Relief for expense otherwise giving rise to carried forward loss***

1261. This section applies if, as the result of a qualifying change in a partner company's interest in the partnership business, a single company succeeds to the partnership business and provides for the carrying forward of the expense incurred by the successor company to later accounting periods. It is based on paragraph 39 of Schedule 10 to FA 2006.

1262. If the successor company makes a loss in the accounting period in which it begins to carry on the business alone, the loss derived from the expense treated as incurred under section 417(5)(a), which could otherwise only be carried forward and applied against the profits of the company's leasing trade, is instead to be treated as an expense of the next accounting period and so available for group relief in that period.

1263. If the company continues to make losses, so much of the loss as derives from the expense can similarly be treated as an expense of subsequent accounting periods which start within the period of five years beginning with the day on which the qualifying change in the partner company's interest in the business occurs, unless there is a subsequent qualifying change of ownership.

1264. The amount of the loss derived from the expense is indexed to up-rate its value and preserve the symmetry between the value of the charge and the value of the relief. See *subsection (2)*.

1265. Paragraph 39 of Schedule 10 to FA 2006 applies for the purposes of:

- paragraph 3 of that Schedule, in a case where the company carries on the leasing business alone; and
- paragraphs 23(4A) and 33 of that Schedule, in a case where the company carries on the business in partnership.

1266. It has been rewritten here for the purposes only of section 417(5). It has also been rewritten in section 386 for the purposes of section 383 and in section 428 for the purposes of section 425. It is considered that it is helpful to paint the complete picture in each Chapter.

*Section 420: **Exception: companies carrying on business ceasing to share in its profits***

1267. This section disapplies section 417 subject to certain conditions where all the companies carrying on the business in partnership cease to be interested in the business on the same day. It is based on paragraph 23A of Schedule 10 to FA 2006.

Section 421: The amount of the income: the basic amount

1268. This section gives the formula (PM – TWDV) for determining the basic amount of income of the partnership which is then to be adjusted in accordance with section 422 or 423 to determine the amount of income of the company for the purposes of section 417 on any day ("the relevant day"). It is based on paragraph 29 of Schedule 10 to FA 2006.

1269. *Subsection (4)* applies the definition of PM in section 400 with modifications.

1270. *Subsection (5)* determines the amount which is TWDV.

1271. The TWDV amount is made up of the unrelieved qualifying expenditure in all single asset pools, class pools and the main pool. This is the amount that would be carried forward assuming that a chargeable period ends on the relevant day and a new one begins on the following day (see *subsection (6)(a)*).

1272. But any expenditure on the acquisition of plant or machinery on the relevant day is excluded, except for plant or machinery acquired from qualifying companies (see *subsection (6)(b)*). This adjustment ensures that amounts in respect of plant or machinery acquired from qualifying companies (as defined in *subsection (7)*) on the relevant day are included in both the PM and the TWDV amounts.

Section 422: Amount to be nil if basic amount negative

1273. This section ensures that, if the formula in section 421(3) produces a negative basic amount, the amount of the company's income for the purposes of section 417 is nil. It is based on paragraph 30 of Schedule 10 to FA 2006.

Section 423: Adjustment to the basic amount

1274. This section limits the amount of the company's income for the purposes of section 417 to a percentage of the basic amount. It is based on paragraph 31 of Schedule 10 to FA 2006.

1275. The percentage of the basic amount is found by deducting the company's percentage share in the profits or loss of the partnership at the end of the day from its percentage share at the beginning of the day.

Section 424: The amount of expense

1276. This section determines the amount of expense treated as incurred by a company in accordance with section 417(2)(b) as the result of a qualifying change in the partner company's interest in the business on any day. It is based on paragraph 32 of Schedule 10 to FA 2006.

1277. Except where a single company is carrying on the business at the end of the day, the amount of the expense is determined by reference to any increase of the company's percentage interest in the profits or loss of the partnership which is attributable to the qualifying change in the interest in the business of the partner company (see *subsections (2)* and *(3)*).

1278. Where a single company is carrying on the business at the end of the day, the amount of the expense is equal to the amount of the income (see *subsection (4)*).

Section 425: Partner company's income and matching expense in different accounting periods

1279. This section provides for an accounting period to end if there is a "qualifying change of ownership" in relation to a company within the charge to corporation tax carrying on a business of leasing plant or machinery in partnership. It is based on paragraph 33 of Schedule 10 to FA 2006.

1280. This section is the equivalent of section 383 which applies where the company is carrying on the business alone. "Qualifying change of ownership" has the same meaning in this section as it does in section 383 (see sections 392 to 398).

1281. On the day the accounting period ends the company is treated as receiving an amount of income which is brought into account in calculating the profits of the company's "notional business" for that accounting period for corporation tax purposes. See *subsections (2)* and *(3)*.

1282. On the following day the company is treated as incurring an expense which is brought into account in calculating the profits of the company's "notional business" for a new accounting period for corporation tax purposes. See *subsections (4)* and *(5)*.

*Section 426: **Amount of income and expense***

1283. This section contains a signpost to the section which contains the provisions for calculating the amount of the income to be brought into account in accordance with section 425(2) and (3) and provides that the amount of the expense to be brought into account in accordance with section 425(4) and (5) is the same as the amount of the income. It is based on paragraph 34 of Schedule 10 to FA 2006.

*Section 427: **No carry back of the expense***

1284. This section prevents any loss which arises in the later accounting period which derives from the expense from being carried back against profits of any earlier accounting period under section 37(3)(b). It is based on paragraph 35 of Schedule 10 to FA 2006.

*Section 428: **Relief for expense otherwise giving rise to carried forward loss***

1285. This section provides for the carrying forward of the expense to later accounting periods. It is based on paragraph 39 of Schedule 10 to FA 2006.

1286. If the company makes a loss in the accounting period which, in accordance with section 425(4)(b), begins on the day after the qualifying change of ownership, the loss derived from the expense treated as incurred under section 425(4)(a), which could otherwise only be carried forward and applied against the profits of the company's leasing trade, is instead to be treated as an expense of the next accounting period and so available for group relief in that period.

1287. If the company continues to make losses, so much of the loss as derives from the expense can similarly be treated as an expense of subsequent accounting periods which start within five years of the qualifying change of ownership, unless there is a subsequent qualifying change of ownership.

1288. The amount of the loss derived from the expense is indexed to up-rate its value and preserve the symmetry between the value of the charge and the value of the relief. See *subsection (2)*.

1289. Paragraph 39 of Schedule 10 to FA 2006 applies for the purposes of:

- paragraph 3 of that Schedule, in a case where the company carries on the leasing business alone; and
- paragraphs 23(4A) and 33 of that Schedule, in a case where the company carries on the business in partnership.

1290. It has been rewritten here for the purposes only of section 425. It has also been rewritten in section 386 for the purposes of section 383 and in section 419 for the purposes of section 417(5). It is considered that it is helpful to paint the complete picture in each Chapter.

Section 429: ***The amount of the income***

1291. This section sets out the rules for determining the amount of the company's income for the purposes of section 425 on any day. It is based on paragraph 36 of Schedule 10 to FA 2006.

1292. The rules adopt concepts from Chapters 3 and 4 for this purpose. The basic amount is found in accordance with section 421 in Chapter 4 and is then adjusted in accordance with sections 404 to 406 in Chapter 3. The "appropriate percentage" of the adjusted amount is then taken.

1293. *Subsection (5)* ensures that, if on the same day there is also a qualifying change in the company's interest in the business carried on by the partnership, the percentage share in relation to which the amount of income under section 417 is calculated is not also taken into account in calculating the income under section 425.

Section 430: ***"Associated company"***

1294. This section gives the meaning of "associated company" for the purposes of Chapter 4 only. It is based on paragraph 26 of Schedule 10 to FA 2006.

1295. This section is substantially similar to section 408 which gives the meaning of "associated company" for the purposes of Chapter 3 but includes additional provisions in *subsection (5)* for the case where the company is a consortium company and there is a qualifying change in its interest in the business carried on by it in partnership.

Section 431: ***"Profits" and "loss"***

1296. This section provides that in calculating the amount of income and expense for the purposes of this Chapter a company's percentage share does not include its share in any chargeable gains or losses. It is based on paragraph 37 of Schedule 10 to FA2006.

1297. In the case of some partnerships, different profit sharing ratios are agreed for income profits and losses and capital profits and losses. This provision ensures certainty in such cases by looking only at the profit sharing ratios for income profits and losses.

Chapter 5: ***Sales of lessors: anti–avoidance provisions***

Overview

1298. This Chapter contains two sets of anti–avoidance provisions.

Section 432: ***Restrictions on relief for Chapter 3 or 4 expenses: introduction***

1299. This section provides for the circumstances in which section 433 applies. It is based on paragraph 38(1), (2), (6) and (7) of Schedule 10 to FA 2006.

1300. Section 433 applies if a company incurs an expense under Chapter 3 or 4 which arises in consequence of or in connection with arrangements the main purpose, or one of the main purposes, of which is to secure that the company is treated as incurring the expense (see *subsection (1)*).

Section 433: ***Restrictions applying to the restricted loss amount***

1301. This section is an anti–avoidance provision. It is based on paragraph 38(2) to(5), (8) and (9) of Schedule 10 to FA 2006.

1302. The section restricts the manner in which the loss derived from the expense referred to in section 432 may be utilised. It ensures that the loss can only be set against income from certain leases of plant or machinery entered into before the day on which the company is treated as incurring the expense.

Section 434: Introduction to sections 435 and 436

1303. This section explains when sections 435 and 436 apply and what is meant by a question as to the application of Chapter 3 or 4. It is based on paragraphs 38A(1) and (4) and 38B(1) of Schedule 10 to FA 2006.

1304. A question as to the application of Chapter 3 or 4 is one which concerns:

- whether a company carries on a business of leasing plant or machinery (whether alone or in partnership); or
- the amount (if any) of any income or expense treated as received or incurred.

Section 435: Disregard of increases and decreases in balance sheet amounts

1305. This section is an anti–avoidance provision. It is based on paragraph 38A(1) to(3) and (5) of Schedule 10 to FA 2006.

1306. The section targets arrangements that increase or reduce the amounts shown in a company's balance sheet in respect of plant or machinery.

1307. *Subsection (1)* provides that this section applies if:

- there is a question as to the application of Chapter 3 or 4 and the answer to the question relies on amounts in respect of plant or machinery shown in any balance sheet of any company;
- there has been an arrangement that results in an increase or reduction of the amount that would otherwise have been shown on the balance sheet; and
- that arrangement had as its main purpose, or one of its main purposes, securing a relevant tax advantage (see *subsection (2)*).

1308. If this section applies the increase or decrease in the amount in respect of plant or machinery is to be ignored (see *subsection (3)*).

Section 436: Balance sheet amounts determined on assumption company has no liabilities

1309. This section is an anti–avoidance provision. It is based on paragraph 38B of Schedule 10 to FA 2006.

1310. The section targets situations where the amount shown in a company's balance sheet in respect of plant or machinery is affected by the liabilities of the company.

1311. It applies if, apart from this section, on any day:

- no amount would fall to be shown in the company's balance sheet in respect of plant or machinery (see *subsection (2)*); or
- the amount which would fall to be shown in the balance sheet of the company in respect of plant or machinery is less than the amount which would fall to be shown on the assumption that the company had no liabilities of any kind on that day (see *subsections (3)* and *(4)*).

1312. In either of those cases, a question as to the application of Chapter 3 or 4 is to be answered applying the assumption that the company had no liabilities of any kind on that day (see *subsection (5)*).

Chapter 6: *Sales of lessors: general interpretation*

Section 437: *Interpretation of the sales of lessors Chapters*

1313. This section defines terms and provides interpretation for the purposes of the sales of lessors Chapters. It is based on paragraph 41 of Schedule 10 to FA 2006.

1314. The definition of connected persons by reference to section 839 of ICTA in paragraph 41(9) of Schedule 10 to FA 2006 has not been rewritten. Section 839 of ICTA is rewritten in section 1122 and section 1176(1) applies the defined term for the purposes of this Act unless otherwise indicated.

1315. Paragraph 42 of Schedule 10 to FA 2006 (index of definitions) has not been rewritten in this Part, but Schedule 4 (Index of defined expressions) contains the principal defined terms used in the sales of lessors Chapters.

Part 10: **Close companies**

Overview

1316. This Part rewrites sections 414 to 417 and 419 to 422 of ICTA and Schedule 12 to FA 1989, which are concerned with close companies.

1317. A company controlled by a small group of persons may arrange its affairs to enable those persons to avoid income tax. The close company provisions in Part 11 of ICTA counter this.

1318. The close company legislation, as such, has two main effects. First, section 418 of ICTA extends the meaning of "distribution" to encompass certain benefits which may be disguised distributions of profit to the shareholders or their families. Section 418 is rewritten in this Act as part of the legislation on distributions. See section 1064. Second, section 419 of ICTA imposes tax in respect of certain loans made to shareholders or their families which could in practice represent the extraction of profits without the payment of tax by those persons. Section 419 is rewritten in Chapter 3 of this Part.

1319. Other legislation imposes further restrictions on close companies. For example, close companies which are "close investment-holding companies" (as defined in section 13A of ICTA) are not entitled to claim to pay the rate of corporation tax for companies with small profits. Section 13A is rewritten in this Act as part of the legislation on relief for companies with small profits. See section 34.

1320. The term "control" is defined for close company purposes in section 416 of ICTA. This definition is also widely used in other contexts. Section 416 is rewritten in Chapter 2 of this Part.

Chapter 1: *Overview of Part*

Section 438: *Overview of Part*

1321. This section introduces the Part. It is new.

1322. In its present form, the close company legislation in Part 11 of ICTA largely dates back to 1965. The opportunity has been taken to disentangle its structure.

1323. The definitions of the key technical terms are located near the beginning of the Part, in Chapter 2.

1324. Chapter 3 imposes the charge to tax in connection with loans or advances by close companies to participators.

1325. Chapter 4 contains a power to obtain information in connection with close companies.

1326. "Participator" is used for the first time in this Part in *subsection (2)*. Its definition is signposted in *subsection (4)*.

Chapter 2: Basic definitions

Overview

1327. This Chapter defines which companies are and are not to be close companies. It has the following structure.

- Sections 439 to 441 define "close company".
- Sections 442 to 447 make exceptions to the rules in sections 439 to 441.
- Sections 448 to 454 define some expressions used in this Part and, in particular, in defining "close company". These definitions are arranged in alphabetical order.

Section 439: "Close company"

1328. This section is the first of a group of three sections defining "close company". It is based on section 414(1), (2) and (2D) of ICTA.

1329. *Subsection (1)* provides that there are two alternative tests to determine whether a company is a close company.

1330. The first test, condition A in *subsection (2)*, focuses on control over the company.

1331. The second test, condition B in *subsection (3)*, focuses on rights to assets in the event that the company is wound up.

1332. *Subsection (4)* gives a signpost to the exceptions to this section in sections 442 to 447.

1333. *Subsections (5)* and *(6)* relate to condition B in subsection (3). Subsection (5) provides for subsection (3) to be supplemented by section 451. Subsection (6) gives a signpost to section 441, which supplements subsection (3).

1334. "Control" and "director" are used for the first time in this Part in subsection (2), and "loan creditor" is used for the first time in subsection (3). Signposts to their definitions are given in *subsection (7)*.

Section 440: Basis of winding up under section 439(3)

1335. This section quantifies the part of the assets available for distribution among the participators which a person is entitled to receive in the notional winding up under section 439(3). It is based on section 414(2A) and (2B) of ICTA.

Section 441: Treatment of some persons as participators or directors for the purposes of section 439(3)

1336. This section supplements section 439(3). It is based on section 414(2C) of ICTA.

Section 442: Particular types of company

1337. This section is the first of a series of sections stipulating that certain companies are not to be treated as close companies. It is based on section 414(1) and (2) of ICTA.

Section 443: Companies controlled by or on behalf of Crown

1338. This section provides that certain companies controlled by or on behalf of the Crown are not to be treated as close companies. It is based on section 414(1) and (4) of ICTA.

1339. *Subsection (1)* provides that "a company is not to be treated as a close company *as a result of section 439(2)* if it is controlled by or on behalf of the Crown." The italicised words are based on "and not otherwise a close company" in section 414(1)(c) of ICTA.

1340. The italicised words leave it open for a company controlled by or on behalf of the Crown to be a close company if condition B in section 439(3) is met. Section 439(3) is based on section 414(2) of ICTA.

1341. The italicised words also leave it open for a company controlled by or on behalf of the Crown to be a close company if condition A in section 439(2) is satisfied by reference to persons acting independently of the Crown. See *subsection (3)*.

1342. In short, section 414(1)(c) of ICTA is a qualified exception to section 414(1) of that Act but not an exception to section 414(2) of that Act.

*Section 444: **Companies involved with non-close companies***

1343. This section provides that certain companies involved with non-close companies are not to be treated as close companies. It is based on section 414(5) and (6) of ICTA.

1344. *Subsections (2)* and *(3)* rewrite section 414(5)(a) and (b) of ICTA respectively.

*Section 445: Section 444: **registered pension schemes***

1345. This section supplements section 444; it is concerned with shares held on trust for registered pension schemes. It is based on section 414(7) of ICTA.

1346. *Subsection (1)* is based on the full-out words at the beginning and end of section 414(7) of ICTA. In summary, a registered pension scheme within subsection (1) is treated as a non-close company.

1347. *Subsection (2)* is based on the "unless"-clause in the full-out words at the beginning of section 414(7) of ICTA. It is the first part of an exception to subsection (1). It focuses on the individuals for whose benefit the scheme is established.

1348. *Subsection (3)* is based on section 414(7)(a) to (c) of ICTA. It is the second part of the exception to subsection (1). It focuses on the companies of which the individuals in subsection (2)(a) are or were directors or employees.

1349. "Associate" and "associated company" appear for the first time in subsection (3). Their definitions are signposted in *subsection (4)*.

*Section 446: **Particular types of quoted company***

1350. This section provides that certain quoted companies are not to be treated as close companies. It is based on section 415(1), (2) and (6) to (8) of ICTA.

1351. *Subsection (1)* lays down the general rule.

1352. *Subsection (2)* makes an exception to the general rule in subsection (1).

1353. Subsection (2) uses the concept of a "principal member" of a company. This term is defined in *subsection (3)*.

1354. *Subsection (4)* qualifies subsection (3).

1355. Subsections (1) to (4) focus on voting power. *Subsection (5)* supplements the references to voting power in those provisions.

*Section 447: Section 446: **meaning of "shares beneficially held by the public" etc***

1356. This interpretative section is based on section 415(3) to (8) of ICTA.

1357. *Subsection (1)* lays down the general rule.

1358. *Subsection (2)* makes an exception to that rule.

1359. *Subsection (3)* specifies the individuals in subsection (2)(e).

1360. *Subsection (4)* rewrites the tail words of section 415(3) of ICTA. It supplements the references to unconditional allotment and unconditional acquisition in section 446(1).

1361. *Subsections (5)* to *(8)* supplement this section or provisions of this section.

Sections 448 and 449: "Associate"; "associated company"

1362. These interpretative sections are based on sections 416(1) and 417(3) and (4) of ICTA.

Section 450: "Control"

1363. This interpretative section is based on section 416(2) and (3) of ICTA.

1364. *Subsection (1)* specifies that this definition of "control" applies for the purposes of this Part. The definition of "control" in section 840 of ICTA is rewritten in section 1124.

1365. *Subsection (2)* rewrites the general proposition in the opening words of section 416(2) of ICTA.

1366. *Subsection (3)* rewrites the specific propositions in section 416(2)(a) to (c) of ICTA.

1367. *Subsection (4)* rewrites as a separate stipulation the words in brackets in section 416(2)(b) of ICTA.

1368. *Subsection (5)* rewrites section 416(3) of ICTA.

Section 451: Section 450: rights to be attributed etc

1369. This section supplements section 450. It is based on section 416(4) to (6) of ICTA.

1370. *Subsections (2)* and *(3)* rewrite, respectively, section 416(4) and (5) of ICTA.

1371. *Subsections (4)* to *(6)* rewrite section 416(6) of ICTA, paragraphing it and breaking it up into sense-units.

1372. Sections 439(5), 446(5) and 447(6) provide for the application of provisions of this section.

Section 452: "Director"

1373. This interpretative section is based on section 417(5) and (6) of ICTA.

1374. Section 417(5) of ICTA refers to "the company's trade or business". Section 6(4)(b) of ICTA provides that, in Part 11 of that Act, "trade" includes "vocation" and also includes an office or employment. A company cannot carry on an employment. In relation to a company, "business" is apt to include an office. *Subsection (2)* therefore does not provide that "trade" includes an office or employment. In addition, *subsection (2)*includes a minor change in the law, in that it does not provide that "trade" includes "vocation". See *Change 4* in Annex 1.

1375. Section 417(5)(b) of ICTA has the phrase "directly or through the medium of other companies or by any other indirect means". It follows from the meaning of "other" that "through the medium of other companies or by any other indirect means" can be compressed to "by any indirect means". Compare Viscount Radcliffe's remarks on "interest, annuities, or other annual payments" in CIR v Frere (1964) 42 TC 125 HL on page 152. And, as a matter of normal English usage, "by any indirect means" is synonymous with "indirectly". *Subsection (2)(b)(ii)* therefore compresses the phrase under review to "directly or indirectly".

1376. In section 417(6) of ICTA, if a person (P) is deemed to own whatever P's associates own or control, then "either on his own or with one or more associates" is otiose. *Subsection (3)* therefore omits it. And subsection (3) goes on to omit as otiose "even if he does not own or control share capital on his own".

Sections 453 and 454 "Loan creditor"; "participator"

1377. These interpretative sections are based on section 417(1), (2) and (7) to (9) of ICTA.

Chapter 3: Charge to tax in case of loan to participator

Section 455: Charge to tax in case of loan to participator

1378. This section imposes a charge to tax if a close company makes a loan, or advances money, to a participator or an associate of a participator. It is based on section 419(1) to (3), (6) and (7) of ICTA.

1379. *Subsection (1)* states when this section applies. It uses the expression "relevant person", which is defined in *subsection (6)*.

1380. *Subsection (2)* imposes the charge.

1381. *Subsection (3)* states when the tax is due and payable.

1382. *Subsection (4)* extends the scope of the charge. It is based on section 419(2) of ICTA, which is expressed to apply for the purposes of that section. Subsection (4) is expressed to apply for the purposes of, among other things, section 456 – that is, including the provisions of that section which are based on section 420 of ICTA. Since section 420 of ICTA makes exceptions to section 419 of that Act, defining the scope of subsection (4) in this way does not change the law.

1383. *Subsection (5)* extends the circumstances in which a person is treated as being a participator in a company.

Section 456: Exceptions to the charge under section 455

1384. This section makes certain exceptions to the charge under section 455. It is based on sections 419(1) and 420 of ICTA.

1385. *Subsection (1)* is an exception for money-lending companies.

1386. *Subsection (2)* is an exception for ordinary supplies of goods and services.

1387. Subsection (2) refers to a company's "trade or business". It does not refer to a company's "vocation". This is a minor change in the law. See the commentary on section 452 and *Change 4*in Annex 1.

1388. *Subsections (3)* to *(8)* are an exception for small amounts.

1389. Subsections (3), (4) and (7) apply not only to loans but also to advances. This is a minor change in the law to bring it into line with practice. See *Change 30* in Annex 1.

Section 457: Section 456: meaning of "material interest in a company"

1390. This interpretative section is based on section 420(2) of ICTA.

1391. The closing sentence of section 420(2) of ICTA attracts, with modifications, section 168(11) of ICTA. Section 168(11) of ICTA has been rewritten in section 68 of ITEPA and repealed. This section largely replicates section 68 of ITEPA.

1392. Section 168(11) of ICTA is reproduced below for the reader's convenience, as it stood before ITEPA and as modified by section 420(2) of ICTA.

"A person shall be treated as having a material interest in a company if he, either on his own or with one or more associates, or if any associate of his with or without such other associates –

(a) is the beneficial owner of, or able, directly or through the medium of other companies, or by any other indirect means, to control more than 5 per cent of the ordinary share capital of the company, or

(b) in the case of a close company, possesses, or is entitled to acquire, such rights as would in the event of the winding up of the company or in any other circumstances, give an entitlement to receive more than 5 per cent of the assets which would then be available for distribution among the participators.

In this subsection "associate" has the same meaning as in section 417(3), except that for this purpose "relative" in that subsection has the meaning given by section 160(6),and "participator" has the meaning given by section 417(1).

1393. The closing sentence of section 420(2) of ICTA provides for the words following "417(3)" to be omitted, and the words in strikethrough reflect this. But this omission merely disapplies the definition of "relative" in section 160(6) of ICTA. It does not extend to the underlined words, because omitting the underlined words would leave "participator" undefined. FA 1989 inserted the underlined words into section 168(11) of ICTA by way of consequential amendment, and it appears that the need to make a further consequential amendment to section 420(2) of that Act was overlooked.

1394. *Subsection (2)(b)* has been compressed for the sake of brevity and consistency with section 452(2)(b)(ii). See the commentary on that provision.

*Section 458: **Relief in case of repayment or release of loan***

1395. This section gives relief from tax in cases in which:

- a loan or advance from a close company has given rise to a charge under section 455, and
- the loan or advance is repaid or the debt in respect of it is released or written off.

1396. It is based on section 419(4) to (4B) of ICTA.

1397. *Subsection (1)* states when the section applies.

1398. *Subsection (2)* specifies the relief and the circumstances in which it is given.

1399. *Subsection (3)* is about claiming the relief. It reflects paragraph 21 of Schedule 39 to FA 2008, which substitutes "4 years" for "six years" in section 419(4) of ICTA with effect from 1 April 2010.

1400. If the company becomes eligible for relief after the tax due under section 455 becomes due and payable, *subsections (4)* and *(5)* defer the relief.

1401. *Subsection (6)* sets the link with TMA.

*Section 459: **Loan treated as made to participator***

1402. This section blocks arrangements to circumvent the charge under section 455. It treats certain loans or advances, which would otherwise be outside the scope of that section, as having been made to a relevant person. It is based on section 419(5) and (7) of ICTA.

1403. *Subsection (1)* states when the section applies.

1404. *Subsection (2)* is the main operative provision.

1405. Section 419(5) of ICTA provides for that section to apply as if the loan or advance had been made to the individual in question. Subsection (2), which is based on section 419(5), provides for sections 455 to 458 to apply. These sections include provisions which are based on section 420 of ICTA. Since section 420 of ICTA makes exceptions to section 419 of that Act, defining the scope of subsection (2) in this way does not change the law.

1406. *Subsection (3)* makes two exceptions to this section.

1407. *Subsection (4)* extends the circumstances in which a person is treated as a participator in a company.

Section 460: ***Loan treated as made by close company***

1408. This section extends the scope of sections 455 to 459 to catch loans or advances made by certain companies which are controlled by other companies. It is based on section 422(1) to (3) and (6) of ICTA.

1409. *Subsection (1)* states when the section applies.

1410. *Subsection (2)* prescribes the consequences if the company (C) making the loan or advance is controlled by a close company.

1411. *Subsection (3)* prescribes the consequences if C is not controlled by a close company but a close company subsequently acquires control of it.

1412. Subsections (2) and (3) operate in relation to section 459, because the references in section 422(1) and (2) of ICTA to section 419 of that Act pick up section 419(5) of that Act.

1413. *Subsection (4)* deals with the case in which two or more close companies control C.

1414. *Subsections (5)* and *(6)* are signposts.

1415. *Subsection (7)* extends the circumstances in which a company is deemed to make a loan.

Section 461: ***Exception to*** *section 460*

1416. This section makes an exception to section 460. It is based on section 422(4) and (6) of ICTA.

Section 462: ***Determination of particular questions as a result of*** *section 460*

1417. This section supplements sections 455 to 459. It is based on section 422(5) and (6) of ICTA.

1418. *Subsection (1)* states when the section applies. It operates in relation to section 459 for the reason given in the commentary on section 460(2) and (3).

1419. *Subsection (2)* lists the questions which come within this section, and requires them to be determined by reference to the company labelled C in section 460(1).

Section 463: ***Taxation of debtor on release of loan to trustees of settlement which has ended***

1420. This section deems income to arise to a company for corporation tax purposes in certain circumstances when a loan or advance from a close company is released or written off. It is based on section 421 of ICTA.

1421. This section deals with the following case, as specified in *subsections (2) to (5)*.

- A close company (X) makes a loan or advance to the trustees of a settlement.
- Another company (Y) becomes the debtor in respect of this loan or advance.

- After the settlement has ended, X releases or writes off the whole or part of the loan or advance.

1422. *Subsection (6)* is the main operative provision.

1423. *Subsection (7)* quantifies the income. Section 421(1)(a) of ICTAuses the word "gross" in a manner analogous to "grossing up" as defined in section 1128(3) of this Act. Subsection (7) therefore uses a formula to rewrite section 421(1)(a) and (b) of ICTA on the lines of the formula in section 1128(3).

Section 464: Section 463: other person treated as releasing or writing off debt

1424. This section supplements section 463. It is based on section 422(5) of ICTA.

1425. *Subsection (1)* states when the section applies. It operates in relation to section 459 for the reason given in the commentary on section 460(2) and (3).

1426. *Subsection (2)* is the operative provision.

Chapter 4: Power to obtain information

Section 465: Power to obtain information

1427. This section gives HMRC power to obtain information about close companies. It is based on Schedule 12 to FA 1989.

Part 11: Charitable companies etc

Overview

1428. This Part contains rules specific to charitable companies. It follows to a large extent the structure of Part 10 of ITA, and, like those provisions, is based on sections 505 to 506C of, and Schedule 20 to, ICTA, section 25 of FA 1990 and section 46 of FA 2000. It also rewrites certain provisions which have only ever applied for corporation tax purposes such as sections 507 and 508 of ICTA.

Chapter 1: Introduction

Overview

1429. This Chapter gives an overview of the Part and provides certain important definitions.

Section 466: Overview of Part

1430. This section sets out the scope of the Part.

Section 467: Meaning of "charitable company"

1431. This section defines "charitable company" for the purposes of this Part and is based on section 506(1) of ICTA, section 25(12) of FA 1990, section 46(6) of FA 2000 and section 83(5) of FA 2004.

1432. The effect of splitting the source legislation between income tax and corporation tax is that the income tax rules apply to charities constituted in the form of charitable trusts while the corporation tax rules apply to charitable companies.

1433. The definition of charitable company therefore includes charities constituted as unincorporated associations and charities incorporated by Royal Charter.

1434. A definition of a "charity" is included in section 1119 of this Act. The definition for income tax is in section 989 of ITA.

Section 468: Meaning of "eligible body"

1435. This section lists the institutions which are referred to in this Part as "eligible bodies". It is based on section 507(1) of ICTA.

Section 469: Conditions for qualifying as a scientific research association

1436. This section sets out the conditions necessary for a company to qualify as a scientific research association (SRA) for the purposes of this Part. It is based on section 508(1) to (3) of ICTA.

Section 470: Meaning of "research and development" in section 469.

1437. This section applies the definition of "research and development" in section 1138. It is based on section 508(3) and (4).

1438. *Subsection (2)* follows the approach taken in section 1138 which draws on the regulatory power in section 1006 of ITA.

Chapter 2: Gifts and other payments

Overview

1439. This Chapter provides the rules on grossing up and exemptions for gifts and other payments paid by individuals and companies to charities and other bodies within this Part.

Section 471: Gifts qualifying for gift aid relief: income tax treated as paid

1440. This section deals with the income tax treated as paid when a charitable company receives gift aid donations from individuals. It is based on section 25(10) and (12) of FA 1990. The corresponding rule for income tax is in sections 520 of ITA.

1441. The company is treated as receiving a grossed up amount, and the tax treated as deducted from the gift is treated as paid by the charitable company.

Section 472: Gifts qualifying for gift aid relief: corporation tax liability and exemption

1442. This section sets out the charge to tax and exemption that can arise on gift aid payments received by a charitable company. It is based on section 505(1) of ICTA, section 25(10) and (12) of FA 1990 and section 83(4) of FA 2004. The corresponding rule for income tax is in section 521 of ITA save that this section incorporates the requirement to make a claim.

1443. The section imposes a freestanding charge to corporation tax on gift aid payments, unlike the source legislation which operates by treating the gifts as annual payments. The charge is on the grossed up amount. The section also sets out the exemption which normally applies if the charitable company uses the gifts for charitable purposes.

1444. *Subsection (4)* provides that a claim is necessary for an exemption.

1445. Claims are made either as required during the accounting period, for example to secure repayments of income tax treated as paid in relation to gift aid payments, or in a corporation tax self-assessment return. The need to make a claim ensures that there is a mechanism for appeals in the event of any dispute about the availability or amount of any exemption.

1446. The corporation tax self-assessment procedure means that a charitable company only need complete a tax return, and make the associated claims, if the charitable company is chargeable to tax or is required to do so by HMRC.

1447. The reference in section 505(1) of ICTA to claims being to the Board of Inland Revenue has been changed. Claims are simply to an officer of Revenue and Customs. See *Change 5* in Annex 1.

1448. *Subsection (5)* provides that if an individual makes a direction in a self-assessment return for a tax repayment to be paid as a gift to a charitable company, the company is treated as having made a claim.

Section 473: Gifts of money from companies: corporation tax liability and exemption

1449. This section sets out the charge to tax that can arise on gifts received by a charitable company from other companies which are not charities. It is based on section 339(4) and 505(1) of ICTA. The corresponding rule for income tax is in section 522 of ITAsave that the requirement to make a claim has been incorporated into the section.

1450. As with section 472, this section imposes a freestanding charge to corporation tax on gifts.

Section 474: Payments from other charities: corporation tax liability and exemption

1451. This section prevents avoidance by charities of the restrictions on exemptions by routing non-charitable expenditure through other charities. It is based on section 505(1) and (2) of ICTA. The corresponding rule for income tax is in section 523 of ITA save that the requirement to make a claim has been incorporated into the section.

1452. The section operates by imposing a charge to tax on certain payments made by a charity to a charitable company. It also sets out the exemption which normally applies if the charitable company uses the payments for charitable purposes.

1453. Earlier drafts of *subsection (1)* added to the conditions (now paragraphs (a) to (c)) a further condition (paragraph (d)) that payment should not arise from a source outside the United Kingdom. This requirement has now been removed. It was unnecessary and subsection (1) now rewrites the law accurately as it stands. CTA 2009 replaced the reference to Schedule D Case III in section 505(2) of ICTA with a reference to the charge to corporation tax on income. The amendment made it clearer that the charge under section 505(2) is not limited to payments from a source in the United Kingdom.

1454. *Subsection (4)* makes it clear that section 494 of ITA, which deals with the grossing up of discretionary payments from trusts, takes precedence over this section where applicable.

Section 475: Gifts qualifying for gift aid relief: income tax treated as paid and exemption

1455. This section gives the treatment that applies when an eligible body receives gift aid donations from individuals. It is based on section 25(10) and (12) of FA 1990 and sections 505(1) and 507(1) of ICTA. The corresponding rule for income tax is in section 520 of ITA save that the exemption and the requirement to make a claim has been incorporated into the section.

1456. The company is treated as receiving a grossed up amount, and the tax treated as deducted from the gift is treated as paid by the charitable company.

1457. Subsection (7) treats eligible bodies as having made a claim for exemption in respect of gifts made under section 429(2) of ITA which are treated as qualifying donations under that Act. See *Change 31* in Annex 1.

Section 476: Gifts of money from companies: exemption

1458. This section gives the exemption that applies where an eligible body receives a gift of money from a company. It is based on sections 339(4), 505(1) and 507(1) of ICTA.

Section 477: Gifts of money from companies: exemption

1459. This section gives the exemption that applies where a scientific research association receives a gift of money from a company. It is based on sections 339(4), 505(1) and 508(1) of ICTA.

Chapter 3: Other exemptions

Overview

1460. This Chapter deals with exemptions other than gifts and payments dealt with in Chapter 2.

Section 478: Exemption for profits etc of charitable trades

1461. This section sets out the exemption for trading profits of charitable companies. It is based on section 505(1) of ICTA. The corresponding rule for income tax is in section 524 of ITA.

1462. The exemption applies only if the trade is a charitable trade. This is defined in section 479.

1463. There is a difference between this section and the corresponding provision in ITA. Adjustment income (arising, for example, on a change of accounting basis) is an integral part of the trading profits of a company – see section 181 of CTA 2009. Charitable companies are entitled to the exemption on adjustment income on the same basis as their trading profits. The consequence is that, in contrast to ITA, there is no need for a change in the law to establish an exemption for adjustment income.

1464. This section does make it clear that, in the same way as the income tax legislation, post-cessation receipts (arising from what was a charitable trade) are exempt, in line with practice. Post-cessation receipt is defined by reference to Chapter 15 of Part 3 of CTA 2009. See *Change 32* in Annex 1.

1465. Exemptions for small-scale trades are dealt with separately in section 480.

Section 479: Meaning of "charitable trade"

1466. This section defines "charitable trade" for the purposes of the Part. It is based on section 505(1) and (1B) of ICTA. The corresponding rule for income tax is in section 525 of ITA.

1467. The source legislation in section 505(1)(e) of ICTA refers to the trade being carried on "in the United Kingdom or elsewhere", and section 505(1)(e)(i) refers to it being exercised in the "actual" carrying out of a primary purpose. The words in inverted commas are omitted as they add nothing.

1468. The section differs slightly from its income tax counterpart in section 525 of ITA. For income tax the conditions must be met throughout the *basis period* for the relevant tax year to reflect the fact that the two time periods are not usually the same, and it clearly makes sense to test the condition by reference to the period in which the activity was being carried on. This is not necessary for corporation tax as the accounting period is both the basis period and the chargeable period.

1469. S*ubsection (4)*, about making apportionments where different parts of a trade are treated as separate trades, makes specific mention of post-cessation receipts, but unlike the equivalent income tax provision there is no need for a specific apportionment for adjustment income. See *Change 32*in Annex 1 and the commentary on section 478.

1470. Any apportionments must be "just" as well as "reasonable". Only the latter term appeared in the source legislation. See *Change 33* in Annex 1.

Section 480: Exemption for profits of small-scale trades

1471. This section provides an exemption for trading income, related adjustment income and post-cessation receipts in circumstances where the amount of income to be exempted under this section and the next is small, and provided the income is applied to the purposes of the charitable company. It is based on section 46 of FA 2000. The corresponding rule for income tax is in section 526 of ITA.

1472. The exemption provided by this section applies only if the income is not otherwise exempt. So profits from primary purpose trading (including related adjustment income and post-cessation receipts) are exempt under section 478, whereas profits from a non-primary purpose trading activity (including related adjustment income and post-cessation receipts) may be exempt under this section.

1473. *Change 32* is not necessary here as post-cessation receipts from a "small trade" are already exempt because of the exemption in section 46 FA 2000 for income chargeable under Schedule D Case VI.

1474. The condition about the limit on the level of income for this exemption to apply is in section 482. For *Change 34* see commentary on section 482.

Section 481: Exemption from charges under provisions to which section 1173 applies

1475. This section provides an exemption for certain miscellaneous income and gains arising to a charitable company and applied to the purposes of the charitable company. It is based on section 46 of FA 2000. The corresponding rule for income tax is in section 527 of ITA.

1476. Section 834A of ICTA, which lists sources of income previously charged to tax under Schedule D Case VI, was inserted by paragraph 273 of Schedule 1 to CTA 2009. It is rewritten in this Act as section 1173. Now that the relief is by reference to the list in section 1173, some of the exclusions from the relief listed in the source legislation no longer need to be mentioned explicitly as they are not within the scope of section 1173. These are sections 703, 788 and 790 of ICTA, and paragraph 52(4) of Schedule 18 to FA 1998.

1477. *Subsection (2)* specifies the particular types of income and gains which cannot benefit from the exemption but which are within section 1173.

1478. The exemption provided by this section applies only if the income or gains are not otherwise exempt. So, for example, post-cessation primary purpose trading receipts are exempt under section 478 and post-cessation trading receipts from a non-primary purpose trading activity are exempt under section 480.

1479. The scope of this provision is therefore narrowed slightly in that post-cessation receipts from a primary purpose trade can now be exempt under section 478 whereas previously they could only be statutorily exempt under section 46 of FA 2000. (See *Change 32* in Annex 1 and the commentary on section 478.)

1480. The condition about the level of the income and gains is in section 482. For *Change 34* see commentary on section 482.

Section 482: Condition as to trading and miscellaneous incoming resources

1481. This section sets out the condition about the limit on the level of trading and miscellaneous incoming resources that has to be met if the exemptions in sections 480 and 481 are to apply. It is based on section 46 of FA 2000. The corresponding rule for income tax is in section 528 of ITA.

1482. The condition operates by reference to the incoming resources associated with the trading activity and miscellaneous transactions whose profits are not exempt under the other exemptions in this Part. The expression "incoming resources" is used instead of "gross income" because this accounting term is a more direct and accessible way of capturing the meaning of the income labelled "gross income" in the source legislation. There are also related points of clarification. See *Change 34* in Annex 1. This change also affects sections 480 and 481 (see following paragraph).

1483. Trading incoming resources and miscellaneous incoming resources are defined in *subsections (2)* and *(4)* respectively. The "requisite limit" is defined in *subsection (6)*. The total incoming resources must not exceed the limit set out in subsection (6)(a), but subsection (6)(b) ensures that the limit is never less than £5000 or greater than £50,000. Accordingly if a charitable company's trading and miscellaneous incoming resources relating to its non-exempt activities for an accounting period are, say, £4500 it would qualify for the exemption (provided that all other conditions are met) under section 480 or 481, even if that amount exceeds 25% of its total incoming resources for the accounting period.

1484. Similarly if the incoming resources related to its non-exempt activities exceed £50,000 in an accounting period, the charitable company cannot benefit from the exemptions in section 480 or 481, even if this figure does not breach the 25% limit in subsection (6)(a).

Section 483: Exemption for profits from fund-raising events

1485. This section gives statutory effect to ESC C4 as it applies to charitable companies and voluntary organisations provided the profits in question are applied to charitable purposes or transferred to a charity. It is new. The corresponding rule for income tax is in section 529 of ITA.

1486. The fund-raising event has to fall within the exemption from VAT under Group 12 of Schedule 9 to the Value Added Tax Act 1994. That Schedule provides an exemption from VAT for the supply by a charity of goods and services in connection with an event that is organised primarily to raise money for itself or other charities. The Schedule defines "event" and places certain limits on the number of events that a charity can hold in the same location in any given year.

1487. See *Change 35* in Annex 1. This change also affects sections 490, 491 and 492.

Section 484: Exemption for profits from lotteries

1488. This section provides an exemption for lottery income provided the income is applied to the purposes of the charitable company. It is based on section 505(1) of ICTA. The corresponding rule for income tax is in section 530 of ITA.

Section 485: Exemption for property income etc

1489. This section sets out the exemption from corporation tax for property income and certain trading income arising from land, provided the income is applied to charitable purposes. It is based on section 505(1) of ICTA. The corresponding rule for income tax is in section 531 of ITA.

1490. The exemption applies if the income is chargeable to tax under either Part 3 or Part 4 of CTA 2009. *Subsection (1)* deals with income chargeable under Part 3 of CTA 2009 and *subsection (2)* with income chargeable under Part 4 of CTA 2009.

1491. There is no requirement for the trade to be exercised in the course of carrying on a primary purpose of the charitable company. Instead, the exemption applies if the income derives from land vested for charitable purposes. But if some of the land is vested for charitable purposes and some vested or held for other purposes (for example, as an investment to generate income for non-charitable purposes) it is necessary to allocate the profits of the single property business between the two parts. This reflects the approach of the exemption in the source legislation that looks to particular interests in land, rather than to one overall property business.

1492. This makes the effect of the source legislation in section 505(1)(a) of ICTA explicit. There is no other income arising from land and chargeable to tax under Part 3 of CTA 2009 which is exempt under that provision.

1493. *Subsection (3)* provides an exemption from corporation tax for distributions from a United Kingdom REIT. The corresponding income tax exemption for this subsection is in section 531(2A) of ITA.

1494. The source legislation in section 505(1)(aa) of ICTA refers to exemption under Part 3 of CTA in respect of distributions to which section 121 of FA 2006 (rewritten in section 548) applies. Distributions to which section 121 of FA 2006 applies cannot be taxed as trading income and the reference to Part 3 of CTA has not therefore been rewritten.

1495. Section 505(1)(aa) of ICTA also refers to charging provisions in ITTOIA. These are not necessary for corporation tax and are not included in the rewritten legislation.

1496. The United Kingdom REIT rules are rewritten in Part 12 of this Act.

*Section 486: **Exemption for investment income and non-trading profits from loan relationships***

1497. This section sets out the various categories of savings and investment income that qualify for exemption from corporation tax, provided the income is applied to charitable purposes. It is based on section 505(1) of ICTA. The corresponding rule for income tax is in section 532 of ITA.

1498. Interest and related amounts are exempted by reference to the loan relationships regime, and the reference to a non-trading profit on a loan relationship also encompasses income from derivative contracts.

1499. The reference to an "Act" in *subsection (1)* is extended to include references to Northern Ireland legislation by section 1119, and to Acts of the Scottish Parliament. See *Change 6* in Annex 1.

1500. Section 56(3)(c) of ICTA disapplies the charge to corporation tax on the disposal of rights to receive amounts under a certificate of deposit where profits or gains (other than trading profits) on the disposal arise to a charitable company and are applied for charitable purposes. But section 56(4A) provides that section 56 does not apply for corporation tax purposes except in relation to rights in existence before 1 April 1996. This is necessary because rights arising in or after April 1996 fall within the loan relationships legislation, now rewritten in Part 5 of CTA 2009. Section 56(3)(c) has been retained as a saving in Schedule 2 so that the disposal of pre-1996 rights are still exempt so far as they are applied to charitable purposes although subsequent rights fall within *subsection (2)(a)* of this section.

*Section 487: **Exemption for public revenue dividends***

1501. This section provides an exemption for public revenue dividends used for the repair of certain places of worship. It is based on section 505(1) and (1A) of ICTA. The corresponding rule for income tax is in section 533 of ITA.

Section 488: Exemption for certain miscellaneous income

1502. This section provides an exemption from corporation tax for certain categories of miscellaneous income, provided the income is applied to charitable purposes. It is based on section 505(1) of ICTA. The corresponding rule for income tax is in section 536 of ITA.

1503. The reference to an "Act" in *subsection (1) (b)* is extended to include references to Northern Ireland legislation by section 1119, and to Acts of the Scottish Parliament. See *Change 6* in Annex 1.

1504. *Subsection (3)(c)* deals with income from intangible fixed assets that does not fall within Part 8 of CTA 2009 because the assets involved are "pre-FA 2002 assets". Previously the only exemption that covered this type of income was the exemption for annual payments. This section broadens the exemption to encompass income that is not covered by another exemption (for example, as a trading receipt) and is not exempted by this section as an annual payment, in the same way as for income tax in section 536 ITA. See C*hange 36* in Annex 1. This change also affects sections 490 and 491.

1505. Note that this extension to pre-FA 2002 assets only applies to what would be regarded as non-trading gains under Part 8 of CTA 2009. If the gains arise in respect of a pre-FA 2002 asset in the course of a non-charitable trade the exemption does not apply.

Section 489: Exemption for income from estates in administration

1506. This section provides an exemption for estate income received by a charitable company provided the income is applied to the purposes of the charitable company. It is new. The corresponding rule for income tax is in section 537.

1507. Estate income is income from property held by the personal representatives of the estate of a deceased person on behalf of the beneficiaries of the estate. The personal representatives are liable to income tax on the income. The exemption provided by this section allows a charitable company to recover any income tax suffered by the personal representatives. See *Change 37*in Annex 1.

Section 490: Eligible bodies

1508. This section extends certain of the exemptions to the five specified bodies defined as "eligible bodies" in section 468. It is based on section 507 of ICTA.

1509. Section 507 of ICTA grants to these bodies the exemptions under section 505 that would fall to be allowed to a charitable company if the whole of the charitable company's income is applied to charitable purposes.

1510. The exemptions are listed in *subsection (3)*. The list includes exemption under section 483 and section 489. These are not part of the source legislation, which refers only to the exemptions under section 505 of ICTA, but they are brought into the purview of the exemptions for these bodies – see *Changes 35*and*37* in Annex 1. The broadening of the exemptions under section 478 in respect of post-cessation receipts, and under section 488 in respect of intangible fixed assets also has an effect – see *Changes 32*and *36* in Annex 1.

1511. The list does not include the exemption under section 487 as the conditions for this exemption are structured in a different way.

Section 491: Scientific research associations

1512. This section brings scientific research associations (SRAs) within most of the exemptions in this Part. It is based on section 508(1) of ICTA.

1513. Like the bodies named in section 490, SRAs are assumed to have met the test regarding the purpose of their expenditure. The relevant exemptions are listed in *subsection (3)*.

An SRA may itself be charitable and able to qualify under its own charitable status by meeting the necessary tests. Exemption under this section does not preclude that possibility, and equally a charitable SRA may still benefit from section 491.

1514. The broadening of the exemptions under section 478 in respect of post-cessation receipts, and under section 488 in respect of intangible fixed assets also has an effect – see *Change 32*and *Change 36* in Annex 1. See also *Changes 36* and *37* in Annex 1 in respect of the exemptions in *subsection (3)*.

*Chapter 4: **Restrictions on exemptions***

Overview

1515. This Chapter sets out the restrictions that may apply to the exemptions under Chapters 2 and 3. Restrictions arise where a charitable company incurs non-charitable expenditure. Non-charitable expenditure may also arise where a company makes payments to "substantial donors" (defined in section 502).

*Section 492: **Restrictions on exemptions***

1516. This section restricts exemptions if income of a charitable company is attributed to non-charitable expenditure. It is based on section 505(3) and (4) of ICTA. The corresponding rule for income tax is in section 539 of ITA.

1517. Certain exemptions have been extended or put onto a statutory footing:

- post-cessation receipts. See *Change 32*in Annex 1 and the commentary on section 478;
- profits of fund-raising events. See *Change 35*in Annex 1 and the commentary on section 483; and
- income from estates in administration. See *Change 37*in Annex 1 and the commentary on section 489.

The restrictions apply to these extended exemptions.

*Section 493: **The non-exempt amount***

1518. This section specifies how the non-exempt amount is calculated. It is based on section 505(3) and (4) of ICTA. The corresponding rule for income tax is in section 540 of ITA.

1519. The term "attributable income and gains" is defined in *subsection (3)*. This label replaces "relievable income and gains" as defined in section 505(3) of ICTA.

1520. *Subsection (5)* specifies that section 256(4) of TCGA is to be ignored in applying subsection (3)(b). Section 256 of TCGA provides the exemption from capital gains tax for certain gains accruing to a charity. Schedule 1 to this Act amends section 256 of TCGA, adding subsections (3A), (7) and (8), and amending subsection (4) so that it applies to charitable companies as well as to charitable trusts. Schedule 1 also inserts sections 256C and 256D of TCGA, to deal with the interaction of this Act and the chargeable gains legislation as regards attributing income and gains to the non-exempt amount. It complements section 494. The headings to sections 256A and 256B of TCGA are amended to make it clear that they apply to charitable trusts only.

*Section 494: **Attributing income to the non-exempt amount***

1521. This section sets out how income is attributed to the non-exempt amount. It is based on section 505(4) of ICTA. The corresponding rule for income tax is in section 541 of ITA.

1522. It specifies that the non-exempt amount is to have attributed to it amounts of attributable income or amounts of attributable gains or a combination of both, until it is used up. The commentary on section 493 contains further detail about the amendments to TCGA 1992.

Section 495: How income is attributed to the non-exempt amount

1523. This section specifies that the charitable company can decide which items of what would otherwise be exempt income or chargeable gains should be treated as taxable. It is based on section 505(7) of ICTA. The corresponding rule for income tax is in section 542 of ITA.

1524. If the restrictions apply, an amount of income (or chargeable gains) equal to the non-exempt amount (of expenditure) must be identified (as calculated in accordance with section 493) in order to enable the charitable company to complete its tax return and self-assess its tax liability. This section provides the mechanism for the charitable company to specify the items or elements of income (such as trading income or investment income) which lose the benefit of exemption.

1525. If the charitable company has not specified the details within a period of 30 days from the date of a request, an officer of Revenue and Customs can decide. References to "the Board" have been replaced with "an officer of Revenue and Customs". See *Change 5* in Annex 1.

Section 496: Meaning of "non-charitable expenditure"

1526. This section defines "non-charitable expenditure". It is based on sections 506(1) and (4) and 506A(3) to (5) of ICTA. The corresponding rule for income tax is in section 543 of ITA.

1527. Section 506(1) of ICTA contains a definition of "charitable expenditure", but neither expenditure itself nor "non-charitable expenditure" is defined explicitly. This section sets out the definition in some detail, to reflect practice and HMRC guidance. See *Change 38*in Annex 1, which also affects sections 497 and 498.

1528. Schedule 2 to this Act contains a transitional provision to ensure that the pre-22 March 2006 rules continue to operate where appropriate.

Section 497: Section 496: supplementary

1529. This section applies relevant material located elsewhere to the definition of "non-charitable expenditure" (eg rules for computing trading losses) and provides interpretative material. It is new. The corresponding rule for income tax is in section 544 of ITA.

1530. *Change 38* in Annex 1 affects this section.

Section 498: Section 496(1)(d): meaning of expenditure

1531. This section provides interpretative material about the meaning of "expenditure". It is new. The corresponding rule for income tax is in section 545 of ITA.

1532. *Change 38* in Annex 1 affects this section.

1533. *Subsection (1)* makes it clear that "expenditure" includes expenditure on the acquisition of capital assets. But expenditure on assets qualifying for capital allowances is taken account of in determining, for example, a trading loss and so is not included in expenditure within section 496(1)(d).

*Section 499: **Section 496(1)(d): accounting period in which certain expenditure treated as incurred***

1534. This section specifies the accounting period to which expenditure relating to commitments (whether or not contractual in nature) that have been entered into is to be allocated for the purpose of operating the restrictions. It is based on section 506(2) of ICTA. The corresponding rule for income tax is in section 546 of ITA.

1535. This rule is rewritten in terms which make explicit reference to UK GAAP. See *Change 39* in Annex 1.

*Section 500: **Section 496(1)(d): payment to body outside the UK***

1536. This section provides interpretative material about payments to a body outside the United Kingdom. It is based on section 506(3) of ICTA. The corresponding rule for income tax is in section 547 of ITA.

1537. The section makes it clear that the onus is on the charitable company to ensure that any payments to a body outside the United Kingdom are applied for charitable purposes. Otherwise the charitable company must classify the payments as "non-charitable expenditure".

*Section 501: **Section 496(1)(g) and (h): investments and loans***

1538. This section provides interpretation about the making of investments or loans. It is based on section 506(5) of ICTA. The corresponding rule for income tax is in section 548 of ITA.

1539. The section makes it clear that it is only the expenditure in the accounting period on making new investments and loans, or expenditure to fund net increases in such investments or loans, that is included in the calculation of non-charitable expenditure.

*Section 502: **Transactions with substantial donors***

1540. This section defines "substantial donor transaction" and explains when a person is a substantial donor to a charitable company. It is based on sections 506A(1) and (2) and 506C(3) of ICTA. The corresponding rule for income tax is in section 549 of ITA.

1541. References to a charitable company include connected charities (see section 509) and references to a substantial donor include persons connected with the donor (see section 510(1)(a)).

*Section 503: **Meaning of "relievable gift"***

1542. This section includes details of the sources of gifts that are "relievable gifts" for the purposes of the preceding section. It is based on section 506C(1) of ICTA. The corresponding rule for income tax is in section 550 of ITA.

*Section 504: **Non-charitable expenditure in substantial donor transactions***

1543. This section specifies that certain amounts relating to substantial donor transactions are to be treated as non-charitable expenditure. It is based on sections 506A(3) to (5) and 506C(2) and (6) of ICTA. The corresponding rule for income tax is in section 551 of ITA.

1544. The source legislation specifies that certain matters are to be determined by the Commissioners for HMRC. References to "the Commissioners for Her Majesty's Revenue and Customs" are replaced with references to "an officer of Revenue and Customs". See *Change 5* in Annex 1, which also affects sections 507 and 510. The source legislation specifies that, on an appeal against an assessment, the tribunal may review a decision of the Commissioners, so section 510 specifies that the tribunal may affirm or replace a decision of an officer.

Section 505: Adjustment if section 504(1) and (2) applied to single transaction

1545. This section makes it clear that if both subsections (1) and (2) of section 504 apply to an amount, the effect is not duplicated to create more "non-charitable expenditure" than the total amount in question. It is based on section 506C(4) of ICTA. The corresponding rule for income tax is in section 552 of ITA.

Section 506: Section 504: certain payments and benefits to be ignored

1546. This section provides that, in determining the amount of non-charitable expenditure, payments or benefits arising from transactions relating to gift aid donations made by individuals or qualifying donations by companies are to be ignored in certain circumstances. It is based on section 506B(7) of ICTA. The corresponding rule for income tax is in section 553 of ITA.

1547. The payments or benefits are ignored if they would not prevent the donation being a "qualifying donation" by virtue of the rules concerning associated benefits provided to donors in section 416(7)(b) of ITA and section 191(7) of this Act.

Section 507: Transactions: exceptions

1548. This section specifies exceptions to the transactions caught by section 502. It is based on section 506B of ICTA. The corresponding rule for income tax is in section 554 of ITA.

1549. In particular, the section carves out of the substantial donor provisions transactions of an ordinary commercial nature between the parties.

1550. References to "the Commissioners for Her Majesty's Revenue and Customs" and "the Commissioners" are replaced with references to "an officer of Revenue and Customs". See *Change 5* in Annex 1.

Section 508: Donors: exceptions

1551. This section specifies exceptions to the donors caught by section 502. It is based on section 506B(8) and (9) of ICTA. The corresponding rule for income tax is in section 555 of ITA.

1552. *Subsection (1)* concerns companies set up by charitable companies, for example to carry on trading activities as a means of generating funds.

1553. *Subsection (2)* concerns registered social landlords and housing associations, which often share services and accommodation with charities as a means of meeting charitable and non-charitable objectives. Section 506B(9) of ICTA is prospectively amended by paragraph 15 of Schedule 9 to the Housing and Regeneration Act 2008 from a day to be appointed by Order (section 325(1) of that Act). This subsection incorporates that amendment with a saving in Schedule 2 to this Act to apply until the amendment made by paragraph 15 has effect.

Section 509: Connected charities

1554. This section extends, for the purposes of sections 502 to 508, the meaning of "charitable company" to include charities connected with the charitable company. It is based on section 506C(5) of ICTA. The corresponding rule for income tax is in section 556 of ITA.

1555. It covers, for example, situations where a charity decides to hold all its properties in one company and organise other charitable activities in another, or where two charities with different objects are managed by the same board of directors.

1556. Note that the term "connected" in this section applies to charities and charitable companies and is different from the use of the term in section 510 where it refers to substantial donors and other persons.

1557. *Subsection (2)* gives the definition of "connected" for subsection (1). The definition of "connected persons" in section 1122 does not apply for this purpose.

Section 510: ***Substantial donor transactions: supplementary***

1558. This section provides interpretation for sections 502 to 508. It is based on section 506C(7) to (9) of ICTA. The corresponding rule for income tax is in section 557 of ITA.

1559. The use of the term "connected" relates to substantial donors and other persons and is different from the use of the term in section 509, where it refers to charities and charitable companies that are connected.

1560. The definition of "connected person" for the purposes of this section is in section 1122 (applied by section 1176).

1561. References to "the Commissioners" are replaced with references to "an officer of Revenue and Customs". See *Change 5* in Annex 1.

Section 511: ***Approved charitable investments***

1562. This section sets out which investments, including loans made by way of investment, count as approved charitable investments for the purposes of the rules restricting exemptions. It is based on Schedule 20 to ICTA. The corresponding rule for income tax is in section 558 of ITA.

1563. The label "approved charitable investment" replaces the label "qualifying investment" in section 506(4) of ICTA.

1564. Paragraph 2 of Schedule 20 to ICTA specifies investments falling within Schedule 1 to the Trustee Investments Act 1961 (TIA 1961) as approved, with a small exception. For trust law purposes TIA 1961 has been largely superseded by the Trustee Act 2000 (TA 2000). So the detail of investments covered by Schedule 1 to TIA 1961 is incorporated into the sections in an updated form, removing the need to refer to a Schedule to an Act (TIA 1961) that trustees no longer need to refer to for investment purposes. See *Change 40* in Annex 1, which also affects section 512 and section 513.

1565. The reference to securities traded on the Unlisted Securities Market has not been reproduced as the Unlisted Securities Market ceased trading in December 1996.

1566. Investments can qualify as approved charitable investments if, despite not falling into any of the specified types not requiring a claim, a claim is made and it is accepted by HMRC. In order to be accepted, the claimant must show that the investment is made for the benefit of the charitable company and is not made for the avoidance of tax.

1567. The source legislation includes a reference in paragraph 7(2) of Schedule 20 to ICTA to an "authorised institution" – which in the context of that paragraph clearly means a "bank". "Authorised institution" was amended to read "bank" in paragraph 7(1) by Schedule 37 to FA 1996, but was not amended in paragraph 7(2) of Schedule 20 to ICTA. This was an oversight and is corrected here.

1568. Type 2 refers to common investment funds established under section 25 of the Charities Act (Northern Ireland) 1964. This section has been prospectively repealed by Schedule 29 of the Charities Act (Northern Ireland) 2008.

1569. The reference to an "Act" in Type 4 is extended to include references to Northern Ireland legislation by section 1119, and to Acts of the Scottish Parliament. See *Change6* in Annex 1.

1570. Paragraph 9(2) of Schedule 20 to ICTA, which explains that a loan in sub-paragraph (1) (rewritten as Type 12 in this section) includes a loan which is secured by a mortgage or charge of any kind over land, has not been rewritten as unnecessary. It adds nothing to the meaning of "loan".

1571. References to "the Board" have been replaced with "an officer of Revenue and Customs". See *Change 5* in Annex 1.

Section 512: Securities which are approved charitable investments

1572. This section sets out details of which investments in securities count as approved charitable investments for the purposes of the rules restricting exemptions. It is based on Schedule 20 to ICTA and Schedule 1 to TIA 1961. The corresponding rule for income tax is in section 559 of ITA.

1573. The details of investments covered by Schedule 1 to TIA 1961 are incorporated into these sections in an updated form. See *Change 40* in Annex 1 and the commentary on section 511.

Section 513: Conditions to be met for some securities

1574. This section sets out details of certain conditions which some of the securities specified in the previous section have to meet to count as approved charitable investments for the purposes of the rules restricting exemptions. It is based on Schedule 1 to TIA 1961. The corresponding rule for income tax is in section 560 of ITA.

1575. The detail of the investments covered by Schedule 1 to TIA 1961 is incorporated into these sections in an updated form. See *Change 40* in Annex 1 and the commentary on section 511.

1576. *Subsection (8)* specifies (among other things) that a company acquiring control of another company or other companies is treated as having paid a dividend or dividends paid by the other company or companies. See *Change 40* in Annex 1.

Section 514: Approved charitable loans

1577. This section sets out which loans (not being made by way of investment) count as approved charitable loans for the purposes of the rules restricting exemptions. It is based on Schedule 20 to ICTA. The corresponding rule for income tax is in section 561 of ITA.

1578. The label "approved charitable loan" replaces the label "qualifying loan" in section 506(4) of ICTA.

1579. References to "the Board" are replaced with references to "an officer of Revenue and Customs". See *Change 5* in Annex 1.

Section 515: Excess expenditure treated as non-charitable expenditure of earlier periods

1580. This section treats "excess expenditure" in an accounting period as non-charitable expenditure for earlier accounting periods. It is based on section 505(3) and (5) of ICTA. The corresponding rule for income tax is in section 562 of ITA.

1581. The "excess expenditure" is the amount of the non-charitable expenditure of the year in excess of the available income and gains of the accounting period.

1582. The term "available income and gains" is defined in *subsection (4)*. This label replaces "total income and gains" as defined in section 505(3) of ICTA.

Section 516: Rules for attributing excess expenditure to earlier periods

1583. This section specifies the earlier accounting periods to which the excess expenditure is to be attributed, later periods taking priority over earlier ones. It is based on section 505(5) and (6) of ICTA. The corresponding rule for income tax is in section 563 of ITA.

1584. The amount of excess expenditure that can be attributed to an accounting period commencing before 22 March 2006 or earlier periods cannot exceed the amount that would have been attributed if the change in the method of calculating excess expenditure resulting from section 55 of FA 2006 had not been introduced. See the transitional provision in Part 12 of Schedule 2.

Section 517: Adjustments in consequence of section 515

1585. This section specifies that any necessary adjustments (eg to tax, interest etc) for earlier years may be made. It is based on section 505(5) of ICTA. The corresponding rule for income tax is in section 564 of ITA.

Part 12: Real Estate Investment Trusts

Overview

1586. This Part sets out the rules applicable to UK REITs.

1587. A UK REIT is:

- a group of companies (a "group UK REIT") the principal company of which gives a notice under section 523; or
- a single company (a "company UK REIT") which gives a notice under section 524.

1588. In either case, the company must not have ceased to be a UK REIT in accordance with section 571, 572 or 578.

1589. Provided that a UK REIT meets certain conditions (see Chapter 2 of this Part and sections 538 (entry charge), and 548 (distributions)), there is no charge to corporation tax (or income tax in the case of certain non-UK companies) on profits or gains of "property rental business" (or "UK property rental business" in the case of non-UK companies). "Property rental business" is defined in section 519(1), "UK property rental business" is defined in section 520 and "non-UK company" is defined in section 521(2).

1590. Distributions made by the principal company of a group UK REIT or company UK REIT of profits and gains of property rental business are subject to deduction of tax at source under regulations made under section 973 of ITA (SI 2009/2036). In the hands of a shareholder, the distribution is treated as if it is UK property business income and is taxed accordingly with a credit for tax which has already been deducted at source.

1591. This Act enacts certain regulations which modify the primary legislation through layers of cross-references. In particular the Act enacts the regulations dealing with joint venture companies (SI 2006/2866)and breach of conditions (SI 2006/2864 and SI 2007/3540), except for regulation 11 of SI 2006/2864.

1592. The Act also enacts the regulations on joint venture groups (SI 2007/3425).

Chapter 1: Introduction

Section 518: Introduction to Part

1593. This section is an overview of the Part. It is based on section 103 of FA 2006.

1594. *Subsection (1)* sets out the "bargain" which is entered into by a group of companies on becoming a UK REIT. If the group meets certain conditions it benefits from an exemption from corporation tax (and, through the operation of section 520(3), an exemption from income tax for non-UK companies) for profits and gains of property rental business. This benefit comes with the following liabilities:

- an entry charge (section 538),
- a requirement that the principal company of a group deducts sums representing income tax in respect of distributions made to shareholders (section 973 of ITA and SI 2009/2036), and
- the treatment of such distributions as profits of a UK property business rather than dividend incomein the hands of shareholders (section 548).

1595. *Subsection (2)* makes similar provision for companies which enter the UK REIT regime other than as part of a group.

1596. *Subsection (3)* contains signposts to the remaining Chapters of the Part.

1597. *Subsection (4)* defines "UK REIT".

Section 519: *"Property rental business"*

1598. This section defines "property rental business" for the purposes of the Part. It is based on section 104 of, and paragraph 32(2) of Schedule 17 to, FA 2006.

1599. *Subsection (1)* defines "property rental business".

1600. *Subsection (4)* provides that, for non-UK companies, business is "property rental business" if it would be property rental business if carried on by a UK company. See section 521 for the definitions of UK company and non-UK company. This provision ensures that the worldwide property rental business of a non-UK company is treated as property rental business for the purposes of the Part.

1601. The definition of "tax-exempt business" in section 107(2) of FA 2006 is not rewritten. Instead reference is made to "property rental business" throughout the Act. This is because "tax-exempt business" suggests that the company must carry on such a business to be within the regime. But sections 563 and 564 allow a company to breach the conditions in section 529 or 530 and remain within the regime.

Section 520: *"UK property rental business" of non-UK companies*

1602. This section defines "UK property rental business" of non-UK companies and treats profits of such business, which would ordinarily be charged to income tax, as chargeable to corporation tax. It is based on paragraph 32(1), (3) and (5) of Schedule 17 to FA 2006.

1603. *Subsection s (2)* and *(3)* provide that profits of UK property rental business of non-UK companies (including non-UK joint venture companies) which are subject to income tax under Chapter 3 of Part 3 of ITTOIA are to be treated as being subject to corporation tax (and not income tax).

1604. Subsections (2) and (3)(a) are needed to bring UK property rental business of non-UK companies within the charge to corporation tax so that provisions such as sections 534 (tax treatment of profits) and 541 (ring-fencing) apply to all non-UK companies.

1605. Paragraph 32(3) of Schedule 17 to FA 2006 does not specify whether it is profits and/ or gains of UK property rental business which are made subject to corporation tax. The Act provides that only *profits* of UK property rental business, which are not already subject to corporation tax, are caught by this section. This approach ensures that gains of non-UK companies with no permanent establishment in the United Kingdom are not brought within the charge to tax in the United Kingdom. See*Change 41* in Annex 1.

1606. In the case of a non-UK company carrying on a UK property rental business, subsections (2) and (3)(b) (based on paragraph 32(5) of Schedule 17 to FA 2006) remove the charge to income tax and replace it with a charge to corporation tax for the purposes of this Part. If the rules in this Part apply, that charge to corporation tax is removed. To the extent that the rules in this Part do not apply, any charge to income tax is undisturbed.

Section 521: "UK company" and "non-UK company"

1607. This section defines "UK company" and "non-UK company" for the purposes of the Part. It is based on section 106(3) of, and paragraph 3(1) of Schedule 17 to, FA 2006.

1608. *Subsection (1)* defines "UK company" for the purposes of the Part as a company which is UK resident and is not resident in any other place for the purpose of taxation. AUK company is not the same as a "UK resident" company (which is defined in section 1119).

Section 522: "Residual business"

1609. This section defines "residual business" for the purposes of the Part. It is based on section 105(3)(c) of, and paragraph 2(c) of Schedule 17 to, FA 2006.

1610. The reason for the definition of residual business is two-fold. First, it is needed to identify the profits and gains which are charged to corporation tax at the main rate under sections 534(3) and 535(6). Second, it is needed to identify items to be included in the financial statements in accordance with section 532(2)(c).

1611. For non-UK companies the definition of residual business is aligned with the definition used for other members of a group. It is based on paragraph 2(c) of Schedule 17 to FA 2006 which provides that residual business is all business other than property rental business.

Chapter 2: Requirements for being a UK REIT

Section 523: Notice for a group of companies to become a UK REIT

1612. This section provides that, in order to be a "group UK REIT", the principal company of the group must give notice of entering the UK REIT regime. It is based on sections 106, 109 and 134 of, and paragraphs 5(1) and 8(1) of Schedule 17 to, FA 2006.

1613. *Subsections (1)* and *(2)* provide that a group of companies may give notice for the UK REIT regime to apply from a specified date. If a group notice is given, all 75% subsidiaries of the group (as defined in section 606) are included in the UK REIT regime. A new accounting period of each company in the group starts on the specified date (see section 536(5)). That new accounting period is called "accounting period 1" – see section 609.

1614. *Subsection (3)* provides that the principal company of a group may give notice only if it is a "UK company" as defined in section 521 and it is not an OEIC.

1615. It is unclear from the source legislation (in particular sections 106(2), 107(1) and 108(1) of FA 2006) whether a group becomes a UK REIT from the date specified in a section 109 of FA 2006 notice or when the various conditions set out in sections 106(2), 107(1) and 108(1) of FA 2006 are satisfied. *Subsection (4)* addresses this by making it clear that a group becomes a UK REIT from the date specified in the notice given under this section.

1616. *Subsection (5)* defines"group UK REIT" as being a group which has given notice under this section.

1617. Section 103(3) of FA 2006, which provides that "a company or group to which this Part applies may be referred to as a Real Estate Investment Trust", is not rewritten as this expression is not used elsewhere in the legislation.

1618. *Subsection (6)* makes clear that merely giving a notice is not enough: the group must also meet the conditions in section 527.

Section 524: Notice for a company to become a UK REIT

1619. This section provides that, in order to be a "company UK REIT", the company must give notice of entering the UK REIT regime. It is based on sections 106 and 109 of FA 2006.

1620. *Subsections (1)* and *(2)* provide that a company may give notice for the UK REIT regime to apply from a specified date. A new accounting period of the company starts on the specified date (see section 536(5)). That new accounting period is called "accounting period 1" – see section 609.

1621. It is possible for a company with a 75% subsidiary to give notice under subsection (3) on its own, in which case none of its 75% subsidiaries is included in the UK REIT regime.

1622. If a company UK REIT gives notice under this section and subsequently wants an existing 75% subsidiary to be brought within the regime, a group notice under section 523 needs to be given. The new notice must comply with all the requirements of section 525.

1623. If a company UK REIT gives notice under section 586(2) for a joint venture company to be treated as forming a group UK REIT with the company UK REIT, the notice does not cause any 75% subsidiaries of the company UK REIT to be brought within the regime.

1624. *Subsection (3)* provides that a company may give notice only if it is a "UK company" as defined in section 521 and it is not an OEIC.

1625. It is unclear from the source legislation (in particular sections 106(2), 107(1) and 108(1) of FA 2006) whether a company becomes a UK REIT from the date specified in a section 109 of FA 2006 notice or when the various conditions set out in sections 106(2), 107(1) and 108(1) of FA 2006 are satisfied. *Subsection (4)* addresses this by making it clear that a group becomes a UK REIT from the date specified in the notice given under this section.

1626. *Subsection (5)* defines"company UK REIT" as being a company which has given notice under this section.

1627. Section 103(3) of FA 2006, which provides that "a company or group to which this Part applies may be referred to as a Real Estate Investment Trust", is not rewritten as this expression is not used elsewhere in the legislation.

1628. *Subsection (6)* makes clear that merely giving a notice is not enough: the company must also meet the conditions in section 527.

Section 525: Notice under section 523 or 524: supplementary

1629. This section makes supplemental provision about a notice given under section 523 or 524. It is based on sections 109(2) to (5) and 134(1) of, and paragraph 8(2) of Schedule 17 to, FA 2006.

1630. *Subsection (1)* lists what the principal company of a group or a single company must provide in order to give a valid notice under section 523 or 524.

1631. Subsection (1)(a) requires the notice to be given in writing to "an officer of Revenue and Customs" rather than to "the Commissionersfor Her Majesty's Revenue and Customs". See *Change 5* in Annex 1.

Section 526: ***Duration of status as UK REIT***

1632. This section provides that once a group or single company becomes a UK REIT, it continues to be a UK REIT until the regime ceases in accordance with section 571, 572 or 578. It is based on sections 110 and 134(1) of, and paragraph 4 of Schedule 17 to, FA 2006.

Section 527: ***Being a UK REIT in relation to an accounting period***

1633. This section makes it clear that once a notice under section 523 or 524 has been given, the principal company of a group, or the company, must meet the conditions set out in the remainder of this Chapter in relation to all accounting periods. It is based on sections 106 to 108 and 134 of, and Schedule 17 to, FA 2006.

1634. *Subsection (2)(e)* provides that the principal company must prepare and submit financial statements to "an officer of Revenue and Customs" rather than to "the Commissionersfor Her Majesty's Revenue and Customs". See *Change 5* in Annex 1.

Section 528: ***Conditions for company***

1635. This section sets out the conditions which the principal company of a group or, in the non-group case, the company, must meet throughout each accounting period. It is based on section 106(3) to (9) of, and paragraph 3(1) of Schedule 17 to, FA 2006.

Section 529: ***Conditions as to property rental business***

1636. This section sets out the conditions which need to be satisfied by a group or company in respect of its property rental business. It is based on sections 107(1), (3), (4) and (6), of, and paragraph 6(1) of Schedule 17 to, FA 2006.

1637. *Subsections (1)* and *(2)* provide that the "property rental business" (defined in section 519) must comprise at least three properties with no single property accounting for more than 40% of the total value of the properties involved in the business.

1638. *Subsection (3)* provides that, for the purposes of this section, the property rental business of a group is treated as single business.

1639. For the purposes of the conditions in subsections (1) and (2), all worldwide properties of non-UK companies are taken into account. This is because paragraph 6(1) of Schedule 17 to FA 2006 provides that "for the purposes of section 107(1) the property rental businesses of the members of the group shall be treated as a single business".

1640. Paragraph 32(2) of Schedule 17 to FA 2006 provides that "business carried on by a non-UK resident company is property rental business for the purposes of this Part if the business would be property rental business within the meaning given by section 104 [of FA 2006] if it were carried on by a UK resident company". So the property rental business includes the worldwide property rental business of non-UK companies. By including the worldwide property rental business of non-UK companies, condition A in section 529 is easier to satisfy. But condition B in section 529 may, depending on the circumstances, be more difficult to satisfy, for example where a non-UK company has an overseas property worth more than 40% of the total value of the properties involved in the property rental business.

1641. *Subsection (5)* excludes a percentage of the property rental business carried on by a subsidiary which is not wholly owned by the group UK REIT. The percentage is the percentage of the business excluded from the financial statements in accordance with section 533. See *Change 42* in Annex 1.

Section 530: Condition as to distribution of profits

1642. This section sets out the distribution condition which needs to be satisfied by the principal company of a group or, in the non-group case, by a company. It is based on section 107(8) and (9) of, and paragraphs 6(4) and (5) and 32(8) of Schedule 17 to, FA 2006.

1643. *Subsection (1)* provides that, in relation to an accounting period of the principal company, the principal company must distribute at least 90% of the group's "UK profits".

1644. *Subsection (2)* defines "UK profits" as the sum of the profits shown in the financial statements under section 532(2)(b). Section 532(3) provides that this is the sum of the profits arising from the property rental business of the UK members of the group together with the profits arising from UK property rental business carried on by non-UK companies. Section 533(3) confirms that if a non-member of the group holds a percentage of the beneficial interest in a member of a group, that percentage is excluded from the financial statements and so also from the calculation of profits which this section requires to be distributed.

1645. *Subsection (4)* provides that, in relation to an accounting period of a company, the company must distribute at least 90% of profits of the company's property rental business.

1646. The distribution requirement in this section also applies to the relevant proportion of profits generated by joint venture companies (regulations 6(1) and 10(3) of SI 2006/2866). See section 588(1)which treats a joint venture company as a member of the group UK REIT and section 588(2) which treats a company UK REIT and a joint venture company as forming a group UK REIT.

1647. The requirement to distribute at least 90% of the group's "UK profits", or "profits" in the case of a company UK REIT, does not extend to chargeable gains. This contrasts with section 121 of FA 2006, rewritten in section 548 (distribution treated as UK property business income in hands of shareholder) and section 973 of ITA (deduction of sums representing income tax at source) which apply to profits *and gains* of property rental business (or UK property rental business in the case of non-UK companies).

Section 531: Conditions as to balance of business

1648. This section sets out the balance of business conditions which need to be satisfied by a group or company. It is based on sections 108(2) and (3) and 134(1) of, and paragraphs 4 and 7 of Schedule 17 to, FA 2006.

1649. *Subsection (1)* provides that at least 75% of the "aggregate profits" of the group or company must relate to property rental business. "Aggregate profits" is defined in *subsection (2)* for groups and *subsection (3)* for companies.

1650. It is not clear from the source legislation whether the balance of business tests should include the worldwide profits and assets of non-UK companies. This section includes the worldwide profits and assets of non-UK companies for the purposes of the balance of business tests.

1651. The balance of business test in this section includes the relevant proportion of property rental business of a joint venture company. See section 588(1)which treats a joint venture company as a member of a group UK REIT and section 588(2) which treats a company UK REIT and a joint venture company as forming a group UK REIT.

Section 532:Financial statements for group UK REITs

1652. This section sets out the requirements which need to be satisfied for the purposes of section 527(2)(e). It is based on paragraphs 3(3), 31(2) and 32(8) of Schedule 17 to FA 2006.

1653. According to paragraph 32(2) of Schedule 17 to FA 2006:

"business carried on by a non-UK resident company is property rental business for the purposes of the Part if the business would be property rental business ... if it were carried on by a UK resident company

1654. It follows that a financial statement required byparagraph 31(2)(a) of Schedule 17 to FA 2006 includes theworldwide property rental business of a non-resident company. This is consistent with the rule about the *profits and gains* of a UK property rental business in paragraph 32(8)(d) of Schedule 17 to FA 2006.

1655. So *subsection (2)(a)* provides that the financial statements should include the worldwide property rental business of the group.

1656. *Subsection (2)(b)* provides that the principal company must prepare financial statements for the group's property rental business in the United Kingdom. *Subsection (3)* defines the group's property rental business in the United Kingdom as property rental business carried on by UK companies and UK property rental business of non-UK companies.

1657. *Subsection (2)(c)* provides that the principal company must prepare financial statements for the group's residual business. Financial statements under subsection(2)(c) relate to all business which is not property rental business. For non-UK companies "residual business" includes*worldwide*business which is not property rental business.

1658. The requirement to prepare financial statements under subsection (2)(a) and (b) also applies to venturing companies and venturing groups (defined in section 585) and the relevant percentage of profits of property rental business of the joint venture company. See section 588(1)which treats a joint venture company as a member of the group UK REIT and section 588(2) which treats a company UK REIT and a joint venture company as forming a group UK REIT.

1659. Financial statements under this section exclude any "non-member percentage" (that is, any percentage of the beneficial interest in a member of the group held by a non-member) – see section 533(3).

Section 533: Financial statements: supplementary

1660. This section sets out further requirements about the preparation of financial statements under section 532 and also contains a regulation-making power. It is based on paragraphs 31(3) to (7) and 32(8) of Schedule 17 to FA 2006.

1661. In *subsection (4)* the expression "equity holder" is not governed by the special definition in section 598.

1662. *Subsection (5)(c)* provides that the Commissioners may make regulations specifying the deadline for submitting a financial statement to an officer of Revenue and Customs. The section refers to an "an officer of Revenue and Customs" in subsection (5)(c) rather than to "the Commissioners". See *Change 5* in Annex 1.

Chapter 3: Tax treatment of profits and gains of UK REITs

Section 534: Profits

1663. This section sets out the tax treatment of profits of property rental business and residual business. It is based on sections 119 and 134(1) of, and paragraphs 17 and 32(4) of Schedule 17 to, FA 2006.

1664. *Subsection (1)* provides that profits of property rental business of a UK company (including a UK joint venture company) which is, or is a member of, a UK REIT are not charged to corporation tax.

1665. *Subsection (2)* provides that profits of UK property rental business of a non-UK member of a group UK REIT (including a non-UK joint venture company) are not charged to corporation tax.

1666. *Subsection (3)* provides that profits of residual business of a UK company which are charged to corporation tax are charged at a rate determined without reference to the small profits reliefs in sections 18 to 23 of this Act: those profits are charged at the main corporation tax rate.

1667. Subsection (3)(b) makes clear that subsection (3) is not a charging provision. The rule in this subsection applies only if the profits are already charged to corporation tax by another rule.

1668. Subsection (3) does not apply to non-UK companies (including non-UK joint venture companies). This is because the whole of section 119 of FA 2006 is disapplied by paragraph 17 of Schedule 17 to FA 2006 but only section 119(1) is reinstated by paragraph 32(4) of the Schedule.

1669. For non-UK companies subject to income tax, the normal tax rule is that they are charged to income tax at the basic rate under Chapter 2 of Part 2 of ITA on profits of residual business.

1670. *Subsection (4)* expands what is treated as profits of residual business for the purposes of corporation tax (and so charged to corporation tax at the main rate) to include the non-member percentage of profits which are excluded from the financial statements under section 533(3).

1671. Subsection (4) also applies to joint venture companies (including non-UK joint venture companies). So a percentage of profits of property rental business attributable to a non-member of a joint venture company is subject to tax at the main rate of corporation tax.

Section 535: ***Gains***

1672. This section sets out how gains of property rental business and residual business are taxed. It is based on section 124, 127 and 134(1) of, and paragraphs 21 and 32(6) of Schedule 17 to, FA 2006.

1673. *Subsections (1)* to*(3)*and *(8)* provide that gains made by a company (including a joint venture company) which is, or is a member of, a UK REIT from property rental business are not chargeable gains.

1674. *Subsections (4), (5)* and (8) provide that if an asset is used partly for the purposes of property rental business (or UK property rental business in the case of a non-UK company), the gain attributable to the property rental business/UK property rental business is not a chargeable gain. These subsections also apply to joint venture companies.

1675. *Subsection (6)* provides that gains of residual business which are subject to corporation tax are charged at the main corporation tax rate.

1676. Subsection (6)(b) makes clear that subsection (6) is not a charging provision. The rule in this subsection applies only if the profits are already charged to corporation tax by another rule. See *Change 41* in Annex 1.

1677. Subsection (6) also applies to joint venture companies (including non-UK joint venture companies). So a percentage of gains arising from property rental business attributable to a non-member of a joint venture company is subject to tax at the main rate of corporation tax.

1678. *Subsection (7)* expands what is treated as gains of residual business (and so potentially subject to corporation tax at the main rate) to include the non-member percentage of gains which are excluded from the financial statements under section 533(3). Subsection (7) applies also to non-UK companies and non-UK joint venture companies.

Chapter 4: *Entering the UK REIT regime*

Section 536: *Effects of entry: corporation tax*

1679. This section provides that, for corporation tax purposes, when a company (including a joint venture company) enters the UK REIT regime its property rental business ceases and recommences and it is deemed to sell and reacquire the assets involved in that business. This section is based on sections 111 and 134 of, and paragraphs 9, 10 and 33 of Schedule 17 to, FA 2006.

1680. *Subsection (1)* provides that property rental business (or UK property rental business of non-UK companies) carried on before entry to the UK REIT regime is treated as ceasing at entry for the purposes of corporation tax. As section 520(3) provides that profits of UK property rental business of non-UK companies are treated as liable to corporation tax, this section applies to all companies whether or not UK resident. See *Change 41* in Annex 1.

1681. *Subsections (2)* to *(4)*provide that, for the purposes of corporation tax, assets involved in property rental business (or UK property rental business of non-UK companies) immediately before entry to the UK REIT regime are treated as being sold and reacquired at market value on entry. Any resulting gain is not chargeable to corporation tax. The only non-UK companies affected by this rule are those that are resident both in the United Kingdom and in another territory. See *Change 41* in Annex 1.

1682. The final words of subsection (2)(b) ensure that the reacquired assets are held by the company within the UK REIT regime.

1683. *Subsection (5)* provides that, for corporation tax purposes, an accounting period ends and begins again on entry to the regime. The subsection also applies to non-UK companies. See *Change 41* in Annex 1.

1684. *Subsection (6)(a)* provides that if a percentage of the assets of a member of a group UK REIT is excluded from the financial statements because that percentage is attributable to a non-member, the percentage is ignored for the purposes of subsection (2).

Section 537: *Effects of entry: CAA 2001*

1685. This section is supplementary to section 536 and modifies how CAA operates when a company (including a joint venture company) enters the UK REIT regime. It is based on sections 111(4) and 134(1) of, and paragraph 9 of Schedule 17 to, FA 2006.

Section 538: *Entry charge*

1686. This section provides for an amount of notional income (calculated in accordance with section 539) to be chargeable to tax on a company on entry to the UK REIT regime. It is based on sections 112(1), (2) and (4) and 134(1) of, and paragraphs 11 and 33 of Schedule 17 to, FA 2006.

1687. *Subsection (2)* provides that the notional amount is treated as arising in the company's residual business. This ensures that the amount is not treated as arising in the company's property rental business and so not chargeable to tax.

1688. It is not clear from section 112(2) of FA 2006 what rate of tax applies to UK joint venture companies. And SI 2006/2866 does not specify the rate of tax applicable for the purposes of section 112 of FA 2006. Subsection (3) of this section and section 539(5)

(a) make it clear that UK joint venture companies are treated in the same way as other UK companies and consequently the rate of tax used is the rate used in section 534(3).

1689. From a practical point of view, this has no effect as the entry charge remains 2% of the market value of assets involved in UK property rental business.

1690. *Subsection (4)* provides that non-UK companies (including non-UK joint venture companies), are chargeable to income tax on the notional amount at the basic rate under section 11 of ITA.

Section 539: Calculation of the notional amount

1691. This section sets out how to calculate the amount of notional income for the purposes of section 538. It is based on sections 112(3) and 134(1) of, and paragraphs 9(4), 10(2) and 11(1) of Schedule 17 to, FA 2006.

1692. *Subsection (3)* defines "MV" as the total market value of assets which are involved in property rental business of the company (or UK property rental business in the case of non-UK companies) immediately before entry to the UK REIT regime.

1693. *Subsection (4)* provides that if a percentage of the assets is excluded from the financial statements because it is attributable to a non-member, that percentage is ignored for the purposes of "MV".

1694. *Subsection (5)(a)* defines "TR" for UK companies as the rate mentioned in section 534(3) (the main rate of corporation tax).

1695. *Subsection (5)(b)* defines "TR" for non-UK companies (including non-UK joint venture companies) as the basic rate of income tax.

Section 540: Election to treat notional income as arising in instalments

1696. This section provides that a company (including a joint venture company) may elect to pay the entry charge in instalments. It is based on sections 112(5) to (7) and 134(1) of, and paragraph 11(1) of Schedule 17 to, FA 2006.

1697. S*ubsection (3)*refers to an "officer of Revenue and Customs" rather than to "the Commissioners for Her Majesty's Revenue and Customs". See *Change 5* in Annex 1.

Chapter 5: Assets etc

Section 541: Ring-fencing of property rental business

1698. This section provides that, for corporation tax purposes, property rental business (or UK property rental business in the case of non-UK companies) is treated as a separate business from any other business carried on by a group UK REIT or by a company UK REIT. Also, to the extent that the UK REIT carries on such a business, it is treated as a separate group or company from the rest of the group or company. This section is based on sections 113(1) to(4) and 134(1) of, and paragraphs 12 and 32(3) of Schedule 17 to, FA 2006.

1699. *Subsections (1)*and *(8)* provide that this section applies to a group UK REIT, each member of the group (including a non-UK company) and a company UK REIT. See *Change 41* in Annex 1.

1700. This section ring-fences the property rental business, rather than the "tax-exempt business". This avoids the problem of how the section applies in a case where the company or group breaches the property rental business conditions in section 529. Such a breach apparently leads to the company or group no longer having "tax-exempt business" for the purpose of section 113 of FA 2006.

1701. This section applies to joint venture companies (including non-UK joint venture companies which are subject to corporation tax).

1702. *Subsection (7)* provides that if a percentage of the profits of property rental business are excluded from the financial statements because they are attributable to a non-member, that percentage is treated as profits of residual business.

Section 542: Disapplication of certain provisions

1703. This section applies to UK companies and allows losses from overseas property rental business to be used against other property rental business income and disapplies the exemption from the transfer pricing rules for small and medium sized enterprises. It is based on sections 113(5) and (6) and 134(1) of, and paragraph 12(2) of Schedule 17 to, FA 2006.

1704. *Subsection (1)* provides that section 66 of this Act (ring-fencing of losses from overseas property business) does not apply to property rental business of a UK company (including a UK joint venture company). The rule applies only to UK companies because non-UK resident companies are not subject to United Kingdom tax on the profits of an overseas property business.

1705. *Subsection (2)* provides that sections 166 to 171 of TIOPA (transfer pricing: exemption for small and medium sized enterprises) do not apply to a UK company. This means that all UK companiesregardless of size, which are subject to this Part, are subject to the transfer pricing rules.

Section 543: Profit: financing-cost ratio

1706. This section provides that if the result of the sum specified in subsection (2) is less than 1.25, "the excess" calculated in accordance with subsection (3) is charged to corporation tax. It is based on sections 115(1) to (3) and 134(1) of, and paragraph 4 of Schedule 17 to, FA 2006.

1707. This section enacts regulations 12 and 13 of SI 2006/2864. See *Change 43* in Annex 1.

1708. *Subsection (2)*sets out the formula to calculate the ratio used to arrive at the "excess" in subsection (3). The definitions of "PP" and "PFC" refer to "property profits" and "property financing costs" and are defined further in section 544.

1709. This section applies to the relevant proportion of a joint venture company's property profits and property financing costs in the same way as for any other member of a group UK REIT. See *Change 43*in Annex 1.

1710. *Subsection (3)*provides that the difference between the actual property financing costs of the UK REIT and the amount that would cause the sum specified in subsection (2) to be 1.25 ("the excess"), is charged to corporation tax. *Subsections (4)* and *(5)* provide that the excess amount is treated as if it were profits of residual business of the principal company of a group UK REIT or a company UK REIT. This means that the rate of tax is the main rate of corporation tax as mentioned in section 534(3).

Section 544: Meaning of "property profits" and "property financing costs"

1711. This section defines "property profits" and "property financing costs" for the purposes of section 543. It is based on sections 115(2) and (4), 120(1) and 134(1) of, and paragraphs 3 and 14 of Schedule 17 to, FA 2006.

1712. *Subsections (1)* and *(3)* define "property profits" and "property financing costs" respectively for the purposes of section 543.

Section 545: Cancellation of tax advantage

1713. This section provides that an officer of Revenue and Customs may counteract a tax advantage obtained by a company which is, or is a member of, a UK REIT (including a joint venture company) if the officer thinks that the company has tried to obtain a tax advantage. It is based on sections 117(1) to (5) and 134(1) of, and paragraph 15(1) of Schedule 17 to, FA 2006.

1714. S*ubsections (1), (4)* and *(6)*refer to "an officer of Revenue and Customs" rather than to "the Commissioners for Her Majesty's Revenue and Customs". See *Change 5* in Annex 1.

1715. *Subsection (3)* sets out how a tax advantage may be counteracted. Subsection (3)(a) provides that an assessment may be made on the company. For non-UK companies, such an assessment may be to income tax or corporation tax.

1716. *Subsection (4)* provides that an officer of Revenue and Customs may assess (in addition to the assessment mentioned in subsection (3)(a)) a UK REIT to an amount of tax to cancel out the tax advantage.

Section 546: Appeal against notice under section 545

1717. This section provides that acompany which is, or is a member of, a UK REIT (including a joint venture company) may appeal against a notice given under section 545. It is based on section 117(6) to (8) and 134(1) of, and paragraph 15(2) of Schedule 17 to, FA 2006.

1718. S*ubsection (2)*refers to "an officer of Revenue and Customs" rather than to "the Commissioners for Her Majesty's Revenue and Customs". See *Change 5* in Annex 1.

Section 547: Funds awaiting reinvestment

1719. This section determines how cash proceeds from the sale of assets used for property rental business are treated. It is based on sections 118 and 134(1) of, and paragraph 16 of Schedule 17 to, FA 2006.

1720. *Subsection (1)* provides that the section applies if a company which is, or is a member of, a UK REIT disposes of an asset used wholly and exclusively for the purposes of property rental business and holds the proceeds in cash.

1721. Section 118 of FA 2006 applies to a company that disposes of an asset and holds cash. Section 134 of FA 2006 applies the rule to a group as it applies to a company. A group cannot dispose of an asset but it may hold cash. There is no justification in section 134 of FA 2006 for saying that the cash has to be held in a particular place in the group.

1722. So this section refers to a member of a group disposing of an asset but makes clear that the proceeds may be held within the group by a company different from that which disposed of the asset.

1723. *Subsection (5)* deals with assets that have had mixed use. The "wholly and exclusively" rule in subsection (1)(a) is relaxed for periods of mixed use that are of at least one year. The section applies the one year test to the aggregate of the periods of mixed use.

1724. This section also applies to:

- the worldwide property rental business of non-UK companies; and
- joint venture companies (including non-UK joint venture companies).

Chapter 6: ***Distributions***

Section 548: ***Distributions: liability to tax***

1725. This section provides that distributions of profits and gains of property rental business in the United Kingdom are treated as income of a UK property business rather than as dividend income in the hands of the shareholder. It is based on sections 121(1), (2) and (8) and 134(1) of, and paragraphs 18(1) and (3) and 32(8) of Schedule 17 to, FA 2006.

1726. *Subsections (1)* and *(3)* provide that the section applies to a distribution of "profits or gains (or both)". This is reflects the inclusion of gains by section 121(8)(b) of FA 2006. The inclusion of gains here contrasts with the rule in section 530 (the distribution of profits test), where the test is concerned only with the (income) profits of property rental business.

1727. *Subsection (5)* provides that if the shareholder is within the charge to corporation tax, the distribution is treated as profits of a UK property business. So the income falls within Part 4 of CTA 2009. Section 931W(2) of CTA 2009 ensures the distribution is not charged to tax under Part 9A of CTA 2009.

1728. *Subsection (6)* (which is based on section 121(1)(b) of FA 2006) provides that if the shareholder is within the charge to income tax, the distribution is treated as profits of a UK property business. So the income falls within Part 3 of ITTOIA. Section 366(2) of ITTOIA ensures that the distribution is not treated as savings and investment income (including dividends).

1729. Section 121(2)(a) of FA 2006 is not rewritten because it deals with a case (non-UK resident company within the charge to corporation tax) that is already covered by section 121(1)(a) (shareholder within the charge to corporation tax).

1730. Section 121(2)(b) of FA 2006 is not rewritten because it deals with a case (non-UK resident not within the charge to corporation tax) that is already covered by section 121(1)(b) (shareholder within the charge to income tax).

1731. *Subsection (7)* provides that in the case of a non-UK resident shareholder, a distribution is not subject to a duty to deduct at source in accordance with regulations made under section 971 of ITA. Schedule 1 to this Act amends section 972(6) of ITA so that it refers to this subsection.

Section 549: ***Distributions: supplementary***

1732. This section makes further provision about section 548. It is based on sections 121(3) to (7) and 134(1) of, and paragraphs 18(1) and (2) and 32(8) of Schedule 17 to, FA 2006.

1733. *Subsection (1)* provides that section 548 does not apply to certain types of shareholders.

1734. *Subsection (2)* (together with *subsection (3)*) provides that neither section 397 of ITTIOA nor section 1109 of this Act (tax credits in respect of (exempt) qualifying distributions) do not apply to distributions made by the principal company of a group UK REIT or by a company UK REIT of profits or gains (or both) of property rental business.

1735. Section 121(8)(b) of FA 2006 applies only to section 121(1) of FA 2006. So it is arguable that it does not apply to the rule in section 121(5). But subsection (4) of this section applies to the same distributions (including distributions of gains) as are dealt with by section 548.

1736. *Subsection (4)* provides that relevant distributions (as defined in subsection (3)) are treated as profits of a single business separate from the businesses mentioned in *subsection (5)*.

Section 550: Attribution of distributions

1737. This section sets out how distributions are attributed between the property rental business of a UK REIT and any other business. It is based on sections 123 and 134(1) of, and paragraph 20 of Schedule 17 to, FA 2006.

Section 551: Tax consequences of distribution to holder of excessive rights

1738. This section sets out the tax consequences of a distribution made to a "holder of excessive rights" (defined in section 553) if the distributing company has not taken steps to prevent it. It is based on section 114 of, and paragraph 13 of Schedule 17 to, FA 2006.

1739. This section enacts regulation 10 of SI 2006/2864. See *Change 43* in Annex 1.

1740. *Subsections (1)*to *(3)* provide that when a distribution is made to a holder of excessive rights and the distributing company has not taken reasonable steps to prevent its being made, the distributing company is treated as receiving an amount of income calculated in accordance with section 552.

1741. *Subsections (4)*to *(6)* provide that the amount is charged to corporation tax as if it were profits of residual business of the distributing company. This means that the rate of tax is the main rate of corporation tax as mentioned in section 534(3).

Section 552: "The section 552 amount"

1742. This section sets out how the "section 552 amount" is calculated for the purposes of section 551. It is based on section 114(2) of, and paragraphs 2 and 13 of Schedule 17 to, FA 2006.

1743. This section enacts regulation 10 of SI 2006/2864. See *Change 43* in Annex 1.

1744. S*ubsections (2)*and *(3)* define "DO" (distribution in respect of ordinary shares) and "DP" (distribution in respect of preference shares) for a group UK REIT by reference to the group's "UK profits" (as defined in section 530(2)). For a company UK REIT,"DO" and "DP" are defined by reference to the "profits of property rental business of the company".

Section 553: Meaning of "holder of excessive rights"

1745. This section defines "holder of excessive rights". It is based on section 114(1) and 134(1) of, and paragraph 13 of Schedule 17 to, FA 2006.

1746. This section enacts regulation 1(2) of SI 2006/2864. See *Change 43* in Annex 1.

Section 554: Regulations: distributions to holders of excessive rights

1747. This section allows the Treasury to make regulations dealing with distributions made to holders of excessive rights. It is based on section 114 of, and paragraph 13 of Schedule 17 to, FA 2006.

1748. The section reproduces neither the general regulation-making power in section 114(1) nor the specific power in section 114(2)(a) of FA 2006. See *Change 43* in Annex 1.

Chapter 7: Gains etc

Section 555: Assets: change of use

1749. This section sets out how gains made on the disposal of an asset used in property rental business (or UK property rental business of non-UK companies) are treated. It also makes provision for repayment of a proportion of the entry charge in certain circumstances. It is based on sections 125 and 134 of, and Schedule 17 to, FA 2006.

1750. *S ubsections (1)* to *(3)* and *(7)* apply if an asset which has been used wholly and exclusively for the purposes of property rental business (or UK property rental business in the case of non-UK companies) begins to be used for the purposes of residual business. The asset is deemed to be sold and reacquired at market value. In accordance with section 535(1) any resulting gain is not a chargeable gain.

1751. *Subsection (4)* provides that any sale and reacquisition under subsection (2) is at written down value for the purposes of CAA.

1752. *Subsection (5)* provides that if a percentage of the gains of property rental business is excluded from the financial statements because the gains are attributable to a non-member, that percentage of the gains is treated as gains of residual business.

1753. This section also applies to joint venture companies, including non-UK resident joint venture companies (see section 588).

*Section 556: **Disposal of assets***

1754. *Subsections (1)* to *(3)* and *(6)* deal with the case where an asset which has been used wholly and exclusively for the purposes of the property rental business (or UK property rental business in the case of non-UK companies) is disposed of in the course of a trade. Usually such a disposal takes place some time after the asset has been removed from the company's property rental business (when there was a deemed disposal and reacquisition under section 555(2)).

1755. Subsection (2) provides that the deemed disposal and reacquisition under section 536(2) is ignored. Instead the asset is treated as disposed of in the course of the company's residual business. In accordance with section 535(6) any resulting gain which is subject to corporation tax is taxed at the main rate of corporation tax.

1756. *Subsection (5)* provides that if a percentage of the gains of property rental business is excluded from the financial statements because the gains are attributable to a non-member, that percentage of the gains is treated as gains of residual business.

1757. This section also applies to joint venture companies, including non-UK resident joint venture companies (see section 588).

*Section 557: **Movement of assets into ring fence***

1758. This section provides that if an asset used by the residual business of a company (including a non-UK company) begins to be used by the company for the purposes of property rental business (or UK property rental business, in the case of a non-UK company), it is treated as disposed of and reacquired at market value. It also provides that, for the purposes of CAA, the transfer of the asset is treated as made at the tax written-down value. It is based on sections 126 and 134(1) of, and paragraphs 21 and 32(6) of Schedule 17 to, FA 2006.

1759. In accordance with section 535(6), if a gain arises under this section and the gain is subject to corporation tax, it is charged at the main rate.

1760. *Subsection (5)* provides that if a percentage of the gains of property rental business is excluded from the financial statements because the gains are attributable to a non-member, that percentage of the gains are treated as gains of a residual business.

1761. This section also applies to joint venture companies, including non-UK resident joint venture companies (see section 588).

*Section 558: **Demergers: disposal of asset***

1762. This section makes provision for a company UK REIT to dispose of an asset to a 75% subsidiary which subsequently becomes a member of a group UK REIT. It is based on section 126A of FA 2006.

Section 559: Demergers: company leaving group UK REIT

1763. This section makes provision for a company to cease to be a member of a group UK REIT but to continue within the UK REIT regime. It is based on paragraph 34 of Schedule 17 to FA 2006.

1764. *Subsection (9)* makes clear that the conditions in the section are to be met by the company giving the notice (not necessarily the exiting company).

Section 560: Interpretation of Chapter

1765. This section provides that the Chapter (apart from section 559) is to be read as if it were contained in TCGA. It is based on section 127 of FA 2006.

Chapter 8: Breach of conditions in Chapter 2

Section 561: Notice of breach of relevant Chapter 2 condition

1766. This section provides that if certain conditions in Chapter 2 are not met, the principal company of a group UK REIT or a company UK REIT must notify an officer of Revenue and Customs of the breach. It is based on sections 116(1) and (2) and 134(1) of FA 2006.

1767. *Subsectio ns (1)*and *(2)*refer to an "officer of Revenue and Customs" rather than to the "Commissioners for Her Majesty's Revenue and Customs". See *Change 5* in Annex 1.

1768. *Subsection (4)* enacts the information requirements in regulation 9 of SI 2006/2864. See *Change 43 in Annex 1.*

Section 562: Breach of conditions C and D in section 528 (conditions for company)

1769. This section makes provision about breaches of conditions C and D in section 528. It is based on sections 116(1) and (3) and 134(1) of, and paragraph 4 of Schedule 17 to, FA 2006.

1770. This section enacts regulations 1 to 4 of SI 2006/2864. See *Change 43*in Annex1.

1771. *Subsection (2)* provides that if a principal company of a group UK REIT or a company UK REIT becomes a member of a pre-existing group UK REIT, and by doing so fails to satisfy condition C (shares are listed) and condition D (not a close company) in section 528, the breaches are ignored.

1772. As indicated in section 569, this section is subject to section 572 which allows an officer of Revenue and Customs to issue a notice of termination of the UK REIT regime in some circumstances.

Section 563: Breach of conditions as to property rental business

1773. This section provides that conditions A or B of section 529 can be breached without causing the UK REIT regime to terminate. It is based on section 116(1) and (3) of FA 2006.

1774. This section enacts regulation 5(1) and (2) of SI 2006/2864. See *Change 43*in Annex 1.

1775. As indicated in section 569, this section is subject tosection 572, which allows an officer of Revenue and Customs to issue a notice of termination of the UK REIT regime in some circumstances.

Section 564: Breach of condition as to distribution of profits

1776. This section sets out how the distribution condition in section 530 can be breached without causing the UK REIT regime to terminate. It is based on section 116(1) and (3) of FA 2006.

1777. This section enacts regulation 6(1) to (3) and (5) to (8) of SI 2006/2864. See *Change 43*in Annex 1.

1778. *Subsection (2)* provides that the breach is ignored if the company does not meet the distribution condition in section 530, but an amount calculated under section 565 is charged to corporation tax. The amount is charged to corporation tax as if it were profits of residual business of the distributing company. Accordingly the rate of tax is the main rate of corporation tax.

1779. As indicated in section 569, this section is subject to section 572 which allows an officer of Revenue and Customs to issue a notice of termination of the UK REIT regime in some circumstances.

Section 565: "The section 565 amount"

1780. This section sets out how to calculate "the section 565 amount" for the purposes of section 564. It is based on section 116(1) and (3) of FA 2006.

1781. This section enacts regulation 6(4) of SI 2006/2864. See *Change 43*in Annex1.

1782. This section provides that an "officer of Revenue and Customs" rather than "the Commissioners" may specify a date before which profits are to be distributed. See *Change 5* in Annex 1.

Section 566: Breach of condition B in section 531 in accounting period 1

1783. This section sets out how condition B in section 531 (balance of business: assets involved in property rental business) can be breached in the first accounting period ("accounting period 1" – see section 609) of a UK REIT without causing the UK REIT regime to terminate. It is based on section 116(1) and (3) of FA 2006.

1784. This section enacts regulations 7 and 7A of SI 2006/2864. See *Change 43*in Annex1.

1785. This section provides that if the balance of business assets test in section 531(5) is not met in accounting period 1, the breach is ignored, but an amount calculated in accordance with section 567 is charged to corporation tax. The amount is charged to corporation tax as if it were profits of residual business of the principal company of the group UK REIT or company UK REIT. Accordingly the rate of tax is the main rate of corporation tax.

1786. As indicated in section 569, this section is subject to section 572 which allows an officer of Revenue and Customs to issue a notice of termination of the UK REIT regime in some circumstances.

Section 567: Meaning of "the notional amount"

1787. This section sets out how to calculate "the notional amount" for the purposes of section 566. It is based on section 116(1) and (3) of FA 2006.

1788. This section enacts regulation 7A(4) to (7) of SI 2006/2864. See *Change 43*in Annex 1.

1789. In regulation 7A(5) of SI 2006/2864. the aggregate market value of assets involved in the UK property rental business excludes assets attributable to any percentage of the assets held by a non-member of the group. *Subsection (4)(c)* of the section makes that exclusion, as in section 539(4). See *Change 44*in Annex 1.

Section 568: Breach of balance of business conditions after accounting period 1

1790. This section sets out how the balance of business conditions in section 531 can be breached in the accounting periods following the first accounting period ("accounting period 1" – see section 609) of the UK REIT without causing the UK REIT regime to terminate. It is based on section 116(1) and (3) of FA 2006.

1791. This section enacts regulation 7B(1) to (3) of SI 2006/2864. See *Change 43*in Annex 1.

1792. As indicated in section 569, this section is subject to section 572 which allows an officer of Revenue and Customs to issue a notice of termination of the UK REIT regimein some circumstances.

Section 569: Chapter subject to section 572

1793. This section provides that this Chapter is subject to section 572 (termination of UK REIT regime by officer of Revenue and Customs). It is based on section 116(4) of FA 2006.

Chapter 9: Leaving the UK REIT regime

Section 570: Overview of Chapter

1794. This section is an overview of the Chapter. It is new.

Section 571: Termination by notice: group or company

1795. This section provides that the principal company of a group UK REIT or a company UK REIT may give notice to an officer of Revenue and Customs for the UK REIT regime to cease for the group or company. It is based on sections 128 and 134(1) of, and paragraph 23 of Schedule 17 to, FA 2006.

1796. *Subsection (3)* requires the notice to be given to an "officer of Revenue and Customs" rather than to "the Commissioners of Her Majesty's Revenue and Customs". *Subsection (4)* requires that the date on the notice must be after the date the "officer" receives the notice. See *Change 5* in Annex 1.

Section 572: Termination by notice: officer of Revenue and Customs

1797. This section provides that, in certain circumstances, an officer of Revenue and Customs may give a notice to the principal company of a group UK REIT or a company UK REIT that the group or company ceases to be within the UK REIT regime. It also provides a right of appeal. It is based on sections 129 and 134(1) of, and paragraphs 23 and 24 of Schedule 17 to, FA 2006.

1798. *Subsections (1), (2)* and *(4)* require the notice to be given by an "officer of Revenue and Customs" rather than by "the Commissioners for Her Majesty's Revenue and Customs". *Subsection (5)* provides that an appeal must be made by the UK REIT by giving notice in writing to an "officer of Revenue of Customs" rather than to "the Commissioners for Her Majesty's Revenue and Customs". See *Change 5* in Annex 1.

Section 573: Notice under section 572: tax advantage

1799. This section provides that if, during a ten year period, two notices have been given under section 545 (cancellation of tax advantage), an officer of Revenue and Customs may give a notice under section 572 terminating the UK REIT regime. It is based on sections 129(2) and 134(1) of FA 2006.

1800. *Subsection (1)* requires the notice to be given by an "officer of Revenue and Customs" rather than by "the Commissioners for Her Majesty's Revenue and Customs". See *Change 5* in Annex 1.

1801. *Subsections (2)* to *(4)* enact regulation 14 of SI 2006/2864. See *Change 43*in Annex 1.

Section 574: Notice under section 572: serious breach

1802. This section provides that if an officer of Revenue and Customs thinks a breach of a condition in sections 529 to 531 is so serious that the UK REIT regime should be terminated, the officer may give a notice under section 572 terminating the regime. It is based on sections 116(1) and (3), 129(2) and 134(1) of FA 2006.

1803. *Subsection (1)* requires the notice to be given by an "officer of Revenue and Customs" rather than by "the Commissioners for Her Majesty's Revenue and Customs". See *Change 5* in Annex 1.

1804. *Subsections (2)* and *(3)* enact regulation 7(4) and (5) of SI 2006/2864. See *Change 43*in Annex 1.

Section 575: Notice under section 572: breach of conditions as to property rental business

1805. This section sets out the circumstances in which an officer of Revenue and Customs may issue a notice under section 572 to terminate the UK REIT regime if there is a breach of either condition A or B in section 529. It is based on sections 116(1) and (3), 129(2) and 134(1) of FA 2006.

1806. *Subsection (1)* requires the notice to be given by an "officer of Revenue and Customs" rather than by "the Commissioners for Her Majesty's Revenue and Customs". See *Change 5* in Annex 1.

1807. This section enacts regulation 5(2) and (5) of SI 2006/2864. See *Change 43*in Annex 1.

Section 576: Notice under section 572: breach of conditions as to balance of business

1808. This section sets out the circumstances in which an officer of Revenue and Customs may issue a notice under section 572 to terminate the UK REIT regime if there is a breach of either condition A or B in section 531. It is based on sections 116(1) and (3), 129(2) and 134(1) of FA 2006.

1809. *Subsection (1)* requires the notice to be given by an "officer of Revenue and Customs" rather than by "the Commissioners for Her Majesty's Revenue and Customs". See *Change 5* in Annex 1.

1810. This section enacts regulation 7B(4) to (7) of SI 2006/2864. See *Change 43*in Annex 1.

Section 577: Notice under section 572: multiple breaches of conditions in Chapter 2

1811. This section provides that if there are multiple breaches of certain Chapter 2 conditions, an officer of Revenue and Customs may issue a notice under section 572 to terminate the UK REIT regime. It is based on sections 129(2) and (3) and 134(1) of FA 2006.

1812. *Subsection (1)* requires the notice to be given by an "officer of Revenue and Customs" rather than by "the Commissioners for Her Majesty's Revenue and Customs". See *Change 5* in Annex 1.

1813. This section enacts regulation 8 of SI 2006/2864. See *Change 43*in Annex 1.

1814. *Subsection (7)(a)* provides that if a member of a group UK REIT or a company UK REIT becomes a member of a pre-existing group UK REIT, and by doing so fails to satisfy condition C (shares are listed) or condition D (not a close company) in section 528, the breaches are ignored.

Section 578: Automatic termination for breach of certain conditions in section 528

1815. This section provides that the UK REIT regime automatically terminates if condition A, B, E or F in section 528 is breached. The company which gave notice under section 523 or 524 must notify an officer of Revenue and Customs of the breach. The section is based on sections 130 and 134(1) of, and paragraphs 4 and 23 of Schedule 17 to, FA 2006.

1816. *Subsection (3)* requires the notice to be given to an "officer of Revenue and Customs" rather than to "the Commissioners for Her Majesty's Revenue and Customs". See *Change5* in Annex 1.

Section 579: Effects of cessation: corporation tax

1817. This section sets out what happens if a group UK REIT, a member of a group UK REIT (including a joint venture company) or a company UK REIT ceases to be within the UK REIT regime. It is based on sections 131 and 134 of, and paragraphs 25, 26 and 33 of Schedule 17 to, FA 2006.

1818. This section also applies to non-UK companies (including non-UK joint venture companies). See *Change 41* in Annex 1.

1819. *Subsections (3)* and *(8)*provide that property rental business (or UK property rental business in the case of a non-UK company) of an exiting company is treated for corporation tax purposes as ceasing immediately before cessation of the UK REIT regime.

1820. *Subsections (4)*and *(8)* provide that assets "involved" in the property rental business (or UK property rental business in the case of a non-UK company) immediately before cessation are treated as being sold immediately before cessation and reacquired immediately afterwards. See section 608(3) for the definition of an asset "involved" in property rental business.

Section 580: Effects of cessation: CAA 2001

1821. This section is supplementary to section 579 and modifies how CAA operates if a company (including a joint venture company) ceases to be in the UK REIT regime. It is based on sections 131(4) and 134(1) of, and paragraphs 25(1) and 26(1) of Schedule 17 to, FA 2006.

Section 581: Early exit by notice

1822. This section sets out what happens if a UK REIT or a member of a group UK REIT (including a joint venture company) that was within the UK REIT regime for less than ten years disposes of an asset within two years of giving notice to leave the UK REIT regime. It is based on sections 132 and 134(1) of, and paragraphs 4, 27 and 28 of Schedule 17 to, FA 2006.

1823. This section applies to UK property rental business of non-UK companies (including non-UK joint venture companies) and subsection (7) applies to non-UK companies. See *Change 41* in Annex 1.

1824. *Subsection (4)* provides that one of the conditions for subsection (6) to apply is that assets "involved" in the property rental business (or UK property rental business in the case of a non-UK company) are disposed of within two years of cessation of the UK REIT regime. See section 608(3) for the definition of an asset "involved" in property rental business.

Section 582: Early exit

1825. This section allows HMRC to make certain directions if a group UK REIT or company UK REIT ceases to be a UK REIT within ten years of entering the regime as a result of section 572 (termination by officer) or section 578 (automatic termination). It is based on sections 133 and 134(1) of, and paragraph 4 and 29 of Schedule 17 to, FA 2006.

1826. *Subsection (2)* allows an "officer of Revenue and Customs" to make the direction rather than "the Commissioners for Her Majesty's Revenue and Customs". See *Change 5* in Annex 1.

Chapter 10: Joint ventures

Section 583: Overview of Chapter

1827. This section is an overview of the Chapter. It is new.

Section 584: Meaning of "joint venture company" and "joint venture group"

1828. This section defines "joint venture company" and "joint venture group" for the purposes of the Chapter. It is based on section 138(1) of FA 2006.

1829. This section enacts parts of SI 2006/2866 and SI 2007/3425. See *Change 43* in Annex 1.

Section 585: Meaning of "venturing group" and "venturingcompany"

1830. This section defines "venturing company" and "venturing group" for the purposes of the Chapter. It is based on section 138(1) of FA 2006.

1831. This section enactsparts of SI 2006/2866 and SI 2007/3425. See *Change 43* in Annex 1.

Section 586: Notice for Part to apply: joint venture company

1832. This section provides that a group UK REIT or a company UK REIT may bring a joint venture company (including a non-UK joint venture company) into the regime if certain conditions are met. It is based on section 138(1) and (3) of FA 2006.

1833. This section enacts parts of SI 2006/2866. See *Change 43* in Annex 1.

1834. *Subsection (1)*provides that the principal company of a group UK REIT may give notice that the Part is to apply in relation to property rental business carried on by a joint venture company. *Subsection (2)* makes similar provision in relation to a company UK REIT.

1835. Giving a notice under subsection (2) does not mean that the company UK REIT is treated as giving a group notice under section 523(1). So it is not required to bring all its subsidiaries into the UK REIT regime.

1836. Condition 7 of regulations 3(1) and 10(1) SI 2006/2866 provides that, in order for a notice to be made in respect of a joint venture company, the joint venture company must satisfy the balance of business tests in section 108 of FA 2006. But a joint venture notice must be made at the beginning of the accounting period and the balance of business tests cannot be satisfied until the end of the accounting period. So it is unclear when a notice can be made.

1837. The balance of business tests are rewritten in section 591, putting joint venture companies on the same basis as joint venture groups. Condition 7 is not rewritten.

1838. *Subsection (6)(b)* requires the "consent" of the joint venture company. This requirement replaces the need for the notice to be "signed by the company secretary or a director". So the section is consistent with the possibilities that the notice may be given electronically and that, following the Companies Act 2006, the company may not have a company secretary or a director.

1839. *Subsection (6)(d)* provides that the notice must be given to an "officer of Revenue and Customs" rather than to "the Commissioners for Her Majesty's Revenue and Customs". See *Change 5* in Annex 1.

Section 587: Notice for Part to apply: joint venture group

1840. This section provides that a group UK REIT or a company UK REIT may bring a joint venture group (including a non-UK member of a joint venture group) into the regime if certain conditions are met. It is based on section 138(1) and (3) of FA 2006.

1841. This section enacts parts of SI 2007/3425. See *Change 43* in Annex 1.

1842. *Subsection (1)*provides that the principal company of a group UK REIT may give notice that the Part is to apply in relation to property rental business carried on by the members of a joint venture group. *Subsection (2)* makes similar provision in relation to a company UK REIT.

1843. Giving a notice under subsection (2) does not mean that the company UK REIT is treated as giving a group notice under section 523(1). So it is not required to bring all its subsidiaries into the UK REIT regime.

1844. *Subsection (6)(b)* requires the "consent" of the principal company of the joint venture group. This requirement replaces the need for the notice to be "signed by the company secretary or a director". So the section is consistent with the possibilities that the notice may be given electronically and that, following the Companies Act 2006, the company may not have a company secretary or a director.

1845. *Subsection (6)(d)* provides that the notice must be given to an "officer of Revenue and Customs" rather than to "the Commissioners for Her Majesty's Revenue and Customs". See *Change 5* in Annex 1.

Section 588: Effect of notice under section 586

1846. This section makes general modifications to the Part to take into account joint venture companies. It is based on section 138(1) and (2) of, and paragraph 3(1) of Schedule 17 to, FA 2006.

1847. This section enacts parts of SI 2006/2866. See *Change 43* in Annex 1.

1848. *Subsection (1)*provides that, if the principal company of a group UK REIT gives notice in relation to a joint venture company, the Part applies in relation to property rental business carried on by the joint venture company as if it were a member of the group UK REIT.

1849. *Subsection (2)* provides that, if a company UK REIT gives notice in relation to a joint venture company, the Part applies in relation to property rental business carried on by the joint venture company as if the company UK REIT and the joint venture company were members of a new group UK REIT.

Section 589: Effect of notice under section 587

1850. This section makes general modifications to the Part to take into account members of a joint venture group. It is based on section 138(1) and (2) of FA 2006.

1851. This section enacts parts of SI 2007/3425. See *Change 43* in Annex 1.

1852. *Subsection (1)*provides that, if the principal company of a group UK REIT gives notice in relation to members of a joint venture group, the Part applies in relation to property rental business carried on by the members of the joint venture group as if they were members of the group UK REIT.

1853. *Subsection (2)* provides that, if a company UK REIT gives notice in relation to members of a joint venture group, the Part applies in relation to property rental business carried on by the members of the joint venture group as if the company UK REIT and the members of the joint venture group were members of a new group UK REIT.

Section 590: ***Duration of notice under*** *section 586* ***or*** *587*

1854. This section provides for a notice under section 586 or 587 to cease to have effect.It is based on section 138(1) and (2) of FA 2006.

1855. This section enacts parts of SI 2006/2886 and SI 2007/3425. See *Change 43* in Annex 1.

1856. *Subsections (1)(b)*and *(2)(b)* provide that if the venturing group or venturing company ceases to be a UK REIT, the notice under section 586 ceases to have effect. For joint venture companies, this is not explicit in regulations 4 and 11 of SI 2006/3425. But it is implicit that a joint venture company ceases to be within the UK REIT regime if the company which made the notice ceases to be a UK REIT. Subsections (1)(b) and (2)(b) make this explicit. So the positions for joint venture companies and joint venture groups are the same.

1857. *Subsection (6)* provides that if a notice under section 586 or 587 ceases to have effect, section 581 (early exit) continues to have effect. The joint venture company regulations do not contain a provision similar to that for joint venture groups. But it is implicit from the regulations that section 581 continues to have effect once the joint venture company ceases to be in the UK REIT regime. So subsection (6) applies to joint venture companies as it does to joint venture groups.

1858. *Subsection (7)* defines "the 40% tests" by reference to the type of notice given. For each of subsections (1) to (4) a different version of the 40% tests applies. See:

- in the case of subsection (1), the tests in section 586(4);
- in the case of subsection (2), the tests in section 586(5);
- in the case of subsection (3), the tests in section 587(4); and
- in the case of subsection (4), the tests in section 587(5).

Section 591: ***Conditions as to balance of business***

1859. This section provides that the balance of business tests in section 531 must be met by the joint venture company or joint venture group. It is based on section 138(1) and (2) of FA 2006.

1860. This section enacts parts of SI 2006/2866 and SI 2007/3425. See *Change 43* in Annex 1.

Section 592: ***Joint venture groups: financial statements***

1861. This section provides that the principal company of a joint venture group must prepare financial statements for the group. It is based on section 138(1) and (2) of FA 2006.

1862. This section enacts parts of SI 2007/3425. See *Change 43* in Annex 1.

1863. *Subsection (5)* provides that the financial statements must be submitted to an "officer of Revenue and Customs" rather than to "the Commissioners for Her Majesty's Revenue and Customs". See *Change 5* in Annex 1.

Section 593: Financial statements under section 532: joint venture groups

1864. This section provides that the amount to be included in the financial statements under section 532 should include only the "relevant percentage" of profits, expenses, gains, losses, assets and liabilities. It is based on section 138(1) and (2) of FA 2006.

1865. This section enacts parts of SI 2007/3425. See *Change 43* in Annex 1.

Section 594: Modifications of Chapter 3

1866. This section makes specific modifications to the Part in relation to property rental business carried on by a joint venture company or by one or more members of a joint venture group. It is based on sections 138(1) and (2) of FA 2006.

1867. This section enacts parts of SI 2006/2866 and SI 2007/3425. See *Change 43* in Annex 1.

Section 595: Joint venture company liable for additional charge

1868. This section provides that a joint venture company is chargeable to an additional amount of entry charge in certain circumstances. It is based on sections 138(1) and (2) of FA 2006.

1869. This section enacts regulation 14 of SI 2006/2866. See *Change 43* in Annex 1.

1870. This sectionprovides that a joint venture company is chargeable to tax under section 538 in respect of the "reduced notional amount" if either:

- a venturing company becomes a principal company of a group UK REIT and it increases its holding in a joint venture company; or
- a venturing group increases its holding in a joint venture company to more than 75%.

1871. *Subsection (7)* defines "reduced notional amount".

1872. If more than 75% of the shares of the joint venture company are held by the company, the joint venture company is a subsidiary and is covered by the section 523(1) notice. It is not possible to give a further notice under section 586.

Section 596: Member of joint venture group liable for additional charge

1873. This section provides that a member of a joint venture group is chargeable to an additional amount of entry charge in certain circumstances. It is based on sections 138(1) and (2) of FA 2006.

1874. This section enacts parts of SI 2007/3425. See *Change 43* in Annex 1.

1875. *Subsections (1)* to *(3)* provide that a member of a joint venture group is chargeable to tax under section 538 in respect of "the reduced notional amount" if a venturing company increases its holding in a member of a joint venture group with the result that it becomes a principal company of a group.

1876. *Subsections (4)* and *(5)*provide that a member of a joint venture group is chargeable to tax under section 538 in respect of the "reduced notional amount" if a venturing group increases its holding in a member of a joint venture group to at least 75% with the result that the member of the joint venture group becomes a member of the venturing group.

1877. Regulation 14(6) of SI 2006/2866 refers to the case where "a venturing group ... increases its shareholding ... to 75% or more" in a joint venture company. These words include the possibility that the 75% comprises smaller shareholdings by members of the venturing group.

1878. Regulation 24(1) of SI 2007/3425 refers to the case where "a member of a venturing group ... increases its shareholding ... to 75% or more" in a member of a joint venture group. These words seem to require that the 75% holding must be by a single member of the venturing group.

1879. The result in each case is that the joint venture company (or member of the joint venture group) becomes a member of a group UK REIT. Chapter 3 of Part 24 of this Act provides that indirect shareholdings are to be taken into account in determining whether a company is a member of a group. So the SI 2006/2866 approach is more logical than that of 2007/3425 and is the one adopted by the section in both cases.

1880. *Subsections (6)* defines "reduced notional amount".

Section 597: Cases where no additional charge due

1881. This section provides that neither a joint venture company nor a member of a joint venture group is chargeable to an additional amount in respect of the entry charge if there is no increase in shareholding. It is based on sections 138(1) and (2) of FA 2006.

1882. This section enacts parts of SI 2006/2866 and SI 2007/3425. See *Change 43* in Annex 1.

Section 598: Chapter 10: supplementary

1883. This section explains what is meant by "equity holder" and percentages of beneficial interest for the purposes of the Chapter. It is based on section 138(1) of FA 2006.

1884. This section enacts parts of SI 2006/2866 and SI 2007/3425.See *Change 43* in Annex 1.

1885. *Subsection (1)(b)* defines "equity holder" for the purposes of the Chapter by reference to a loan creditor other than a loan in relation to a "normal commercial loan". This is based on regulation 4(1) of SI 2007/3425. SI 2006/2866 does not define "normal commercial loan" for joint venture companies. This section applies the definition for both joint venture groups and joint venture companies.

1886. The exclusions for "owner-occupied" property in Condition 6 of regulations 3(1) and 10(1) of SI 2006/2866 are rewritten in *subsection (3)*. These exclusions are the equivalent of the exclusion for owner-occupied property in section 604(2), which may not apply to a joint venture company or a joint venture group.

Chapter 11: Part 12: supplementary

Section 599: Calculation of profits

1887. This section provides for the calculation of profits for the purposes of certain provisions in the Part. It is based on section 120 of FA 2006.

1888. This section applies to non-UK companies and joint venture companies (including non-UK ones).

1889. *Subsection (7)* requires income and expenditure to be "apportioned on a just and reasonable basis". It is based on section 120(6) of FA 2006 which states that income and expenditure be "apportioned reasonably". See *Change 33* in Annex 1.

Section 600: Power to make regulations about cases involving related persons

1890. This section allows the Treasury, by order, to treat persons as forming part of a group REIT. It is based on section 136A of FA 2006.

1891. An order under this section is intended to counteract arrangements by which a company with non-qualifying activities is artificially excluded from a group of companies with the result that the balance of business tests are satisfied.

1892. In *subsection (2)* "REIT company" is defined, for the purpose of subsection (1) only, to include the members of a group UK REIT. In this respect it differs from the definitions in section 518(4).

1893. *Subsection (5)* ensures that this section is an exception to the general rule about orders and regulations in section 1171(4).

Section 601: Availability of group reliefs

1894. This section provides that the part of a group UK REIT that carries on property rental business is treated as a separate group from the part that carries on other business for the purposes of various group-related provisions. It is based on section 136 of FA 2006.

Section 602: Effect of deemed disposal and reacquisition

1895. This section provides that a deemed disposal and reacquisition of an asset under this Part has effect for any future disposal. It is based on section 141 of FA 2006.

Section 603: Regulations

1896. This section provides that regulations made under the Part may make provision for various other purposes. It is based on section 144 of FA 2006.

1897. This section is in line with other general regulation-making provisions and includes a specific reference to the making of "supplemental" provision.

Section 604: Property rental business: exclusion of listed business

1898. This section provides a list of classes of businesses that are not property rental business. It is based on section 104(2) of, and paragraphs 1 to 5 and 14 of Schedule 16 to, FA 2006.

Section 605: Property rental business: exclusion of business producing listed income

1899. This section provides that business is not property rental business in so far as it gives rise to certain income. It is based on section 104(2) of, and paragraphs 6 to 14 of Schedule 16 to, FA 2006.

1900. *Subsection (1)* provides that business is not property rental business in so far as it gives rise to income of a class referred to in *subsection (2)*. Section 104(2)(b) of FA 2006 refers to "income *or profits*...". It is unclear what the reference to "profits" is intended to catch. So this section omits the reference to profits.

Section 606: Groups

1901. This section sets out which companies are treated as part of a group for the purposes of the Part. It is based on section 134(2) to (6) of FA 2006.

1902. *Subsection (3)* provides that a company cannot be a member of more than one group. But that rule is disapplied for the joint venture Chapter by*subsection (4)*.So a company may be a member of a joint venture group (see section 584(2)) and a member of another group. And a company may be a member of more than one group UK REIT.

Section 607: Meaning of "entry" and "cessation" etc

1903. This section contains definitions related to a company or group becoming, or ceasing to be, a UK REIT. It is based on sections 105(1) and (2) and 134(1) of, and paragraphs 4 and 10 to 12 of Schedule 17 to, FA 2006.

Section 608: References to assets

1904. This section explains what is meant by a reference to an asset and when that asset is "involved" in a business. It is based on sections 108(3), 111(6), 131(6), 132(3) and 142 of FA 2006.

Section 609: Definitions

1905. This section contains a list of definitions for this Part. It is based on section 142 of FA 2006.

Part 13: Other special types of company etc

Overview

1906. This Part contains rules for special types of company etc.

1907. Chapter 1 is about corporate beneficiaries under trusts.

1908. Chapter 2 is about authorised investment funds.

1909. Chapter 3 is about unauthorised unit trusts.

1910. Chapter 4 is about securitisation companies.

1911. Chapter 5 is about companies in liquidation or administration.

1912. Chapter 6 is about banks in compulsory liquidation.

1913. Chapter 7 is about co-operative housing associations.

1914. Chapter 8 is about self-build societies.

1915. Chapter 9 is about community amateur sports clubs.

Chapter 1: Corporate beneficiaries under trusts

Overview

1916. This Chapter contains rules that apply to the income of corporate beneficiaries of settlements. The first section concerns payments made at the discretion of the trustees. The second section concerns cases where the beneficiary is entitled to a share of the settlement income as it arises (often described as having an "interest in possession").

Section 610: Discretionary payments by trustees to companies

1917. This section provides that discretionary payments by trustees to which sections 494 and 495 of ITA apply are ignored in calculating the beneficiary's liability to corporation tax. It is based on section 687A of ICTA.

1918. Under *subsection (2)*, this provision does not apply to payments made to charitable and similar bodies. These bodies have their own rules (see Part 11).

1919. The word "profits" in section 687A of ICTA does not have a defined meaning: the interpretation in section 6(4)(a) of ICTA does not apply to this section. *Subsections (3)* and *(4)* of this section refer to the "income" of the company for corporation tax purposes instead as this fits with the charge to corporation tax on income (see for example section 4(3) of this Act) and with Chapter 7 of Part 9 of ITA (discretionary payments).

1920. Under *subsection (3)(b)*, the payments are income for corporation tax purposes under section 493 of ITA but are ignored for the purpose of determining the income that is chargeable to corporation tax.

1921. The beneficiary is treated under section 494 of ITA as having paid income tax on the grossed-up amount of the discretionary payment and the trustees are liable for that tax under section 496 of ITA. But *subsection (3)(a)* provides that the tax is not available for set-off against corporation tax or any other income tax for which the beneficiary has to account and *subsection (3)(c)* provides that the deemed income tax is not repaid to the company.

Section 611: Income tax provisions to apply in relation to trustees' expenses

1922. This section applies the rules in sections 500 and 503 of ITA. It is based on section 698B of ICTA. These provisions are concerned with the treatment of trustees' expenses in a case where the beneficiary is entitled to trust income as it arises. This is where the beneficiary has an interest in possession (IIP).

1923. It is very rare for a company to be an IIP beneficiary of a trust so this is a case where it seems preferable to have this section read across to, rather than duplicate, the income tax provisions.

1924. Much of the content of sections 500 and 503 ITA was new as there was very little statutory guidance about how trustees' expenses affect the measure of a beneficiary's income. The principles were mainly derived from trust and tax law, but are well understood and are the subject of guidance issued by HMRC. See *Change 45*in Annex 1.

Chapter 2: Authorised investment funds

Overview

1925. This Chapter rewrites sections 468, 468A and 469A of ICTA and provides rules about authorised investment funds.

1926. The term "authorised investment funds" is not defined in this Chapter because it is not used in the body of the sections. But it is defined in other legislation and is commonly understood to refer to both open-ended investment companies (OEICs) and authorised unit trusts (AUTs). The Chapter also provides rules about court investment funds, which are treated as AUTs.

Section 612: Overview of Chapter

1927. This section provides an overview of what is in the Chapter. It is new.

Section 613: Meaning of "open-ended investment company"

1928. This section sets out the definition of an "open-ended investment company" (an OEIC). It is based on section 468A(2) of ICTA.

Section 614: Applicable corporation tax rate

1929. This section, which is based on section 468A(1) of ICTA, provides that the rate of corporation tax applicable to an OEIC is the income tax basic rate (see section 6 of ITA).

Section 615: Umbrella companies

1930. This section sets out the definition of "umbrella company" and how such a company is treated. It is based on section 468A(3) and (4) of ICTA.

1931. An umbrella company is an OEIC whose investments are pooled separately in sub-funds which may have different investment objectives. As in section 235 of FISMA, this practice is referred to in this section in terms of separate pooling and separate parts. References in the section to a part of an umbrella company are to a separate pool (*subsection (2)*).

1932. Each separate part of an umbrella company is treated as a separate OEIC while the umbrella company as a whole is not treated as an OEIC. This mirrors the provision made for umbrella schemes by section 619.

Section 616: Meaning of "authorised unit trust" and "unit holder"

1933. This section defines these terms for the purposes of the Chapter. It is based on section 468(6) of ICTA.

Section 617: Authorised unit trust treated as UK resident company

1934. This section provides that the Tax Acts have effect as if the trustees of an AUT were a UK resident company, and as if the rights of the unit holders were shares in the company. It is based on section 468(1) and (3) of ICTA.

1935. Detailed rules for the taxation of both an AUT as an institution, and unit holders as investors, are set out in the Authorised Investment Funds (Tax) Regulations 2006 (SI 2006/964).

1936. *Subsection (3)* makes it clear that the treatment in *subsection (1)(b)* does not affect the rules which enable an AUT to make distributions which are interest distributions to unit holders. The term "interest distribution" is currently defined in regulation 18(3) of SI 2006/964.

Section 618: Applicable corporation tax rate

1937. This section states that a special rate of corporation tax is applicable to AUTs. It is based on section 468(1A) of ICTA.

1938. The applicable rate is the income tax basic rate (see section 6 of ITA).

Section 619: Umbrella schemes

1939. This section sets out the definition of an "umbrella scheme" and how such a scheme is treated. It is based on section 468(7), (8) and (9) of ICTA.

1940. An umbrella scheme is a fund which is divided into sub-funds which may have different investment objectives. As in section 235 of FISMA, this practice is referred to in this section in terms of separate pooling and separate parts. References in the section to a part of an umbrella scheme are to the pooling arrangements that relate to a separate pool.

1941. Each separate part of an umbrella scheme is treated as a separate AUT while the umbrella scheme as a whole is not treated as an AUT. This mirrors the provision made for umbrella companies by section 615.

Section 620: Court investment funds

1942. This section sets out the treatment of court investment funds. It is based on section 469A of ICTA.

1943. In section 469A of ICTA the fund is described as a court common investment fund but for capital gains tax purposes (see section 100(3) of TCGA) the same kind of account is named a court investment fund. We have changed the term to be consistent with the simpler and clearer description in TCGA.

1944. A court investment fund is defined in *subsection (1)* as a fund set up under section 42 of the Administration of Justice Act 1982.

1945. The effect of the section is that the Tax Acts apply to a court investment fund as if it were an AUT (with the investment manager of the fund in the role of trustee) and as if the persons with qualifying interests in the fund (see the table in*subsection (3)*) were unit holders in the AUT.

Chapter 3: Unauthorised unit trusts

Overview

1946. This Chapter contains special rules relating to the income and capital expenditure of unit trusts. It is based on section 469 of ICTA. The corresponding income tax provisions are in Chapter 9 of Part 9 of ITA.

Section 621: Treatment of income

1947. This section is based on sections 469(1) and (2) of ICTA. The corresponding rule for income tax is in section 504 of ITA.

1948. *Subsection (2)* provides that for the purposes of the Corporation Tax Acts income arising to the trustees is treated as their income and not as the income of the unit holders.

Section 622: Treatment of capital expenditure

1949. This section is based on sections 469(1) and (2) of ICTA. The corresponding rule for income tax is in section 504A of ITA, as inserted by the Income Tax Act 2007 (Amendment) Order 2009 (SI 2009/23).

1950. The effect of this special rule is that all allowances and charges under rules relating to capital expenditure are enjoyed or suffered by the trustees and not the unit holders.

Chapter 4: Securitisation companies

Overview

1951. This Chapter deals with securitisation companies. It is based on section 84 of FA 2005.

1952. Section 84 of FA 2005 consisted primarily of a Treasury power to determine how the Corporation Tax Acts were to apply to securitisation companies. It also contained a Treasury power to refine, for the purposes of those regulations, the basic section 84 definition of a securitisation company .

1953. The rewritten sections separate the two regulation making powers. The power to refine the definition of a securitisation company is in subsection (2)(b) of section 623. The power to make regulations governing the taxation of securitisation companies comprises the whole of section 624.

1954. Section 83 of FA 2005 also deals with securitisation companies although the definition of "securitisation companies" for the purposes of section 83 is not the same as that for section 84. Section 83 governs the application of accounting standards to certain securitisation companies for periods of account beginning on or after 1January2005 and ending before 1January 2008. That period has,however, now been extended, (in accordance with the power in subsection (7A)) by the Securitisation Companies (Application of section 83(1) of the Finance Act 2005: Accounting Standards) Regulations 2007(SI 2007/3338), to 1 January 2017 in a limited number of cases. As section 83 has a finite life and a limited application it is not rewritten.

Section 623: Meaning of "securitisation company"

1955. This section provides a definition of "securitisation company". It is based on section 84(2) and (6) of FA 2005.

1956. *Subsections (3) to (5)* set out the conditions that must be met if a company is to be a "securitisation company". *Subsection (2)* includes the proviso that in addition to meeting the conditions in subsections (3) to (5) the company must also meet any conditions set out in regulations. Such conditions are in regulation 4 of the Taxation of Securitisation Companies Regulations 2006 (SI 2006/3296).

Section 624: Power to make regulations about the taxation of securitisation companies

1957. This section sets out how the Treasury may make regulations governing the taxation of securitisation companies. It is based on section 84(1), (3) and (6) of FA 2005.

Section 625: Regulations: supplementary

1958. This section contains provisions that supplement the regulation-making powers conferred by sections 623 and 624. It is based on section 84(4) and (5) of FA 2005.

Chapter 5: Companies in liquidation or administration

Overview

1959. This Chapter deals with the taxation of companies in liquidation or administration. It is based on sections 342 and 342A of ICTA.

1960. The rules governing the accounting periods of such companies are in Chapter2 of Part 2 of CTA 2009.

Section 626: Meaning of "final year", "penultimate year" etc

1961. This section defines a number of the terms used in the Chapter. It is based on sections 6(4), 342(1) and 342A(1) of ICTA.

Section 627: Meaning of "rate of corporation tax" in case of companies with small profits

1962. This section defines "rate of corporation tax" for companies with small profits subject to this Chapter. It is based on section 342(2) and (3) and section 342A(2) and (3) of ICTA.

Section 628: Company in liquidation: corporation tax rates

1963. This section sets out the corporation tax rates that are to be applied in the final or penultimate year of the liquidation period of a company that is being wound up. It is based on section 342(2), (3) and (8) of ICTA.

1964. If the rates of corporation tax have been either fixed or proposed for the final year or the penultimate year then the proposed or fixed rates are to be used. Accordingly in the vast majority of cases the normal corporation tax rates apply.

1965. Corporation tax rates are generally proposed in the PBR (Pre-Budget Report). The PBR takes place in autumn. The PBR in the autumn of Financial Year 1 proposes corporation tax rates for Financial Year 3. The same PBR proposes the rate of corporation tax for companies with small profits and fractions for Financial Year 2. The associated Finance Act usually becomes law in July of Financial Year 2. The corporation tax rates for Financial Year 3 become fixed in Financial Year 2 and the rate for companies with small profits and fractions for Financial Year 2 also become fixed in Financial Year 2.

1966. The section assists liquidators seeking to finalise a company's liability in advance of a formal winding up by setting out the rates to be used even in those rare cases where corporation tax rates have not been fixed at the time when a liquidator wishes to make an assessment to tax.

Section 629: Company in liquidation: making of assessment to tax

1967. This section enables a liquidator to make a corporation tax self-assessment for an accounting period that has not finished. It is based on section 342(4), (5) and (6) of ICTA.

1968. In normal circumstances it is not possible to make a corporation tax self-assessment before the end of an accounting period. In the majority of instances the profits for the period are not known in advance and the relevant corporation tax rates may not have been fixed.

1969. Liquidators may seek to finalise a company's liability to corporation tax in advance of the completion of a formal winding up. This section enables the liquidator to do so by making a corporation tax self-assessment before the end of an accounting period.

1970. The rules about accounting periods for companies being wound up are in section 12 of CTA 2009 (see in particular subsection (3)).

*Section 630: **Company in administration: corporation tax rates***

1971. This section sets out the corporation tax rates that are to be applied in the final year and the penultimate year of an administration period that concludes with the company's dissolution. It is based on section 342A(2), (3) and (10) of ICTA.

1972. If the rates of corporation tax have been either fixed or proposed for the final year or the penultimate year then the proposed or fixed rates are to be used. Accordingly in the vast majority of cases the normal corporation tax rates apply.

1973. The section assists administrators seeking to finalise a company's liability in advance of an anticipated dissolution date by setting out the rates to be used even in those rare cases where corporation tax rates have not been fixed at the time when the administrator wishes to make an assessment to tax.

*Section 631: **Company in administration: making of assessment to tax***

1974. This section enables an administrator to make a corporation tax self-assessment for an accounting period that has not finished. It is based on section 342A(6), (7) and (8) of ICTA.

1975. In normal circumstances it is not possible to make a corporation tax self-assessment before the end of an accounting period. In the majority of instances the profits for the period are not known in advance and the relevant corporation tax rates may not have been fixed.

1976. Administrators may seek to finalise a company's liability to corporation tax in advance of an anticipated dissolution date. This section enables the administrator to do so by making a corporation tax self-assessment before the end of an accounting period.

1977. The rules about determining the end of an accounting period are in section 10 of CTA 2009 (see particularly subsection (3)).

*Section 632: **Meaning of rate being "fixed" or "proposed"***

1978. This section defines terms used in the previous sections. It is based on section 342(7) and 342A(9) of ICTA.

*Section 633: **Exemption for interest on overpaid tax in final accounting period***

1979. This section provides a limited exemption for interest on overpaid tax received or paid in the final accounting period. It is based on sections 342(3A) and 342A(4), (5) of ICTA.

1980. The rules about accounting periods for companies being wound up are in section 12 of CTA 2009 (see in particular subsection (4)).

Chapter 6: Banks etc in compulsory liquidation

Overview

1981. This Chapter deals with the taxation of banks in compulsory liquidation. It is based on Schedule 12 to F(No 2)A 1992.

Section 634: Overview of Chapter

1982. This section gives an overview of the Chapter. It is new.

Section 635: Application of Chapter

1983. This section sets out the conditions that a company must meet in order for the Chapter to apply. It is based on paragraph 1 of Schedule 12 to F(No 2)A 1992.

1984. *Subsection (6)* refers to an EEA firm with permission under paragraph 15 of Schedule 3 to FISMA. The source qualified this by adding "(as a result of qualifying for authorisation by virtue of paragraph 12 of that Schedule)". This qualification is considered unnecessary as the only way in which permission under paragraph 15 may be given is by virtue of paragraph 12. These words are therefore repealed without replacement.

Section 636: Charge to corporation tax on winding up receipts

1985. This section charges amounts received during the winding up period. It is based on paragraph 3(1), (1A), (2) and (3) of Schedule 12 to F(No 2)A 1992.

Section 637: Transfer of rights to payment

1986. This section charges sums received in respect of transfers of rights as if those sums were winding up receipts. It is based on paragraph 5 of Schedule 12 to F(No 2)A1992.

1987. In the case of a non-arm's length transaction the source provided that market value was to be substituted for the consideration received. However, the tax charge was based on amounts received. In relation to the deemed amounts arising from non-arm's length transactions the source,therefore, stated that "references ... to sums received shall be construed accordingly."

1988. Although the meaning was not in doubt the source was not as clear as it might have been. In the rewritten section a slightly different approach is adopted by explicitly treating the value of transferred rights as winding up receipts.

Section 638: Allowable deductions

1989. This section provides rules for setting allowable deductions against winding up receipts. It is based on paragraph 4 of Schedule 12 to F(No 2)A 1992.

Section 639: Election to carry back

1990. This section gives a company the right to elect to carry back a winding up receipt to the date that the business ceased. It is based on paragraph 6 of Schedule 12 to F(No 2)A 1992.

Section 640: Relationship of Chapter with other corporation tax provisions

1991. This section gives priority to a charge under this Chapter over potential charges arising under other provisions. It is based on paragraph 3(4) and (5) of Schedule 12 to F(No 2)A 1992.

Section 641: Interpretation of Chapter

1992. This section sets out a number of definitions and interpretations relevant to the Chapter. It is based on paragraph 2 of Schedule 12 to F(No 2)A 1992.

Chapter 7: Co-operative housing associations

Overview of Chapter

1993. This Chapter rewrites section 488 of ICTA. It provides tax rules forco-operative housing associations and an approvals process that underpins those rules. The approvals process has been modified significantly for Scotland and Wales as a result of devolution. The rewritten legislation incorporates these effects.

Section 642: Disregard of rent from members and of interest payable

1994. This sectionprovides that, where an approved housing association makes a claim, any rent that it receives from its members is ignored for tax purposes and any interest that it pays is treated by the association as not payable. It is based on section 488(1) and (2) of ICTA.

1995. The source legislation is based on tax years, but as these bodies are subject to corporation tax it is more appropriate to operate on the basis of accounting periods. Moving to this basis also brings the disregard of rent and interest into line with the chargeable gains exemption in section 643. See *Change 46* in Annex 1.

Section 643: Exemption for gains on a sale of property

1996. This section exempts an approved housing association from corporation tax on gains on sales of property to its members. It is based on section 488(5) of ICTA.

Section 644: Approval of housing associations

1997. This section sets out the process by which housing associations are approved for the purposes of this Chapter. It is based on section 488(6) and (7) of ICTA.

1998. Since section 488 of ICTA was enacted, a number of changes to the approvals regime have been made as a result of devolution.

1999. Specified functions have been transferred:

- to the Scottish Ministers by the Scotland Act 1998 (Transfer of Functions to the Scottish Ministers etc) Order 2004 (SI 2004/2030), articles2(1) and 3; and
- to the Welsh Ministers by the National Assembly for Wales (Transfer of Functions) Order 1999 (SI 1999/672), article 2 and Schedule 1 and by the Government of Wales Act2006,paragraphs 30(1) and (2) of Schedule 11.

2000. The effects of these modifications are included explicitly in this Chapter.

2001. In order to reflect changes in the responsibilities of the Department of the Environment and the Department for Social Development, the approvals process for Northern Ireland refers to the Department for Social Development instead of the Head of the Department of the Environment for Northern Ireland. See *Change 47* in Annex 1.

2002. *Subsection (4)* provides a signpost to a saving provision in Schedule 2 concerning the concurrent exercise of these functions in relation to Wales by the Secretary of State and the Welsh Ministers where the association is a "cross-border body".

Section 645: Tests to be satisfied by the association

2003. This section sets out the tests which housing associations have to satisfy in order to be approved for the purposes of this Chapter. It is based on section 488(6) of ICTA.

2004. As mentioned in relation to section 644, since section 488 of ICTA was enacted, a number of changes to the approvals regime have been made as a result of devolution.

2005. So far as exercisable in relation to Wales, the functions under section 488(6) have been transferred to the Welsh Ministers by the National Assembly for Wales (Transfer of Functions) Order 1999 (SI 1999/672), article 2 and Schedule 1 and by the Government of Wales Act 2006, paragraphs 30(1) and(2) of Schedule 11.

2006. Article 5 of the Scotland Act 1988 (Transfer of Functions to the Scottish Ministers etc) Order 2004 (SI 2004/2030) amended section 488(6)(iii). The effect of the amendment on the approvals process for Northern Irelandis discussed in*Change 47* in Annex 1.

Section 646: Delegation of powers to the Regulator of Social Housing

2007. This section permits the Secretary of State's functions under section 644 or 645 to be delegated to the Regulator of Social Housing. It is based on section 488(7A) of ICTA.

2008. The Housing and Regeneration Act 2008 established the Regulator of Social Housing in place of the Housing Corporation as the body responsible for regulating social housing in England. This section incorporates the prospective amendments made by paragraph 13 of Schedule 9 to the Housing and Regeneration Act 2008 which come into force from a day to be appointed by Order (section 325(1) of that Act). Until the Order is made this section is subject to the provisions for co-operative housing associations and self-build societies in Schedule 2.

Section 647: Claims under section 642 or 643

2009. This section sets out the conditions that must be met for a claim under section 642 or 643 to be made. It is based on section 488(9), (10) and (11) of ICTA.

2010. Claims under the source legislation in relation to rent and interest are based on tax years, but as these bodies are subject to corporation tax it is more appropriate to operate on the basis of accounting periods. Moving to this basis also brings those claims into line with the claim for the chargeable gains exemption in section 643. See *Change 46* in Annex 1.

Section 648: Adjustments of liability

2011. This section sets out how adjustments to an association's corporation tax liability may be made as a result of a claim or an amendment of a claim. It is based on section 488(4) and (11A) of ICTA.

2012. Adjustments under the source legislation as a result of claims in relation to rent and interest may be based on tax years or accounting periods, but as these bodies are subject to corporation tax it is more appropriate to operate on the basis of accounting periods. See *Change 46* in Annex 1.

Section 649: Power to make further provision

2013. This section sets out the power to make further provision by statutory instrument or, in Northern Ireland, by statutory rule. It is based on section 488(8) of ICTA.

2014. Powers to make regulations under this provision in relation to Wales were transferred to the Welsh Ministers by the National Assembly for Wales (Transfer of Functions) Order 1999 (SI 1999/672), article 2 and Schedule 1 and by the Government of Wales Act 2006, paragraphs 30(1) and (2) of Schedule 11.

2015. In order to reflect changes in the responsibilities of the Department of the Environment and the Department for Social Development,the powers to make regulations under this provision for the purposes of housing associations in Northern Ireland refer to the Department for Social Development rather than the Head of the Department of the Environment for Northern Ireland. See *Change 47* in Annex 1.

Chapter 8: Self-build societies

Overview of Chapter

2016. This Chapter rewrites section 489 of ICTA. It provides tax rules for self-build societies and an approvals process that underpins those rules. The approvals process has been modified significantly for Wales as a result of devolution. The draft legislation incorporates these effects on the face of the legislation.

Section 650: Meaning of "self-build society"

2017. This section sets out the meaning of "self-build society" for the purposes of the Chapter. It is based on section 489(11) of ICTA.

Section 651: Disregard of rent from members

2018. This section sets out that where a self-build society is approved and makes a claim, any rent that it receives from its members is ignored for tax purposes. It is based on section 489(1) and (11) of ICTA.

2019. The source legislation is based on tax years, but as these bodies are subject to corporation tax it is more appropriate to operate on the basis of accounting periods. Moving to this basis also brings the disregard for rent into line with the chargeable gains exemption in section 652. See *Change 46* in Annex 1.

Section 652: Exemption for gains on disposals of land to members

2020. This section exempts an approved society from corporation tax on chargeable gains on sales of property to its members. It is based on section 489(3) of ICTA.

Section 653: Approval of self-build societies

2021. This section sets out the process by which self-build societies become approved for the purposes of this Chapter. It is based on section 489(4), (5) and (12) of ICTA.

2022. Approvals under this section for self-build societies in Wales have been transferred to the Welsh Ministers by article 2 of and Schedule 1 to the National Assembly for Wales (Transfer of Functions) Order 1999 (SI 1999/672), and paragraphs 30(1) and (2) of Schedule 11 to the Government of Wales Act 2006.The effects of these modifications are included explicitly in this Chapter.

2023. In order to reflect changes in the responsibilities of the Department of the Environment and the Department for Social Development, the approvals process for Northern Ireland refers to the Department for Social Development instead of the Department of the Environment for Northern Ireland. See *Change 47* in Annex 1.

2024. *Subsection (5)* provides a signpost to a saving provision in Schedule 2 concerning the concurrent exercise of these functions in relation to Wales by the Secretary of State and the Welsh Ministers where the society is a "cross-border body".

Section 654: Delegation of powers to the Regulator of Social Housing

2025. This section permits the Secretary of State's functions under section 653 to be delegated to the Regulator of Social Housing. It is based on section 489(5A) of ICTA.

2026. The Housing and Regeneration Act 2008 established the Regulator of Social Housing in place of the Housing Corporation as the body responsible for regulating social housing in England. This section incorporates the prospective amendments made by paragraph 14 of Schedule 9 to the Housing and Regeneration Act 2008 which come into force from a day to be appointed by Order (section 325(1) of that Act). Until the Order is made this section is subject to the provisions for co-operative housing associations and self-build societies in Schedule 2.

Section 655: Claims under section 651 or 652

2027. This section sets out the conditions that must be met for a claim under section 651 or 652 to be made. It is based on section 489(7) to (10) of ICTA.

2028. Claims under the source legislation in relation to rent are based on tax years, but as these bodies are subject to corporation tax it is more appropriate to operate on the basis of accounting periods. Moving to this basis also brings those claims into line with the claim for the chargeable gains exemption in section 652. See *Change 46* in Annex 1.

Section 656: Adjustments of liability

2029. This section sets out how adjustments to a society's corporation tax liability may be made as a result of a claim or an amendment of a claim. It is based on section 489(2) and (9A) of ICTA.

2030. Adjustments under the source legislation as a result of claims in relation to rent may be based on tax years or accounting periods, but as these bodies are subject to corporation tax it is more appropriate to operate on the basis of accounting periods. See *Change 46* in Annex 1.

Section 657: Power to make further provision

2031. This section sets out the power to make further provision by statutory instrument or, in Northern Ireland, by statutory rule. It is based on section 489(6) and (12) of ICTA.

2032. Powers to make regulations under this provision for the purposes of self-build societies in Wales were transferred to the Welsh Ministers by the National Assembly for Wales (Transfer of Functions) Order 1999 (SI 1999/672), article 2 and Schedule 1 and by the Government of Wales Act 2006, paragraphs 30(1) and (2) of Schedule 11.

2033. In order to reflect changes in the responsibilities of the Department of the Environment and the Department for Social Development,powers to make regulations under this provision for the purposes of self-build societies in Northern Irelandrefer to the Department for Social Development instead of the Head of the Department of the Environment for Northern Ireland. See *Change 47* in Annex 1.

Chapter 9: Community amateur sports clubs

Overview

2034. This Chapter provides for the registration of community amateur sports clubs (CASCs) and exemptions from tax of registered clubs. It is based on Schedule 18 to FA 2002.

2035. Paragraph 9 of that Schedule has not been rewritten in this Chapter.

2036. Paragraph 9(1) is merely a signpost to Chapter 2 of Part 8 of ITA (gift aid) which treats a registered club as a charity (see section 430 of ITA). Paragraph 9(1) is not rewritten as it is unnecessary.

2037. The remaining provisions of paragraph 9 are rewritten in this Act by amending the provisions of IHTA, TCGA and CAA to which they cross–refer. See Schedule 1.

Section 658: *Meaning of "community amateur sports club" and "registered club"*

2038. This section sets out the three qualifying conditions which must be met for a club to be entitled to be registered as a CASC and be able to obtain an exemption from tax on relevant income or gains. It is based on paragraphs 1, 11(1) to (3) and (5) and 15(2) of Schedule 18 to FA 2002.

2039. In *subsections (2)* to *(4)* there is a reference to "an officer of Revenue and Customs". This is a change from the source legislation in Schedule 18 to FA 2002 where the reference is to "the Inland Revenue" which is a reference to "the Board" under paragraph 15(2) of Schedule 18 to FA 2002. See *Change 5* in Annex 1.

2040. There is also a change in the words used in *subsection (5)*. In this case the change is to replace a reference to "Inland Revenue" which is a reference to "the Board" under paragraph 15(2) in the source legislation witha reference to "Her Majesty's Revenue and Customs" for the publication of the names and addresses of clubs.See *Change 5* in Annex 1.

Section 659: *Meaning of "open to the whole community"*

2041. This section defines the term "open to the whole community", which is the first of the qualifying conditions for being a registered club. It is based on paragraph 2 of Schedule 18 to FA 2002.

Section 660: *Meaning of "organised on an amateur basis"*

2042. This section defines the term "organised on an amateur basis", which is the second of the qualifying conditions for being a registered club. It is based on paragraph 3 of Schedule 18 to FA 2002.

2043. "Match officials" in *subsection (4)(h)* includes coaches.

2044. This section does not rewrite the requirement in paragraph 3 of Schedule 18 to FA 2002 for certain formalities to apply if a club member supplies goods or services to the club or is employed by the club. See *Change 48* in Annex 1.

Section 661: *Meaning of "eligible sport", "qualifying purposes" etc*

2045. This section sets out the definitions of "eligible sport", "qualifying purposes", "non-qualifying purposes" and "non-qualifying expenditure" specific to this Chapter. It is based on paragraphs 8(1) and (7), 14(1), and 16 of Schedule 18 to FA 2002.

2046. There is an additional definition for "non-qualifying expenditure" which is implicit in the source legislation but this is now made explicit in the rewritten legislation.

2047. This section omits the provision in paragraph 14(2) of Schedule 18 to FA 2002 that a Treasury order designating a sport as an "eligible sport" is subject to annulment in pursuance of a resolution of the House of Commons. That provision is unnecessary as this Act contains general provisions to the same effect in section 1171.

Section 662: *Exemption for UK trading income*

2048. This section provides for the trading income of a registered club to be exempt from tax if the relevant conditions are met. It is based on paragraph 4 of Schedule 18 to FA 2002.

Section 663: *Exemption for UK property income*

2049. This section provides for the property income of a registered club to be exempt from tax if the relevant conditions are met. It is based on paragraph 6 of Schedule 18 to FA 2002.

*Section 664: **Exemption for interest and gift aid income***

2050. This section provides for the interest and gift aid income of a registered club to be exempt from tax if the relevant conditions are met. It is based on paragraph 5 of Schedule 18 to FA 2002.

2051. *Subsection (2)* provides that if a club is registered for only part of an accounting period, that part is treated as a separate accounting period and the club's interest income for that separate period is proportionately reduced. This approach follows that of the source legislation.

2052. In *subsection (3)* thedefinition of "gift aid income" now relies on Chapter 2 of Part 8 of ITA rather than section 25(10) of FA 1990 (see paragraph 5(3)(b) of Schedule 18 to FA 2002). Paragraph 5(4) of that Schedule is not now necessary because section 430 of ITA itself includes CASCs within the definition of charities for the purposes of gift aid.

*Section 665: **Exemption for chargeable gains***

2053. This section provides for the chargeable gains of a registered club to be exempt from tax. It is based on paragraphs 7 and 16 of Schedule 18 to FA 2002.

*Section 666: **Exemptions reduced if non-qualifying expenditure incurred***

2054. This section provides for exemptions to be restricted if the club incurs expenditure for non-qualifying purposes. It is based on paragraphs 8 and 16 of Schedule 18 to FA 2002.

2055. The reference to "income receipts" replaces the reference in paragraph 8 to "income (whether taxable or not and before deduction of expenses)".

2056. Paragraph 8(5) of Schedule 18 to FA 2002 provides a formula to ascertain the relevant surplus amount of non-qualifying expenditure. This is unpacked and set out in narrative form.

*Section 667: **Rules for attributing surplus amount to earlier periods etc***

2057. This section supplements section 666. It is based on paragraph 8(5) to (8) of Schedule 18 to FA 2002.

*Section 668: **How income and gains are attributed***

2058. This section provides that a club may specify or be required to specify how the exempted income and gains are to be reduced in accordance with section 666. It is based on paragraphs 8(9) and 15(1) of Schedule 18 to FA 2002.

*Section 669: **Asset ceasing to be held for qualifying purposes etc***

2059. This section provides that the exemption for chargeable gains on assets is not available if the club ceases to be registered or to hold the asset for qualifying purposes. It is based on paragraphs 10 and 16 of Schedule 18 to FA 2002.

2060. Paragraph 10 of Schedule 18 to FA 2002 refers to "property" but TCGA refers to disposals of "assets". Consequently, the section refers to disposals of "assets" for the purposes of TCGA rather than disposals of "property".

2061. *Subsections (5)* and *(6)* separate and clarify the process for making assessments and the time limit for doing so. These are dealt with together in paragraph 10(3) of Schedule 18 to FA 2002.

Section 670: Notification of HMRC decision

2062. This section provides for the notification of the decision by HMRC for registering a club, the refusal to register a club and the cancellation of the registration of a club. It is based on paragraphs 11(4) and 15(2) of Schedule 18 to FA 2002.

2063. Reference to "the Inland Revenue", which is a reference to "the Board" under paragraph 15(2) in the source legislation,is replaced with a reference to "an officer of Revenue and Customs". See *Change 5* in Annex 1.

Section 671: Appeals

2064. This section sets out the provisions relating to appeals against decisions concerning a club's application or registration. It is based on paragraphs 13 and 15 of Schedule 18 to FA 2002.

2065. In *subsections (1), (5)* and *(6),* reference to "the Inland Revenue",which is a reference to "the Board" under paragraph 15(2) in the source legislation, has been replaced with a reference to "an officer of Revenue and Customs". See *Change 5*in Annex 1.

Part 14: Change in company ownership

Overview

2066. Sections 767A to 769 of, and Schedule 28A to, ICTA have been enacted and amended piecemeal over many years; what is now section 768 of ICTA made its first appearance as section 30(1) to (4) of FA 1969 and paragraphs 8 to 10 of Schedule 15 to that Act. The structure of the legislation is tight and intricate – see, for example, section 768C(5).

2067. The opportunity has been taken to restructure the source legislation to make it easier for users to navigate. In summary, this Part of the Act has the following structure.

2068. Chapter 1 provides a bird's eye view of the Part.

2069. Chapter 2 disallows trading losses in defined situations. It applies both to companies with investment business and to companies without investment business. It is based on sections 768 and 768A of ICTA.

2070. Chapters 3 and 4 apply to companies with investment business. They impose restrictions on corporation tax relief. Chapter 3 provides the general rules and Chapter4 deals with special circumstances involving the transfer of an asset within a corporate group. Chapter 3 is chiefly based on sections 768B, 768D and 768E of ICTA and paragraphs 1 to 9A of Schedule 28A to that Act. Chapter 4 is based on sections 768C to 768E of, and paragraphs 10, 10A and 13 to 17 of Schedule 28A to, ICTA.

2071. Chapter 5 applies to companies without investment business. It disallows property losses. It is based on section 768D of ICTA.

2072. Chapter 6 is concerned with recovery of unpaid corporation tax. It is based on sections 767A to 767B of ICTA.

2073. Chapter 7 defines the key expression "change in the ownership of a company" for the purposes of the Part. It is based on section 769 of ICTA.

2074. Chapter 8 is supplementary.

Chapter 1: Introduction

Section 672: Overview of Part

2075. This section introduces the Part. It is new.

2076. *Subsection (6)* signposts the Chapter on recovery of unpaid corporation tax due from non-UK resident companies. It is similar to Chapter 6, but is not located in this Part because it applies whether or not there is a change in company ownership.

2077. *Subsection (7)* signposts three important definitions.

Chapter 2: Disallowance of trading losses

Overview

2078. Chapter 2 is the first of four Chapters dealing with variations on the theme of "loss buying".

2079. Companies can obtain corporation tax relief for various expenses and losses in different periods from the periods in which the expenses or losses arise. They can,however, only turn these reliefs into a reduction in tax liability if they have taxable profits against which the expenses or losses can be set. The shareholders of an unsuccessful company might therefore wish to monetise these tax reliefs by selling the company to people who might be able to make use of them. Sections 768 to 768E of, and Schedule 28A to, ICTA are directed against such "loss buying".

2080. This Part of the Act does not deal with the buying in of group relief. Section 142, which is based on section 403A(9) and (10) of ICTA, prevents companies claiming group relief in relation to expenses and losses arising before a company joined the group.

2081. The loss buying provisions of TCGA are outside the scope of this Act. See, however, the commentary on section 694.

Section 673: Introduction to Chapter

2082. This section introduces the Chapter. It is based on sections 6, 768, 768A and 834 of ICTA.

2083. *Subsections (1)* to *(3)* lay down the conditions for the Chapter to apply.

2084. Subsection (2) omits as otiose the words "either earlier or later in the period, or at the same time" in sections 768(1) and 768A(1) of ICTA.

2085. Section 767A(4)(b) of ICTA refers to a "significant revival" of activities; sections 768(1)(b) and 768B(1)(c) of ICTA refer to a "considerable revival" of a trade or business. Sections 768(1)(b) and 768B(1)(c) contrast "considerable" with "small or negligible"; in section 767A(4)(b), the contrast is not only with "small or negligible" but also with cessation. The rewrite of these provisions eliminates this variation by consistently using "significant" in subsection (3)and sections 677(2) and (4), 704(3) and 705(3).

2086. *Subsection (4)* defines, non-exhaustively, "major change in the nature or conduct of a trade". The phrase "major change" has been retained in this definition, because there is case law on it: Willis v Peeters Picture Frames Ltd(1982), 56 TC 436 CA(NI)[3] and Purchase v Tesco Stores Ltd (1984), 58 TC 46 HC.[4] For the same reason, the phrase "major change" has also been retained in the similar definitions in sections 677(5), 704(10) and 705(9).

2087. *Subsection (5)* defines "the change in ownership", "the company" and "trade" for the purposes of this Chapter. It defines "trade" to include an office, but does not define "trade" to include "vocation". This is a minor change in the law. See *Change 4* in Annex 1.

---

3 [1983] STC 453.
4 [1984] STC 304.

Section 674: *Disallowance of trading losses*

2088. This section restricts relief for trading losses in cases in which this Chapter applies. It is based on sections 768 and 768A of ICTA.

2089. *Subsection (1)* restricts relief under sections 37 and 42(relief for trade losses). It is aimed at the abuse known as "profits buying" or "loss capacity buying" whereby a trading company with large profits is sold to new owners who feed new activities into the trade which result in heavy initial losses for which early relief would not otherwise be available. The price paid to the old owners would reflect the tax benefit expected to accrue to the new owners.

2090. *Subsection (2)* restricts relief under section 45(carry forward of trade loss against subsequent trade profits).

2091. Section 768(1) of ICTA refers to "relief … given under section 393 [of that Act] by setting a loss incurred by the company … against any income or other profits …". But section 393 of ICTA only gives relief for losses against "trading income" (as defined in section 393(8) of that Act). The reference to "other profits" is a missed consequential amendment. The words should have been omitted when FA1991 replaced section 393(2) of ICTA with section 393A of ICTA. Subsection (2) of this section therefore omits the reference to "other profits".

2092. Section 768(3) of ICTA provides:

> "The apportionment under subsection (2) above shall be on a time basis according to the respective lengths of those parts except that if it *appears* that that method would work unreasonably or unjustly such other method shall be used as *appears* just and reasonable. (emphasis added)

2093. *Subsection (5)* omits the first instance of "appears" in section 768(3) of ICTA for the sake of consistency with sections 685(3) and 702, which are based on paragraphs 8 and 17 respectively of Schedule 28A to ICTA, and sections 704(7) and 705(7), which are based on section 768D(4) of ICTA. It also omits the second instance of "appears" in section 768(3) of ICTA to sharpen the drafting.

Section 675: *Disallowance of trading losses: calculation of balancing charges*

2094. This section prevents double taxation in cases in which this Chapter applies. It is based on section 768 of ICTA.

2095. If section 674(2) restricts relief for trading losses carried forward under section 45, the underlying computations of capital allowances are not affected, because the trade itself does not cease. This means that if, at the time of the change of ownership, a company owns assets on which capital allowances have been given, it can be effectively penalised twice by:

- disallowance of any unused capital allowances included in the losses disallowed; and
- a balancing charge when the assets are disposed of.

2096. *Subsections (2)* and *(3)* solve this problem. If an extinguished loss includes unallowed capital allowances, those capital allowances are treated as not having been given when calculating the balancing charges on an asset owned at the date of the change in ownership and disposed of later.

2097. *Subsection (4)* sets an identification rule. If, in any period, both losses and capital allowances were available for setting against profits, capital allowances are treated as set off before other losses. As requested by respondents, we have sharpened the drafting of this subsection.

2098. Section 768(6) and (7) of ICTA use the expression "allowance or deduction". Since "or deduction" adds nothing to "allowance", subsections (2) to (4) omit "or deduction" as otiose.

*Section 676: **Disallowance of trading losses where company reconstruction without change in ownership***

2099. This section deals with the interaction between sections 674(2) and 944(3). It is based on section 768 of ICTA.

2100. When a trade is transferred from a predecessor company to a successor company, and the relevant conditions are met for a company reconstruction without a change in ownership, section 944(3) provides for the successor to be entitled to relief under section 45 for a trading loss made by the predecessor. Section 674(2) restricts relief under section 45 if there is a change in company ownership. If there is both a company reconstruction without a change in ownership (such that section 944(3) applies) and, separately, a change in ownership (such that section 674(2) applies), then this section extends section 674(2) to restrict relief given under section 944(3).

2101. Section 768(5) of ICTA refers to "section 343" of that Act. But section 768(5) only operates on section 768(1) of ICTA, and section 768(1) only restricts relief under section 393 of that Act. The only provision of section 343 of ICTA which gives relief under section 393 of that Act is section 343(3).This section refers precisely to section 944(3), which is based on section 343(3) of ICTA.

*Chapter 3: **Company with investment business: restrictions on relief: general provision***

Overview

2102. Chapter 3 is the second of four Chapters dealing with various kinds of loss buying. It has the following structure.

- Section 677 (introduction) lays down the conditions for the Chapter to apply and defines some key terms.
- If the Chapter applies, section 678 (notional split of accounting period in which change in ownership occurs) sets the stage. It splits the period in which the change in ownership occurs into two notional accounting periods, and indicates that certain amounts need to be apportioned between these two periods.
- Sections 679 to 684 are a group of six sections restricting various kinds of corporation tax relief. If, having reviewed them, the reader is satisfied that in the case under review these sections make no practical difference, the reader is able to conclude that there is in practice no need to make the apportionments required by section 678.
- Sections 685 and 686 are the detailed rules for making apportionments of amounts for the purposes of this Chapter.
- Section 687 provides for the adjustment of balancing charges in certain cases in which corporation tax relief is restricted.
- Sections 688 to 691 define "significant increase in the amount of a company's capital".

*Section 677: **Introduction to Chapter***

2103. This section introduces the Chapter. It is based on sections 768B, 768D and 768E of ICTA. If, having read this section, the reader is satisfied that the conditions for this Chapter to apply are not met, the reader need read no further in this Chapter.

2104. *Subsections (1)* to *(4)* lay down the conditions for the Chapter to apply.

2105. Subsection (1) is based on, among other things, section 768D(1)(a)(i) of ICTA. Unlike section 768D(1) of ICTA, subsection (1) does not refer to a change in the ownership of a company carrying on a UK property business; it refers to a change in the ownership of a company with investment business. The reason is that, if section 768D(1)(a)(i) of ICTA applies, then:

- There is a change in the ownership of a company carrying on a UK property business (see the opening words of section 768D(1)); and
- The company whose ownership has changed is a company with investment business (see the opening words of section 768D(1)(a)).

2106. Accordingly, if section 768D(1)(a)(i) of ICTA applies, there is by implication a change in the ownership of a company with investment business. There is therefore no need for section 768D(1)of ICTA to pick up the opening words of section 768B of that Act.

2107. *Subsection (5)* defines, non-exhaustively, "major change in the nature or conduct of a business".

*Section 678: **Notional split of accounting period in which change in ownership occurs***

2108. This section deems the accounting period in which the change in ownership occurs to be split into two notional accounting periods for the purposes of this Chapter. It is based on sections 768B, 768D and 768E of ICTA.

2109. *Subsection (3)* requires amounts for the actual accounting period to be apportioned between the two notional accounting periods in accordance with section 685.

*Section 679: **Restriction on debits to be brought into account***

2110. This section restricts debits on the company's loan relationships in cases in which this Chapter applies. It is based on section 768B of ICTA and paragraph 9 of Schedule 28A to that Act.

2111. This section is the first of a group of six sections (sections 679 to 684) imposing restrictions on corporation tax relief. The first four of these sections restrict reliefs given by CTA 2009, and are arranged in the order in which those reliefs appear in that Act. The fifth and sixth of those sections restrict relief for property business losses, and are arranged in the order in which those reliefs appear in Chapter 4 of Part 4 of this Act.

2112. Section 574 of CTA 2009 provides that non-trading credits and debits from derivative contracts are to be brought into account as if they were non-trading credits or non-trading debits for the purposes of Part 5 of CTA 2009 in respect of loan relationships of the company. The reference to that section in section 768B(10) of ICTA is otiose. *Subsection (1)* therefore omits it.

2113. *Subsections (2)* to *(4)* set out the consequences of the apportionment made under section 678.

2114. "Relevant non-trading debits" in subsections (2) and (3) translates "debitsfalling within paragraph 11 below" in paragraph 9(2) of Schedule 28A to ICTA. *Subsection (5)* tells the reader where this expression is defined.

*Section 680: **Restriction on the carry forward of non-trading deficit from loan relationships***

2115. This section restricts relief for the company's non-trading deficit on its loan relationships in cases in which this Chapter applies. It is based on section 768B of, and paragraph 9A of Schedule 28A to, ICTA.

2116. Debits and deficits have different functions in the loan relationships regime, therefore this Chapter imposes different restrictions on them.

2117. Section 574 of CTA 2009 provides that non-trading credits and debits from derivative contracts are to be brought into account as if they were non-trading credits or non-trading debits for the purposes of Part 5 of CTA 2009 in respect of loan relationships of the company. The reference to that section in section 768B(10) of ICTA is otiose. *Subsection (1)* therefore omits it.

*Section 681: **Restriction on relief for non-trading loss on intangible fixed assets***

2118. This section restricts relief for the company's non-trading loss on its intangible fixed assets in cases in which this Chapter applies. It is based on section 768E of ICTA.

2119. *Subsection (3)* corrects a drafting error in section 768E(5) of ICTA. This is a minor change in the law. See *Change 49* in Annex 1. A similar correction is made in section 698(4).

*Section 682: **Restriction on the deduction of expenses of management***

2120. This section restricts relief for the company's expenses of management in cases in which this Chapter applies. It is based on section 768B of ICTA.

2121. In rewriting section 768B(6), *subsection (2)* inserts "as" before the second occurrence of "expenses of management", to correct a drafting slip in paragraph 3(3)(b) of Schedule 6 to FA 2004.

2122. Section 768B(7) and (9)(b) of ICTA are not rewritten. See the commentary on the amendments made to that section by Schedule 1.

*Section 683: **Disallowance of UK property business losses***

2123. This section restricts relief for the company's UK property business loss in cases in which this Chapter applies. It is based on section 768D of ICTA.

*Section 684: **Disallowance of overseas property business losses***

2124. This section restricts relief for the company's overseas property business loss in cases in which this Chapter applies. It is based on section 768D of ICTA.

2125. Section 768D(9) of ICTA has to be read as implying that, in a case in which section 768D applies in relation to an overseas property business, references to section 392A of ICTA have to be read as references to the corresponding provisions of section 392B of ICTA. Otherwise section 768D of ICTA applies in such a case but does not actually do anything. This section therefore refers to section 66, which is based on section 392B of ICTA.

2126. Section 768D(5) of ICTA can have no application in relation to an overseas property business, and is therefore not rewritten in this section.

*Section 685: **Apportionment of amounts***

2127. This section stipulates how various amounts are to be apportioned for the purposes of this Chapter. It is based on section 768E of, and paragraphs 6, 7 and 8 of Schedule 28A to, ICTA.

2128. The source legislation obliges the reader to tally sub-paragraphs of paragraph 6 of Schedule 28A to ICTA with sub-paragraphs of paragraph 7(1) of that Schedule. This is inconvenient, as the sub-paragraphs are not always in one-to-one correspondence and the legislation has been amended several times. Paragraphs 6 and 7(1) of that Schedule have therefore been rewritten in *subsection (2)* as a two-column table.

2129. Detailed comments on the table are given below.

Row	*Origin*
1 and 2	Paragraphs 6(da) and 7(1)(c) of Schedule 28A to ICTA. In rows 1 and 2, the opportunity has been taken to deal with profits and deficits separately.
3	Paragraphs 6(db) and 7(1)(d)(i) and (e)(i) of Schedule 28A to ICTA.
4	Paragraphs 6(dc) and 7(1)(b) of Schedule 28A to ICTA.
5	Paragraphs 6(de) and 7(1)(g) of Schedule 28A to ICTA.
6	Paragraphs 6(df) and 7(1)(h) of Schedule 28A to ICTA.
7	Paragraphs 6(a) and 7(1)(a) of Schedule 28A to ICTA.
–	Paragraphs 6(b) and 7(1)(aa) of Schedule 28A to ICTA are repealed as obsolete. See the commentary on the amendments made to section 768B of ICTA by Schedule 1.
8	Paragraphs 6(c) and 7(1)(b) of Schedule 28A to ICTA.
9	Paragraphs 6(d) and 7(1)(c) of Schedule 28A to ICTA.
10	Paragraphs 6(e) and 7(1)(c) of Schedule 28A to ICTA.

2130. In rewriting paragraph 8 of Schedule 28A to ICTA, *subsection (3)* omits both instances of "appears". See the commentary on section 674.

Section 686: Meaning of certain expressions in section 685

2131. This interpretative section is based on paragraphs 6, 6A and 7 of Schedule 28A to ICTA. The subsections of this section are arranged in the order of the rows to which they refer in the table in section 685(2).

Section 687: Adjustment to balancing charges if relief is restricted

2132. This section prevents double taxation in certain cases within sections 679, 680 and 682. It is based on sections 768 and 768B of ICTA.

2133. This section has the same function in this Chapter as section 675 has in Chapter 2. See the commentary on that section.

2134. Section 574 of CTA 2009 provides that non-trading credits and debits from derivative contracts are to be brought into account as if they were non-trading credits or non-trading debits for the purposes of Part 5 of that Act in respect of loan relationships of the company. The reference to that section in section 768B(13) of ICTA is otiose. *Subsection (2)* therefore omits it.

2135. Section 768(6) and (7) of ICTA use the expression "allowance or deduction". Since "or deduction" adds nothing to "allowance", *subsections (4)* to *(6)* omit "or deduction" as otiose.

Section 688: Meaning of "significant increase in the amount of a company's capital"

2136. This section is the first of a group of four sections which together define "significant increase in the amount of a company's capital" for the purposes of condition A in section 677(2). It is based on paragraphs 1 and 2 of Schedule 28A to ICTA.

Sections 689 and 690: Amount A; amount B

2137. Theseinterpretative sectionsare based on paragraphs 3 and 4 of Schedule 28A to ICTA.

Section 691: ***Meaning of "amount of capital"***

2138. This interpretative section is based on paragraph 5 of Schedule 28A to ICTA.

2139. In paragraph 5(1) of Schedule 28A to ICTA, "the capital of a company" has to be read as "the amount of the capital of a company". Otherwise, in paragraph 3(1) of that Schedule, "the amount of the company's capital" has to be read as "the amount of the aggregate of (a) the amount of …". *Subsection (2)* makes this clear.

2140. Paragraph 5(3) of Schedule 28A to ICTA provides for amounts of capital to be rounded up to the nearest pound.*Subsection (4)* omits this requirement because it has no practical effect.

Chapter 4: ***Company with investment business: restrictions on relief: asset transferred within group***

Overview

2141. Chapter 4 is the third of four Chapters dealing with various kinds of loss buying. It rewrites section 768C of ICTA and the corresponding provisions of sections 768D and 768E of ICTA.

2142. Section 768C of ICTA was inserted by FA 1995 to block the following scheme. A company is about to realise a chargeable gain on an asset. The company purchases a company with excess management expenses. Relief for these is not restricted by section 768B of ICTA, because the conditions in section 768B(1)(a) to (c) are not met. The asset is transferred to the newly purchased company at no gain/no loss under section 171 of TCGA. When the transferee company disposes of the asset and crystallises the chargeable gain, it can use its pre-acquisition management expenses to shelter the gain.

2143. Sections 768D and 768E of ICTA (inserted by FA 1998 and FA 2002 respectively) included provisions corresponding to section 768C to cover pre-acquisition property losses and pre-acquisition non-trading losses on intangible fixed assets: see sections 768D(1)(a)(ii) and 768E(1)(b).

2144. Section 768C(13) (inserted by FA 2002) extended section 768C to cover tax-neutral intra-group transfers of intangible fixed assets.

2145. Chapter 4 is similar in many respects to Chapter 3, but there are important differences of detail because, unlike Chapter3, Chapter 4 needs to cater for chargeable gains and realisation gains on intangible fixed assets.

2146. Chapter 4 has the following structure.

- Sections 692 to 694 lay down the conditions for the Chapter to apply and define some key terms.
- If the Chapter applies, section 695 (notional split of accounting period in which change in ownership occurs) sets the stage. It splits the period in which the change in ownership occurs into two notional accounting periods, and indicates that certain amounts need to be apportioned between these two periods.
- Sections 696 to 701 are a group of six sections restricting various kinds of corporation tax relief. If, having reviewed them, the reader is satisfied that in the case under review these sections makes no practical difference, the reader is able to conclude that there is in practice no need to make the apportionments required by section 695.
- Sections 702 and 703 contain the detailed rules for making apportionments of amounts for the purposes of this Chapter.

*Section 692: **Introduction to Chapter***

2147. This section introduces the Chapter. It is based on sections 768C, 768Dand 768E of ICTA. If, having read this section, the reader is satisfied that the conditions for this Chapter to apply are not all met, the reader need read no further in this Chapter.

2148. *Subsections (1)* to *(4)* lay down the conditions for the Chapter to apply.

2149. Subsection (1) is based on, among other things, section 768D(1)(a)(ii) of ICTA. Unlike section 768D(1) of ICTA, subsection (1) does not refer to a change in the ownership of a company carrying on a UK property business; it refers to a change in the ownership of a company with investment business. The reason is that, if section 768D(1)(a)(ii) of ICTA applies, then:

- There is a change in the ownership of a company carrying on a UK property business (see the opening words of section 768D(1)); and
- The company whose ownership has changed is a company with investment business (see the opening words of section 768D(1)(a)).

2150. Accordingly, if section 768D(1)(a)(ii) of ICTA applies, there is by implication a change in the ownership of a company with investment business. There is therefore no need for section 768D(1)of ICTA to pick up the opening words of section 768B of that Act.

2151. *Subsections (5)* and *(6)* supplement subsection (4).

2152. *Subsection (7)* defines "the change in ownership", "the company", "non-trading chargeable realisation gain" and "the relevant gain" for the purposes of this Chapter.

*Section 693: **Meaning of "amount of profits which represents a relevant gain"***

2153. This interpretative section is based on section 768C of ICTA.

*Section 694: **Meaning of "the relevant provisions"***

2154. This interpretative section is based on section 768C of, and paragraph 13 of Schedule 28A to, ICTA.

2155. *Paragraph (a)* refers to section 8(1) of TCGA, which provides (in summary) that the chargeable gains included in a company's total profits are its chargeable gains after deducting allowable losses. Paragraph (a) also refers to Schedule 7A to that Act. That Schedule is directed against another kind of loss buying, namely the purchase of allowable losses for the purposes of corporation tax on chargeable gains. In summary, if that Schedule bites, relief for allowable losses is restricted to the extent that (1) they accrued before the company joined the relevant group and (2) they cannot be deducted from chargeable gains accruing before that date. Defining "the relevant provisions" in this way ensures that Schedule 7A to TCGA is applied before the provisions of this Chapter are applied.

2156. The concept of "the relevant provisions" is used, in particular, in row 1 in the table in section 702(2).

2157. In a case in which section 768C of ICTA applies in relation to an asset to which Part 8 of CTA 2009 (intangible fixed assets) applies, section 768C(13)(d) of ICTA applies not only to section 768C(12) of that Act but also to paragraph 13(2) of Schedule 28A to that Act.

*Section 695: **Notional split of accounting period in which change in ownership occurs***

2158. This section deems the accounting period in which the change in ownership occurs to be split into two notional accounting periods for the purposes of this Chapter. It is based on sections 768C, 768D and 768E of ICTA.

2159. *Subsection (3)* requires amounts for the actual accounting period to be apportioned between the two notional accounting periods in accordance with section 702.

*Section 696: **Restriction on debits to be brought into account***

2160. This section restricts debits on the company's loan relationships in cases in which this Chapter applies. It is based on section 768C of, and paragraph 10 of Schedule 28A to, ICTA.

2161. This section is the first of a group of six sections (sections 696 to 701) imposing restrictions on corporation tax relief. The first four of these sections restrict reliefs given by CTA 2009, and are arranged in the order in which those reliefs appear in that Act. The fifth and sixth of these sections restrict relief for property losses, and are arranged in the order in which those reliefs appear in Chapter 4 of Part 4 of this Act.

2162. *Subsection (1)* states the purpose of the section.

2163. Section 574 of CTA 2009 provides that non-trading credits and debits from derivative contracts are to be brought into account as if they were non-trading credits or non-trading debits for the purposes of Part 5 of CTA 2009 in respect of loan relationships of the company. The reference to that section in section 768C(9) of ICTA is therefore otiose. Subsection (1) therefore omits it.

2164. *Subsection (2)* limits the scope of the section to cases in which gains arise or accrue as discussed in the 'overview' paragraphs of thecommentary on this Chapter. Its inclusion here emphasises the point that the section only makes a difference in practice if there are *both* debits to be restricted *and* a gain to be sheltered by those debits.

2165. *Subsections (3)* to *(5)* set out the consequences of the apportionment made in accordance with section 702.

2166. The other five sections in this group have a similar structure.

*Section 697: **Restriction on the carry forward of non-trading deficit from loan relationships***

2167. This section restricts relief for the company's non-trading deficit on its loan relationships in cases in which this Chapter applies. It is based on section 768C of, and paragraph 10A of Schedule 28A to, ICTA.

2168. Debits and deficits have different functions in the loan relationships regime, therefore this Chapter imposes different restrictions on them.

*Section 698: **Restriction on relief for non-trading loss on intangible fixed assets***

2169. This section restricts relief for the company's non-trading loss on its intangible fixed assets in cases in which this Chapter applies. It is based on section 768E of ICTA.

2170. *Subsection (2)* makes it clear that section 768E(5)(b) of ICTA refers to section 768C(6) of that Act by implication. This clarification is a minor change in the law: see *Change 50* in Annex 1.

2171. *Subsections (4)*and *(5)* include a minor change in the law. See *Change 49* in Annex 1 and the commentary on section 681.

Section 699: ***Restrictions on the deduction of expenses of management***

2172. This section restricts relief for the company's expenses of management in cases in which this Chapter applies. It is based on section 768C of ICTA.

2173. *Subsection (4)* only operates on *subsection (5)*. The corresponding provision in the other sections in this group operates, in each case, on the whole section.

Section 700: ***Disallowance of UK property business losses***

2174. This section restricts relief for the company's UK property business loss in cases in which this Chapter applies. It is based on section 768D of ICTA.

2175. *Subsection (2)* makes it clear that section 768D(6)(b) of ICTA refers by implication to section 768C(6) of that Act. This clarification is a minor change in the law: see *Change 50* in Annex 1.

Section 701: ***Disallowance of overseas property business losses***

2176. This section restricts relief for the company's overseas property business loss in cases in which this Chapter applies. It is based on section 768D of ICTA.

2177. Section 768D(9) of ICTA has to be read as implying that, in a case in which section 768D of ICTA applies in relation to an overseas property business, references to section 392A of ICTA have to be read as references to the corresponding provisions of section 392B of that Act. Otherwise section 768D of that Act applies in such a case but does not actually do anything. *Subsections (1)* and *(3)* therefore refer to section 66, which is based on section 392B of ICTA.

2178. *Subsection (2)* includes a minor change in the law. See *Change 50* in Annex 1 and the commentary on section 700.

Section 702: ***Apportionment of amounts***

2179. This section stipulates how various amounts are to be apportioned for the purposes of this Chapter. It is based on sections 768C and 768E of, and paragraphs 13 to 17 of Schedule 28A to, ICTA.

2180. The source legislation obliges the reader to tally sub-paragraphs of paragraph 13(1) of Schedule 28A to ICTA with sub-paragraphs of paragraphs 15 and 16(1) of that Schedule. This is inconvenient, as the sub-paragraphs are not always in one-to-one correspondence and the legislation has been amended several times. Paragraphs 13(1), 15 and 16(1) of that Schedule have therefore been rewritten in *subsection (2)* as a two-column table.

2181. Detailed comments on the table are given below.

Row	***Origin***
1	*Paragraphs 13(1)(a) and 15 of Schedule 28A to ICTA.*
2 and 3	*Paragraphs 13(1)(ea) and 16(1)(c) of that Schedule. The opportunity has been taken to deal with profits and deficits separately.*
4	*Paragraphs 13(1)(eb) and 16(1)(d) and (e) of that Schedule.*
5	*Paragraphs 13(1)(ec) and 16(1)(b) of that Schedule.*
6	*Paragraphs 13(1)(ee) and 16(1)(g) of that Schedule.*
7	*Paragraphs 13(1)(ef) and 16(1)(h) of that Schedule.*
8	*Paragraphs 13(1)(b) and 16(1)(a) of that Schedule.*

Row	*Origin*
–	*Paragraphs 13(1)(c) and 16(1)(aa) of that Schedule are repealed as obsolete. See the commentary on the amendments made to section 768B of ICTA by Schedule 1.*
9	*Paragraphs 13(1)(d) and 16(1)(b) of Schedule 28A.*
10	*Paragraphs 13(1)(e) and 16(1)(c) of that Schedule.*
11	*Paragraphs 13(1)(f) and 16(1)(c) of that Schedule.*

Section 703: Meaning of certain expressions in section 702

2182. This interpretative sectionis based on paragraphs 13, 13A and 16 of Schedule 28A to ICTA.

Chapter 5: Company without investment business: disallowance of property losses

Overview

2183. Chapter 5 is the fourth of four Chapters dealing with various kinds of loss buying.

Section 704: Company carrying on UK property business

2184. This section restricts relief for UK property losses in cases in which this Chapter applies. It is based on section 768D of ICTA.

2185. *Subsections (1)* to *(3)* lay down the conditions for the section to apply.

2186. *Subsection (4)* states the purpose of the section. In subsection (4), "the company" has the meaning given by subsection (1).

2187. *Subsection (5)* deems the accounting period in which the change of ownership occurs to be two separate accounting periods. The profits or losses of the actual accounting period must then be apportioned to the two notional accounting periods in accordance with *subsections (6)* and *(7)*.

2188. *Subsections (8)* and *(9)* set out the consequences of this apportionment.

2189. *Subsection (10)* defines "major change in the nature or conduct of a trade or UK property business".

Section 705: Company carrying on overseas property business

2190. This section restricts relief for the company's overseas property business loss in cases in which this Chapter applies. It is based on section 768D of ICTA, and has a similar structure to section 704 of this Act.

2191. Section 768D(9) of ICTA has to be read as implying that, in a case in which section 768D applies in relation to an overseas property business, references to section 392A of ICTA have to be read as references to the corresponding provisions of section 392B of that Act. Otherwise section 768D of that Act applies in such a case but does not actually do anything. *Subsections (4)* and *(8)* therefore refer to section 66, which is based on section 392B of ICTA.

2192. Section 768D(5) of ICTA can have no application in relation to an overseas property business, and is therefore not rewritten in this section.

Chapter 6: Recovery of unpaid corporation tax

Overview

2193. This Chapter is based on sections 767A to 767B of ICTA.

2194. Sections 767A and 767B of ICTA were introduced by FA 1994 to counter the use of company purchase schemes to avoid the payment of corporation tax. In a typical case a profitable company is stripped of its trade or business, usually by way of transfer to another member of its group, leaving it only with sufficient cash to settle its outstanding corporation tax. The company is then sold – for a sum equivalent to a proportion of the tax outstanding – to a third party (often non-resident) who arranges for the company to participate in arrangements intended to eliminate the tax liability. On the assumption that the arrangements will be successful, the new owner then arranges for the cash to be withdrawn.

2195. If the avoidance arrangements are effective, the company has no corporation tax to pay. But if they are found to be ineffective, HMRC have little or no prospect of collecting the unpaid tax from the company, because the company is left with no funds. Sections 767A and 767B of ICTA enable HMRC to collect the unpaid corporation tax from a person linked with the company as mentioned in section 767A(2).

2196. Subsequently, alternative schemes were developed that attempted to find ways around sections 767A and 767B of ICTA. For example, as sections 767A and 767B of ICTA only applied to tax liabilities for accounting periods beginning before the change in ownership, the new schemes ensured that the tax liability crystallised in an accounting period beginning after that date. They did this by using provisions such as rollover relief that postponed the tax charge or other provisions that involved income or gains being taxed in periods other than that in which they accrued. Section 767AA of ICTA was introduced by FA 1998 to block such schemes. If it bites, HMRC can collect the unpaid corporation tax from a person linked with the company as mentioned in section 767AA(4).

2197. This Chapter has the following structure.

- Sections 706 to 709 define some key expressions for the purposes of the Chapter.
- Sections 710 to 712 enable HMRC to recover unpaid corporation tax for an accounting period beginning before the change in ownership. They are based on sections 767A and 767B of ICTA.
- Sections 713 to 715 enable HMRC to recover unpaid corporation tax for an accounting period ending on or after the change in ownership. They are based on section 767AA of ICTA.
- Sections 716 to 718 are miscellaneous provisions.

Section 706: Meaning of "linked" person

2198. This interpretative section explains when a person is "linked" to a company for the purposes of this Chapter. It is based on sections 767A and 767AA of ICTA.

2199. If the statutory conditions are met, such a person may be assessed and charged to an amount of unpaid corporation tax under section 710(2) or, as the case may be, section 713(2).

Section 707: Meaning of "control"

2200. This interpretative section is based on section 767B of ICTA.

*Section 708: **Rights to be attributed for the purposes of section 707***

2201. This section supplements section 707. It is based on section 767B of ICTA.

*Section 709: **Meaning of "the relevant period"***

2202. This interpretative section is based on sections 767A and 767AA of ICTA.

2203. *Subsection (3)* makes an exception to the general rule laid down by *subsection (2)*. Suppose A sells a company to B without intending to avoid tax and B enters into a company purchase scheme with C: B may be liable under this Chapter but A may not. The rationale is that A can be expected to ensure, when selling the company to B, that B does not behave in a way which would trigger this Chapter, but A cannot be expected to ensure that B does not enter into arrangements with C whereby C triggers this Chapter. Subsection (3) begins "But if …" to make it clear that subsection(2) is subject to subsection (3).

*Section 710: **Recovery of unpaid corporation tax for accounting period beginning before change***

2204. This section enables an officer of Revenue and Customs to assess and charge a linked person to an amount of unpaid corporation tax for an accounting period beginning before the change in the ownership of a company. It is based on section 767A of ICTA.

2205. Section 767A(1) of ICTA gives this assessment function to "the Board", ie to the Commissioners for HMRC. In practice, the Commissioners delegate this function to officers of Revenue and Customs, and *subsections (1)* and *(2)* reflect this. This is a minor change in the law. See *Change 5* in Annex1. In practice, the administration of sections 767A and 767AA of ICTA and the provisions which supplement them is restricted to a specialist group of officers. *Change 5* has no effect on this practice.

2206. Like the source legislation, subsection (2) provides that "[a person]… *may* be assessed …". This gives officers the power, but not the obligation, to assess linked persons, and therefore allows HMRC to exercise managerial discretion.

*Section 711: **Conditions relating to company's trade or business***

2207. This section lists three conditions which relate to the company's trade or business; if none of these conditions is met, section 710 does not apply. This section is based on sections 767A and 767B of ICTA.

2208. The meaning of "connected" in *subsection (5)* is given by section 1176(1). Section 767B(9) of ICTA is therefore not rewritten as a separate proposition.

*Section 712: **Meaning of "a major change in the nature or conduct of a trade or business"***

2209. This interpretative section is based on section 767B of ICTA.

2210. Section 767B(7) of ICTA refers to section 245 of that Act. In repealing section 245 of ICTA, FA 1998 inadvertently omitted to make the necessary consequential amendment to section 767B(7) of ICTA.

2211. As it stood before its repeal, section 245(4)(a) of ICTA read:

"In subsection (1) above "a major change in the nature or conduct of a trade or business" includes –

(a) a major change in the type of property dealt in, or services or facilities provided, in the trade or business; or

(b) a major change in customers, outlets or markets of the trade or business; or

(c) a change whereby the company ceases to be a trading company and becomes an investment company or vice versa; or

(d) where the company is an investment company, a major change in the nature of the investments held by the company.

2212. Before its repeal, section 245(5) of ICTA defined "trading company" and "investment company" for the purposes of that section:

> ""trading company" means a company whose business consists wholly or mainly of the carrying on of a trade or trades and
>
> "investment company" means a company (other than a holding company) whose business consists wholly or mainly in the making of investments and the principal part of whose income is derived therefrom;
>
> "holding company" means a company whose business consists wholly or mainly in the holding of shares or securities of companies which are its 90 per cent subsidiaries and which are trading companies.

2213. Departmental practice in applying section 767B(7) of ICTA has not changed since 1998.

2214. If the repeal of section 245(4) of ICTA repealed section 767B(7) of that Act by implication, then it enabled the taxpayer to argue that a change which used to be mentioned in section 245(4) was not necessarily a major change in the nature or conduct of a trade or business.

2215. Section 245 of ICTA was one of a number of provisions repealed by Schedule 3 to FA 1998 as part of the abolition of advance corporation tax (ACT). It would be anomalous if, as part of the abolition of ACT, Parliament implicitly repealed section 767B(7) of ICTA and thereby weakened section 767A of that Act. It would be particularly anomalous if Parliament did this in FA 1998, since FA 1998 inserted section 767AA of ICTA to catch schemes which section 767A of that Act did not. In statutory interpretation, there is a presumption that Parliament wishes to avoid an anomalous result. Accordingly, the repeal of section 245 of ICTA did not by implication repeal section 767B(7) of that Act.

2216. Accordingly, this section draws on section 245 of ICTA (repealed) to rewrite section 767B(7) of ICTA.

Section 713: ***Recovery of unpaid corporation tax for accounting period ending on or after change***

2217. This section enables an officer of Revenue and Customs to assess and charge a linked person to an amount of unpaid corporation tax for an accounting period ending on or after the change in the ownership of a company. It is based on section 767AA of ICTA.

2218. Section 767AA(1) of ICTA gives this assessment function to "the Board", ie to the Commissioners for HMRC. In practice, the Commissioners delegate this function to officers of Revenue and Customs, and *subsections (1)* and *(2)* reflect this. This is a minor change in the law. See *Change 5* in Annex1. In practice, the administration of sections 767A and 767AA of ICTA and the provisions which supplement them is restricted to a specialist group of officers.*Change 5*has no effect on this practice.

2219. Like the source legislation, subsection (2) provides that "[a person]… *may* be assessed …". This gives officers the power, but not the obligation, to assess linked persons, and therefore allows HMRC to exercise managerial discretion.

2220. For the sake of consistency, subsection (1)(b) has been brought into line with section 710(1)(b).

Section 714: The expectation condition

2221. This section spells out the expectation condition mentioned in section 713(1)(d). It is based on section 767AA of ICTA.

2222. *Subsection (2)* omits as otiose "either or both of" in section 767AA(2) of ICTA.

2223. In *subsection (4)(a)*, the words in brackets warn the reader that "an associated company" is not necessarily the "associated company" mentioned in section 713(1)(b). Which company in a group has a corporation tax liability may depend on (for example) how the group allocates its group relief.

Section 715: Meaning of "transaction entered into in connection with change in ownership"

2224. This interpretative section is based on section 767AA of ICTA.

Section 716: Interest

2225. This section imposes interest on tax which has been assessed under section 710 or section 713 and is overdue. It is based on section 767B of ICTA.

Section 717: Effect of payment in pursuance of assessment under section 710 or713

2226. This section is about payments in pursuance of an assessment under section 710 or 713. It is based on section 767B of ICTA.

2227. *Subsection (1)* disallows such a payment. *Subsection (2)* gives the maker of such a payment a right of recovery.

Section 718: Meaning of "associated company"

2228. This interpretative sectionis based on section 767AA of ICTA.

Chapter 7: Meaning of "change in the ownership of a company"

Overview

2229. This Chapter defines "change in the ownership of a company" for the purposes of this Part. It applies both for the purposes of Chapters 2 to 5 (restriction of corporation tax reliefs) and for the purposes of Chapter 6 (recovery of unpaid corporation tax).

2230. This Chapter is based on section 769 of ICTA. Section 769 of ICTA does not expressly mention section 768E of that Act, but the references in section 769 of ICTA to sections 768B and 768C of that Act include by implication references to section 768E of that Act.

Section 719: Meaning of "change in the ownership of a company"

2231. This section gives the basic definition of "change in the ownership of a company" for the purposes of this Part of the Act. It is based on section 769 of ICTA.

2232. Section 769(1)(a) of ICTA is satisfied "if a single person acquires more than half the ordinary share capital of the company". This raises the question: is this a reference to acquiring:

- An additional holding (A);
- The existing holding (X);
- The total holding after the acquisition (T = A + X); or
- T, but only if X<50%?

2233. Section 769(1)(a) of ICTA cannot be read as referring to the acquisition of X. Otherwise, a person who held more than 50% of the ordinary share capital and did not acquire any more shares would "acquire more than half the ordinary share capital". As a matter of normal English usage, "acquires" cannot imply that.

2234. Section 769(1)(a) of ICTA cannot be read as referring to the acquisition of T, whether or not X<50%. According to Bramwell et al.[5]:

"If one person owns 50 per cent. of a company's shares and then buys 1 per cent. more, he does not thereby "acquire more than half" of the shares – he acquires 1 per cent. [Section 769(1)(b) and (c) of ICTA] refers to any number of persons acquiring holdings of shares that together amount to more than half of the ordinary shares in a company, but [section 769 (1)(c)] makes it clear that acquired holdings must be distinguished from existing holdings.

2235. Bramwell et al. are correct on this point, because:

- There is no indication that "acquire" has to have a different scope in section 769(1)(a) and (c) of ICTA;
- Since Parliament has not said "acquires *a total of* more than half the ordinary share capital" it is not legitimate for any such words to be read in; and
- Section 769(2)(b) of ICTA says "... may be regarded as having acquired a percentage holding *equal to the increase*" (emphasis added).

2236. The acquisition of "more than half the ordinary share capital" in section 769(1)(a) of ICTA is therefore a reference to the acquisition of the additional holding, A. Accordingly, to sharpen the drafting, *subsection (2)* expressly refers to the acquisition of "a holding of more than half the ordinary share capital".

2237. Section 769(1)(c) of ICTA says "less that 5 per cent".*Subsection (5)* corrects this typo.

Section 720: Section 719: supplementary

2238. This interpretative sectionis based on section 769 of ICTA.

2239. The meaning of "connected" in *subsection (4)* is given by section 1122, which is applied "for the purposes of this Act" by section 1176(1). Unlike section 769(2)(c) of ICTA, therefore, subsection (4) does not specifically apply the definition of "connected persons" in section 839 of that Act.

2240. Section 769(2)(d) of ICTA has the expression "under the will or on the intestacy *of a deceased person*". The words "*of a deceased person*" add nothing and so *subsection (5)* compresses that expression to "under a will or on intestacy".

Section 721: When things other than ordinary share capital may be taken into account: Chapters 2 to 5

2241. This section allows other interests in a company, such as voting power attaching to shares, to be taken into account in determining whether there has been a change in ownership. It applies in cases when applying the "ordinary share capital" test in section 719 would give anomalous results. It is based on section 769 of ICTA.

2242. Section 769(3) of ICTA uses the expression "under the articles of association or under any other document regulating the company". *Subsection (2)* compresses this to "under any document regulating the company".

2243. Section 769(3) of ICTA uses the old-fashioned term "enure". In response to representations, the term "enure" was retained in section 723(1) of ITA (transfer of

5 Bramwell et al. *Taxation of Companies and Company Reconstructions* (Thomson, Sweet & Maxwell, November 2002) paragraph A 9.2.7 footnote 3.

assets abroad: charge where power to enjoy income: enjoyment conditions). It has therefore also been retained in *subsection (3)*.

2244. Section 769(3) of ICTA uses the expression "all kinds of share capital, including preference shares". *Subsection (4)(a)* compresses this to "all kinds of share capital".

Section 722: When things other than ordinary share capital may be taken into account: Chapter 6

2245. In cases when applying the "ordinary share capital" test in section 719 would give anomalous results, this section allows other interests in a company, such as voting power attaching to shares, to be taken into account in determining whether there has been a change in ownership. It is based on section 769 of ICTA.

Section 723: Changes in indirect ownership

2246. This section extends the basic rule about changes in company ownership in section 719. It is based on section 769 of ICTA.

2247. The basic rule in section 719 only relates to the direct ownership of a company. It does not capture a change in the ultimate ownership of a company, so this section contains additional rules for groups of companies.

Section 724: Disregard of change in company ownership

2248. This section excludes certain changes in company ownership from the scope of Chapters 2 to 6. It is based on section 769 of ICTA.

Section 725: Provision applying for the purposes of Chapters 2 to 5

2249. This supplementary section is based on section 769 of ICTA.

2250. *Subsection (2)* is a "tie-breaker" provision, to deal with shareholdings being acquired piecemeal.

2251. *Subsections (3)* to *(6)* explain how the three-year maximum in section 720(2)is to be applied in cases involving (for example) options or contracts for future delivery.

Section 726: Interpretation of Chapter

2252. This interpretative section is based on section 769 of ICTA.

Chapter 8: Supplementary provision

Sections 727 to 730: Extended time limit for assessment; provision of information about ownership of shares etc; meaning of "company with investment business"; meaning of "relevant non-trading debit"

2253. Thesesections extend the time limit for assessments giving effect to the provisions of Chapters 2 to 6 of this Part of the Act, enable officers of Revenue and Customs to obtain information about the ownership of shares, stock and securities for the purposes of this Part, and define "company with investment business" and "relevant non-trading debit". They are based on sections 767B and 768 to 768E of,and paragraphs 11 and 12 of Schedule 28A to, ICTA.

Part 15: Transactions in securities

Overview

2254. This Part rewrites sections 703 to 705 and 707 to 709 of ICTA for the purposes of corporation tax.

2255. Sections 703 to 709 of ICTA were enacted as a wide-ranging anti-avoidance rule which would enable the Crown to counter all manner of devices to avoid tax involving transactions in shares or other securities or the manipulation of a company's assets or both, and to forestall the creation of such devices in future.

2256. Chapter 1 of Part 13 of ITA rewrote sections 703 to 709 of ICTA for the purposes of income tax, and paragraphs 154 to 161 of Schedule 1 to ITA consequentially amended those sections to apply solely for the purposes of corporation tax.

2257. This Part replicates Chapter 1 of Part 13 of ITA as far as possible. It differs from Chapter 1 of Part 13 of ITA in two respects.

2258. First, where this Part rewrites provisions of ICTA which are corporation tax specific there are no corresponding provisions in ITA. These are noted in detail in the commentary on section 735. In addition there are some provisions in ITA which are not reflected in this Part. Sections 703 to 709 of ICTA, as amended, do not include any provisions corresponding to sections 699 and 712 of ITA (limit on amount assessed in section 689 and 690 cases; application of Chapter where individual within section 684 dies), because these sections are income tax specific; accordingly, no such provisions appear in this Part.

2259. Second, where necessary this Part uses terminology specific to corporation tax where Chapter 1 of Part 13 of ITA uses terminology specific to income tax. For example, since persons other than companies are not liable to corporation tax, this Part uses the word "company" to refer to the taxpayer where Chapter 1 of Part 13 of ITA uses the word "person".

Sections 731 to 734: Overview of Part; meaning of "corporation tax advantage"; company liable to counteraction of corporation tax advantages; exception where no tax avoidance object shown

2260. These sections introduce the Part and provide definitions of "corporation tax advantage" and the company liable to counteraction. They are based on sections 703(1) and (2) and 709(1) and (2A) of ICTA.

2261. Except as noted in the Overview above, these sections replicate exactly sections 682 to 685 of ITA.

Section 735: Abnormal dividends used for exemptions or reliefs (circumstance A)

2262. This sectionis the first in a sequence of sections in which the sets of circumstances in section 704 of ICTA are laid out and expanded in five separate sections. It is based on sections 704 A and 709(3) of ICTA.

2263. This section is similar to section 686 of ITA. The main change is in *subsection (4)* wherethepurpose stated differs from those listed in section 686(4) of ITA to cater for the application of the section to companies.

2264. Section 704 A(a) to (c) of ICTA are no longer capable of having any practical effect for corporation tax purposes and are therefore not rewritten.

2265. To avoid confusion, this sequence of sections has been given the same titles as the corresponding provisions of Chapter 1 of Part 13 of ITA. There is accordingly no mention of "circumstance B", because section 704 B of ICTA was repealed by FA 2008.

Sections 736 to 738: Receipt of consideration representing company's assets, future receipts or trading stock (circumstance C); receipt of consideration in connection with relevant company distribution (circumstance D); receipt of assets of relevant company (circumstance E)

2266. These sections are based on sections 704 C, D and E and 709 of ICTA.

2267. Except as noted in the Overview above, these sections replicate exactly sections 688 to 690 of ITA.

Section 739: Meaning of "relevant company" in sections 737 and 738

2268. This section defines "relevant company" in the same way as section 691 of ITA. It is based on section 704 D of ICTA.

Section 740: Abnormal dividends: general

2269. This sectionis the first of three interpretative sections about abnormal dividends. It is based on section 709(4) of ICTA. This section and section 692 of ITA are identical.

2270. This section replaces the reference to "the Board" with a reference to "an officer of Revenue and Customs". See *Change 5* in Annex 1.

2271. HMRC internal procedures restrict the exercise of the Commissioners for HMRC' functions under Chapter 1 of Part 17 of ICTA to a small group of specialist officers. This change in the law has no effect on this practice.

Sections 741 and 742: Abnormal dividends: the excessive return condition and the excessive accrual condition

2272. These interpretative sections are based on section 709(4) to (6) of ICTA.

2273. Except as noted in the Overview above, these sections replicate exactly sections 693 and 694 of ITA.

Sections 743 to 746: Preliminary notification that section 733 may apply, opposed notifications and counteraction notices

2274. These sections are concerned with the procedure for counteraction of corporation tax advantages. They are based on sections 703(3), (9), (10) and (12) of ICTA. Apart from differences of the kind described in the Overview, they replicate sections 695 to 698 and 700 of ITA.

2275. Sections 743 to 746 replace references to "the Board" with references to "an officer of Revenue and Customs". See *Change 5* in Annex 1.

Sections 747 to 751: Timing of assessments in section 738 cases; application for clearance of transactions; effect of clearance notification under section 748; appeals against counteraction notices; interpretation of Part

2276. These sectionsmake a special rule for the timing of assessments in section 738 cases, provide a clearance procedure and deal with appeals against counteraction notices, and define certain expressions. They are based on sections 704 E(2) and (3), 705(1) and (5), 707 and 709(2) of ICTA.

2277. Except as noted in the Overview above, these sections replicate exactly sections 700 to 702, 705 and 713 of ITA.

Part 16: Factoring of income etc

Overview

2278. This Part rewrites sections 774A to 774G and 786 of ICTA (for the purposes of corporation tax) and paragraphs 1 to 6 of Schedule 25 to FA 2009.

2279. Chapter 1 of this Part (transfers of income streams) is based on paragraphs 1 to 6 of Schedule 25 to FA 2009. Chapter 2 of this Part (finance arrangements) is based on sections 774A to 774G of ICTA. Chapter 3 of this Part (loan or credit transactions) is based on section 786 of ICTA.

2280. Paragraph 7 of Schedule 25 to FA 2009 inserted Chapter 5A of Part 13 of ITA, which makes provision for income tax corresponding to Chapter 1 of this Part. Sections 774A to 774G and 786 of ICTA are rewritten for income tax purposes in Chapters 5B and 5C of Part 13 of ITA. These Chapters are inserted by Schedule 5 to TIOPA. See the commentary on that Schedule.

*Chapter 1: **Transfers of income streams***

Overview

2281. This Chapter is concerned with transfers of income streams. It is based on paragraphs 1 to 6 of Schedule 25 to FA 2009.

*Sections 752 to 757: **Application of Chapter; value of transferred income treated as income; exception: amount otherwise taxed; exception: transfer by way of security; partnership shares; interpretation***

2282. These sections are concerned with transfers of income streams. They are based on paragraphs 1 to 6 of Schedule 25 to FA 2009. They replicate the source legislation, except in two respects.

2283. First, the statutory references have been updated. In consequence, section 755 (exception: transfer by way of security) is worded differently from the source legislation, paragraph 4 of Schedule 25 to FA 2009. But it has the same effect.

2284. Second, section 757 (interpretation) omits the express Scottish modifications in the source legislation, paragraph 6 of Schedule 25 to FA 2009, because section 1166(1) provides that in the application of the Corporation Tax Acts to Scotland "assignment" means assignation and "surrender" includes renunciation.

*Chapter 2: **Finance arrangements***

Overview

2285. This Chapter is based on sections 774A to 774G to ICTA (structured finance arrangements). It stops a number of schemes which are intended to enable taxpayers to borrow money and obtain effective tax relief for both interest and repayment of principal.

2286. A "finance arrangement", within this Chapter, is an arrangement where in accordance with GAAP a person ("the borrower") records in its accounts a financial liability in respect of a sum ("advance") paid by "the lender", and that sum is paid to acquire assets (for example an incomestream), which will be used to repay the advance.

2287. Where there is a finance arrangement which would have had theeffect that either:

- income or receipts that would have been brought into account by the borrower for tax purposes, but for this arrangement, are not brought into account; or
- the borrower would have become entitled to a deduction incomputing its income or profits for tax purposes,

then

- the finance arrangement does not have that effect, with the result that the income from the transferred asset continues to be taxed on theborrower; and
- any disposal or reacquisition of the asset is disregardedfor the purposes of TCGA.

2288. Corporation tax relief is allowed for the amount of any interest or "finance charge" in respect of the finance agreement shown in theborrower's accounts. This amount is treatedas interest payable on a debtor loan relationship to which it is party.

2289. This Chapter has the following structure.

- Sections 758 to 762 deal with "type 1 finance arrangements": the simple case, not necessarily involving a partnership.
- Sections 763 to 766 deal with "type 2 finance arrangements": the first of two complex partnership cases.
- Sections 767 to 769 deal with "type 3 finance arrangements": the second of two complex partnership cases.
- Sections 770 to 773 make exceptions to these rules.
- Sections 774 to 776 are interpretative.

*Section 758: **Type 1 finance arrangement defined***

2290. This section defines a form of arrangement, labelled a "type 1 finance arrangement", which falls within this legislation. It is based on section 774A of ICTA.

2291. *Subsection (1)* provides that two conditions must be met if an arrangement is to be a type 1 finance arrangement.

2292. The word "arrangement" appears in subsection (1) for the first time in this Chapter. See section 775.

2293. *Subsection (2)* specifies condition A, which concerns the terms of the arrangement. There are three tests in condition A, all of which must be passed if the condition is to be met. To summarise:

- A borrower must "receive" an advance from a lender;
- the borrower (or a person "connected" with the borrower) must "dispose" of an asset (the security) to, or for the benefit of, a lender (or a person "connected" with the lender); and
- the lender (or a person "connected" with the lender) must be entitled to "payments in respect of" the security.

2294. An ordinary secured loan would not be a type 1 finance arrangement, because it would not satisfy subsection (2)(b) or, if it did, it would not satisfy subsection (2)(c).

2295. The first reference in this Chapter to a person receiving an asset is in subsection (2)(a). See section 776(2).

2296. Subsection (2)(b) is the first of a number of provisions in this Chapter which refer to persons being "connected". The meaning of "connected" in those provisionsis given by section 1176(1). Section 774G(4) of ICTA is therefore not rewritten as a separate proposition.

2297. The first reference in this Chapter to a disposal of an asset is in subsection(2)(b). See section 776(3).

2298. The first reference in this Chapter to payments in respect of an asset is in subsection (2)(c). See section 776(4).

2299. *Subsection (3)* specifies condition B, which is about accounting. To summarise, the payments mentioned in subsection (2)(c) must be, for accounting purposes, payments of principal rather than interest.

2300. The first reference in this Chapter to a person's accounts is in subsection(3)(a). See section 774(2) and (4).

2301. The first reference in this Chapter to an amount being recorded in accounts as a financial liability is in subsection (3)(a). See section 774(3).

Section 759: Certain tax consequences not to have effect

2302. This section disapplies certain tax consequences of a type 1 finance arrangement if certain conditions are met. It is based on sections 774A(4), 774B(1), (1A) and (2) to (4) and 774G(2) of ICTA.

2303. Under *subsections (1)* and *(2)*, if – but for this section – a type 1 finance arrangement would have the "relevant effect", then it does not.

2304. *Subsection (3)* defines the "relevant effect", and *subsection (4)* defines the "relevant effect" if the borrower is a partnership. Each of those subsections specifies three alternative effects.

Section 760: Payments treated as borrower's income

2305. This section treats the payments mentioned in section 758(2)(c) as income of the borrower. It is based on sections 774A(4), 774B(1) and (1B) to (3) and 774G(2) of ICTA.

2306. Under *subsection (1)*, this section only applies if:

- there is a type 1 finance arrangement;
- section 759(2) and the corresponding income tax provision do not stop this arrangement having the relevant effect because it would not have the relevant effect in the first place; and
- the borrower is either (a) a company within the charge to corporation tax or (b) a partnership at least one member of which is a company within the charge to corporation tax.

Section 761: Deemed loan relationship if borrower is a company

2307. This section brings the loan relationship provisions into play if there is a type 1 finance arrangement and the borrower is a company. It is based on section 774B(5), (7) and (8) of ICTA.

2308. If there is a type 1 finance arrangement and the borrower is a company, then either section 759 prevents it having the relevant effect in relation to the company, in which case *subsection (1)(c)(i)* applies this section, or else section 760 applies to the company, in which case *subsection (1)(c)(ii)* applies this section.

2309. *Subsection (2)* applies the loan relationship provisions of CTA 2009 to the company mentioned in subsection (1), deeming the advance to be a money debt owed by the company and the arrangement to be a debtor relationship of the company. "Money debt" and "debtor relationship" have the meanings given by, respectively, sections 303 and 302(6) of CTA 2009.

2310. Under *subsection (3)*, any finance charge recorded in the company's accounts is deemed to be interest payable under the deemed loan relationship.

2311. If subsection (3) deems there to be interest payable, *subsection (4)* determines when it is deemed to be paid.

Section 762: Deemed loan relationship if borrower is partnership with corporate member

2312. This section brings the loan relationship provisions into play if there is a type 1 finance arrangement and the borrower is a partnership with at least one corporate member. It is based on section 774B(5) to (8) of ICTA, and has a similar structure to section 761. See the commentary on that section.

Section 763: Type 2 finance arrangement defined

2313. This section defines a form of arrangement, labelled a "type 2 finance arrangement", which falls within this legislation. It is based on section 774C(1) to (3) of ICTA.

2314. A type 2 finance arrangement works like this.

- Under the arrangement, atransferor disposes of an asset to a partnership.
- This partnership is one of which the transferoris a member immediately after that disposal – it doesnot matter whether it was a partner before the disposal.
- The partnership receivesan advance from a lender.
- The accounts of the partnership record inaccordance with GAAP for that period a financial liability inrespect of the advance.
- There is a "relevant change" in relation to the partnership. Broadly speaking, a "relevant change" affects the lender. Either the lender (or a person connected with the lender) becomes a member of the partnership, or else there is a change in the profit share of the lender (or of a person connected with the lender). See section 764.
- The share of the lender (or other person involved in the relevant change) in the profits of the partnership is determined (wholly or partly) byreference to payments in respect of the asset disposed of.
- In accordance with GAAP the payments reduce the amount ofthe financial liability.

2315. The lender's advance is thus madein the form of a contribution to the partnership and its profit shareis such that payments are made to it which repay that contributiontogether with interest. Once the repayment with interest has beenmade it is likely that there are arrangements under which the lenderceases to be a member of the partnership or to share in the profitsof it.

2316. If the relevant change would (but for section 765) have the "relevant effect" (as defined in subsection (3) of that section), then that section negates the relevant effect.

2317. *Subsection (1)* provides that two conditions must be met if an arrangement is to be a type 2 finance arrangement.

2318. *Subsection (2)* specifies condition A, which concerns the terms of the arrangement. There are five tests in condition A, all of which must be passed if the condition is to be met.

2319. *Subsection (3)* specifies condition B, which is about accounting. To summarise, the payments mentioned in subsection (2)(e) must be, for accounting purposes, payments of principal rather than interest.

Section 764: Relevant change in relation to partnership

2320. This section defines "relevant change". It is based on section 774C(2), (4), (6) and (7) of ICTA.

2321. This section applies for the purposes of this Chapter and, therefore, is used in defining both "type 2 finance arrangement" and "type 3 finance arrangement". See sections 763(2)(d) and 767(2)(c).

2322. *Subsection (5)* defines "person involved in a relevant change" for the purposes of this Chapter.

Section 765: Certain tax consequences not to have effect

2323. This section disapplies certain tax consequences of a type 2 finance arrangement if certain conditions are met. It is based on sections 774D(1) to (4) and 774G(2) of ICTA.

2324. Under *subsections (1)* and *(2)*, if – but for this section – a relevant change in relation to the partnership would have the "relevant effect", then it does not.

2325. *Subsection (3)* defines the "relevant effect". It specifies three alternative effects.

Section 766: Deemed loan relationship

2326. This section brings the loan relationship provisions into play if there is a type 2 finance arrangement. It is based on section 774D(7), (8), (12) and (13) of ICTA.

2327. *Subsection (2)* has the effect of deeming a loan relationship to exist for the purposes of Part 5 of CTA 2009. The wording of subsection (2) chimes with the definition of "loan relationship" in section 302(1) of CTA 2009 to define a loan relationship. See also Chapter 9 of Part 5 of CTA 2009 (loan relationships: partnerships involving companies).

2328. Under *subsection (3)*, any finance charge recorded in respect of the advance in the partnership's accounts is deemed to be interest payable under the deemed loan relationship.

2329. If subsection (3) deems there to be interest payable, *subsection (5)* determines when it is deemed to be paid.

Section 767: Type 3 finance arrangement defined

2330. This section defines a form of arrangement, labelled a "type 3 finance arrangement", which falls within this legislation. It is based on section 774C(1), (4) and (5) of ICTA.

2331. A type 3 finance arrangement is similar to a type 2 finance arrangement. See the commentary on section 763. A type 3 finance arrangement, however, deals with a casewhere an existing partnership enters into an arrangement underwhich the lender becomes a partner and shares in the profits to anextent sufficient to repay its contribution with interest. It differsfrom a type 2 finance arrangement in that (a) the partnership cannot be one formed for the purposes of the arrangement and (b) there is no reference to a transfer of an asset or a transferor.

2332. *Subsection (1)* provides that two conditions must be met if an arrangement is to be a type 3 finance arrangement.

2333. *Subsection (2)* specifies condition A, which concerns the terms of the arrangement. There are four tests in condition A, all of which must be passed if the condition is to be met.

2334. *Subsection (3)* specifies condition B, which is about accounting. To summarise, the payments mentioned in subsection (2)(d) must be, for accounting purposes, payments of principal rather than interest.

2335. Conditions A and B in this section are very similar to conditions A and B in section 763 (type 2 finance arrangement defined). For the provisions which differ, see sections 763(2)(a) and (b) and 767(2)(a).

Section 768: Certain tax consequences not to have effect

2336. This section disapplies certain tax consequences of a type 3 finance arrangement if certain conditions are met. It is based on sections 774D(1) to (4) and 774G(2) of ICTA.

2337. Under *subsections (1)* and *(4)*, if – but for this section – a relevant change in relation to the partnership would have the "relevant effect", then it does not.

2338. *Subsection (2)* defines the "relevant effect". It specifies three alternative effects. The "relevant effect" in subsection (2) is very similar to the "relevant effect" in section 765(3), which makes corresponding provision for type 2 finance arrangements. But the "relevant effect" in subsection (2) is an effect on a "relevant member" (as defined in *subsection (3)*), whereas the "relevant effect" in section 765(3) is an effect in relation to the transferor.

*Section 769: **Deemed loan relationship***

2339. This section brings the loan relationship provisions into play if there is a type 3 finance arrangement. It is based on section 774D(3) and (10) to (13) of ICTA.

2340. This section is very similar to section 766. But this section focuses on a "relevant member" (as defined in *subsection (6)*), whereas section 766 focuses on the transferor.

*Section 770: **Exceptions: preliminary***

2341. This section introduces a group of sections which make exceptions to sections 758 to 769. It is new.

*Section 771: **Exceptions***

2342. This section specifies exceptions to sections 758 to 769. It is based on section 774E(1) to (6) of ICTA.

2343. *Subsection (6)* refers to Part 10A of ITA (alternative finance arrangements), which is inserted by Schedule 2 to TIOPA and is based on Chapter 5 of Part 2 of FA 2005.

*Section 772: **Exceptions: relevant person***

2344. This section defines "relevant person" for the purposes of section 771. It is based on section 774E(7) of ICTA.

2345. Section 774E of ICTA contains priority rules which prevent sections 774B and 774D of ICTA applying if other tax enactments apply. The definition of "relevant person" in section 774E(7) of ICTA interprets the references to a relevant person in section 774E(1) and (3) of ICTA. The wider the meaning of "relevant person", the more likely it is that section 774E(1) and (3) of ICTA disapply the anti-avoidance rules in sections 774B and 774D of ICTA. The only possibly uncertain element of the meaning of "relevant person" is the reference to a person connected with the borrower. Section 774G(4) of ICTA provides that the definition of "connected" in section 839 of ICTA applies "for the purposes of sections 774A to 774D". It is not clear whether the use of "connected" in section 774E(7) of ICTA can be said to be "for the purposes of sections 774A to 774D". But it is at any rate clear that section 774E only operates effectively as a priority rule if, at the very least, the reference in section 774E(7) of ICTA to persons connected with the borrower includes all persons who as a result of section 839 of ICTA would be treated as connected to the borrower. Whether the reference goes (or needs to go) wider than that group is open to argument. The inclusive definition in *subsection (5)* preserves the scope for making that argument while giving the maximum possible certainty.

*Section 773: **Power to make further exceptions***

2346. This section enables the Treasury to make further exceptions to sections 758 to 769. It is based on section 774F of ICTA.

*Sections 774 to 776: **Accounts; arrangements; assets***

2347. These interpretative sections are based on section 774G(1), (3) and (5) to (6) of ICTA.

Chapter 3: Loan or credit transactions

Overview

2348. This Chapter is based on section 786 of ICTA. It deals with certain loan or credit transactions.

Section 777: Loan or credit transaction defined

2349. This section defines "loan or credit transaction" for the purposes of sections 778 and 779. It is based on section 786(1) and (2) of ICTA.

2350. What is now section 786 of ICTA originally appeared as paragraph 12 of Schedule 13 to FA 1969. It is aimed at artificial arrangements for dressing up payments of interest in another form – for example, arrangements whereby X grants Y an interest-free loan and:

- Y grants X an annuity while the loan is outstanding; or
- Y transfers income-bearing assets to X on the understanding that X will return them when the loan is paid off.

2351. *Subsection (1)* states the scope of the definition.

2352. *Subsections (2)* and *(3)* focus on, respectively, the lending of money and the giving of credit.

2353. *Subsections (4)* and *(5)* supplement subsections (2) and (3) respectively.

Section 778: Certain payments treated as interest

2354. This section deems annual payments under loan or credit transactions to be interest. It is based on section 786(3) and (3A) of ICTA.

2355. For corporation tax purposes, the word "annual" adds nothing to the sense of "annual interest" in section 786(3) of ICTA. It is therefore not rewritten in *subsection (2)*.

Section 779: Tax charged on income transferred

2356. This section imposes a charge to corporation tax in certain cases in which, under a loan or credit transaction, a company transfers income arising from property without a sale or transfer of the property. It is based on section 786(5) to (7) of ICTA.

2357. *Subsection (1)* states when this section applies.

2358. *Subsection (2)* imposes the charge to corporation tax on income and quantifies the amount taxable.

2359. *Subsections (3)* to *(7)* are supplementary.

Part 17: Manufactured payments and repos

Overview

2360. This Part contains provisions about stock lending and other transactions in the financial markets giving rise to manufactured payments. It is based on sections 231AA, 231AB, 254 and 736B of, and Schedule 23A to, ICTA, sections 263B and 263C of TCGA, section 139 of FA 2006 and paragraph 30 of Schedule 17 to that Act.

2361. Manufactured payments normally arise under stock loan and repo agreements, but they may also occur if there has been a short sale of securities. A short sale is a sale of securities by someone who does not own the securities at the time of selling them, so is required to acquire them at a time between the date of the bargain and the date when the seller has to deliver them to the purchaser. Dealers may sell short for a variety of reasons. For example, dealers may expect the market price of the securities to fall between the time of the sale bargain and the time at which they expect to buy and so may choose to delay acquiring securities.

2362. A consequence of short selling can be that the dealer sells the securities cum-div (with dividend) but buys them ex-div (without dividend – leaving the right to the next dividend with the seller). The dealer pays the buyer a sum as compensation for the dividend that the buyer expected to receive, but did not. This sum is a manufactured payment.

2363. Many of the detailed rules, especially as regards manufactured overseas dividends (MODs), are laid down in regulations. This Act does not rewrite any of these regulations.

Chapter 1: Introduction

Section 780: Overview of Part

2364. This section gives an overview of the Part. It is new.

Section 781: Key definitions

2365. This interpretative section is based on sections 231AA and 231AB of ICTA, paragraphs 2 and 4 of Schedule 23A to that Act and section 139 of FA 2006.

2366. The key expressions "manufactured dividend" and "manufactured overseas dividend" are defined at the beginning of, respectively, Chapters 2 (manufactured dividends) and 3 (manufactured overseas dividends). This section applies those definitions throughout the Part.

2367. As noted in section 780(4), Part-wide definitions are located in Chapter 6.

Chapter 2: Manufactured dividends

Overview

2368. This Chapter is concerned with:

- the taxability of manufactured dividends in the hands of the recipient (or, if different, the owner);
- tax relief for the payer of manufactured dividends; and
- taxes management.

Section 782: Meaning of "manufactured dividend"

2369. This interpretative section is based on paragraph 2 of Schedule 23A to ICTA and section 139 of FA 2006.

2370. The expression "UK shares" is used in this section for the first time in this Part. It is defined in section 814.

Section 783: Treatment of payer of manufactured dividend

2371. This section gives corporation tax relief for the payer of a manufactured dividend. It is based on paragraphs 2(1A) to (1F) of Schedule 23A to ICTA.

2372. Paragraph 2(1C) of Schedule 23A to ICTA envisages that a particular manufactured dividend may relate both to a trade carried on by the dividend manufacturer and to life assurance business carried on by the dividend manufacturer. *Subsection (4)* makes it clear that the words about paragraph 2(1E) in paragraph 2(1C) are intended to exclude relief under paragraph 2(1C) only so far as relief is given under paragraph 2(1E). This drafting clarification does not change the law.

*Section 784: **Treatment of recipient of manufactured dividends***

2373. This section deals with the corporation tax treatment, in the hands of the recipient (or, if different, the owner), of a manufactured dividend. It is based on paragraph 2 of Schedule 23A to ICTA.

*Section 785: **Treatment of payer: Real Estate Investment Trusts***

2374. This section gives corporation tax relief for the payer of a manufactured dividend, to the extent that it is representative of a dividend (a property income dividend or PID) paid by a company UK REIT or by the principal company of a group UK REIT. It is based on section 139 of FA 2006 and paragraph 30 of Schedule 17 to that Act.

*Section 786: **Treatment of recipient: Real Estate Investment Trusts***

2375. This section deals with the corporation tax treatment of a manufactured dividend, in the hands of the recipient (or, if different, the owner), to the extent that the manufactured dividend is representative of a PID. It is based on section 139 of FA 2006 and paragraph 30 of Schedule 17 to that Act.

*Section 787: **Exemption of manufactured dividends***

2376. This section provides that a manufactured dividend is exempt from corporation tax to the extent that the dividend of which it is representative is (or would be) so exempt. It is based on paragraph 2(3A) and (3B) of Schedule 23A to ICTA.

*Section 788: **Statements about manufactured dividends***

2377. This section imposes an obligation on the payer of a manufactured dividend to give the recipient a statement setting out information which may be relevant for tax purposes. It is based on paragraph 2 of Schedule 23A to ICTA and section 139 of, and paragraph 30 of Schedule 17 to, FA 2006.

*Section 789: **Powers about administrative provisions***

2378. This section is a general regulation-making power about manufactured dividends. It is based on paragraph 8 of Schedule 23A to ICTA.

*Chapter 3: **Manufactured overseas dividends***

2379. This Chapter is concerned with:

- the taxability of MODs in the hands of the recipient (or, if different, the owner);
- tax relief for the payer of MODs; and
- taxes management.

*Section 790: **Meaning of "manufactured overseas dividend"***

2380. This interpretative section is based on paragraph 4 of Schedule 23A to ICTA.

2381. The expressions "overseas dividend" and "overseas securities" are used in *paragraph (a)* for the first time in this Part. They are defined in section 814.

*Section 791: **Treatment of payer of manufactured overseas dividend***

2382. This section deals with the corporation tax treatment of a payer of MODs. It is based on paragraph 4 of Schedule 23A to ICTA.

Section 792: Company receiving manufactured overseas dividend from UK resident etc

2383. This section deals with the corporation tax treatment of MODs in the hands of the recipient (or, if different, the owner) when tax has been deducted under section 922(1) of ITA. It is based on paragraph 4 of Schedule 23A to ICTA.

2384. The expression "gross amount of the manufactured overseas dividend" is used in *subsection (3)(a)* for the first time in this Part. It is defined in section 813.

2385. The expression "overseas tax" is used in *subsection (3)(b)* for the first time in this Part. It is defined in section 814.

Section 793: Section 792: amount treated as withheld

2386. This section quantifies the amount treated as withheld under section 792(3)(b). It is based on paragraph 4A of Schedule 23A to ICTA.

2387. *Subsection (2)* refers to section 925A of ITA, which is based on paragraph 13 of Schedule 13 to FA 2007 and is inserted by Schedule 7 to TIOPA.

Section 794: Company receiving manufactured overseas dividend from foreign payer

2388. This section deals with the corporation tax treatment of MODs in the hands of the recipient (or, if different, the owner) when tax has been accounted for and paid under section 923(1) of ITA. It is based on paragraph 4 of Schedule 23A to ICTA.

Section 795: Exemption of manufactured overseas dividends

2389. This section provides that a MOD is exempt from corporation tax to the extent that the overseas dividend of which it is representative is (or would be) so exempt. It is based on paragraph 4 of Schedule 23A to ICTA.

Chapter 4: Further provision about manufactured payments

Overview

2390. This Chapter makes further provision about manufactured payments. The detailed structure of the Chapter is as follows:

- Sections 796 to 798 – manufactured payments exceeding, or less than, underlying payments;
- Sections 799 to 801 – manufactured payments under arrangements with unallowable purpose;
- Sections 802 to 804 – miscellaneous.

Sections 796 and 797: Manufactured dividends and manufactured overseas dividends: amounts exceeding underlying payments

2391. These sections deal with cases in which an amount paid by way of manufactured dividend or MOD would otherwise exceed the amount of the payment of which it is representative. They are based on paragraph 7 of Schedule 23A to ICTA.

2392. If either of these sections applies, the excess is taken out of the scope of the rules about manufactured payments and is treated as a fee. This may affect (a) relief for the payer, (b) taxability for the recipient (or, if different, the owner) or (c) both, if the person concerned is a corporation tax payer.

2393. In paragraph 7(1) of Schedule 23A to ICTA, the words "notwithstanding anything in paragraph 2 above or anything in paragraph 4 other than in sub-paragraph (1A)" signal that the treatment of the excess element of manufactured dividend or MOD as a fee does not prevent it from being eligible for relief as (for example) a trading expense (even though it does not qualify for such relief under paragraph 4(1A) of that Schedule). These words are not rewritten, as they add nothing except emphasis.

Section 798: Manufactured overseas dividends less than underlying payments

2394. This section overrides section 813(2) of this Act (the general rule quantifying the gross amount of a MOD). It is based on paragraph 7 of Schedule 23A to ICTA.

Section 799: Manufactured payments under arrangements with unallowable purpose

2395. This section denies tax relief for manufactured payments made under arrangements having an unallowable purpose. It is based on paragraph 7A of Schedule 23A to ICTA.

2396. *Subsection (1)* states when the section applies.

2397. *Subsection (2)* sets out the consequences of the section applying.

2398. *Subsection (3)* defines "relevant tax relief".

2399. *Subsections (4)* and *(5)* state when a company is subject to another relevant tax relief restriction for the purposes of this section. See the priority rule in subsection (1)(d).

2400. *Subsection (6)* requires the manufactured payment to be justly and reasonably apportioned in order to determine the part which is attributable to the unallowable purpose.

2401. *Subsection (7)* is a signpost to the definition of "arrangements" in section 801 of this Act.

Section 800: Arrangements with an unallowable purpose

2402. This section states when arrangements have an unallowable purpose for the purposes of section 799 of this Act. It is based on paragraph 7A of Schedule 23A to ICTA.

2403. *Subsections (2)* and *(3)* define arrangements having an unallowable purpose.

2404. *Subsection (5)* restricts the business and other commercial purposes of a company to the purposes of activities in respect of which it is within the charge to corporation tax.

2405. *Subsections (6)* and *(7)* limit the extent to which a tax avoidance purpose can be a business or other commercial purpose of the company.

Section 801: Sections 799 and 800: supplementary

2406. This supplementary section is based on paragraph 7A of Schedule 23A to ICTA.

2407. *Subsection (1)* adopts the corporation tax definition of "manufactured interest" used in Chapter 9 of Part 6 of CTA 2009 (relationships treated as loan relationships etc: manufactured interest). This is a minor change in the law. See *Change 51* in Annex 1.

Section 802: Powers about amounts representative of overseas dividends

2408. This section is concerned with double taxation relief. It is based on paragraph 8 of Schedule 23A to ICTA.

Section 803: Power to deal with special cases

2409. This section is a general power to modify the rules about manufactured payments contained in sections 783 to 788, 791, 792, 794 and 795. It is based on paragraph 8 of Schedule 23A to ICTA.

2410. *Subsection (2)* does not refer to section 793, which is based on paragraph 4A of Schedule 23A to ICTA, because paragraph 8(1) of that Schedule does not refer to that paragraph. Section 793 merely specifies an amount for the purposes of section 792, which is within the scope of this section.

Section 804: Regulation-making powers: general

2411. This section is a general provision about powers to make regulations. It is based on paragraph 8 of Schedule 23A to ICTA.

Chapter 5: Stock lending arrangements and repos

Overview

2412. This Chapter contains rules concerning stock lending arrangements and repos.

2413. The detailed structure of the Chapter is as follows:

- Sections 805 to 807 – interpretation;
- Sections 808 to 811 – tax credits: stock lending arrangements and repos;
- Section 812 – deemed manufactured payments.

Sections 805 to 807: "Stock lending arrangement"; section 805: supplementary; "creditor repo", "creditor quasi-repo", "debtor repo" and "debtor quasi-repo"

2414. These interpretative sections are based on sections 231AA and 736B of ICTA, paragraph 1 of Schedule 23A to that Act and sections 263B and 263C of TCGA.

Section 808: No tax credits for borrower under stock lending arrangement

2415. This section prevents the borrower under a stock lending arrangement from claiming a tax credit when that person in economic terms does not retain a dividend on the securities, but passes it on to the lender, by way of a manufactured dividend or other means. It is based on section 231AA of ICTA and section 263B of TCGA.

Section 809: No tax credits for lender under creditor repo or creditor quasi-repo

2416. This section prevents the lender under a creditor repo or creditor quasi-repo from claiming a tax credit when that person in economic terms does not retain a dividend on the shares, but passes it on to the counterparty, by way of a manufactured dividend or other means. It is based on section 231AA of ICTA.

2417. *Subsection (3)(b)* refers to section 925A of ITA, which is based on paragraph 13 of Schedule 13 to FA 2007 and is inserted by Schedule 7 to TIOPA.

Section 810: No tax credits for borrower under debtor repo or debtor quasi-repo

2418. This section counters unusual repo arrangements where the borrower does not pass entitlement to the dividends to the counterparty but the borrower nonetheless receives a manufactured dividend. It is based on section 231AB of ICTA.

Section 811: Arrangements between companies to make distributions

2419. This section extends the meaning of distribution to encompass arrangements between two or more companies to make distributions to each other's members. It is based on section 254(8) of ICTA.

Section 812: Deemed manufactured payments: stock lending arrangements

2420. This section deems the borrower in a stock lending arrangement to make a manufactured payment in certain circumstances. It is based on sections 231AA, 231AB and 736B of ICTA.

2421. Usually, a stock lending arrangement requires the borrower to make a manufactured payment to the lender, in which case Chapter 2 of this Part applies for corporation tax purposes.

2422. Exceptionally, a stock lending arrangement may be structured in such a way that the lender is not entitled to receive a manufactured payment, even though the lender has forgone interest or dividends on the securities transferred. In such a case, this section deems the borrower to make a manufactured payment. In consequence, Chapters 2 to 4 of this Part applies and, in particular, if the securities are overseas securities, the lender is deemed to receive a MOD. But the borrower is denied any tax relief for the deemed manufactured payment.

Chapter 6: Interpretation of Part

Sections 813 and 814: The gross amount of a manufactured overseas dividend etc; other interpretation

2423. These interpretative sections are based on sections 736B and 736C of ICTA, paragraphs 1, 4 and 7 of Schedule 23A to that Act and section 263B of TCGA.

Part 18: Transactions in land

Overview

2424. This Part rewrites sections 776 to 778 of ICTA for the purposes of corporation tax.

2425. Sections 776 to 778 of ICTA were enacted as a wide-ranging anti-avoidance rule specifically aimed at transactions in land.

2426. Chapter 3 of Part 13 of ITA rewrote sections 776 to 778 of ICTA for the purposes of income tax, and paragraphs 184 to 186 of Schedule 1 to ITA consequentially amended those sections to apply solely for the purposes of corporation tax.

2427. This Part replicates Chapter 3 of Part 13 of ITA as far as possible. It differs from Chapter 3 of Part 13 of ITA in two respects.

2428. First, sections 776 to 778 of ICTA, as amended by ITA, do not include any provisions corresponding to section 759(8) of ITA (person liable: territorial scope), section 767 of that Act (exemption: private residences) or section 768(6) to (8) of that Act (income treated as highest part of individual's total income), because those provisions are income tax specific. Accordingly, no such provisions appear in the corporation tax version of the legislation.

2429. Second, where necessary this Part uses concepts specific to corporation tax where Chapter 3 of Part 13 of ITA uses concepts specific to income tax. For example, since persons other than companies are not liable to corporation tax, this Part uses the word "company" to refer to the taxpayer where Chapter 3 of Part 13 of ITA uses the word "person".

2430. In rewriting sections 776 to 778 of ICTA for the purposes of income tax, Chapter 3 of Part 13 of ITA included some minor changes in the law. Some of the same changes are made in this Part, for the purposes of corporation tax. They are highlighted in the commentary on sections 821, 831 and 832.

2431. The rewrite of this legislation for the purposes of corporation tax raises three new points of detail, which are highlighted in the commentary on sections 817 and 821 and Schedule 1.

Sections 815 and 816: Introduction to Part; meaning of disposing of land

2432. These sections are based on sections 776(1), (2) and (4) of ICTA.

2433. Except as noted in the Overview above, these sections replicate exactly sections 752 and 753 of ITA.

Section 817: Priority of other tax provisions

2434. This section is based on section 777(10) of ICTA. It replicates exactly section 754 of ITA.

2435. *Paragraph (a)* gives Chapter 5 of Part 5 of ITTOIA (which is an income tax provision) priority over this Part (which is a corporation tax provision). This is necessary because without it there might be the possibility of a double charge. The possibility arises because the company liable to corporation tax under this Part is not necessarily the person to whom the gain has accrued; see section 821.

2436. Chapter 5 of Part 5 of ITTOIA treats any capital sum paid directly or indirectly by the trustees of a settlement to the settlor as the settlor's income. If such a capital sum became available for payment because a gain of a capital nature had accrued, and the gain was derived from value provided by a company, then (but for paragraph (a)) the company and the settlor could both be taxed by reference to the same income.

2437. It may well be that such a case would be unlikely to arise in practice. But omitting paragraph (a) would remove a potential safeguard against double taxation and so it has been retained.

2438. Similarly, *paragraph (b)* refers to "the Tax Acts" (ie both the Corporation Tax Acts and the Income Tax Acts) both to ensure that there is no unintended change and for the sake of consistency with section 754(b) of ITA.

Section 818: Charge to tax on gains from transactions in land

2439. This section imposes the charge to corporation tax on income and stipulates when the charge applies. It is based on section 776(3) and (3A) of ICTA, and is similar to section 755 of ITA.

Sections 819 and 820: Gains obtained from land disposals in some circumstances; person obtaining gain

2440. These sections are based on section 776(2) to (5), (13) and (14) of ICTA.

2441. Except as noted in the Overview above, these sections replicate exactly sections 756 and 757 of ITA.

Section 821: Company chargeable

2442. This section is based on section 776(3) and (8) of ICTA. It is very similar to section 759 of ITA.

2443. *Subsection (1)* lays down the general rule for determining the company chargeable to corporation tax under this Chapter. *Subsections (3)* and *(5)*make exceptions to this general rule.

2444. *Subsection (4)* backs up subsection (3). But there is no equivalent of subsection (4) to back up subsection (5), because none is needed. This is a change in the law but not in practice. See *Change 52* in Annex 1.

2445. As a separate matter, there is no equivalent in this section of section 759(8) of ITA, because there is no corporation tax equivalent of section 1015 of that Act, to which section 759(8) of that Act refers.

2446. The table below summarises the territorial scope of the corporation tax legislation on transactions in land.

Residence of company	***Where land is located***	***Application of the legislation***
United Kingdom	Wholly in the United Kingdom	The legislation applies (assuming all the other conditions are met).
United Kingdom	Wholly outside the United Kingdom	The legislation does not apply.
United Kingdom	Partly in the United Kingdom, partly outside the United Kingdom	The legislation applies to the whole of the gain (assuming all the other conditions are met).
Non-UK	Wholly in the United Kingdom	The legislation applies (assuming all the other conditions are met, including Chapter 4 of Part 1 of CTA 2009).
Non-UK	Wholly outside the United Kingdom	The legislation does not apply.
Non-UK	Partly in the United Kingdom, partly outside the United Kingdom	The legislation applies to the whole of the gain (assuming all the other conditions are met, including Chapter 4 of Part 1 of CTA 2009).

2447. This section and section 819 are drafted on this basis.

*Sections 822 to 826**: Method of calculating gain; transactions, arrangements, sales and realisations relevant for Part; tracing value; meaning of "another person"; valuations and apportionments***

2448. These sections are based on sections 776(6) and 777(2), (3) and (5) to (7) of ICTA. Except that section 822 refers to CTA 2009 rather than to ITTOIA, they replicate exactly sections 760 to 764 of ITA.

Section 827 ***and*** *828**: Gain attributable to period before intention to develop formed and disposals of shares in companies holding land as trading stock***

2449. These sections are based on section 776(7) and (10) of ICTA. Apart from differences of the kind described in the Overview and the fact that section 827 refers to CTA 2009 rather than to ITTOIA, they replicate sections 765 and 766 of ITA.

Sections 829 and 830: Cases where consideration receivable by person not assessed; certificates of tax paid etc

2450. These sections are based on section 777(8) of ICTA. They replicate exactly sections 768(1) to (5) and 769(1) and (2) of ITA.

2451. There is no equivalent in these sections of sections 768(6) to (8) and 769(3) of ITA, which are income tax specific.

Section 831: Clearance procedure

2452. This section is based on section 776(11) of ICTA; apart from differences of the kind described in the Overview, it replicates exactly section 770 of ITA.

2453. This section includes a minor change in the law. Section 776(11) of ICTA gives the clearance function to "the inspector to whom [the taxpayer] makes its return of income". In practice, HMRC do not interpret this restrictively. This section gives the clearance function to the Commissioners for HMRC. See *Change 53* in Annex 1, which corresponds to *Change 118* in Annex 1 to the explanatory notes on ITA.

Section 832: Power to obtain information

2454. This section is based on section 778 of ICTA. It replicates exactly section 771 of ITA.

2455. *Subsection (1)* includes a minor change in the law: it expressly restricts the particulars to be provided to those which an officer of Revenue and Customs may reasonably require. See *Change 54* in Annex 1, which corresponds to *Change 114* in Annex 1 to the explanatory notes on ITA.

Section 833: Interpretation of Part

2456. This section is based on sections 776(13) and 777(13) of ICTA. Except as noted in the Overview above, it replicates exactly section 772 of ITA.

Part 19: Sale and lease-back etc

Overview

2457. This Part rewrites sections 779 to 785 of ICTA (sales and lease-backs) for the purposes of corporation tax.

2458. Sections 779 and 781 to 785 of ICTA first appeared as sections 17 to 19 of, and Schedule 7 to, FA 1964. Section 780 of ICTA first appeared as section 80 of FA 1972. There have been numerous changes to the taxation of leasing since 1972, but sections 779 to 785 of ICTA are still capable of applying.

2459. The four main operative sections of the source legislation – sections 779, 780, 781 and 782 of ICTA – have been rewritten in separate Chapters. Within each Chapter, the detailed provisions have been laid out in sections arranged in a rational order. The legislation is also being split between the corporation tax and income tax codes.

2460. This Part has the following structure.

- Chapter 1 (payments connected with transferred land) is based on section 779 of ICTA.
- Chapter 2 (new lease of land after assignment or surrender) is based on section 780 of ICTA.
- Chapter 3 (leased trading assets) is based on sections 782 and 785 of ICTA.
- Chapter 4 (leased assets: capital sums) is based on sections 781, 782(1) and 783 to 785 of ICTA.

2461. Chapters 1 and 2 apply to certain transactions in land. Chapters 3 and 4 apply to certain transactions in assets other than land.

2462. If Chapter 1 or Chapter 3 applies, tax relief for lease rental (or similar) expenditure is deferred (and may in certain circumstances be denied).

2463. If Chapter 2 or Chapter 4 applies, a capital sum is taxed as income.

Chapter 1: Payments connected with transferred land

Overview

2464. This Chapter is based on section 779 of ICTA. It counters certain avoidance devices based on arrangements for the sale and lease-back of land or on analogous arrangements, such as arrangements for sale of land with reservation of a rentcharge. It restricts tax relief for lease rental expenditure.

2465. The Chapter has the following structure.

- Section 834 summarises the Chapter.
- Sections 835 to 837 say when the Chapter applies and define "relevant corporation tax relief".
- Section 838 restricts relevant corporation tax relief and carries forward relief which has been denied.
- Sections 839 to 842 restrict corporation tax relief for certain insurance company expenses and carry forward relief which has been denied.
- Sections 843 to 848 are interpretative.

Section 834: Overview

2466. This section summarises this Chapter. It is new.

Section 835: Transferor or associate becomes liable for payment of rent

2467. This section sets out the conditions for section 838 or, as the case may be, section 839 to apply in a case involving the payment of rent. It is based on section 779(1), (3), (13) and (14) of ICTA.

2468. *Subsection (1)* lists the conditions which must be met if section 838 (relevant corporation tax relief: deduction not to exceed commercial rent) is to apply.

2469. The words "rent" and "lease" appear for the first time in this Chapter in subsection (1)(b). They are defined in section 846.

2470. *Subsection (2)* lists the conditions which must be met if section 839 (deduction under section 76 of ICTA not to exceed commercial rent) is to apply.

2471. *Subsection (3)* explains what is meant in subsections (1)(a) and (2)(a) by "transferring" an estate or interest in land.

2472. *Subsection (4)* explains what is meant in this Chapter by the "transferor".

2473. *Subsections (5)* and *(6)* explain what is meant in subsections (1)(b) and (2)(b) by becoming "liable" to make a payment.

2474. *Subsection (7)* preserves the rule that, if the transfer was made before the legislation was first introduced, a lease-back after that date does not activate the legislation.

Section 836: Transferor or associate becomes liable for payment other than rent

2475. This section sets out the conditions for the Chapter to apply in a case involving a payment other than rent. It is based on section 779(2), (3), (13) and (14) of ICTA. It is very similar in structure to section 835. See the commentary on that section.

2476. If, in a given case, the reader is satisfied that at least one of the conditions in section 835 is not met and at least one of the conditions in this section is not met, the reader can conclude that as this Chapter does not have effect there is no need to read any further in it.

Section 837: Relevant corporation tax relief

2477. This section lists, for the purposes of this Chapter, the deductions by way of "relevant corporation tax relief". It is based on section 779(13) of ICTA.

2478. *Paragraph (a)*omits references to a profession and to a vocation where the source legislation refers to the carrying on by a company of a trade, profession or vocation. See *Change 4*in Annex 1. The same change is being made in sections 851, 860, 864, 880, 883 and 886.

Section 838: Relevant corporation tax relief: deduction not to exceed commercial rent

2479. This section restricts relevant corporation tax relief for payments falling within section 835(1) or 836(1) and, in certain cases, provides for such relief to be carried forward. It is based on section 779(1), (2) and (4) to (6) of ICTA.

2480. *Subsection (3)* puts on a clear statutory footing the practice of spreading lease rental expenditure in accordance with GAAP before applying section 779 of ICTA. This is a minor change in the law, in favour of the taxpayer. See *Change 55* in Annex 1.

2481. Section 865 makes the same change in rewriting section 782 of ICTA.

Section 839: Deduction under section 76 of ICTA not to exceed commercial rent

2482. This section is a special rule restricting deductions under section 76 of ICTA (relief for certain insurance company expenses) in relation to payments falling within section 835(2) or 836(2). It is based on section 779(1), (2), (4) and (6) of ICTA.

2483. Section 76 of ICTA does not use GAAP. Accordingly, cases within section 76 of ICTA are excluded from the main rule in section 838, and sections 840 to 842 supplement this section.

Section 840: Carrying forward parts of payments

2484. This section permits amounts which have been disallowed under section 839 to be carried forward to a later period (and thus, potentially, relieved). It is based on section 779(5) and (6) of ICTA, and is the first of three sections supplementing section 839.

2485. *Subsections (1)* to *(3)* specify the conditions which must be met if this section is to apply.

2486. *Subsection (4)* is the main operative provision.

2487. *Subsection (5)* permits the section to be applied repeatedly.

Section 841: Aggregation and apportionment of payments

2488. This section is concerned with the aggregation and apportionment, for the purposes of section 839, of payments under the lease or rentcharge etc. It is based on section 779(6) of ICTA, and is the second of three sections supplementing section 839.

Section 842: ***Payments made for later periods***

2489. This section prevents the taxpayer escaping section 839 by labelling the bunched-up payments as payments *for* later periods. It is based on section 779(7) of ICTA, and is the third of three sections supplementing section 839.

Section 843: ***Exclusion of service charges etc***

2490. This section is concerned with service charges and the like. It is based on section 779(6) and (12) of ICTA. It applies for the purposes of both the main rule in section 838 and the special rule for certain insurance company expenses in section 839.

2491. Leases commonly provide for the tenant to pay the landlord not only rent but also service charges and the like, and these may be paid in a single sum; the definitions of "commercial rent" in sections 844 and 845 of this Act do not include service charges etc and so this section correspondingly excludes them from the amount with which the commercial rent is compared.

2492. *Subsections (3)* and *(4)* prevent the taxpayer escaping this Chapter by agreeing to pay an excessive amount by way of service charge. They include a minor change in the law to bring it into line with Self Assessment. See *Change 56* in Annex 1.

2493. The source legislation uses the term "asset", which is defined to exclude land and interests in land. Since many readers may find this counter-intuitive, *subsection (2)(b)* refers to "relevant assets". The term "relevant asset" is defined in *subsection (5)*. Chapters 3 and 4 of this Part also use the term "relevant asset", for the same reason. See sections 869 and 885 of this Act.

Section 844: ***Commercial rent: comparison with rent under a lease***

2494. This section defines "commercial rent" for the purpose of comparison with rent under a lease. It is based on section 779(8) of ICTA.

2495. Commercial rent is the rent payable under a hypothetical lease. Under *subsection (3)(d)*, the hypothetical lease provides for rent to be payable "at an appropriate rate". This expression is defined in *subsection (4)*.

Section 845: ***Commercial rent: comparison with payments other than rent***

2496. This section defines "commercial rent" for the purpose of comparison with payments other than rent. It is based on section 779(9) and (12) of ICTA.

2497. Commercial rent is the rent payable under a hypothetical lease. Under *subsection (2)(b)*, the hypothetical lease is "a tenant's repairing lease". This expression is defined in *subsection (3)*.

2498. Under *subsection (2)(c)*, the hypothetical lease is "of an appropriate duration". The rules for determining whether a lease is of an appropriate duration are laid down in *subsection (4)*.

Section 846: ***Lease and rent***

2499. This section defines "lease" and "rent" for the purposes of this Chapter. It is based on section 779(10) and (12) of ICTA.

Section 847: ***Associated persons***

2500. This section defines "associated persons" for the purposes of this Chapter. It is based on section 779(11) of ICTA.

*Section 848: **Land outside the UK***

2501. This section explains how expressions in this Chapter relating to interests in land in the United Kingdom and their disposition are to be interpreted in cases involving land outside the United Kingdom. It is based on section 779(12) of ICTA.

*Chapter 2: **New lease of land after assignment or surrender***

Overview

2502. This Chapter is based on section 780 of ICTA. It deals with the situation where the existing occupier of premises incurs additional rental liability in return for the payment of a lump sum.

2503. In form, the lump sum is the consideration received for assigning the lease, usually to a charity or a pension fund, and the lease-back is at an increased rent.

2504. In substance, however, the lump sum is a loan and the additional rent represents the repayment of principal and interest.

2505. Where the Chapter applies, a proportion of the lump sum is to be treated as income of the recipient.

2506. The Chapter has the following structure.

- Section 849 summarises the Chapter.
- Section 850 states when the Chapter applies.
- Sections 851 and 852 tax some or all of the consideration as income.
- Section 853 concerns relief for rent under the new lease.
- Sections 854 to 858 deal with cases in which the new lease is deemed to end.
- Section 859 deals with a case in which a lease is varied to provide for increased rent.
- Sections 860 to 862 are interpretative.

*Section 849: **Overview***

2507. This section summarises this Chapter. It is new.

2508. The word "lease" appears in *subsection (1)* for the first time in this Chapter. On the meaning of "lease" in this Chapter, see section 862.

*Section 850: **New lease after assignment or surrender***

2509. This section states when this Chapter applies. It is based on section 780(1), (7) and (9) of ICTA.

2510. *Subsection (1)* provides that five conditions must be met if the Chapter is to apply. If, in a given case, the reader is satisfied that at least one of these conditions is not met, the reader need read no further in this Chapter.

2511. *Subsection (2)* specifies condition A, concerning the original lease.

2512. The word "lessee" appears in subsection (2)(a) for the first time in this Chapter. On the meaning of "lessee" in this Chapter, see section 862.

2513. The expression "a deduction by way of relevant corporation tax relief" appears in subsection (2)(b) for the first time in this Chapter. It is defined in section 860.

2514. *Subsection (3)* specifies condition B, concerning the assignment or surrender of the original lease. Section 1166 provides that in the application of the Corporation Tax

Acts to Scotland "assignment" means assignation. This gives effect to the application of section 24(5) of ICTA by section 780(8) of that Act. Section 1166 also provides that in the application of the Corporation Tax Acts to Scotland "surrender" includes renunciation.

2515. *Subsection (4)* specifies condition C, concerning the new lease.

2516. The expression "a person linked to L" appears for the first time in this Chapter in subsection (4)(a). It is defined in section 861. See further the commentary on section 851(6) and (7).

2517. *Subsection (5)* specifies condition D, concerning the relationship between the new lease and the original lease.

2518. Condition E in *subsection (6)* preserves the rule that, if, before the legislation was introduced, there was a legal or equitable right to the grant of a new lease, then the grant of the new lease does not activate the legislation.

2519. *Subsection (7)* signposts the transitory provision based on the second limb of section 780(9) of ICTA. The "relevant provisions" are the paragraphs headed "New lease of land after assignment or surrender: right to new lease existed pre-22 June 1971 " in the "sale and lease-back etc" Parts of Schedule 2 to this Act and Schedule 9 to TIOPA.

Section 851: ***Taxation of consideration***

2520. This section taxes, as if it were income, some or all of the consideration received by the lessee. It is based on section 780(1), (3), (3A), (7) and (8) of ICTA.

2521. *Subsection (1)* requires an "appropriate amount" of the consideration to be found.

2522. Subsection (1)(a) refers to the assignment of the original lease. Section 1166 provides that in the application of the Act to Scotland "assignment" means assignation. This gives effect to the application of section 24(5) of ICTA by section 780(8) of that Act. Section 1166 also provides that in the application of the Act to Scotland "surrender" includes renunciation.

2523. *Subsection (2)* provides that the appropriate amount is not to be treated as a capital receipt.

2524. *Subsection (3)* defines the appropriate amount if the term of the new lease is not more than one year. *Subsection (4)* defines the appropriate amount if the term of the new lease is more than one year.

2525. In a case in which the term of the new lease (a) exceeds one year and (b) is not for a whole number of years, the formula in section 780(3) of ICTA does not expressly say how to deal with parts of years. *Subsection (5)* makes it clear that, in such a case, a part of a year is to be taken as an appropriate proportion of a year.

2526. *Subsection (6)* provides that the way in which the appropriate amount is treated depends on whether certain specified conditions are met.

2527. If these conditions are met, *subsection (7)* treats the appropriate amount as a receipt of the trade mentioned in subsection (6)(a).

2528. Subsections (6)(a) and (7) omit references to a profession and to a vocation where the source legislation refers to the carrying on by a company of a trade, profession or vocation. See the commentary on section 837 and *Change 4* in Annex 1. This Change is not made in subsection (6)(b), because a person linked to L is not necessarily a corporation tax payer.

2529. If the conditions in subsection (6) are not met, *subsection (8)* treats the appropriate amount as chargeable to corporation tax under the charge to corporation tax on income.

*Section 852: **Position where new lease does not include all original property***

2530. This section deals with the position where the new lease does not include all the original property. It is based on section 780(4) of ICTA.

*Section 853: **Relief for rent under new lease***

2531. This section makes it clear that the normal rules for tax relief apply to rent under the new lease. It is based on section 780(1) of ICTA.

*Section 854: **New lease treated as ending***

2532. This section introduces three sections which treat the new lease as ending in certain circumstances. It is based on section 780(2) of ICTA.

2533. *Subsection (2)* is a tie-breaker rule. Section 780(2) of ICTA indicates that if section 780(2)(a) and (2)(b) could both apply then only one of them applies, namely the one that produces the earlier date. But section 780(2)(b) might on its own produce different dates, and it seems to take section 780(2)(b)(i) and (ii) separately (see "as the case may be") without expressly providing which prevails. But it would be anomalous if section 780(2) included a tie-breaker rule for some but not all of the possible cases, or if it had different tie-breaker rules for different cases. Subsection (2) therefore makes it clear that the earliest date prevails in all cases.

*Section 855: **Position where rent reduces***

2534. This section deals with the position where the rent is reduced. It is based on section 780(2) and (8) of ICTA.

2535. *Subsection (1)* uses the expressions "rent for a relevant period" and "following comparable period". *Subsection (2)(a), (b)* and *(c)* define "relevant period", "following comparable period" and "rent for a period" respectively.

2536. Subsection (2)(a) uses the expressions "rental period" and "fifteenth anniversary [of the new lease]". These expressions are defined in *subsection (2)(d)* and *(e)* respectively.

2537. *Subsection (3)* supplements the definition of "rental period" in subsection (2)(d).

*Section 856: **Position where lease may be ended***

2538. This section deals with the position where the lease has a provision for early termination. It is based on section 780(2) and (7) of ICTA.

*Section 857: **Position where lease may be varied***

2539. This section deals with the position where the lessee has the power to vary the terms of the lease in the lessee's favour (for example, by reducing the rent which the lessee would otherwise have to pay). It is based on section 780(2) and (7) of ICTA.

*Section 858: **Lease treated as ending: rentcharge***

2540. This section supplements the previous three; it deals with rentcharges. It is based on section 780(2) and (7) of ICTA.

*Section 859: **Lease varied to provide for increased rent***

2541. This section deals with a case in which a lease is varied to provide for increased rent. It is based on section 780(6) of ICTA.

2542. *Subsection (1)* provides that four conditions must all be met if this section is to apply.

2543. *Subsection (2)* specifies condition A, concerning the original lease.

2544. *Subsection (3)* specifies condition B, concerning the variation of the lease.

2545. *Subsection (4)* specifies condition C, concerning the increase in the rent.

2546. *Subsection (5)* specifies condition D, concerning the period within which the increased rent is to be paid.

2547. *Subsection (6)* is the main operative provision. Condition A in subsection (2) is the same as condition A in section 850 (new lease after assignment or surrender). In consequence of subsection (6)(a), condition B in that section is met. In consequence of subsection (6)(b), conditions C and D in that section are met. Accordingly, if conditions A to D in this section are met, conditions A to D in that section are met and this Chapter therefore has effect.

Section 860: Relevant corporation tax relief

2548. This section defines deductions by way of relevant corporation tax relief. It is based on sections 779(13) and 780(1) of ICTA.

2549. This section omits references to a profession and to a vocation where the source legislation refers to the carrying on by a company of a trade, profession or vocation. See the commentary on section 837 and *Change 4* in Annex 1.

Section 861: Linked persons

2550. This section defines "a person linked to L" in this Chapter. It is based on section 780(7) of ICTA.

Section 862: Lease, lessee, lessor and rent

2551. This section concerns the meaning of "lease", "lessee", "lessor" and "rent". It is based on sections 24(1) and (6) and 780(8) of ICTA.

2552. *Section (3)* says that "lease" does not include a mortgage. This is based on section 24(1) of ICTA as applied by section 780(8) of ICTA. In fact, section 24(1) of ICTA says that a lease includes neither a mortgage nor a heritable security. A "heritable security" is the Scottish equivalent of a mortgage, although post-1970 heritable securities take the form of a standard security. Section 1166 contains a general provision to the effect that, in the application of the Act to Scotland, "mortgage" includes the Scottish equivalents. Accordingly, subsection (3) has to be read as if it said that a lease includes neither a mortgage nor the Scottish equivalents. Subsection (3) therefore achieves the same effect as the source legislation, even though section 1166 has a definition of the Scottish equivalents that contains more detail than the words "mortgage or heritable security" in section 24(1) of ICTA. The approach is the same as that taken for income tax purposes when the definition of "lease" in section 24(1) of ICTA was rewritten to sections 364(1) and 879(1) of ITTOIA.

Chapter 3: Leased trading assets

Overview

2553. This Chapter is based on sections 782 and 785 of ICTA.

2554. This Chapter applies where a company carrying on a trade pays rent under a lease of an asset other than land or buildings and at any time before the lease was created the asset was used either (a) in that trade or (b) in another trade carried on by the person who then or later was carrying on the first trade and, in either case, when so used was owned by the company carrying on the trade in which it was used.

2555. If this Chapter applies, it provides that in computing the profits and gains of the trade the deduction in respect of a payment under the lease shall not exceed the commercial rent of the asset for the period for which the payment was made.

2556. This Chapter has the following structure.

- Section 863 summarises the Chapter.
- Section 864 states when the Chapter applies.
- Section 865 restricts corporation tax relief and carries forward relief which has been denied.
- Sections 866 and 867 supplement section 865.
- Sections 868 and 869 are interpretative.

*Section 863: **Overview of Chapter***

2557. This section summarises this Chapter. It is new.

2558. The word "lease" appears in this section for the first time in this Chapter. It is defined in section 868.

*Section 864: **Leased trading assets***

2559. This section states when this Chapter applies to a payment. It is based on section 782(1) and (8) to (10) of ICTA.

2560. *Subsection (1)* introduces the three conditions relating to the application of this Chapter and explains their logical relationship.

2561. *Subsection (2)* specifies condition A, concerning the payment.

2562. In particular, under subsection (2)(a) the payment must be made under the lease of a "relevant asset". The expression "relevant asset" appears in subsection (2)(a) for the first time in this Chapter. It is defined in section 869.

2563. *Subsections (3)* and *(4)* specify conditions B and C. These are two alternative conditions concerning the use to which the leased asset was put before it was leased.

2564. Subsections (2)(b), (3)(a) and (b)and (4)(c) omit references to a profession and to a vocation where the source legislation refers to the carrying on by a company of a trade, profession or vocation. See the commentary on section 837 and *Change 4* in Annex 1.

2565. *Subsection (5)* preserves the rule that, if the lease was created before the legislation was first introduced, a lease-back after that date does not activate the legislation.

*Section 865: **Tax deduction not to exceed commercial rent***

2566. This section restricts corporation tax relief and carries forward relief which has been denied. It is based on section 782(1) to (4) of ICTA.

2567. *Subsection (3)* brings the law into line with practice. See the commentary on section 838 and *Change 55* in Annex 1.

*Section 866: **Long funding finance leases***

2568. This section makes an exception for long funding finance leases. It is based on section 782(1A) of ICTA.

*Sections 867 **and** 868: **Commercial rent; lease***

2569. These interpretative sections are based on sections 782(6) and (7) and 785 of ICTA.

Section 869: ***Relevant asset***

2570. This section defines "relevant asset" for the purpose of this Chapter. It is based on the definition of "asset" in section 785 of ICTA.

2571. The source legislation uses the term "asset", which is defined to exclude land and interests in land. Since many readers may find this counter-intuitive, this section uses the new term "relevant asset".

Chapter 4: ***Leased assets: capital sums***

Overview

2572. This Chapter is based on section 781 of ICTA.

2573. It deals with cases such as that of a taxpayer which, having had tax relief in respect of a payment under a lease of an asset other than land or buildings, receives or has received at any time a capital sum in respect of the lessee's interest in the lease.

2574. If the Chapter applies, corporation tax is charged on (broadly speaking) the amount on which relief has been obtained or, if less, on the capital sum.

2575. The Chapter has the following structure.

- Section 870 summarises the Chapter.
- Sections 871 to 873 state when the Chapter applies.
- Sections 874 to 876 concern the charge to corporation tax.
- Sections 877 to 879 deal with obtaining the capital sum.
- Sections 880 and 881 are about apportionment.
- Sections 882 to 886 are interpretative.

Section 870: ***Overview***

2576. This section summarises the Chapter. It is new.

2577. The expressions "capital sum" and "lease" appear in this section for the first time in this Chapter. They are defined in sections 883 and 884 respectively.

Section 871: ***Application of the Chapter***

2578. This section introduces the five conditions relating to the application of this Chapter and explains their logical relationship. It is based on section 781(1) of ICTA.

Section 872: ***Payment under lease***

2579. This section specifies a necessary condition (condition A) for the Chapter to apply, namely that a tax-deductible payment is made under a lease of a relevant asset. It is based on sections 781(1) and (3) and 782(1) of ICTA.

2580. The expressions "relevant asset" and "relevant tax relief" appear in *subsection (1)(a)* and *(b)* respectively for the first time in this Chapter. They are defined in sections 885 and 886 respectively.

2581. The person entitled to a deduction by way of tax relief under section 781(1)(a) of ICTA is not necessarily the person obtaining the capital sum and charged to tax under that subsection. It follows that, if the person obtaining the capital sum is charged to corporation tax, the person entitled to a deduction by way of tax relief is not necessarily a corporation tax payer. Subsection (1)(b) of this section therefore refers to "relevant tax relief", rather than "relevant corporation tax relief".

2582. *Subsection (2)* stipulates that if Chapter 3 of this Part applies to the payment then condition A is not met (and, therefore, this Chapter does not apply to the payment). For that reason, Chapter 3 appears in this Part before this Chapter, reversing the order of the source legislation.

2583. *Subsection (3)* similarly stipulates that if Chapter 3 of Part 12A of ITA (the income tax provision corresponding to Chapter 3 of this Part) applies to the payment then condition A is not met (and, therefore, this Chapter does not apply to the payment). Subsection (3) is unlikely to apply in practice, but omitting it would change the law to the taxpayer's disadvantage.

2584. *Subsection (4)* preserves the rule that, if the lease was created before the legislation was first introduced, receiving a capital sum after that date does not activate the legislation.

*Section 873: **Sum obtained***

2585. This section specifies four alternative additional conditions for the Chapter to apply. It is based on sections 781(1) and (9) and 783(3) of ICTA.

2586. All four of the conditions concern the obtaining of a capital sum by a person of the description specified in the condition. In particular, the person obtaining the capital sum need not be the person making the tax-deductible payment.

2587. In conditions B and C in *subsections (1)* and *(2)*, the capital sum is obtained in respect of the lessee's interest in the lease. In condition B, the capital sum is obtained by the person making the payment. In condition C, the capital sum is obtained by an associate of that person.

2588. Subsection (1)(a) is the first provision in this Chapter which refers to obtaining a sum in respect of an interest in a lease and, specifically, to obtaining a sum in respect of the lessee's interest in a lease. The former expression is defined in section 877. The latter expression is defined in section 878.

2589. The word "associate" appears in subsection (2) for the first time in this Chapter. It is defined in section 882.

2590. In conditions D and E in *subsections (3)* and *(4)*, the capital sum is obtained in respect of the lessor's interest in the lease, or of any other interest in the asset. In condition D, the capital sum is obtained by an associate of the person making the payment. In condition E, the interest belongs to an associate of that person and the capital sum is obtained by an associate of that associate.

2591. *Subsection (5)* makes it clear that, for the purposes of this section, it is irrelevant when the payment is made.

2592. *Subsections (6)>* and *(7)* relate to hire-purchase agreements for plant and machinery. Subsection (6) makes an exception to conditions B and C. Subsection (7) makes an exception to conditions D and E.

*Section 874: **Charge to corporation tax***

2593. This section imposes the charge to corporation tax on the company obtaining the capital sum. It is based on sections 781(1), (1B), (2) and (6) of ICTA.

2594. Under *subsection (1)*, there is a charge to corporation tax on income for the accounting period in which the sum is obtained.

2595. *Subsection (2)* measures the amount on which tax is charged.

2596. *Subsection (3)* introduces four subsections limiting the effect of subsections (1) and (2).

2597. *Subsection (4)* caps the amount on which tax is charged.

2598. To prevent double taxation, *subsections (5)* and *(6)* ensure that once a payment (or part of a payment) has been taken into account in making a charge under this section it cannot be taken into account in making a further charge in respect of another sum.

2599. *Subsection (7)* is a timing rule supplementing subsections (5) and (6).

Section 875: ***Hire-purchase agreements***

2600. This section concerns hire-purchase agreements. It is based on section 784 of ICTA.

2601. This section may be in point if section 873(6) and (7) (sum obtained: exceptions for hire-purchase agreements) do not prevent this Chapter from applying. If this Chapter applies, *subsection (1)* states the conditions for this section to apply.

2602. *Subsection (2)* requires the total to be found of:

- non-tax-deductible payments under the lease; and
- if the lessee's interest in the lease was assigned to the company before it obtained the capital sum in respect of that interest, any capital payment made by the company as consideration for the assignment.

2603. This total is then compared with the capital sum. If it is equal to or greater than the capital sum, then under *subsection (3)* the capital sum is treated for the purposes of section 874(4) as £nil. If the total found under subsection (2) is less than the capital sum, then under *subsection (4)* it is deducted from the capital sum in applying section 874(4).

2604. *Subsection (5)* covers the special case in which the capital sum is the consideration for part onlyof the lessee's interest in the lease.

2605. Section 784(4) of ICTA provides that:

""“the amount to be deducted ... shall be such proportion of the capital expenditure which is still unallowed *as is reasonable*” (emphasis added).

2606. Rewriting this, subsection (5)(a) requires the unallowed amount to be reduced to a proportion which is not only reasonable but also just. This is a minor change in the law: see *Change 33* in Annex 1.

2607. To prevent double relief, *subsections (6)* and *(7)* ensure that if a payment has been taken into account under subsection (2) in respect of a capital sum it cannot be taken into account in respect of another capital sum.

2608. *Subsection (8)* is a timing rule supplementing subsections (6) and (7).

Section 876: ***Adjustments where sum obtained before payment made***

2609. This section provides for adjustments to be made if a capital sum is obtained as mentioned in section 873 and later a payment is made as mentioned in section 872. It is based on section 781(7) to (8A) of ICTA.

Section 877: ***Sum obtained in respect of interest***

2610. This section is concerned with the meaning, in this Chapter, of “a sum obtained in respect of an interest in an asset”. It is based on section 783(1) and (2) of ICTA.

Section 878: ***Sum obtained in respect of lessee's interest***

2611. This section is concerned with the meaning, in this Chapter, of “a sum obtained in respect of the lessee's interest in a lease of an asset”. It is based on section 783(1) and (2) of ICTA.

Section 879: ***Disposal of interest to associate***

2612. This section determines the amount which a company is deemed to obtain if it disposes of an interest in an asset to a person who is the company's associate. It is based on sections 781(1) and 783(4) and (5) of ICTA.

Section 880: ***Apportionment of payments made and of sums obtained***

2613. This section provides for apportionments to be made of payments made and sums obtained. It is based on section 783(6) to (8) of ICTA.

2614. *Subsection (3)* requires apportionments to be not only just but also reasonable. This is a minor change in the law. See *Change 33* in Annex 1.

2615. *Subsections (4)* and *(5)*omit references to a profession and to a vocation where the source legislation refers to the carrying on by a company of a trade, profession or vocation. See the commentary on section 837 and *Change 4* in Annex 1. This Change is not made in *subsection (2)*, as the reference in that subsection to "relevant tax relief" is not limited to corporation tax.

Section 881: ***Manner of apportionment***

2616. This section provides for apportionments to be made by the tribunal in certain circumstances. It is based on section 783(9) of ICTA.

Section 882: ***Associates***

2617. This section defines "associates" for the purposes of this Chapter. It is based on section 783(10) and (11) of ICTA.

Section 883: ***Capital sum***

2618. This section defines "capital sum" for the purposes of this Chapter. It is based on the definition of "capital sum" in section 785 of ICTA.

2619. *Paragraph (a)*omits references to a profession and to a vocation where the source legislation refers to the carrying on by a company of a trade, profession or vocation. See the commentary on section 837 and *Change 4* in Annex 1.

Section 884: ***Lease***

2620. This section defines "lease" for the purposes of this Chapter. It is based on the definition of "lease" in section 785 of ICTA.

Section 885: ***Relevant asset***

2621. This section defines "relevant asset" for the purposes of this Chapter. It is based on the definition of "asset" in section 785 of ICTA.

2622. The source legislation uses the term "asset", which is defined to exclude land and interests in land. Since many readers may find this counter-intuitive, this section uses the new term "relevant asset".

Section 886: ***Relevant tax relief***

2623. This section defines "relevant tax relief" for the purposes of this Chapter. It is based on section 781(4) of ICTA.

2624. *Paragraph (a)* omits references to a profession and to a vocation where the source legislation refers to the carrying on by a company of a trade, profession or vocation. See the commentary on section 837 and *Change 4* in Annex 1.

Part 20: Tax avoidance involving leasing plant or machinery

Overview

2625. This Part rewrites certain provisions of Part 17 of ICTA (tax avoidance) relating to leasing plant or machinery.

Chapter 1: Restrictions on use of losses in leasing partnerships

Overview

2626. This Chapter rewritessections 785ZA and 785ZB of ICTA, which were introduced by FA 2006 as an adjunct to the provisions of Schedule 10 to FA 2006 (sale etc of lessor companies etc) rewritten in Chapters 3 to 6 of Part 9.

2627. These sections of ICTA address an alternative arrangement designed to achieve a similar effect to a disposal of an interest in a leasing business carried on in partnership, throughdiffering allocations of profits and lossesand of capital allowances in the leasing business.

Section 887: When restrictions on leasing partnership losses under this Chapter apply

2628. This section sets out the circumstances in which the restrictions on the use of losses in section 888 apply. It is based on sections 785ZA(1) to (4) and 785ZB(1) and (2) of ICTA.

2629. The restrictions apply where a company carries on a "business of leasing plant or machinery" in partnership and the company's profit sharing arrangements are unusual. *Subsection (1)(e)* achieves this by providing that the restrictions only apply if the profit sharing arrangements are not determined "on an allowable basis" as defined in *subsections (2)*to *(4)*.

2630. "Business of leasing plant or machinery" has the same meaning as it has for the purposes of Chapter 4 of Part 9 (see *subsection (5)*).

Section 888: Restrictions on leasing partnership losses

2631. This section restricts the use of losses incurred by a company in the partnership leasing business. It is based on sections 785ZA(5) to (9) and 785ZB(1), (7) and (8) of ICTA.

2632. A loss which derives from capital allowances on the leased plant or machinery may only be set off against the company's income from leases of plant or machinery entered into by the partnership no later than the end of the accounting period in which the loss is incurred. It can be carried forward, but only against such leasing income (see *subsection (2)*). It cannot be set sideways (see *subsection(3)*) or surrendered as group relief (see *subsection (4)*).

Section 889: Interpretation of Chapter

2633. This defines certain terms used in the Chapter. It is based on section 785ZB(1) and (3) to (6) of ICTA.

Chapter 2: Capital payments in respect of leases treated as income

Overview

2634. This Chapter rewrites sections 785B to 785E of ICTA introduced by FA 2008.

2635. Only minor changes in language have been made but the provisions have been restructured to improve accessibility. In particular, section 785C (section 785B:

interpretation) has been rewritten in two sections. The first section deals with the meaning of the primary terms "capital payment" and "relevant capital payment", while the other defined terms are relegated to the second section.

Section 890: Capital payments in respect of leases treated as income

2636. This section taxes certain capital receipts arising in connection with leases of plant or machinery (such as premiums and similar sums) as income of the lessor. It is based on section 785B of ICTA.

2637. The accounting period in which the charge to tax arises depends upon whether or not an unconditional obligation to make a "relevant capital payment" (see section 893) is entered into before the relevant capital payment is made. See *subsections (3)* and *(4)*.

Section 891: Apportionments for leases of plant or machinery and other property

2638. This section ensures that section 890 applies in a just and reasonable manner where the lease includes (but is not limited to) plant or machinery that is not a fixture. It is based on section 785D of ICTA.

2639. *Subsection (3)* ensures that where the capital payment refers to plant or machinery, any income from which would be charged as profits of a UKproperty business, it is treated as referring to "other property" for the purpose of arriving at an apportionment under *subsection (2)*. For example, if a lease of property includes furniture (and the income in respect of the furniture is taxed as property income) any element of the capital payment that refers to the furniture is outside the scope of section 890.

2640. The words "if the income (if any) ... is chargeable" in section 785D(3) of ICTA have been rewritten as "any income ... would be chargeable" in subsection (3), in order to remove any doubt that this treatment applies whether or not any income actually arises. This conforms the wording of subsection (3) with that of section 785C(4)(a) of ICTA rewritten in section 894(4).

Section 892: Deduction where failure to make relevant capital payment expected

2641. This section gives relief for bad debts, or debts which are expected to be bad. It is based on section 785E of ICTA.

2642. As section 890 may tax a relevant capital payment before it is received, relief is to be given at the time the lessor reasonably expects that some or all of the relevant capital payment will not be paid. This rule applies whether the payment was due to be made to the lessor or to someone on their behalf.

Section 893: Meaning in Chapter of "Capital payment", "relevant capital payment" etc

2643. This section defines "relevant capital payment" and related terms. It is based on section 785C(2) and (6) to (10) of ICTA.

2644. *Subsection (2)* defines the term "capital payment". It excludes any payment that would fall to be included in calculating the lessor's income for corporation tax purposes or any payment in respect of a long funding finance lease which would be so included but for the fact thatsection 360 ensures that only sums treated asthe gross return on investment or as interest in respect ofthe lease are taxed. Subsection (2), therefore, ensures that no part of the rentals under a long funding finance lease triggers section 890.

2645. Section 890 is only triggered if the capital payment is "relevant" as defined in *subsections (3)* to *(5)*. But a capital payment which falls within those subsections is not relevant to the extent that it falls within *subsection (6)* and is only relevant to a limited extent if it falls within *subsection (7)*.

2646. Payment is given an extended meaning for the purposes of the Chapter (see *subsections (8)* and *(9)*).

Section 894: Other interpretation of Chapter

2647. This section defines other terms used in the Chapter. It is based on section 785C(1) and (3) to (5).

2648. The effect of *subsections (3)* to *(5)* is that a "lease of plant or machinery" includes:

- a lease of plant or machinery only;
- a lease of plant or machinery that is not a fixture where it is leased with land or other assets in circumstances where income attributable to the plant or machinery would not be chargeable to tax as profits of a UKproperty business (in which case see section 891).

but does not include:

- a lease of land and buildings, including fixtures and other plant or machinery the income from which would be taxed as property income; or
- plant or machinery leased out under a long funding lease where the lessor would have been entitled to claim capital allowances but for section 34A of CAA.

Part 21: Leasing arrangements: finance leases and loans

Overview

2649. This Part is based on Schedule 12 to FA 1997.

2650. Schedule 12 to FA 1997 has effect for both corporation tax purposes and income tax purposes. Schedule 12 is rewritten for corporation tax purposes in this Act and for income tax purposes in Part 11A of ITA (see Schedule 3 to TIOPA, which also rewrites provisions of Schedule 12 relating to chargeable gains in TCGA).

2651. Schedule 12 to FA 1997 was introduced to deal with two finance leasing arrangements. Schedule 12 achieves its aims by aligning the tax treatment of the return in respect of finance leases and loans more closely with the commercial accounting treatment.

2652. Part 1 of Schedule 12 (rewritten in Chapter 2) counters tax avoidance by finance lessors trying to turn some of their lease rental income into capital receipts (taxed later and at lower effective rates, if at all). It ensures that any part of the capital receipt which is recognised as return on investment under GAAP is brought into account for tax purposes as income.

2653. Part 2 of Schedule 12 to FA 1997 (rewritten in Chapter 3) deals with a possible deferral of tax liability by means of leases under which rentals are concentrated towards the end of the lease term. But for the provisions of Schedule 12, rental income in the case of such a finance lease could be recognised for tax purposes later than it is recognised in accordance with GAAP.

Chapter 1: Introduction

Overview

2654. This Chapter not only gives an overview of the Part but also brings to prominence the definitions of certain terms fundamental to its provisions.

Section 895: Overview of Part

2655. This section describes the Part and the contents of each Chapter. It is new.

*Section 896: **Normal rent***

2656. This section defines "normal rent". It is based on paragraph 20 of Schedule 12 to FA 1997.

2657. Normal rent is the amount which but for this Part a lessor would bring into account as rent from a lease for the purposes of corporation tax.

*Section 897: **Accountancy rental earnings***

2658. This section defines "accountancy rental earnings". It is based on paragraph 21 of Schedule 12 to FA 1997.

2659. This Part provides that the accountancy rental earnings of a lessor in relation to a lease are, in certain circumstances, to be brought into account for corporation tax purposes instead of the normal rent from the lease.

2660. *Subsections (1)* and *(2)* provide that in relation to a lease "accountancy rental earnings" are the highest of the following three figures for a period of account:

- the rental earnings (see section 898) of the lessor in relation to the lease;
- the rental earnings of a connected person of the lessor in relation to the lease; or
- the rental earnings in relation to the lease for the purposes of consolidated accounts of the group of which the lessor is a member.

2661. The purpose of taking the highest of the three figures is to ensure that the earnings fully reflecting the economic substance of the transaction are taxed. This is especially important when the capital sum which is an essential part of a leasing arrangement within Chapter 2 may be received not by the lessor but by a related party. In such a case it is only by considering the lessor's position and that of the related party together that the true economic substance of the transaction can be appreciated. That is likely to be in the consolidated accounts of the group as a whole, or possibly in the accounts of the related party, rather than in those of the lessor company itself.

*Section 898: **Rental earnings***

2662. This section defines "rental earnings". It is based on paragraph 22 of Schedule 12 to FA 1997.

*Chapter 2: **Finance leases with return in capital form***

Overview

2663. This Chapter is concerned with finance leases intended to turn part of the associated rental income into capital receipts.

*Section 899: **Arrangements to which this Chapter applies***

2664. This section describes the leasing arrangements that fall within Chapter 2. It is based on paragraphs 1(1) and 2(1) of Schedule 12 to FA 1997.

2665. The arrangements fall within the Chapter if they involve the lease of any property or rights (see *subsection (1)* and the definition of "asset" in section 937). Contrast Parts 9 and 20 which apply only to leases of plant or machinery.

2666. The Chapter is only capable of applying if two conditions are met. First, the arrangements must fall to be treated under GAAP as a finance lease or loan (see *subsection (2)*). Second, it is necessary that some or all of the lessor's return on investment in respect of the finance lease or loan is not in the form of rent and would not, apart from this Part or Part 11A of ITA, be brought into account for tax purposes as rent (see *subsection (3)*).

2667. References to Part 11A of ITA and to tax purposes (rather than only corporation tax purposes) have been included in subsection (3) to ensure that the division between that Part of ITA and this Part works as intended.

2668. The Chapter is capable of applying to arrangements entered into before the commencement date of Schedule 12 to FA 1997 (see *subsection (4)(a)* and the commentary on section 923).

Section 900: ***Purposes of this Chapter***

2669. This section sets out the main purposes of Chapter 2. It is based on paragraph 1(2) of Schedule 12 to FA 1997.

2670. The first purpose (in *subsections (2)* to *(4)*) is to substitute for the ordinary tax measure of income from the lease the amount recognised in accordance with GAAP where this is larger than the normal measure (see section 905).

2671. Under GAAP, part of the sum mentioned in section 899(3) is recognised as annual income over the course of the lease and thus taken into account in computing commercial profits. Income is recognised in this way because in substance the lease is tantamount to a loan, the interest on which needs to be matched with the lessor's own borrowing costs in order properly to reflect the lessor's profit.

2672. The income recognised in accordance with GAAP may be that shown in consolidated accounts of the lessor's group or in those of a company which is a "connected person" of the lessor. The reason for looking wider than the lessor (see subsection (4)) is that the full earnings from the lease may only be shown in, say, the accounts of the parent or in the consolidated group results.

2673. The second purpose of Chapter 2 (in *subsections (5)* and *(6)*) is to recover appropriately any tax reliefs for capital expenditure already given.

Section 901: ***Application of this Chapter***

2674. This section, together with section 902, determines whether Chapter 2 applies to a particular lease. It is based on paragraph 2 of Schedule 12 to FA 1997.

2675. For the Chapter to apply, the conditions in section 902 must have been met in relation to the lease at some time in a period of account of the current lessor (see *subsection (1) (b)*). But once they have been met in relation to the lessor at the time, they are treated as continuing to be met as regards any subsequent lessor unless and until the lease is assigned to a wholly unrelated person (see *subsections (3)* to *(5)*).

2676. *Subsection (2)* provides that the Chapter does not apply to long funding leases of plant or machinery in relation to which Part 2 of CAA gives capital allowances to the lessee instead of the lessor. The provisions rewritten in Chapter 2 of Part 9 of this Act set out the basis of taxation of rental earnings under such leases.

2677. *Subsection (6)* is a necessary consequence of the split into separate provisions for corporation tax purposes and income tax purposes.

Section 902: ***The conditions referred to in section 901(1)***

2678. This section sets out the five conditions, A to E, all of which must be met if Chapter 2 is to apply to a specific lease. It is based on paragraph 3(1) to (5) of Schedule 12 to FA 1997.

2679. Condition A in *subsections (2)* to *(4)* requires the lease to fall to be treated under GAAP as a finance lease or loan.

2680. Condition B in *subsection (5)* requires a "major lump sum" which is not rent to be payable and for part of that sum to be treated under GAAP as return on investment in respect of the finance lease or loan.

2681. Condition C in *subsection (6)* is that not all of that part of the major lump sum would apart from Chapter 2 be brought into account for corporation tax purposes as the "normal rent" (see sections 896 and 903(3)) from the lease for accounting periods ending with "the relevant accounting period" (see section 903(1)).

2682. Condition D in *subsection (7)* is that for the period of account of the lessor in which "the relevant time" (see section 903(1)) falls or for an earlier period of account of the lessor, the "accountancy rental earnings" (see section 897) in respect of the lease exceed the normal rent for the period. The point of this condition is that, if a lessor is consistently being taxed on at least as much income as the commercial accounts show, then the terms of the lease are not ones which are designed to turn rental income into a capital receipt.

2683. Condition E in *subsection (8)* is that at the relevant time there exist such arrangements or circumstances as are mentioned in section 904.

2684. The arrangements and circumstances are set out in detail in section 904, but essentially there must be some likelihood that the lessee or a connected person of the lessee will buy out the lessor's interest in the leased asset for a major lump sum.

2685. Condition E is intended to ensure that a lease does not come within Chapter 2 solely because there is a possibility that the lessor may obtain a major capital sum otherwise than from the lessee or a connected person. This might happen for example on the unplanned sale of the leased asset to a third party or on a claim under an insurance policy on the destruction of the asset.

Section 903: ***Provisions supplementing section 902***

2686. This section provides the meanings of "the relevant accounting period" and "the relevant time" and sets out how the normal rent is to be determined, for the purposes of section 902. It is based on paragraph 3(7) and (8) of Schedule 12 to FA1997.

Section 904: ***The arrangements and circumstances referred to in section 902(8)***

2687. This section sets out the arrangements and circumstances which constitute Condition E in section 902(8). It is based on paragraph 4 of Schedule 12 to FA 1997.

2688. See the commentary on section 902.

Section 905: ***Current lessor taxed by reference to accountancy rental earnings***

2689. This section provides for the lessor to bring into account for corporation tax purposes the accountancy rental earnings in respect of the lease for a period of account if they exceed the normal rent for the period. It is based on paragraph 5 of Schedule 12 to FA 1997.

Sections 906 to 910: ***Reduction of taxable rent by cumulative rental excesses***

Overview

2690. These sections ensure that the rule in section 905 that the higher of the accountancy rental earnings and the normal rents (ordinary taxable rents) are taxeddoes not overall cause more rent to be taxed as income than is actually due to the lessor. They are based on paragraph 6 of Schedule 12 to FA 1997.

2691. These sections achieve their purpose by requiring running totals to be kept of aggregate differences between accountancy rental earnings and the normal rents. Any aggregate excess of accountancy rental earnings over normal rents arising in past periods can then be set against any current excess of normal rents over accountancy rental earnings. Conversely, any aggregate excess of normal rents over accountancy rental earnings arising in past periods can be set against any current excess of accountancy rental earnings over normal rents.

2692. The provisions of paragraph 6 of Schedule 12 to FA 1997 have been unpacked into five sections to provide greater clarity.

*Section 906: **Reduction of taxable rent by cumulative rental excesses: introduction***

2693. This section introduces sections 907 to 910. It is based on paragraph 6(5) to(9) of Schedule 12 to FA 1997.

*Section 907: **Meaning of "accountancy rental excess" and "cumulative accountancy rental excess"***

2694. This section defines the terms "accountancy rental excess" and "cumulative accountancy rental excess". It is based on paragraph 6(3), (4) and (8) of Schedule 12 to FA 1997.

*Section 908: **Reduction of taxable rent by the cumulative accountancy rental excess***

2695. This section applies if in relation to a lease for a period of account the normal rent exceeds the accountancy rental earnings (so it is the normal rent that is taxed) and there is a cumulative accountancy rental excess. It is based on paragraph 6(5) and (6) of Schedule 12 to FA 1997.

2696. The rent that is brought into account for corporation tax purposes is found by reducing normal rent by the cumulative accountancy rental excess but not so as to bring into account an amount less than the accountancy rental earnings for the period.

*Section 909: **Meaning of "normal rental excess" and "cumulative normal rental excess"***

2697. This section defines the terms "normal rental excess" and "cumulative normal rental excess". It is based on paragraph 6(1), (2) and (6) of Schedule 12 to FA 1997.

*Section 910: **Reduction of taxable rent by the cumulative normal rental excess***

2698. This section applies if in relation to a lease for a period of account the taxable rent under section 905 would be the amount of the accountancy rental earnings and there is a cumulative normal rental excess. It is based on paragraph 6(7) and (8) of Schedule 12 to FA 1997.

2699. Section 905 only applies if the accountancy rental earnings exceed the normal rent. To avoid more rent being taxed as income for the period than is actually due to the lessor where there is a cumulative normal rental excess for the period, the rent that is brought into account for corporation tax purposes is found by reducing the accountancy rental earnings by the cumulative normal rental excess, but not so as to bring into account an amount less than the normal rent for the period.

*Sections 911 to 914: **Relief for bad debts by reduction of cumulative rental excesses***

Overview

2700. These sections are concerned with bad debts. Broadly, the aim is to ensure that any bad debts are sensibly taken into account in calculating taxable profits and accountancy rental excesses and normal rental excesses. If the lease runs its course, the net rents taxed should equal the net rents payable after allowing for any bad debts.

Section 911: Relief for bad debts: reduction of cumulative accountancy rental excess

2701. This section deals with a bad debt deduction in respect of rent under a lease for a period of account if there is a cumulative accountancy rental excess for the period. It is based on paragraph 9(1) to (4) and (7) of Schedule 12 to FA 1997.

2702. *Subsection (2)* reduces the cumulative accountancy rental excess for a period where the accountancy rental earnings exceed normal rent by an amount equal to the excess of the bad debt deduction over the accountancy rental earnings.

2703. *Subsection (3)* deals with the converse situation if, for a period of account, normal rent is at least equal to accountancy rental earnings (so that it is the normal rent which is taxed). In those circumstances there are two restrictions.

2704. *Subsection (4)* provides that relief otherwise available under section 908(2) in a period for any cumulative accountancy rental excess brought forward from previous periods is restricted to any excess of the normal rent over any bad debt deduction given in respect of rents from the lease. That is because only the normal rent net of bad debt relief is in effect being brought into account for tax.

2705. *Subsection (5)* applies if the bad debt deduction exceeds the normal rent for a period of account. In such a case any cumulative accountancy rental excess brought forward from previous periods is reduced by the amount by which the bad debt deduction exceeds the normal rent. That is because the excess of the bad debt deduction over the normal rent for the period of account already represents relief for rents taxed in previous periods.

Section 912: Recovery of bad debts following reduction under section 911

2706. This section reinstates any relief for cumulative accountancy rental excess reduced under section 911 if the bad debt deduction is subsequently reversed (because the debt is recovered or prospects for its recovery improve). It is based on paragraph 9(5) to (7) of Schedule 12 to FA 1997.

Section 913: Relief for bad debts: reduction of cumulative normal rental excess

2707. This section deals with the interaction of bad debt deductions and relief for cumulative normal rental excess under section 910. It is based on paragraph 10(1) to(4) and (7) of Schedule 12 to FA 1997.

2708. As with section 911, the rationale is that the relief should only represent an excess of normal rent over accountancy rental earnings which have effectively been brought into account for tax and that the relief should only be given against rents similarly brought into account.

2709. The structure of the detailed rules is identical with that in section 911.

Section 914: Recovery of bad debts following reduction under section 913

2710. This section reinstates any relief for cumulative normal rental excess reduced under section 913 if the bad debt deduction is subsequently reversed (because the debt is recovered or prospects for its recovery improve). It is based on paragraph 10(5) to (7) of Schedule 12 to FA 1997.

Section 915: Effect of disposals of leases: general

2711. This section treats a period of account of the lessor as coming to an end for the purposes of this Part immediately before any disposal of the lessor's interest under the lease, the leased asset or an asset representing the leased asset. It is based on paragraph 12(5) to (7) of Schedule 12 to FA 1997.

2712. This enables the cumulative accountancy rental excess or the cumulative normal rental excess for the period of account of the lessor that then begins, and in which the disposal takes place, to be calculated.

2713. The remaining sub-paragraphs of paragraph 12 of Schedule 12 to FA 1997 are rewritten as section 37A of TCGA by Part 2 of Schedule 3 to TIOPA. See the commentary on that Schedule to TIOPA. *Subsection (5)* provides a signpost to that section.

*Section 916: **Assignments on which neither a gain nor a loss accrues***

2714. This section deals with the assignment of a lease in circumstances which are regarded for the purposes of corporation tax on chargeable gains as giving rise to neither a gain nor a loss. It is based on paragraph 7 of Schedule 12 to FA 1997.

2715. Paragraph 7(2) of Schedule 12 to FA 1997, on which *subsection (2)* is based, provides for a period of account of the assignor to end and a period of account of the assignee to begin with the assignment.

2716. Paragraph 7(3) of Schedule 12 to FA 1997 provides that the assignee takes over the assignor's "unused cumulative accountancy rental excess" or "unused cumulative normal rental excess".

2717. These "unused" cumulative excesses are the aggregate of the cumulative rental excess for the period of the assignor which ends with the assignmentand any rental excess for that period.

2718. But the combined effect of section 915(2) (basedon paragraph 12(5) of Schedule 12 to FA 1997) and subsection (2) is that the period of account of the assignor which ends with the assignment is infinitesimally short. There can, therefore, in practice be no accountancy rental excess or normal rental excess for that period.

2719. Accordingly, in rewriting paragraph 7(3) of Schedule 12 to FA 1997 in *subsections (3)* and *(4)*, the provision has been simplified by referring only to the cumulative accountancy rental excess or the cumulative normal rental excess for that period.

2720. *Subsection (5)* ensures that the division of the income tax provisions in Part 11A of ITA and the corporation tax provisions in this Part works as intended.

*Sections 917 to 922: **Capital allowances: clawback of major lump sums***

Overview

2721. These sections unpack paragraph 11 of Schedule 12 to FA 1997 to improve its accessibility.

*Section 917: **Effect of capital allowances: introduction***

2722. This section introduces sections 918 to 922 and provides that they apply if a major lump sum (see section 902(5)) falls to be paid in relation to a lease. It is based on paragraph 11(1) and (2) of Schedule 12 to FA 1997.

*Section 918: **Cases where expenditure taken into account under Part 2, 5 or 8 of CAA 2001***

2723. This section deals with capital allowances in respect of plant or machinery, mineral extraction and patent rights. It is based on paragraph 11(3) to (7) of Schedule 12 to FA 1997.

2724. *Subsection (2)* brings into account as disposal value for the purposes of CAA an amount equal to the amount or value of the major lump sum. This is subject to adjustment under *subsections (3)* to *(6)* if the disposal value is limited in accordance with CAA.

Section 919: Cases where expenditure taken into account under other provisions of CAA 2001

2725. This section deals with capital allowances given under any provision of CAA other than those mentioned in section 918. It is based on paragraph 11(8) and (14) of Schedule 12 to FA 1997.

2726. In these cases, an amount equal to the allowances given or, if less, the amount or value of the major lump sum is treated as a balancing charge.

2727. Following the repeal of section 532 of ICTA by CTA 2009, the extended definition of the Capital Allowances Act in paragraph 11(14) of Schedule 12 to FA 1997 is otiose and has not been rewritten.

Section 920: Capital allowances deductions: waste disposal and cemeteries

2728. This section deals with deductions for capital expenditure allowed under section 142, 145 or 147 of CTA 2009. It is based on paragraph 11(11) and (12) of Schedule 12 to FA 1997.

2729. In these cases, an amount equal to the deductions allowed or, if less, the amount or value of the major lump sum is treated as a trading receipt.

Section 921: Capital allowances deductions: films

2730. This section deals with deductions in respect of films allowed under section 40B(1) or 42 of F(No 2)A 1992. It is based on paragraph 11(9) and (10) of Schedule 12 to FA 1997.

2731. In these cases, if the amount or value of the major lump sum exceeds so much of that sum as was treated as a receipt of a revenue nature under section 40A(2) of F(No 2)A 1992, the excess is also treated as a receipt of a revenue nature.

Section 922: Contributors to capital expenditure

2732. This section deals with the case where capital allowances have been made to a person making contributions to capital expenditure on the provision of a leased asset under sections 537 to 542 of CAA. It is based on paragraph 11(13) of Schedule 12 to FA 1997.

2733. *Subsection (2)* provides that sections 918 and 919 have the same effect in relation to the contributor and those allowances as they do in relation to the lessor and allowances given to the lessor for such expenditure by the lessor.

Section 923: Pre-26 November 1996 schemes where this Chapter does not at first apply

2734. This section makes provision for recognising income from some finance leases which form part of a "pre–26 November 1996 scheme" as defined in section 930(1)(a). It is based on paragraph 13 of Schedule 12 to FA 1997.

2735. A lease which forms part of a pre–26 November 1996 scheme only falls within this Part if it meets all the conditions in section 902. It does not fall within Chapter 3 as that Chapter only applies to leases which do not form part of a pre–26 November 1996 scheme (see section 927(1)(b) and the definition of a post–25 November 1996 scheme in section 930(1)(b)).

2736. If a lease forming part of a pre–26 November 1996 scheme met all the conditions in section 902 on 26 November 1996, it falls within Chapter 2 for all periods of account beginning, or treated under section 932 as beginning, on or after that date, subject to section 901(3).

2737. But such a lease may not meet all those conditions until after 26 November1996. In that case, this section effects a catching up exercise by taxing under section 905 in the period when the lease is first subject to the rules in Chapter 2 the accumulated excess (if any) of the accountancy measure of income from the lease over the income actually taxed in earlier periods. No such excess relating to periods prior to 26 November 1996 can be taxed in this way nor are the assessments for earlier periods of account actually re–opened. The catching up is done in the period in which the conditions are met.

2738. *Subsection (3)(b)* provides that for the purposes of this Part the time when the conditions are satisfied forms its own brief period of account. This ensures that the computational provisions in this section work correctly.

2739. *Subsection (10)* provides for the case where for example there has been an assignment within section 916 and the lessor at an earlier time was within the charge to income tax.

*Section 924: **Post-25 November 1996 schemes to which Chapter 3 applied first***

2740. This sectionprovides continuity of reliefs when a lease changes status. It is based on paragraph 14 of Schedule 12 to FA 1997.

2741. It applies if a lease which is initially subject to the rules of Chapter 3 subsequently comes within those of Chapter 2. Any cumulative accountancy rental excess or any cumulative normal rental excess for the purposes of Chapter 3 counts for the purposes of Chapter2.

2742. *Subsection (4)* provides for the case where for example there has been an assignment within section 916 and the lessor at an earlier time was within the charge to income tax.

*Chapter 3: **Other finance leases***

Overview

2743. This Chapter is concerned with cases outside Chapter 2 where any assets are leased in such a way that they are a finance lease or loan in accordance with GAAP.

*Section 925: **Introduction to Chapter***

2744. This section introduces the Chapter. It is based on paragraph 15(1) of Schedule 12 to FA 1997.

*Section 926: **Purpose of this Chapter***

2745. This section sets out the main purpose of the Chapter. It is based on paragraph 15(2) of Schedule 12 to FA 1997.

2746. That purpose is to ensure that the taxable measure of earnings from the lease is not less than the accountancy measure. In effect, the rules take as the taxable earnings the amount which, but for this Part, the lessor would bring into account as rent from the lease for the purposes of corporation tax or the amount of the return on investment from the lease in accordance with GAAP, whichever is the higher. Unlike Chapter 2, this Chapter contains no special rules relating to reliefs for capital expenditure.

*Section 927: **Leases to which this Chapter applies***

2747. This section determines whether Chapter 3 applies to a particular lease. It is based on paragraph 16 of Schedule 12 to FA 1997.

2748. The Chapter only applies to leases granted on or after 26 November 1996 and then only if they form part of a post–25 November 1996 scheme as defined in section 930(1)(b) (see *subsection (1)(a)* and *(b)*).

2749. The lease may be of any property or rights (see subsection (1)(a) and the definition of "asset" in section 937). Contrast Parts 9 and 20 which apply only to leases of plant or machinery.

2750. In addition, for the Chapter to apply, condition A, but not all of conditions B to E, in section 902 must have been met in relation to the lease at some time on or after26 November 1996 in a period of account of the current lessor (see *subsection (1)(c)* and *(d)*). But once condition A has been met in relation to the lessor at the time, it is treated as continuing to be met as regards any subsequent lessor unless and until the lease is assigned to a wholly unrelated person (see *subsections (4)* to *(6)*).

2751. *Subsection (3)* provides that Chapter 2 does not apply to long funding leases of plant or machinery in relation to which Part 2 of CAA gives capital allowances to the lessee instead of the lessor. Chapter 2 of Part 9 of this Act sets out the basis of taxation of rental earnings under such leases.

2752. *Subsection (7)* is a necessary consequence of the split into separate provisions for corporation tax purposes and income tax purposes.

*Section 928: **Current lessor taxed by reference to accountancy rental earnings***

2753. This section provides for the lessor to bring into account for income tax purposes the accountancy rental earnings in respect of the lease for a period of account if they exceed the normal rent for the period. It is based on paragraph 17 of Schedule 12 to FA 1997.

2754. Paragraph 17 applies paragraph 5 of Schedule 12 to FA 1997 for the purposes of Part 2 of that Schedule by cross-reference. This section restates section 905 (based on paragraph 5 of Schedule 12 to FA 1997) in full for the purposes of Chapter 3.

*Section 929: **Application of provisions of Chapter 2 for purposes of this Chapter***

2755. This section applies the provisions of sections 906 to 916 for the purposes of this Chapter. It is based on paragraph 17 of Schedule 12 to FA 1997.

*Chapter 4: **Supplementary provisions***

Overview

2756. This Chapter contains supplementary and interpretative provisions.

*Section 930: **Pre-26 November 1996 schemes and post-25 November 1996 schemes***

2757. This section defines a "pre–26 November 1996 scheme" and a "post–25 November 1996 scheme". It is based on paragraph 27 of Schedule 12 to FA 1997.

2758. For the significance of these terms see the commentary on sections 923 and 927.

*Section 931: **Time apportionment where periods of account do not coincide***

2759. This section deals with situations where the measure of the accountancy rental earnings taxed under this Part on the lessor is that shown in the accounts of a connected person or the group as a whole and the period for which those accounts are drawn up is different from the period for which the lessor's accounts are drawn up. It is based on paragraph 24 of Schedule 12 to FA 1997.

2760. In these circumstances the figures are time–apportioned as necessary to arrive at the measure of accountancy rental earnings for the lessor's period of account.

Section 932: Periods of account and related periods of account and accounting periods

2761. This section sets out the definition of "period of account". It is based on paragraphs 23 and 30 of Schedule 12 to FA 1997.

Section 933: Connected persons

2762. This section provides that persons are regarded as connected throughout the period beginning at the time the leasing arrangements are made and ending with the termination of the current lessor's interest, if they are connected at some point during that period. It is based on paragraph 25(1) of Schedule 12 to FA 1997.

2763. Section 1176(1) provides that section 1122 ("connected" persons) applies for the purposes of this Act unless otherwise indicated (whether expressly or by implication). Accordingly it is unnecessary to rewrite paragraph 25(2) of Schedule 12 to FA 1997 here.

Section 934: Assets which represent the leased asset

2764. This section defines assets which represent leased assets. It is based on paragraph 26 of Schedule 12 to FA 1997.

2765. The purpose is to identify assets which in economic terms are essentially the same asset, in whole or in part, as the leased asset. This Part provides broadly that transactions in such assets are treated as transactions involving the leased asset itself.

Section 935: Parent undertakings and consolidated group accounts

2766. This section sets out an assumption about consolidated accounts of companies which would count as "parent undertakings" for the purposes of the Companies Act2006 but are not required for accounting purposes to prepare consolidated accounts in accordance with GAAP. It is based on paragraph 28 of Schedule 12 to FA1997.

2767. Such companies are regarded for the purposes of this Part as having to draw up consolidated accounts whether or not they are actually required to do so for accounting purposes. So parent companies incorporated outside the United Kingdom are treated, for the purpose of identifying leases within the Part and calculating the rental income from them, as having to draw up consolidated accounts if they would not be so required for accounting purposes.

Section 936: Assessments and adjustments

2768. This section ensures that all assessments and adjustments necessary to give effect to the provisions of this Part are made. It is based on paragraph 29 of Schedule 12 to FA 1997.

Section 937: Interpretation of Part

2769. This section provides definitions and interpretative rules. It is based on paragraph 30 of Schedule 12 to FA 1997.

Part 22: Miscellaneous provisions

Overview

2770. This Part contains miscellaneous rules about corporation tax liability.

2771. Chapter 1 is about transfers of trade without a change of ownership.

2772. Chapter 2 is about transfers of trade to obtain balancing allowances.

2773. Chapter 3 is about transfer of relief within partnerships.

2774. Chapter 4 is about surrenders of tax refunds within groups.

2775. Chapter 5 is about the set off of income tax deductions against corporation tax.

2776. Chapter 6 is about collection of tax from UK representatives of non-UK resident companies.

2777. Chapter 7 is about recovery of unpaid corporation tax due from non-UK resident companies.

2778. Chapter 8 contains provisions exempting certain bodies from corporation tax on some or all of their income.

2779. Chapter 9 contains provisions about European Economic Interest Groupings, harbour reorganisation schemes andthe use of different accounting practices within a group of companies.

Chapter 1: Transfers of trade without a change of ownership

Overview

2780. The Chapter rewrites sections 343, 343A and 344 of ICTA (company reconstructions without a change of ownership).

2781. It is possible (and common) for the trade, assets and liabilities of one company ("the predecessor") to be transferred to another ("the successor"). As a rule, on such a transfer the predecessor's trade ceases. This has two consequences in particular.

2782. First, if the predecessor has incurred qualifying expenditure on plant and machinery, a balancing charge is imposed or a balancing allowance is given under Part2 of CAA (plant and machinery allowances). Also, the successor is entitled to plant and machinery allowances on the amount paid to the predecessor for the plant and machinery. Similar rules apply to the other types of capital allowance.

2783. Second, if the predecessor has incurred losses in its trade they cannot be carried forward under section 393 of ICTA. To the extent that they cannot be relieved under section 393A of ICTA or by group relief, they are wasted.

2784. But the predecessor and the successor are not necessarily independent. If they are under common ownership, the owners of the companies may have commercial reasons for transferring the trade and net assets from one to another. Where this is the case, section 343 of ICTA makes it possible for:

- capital allowances to be given to the successor as if the trade was still being carried on by the predecessor; and
- the predecessor's unrelieved trade losses to be carried forward to the successor.

2785. Sections 343 and 344 of ICTA were based on section 61 of FA 1965, which was itself modelled on section 17 of FA 1954 and Schedule 3 to that Act.

2786. Section 343A of ICTA was inserted by paragraph 1 of Schedule 6 to FA 2007.

2787. The sections rewriting sections 343, 343A and 344 of ICTA are laid out in the following order.

- Sections 938 and 939 are introductory.
- Sections 940 to 943 specify the transfers to which the Chapter applies.
- Sections 944 to 950 specify the effect of the Chapter in relation to transfers to which it applies.
- Sections 951 to 953 are supplementary.

Section 938: Overview of Chapter

2788. This section gives an overview of the Chapter. It is new.

Section 939: Meaning of "transfer of a trade" and related expressions

2789. This interpretative section is based on section 343(1) of ICTA.

Section 940: Transfers to which Chapter applies

2790. This section states that there are two conditions which must be met if the Chapter is to apply to a transfer of a trade: the ownership condition and the tax condition. It is based on section 343(1) of ICTA.

Section 941: The ownership condition

2791. This section lays down the first of the two conditions which need to be met if the Chapter is to apply to a transfer. It is based on sections 343(1) and 344(1), (2) and (4) of ICTA.

2792. The ownership condition works in the following way. First, it is necessary to identify persons having a 75% interest in the transferred trade at the time of the transfer or at any time in the two-year period beginning immediately after the transfer. Then, it is necessary to see whether those same persons have a 75% interest in the transferred trade at any time in the one-year period beginning immediately before the transfer. If they do, the ownership condition is met.

2793. *Subsections (3)* and *(4)* are based on the second sentence of section 343(1) of ICTA; in that context, "comprise" is non-exhaustive.

2794. *Subsection (5)(a)* is based on section 344(1)(a) of ICTA. Section 344(1)(a) refers to "a trade carried on by two or more persons", but does not actually need to cover trades carried on by non-corporates. Subsection (5)(a) therefore says, more precisely, "if two or more companies carry on a trade".

Section 942: Options that may be applied for the purposes of the ownership condition

2795. This section sets out various options that may be applied to see whether the ownership condition is met. It is based on section 344(2) and (3) of ICTA.

2796. Schedule 1 to the Interpretation Act 1978 defines "person" as including a body of persons corporate or unincorporate. Option 3 in *subsection (1)* therefore compresses "person or body of persons" in the tail words of section 344(2) of ICTA to "person".

2797. Option 3 in subsection (1)is more focused on the final result than the tail words of section 344(2) of ICTA. But this difference is merely verbal.

2798. It is implicit in section 344(3)(c) of ICTA that ownership includes indirect ownership; *subsection (6)* makes this implication explicit and, therefore, applies to the whole of the section.

Section 943: The tax condition

2799. This section lays down the second of the two conditions which need to be met if the Chapter is to apply to a transfer. It is based on section 343(1) of ICTA.

2800. Briefly, the tax condition is that the trade has been subject to United Kingdom corporate taxation at all material times.

2801. Section 343(1)(b) of ICTA has a cryptic reference to "the period taken for the comparison under paragraph (a) above". *Subsection (2)* expressly defines this period. Subsection (2) refers to section 941(1)(a) and (b) in reverse order. This is deliberate.

Section 941 (the ownership condition) starts with the new owners of the transferred trade and moves from there to see whether common ownership can be established. By contrast, section 943 (the tax condition) is seeking to establish whether the trade has been subject to United Kingdom corporate taxation throughout the relevant period and so starts at the beginning of that period and works forwards.

*Section 944: **Modified application of Chapter 2 of Part 4***

2802. This section modifies the application of the Chapter of this Act giving relief for trade losses. It is based on section 343(1), (3) and (4A) of ICTA.

2803. If this Chapter applies to a transfer of a trade, *subsection (2)* disapplies the terminal loss rules and *subsection (3)* entitles the successor to relief for trade losses carried forward.

*Section 945: **Cases in which predecessor retains more liabilities than assets***

2804. This section restricts the relief given to the successor under section 944(3) to the extent that (a) the successor does not take over the predecessor's liabilities and (b) the predecessor does not have enough assets to meet them in full. It is based on sections 343(4) and 344(5) to (7) of ICTA.

2805. The aim of this section is to stop tax relief being given twice for the same expenditure. It is fairly common, especially in receivership cases, for the liabilities of the business not to be transferred with the trade. Those liabilities are then left stranded in the predecessor company, and the creditors stand little or no chance of being paid. In such a case, the creditors have to write off the debts owed to them by the predecessor. If these creditors have incurred these debts in the course of their trades of (a) supplying goods or services or (b) lending money, the write-offs are tax deductible as trading expenses.

2806. But for this section, the successor could also claim tax relief for the same expenditure under the heading of losses carried forward. Under this section, broadly speaking, the losses disallowed in the successor's hands equate to the amount of the debts which the predecessor is unable to pay.

2807. *Subsection (1)* states when the section applies, using the terms "L" and "A".

2808. *Subsections (2)* and *(3)* define "L" and "A" respectively.

2809. *Subsections (4)* and *(5)* use a formula to determine the amount by which the successor's relief is restricted. That formula uses "L" and "A" to define "E".

*Section 946: **Rules for determining "L"***

2810. This section supplements section 945 of this Act. It is based on section 344(6), (8), (9), (11) and (12) of ICTA.

2811. This section recasts section 344(9) of ICTA to remove the curious expression "a liability *representing* the predecessor's share capital, share premium account, reserves or relevant loan stock".

2812. In *subsection (6)(a)*, the expression "issued or otherwise originated" is broad enough to cover a transfer to reserves.

2813. The wording of section 344(9) of ICTA is broad enough to cover a series of conversions of capital. Subsection (6)(a) makes this point explicit. In practice, however, such a series would be unlikely to meet the temporal condition imposed by *subsection (6)(b)*.

2814. In section 344(11) of ICTA, the words "(whether secured or unsecured)" block the argument that unsecured loan notes cannot be "relevant loan stock" because if they are not secured they cannot be securities. *Subsection (8)* therefore retains this parenthesis.

*Section 947: **Rules for determining "A"***

2815. This section supplements section 945 of this Act. It is based on section 344(5), (7) and (10) of ICTA.

2816. Section 344(7)(a) of ICTA defines "the value of assets (other than money)". *Subsection (3)* omits as unnecessary the reference to money.

*Section 948: **Modified application of CAA 2001***

2817. This section modifies the application of CAA. It is based on section 343(1) and (2) of ICTA.

2818. Under *subsections (2)* to*(4)*, for capital allowances purposes, the successor stands in the predecessor's shoes.

2819. Section 561A(2)(c) of CAA refers to section 343 of ICTA, whereas section 561(5) of CAA refers to section 343(2). Nothing turns on this distinction, so *subsection (6)* simply refers to sections 561 and 561A of CAA.

*Section 949: **Dual resident investing companies***

2820. This section prevents the successor from benefiting from section 948 if it is a dual resident investing company. It is based on section 343(2) of ICTA.

2821. The source legislation refers to section 404 of ICTA. Section 404 of ICTA is rewritten in section 109. As far as possible, this section is conformed to that section.

2822. The source legislation defines "dual resident investing company" by reference to section 404 of ICTA but does not spell out how the reference in that section to "the material accounting period" is to be applied in the context of transfers of trade. This section uses the concept of "the transfer accounting period" to bring out the implicit requirements of the source legislation. This is a drafting clarification which does not change the law.

2823. *Subsection (1)* is the main operative provision.

2824. *Subsection (2)* specifies when a company is a dual resident investing company.

2825. *Subsection (3)* defines the expression "dual resident company", which is used in subsection (2)(a), and *subsections (4)* to *(6)* specify the conditions mentioned in subsection (2)(b).

2826. *Subsection (7)* defines "non-UK tax", "trading company" and "the transfer accounting period".

*Section 950: **Transfers of trades involving business of leasing plant or machinery***

2827. This section deals with transfers of trades involving businesses of leasing plant or machinery. It is based on section 343A of ICTA.

*Section 951: **Part of trade treated as separate trade***

2828. This section deals with transfers of parts of trade. It is based on section 343(1) and (8) of ICTA.

2829. This section refers to "activities" of a trade and "part" of a trade, as these expressions have been the subject of judicial comment: see Falmer Jeans Ltd v Rodin (1990), 63 TC 55.[6]

---

6 [1990] STC 270.

2830. Section 344(5) and (6) of ICTA do not expressly provide that, if there has been an apportionment, only the assets and liabilities apportioned to the transferred trade are to be taken into account. *Subsection (6)* makes these points explicit.

Section 952: Apportionment if part of trade treated as separate trade

2831. This section provides for apportionments to be made if, in accordance with section 951(2) or (4), part of a trade is treated as a separate trade. It is based on section 343(9) and (10) of ICTA.

2832. *Subsection (1)* expressly requires apportionments to be reasonable as well as just. This is a minor change in the law: see *Change 33*in Annex 1. The same change has been made in previous rewrite Acts.

Section 953: Application of Chapter to further transfers of a trade

2833. This section deals with further transfers of trades. It is based on section 343(7) of ICTA.

2834. *Subsection (1)* spells out when the section applies.

2835. Under subsection (1)(a), there must be a transfer (the original transfer) which meets the ownership condition and the tax condition. Under section 940 of this Act, this Chapter applies to the original transfer.

2836. Under subsection (1)(b), there must be a further transfer (as defined).

2837. Under subsection (1)(c), the further transfer must take place at some time before the end of the period specified in *subsection (7)*.

2838. It is implicit in section 343(7) that the ownership condition was met in relation to the original transfer only on or after the further transfer. Subsection (1)(d) lays this down as an express condition for this section to apply.

2839. If section 343(2) to (5) of ICTA already apply in relation to a transfer, there is no need to rely on section 343(7) of that Act. Accordingly, subsection (1)(e) lays down, as an express condition for this section to apply, that, were it not for this section, this Chapter would not apply to the further transfer.

2840. *Subsection (2)* applies the Chapter to the further transfer as well as to the original transfer.

2841. *Subsection (3)* explains how the references to "the successor" and "the predecessor" in this Chapter are to be interpreted in cases where the Chapter applies to a transfer by virtue of this section.

2842. *Subsection (4)* extends the scope of "the successor" in relation to the original transfer.

2843. *Subsection (5)* extends the scope of "the predecessor" in relation to the further transfer.

2844. *Subsection (6)* covers successive further transfers.

2845. *Subsection (7)* defines the period mentioned in subsection (1)(c).

Chapter 2: Transfers of trade to obtain balancing allowances

Overview

2846. This Chapter counters certain schemes for accelerating relief for expenditure qualifying for capital allowances. Such schemes involve a trading company being acquired by a profitable group and, as part of the arrangements, the trading company selling its trade to an unconnected buyer a short time later.

2847. This Chapter is based on section 343ZA of ICTA.

Section 954: Transfer of activities on complete cessation of trade

2848. This section deals with capital allowance schemes involving the transfer of activities on the complete cessation of a trade. It is based on section 343ZA(1), (4), and (5) of ICTA.

2849. *Subsection (1)* states when this section applies.

2850. *Subsection (2)* modifies the application of CAA in cases in which this section applies.

2851. Section 343ZA(4) of ICTA modifies the application of section 343(2) of that Act. Section 343(2) is rewritten in section 948. *Subsections (3)* to *(5)* are based on section 343ZA(4) of ICTA; for the convenience of the reader, they restate the propositions in section 948(2) to (4) rather than applying those provisions with modifications.

2852. *Subsection (6)* applies if the successor carries on the activities of the trade as part of its trade.

Section 955: Transfer of activities on part cessation of trade

2853. This section deals with capital allowance schemes involving the transfer of activities on the part cessation of a trade. It is based on section 343ZA(2), (4) and (6) of ICTA.

2854. *Subsection (1)* states when this section applies.

2855. *Subsection (2)* modifies the application of CAA in cases in which this section applies.

2856. Section 343ZA(4) of ICTA modifies the application of section 343(2) of that Act. Section 343(2) is rewritten in section 948. *Subsections (4)* to *(6)* are based on section 343ZA(4); for the convenience of the reader, they restate the propositions in section 948(2) to (4) rather than applying those provisions with modifications.

2857. *Subsection (7)* applies if the successor carries on the activities of the trade as part of its trade.

Section 956: Apportionment if part of trade treated as separate trade

2858. This section requires apportionments to be made if part of a trade is treated as a separate trade under section 954(6) or 955(7). It is based on section 343ZA(7) and (8) of ICTA.

2859. *Subsection (1)*requires apportionments to be made in such cases. In expressly requiring the apportionments to be reasonable as well as just, subsection (8) makes a minor change in the law. See *Change 33* in Annex 1 and the commentary on section 952.

Section 957: Supplementary and interpretative provisions

2860. This section provides that if Chapter 1 of this Part applies then this Chapter does not. It is based on section 343ZA(3) of ICTA.

Chapter 3: Transfer of relief within partnerships

Overview

2861. This Chapter deals with arrangements within firms for transferring relief between partners.

Section 958: Application

2862. This section sets the scope of the Chapter. It is based on section 116 of ICTA.

*Section 959: **Arrangements for transfer of relief***

2863. This section sets out the sorts of arrangements to which the Chapter applies. It is based on section 116 of ICTA.

2864. *Subsection (1)* identifies four effects that the arrangements may have. Effects 1 and 2 correspond to paragraph (b) of section 116(1) of ICTA; Effects 3 and 4 correspond to paragraph (a) of section 116(1) of ICTA.

2865. *Subsection (2)* makes clear that the Chapter operates by reference to *part* of a company's share of the firm's profits or losses as it operates by reference to the whole of the profits or losses. So the Act does not reproduce from section 116(1) of ICTA "any portion of" any of the profits or losses.

2866. *Subsection (4)* is the rule that a payment for group relief (see also section 183) does not trigger the anti-avoidance rules in this Chapter.

*Section 960: **Restrictions on use of reliefs***

2867. This section sets out the results if this Chapter applies. It is based on section 116 of ICTA.

2868. *Subsection (1)* is the rule about the firm's losses. The partner company's share of the firm's trading loss is available only against its share of profits from the same trade. This means that a claim may be made under section 45 (losses carried forward) but not under section 37 (relief against total profits).

2869. *Subsection (3)* is the rule about the firm's profits. It isolates the partner company's share of the profits from reliefs that would otherwise be available (unless they are losses of the firm's trade available in accordance with subsection (1)). So the partner company may not set against its share of the firm's profits either:

- trading losses of another trade (paragraph (a) of the subsection); or
- other reliefs (paragraph (b) of the subsection).

*Section 961: **Non-trading profits and losses***

2870. This section extends the Chapter so that it applies to non-trading activities carried on in partnership as it applies to trades. It is based on section 116 of ICTA.

2871. *Subsection (1)* identifies the non-trading profits to which the Chapter applies. They are the profits from the sources listed in section 1173.

2872. *Subsection (3)* is a rule for "special leasing" allowances within section 259 or 260 of CAA. The partner company's share of the allowances is not available against the partner company's other profits.

*Section 962: **Interpretation of Chapter***

2873. This section provides some definitions. It is based on section 116 of ICTA.

2874. *Subsection (2)* is a link to Part 17 of CTA 2009 (partnerships). In particular, "accounting period of a firm" is explained in section 1261 of that Act as meaning the accounting period of the company that is deemed to carry on the firm's trade.

2875. The definition of "connected person" is in section 1122 of this Act, as applied by section 1176(1).

Chapter 4: Surrender of tax refund within group

Overview

2876. Section 102 of FA 1989 enables a group of companies to mitigate the differential between the rates of interest on unpaid and overpaid tax. In the absence of section 102, a group which, overall, had paid the correct amount of tax on the correct dates could still suffer a net interest charge if it split those payments incorrectly between members of the group at the time of payment. Section 102 allows the group to mitigate this by applying hindsight to reallocate the tax payments to the right companies with effect from the date of payment.

2877. Regulation 9 of the Corporation Tax (Instalment Payments) Regulations 1998[7] applies section 102 of FA 1989 with modifications in cases where a tax refund falls to be made to the surrendering company in respect of an amount paid in respect of its total liability for an accounting period and (a) either the surrendering company or the recipient company is a large company (within the meaning of regulation 3 of those Regulations) as respects that accounting period or (b) both the surrendering company and the recipient company are large companies as respects that accounting period. The continuity of the law provisions in Part 1 of Schedule 2 ensure that this regulation continues to apply undisturbed.

Section 963: Power to surrender tax refund

2878. This section lays down the conditions to be met if a tax refund is to be surrendered within a group of companies. It is based on section 102(1) to (3) and (8) of FA 1989.

Section 964: Effects of surrender of tax refund

2879. This section sets out the effects of a surrender of a tax refund for the surrendering company and the recipient company. It is based on section 102(4), (5) and (6) of FA 1989.

Section 965: Interest on tax overpaid or underpaid

2880. This section deals with the consequences of a surrender of a tax refund for interest on unpaid and overpaid tax. It is based on section 102(4A) of FA 1989.

2881. *Subsection (1)(b)* omits as spent the reference in section 102(4A) of FA 1989 to section 826(7) of ICTA, which has been repealed.

Section 966: Payments for surrendered tax refunds

2882. This section concerns the consequences of making payments for the transfer of tax refunds. It is based on section 102(7) of FA 1989.

Chapter 5: Set off of income tax deductions against corporation tax

Section 967: Deductions from payments received by UK resident companies

2883. This section explains how income tax deducted from payments received by UK resident companies is set off against corporation tax. It is based on section 7(2) and (4) of ICTA.

2884. The exception for relevant loan interest in section 7(3) is rewritten by consequential amendment to section 369(6) of ICTA. Section 369 has not been repealed because the relief for certain life annuity payments continues to be in force.

---

7 SI 1998/3175.

Section 968: Deductions from payments received by non-UK resident companies

2885. This section explains how income tax deducted from payments received by non-UK resident companies is set off against corporation tax. It is based on section 11(3) of ICTA.

2886. As is the case for section 7(3) of ICTA, the exception for relevant loan interest in section 11(4) is rewritten by consequential amendment to section 369(6) of ICTA.

Chapter 6: Collection etc of tax from UK representatives of non–UK resident companies

Overview

2887. This Chapter sets out the obligations and liabilities of a UK representative of a non-UK resident company carrying on a trade through a permanent establishment in the United Kingdomin relation to the assessment, collection and recovery of corporation tax on the chargeable profits of the non-UK resident company attributable to the permanent establishment. As to "chargeable profits" see section 19 of CTA 2009.

Section 969: Introduction to Chapter

2888. This section introduces the Chapter and sets out the rules for determining the extent to which and the period for which a permanent establishment is a UK representative. It is based on section 150(1) and (2) of FA 2003.

2889. A permanent establishment in the United Kingdom through which a non-UK resident company carries on a trade is the UK representative of the non-UK resident company in relation to the chargeable profits attributable to the permanent establishment. See *Rule 1* in *subsection (3)*.

2890. If a permanent establishment in the United Kingdom of a non-UK resident company ceases to be a permanent establishment through which the company carries on a trade, it nevertheless continues thereafter to be the UK representative of the non-UK resident company in relation to the chargeable profits attributable to the permanent establishment. See *Rule 2* in subsection (3).

Section 970: Obligations and liabilities in relation to corporation tax

2891. This section treats the obligations and liabilities of the non-UK resident company in respect of the chargeable profits of the trade carried on through a permanent establishment in the United Kingdom as also being the obligations and liabilities of the UK representative. It is based on section 150(1) and (3) of FA 2003.

Section 971: Exceptions

2892. This section sets out circumstances in which:

- certain obligations or liabilities of a non-UK resident company attach to its UK representative (*subsections (1)* and *(2)*);
- a non-UK resident company is bound by the mistakes of its UK representative (*subsection (3)*); and
- a UK representative may be proceeded against for a criminal offence (*subsection (4)*).

2893. It is based on section 150(4) to (6) of FA 2003.

Section 972: Interpretation of Chapter

2894. This section defines terms used in the Chapter. It is based on section 150(7) and(7A) of FA 2003.

2895. In the definition of "information" in *subsection (1)*, the words "to the Commissioners for Her Majesty's Revenue and Customs or to any officer of Revenue and Customs" have been substituted for the words "to the Board or any officer of the Board" in the source legislation. This gives effect to section 50(1) and (2) of CRCA which require references to the terms in the source legislation to be taken as references to the substituted terms.

Chapter 7: Recovery of unpaid corporation tax due from non–UK resident company

Overview

2896. This Chapter enables unpaid corporation tax due from a non-UK resident company to be recovered from a related company.

Section 973: Introduction to Chapter

2897. This section introduces the Chapter and defines "company" for the purposes of sections 973(1) and (4) and 974 to 980. It is based on paragraph 6 of Schedule 28 to FA 2000.

Section 974: Case in which this Chapter applies

2898. This section states when this Chapter applies. It is based on paragraph 1 of Schedule 28 to FA 2000.

2899. *Subsection (2)* defines "the taxpayer company" for the purposes of this Chapter.

Sections 975 and 976: Meaning of "the relevant period"; meaning of "related company"

2900. These interpretative sectionsare based on paragraph 2 of Schedule 28 to FA2000.

Section 977: Notice requiring payment of unpaid tax

2901. This section enables an officer of Revenue and Customs to serve notice on a related company requiring it to pay unpaid corporation tax due from the taxpayer company. It is based on paragraph 3 of Schedule 28 to FA 2000.

2902. Paragraph 3(1) of Schedule 28 to FA 2000 gives "the Board" (that is, the Commissioners for HMRC) the power to serve notice to pay unpaid corporation tax due from the taxpayer company. In practice, the Commissioners delegate this function to officers of Revenue and Customs, and *subsection (1)* reflects this. This is a minor change in the law without any practical implications; see *Change 5* in Annex 1.

2903. Like the source legislation, subsection (1) provides that an officer "… *may* serve a notice …". This gives officers the power, but not the obligation, to serve notice on related companies, and therefore allows HMRC to exercise managerial discretion.

Section 978: Time limit for giving notice

2904. This section sets the time limit for giving notice under section 977. It is based on paragraph 4 of Schedule 28 to FA 2000.

2905. Paragraph 4(3)(d) of Schedule 28 to FA 2000 says: "if … the Inland Revenue amend the return …". In this context, "the Inland Revenue" is not expressly defined; however, the reference is to amendment under paragraph 34(2) of Schedule 18 to FA1998. As originally enacted, paragraph 34(2) of that Schedule referred to amendments being made by "the Inland Revenue", which was defined in paragraph 95(1) of that Schedule to mean any officer of the Board; by implication, therefore, "the Inland Revenue" in paragraph 4(3)(d) of Schedule 28 to FA 2000 had the same meaning.

2906. Paragraph 68(a) and (b) of Schedule 4 to CRCA (a) substituted "an officer of Revenue and Customs" for "the Inland Revenue" in paragraph 34(2) of Schedule 18 to FA 1998 and (b) consequentially repealed paragraph 95 of that Schedule. Also, section 50(2) of CRCA provided that any reference in an enactment (however expressed) to an officer of the Board was to be taken as a reference to an officer of Revenue and Customs. By implication, therefore, CRCA substituted "an officer of Revenue and Customs" for "the Inland Revenue" in paragraph 4(3)(d) of Schedule 28 to FA 2000. In rewriting paragraph 4(3)(d) of that Schedule, *subsection (3)(d)* explicitly refers to "an officer of Revenue and Customs".

*Section 979: **Amount payable in consortium case***

2907. This section determines for the purposes of section 977(1)(b) the amount payable in a consortium case. It is based on paragraph 5 of Schedule 28 to FA2000.

2908. In paragraph 5(1) of Schedule 28 to FA 2000, the words "limited to" merely repeat the point that the amount to be charged in a consortium case is "the appropriate proportion" in paragraph 3(1)(b) of that Schedule. *Subsection (1)* therefore omits them as otiose.

*Section 980: **Chapter 7: supplementary***

2909. This supplementary section is based on paragraph 6 of Schedule 28 to FA2000.

2910. For the sake of consistency with section 717(1) of this Act, *subsection (2)* refers not only to income and profits but also to losses. This verbal change has no substantive effect.

*Chapter 8: **Exemptions***

Overview

2911. This Chapter provides exemption from corporation tax for certain bodies.

2912. This Chapter rewrites some, but not all, of the provisions in Chapter 6 of Part 12 of ICTA. The sections dealing with exemptions for charities, and for bodies that are treated as charities, which form part of Chapter 6 have been included with the rules for charitable companies etc in Part 11 of this Act.

2913. A number of sections of Part 12 of ICTA are obsolete and this Act repeals these redundant sections.

*Section 981: **Exemption for trade unions and eligible employers' associations***

2914. This section provides a limited relief for trade unions and employers' associations. It is based on section 467(1), (3) and (3A) of ICTA.

2915. Section 467 is drafted in terms of "a trade union" and provides a definition of the meaning of "trade union". This definition includes specified employers' associations. The inclusion of employers' associations in the definition of "trade union" reflects the old system under which there was a single system of registration for trade unions and employers' associations. Following the Industrial Relations Act 1971 - or, in Northern Ireland, the Industrial Relations (Northern Ireland) Order 1992 (SI 1992/807 (N.I.5)), - there are separate systems of registration for the two kinds of organisation, which are accordingly separately defined.

2916. The approach in section 981 reflects this change in the arrangements for registration and includes references to both "trade union" and "eligible employers' association". The use of "eligible" is intended to flag at the outset that not all employers' associations qualify for the exemption. Only those employers' associations that were in existence and qualified for the exemption in 1971 (1992 for Northern Ireland employers' associations) qualify.

*Section 982: **Qualifying income or gains***

2917. This section defines the types of income subject to relief and provides a partial definition of what provident benefits are. It is based on section 467(1) and (2) of ICTA.

*Section 983: **Meaning of "trade union" and "eligible employers' association"***

2918. This section defines trade union and eligible employer's association. It is based on section 467(4) of ICTA.

*Section 984: **Local authorities and local authority associations***

2919. This section exempts United Kingdom local authorities and local authority associations from corporation tax. It is based on section 519 of ICTA.

2920. The definitions of "local authority" and "local authority association" are in section 1130 and section 1131 respectively.

*Section 985: **Health service bodies***

2921. This section exempts health service bodies from corporation tax. It is based on section 519A(1) of ICTA.

2922. It is the first of three sections that deal with the exemption from corporation tax of health service bodies. The exemption is straightforward except in the case of NHS foundation trusts where under certain circumstances the exemption does not apply. The sections are based on section 519A of ICTA.

*Section 986: **Meaning of "health service body"***

2923. This section provides a definition of "health service body". It is based on section 519A(2).

2924. Section 519A(2) of ICTA states that the definition of "health service body" included a National Health Service trust constituted under section 12A of the National Health Service (Scotland) Act 1978. However, there are no longer any "National Health Service trusts" in Scotland (they were abolished as at 1 April 2004) and the NHS Reform (Scotland) Act 2004 repealed section 12A of the 1978 Act. The reference to section 12A is therefore not reproduced in this provision.

2925. Section 519A(2) of ICTA also states that the definition of "health service body" included a Health and Social Services trust established under the Health and Personal Social Services (Northern Ireland) Order 1991. However such trusts were renamed by section 1 of the Health and Social Care (Reform) Act (Northern Ireland) 2009. The table accordingly refers to Health and Social Care trusts.

2926. The table includes references to Health and Social Services Boards and the Northern IrelandCentral Services Agency for the Health and Social Services. These bodies were dissolved from 1 April 2009 by the Health and Social Care (Reform) Act (Northern Ireland) 2009.

2927. The 2009 Act makes provision about the transfer of functions of Health and Social Services Boards and of the Northern Ireland Central Services Agency for the Health and Social Services to other bodies. Section 27 of the that Act makes provision about the translation of legislative references to the old bodies into references to bodies to whom functions of the old bodies have been transferred. Subsections (2) and (4) of that section deal with the transfers of functions of the bodies referred to in section 519A(2) of ICTA.

The translations of the references do not operate generally, but only "in relation to" functions that have been transferred from the old bodies to the new bodies.

2928. Legislative references to the old bodies do not therefore include references to functions which were not carried on previously by those bodies.

2929. In order to preserve the current law this Act retains the references to the old bodies.

Section 987: NHS foundation trusts

2930. This section removes some classes of activity carried on by NHS foundation trusts from the exemption to corporation tax in section 985. It is based on section 519A(3), (4), (5), (6), (7), and (8) of ICTA.

2931. The exception from the exemption broadly applies to commercial activities.

2932. *Subsection (1)* provides that an order must be made by the Treasury for the exception to apply.

2933. Under the terms of Health and Social Care (Community Health and Standards) Act 2003 an NHS foundation trust is not obliged to carry on commercial activity through a separate company. Such activity may be subject to corporation tax if the conditions set out in *subsections (2)* and *(3)* are met.

2934. The taxation treatment of NHS foundation trusts may be contrasted with that for local authorities and local authority associations (see section 984). Using powers under section 99(4) of the Local Government Act 2003, the Government issued the Local Government (Best Value Authorities) (Power to Trade) (England) Order 2004 (SI 2004/1705). This order allows local authorities to trade but provides that the trade must be carried on by a company.

Section 988: Issue departments of the Reserve Bank of India and the State Bank of Pakistan

2935. This section exempts from corporation tax the income of the issue departments of the central banks of India and Pakistan. It is based on section 517 of ICTA.

Section 989: Agricultural societies

2936. This section exempts profits made by an agricultural society from exhibitions or shows where those profits are applied solely to the purposes of the society.It is based on section 510 of ICTA.

2937. The section gives statutory effect to the decision in Peterborou gh Royal Foxhound Show Society v CIR (1936), 20 TC 249 HC, by replacing the reference in section 510 ICTA to livestock breeding with a reference to the breeding of any kind of animal.

2938. Section 510 ICTA includes "livestock breeding" among the activities that define an agricultural society for the purpose of the exemption under that section. In the case mentioned above it was held that "livestock breeding" in section 23 FA 1924 (which became section 510 ICTA) includes foxhound breeding. The judge in that case said that,

> The words "live stock" are ordinarily and properly used in contrast with dead stock and include all live animals and birds the breeding of which is regulated by man.

2939. The decision in that case was applied in CIR v Glasgow (City) Ornithological Association (1938), 21 TC 445 Court of Session, in which it was held that "livestock" in section 23 of FA 1924 included caged birds.

Chapter 9: Other miscellaneous provisions

Overview

2940. This Chapter amends in certain cases the way in which the normal corporation tax rules apply.

Section 990: European Economic Interest Groupings

2941. This section sets out the basic rules that determine how corporation tax is to be charged on the members of a European Economic Interest Grouping (EEIG). It is based on section 510A of ICTA.

2942. Members of a grouping may be companies, individuals or partnerships. See section 842 of ITA for the income tax rules that apply to the non-corporate members of an EEIG.

Section 991: Harbour reorganisation schemes: corporation tax

2943. This section provides that if certain conditions are met, a trade transferred to a harbour authority as a result of a harbour reorganisation scheme is certified as not having ceased; and losses which would have been available to the transferor for relief may be used by the transferee. It is based on section 518(1), (2) and (3) of ICTA.

2944. The section is the first of five sections that deal with the corporation tax consequences of the transfer of a trade under a harbour reorganisation scheme.

2945. One of the conditions set out in *subsection (1)* is that the section applies only if the trade is transferred from a body corporate that is not a limited liability company. It is therefore clear that the section and those that follow can apply only in very limited circumstances.

Section 992: Harbour reorganisation schemes: capital allowances etc

2946. This section sets out the rules relating to capital allowances that apply when a trade is transferred to a harbour authority under a harbour reorganisation scheme. It is based on section 518(4) and (5) of ICTA.

Section 993: Harbour reorganisation schemes: chargeable gains

2947. This section sets out the rules relating to loss relief against chargeable gains that apply when a trade is transferred to a harbour authority under a harbour reorganisation scheme. It is based on section 518(7) of ICTA.

Section 994: Transfer of part of trade

2948. This section modifies the rules in section 991 if only part of a trade is transferred to a harbour authority under a certified harbour reorganisation scheme. It is based on section 518(8) and (9) of ICTA.

2949. *Subsection (4)(b)* refers to the need to make "just and reasonable apportionments" in certain circumstances and includes a minor change in the law. The change is made to bring the corporation tax code into line with that for income tax. See *Change 33* in Annex 1.

Section 995: Interpretation of sections 991 to 994

2950. This section provides a number of definitions for sections 991 to 994. It is based on section 518(10) of ICTA.

Section 996: Use of different accounting practices within a group of companies

2951. This section deals with the use of different accounting practices within a group of companies. It is based on section 51 of FA 2004.

2952. If the accounting treatments for a transaction under international accounting standards and UK GAAP are different, this could give rise to a tax mismatch: for example, one company might recognise a (deductible) loss before the other company recognised the corresponding (taxable) gain. If the two companies were members of the same group, the intra-group gain and loss would be cancelled out in arriving at the group's consolidated profit before tax – but the group would still have the tax advantage of obtaining the deduction before having to recognise the taxable income.

2953. Accordingly, a tie-breaker provision is needed to deal with such cases. This section of the Act gives UK GAAP the priority, whether the tax advantage arises by accident or design.

Part 23: Company distributions

Overview

2954. This Part sets out what is and what is not a company distribution for the purposes of the Corporation Tax Acts. It rewrites Part 6 and section 418 of ICTA and elements of sections 477A, 486 and 490 of ICTA.

2955. The definition of "the Corporation Tax Acts" in the Interpretation Act 1978 refers to enactments relating to the taxation of company distributions and associated income tax provisions. Some income tax rules are included in this Act. But the income tax effect of some provisions (notably sections 249 and 252 of ICTA) are relocated in ITTOIA.

2956. Provisions of an administrative nature relating to specific aspects of distributions have been located alongside the provisions to which they relate. More general provisions about returns and information are in Chapter 6.

2957. The structure of the Part is as follows.

- Chapter 2 sets out what is treated as a distribution.
- Chapter 3 sets out what is not a distribution.
- Chapter 4 deals with certain special cases.
- Chapter 5 deals with demergers.
- Chapter 6 contains provisions about returns and information.
- Chapter 7 deals with tax credits in connection with distributions.
- Chapter 8 provides interpretation.

Chapter 1: Introduction

Section 997: Overview of Part

2958. This section sets out the scope of the Part. It is new.

2959. The section provides signposts to rules that define what is and is not a distribution, to rules that extend the meaning of distribution, and to the power in section 152 of FA 1995 to make modifications in relation to open-ended investment companies. Section 152 of FA 1995 is not being rewritten.

Chapter 2: Matters which are distributions

Section 998: Overview of Chapter

2960. This section sets out the scope of Chapter 2 and provides signposts to other provisions in the Chapter, including those setting out exceptions. It is new.

Section 999: ***Priority of negative rules***

2961. This section directs that the Chapter is subject to any express exceptions, and lists some of those that most commonly affect what is to be treated as a distribution. It is based on section 209(1) of ICTA.

2962. The section specifically refers to paragraph 6 of Schedule 12 to FA 1988, which sets out a number of tax matters connected with the transfer of the whole of the business of a building society to a successor company. It was decided to keep this material together rather than take out one small part. The Schedule has, therefore, not been rewritten.

Section 1000: ***Meaning of "distribution"***

2963. This section sets out the main circumstances that give rise to a distribution. It is based on sections 209(2) and (4) and 418 of ICTA.

2964. The section sets out the circumstances that give rise to a distribution in paragraphs A to H. A number of later sections refer to one or more of these paragraphs.

2965. The references to the source legislation are as follows:

Paragraph	***Origin (in ICTA).***
A	section 209(2)(a).
B	section 209(2)(b).
C	section 209(2)(c).
D	section 209(2)(c).
E	section 209(2)(d).
F	section 209(2)(e).
G	section 209(4).
H	section 209(2)(f).

2966. The section also provides signposts to extensions to the meaning of distribution in section 1064 and section 1072.

Section 1001: ***Provisions related to paragraphs A to H in section 1000(1)***

2967. This section provides information and signposts to bring together in one place a table of the main provisions that explain, supplement or limit each of the categories of distribution. It is new.

2968. It is not exhaustive, but provides a set of signposts to aid navigation through the legislation.

Section 1002: ***Exceptions for certain transfers of assets or liabilities between a company and its members***

2969. This section excludes two circumstances from the scope of paragraph B in section 1000. It is based on section 209(5) and (6) of ICTA.

2970. Section 209(5) and (6) of ICTA are written in slightly different terms. Subsection (5) first qualifies section 209(4) of ICTA. This qualification is rewritten in section 1021(1). Subsection (5) then goes on to disapply section 209(2)(b) of ICTA. Section 1002(1) picks up this link, which brings with it the interpretation material of section 209(7) of ICTA, rewritten in section 1021(2) and (3).

2971. Section 209(6) of ICTA is rewritten in section 1002(2) and section 1021(4). This ensures that the qualifications are located close to the rewritten provisions that they modify.

Section 1003: Redeemable share capital

2972. This section explains how the amount of a distribution is identified when a distribution falls within paragraph C in section 1000 because redeemable share capital is issued partly for new consideration. It is based on section 209(2) and (8) of ICTA.

2973. If a premium is payable to the holder of this type of share capital, either on redemption or otherwise, the amount of the premium is added to the value of the share capital for the purposes of calculating the amount of the distribution.

2974. For example, the nominal value of the share capital is £1000 and the premium payable on redemption is £100. The total value calculated by section 1003 is therefore £1100. If the recipient gives, say, £900 for those shares the amount of the distribution is £200.

Section 1004: Securities issued otherwise than for new consideration

2975. This section performs a role similar to that of section 1003, but in this case in relation to paragraph D in section 1000 – securities issued partly for new consideration. It is based on section 209(2) and (8) of ICTA.

Section 1005: Meaning of "non-commercial securities"

2976. This section sets out the definition of a non-commercial security for the purposes of paragraph E in section 1000. It is based on section 209(2)(d) of ICTA.

2977. Sections 1006 to 1014 also affect the scope and amount of a distribution within paragraph E in section 1000.

Section 1006: Distributions exceeding consideration received for issue of security

2978. This section qualifies the meaning of "the principal secured" for the purposes of section 1005 and of paragraph E in section 1000. It is based on section 209(3) of ICTA.

2979. The basic meaning of "principal secured" is not defined in tax statute and takes its general meaning, subject to any relevant specific tax rules.

2980. In measuring the extent to which there is more than a reasonable commercial return for the use of the principal, the "principal secured" cannot be greater than the amount given for the issue of the security.

2981. Section 1117(6) provides a further qualification if securities are issued at a price less than the amount repayable on them, and are not listed on a recognised stock exchange.

Section 1007: Securities issued at premium representing new consideration

2982. This section sets out the effect on the measurement of the "principal secured" if a security is issued at a premium representing new consideration. It is based on section 209(3A) of ICTA.

2983. The amount of the premium is taken into account in determining both the amount of the principal secured and the extent to which the return on the securities is more than a reasonable commercial return.

2984. Section 1008 qualifies this section, and there is a table at the end of the note on section 1013 summarising the interaction of sections 1006 to 1013.

Section 1008: Consideration for issue of security exceeding amount of principal

2985. This section explains what happens when the amount of the consideration paid for securities exceeds the principal secured. It is based on section 209(3AA) of ICTA.

2986. In such a case the principal secured is deemed to be increased to the amount of the consideration, for the purposes of determining whether or to what extent paragraph E in section 1000 applies. The rules in section 1007 concerning issue at a premium do not apply.

2987. An example is where the security is linked to movement in the value of a basket of shares. The amount received back by the investor could be lower than the amount paid for the security, so the value of the principal secured could be very small in such an example. This could on one view appear to be above a commercial return for that principal, but not so when viewed in relation to the amount actually paid by the investor for the security.

Section 1009: Securities reflecting dividends on certain shares etc: exclusion of section 1008

2988. This section is the first of two that qualify section 1008. It is based on section 209A(1), (2) and (4) of ICTA.

2989. The section applies where a security is linked to shares of the issuing company or any of its associated companies. The effect is that if the consideration given for the security exceeds the principal secured, the increase provided for by section 1008 is not made, but the rules in section 1007 concerning issue at a premium do apply.

2990. Section 1009 does not apply if the link to shares of a company or its associated companies arises solely because a bank or securities house has issued, as part of its normal business, securities based on a "qualifying index". This could happen if the basket of shares forming the subject matter of the index includes shares in the issuing bank itself or in one of its associated companies.

2991. The second qualification is in section 1012.

Section 1010: Meaning of "qualifying index" in section 1009

2992. This section defines "qualifying index". It is based on section 209A(3) of ICTA.

2993. The index must include shares of at least one company that is not either the issuing company or one of its associated companies, and those shares must be a "significant proportion" of the market value of the shares that make up the index.

Section 1011: Meaning of "associated company" in section 1009

2994. This section defines the term "associated company" as it applies in section 1009. It is based on section 209A(5) to (7) of ICTA.

2995. The section sets out how a person can control a company for this purpose. Any shares held on trading account (but not as part of an insurance company's long-term insurance fund) are disregarded for this purpose.

Section 1012: Hedging arrangements

2996. This section provides the second exception to section 1008. It disapplies section 1008 if there are "hedging arrangements" in place. It is based on section 209B(1) and (3) of ICTA.

2997. Section 1012 takes effect either from the time when the hedging arrangements come into effect, or from a later time in relation to earlier hedging arrangements (but only if those arrangements were in place on or after 17 April 2002). An example of the latter is where a distribution in respect of a security did not initially fall within paragraph E in section 1000, but did so subsequently and there were hedging arrangements in place before the distribution fell within paragraph E.

2998. At any time when section 1012 takes effect, paragraph E in section 1000 operates from that time as if the adjustment under section 1008, increasing the principal secured to the consideration given on issue, had not been made.

2999. For example, a security with principal secured of £100 is issued for £120. Section 1008 would normally deem the principal secured to be increased to £120, and the return would be evaluated against that amount for the purposes of paragraph E in section 1000. If hedging arrangements are subsequently put in place, the principal secured from that point onwards is £100.

3000. The definition of "hedging arrangements" is in section 1014.

Section 1013: ***Exception to*** *section 1012*

3001. This section sets out a series of circumstances in which section 1012 does not apply, and hence section 1008 does apply. It is based on section 209B(2), (4), (5), (6), (7) and (9) of ICTA.

3002. All the four conditions A to D must be met and have been met at all times in which any hedging arrangements have been in place in relation to that security (but only on or after 17 April 2002).

3003. Once any one of the conditions A to D in this section is not met, section 1012 applies from that point onwards, and continues to apply even if all the conditions are subsequently satisfied.

3004. The following table summarises the interaction of sections 1006 to 1013.

	Section 1008 applies?	***Section 1007applies?***
Security issued at a premium representing new consideration and the consideration is not greater than the principal secured – section 1007(1)	NO	YES
New consideration received exceeds the principal secured	YES	NO
Section 1009(1) applies – securities linked to shares	NO	YES
Section 1009(2) applies, overrides section 1009(1)	YES	NO
Section 1012 applies – hedging arrangements	NO	YES
Section 1013 applies, overrides section 1012	YES	NO

Section 1014: ***Meaning of "hedging arrangements"***

3005. This section defines "hedging arrangements" for the purposes of sections 1012 and 1013. It is based on section 209B(8) of ICTA.

3006. The "hedging arrangements" are looked at from the point of view of the issuing company. The essence of the definition is that there is an amount of income or gain that offsets amounts that the company has to meet in relation to the security.

Section 1015: Meaning of "special securities"

3007. This section defines "special securities" for the purpose of paragraph F in clause 1000. It is based on, and covers, the various circumstances that are set out in section 209(2)(e) of ICTA.

3008. There are five sets of circumstances listed, corresponding as follows to the provisions in section 209(2)(e) of ICTA:

Condition A	section 209(2)(e)(i).
Condition B	section 209(2)(e)(ii).
Condition C	section 209(2)(e)(iii).
Condition D	section 209(2)(e)(vi).
Condition E	section 209(2)(e)(vii).

Section 1016: Meaning of "equity note" in section 1015

3009. This section provides the definition of "equity note". It is based on section 209(9) of ICTA.

Section 1017: Section 1015: other interpretation

3010. This section provides additional definitions for the purpose of section 1015. It is based on section 209(2), (3B), (10) and (11) of ICTA.

3011. *Subsection (1)* qualifies condition C in section 1015 if the return on a security is dependent on the results of the company's business. This is based on section 209(3B) of ICTA.

3012. *Subsection (2)* expands the meaning of "securities connected with shares in the company" for the purpose of condition Din section 1015. It is based on section 209(2)(e)(vi) of ICTA.

Section 1018: The principal secured: special securities

3013. This section qualifies the meaning of "principal secured" for the purposes of section 1015 if securities are issued at a premium. It is based on section 209(3) and (3A) of ICTA.

3014. The section performs the same function in relation to securities as section 1007(2) does in relation to shares. Note however that there is no equivalent of section 1007(3).

Section 1019: Relevant alternative finance return

3015. This section ensures that returns from certain alternative finance arrangements are not treated as distributions for the purposes of the Corporation Tax Acts. It is based on section 209(6A) of ICTA.

Section 1020: Transfers of assets or liabilities treated as distributions

3016. This section treats a company as making a distribution, and describes how to calculate the amount of the distribution, if assets or liabilities are transferred by a company to its members or vice versa (paragraph G in section 1000). It is based on section 209(4) of ICTA.

3017. The value of the benefit to the member is determined, and is then compared with the amount of any new consideration. If the amount given by the member is less than the value provided to the member, a distribution arises equal to the difference.

3018. This section is subject to the exceptions in section 1021.

Section 1021: Section 1020 ***exceptions***

3019. This section sets out two circumstances where section 1020 does not apply. It is based on section 209(5) to (7) of ICTA.

3020. *Subsection (1)* sets out the two exceptions. *Subsections (2)* to *(5)* contain further interpretation.

3021. Note that if subsection (1) disapplies section 1020 and thereby takes something out of being a distribution, it is not to be treated as a distribution under paragraph B in section 1000. Section 1002(2) makes the necessary link.

Section 1022: ***Bonus issue following repayment of share capital treated as distribution***

3022. This section sets out how a distribution can arise when a company makes a bonus issue of shares following a repayment of share capital. It is based on section 210(1) of ICTA.

3023. This section is qualified by section 1023.

3024. The rules for a repayment of share capital following a bonus issue of shares are in section 1026.

Section 1023: ***Exceptions to*** *section 1022*

3025. This section sets out certain exceptions to section 1022. It is based on section 210(2) to (4) of ICTA.

Section 1024: ***Premiums paid on redemption of share capital***

3026. This section works with section 1025 to determine what is treated as a repayment of share capital. It is based on section 211(7) of ICTA.

3027. The starting point is that a premium paid on redemption of share capital is not treated as a repayment of share capital. This is further qualified by section 1025.

3028. The source legislation in section 211(7) of ICTA is not expressly limited in its application, but analysis of the legislation has shown that its practical application is limited to matters within the distributions legislation. This has now been made explicit by limiting its effect to this Chapter. See *Change 57*in Annex 1.

Section 1025: ***Share capital issued at a premium representing new consideration***

3029. This section provides further interpretation of what constitutes a repayment of share capital. It is based on section 211(5) and (6) of ICTA.

3030. If a premium is paid by the purchaser on the issue of share capital, the amount of the premium is considered to be part of the value of that share capital for the purpose of determining what is subsequently to be treated as a repayment of share capital or as a distribution.

3031. For example, taking sections 1024 and 1025 together, if share capital with a nominal value of £100 is issued at par and is later repaid with a redemption premium of £20 then only £100 is considered to be a repayment of share capital.

3032. If, however, that same share capital was issued at an issue premium of £10, then £110 of the £120 would be regarded as a repayment of that share capital. However, all or part of the £10 issue premium is not regarded as a repayment of share capital to the extent that it has already been applied in paying up any share capital – see *subsection (3)*.

Section 1026: Distributions following a bonus issue

3033. This section sets out the circumstances in which certain distributions are not treated as repayments of share capital because they follow an earlier issue of bonus shares. It is based on section 211(1), (2) and (4) of ICTA.

3034. The section applies only if the issue of bonus shares does not fall to be treated as a qualifying distribution under another provision. A qualifying distribution is any distribution other than one that is a distribution solely because of paragraph C or D in section 1000 (see section 1136 for the definition).

3035. Distributions made more than ten years after any bonus issue can be treated as repayments of share capital provided that section 739 does not apply to the company, and provided that the shares are not redeemable share capital.

3036. Section 1027 contains a further qualification.

3037. Schedule 2 contains savings for certain bonus issues that took place before 7 April 1973.

Section 1027: Cap on amount of distributions affected by section 1026

3038. This section qualifies section 1026. It is based on section 211(1) and (3) of ICTA.

3039. The section limits the amount of the distribution to the total value of any previous bonus issues that:

- have not already been treated as distributions, and
- have not been met by new consideration (defined as the "cap").

Section 1028: Certain payments connected with exempt distributions

3040. This section affects section 1022 by treating chargeable payments made within five years of an exempt distribution as not being repayments of share capital for the purposes of those sections. It is based on sections 214 and 218(1)of ICTA.

3041. Exempt distributions and chargeable payments are dealt with in Chapter 5 (demergers). Chargeable payments are charged to income tax and corporation tax by section 1086.

Chapter 3: Matters which are not distributions

Section 1029: Overview of Chapter

3042. This section sets out the scope of the Chapter. It is new.

3043. The section refers to paragraph 6 of Schedule 12 to FA 1988. This Schedule is about change of status of building societies. It was decided to keep this material together rather than take out one small part. The Schedule has, therefore, not been rewritten.

Section 1030: Distribution in respect of share capital in a winding up

3044. This section excludes distributions made in a winding up from the scope of distributions for the purposes of the Corporation Tax Acts. It is based on section 209(1) of ICTA.

Section 1031: Distribution as part of a cross-border merger

3045. This section ensures that certain distributions made in the course of a cross-border merger are not treated as distributions for the purposes of the Corporation Tax Acts. It is based on section 209(1A) of ICTA.

3046. Provided certain conditions are met, if a company makes a distribution as part of a cross-border merger and then ceases to exist without being formally wound up, that distribution is not treated as a distribution.

*Section 1032: **Interest etc paid in respect of certain securities***

3047. This section qualifies paragraph F in section 1000. It is based on section 212(1) and (3) of ICTA.

3048. The section excludes from the meaning of a distribution amounts paid to companies within the charge to corporation tax, but not if the distribution falls within the rules for non-commercial securities in paragraph E in section 1000.

3049. Schedule 2 contains savings for certain obligations entered into before 9 March 1982, or entered into before 1 July 1982 as a result of negotiations that were in progress before 9 March 1982.

*Section 1033: **Purchase by unquoted trading company of own shares***

3050. This section sets out the conditions that must apply so that the purchase by an unquoted trading company of its own shares is not treated as a distribution for the purposes of the Corporation Tax Acts. It is based on sections 219 and 229(3) of ICTA.

3051. The consideration for the purchase of own shares potentially falls into the computation of a chargeable gain in the hands of the seller, subject to any necessary matters to be taken into account under the chargeable gains legislation. This was confirmed by the judgement in the Court of Appeal in Strand Options and Futures Ltd v Vojak [2004] STC 64.

3052. This section is supplemented by sections 1034 to 1048.

*Section 1034: **Requirements as to residence***

3053. This section sets out requirements relating to the residence and ordinary residence (for tax purposes) of the seller, and includes cases where the shares are held through a nominee or by a personal representative. It is based on section 220(1), (3) and (4) of ICTA.

*Section 1035: **Requirement as to period of ownership***

3054. This section sets a minimum period throughout which the shares disposed of must have been held, and contains rules to determine, in certain circumstances, when those shares were acquired. It is based on section 220(5), (8) and (9) of ICTA.

*Section 1036: **Determining the period of ownership***

3055. This section deems the seller to own the shares in certain periods. It is based on section 220 (6) and (7) of ICTA.

3056. Subject to certain conditions, periods of ownership by a spouse or civil partner of the seller, or by a person whose shares are transferred to the seller under a will or intestacy, are treated as periods of ownership by the seller.

3057. The definition in section 1011 of ITA relating to married persons or civil partners living together applies for the purposes of the Income Tax Acts, which in turn include corporation tax provisions which relate to income tax. The purchase of own share rules fall within that scope. The definition of persons "living together" has been provided in this legislation to avoid the need to refer to section 1011 of ITA - see section 1116.

*Section 1037: **Requirement as to reduction of seller's interest as shareholder***

3058. This section is the first of two that place conditions on the seller's interest in the company after the purchase by the company of its own shares. It is based on section 221(1), (2), (3) and (4) of ICTA.

3059. The seller's shareholding in the company must be reduced to no more than 75% of what it was before the company's purchase of its own shares took place. For this purpose, the shareholdings of the seller and any shareholdings of the seller's associates are looked at as one. The meaning of "associate" is provided by sections 1059 to 1061.

3060. The section is qualified generally by sections 1038 and 1043, and by sections 1039 to 1042 if the company making the purchase is a member of a group.

*Section 1038: Section 1037: **effect of entitlement to profits***

3061. This section sets out the second condition concerning the seller's interest in the company after the purchase of its own shares. It is based on section 221(5), (6), (7) and (8) of ICTA.

3062. The seller's entitlement to the profits of the company after the purchase must be no more than 75% of what it was before the purchase. There are further requirements in section 1039 where the company is a member of a group.

*Section 1039: **Requirements where purchasing company is a member of a group***

3063. This section supplements the requirements of sections 1037 and 1038 where the company is a member of a group. It is based on section 222(1) and (3) of ICTA.

3064. The seller's shareholding in all companies in the group must be substantially reduced after the purchase of own shares, taking into account any shares in the group held by any of the seller's associates – even if the seller holds no shares in the company making the purchase after the purchase has taken place.

3065. There are further qualifications in sections 1040 and 1043.

*Section 1040: **Determining whether interests as shareholders in a group are substantially reduced***

3066. This section sets out how to determine whether the seller's shareholding in the purchaser's group is substantially reduced. It is based on section 222(2), (4), (5) and (6) of ICTA.

3067. The seller's shareholding in the group, taken together with any shareholdings of the seller's associates, must be no greater than 75% of what it was before the purchase of own shares took place.

*Section 1041: Section 1040: **effect of entitlement to profits***

3068. This section stipulates that the seller's entitlement to the profits of the group must be no greater than 75% of what it was before the purchase of shares took place. It is based on section 222(7) and (8) of ICTA.

*Section 1042: **Other requirements***

3069. This section places certain further requirements on the seller and on the transaction. It is based on section 223 of ICTA.

3070. The definition of "connected" for this purpose is in section 1062.

Section 1043: Relaxation of requirements in certain cases

3071. This section treats the seller as meeting the necessary conditions if the seller agreed to the purchase in order to permit an associate's shareholding to be substantially reduced. It is based on section 224 of ICTA.

Section 1044: Advance clearance of payments by Commissioners

3072. This section permits the company to apply to the Commissioners for HMRC for a decision whether or not section 1033 applies in respect of a particular purchase of own shares. It is based on section 225(1) of ICTA.

3073. The words "the Commissioners for Her Majesty's Revenue and Customs" have been substituted for the words "the Board" in the source legislation. This gives effect to section 50(1) and (2) of CRCA which requires references to the terms in the source legislation to be taken as references to the substituted terms.

Section 1045: Advance clearance: supplementary

3074. This section sets out time limits and further procedural rules in relation to the consideration of an application under section 1044. It is based on section 225(2) to (5) of ICTA.

Section 1046: Information and returns

3075. This section requires a company to make a return of a payment that it considers is within section 1033. It also provides fora company or any person connected with it to provide information about schemes or arrangements in relation to payments treated as falling within that section and for certain information to be provided where a payment falling within that section is received on behalf of another person It is based on section 226(1), (2) and (4) of ICTA.

Section 1047: Meaning of "group" and "51% subsidiary" in sections 1033 to 1047

3076. This section widens the general meaning of "group" and "51% subsidiary" for the purpose of the purchase of own share rules. It is based on section 222(9) to (12) of ICTA.

Section 1048: Sections 1033 to 1047: other interpretation

3077. This section contains definitions. It is based on section 229 of ICTA.

3078. The term "personal representatives" (used in *subsection (3)*)is defined for all purposes of this Act in section 1119.

3079. The reference to "trading activities" in the source is omitted as that term is not used in this part of the legislation.

Section 1049: Stock dividends

3080. This section sets out the treatment of a dividend taken in shares instead of cash, and an issue of bonus shares derived from rights attaching to those shares. It is based on sections 230 and 249 of ICTA.

3081. If the value of the shares is charged to tax as income of the recipient under ITTOIA, the issue of those shares is not treated as a distribution.

3082. The section is supplemented by sections 1050 and 1051, and there are special rules in Schedule 2 for share capital issued before 6 April 1975.

3083. Section 249(3) of ICTA is not rewritten as it is no longer needed. It introduces specific rules for income tax where two or more persons are entitled to the share capital that has been issued and provides how those rules are applied in such a case. This provision is already made for income tax by section 413(5) of ITTOIA, for the purposes of the rules in Chapter 5 of Part 4 of that Act, and has no effect for corporation tax.

3084. Schedule 1 contains consequential amendments to the provisions of ITTOIA that deal with the income tax provisions for stock dividends.

Section 1050: Application of section 1049 where bonus share capital is converted etc

3085. This section sets out the tax treatment of the shares issued in an exchange or conversion of shares that were themselves bonus shares taxed as a stock dividend. It is based on section 249(9) of ICTA.

3086. If the stock dividend was taxed as income then the issue of the replacement shares:

- is not taxed as a stock dividend,
- is not treated as a distribution, and
- is not regarded as issued for new consideration – *subsection (5)*.

3087. Some bonus issues do not fall within the rules of the provisions that section 1049 rewrites, either because they were issued before the original rule was introduced (section 34 of the F(No 2)A 1975) or because the rights to the bonus issue were contained in shares issued before 6 April 1975 (the transitional rule in section 249(8) of ICTA, rewritten as paragraph 78A of Schedule 2 to ITTOIA).

3088. If this is the case, section 1049 does not apply to the replacement shares. Therefore, the issue of those shares is treated as a distribution and they are not treated as issued for new consideration – see *subsection (3)*.

Section 1051: "Bonus share capital" and "in lieu of a cash dividend"

3089. This section provides interpretation for the stock dividend rules. It is based on sections 249(1) and 251(1) of ICTA.

Section 1052: Share capital to which section 1049 applies: returns

3090. This section makes provision for certain returns to be made in relation to stock dividends. It is based on section 250(1), (3), (4), (5) and (6) of ICTA.

Section 1053: Return periods

3091. This section sets out the return periods for the purposes of section 1052. It is based on section 250(2) of ICTA.

Section 1054: Building society payments

3092. This section ensures that interest or dividends paid in respect of accounts held with a building society are not treated as distributions for corporation tax purposes. It is based on section 477A(3)(b) and (9) of ICTA.

3093. Such payments are charged to income tax as interest by section 372 of ITTOIA, and to corporation tax by section 498 of CTA 2009.

Section 1055: Industrial and provident societies: interest and share dividends

3094. This section states that payments made to members by an industrial or provident society in the form of a share of profits – for example the traditional "divi" from the Co-op – is not treated as a distribution for corporation tax purposes. It is based on section 486(1) and (12) of ICTA.

3095. Such payments are charged to income tax as interest by section 379 of ITTOIA, and to corporation tax, as interest under a loan relationship, by section 499 of CTA 2009.

Section 1056: ***Dividend or bonus relating to transactions***

3096. This section ensures that any payment made by an industrial and provident society that is deductible for corporation tax by virtue of section 132 of CTA 2009 is not treated as a distribution. It is based on section 230A of ICTA.

Section 1057: ***UK agricultural or fishing co-operatives: interest and share dividends***

3097. This section provides the same treatment for payments made to members in the case of UK agricultural or fishing co-operatives as section 1055 provides for an industrial and provident society. It is based on section 486(1), (9) and (12) of ICTA.

Section 1058: ***Meaning of "UK agricultural or fishing co-operative"***

3098. This section provides definitions for the purpose of section 1057. It is based on section 486(9) and (12) of ICTA.

3099. The reference in section 486(12) of ICTA to "the Department for Agriculture for Northern Ireland" is rewritten in *subsection (4)* as "the Department of Agriculture and Rural Development", its current title.

Section 1059: ***Associated persons***

3100. This section contains the basic definition of "associate" for the provisions contained in Chapter 3. It is based on section 227(1), (2), (3), (4) and (7) of ICTA. As for section 1036 the definition of persons "living together" has been brought directly into the legislation – see section 1116.

3101. Further rules in sections 1060 and 1061 extend the meaning in the case of trustees and personal representatives.

Section 1060: ***Associated persons: trustees***

3102. This section supplements the definition of "associate" in section 1059. It is based on section 227(5), (8) and (9) of ICTA.

Section 1061: ***Associated persons: personal representatives***

3103. This section also supplements the definition of "associate" in section 1059. It is based on section 227(6) and (9) of ICTA.

3104. The term "personal representatives" is defined for all purposes of this Act in section 1119.

Section 1062: ***Connected persons***

3105. This section sets out rules for identifying a "connected person" for the purposes of Chapter 3. It is based on section 228(1) to (5) of ICTA.

3106. These rules are supplemented by section 1063.

Section 1063: *Section 1062*: ***supplementary***

3107. This section supplements the definitions in section 1062. It is based on section 228(6), (7) and (8) of ICTA.

Chapter 4: Special rules for distributions made by certain companies

Section 1064: Certain expenses of close companies treated as distributions

3108. This section extends the meaning of "distribution" to include certain expenses incurred by a close company in providing benefits for participators. It is based on section 418(1), (2) and (4) of ICTA.

3109. Expenses that fall within the rules are treated as distributions, the amount of the distribution being measured in the same way as under the income tax code if a benefit is provided to an employee.

3110. Clarification has been provided in *subsection (2)(b)* in relation to the question of amounts "made good" by the participator. The source legislation measures the amount of the "expense" in section 418(4) of ICTA by reference to the income tax legislation relating to employee benefits in kind – see *subsection (3)*. The amount found under those rules is the net amount after any amounts made good or contributed by the employee.

3111. The purpose of section 418(2) of ICTA is to set out the conditions for an amount to be treated as a distribution. Section 418(2) also provides that the amount of the "expense" is reduced by any amount "made good". In plain words, an amount can only be "made good" if it has been borne by the company – and if the participator has already made good any amount in arriving at the calculation in section 418(4) of ICTA then it is not possible to make it good again because the company has not borne the expense (or that part of it). Subsection (2)(b) makes this explicit.

3112. Where an amount contributed by the participator is not taken into account in the computation made using the employee benefit in kind rules, the reduction provided for in section 418(2) of ICTA can then take effect.

3113. Sections 1065 and 1066 set out two exceptions. Section 1067 contains supplementary material.

Section 1065: Exception for benefits treated as employment income etc

3114. This section sets out the first circumstance where section 1064 does not apply. It is based on section 418(3) of ICTA.

3115. The exceptions are set out in a table. The exceptions arise where the participator is also an employee within the benefit in kind rules of ITEPA (the benefits in kind rules apply instead), or in the case of certain death or retirement benefits for dependents of participators.

Section 1066: Exception for certain transfers between UK resident companies

3116. This section sets out the second exception to section 1064. It is based on section 418(5) and (6) of ICTA.

Section 1067: Companies acting in concert or under arrangements

3117. This section deals with the situation where two or more close companies act together to provide benefits to each other's participators. It is based on section 418(7) of ICTA.

3118. In such a case the benefits are deemed to be provided by a close company to its own participator and hence treated as a distribution.

3119. *Subsection (2)* makes clear that this provision applies only for the purposes of the sections rewriting section 418 of ICTA.

Section 1068: Meaning of "participator" in sections 1064 to 1067

3120. This section defines "participator" for the purposes of sections 1064 to 1067. It is based on section 417(1) and (2) of ICTA.

Section 1069: Additional persons treated as participators

3121. This section makes two extensions to the meaning of "participator" in section 1068. It is based on sections 416(2) to (6), 417(1) and (3) and 418(8) of ICTA.

Section 1070: Companies carrying on a mutual business

3122. This section restricts the application of the rules about distributions in the case of a company carrying on a mutual business. It is based on sections 6(4), 490(1) to (3) and 834(2) of ICTA.

3123. The rules about distributions only apply to such a company to the extent that distributions are made out of taxable profits or franked investment income (FII). But this limitation applies only if the distribution is made to persons who participate in the mutual business.

3124. The inclusion of FII allows the company in effect to pass dividend income to its members as its own distribution so that the members are taxable on the amount received as if they had received the dividends directly instead of earning them "through" the mutual company.

3125. If the business is a mutual life business then the distribution rules do not apply at all (that is, there is no qualification in terms of being made out of taxable profits or FII) in the case of distributions made to persons participating in that business.

Section 1071: Companies not carrying on a business

3126. This section restricts the application of the rules about distributions in the case of a company that does not carry on, or has never carried on, a trade or a business of holding investments nor has held an office. It is based on sections 6(4), 490(4) and 834(2) of ICTA.

3127. In such a case the rules about distributions are limited to amounts distributed out of taxable profits or franked investment income.

3128. Although the section reflects the application of the definition of "trade" in section 6(4) of ICTA, as applied to section 490 of ICTA by section 834(2) of ICTA, the term does not include any reference to a profession or vocation. See *Change 4* in Annex 1.

Section 1072: Members of a 90% group

3129. This section extends the meaning of distribution in the case of a company and its 90% subsidiaries. It is based on section 254(1), (3) and (4) of ICTA.

3130. If this provision applies, the distribution rules are expanded to encompass anything distributed out of assets of the company in respect of shares or securities of any company in the group, unless the distribution is to another company in the group which is UK resident.

Chapter 5: Demergers

Overview

3131. This Chapter rewrites the provisions concerning exempt distributions and chargeable payments in sections 213 to 218 of ICTA.

Section 1073: Key terms etc

3132. This section provides signposts to the key terms used in this Chapter, and to the reference to chargeable payment in section 1028. It is new.

Section 1074: Purpose of provisions about demergers

3133. This section explains the purpose of the rules concerning demergers and explains what provisions are included within the term "the provisions about demergers". It is based on section 213(1) of ICTA.

Section 1075: Exempt distributions

3134. This section states that an exempt distribution is not a distribution for the purposes of the Corporation Tax Acts, and provides a signpost to the categories of exempt distribution set out in the following three sections. It is based on sections 213(2) and (3), 213A(1) and (2) and 218(1) of ICTA.

Section 1076: Transfer of shares in subsidiaries to members

3135. This section defines the circumstances giving rise to the first type of exempt distribution. It is based on section 213(2) and (3) of ICTA.

3136. Conditions A to D are in section 1081, conditions E and F are in section 1082 and conditions L and M are in section 1085.

Section 1077: Transfer by distributing company and issue of shares by transferee company

3137. This section defines the circumstances giving rise to the second type of exempt distribution. It is based on section 213(2) and (3) of ICTA.

3138. Conditions A to D are in section 1081, conditions G to K are in section 1083 and conditions L and M are in section 1085.

Section 1078: Division of business in a cross-border transfer

3139. This section defines the circumstances giving rise to the third type of exempt distribution. It is based on section 213A(1) of ICTA.

Section 1079: "The distributing company"

3140. This section defines the term "the distributing company" for the purposes of sections 1080 to 1099. It is based on sections 213(3) and 213A(3) of ICTA.

Section 1080: Meaning of "relevant company"

3141. This section defines the term "relevant company" for the purposes of sections 1076, 1077 and 1078. It is based on sections 213(3) and 213A(3) of ICTA.

Section 1081: General conditions

3142. This section sets out the conditions (A to D) for an exempt distribution to be treated as such, and covers all exempt distributions of the first or second type – see sections 1076 and 1077. It is based on section 213(4), (5), (10) and (11) of ICTA.

3143. *Subsection (1)* reflects the amendment of section 213(4) of ICTA by the Corporation Tax (Implementation of the Mergers Directive) Regulations 2009 (SI 2009/2797). The regulations substituted the words "resident in a memberState" for the words "UK resident" to ensure that the United Kingdom is fully compliant in this context with its obligations under Directive 90/434/EEC of the European Council on cross-border mergers etc of limited liability companies.

3144. The section is supplemented by sections 1082 and 1083 which set out conditions that must be met in relation to specific types of exempt distribution.

Section 1082: Conditions for distributions within section 1076(a)

3145. This section supplements section 1081 by requiring additional conditions (E and F) to be met if the exempt distribution is of a type involving the distribution by a company to its members of shares in one or more of its 75% subsidiaries. It is based on section 213(6), (7) and (12) of ICTA.

3146. *Subsection (1)* sets out conditions relating to the company whose shares are transferred and *subsection (2)* sets out conditions relating to the company making the transfer.

3147. Condition F in *subsection (2)*, the requirement for the company making the transfer to be a trading company after the distribution, does not apply if that company is itself a 75% subsidiary. Instead, section 1085 applies.

Section 1083: Conditions for distributions within section 1077

3148. This section supplements section 1081 by requiring additional conditions (G to K) to be met if the exempt distribution consists of the transfer of a trade or trades, or shares in one or more 75% subsidiaries, followed by the issue of shares in the receiving company to the members of the company making the transfer. It is based on section 213(8) of ICTA.

3149. The company making the transfer must dispose of substantially the whole of its interest in the trade or shareholding that it transfers.

3150. Section 1084 further qualifies this section.

Section 1084: Cases where condition K does not apply

3151. This section qualifies section 1083 by setting out circumstances where one of its conditions, condition K, does not apply. It is based on section 213(9) and (12) of ICTA.

Section 1085: Conditions to be met if the distributing company is a 75% subsidiary

3152. This section applies instead of either condition F in section 1082 or condition K in section 1083 if the distributing company is itself a 75% subsidiary. It is based on section 213(12) of ICTA.

3153. Without this section a 75% subsidiary would not be able to meet the overarching requirement in section 1074(1), namely that the outcome of an exempt distribution is that a trade must be divided between two companies not in the same group or two independent groups. The categories of exempt distribution all involve transfers of shares to the members of the distributing company, and in the case of a 75% subsidiary the members would be the immediate holding company. Hence the conditions could not be met as everything would remain within the one group.

3154. The "trading company or group" condition in condition F or K of the relevant section is replaced by a requirement in *subsection (1)*about the group to which the company belongs.

3155. This section then requires further distributions, each of which must meet all the relevant tests – apart from condition F or K where the distributing company is a 75% subsidiary. The final exempt distribution in this process must therefore be made by a company which is not itself a 75% subsidiary and which is capable of meeting the requirements of section 1074(1).

Section 1086: Chargeable payments connected with exempt distributions

3156. This section sets out how a chargeable payment is charged to corporation tax or income tax, together with the condition that the charge only applies where the payment is made within five years after an exempt distribution. It is based on sections 214(1), (1A), (1B), and (6) and 215(4) of ICTA.

*Section 1087: **Chargeable payments not deductible in calculating profits***

3157. This section sets out the corporation tax treatment for the payer of a chargeable payment made within five years after an exempt distribution. It is based on section 214(1) of ICTA.

3158. The chargeable payment is treated as a distribution for corporation tax purposes in the case of the payer. That is, the payer does not get a deduction for the payment. If the recipient is a company it is chargeable to corporation tax on the receipt – see section 1086 – despite the treatment in the hands of the payer as a distribution.

*Section 1088: **Meaning of "chargeable payment"***

3159. This section sets out four conditions A to D, all of which must be met for a payment to be treated as a chargeable payment. It is based on section 214(2) and (3) of ICTA.

3160. This section is supplemented by section 1089 if any company concerned in the exempt distribution is an unquoted company.

*Section 1089: **Meaning of "chargeable payment": unquoted companies***

3161. This section expands the circumstances in which Condition A in section 1088 is met if a company concerned in an exempt distribution is an unquoted company. It is based on section 214(2) and (3) of ICTA.

3162. The section sets out conditions B1, C1 and D1. These are the parallel conditions to conditions B, C and D of section 1088. They have been given different but related labels to highlight the relationship.

*Section 1090: **Meaning of "company concerned in an exempt distribution"***

3163. This section defines the term "company concerned in an exempt distribution" for the purposes of the Chapter. It is based on section 214(4) and (5) of ICTA.

3164. This term is used in the conditions in section 1088 and the extension in section 1089.

*Section 1091: **Advance clearance of distributions***

3165. This section allows a company to seek a ruling from the Commissioners for HMRC as to whether a distribution is treated as an exempt distribution. It is based on section 215(1) of ICTA, and is supplemented by section 1093.

3166. The words "the Commissioners for Her Majesty's Revenue and Customs" have been substituted for the words "the Board" in the source legislation. This gives effect to section 50(1) and (2) of CRCA which require references to the terms in the source legislation to be taken as references to the substituted terms.

*Section 1092: **Advance clearance of payments***

3167. This section provides companies with an opportunity to seek advance clearance that a payment is not treated as a chargeable payment. It is based on section 215(2) and (3) of ICTA.

*Section 1093: **Requirements relating to applications for clearance***

3168. This section sets out how an application under section 1091 or section 1092 must be made and the time limits that must be observed by the Commissioners and the company. It is based on section 215(5) of ICTA.

Section 1094: Decision of the Commissioners or tribunal

3169. This section sets out the time limit in which the Commissioners must make a decision on an application under section 1091 or section 1092 and the process for referring the application to the tribunal. It is based on section 215(6) to (8) of ICTA.

Section 1095: Exempt distributions: returns

3170. This section requires a company to make a return of an exempt distribution. It is based on section 216(1) of ICTA.

Section 1096: Chargeable payments etc: returns

3171. This section requires returns to be made in relation to chargeable payments connected with an exempt distribution. It is based on section 216(2), (3) and (4) of ICTA.

Section 1097: Information about person for whom a payment is received

3172. This section enables an officer of Revenue and Customs to require certain information of a person who receives a chargeable payment on behalf of another person, or the person on whose behalf it is received. It is based on section 217(4) of ICTA.

Section 1098: "Unquoted company"

3173. This section defines "unquoted company" for the purposes of the Chapter. It is based on section 218(1) of ICTA.

Section 1099: Other definitions etc

3174. This section contains further interpretation for the purposes of the Chapter. It is based on section 218(1), (2) and (3) of ICTA.

Chapter 6: Information and returns: further provisions

Overview

3175. This Chapter contains sections of an administrative nature that apply generally across the distributions legislation.

Section 1100: Qualifying distributions: right to request a statement

3176. This section enables the recipient of a qualifying distribution to require certain information from the payer. It is based on section 234(1) and (2) of ICTA.

Section 1101: Non-qualifying distributions etc: returns and information

3177. This section requires the payer of a distribution that is not a qualifying distribution to make certain returns and provide certain information to HMRC. It is based on section 234(5) to (8) of ICTA.

3178. The definition of what is and is not a qualifying distribution is in section 1136.

Section 1102: Non-qualifying distributions etc: additional information

3179. This section enables an officer of Revenue and Customs to require the provision of certain information in relation to distributions that are not qualifying distributions. It is based on section 234(9) of ICTA, and paragraphs 3 and 4 of Schedule 12 to FA 1989.

3180. Paragraphs 3 and 4 of Schedule 12 to FA 1989 have been rewritten here rather than being applied by cross-reference.

Section 1103: ***Power to modify or replace sections 1101 and 1102***

3181. This section enables the Commissioners for HMRC to lay regulations amending sections 1101 and 1102. It is based on section 253 of ICTA.

Section 1104: ***Company distributing dividend or interest: duty to provide tax certificates***

3182. This section requires a company to provide a tax certificate when it makes a distribution. It is based on section 234A(1), (2) and (3) of ICTA.

3183. The meaning of "company" is that in section 1 of the Companies Act 2006, which came into effect from 1 October 2009 as a result of article 3(a) of The Companies Act 2006 (Commencement No 8, Transitional Provisions and Savings) Order 2008, SI 2008/2860. The Companies Act 2006 (Consequential Amendments) (Taxes and National Insurance) Order 2009, SI 2009/1890 article 3 made the necessary amendment of section 234A of ICTA.

3184. Section 234A(6) has been omitted as having no effect because interest that is treated as a distribution can only be a qualifying distribution. See *Change*58 in Annex 1.

Section 1105: ***Duties of nominees***

3185. This section places certain duties on nominees who receive distributions on behalf of others. It is based on section 234A(4) and (5) of ICTA.

Section 1106: ***Meaning of "tax certificate" etc***

3186. This section sets out what is required in a "tax certificate" in this Chapter and provides certain other definitions. It is based on section 234A(7), (8) and (8A) of ICTA.

3187. Section 234A(6) has been omitted as having no effect because interest that is treated as a distribution can only be a qualifying distribution. See *Change*58 in Annex 1.

Section 1107: ***Penalties***

3188. This section provides for penalties to be charged for failure to provide a tax certificate. It is based on section 234A(9) of ICTA.

Section 1108: ***Alternative means of compliance with sections 1104 and 1105***

3189. This section enables the Commissioners for HMRC to lay regulations providing for alternative methods by which a person may comply with obligations under section 1104 or section 1105. It is based on section 234A(10) and (11) of ICTA.

Chapter 7: ***Tax credits***

3190. This Chapter provides the rules under which a company is entitled to a tax credit and related administrative provisions. It is based on sections 231 and 252 of ICTA and paragraphs 3 and 4 of Schedule 12 to FA 1989.

3191. Sections 231AA and 231AB of ICTA are rewritten in Part 17 of this Act (see sections 808, 809 and 810). Section 231B of ICTA is not rewritten as it has only a very limited future application.

Section 1109: ***Tax credits for certain recipients of exempt qualifying distributions***

3192. This section sets out the conditions to be met for a company to be entitled to a tax credit in relation to a distribution that it receives. It is based on section 231 of ICTA and paragraphs 3 and 4 of Schedule 12 to FA 1989. The corresponding provision for income tax is section 397 of ITTOIA.

3193. One of the conditions is that the distribution is a qualifying distribution. This term is defined in section 1136.

Section 1110: Recovery of overpaid tax credit etc

3194. This section enables an officer of Revenue and Customs to make assessments to recover tax and/or interest where a tax credit has been overpaid or a set-off of tax credit is excessive. It is based on section 252(1) and (2) of ICTA.

3195. Schedule 1 inserts the equivalent income tax provision into ITTOIA as section 401A.

Section 1111: Section 1110: supplementary

3196. This section makes further provision relating to the recovery provisions in section 1110. It is based on section 252(3) and (5) of ICTA.

Chapter 8: Interpretation of Part

Section 1112: Arrangements between companies

3197. This section extends the meaning of distribution to encompass arrangements between two or more companies to make distributions to each other's members. It is based on section 254(8) of ICTA.

Section 1113: "In respect of shares"

3198. This section provides interpretation of the term "in respect of shares in the company". It is based on section 254(1), (2), (4) and (12) of ICTA.

Section 1114: "In respect of securities"

3199. This section provides interpretation of the term "in respect of securities in the company". It is based on section 254(1), (2), (4) and (12) of ICTA.

Section 1115: "New consideration"

3200. This section provides interpretation of the term "new consideration". It is based on section 254(1), (5), (6) and (7) of ICTA.

Section 1116: References to married persons, or civil partners, living together

3201. This section contains the definition of "living together". It is based on section 1011 of ITA.

Section 1117: Other interpretation

3202. This section provides further interpretation. It is based on sections 218(1) and 254(1), (9), (10), (11) and (12) of ICTA.

Part 24: Corporation Tax Acts definitions etc

Overview

3203. This Part sets out definitions and related material applying for the purposes of the Corporation Tax Acts generally.

3204. Chapters 1 and 5 are based on a number of provisions in Part 19 of ICTA. Chapter 2 (permanent establishments) is based on sections 148 and 152 of, and Schedule 26 to, FA 2003. Chapter 3 (subsidiaries) is based on section 838 of ICTA. Chapter 4 (investment trusts) is based on section 842 of ICTA.

3205. Definitions have been rewritten using the following principles (which were also used in ITA):

- if definitions are relatively short or straightforward, they are duplicated in the legislation about each of the taxes to which they apply;
- if a definition is longer and more complicated, and is mainly concerned with one tax, it is set out in full in the legislation about that tax and defined by cross-reference for the purposes of any other taxes that are relevant;
- if a definition is longer and more complicated but is made substantial use of in relation to more than one tax, again it is normally duplicated.

Chapter 1: ***Definitions***

Section 1118: ***Introduction to Chapter***

3206. This section introduces Chapter 1 which contains definitions applying for the purposes of the Corporation Tax Acts. Where it is not new, it is based on section 832 of ICTA. The corresponding provision for income tax is in section 988 of ITA.

3207. A number of terms that are defined by ITA for the purposes of the Income Tax Acts are used without definitionin this Act. As that use is in an income tax context, the ITA definition applies in this Act.

3208. *Subsections (3)* to *(5)*indicate the extent to which the definitions apply.

3209. Subsection (5) makes clear that the application of a definition is also subject to any contrary indication.

Section 1119: ***The definitions***

3210. This section sets out the definitions in alphabetical order. It is based on a number of provisions in ICTA, in particular sections 832 and 834, and on section 1319 of CTA 2009. The corresponding provision for income tax is in section 989 of ITA.

3211. The definition of "Act" uses the term "Northern Ireland legislation", which is defined in section 24(5) of the Interpretation Act 1978, rather than a list of categories of relevant legislation as in the source legislation. See *Change 6* in Annex 1.

3212. The definition of "capital allowance" does not include, as specified by section 832(1) of ICTA, allowances under enactments which under ICTA are treated as contained in CAA. The only such enactment was section 532 of ICTA, which was repealed by CTA 2009.

3213. The definition of "period of account" omits the reference in the source legislation to "profession, vocation". See *Change 4* in Annex 1.

3214. The definition of "personal representatives" is new. It follows the approach adopted in ITTOIA and ITA. See *Change 59*in Annex 1.

3215. The definition of "tax" does not rewrite the words "and in any enactment passed after 12th March 1970 which by any express provision is to be construed as one with the Tax Acts, the Corporation Tax Acts or the Income Tax Acts" in section 832(3) of ICTA as the definition already applies in a case which is to be construed as one with the Corporation Tax Acts. The effect of the opening words of section 832(3) of ICTA ("except so far as the context otherwise requires") is included in section 1118(4).

3216. The definition of "trade" has been streamlined in line with the approach in ITA.

3217. A number of definitions in section 832(1) of ICTA have not been rewritten. The definitions of "the Board", "collector" and "inspector" were superseded by the interpretative rules in CRCA (see sections 5 to 7 and 50 of that Act). The terms "farm land" and "market garden land" no longer appear in corporation tax provisions but the substance of these definitions is included in the definitions in section 1125 ("farming" and related expressions). The term "qualifying policy" is no longer relevant to corporation tax provisions.

Section 1120: "Bank"

3218. This section defines "bank". It is based on section 840A of ICTA. The corresponding provision for income tax is in section 991 of ITA.

3219. The definition operates only where specifically applied.

3220. The regulatory power mentioned in *subsection (2)(e)* differs from that in ITA, in that *subsection (5)* preserves the possibility in the source legislation that an organisation is designated for the purposes of only some provisions that deploy this definitionrather than all such provisions. Schedule 1 to this Act makes a corresponding consequential amendment to section 991 of ITA which brings the income tax and corporation tax codes back in line.

Section 1121: "Company"

3221. This section defines "company". It is based on section 832(1) and (2) of ICTA. The corresponding provision for income tax is in section 992 of ITA.

3222. *Subsection (2)* indicates that an "authorised unit trust" is treated as a company for specified purposes of the Corporation Tax Acts.

3223. The section does not rewrite the tail words of section 832(2) of ICTA as section 1118(4) fulfils the function, so far as now necessary (given the redundancy or repeal of some of the provisions mentioned in section 832(2) of ICTA), of ceding priority to a different definition.

3224. The reference to "sections 774 to 777" in the provisions listed in section 832(2) of ICTA implies the inclusion of sections 774A to 774G of ICTA. Those new sections were inserted by FA2006, i.e. after that list was drafted for ICTA in 1988. Those sections (rewritten in Chapter 2 of Part 16 of this Act) do not provide a bespoke definition of "company" nor did the drafter making the FA 2006 insertion provide that the exclusions in section 832(2) of ICTA should include those sections. Having regard to all that, and to give sensible effect in particular to the former section 774G(5) of ICTA (see section 774), the general definition in this section applies in those sections (so far as the use of the term in Chapter 2 of Part 16 of this Act needs a definition).

Section 1122: "Connected" persons

3225. This sectionsets out when various persons are regarded as "connected". It is based on section 839 of ICTA. The corresponding provision for income tax is in section 993 of ITA.

3226. The definition operates only where specifically applied. Section 1176 applies the definition for the purposes of this Act unless otherwise indicated.

Section 1123: "Connected" persons: supplementary

3227. This sectioncontains interpretative material for section 1122. It is based on section 839 of ICTA. The corresponding provision for income tax is in section 994 of ITA.

Section 1124: "Control"

3228. This section defines what "control" of a company or partnership means. It is based on section 840 of ICTA. The corresponding provision for income tax is in section 995 of ITA.

3229. The drafting largely follows the approach adopted in section 574 of CAA.

3230. The definition operates only where specifically applied. Section 1176 applies the definition for the purposes of this Act unless otherwise indicated.

Section 1125: "Farming" and related expressions

3231. This section defines "farming" and "market gardening" and modifies the meaning of "forestry" and "woodlands". It is based on section 832 of ICTA and section 154 of FA 1995. The corresponding provision for income tax is in section 996 of ITA.

3232. *Subsection (3)* provides that the cultivation of short rotation coppice is to be regarded as husbandry. To be then regarded as farming, within the meaning given by *subsection (1)*, the cultivation of short rotation coppice must involve the occupation of land. As it is impossible to cultivate short rotation coppice without occupying land, such cultivation is also regarded as farming.

3233. As with section 996 of ITA, there is no territorial restriction in the definitions in this section. There is therefore no needin section 48, which rewrites section 397 of ICTA (restriction of loss relief in farming and market gardening cases), to apply the provision to farming outside the United Kingdom as was the case in section 397(5) of ICTA. Similarly, the cultivation of short rotation coppice on land outside the United Kingdomis regarded as husbandry and therefore as farming.

3234. If a territorial restriction is required, it is applied to a particular section (following the pattern in ITA). So *subsection (7)* restricts the definitions, in their application to paragraph 26 of Schedule 15 to FA 2000 (corporate venturing scheme), to farming or market gardening in the United Kingdom.

Section 1126: "Franked investment income"

3235. This section defines "franked investment income" and provides for the construction of references to an amount of franked investment income. It is based on sections 13(8AB) and 832(1) and (4A) of ICTA.

Section 1127: "Generally accepted accounting practice" and related expressions

3236. This section defines a number of terms referring to accounting practice. It is based on the definition of "for accounting purposes" in section 832(1) of ICTA and on section 50 of FA 2004. The corresponding provision for income tax is in section 997 of ITA.

Section 1128: "Grossing up"

3237. This section sets out how to calculate the gross amount of an amount from which income tax has been deducted. To the extent it is not new, it is based on section 25(12) of FA 1990. The corresponding provision for income tax is in section 998 of ITA.

Section 1129: "Hire-purchase agreement"

3238. This section defines a "hire-purchase agreement". It is based on section 784(6) of ICTA and section 57(3), (4) and (6) of CTA 2009.

Section 1130: "Local authority"

3239. This section defines a "local authority" in relation to the constituent parts of the United Kingdom. It is based on section 842A of ICTA. The corresponding provision for income tax is in section 999 of ITA.

3240. The definition, in its application to Northern Ireland, is restricted to bodies of a local rather than central government character. See *Change 60* in Annex 1. An amendment in Schedule 1 makes the equivalent restriction in section 999 of ITA.

Section 1131: "Local authority association"

3241. This section defines a "local authority association". It is based on section 519(3) of ICTA. The corresponding provision for income tax is in section 1000 of ITA.

Section 1132: "Offshore installation"

3242. This section defines an "offshore installation". It is based on section 837C(1) to (4) of ICTA. The corresponding provision for income tax is in section 1001 of ITA.

Section 1133: Regulations about the meaning of "offshore installation"

3243. This section provides regulatory power for the purposes of section 1132. It is based on section 837C(5) and (6) of ICTA. The corresponding provision for income tax is in section 1002 of ITA.

Section 1134: "Oil and gas exploration and appraisal"

3244. This section defines the expression "oil and gas exploration and approval". It is based on section 837B of ICTA. The corresponding provision for income tax is in section 1003 of ITA.

Section 1135: "Property investment LLP"

3245. This section defines a "property investment LLP". It is based on section 842B of ICTA. The corresponding provision for income tax is in section 1004 of ITA.

Section 1136: "Qualifying distribution"

3246. This section defines a "qualifying distribution". It is based on sections 14(2) and 832(1) of ICTA.

Section 1137: "Recognised stock exchange"

3247. This section defines a "recognised stock exchange". It is based on section 841 of ICTA. The corresponding provision for income tax is in section 1005 of ITA.

3248. This section operates by cross-reference to the definition in section 1005 of ITA. This guards against any risk of orders being made (under powers in that section) which might inadvertently result in the two definitions getting out of step.

Section 1138: "Research and development"

3249. This section defines the expression "research and development". It is based on section 837A of ICTA. The corresponding provision for income tax is in section 1006 of ITA.

Section 1139: "Tax advantage"

3250. This section defines "tax advantage". It is based on section 840ZA of ICTA. The section is modelled on the definition of "income tax advantage" in section 683 of ITA.

Section 1140: "Unauthorised unit trust"

3251. This section defines an "unauthorised unit trust". It is based on section 832(1) of ICTA. The corresponding provision for income tax is in section 989 of ITA.

3252. *Subsection (2)* applies the effect of regulations made under section 1007 of ITA that exclude certain unit trust schemes from those that would otherwise meet the definition in *subsection (1)*.

Chapter 2: ***Permanent establishments***

Overview

3253. This Chapter determines what constitutes a permanent establishment in a territory of a company which is not resident in that territory. It is based on sections 148 and 152 of, and Schedule 26 to, FA 2003.

3254. The determination is in line with various internationally recognised characteristics commonly used in the United Kingdom's double tax agreements.

3255. If a non-UK resident company trades in the United Kingdom through a permanent establishment here, it is chargeable to corporation tax on its "chargeable profits". Section 19 of CTA 2009 defines "chargeable profits" as the trading income arising directly or indirectly through or from the permanent establishment and the other income and chargeable gains referred to in section 19(3) attributable to the permanent establishment in accordance with sections 20 to 32 of that Act.

3256. If a non-UK resident company is chargeable to tax in respect of any other income from a United Kingdom source, it is charged to income tax and its liability is limited in accordance with Chapter 1 of Part 14 of ITA. The extent to which the non-UK resident company is chargeable to tax in respect of such income may be limited by the terms of any applicable DTA.

Section 1141: ***Permanent establishments of companies***

3257. This section sets out the basic tests for determining whether a company resident in a territory has a permanent establishment in another territory. It is based on section 148(1) and (2) of FA 2003.

3258. This section is not limited to permanent establishments in the United Kingdom of non-UK resident companies but also serves to determine whether a UK resident company has a permanent establishment in another territory. Under DTAs adopting the OECD model convention, primary taxing rights in relation to the profits of a trade carried on by a company resident in the territory of one of the contracting states, through a permanent establishment in the territory of the other contracting state, are accorded to the fiscal authorities of the other contracting state.

3259. *Subsection (3)* refers to the following three sections which set out circumstances in which there is no permanent establishment, notwithstanding that the conditions in *subsection (1)* are met.

Section 1142: ***Agent of independent status***

3260. This section prevents a company which is not resident in a territory from being treated as having a permanent establishment in that territory merely because it carries on business in that territory through an agent of independent status there. It is based on sections 148(3) and 152 of, and paragraph 1 of Schedule 26 to, FA 2003.

3261. *Subsection (2)* introduces sections 1145 to 1151 which contain special provisions in relation to non-UK resident companies concerning transactions carried out through a broker in the United Kingdom, investment transactions carried out through an investment manager in the United Kingdom and Lloyd's underwriting business.

Section 1143: ***Preparatory or auxiliary activities***

3262. This section treats a company which is not resident in a territory as not having a permanent establishment in that territory if the activities carried on in that territory are only of a preparatory or auxiliary character. It is based on section 148(4) and (5) of FA 2003.

3263. *Subsection (3)* sets out a non–exhaustive list of activities of a preparatory or auxiliary character.

*Section 1144: **Alternative finance arrangements***

3264. This section provides that a non-UK resident company that receives sums treated as alternative finance return is not treated as having a permanent establishment in the United Kingdom merely because of anything done by the counter–party to the alternative finance arrangements under which the return is paid or by any other person acting for the non-UK resident company in relation to the arrangements. It is based on section 148(5A) of FA 2003.

3265. Alternative finance return is defined in *subsection (3)* by cross–reference to the application of provisions, in identical terms, contained in Part 10A of ITA (which is insertedby Schedule 2 to TIOPA andapplies for income tax purposes) and in Chapter 6 of Part 6 of CTA 2009 (which applies for corporation tax purposes). See the transitional provisions in Schedule 9 to TIOPA and Schedule 2 to CTA 2009 which provide in like terms for the application of the treatment of sums received as alternative finance return for the purposes of that Part and that Chapter.

*Section 1145: **The independent broker conditions***

3266. This section sets out the conditions to be met if a broker in the United Kingdom is to be treated as an agent of independent status for the purposes of section 1142(1), and therefore not a permanent establishment, in relation to a transaction carried out on behalf of a non-UK resident company by the broker. It is based on paragraphs 1(1) and 2 of Schedule 26 to FA 2003.

3267. In *subsection (6)* the words "(apart from this subsection)" have been added for the reasons given in *Change 61*in Annex 1.

*Section 1146: **The independent investment manager conditions***

3268. This section sets out the conditions to be met if an investment manager in the United Kingdom is to be treated as an agent of independent status for the purposes of section 1142(1), and therefore not a permanent establishment, in relation to an investment transaction carried out on behalf of a non-UK resident company by the investment manager. It is based on paragraphs 1(1), 3 and 7(2) of Schedule 26 to FA 2003.

*Section 1147: **Investment managers: the 20% rule***

3269. This section sets out the "20% rule" for investment managers. It is based on paragraph 4(1) of Schedule 26 to FA 2003.

3270. The 20% rule has two requirements. The first requirement is that the investment manager and connected persons must intend that any interest that they may have in the non-UK resident's "relevant disregarded income" does not exceed 20% of that income. The second requirement applies if that intention is not fulfilled. The 20% rule continues to be met if the only reason why it is not fulfilled is because of matters outside the control of the investment manager or connected persons despite their having taken reasonable steps to mitigate the effect of those matters.

3271. In *subsection (2)* the term "relevant disregarded income" has been substituted for the term "relevant excluded income" which appears in paragraph 4(1) of Schedule 26 to FA 2003. The same substitution was made in section 819(2) of ITA which is also based on paragraph 4(1) of Schedule 26 to FA 2003.

*Section 1148: Section 1147: **interpretation***

3272. This section defines three terms used in section 1147. It is based on paragraph 4(2) to (4) of Schedule 26 to FA 2003.

3273. *Subsection (2)* makes explicit that the accounting periods referred to in paragraph 4(2) of Schedule 26 to FA 2003 are those of the non-UK resident company.

3274. *Subsection (3)* adopts the term "relevant disregarded income" in preference to the term "relevant excluded income" in paragraph 4(3) of Schedule 26 to FA 2003. Section 821 of ITA, which is also based on paragraph 4(3) of Schedule 26 to FA 2003, similarly adopts the term "relevant disregarded income".

3275. In subsection (3), a reference to "the total of the non-UK resident company's income" has been substituted for the reference in paragraph 4(3) of Schedule 26 to FA 2003 to "the aggregate of such of the chargeable profits of the company". See *Change 62* in Annex 1.

*Section 1149: **Application of 20% rule to collective investment schemes***

3276. This section modifies the 20% rule where the non-UK resident company is a participant in a collective investment scheme. It is based on paragraph 5 of Schedule 26 to FA 2003.

3277. This section applies at the level of the scheme itself, treating the scheme as if it were a non-UK resident company, see *subsection (3)*.

3278. A minor drafting change has been made in subsection (3) by substituting reference to a non-UK resident company for the reference in paragraph 5(2) of Schedule 26 to FA 2003 to a company resident outside the United Kingdom. This has been done to clarify the assumption and in this context does not change the effect of the law. The same minor drafting change was made in section 824(3) of ITA.

3279. *Subsection (4)* applies to a scheme which, if it was assumed to be a non-UK resident company, would *not* be regarded as carrying on a trade in the United Kingdom. The 20% rule is treated as satisfied in relation to such a scheme.

3280. *Subsection (5)* applies to a scheme which, if it was assumed to be a non-UK resident company, would be regarded as carrying on a trade in the United Kingdom. The 20% rule applies to such a scheme with the modifications in *subsection (6)*.

*Section 1150: **Meaning of "investment manager" and "investment transaction"***

3281. This section defines the terms "investment manager" and "investment transaction" which underlie the independent investment manager conditions. It is based on paragraph 3(1), (3) and (4) of Schedule 26 to FA 2003.

3282. The transactions currently specified as "investment transactions" are set out in the Investment Manager (Specified Transactions) Regulations 2009 made under the powers in paragraph 3(3) and (4) of Schedule 26 to FA 2003 and which came into force on 12 May 2009.

*Section 1151: **Lloyd's agents***

3283. This section applies if a person in the United Kingdom acts as the members' agent of a non-UK resident company which is trading as a corporate member of Lloyd's or if the person acts as the managing agent of a Lloyd's syndicate of which the non-UK resident company is a member. It is based on paragraphs 1(1) and 6 of Schedule 26 to FA 2003.

3284. This section provides that the members' agent or managing agent is to be treated as an agent of independent status for the purposes of section 1142(1), and therefore not a permanent establishment, in relation to a transaction carried out on behalf of the non-

UK resident company in the course of the non-UK resident company's underwriting business at Lloyd's.

Section 1152: ***Investment managers: disregard of certain chargeable profits***

3285. This section applies if an investment manager falls to be treated as a permanent establishment in the United Kingdom of a non-UK resident company. It is based on paragraph 5A of Schedule 26 to FA 2003.

3286. The section provides that in the two cases specified in *subsection (2)* some or all of the profits derived from an investment transaction carried out by the investment manager on behalf of the non-UK resident company are disregarded when attributing profits to the permanent establishment.

3287. If Case 2 applies, the disregard is only of that part of the non-UK resident company's income from the transaction to which the investment manager and persons connected with the investment manager are not beneficially entitled (see *subsection (3)*).

Section 1153: ***Miscellaneous***

3288. This section explains when a person is to be regarded as carrying out a transaction on behalf of another and makes provision for a person part only of whose business is as a broker or investment manager. It is based on paragraph 7(1) and (4) of Schedule 26 to FA 2003.

3289. Paragraph 7(3) of Schedule 26 to FA 2003, which provides that section 839 of ICTA (connected persons) applies for the purposes of that Schedule, has not been rewritten. This provision is not required, as section 1176(1) applies section 1122 (rewriting section 839 of ICTA) for the purposes of this Act unless otherwise indicated.

Chapter 3: ***Subsidiaries***

Overview

3290. This Chapter sets out the circumstances in which one body corporate is regarded for the purposes of the Corporation Tax Acts as a "51% subsidiary", "75% subsidiary" or "90% subsidiary" of another. It is based on section 838 of ICTA.

3291. The definitions apply in respect of a "body corporate" rather than a "company" as the definition of the latter term in section 1121 includes other types of body to whom these definitions are not relevant. But all bodies corporate in relation to whom the definitions are relevant are companies.

Section 1154: ***Meaning of "51% subsidiary", "75% subsidiary" and "90% subsidiary"***

3292. This section defines "51% subsidiary", "75% subsidiary" and "90% subsidiary" in terms of beneficial ownership of the subsidiary's ordinary share capital. It is based on section 838(1), (2) and (3) of ICTA.

3293. In the case of the definitions of "51% subsidiary" and "75% subsidiary" (but not "90% subsidiary"), "indirect ownership"counts towards meeting the test. Indirect ownership means the attribution to one company ("A") of all or part of the ordinary share capital in the subsidiary in question held by a company in which A has an interest. The remainder of the Chapter sets out how such indirect ownership is identified and quantified.

Section 1155: ***Indirect ownership of ordinary share capital***

3294. This section explains indirect ownership. It is based on section 838(2), (4) and (5) of ICTA.

Section 1156: ***Calculation of amounts owned indirectly: main rules***

3295. This section sets out how to find how much of the ordinary share capital of a company that may be a "51% subsidiary" or "75% subsidiary" of another company ("A") is owned indirectly by A. It is based on section 838(6), (7), (8) and (9) of ICTA.

Section 1157: ***Adding fractions together***

3296. This section supplements section 1156 for the case where A owns part of the ordinary share capital of the potential "51% subsidiary" or "75% subsidiary" directly as well as having an indirect holding, or where a number of indirect holdings arise because of chains of ownership that have one or more different members. It is based on section 838(6) and (10) of ICTA.

Chapter 4: ***Investment trusts***

Overview

This Chapter sets out the meaning of "investment trust" for the purposes of the Corporation Tax Acts.

Section 1158: ***Meaning of "investment trust"***

3297. This section explains that an investment trust is a company that is not a close company and is approved by the Commissioners for HMRC as an investment trust. It is based on section 842(1) of ICTA.

3298. *Paragraph (b)* makes it explicit that the requirement that the company is not a close company relates to the whole of the accounting period for which approval is sought.

Section 1159: ***Conditions for approval***

3299. This section sets out conditions A to F which a company must meet for an accounting period in order for it to be approved by the Commissioners for HMRC. It is based on section 842(1) of ICTA.

3300. Conditions A, B and E make it clear that the conditions concerned relate to the whole of the accounting period for which approval is sought. This is implicit in section 842(1) of ICTA. Similarly, the reference in condition C to the income of the accounting period aims to state more clearly what is implied by the reference to "the company's income" in section 842(1)(a).

Section 1160: ***Calculation of income***

3301. This section provides additional information on conditions C and D. It is based on section 842(1AB), (1AC), (2D), (2E) and (3A) of ICTA.

3302. Some references to income in section 842 of ICTA, for example references to income derived from shares or securities, are in a context which implies that the term "income" is to be interpreted in the framework of tax language and principles. References to income in the context of the retention of income in section 842(2A) and (2B), on the other hand, do not appear to invoke the tax-based meaning of income.

3303. Section 842(1AB) of ICTA, on which *subsection (2)* is based, makes provision for determining amounts of "income" for the purposes of subsections (1)(a) and (e) of that section (and accordingly of subsection (2A)(b)). The requirements in section 842(1)(a) and (e) are conditions C and D in section 1159.

3304. In contrast section 842(2D) and (3A) of ICTA are expressed to apply to section 842 as a whole. But it appears that those subsections also presuppose a tax-based measure of income and that their application is accordingly limited to the purposes for which section 842(1AB) applies.

3305. Therefore *subsection (1)* provides that *subsections (3)* and *(4)*of this section, based on section 842(2D) and (2E) and section 842(3A) respectively, as well as subsection (2), apply in determining what is to be included as the amount of the company's income or the amount of income which a company derives from shares or securities for the purposes of conditions C and D (and accordingly of section 1161(2)(a)).

3306. *Subsection (5)* is concerned specifically with what is to be included as income of the company for the purpose of condition C.

*Section 1161: **The income retention condition: exceptions***

3307. This section qualifies the application of condition D. It is based on section 842(2A), (2B) and (2C) of ICTA.

*Section 1162: **The 15% holding limit: exceptions***

3308. This section qualifies the application of condition E. It is based on section 842(1), (2) and (3) of ICTA.

3309. A well-known HMRC practice with regard to the disposal of shares or securities from a holding is legislated for in *subsections (4)* and *(5)*. See *Change 63*in Annex 1.

*Section 1163: **Basic meaning of "holding in a company"***

3310. This section explains references to "holding in a company"for the purposes of condition E. It is based on section 842(3) of ICTA.

3311. *Subsection (2)* explains the reference to a holding being "enlarged" in section 1162.

*Section 1164: **More about the meaning of "holding in a company"***

3312. This section gives more information about how to interpret a holding in a company for the purposes of condition E. It is based on section 842(1A), (3) and (4) of ICTA.

3313. *Subsections (1)* and *(2)* deal with certain cases involving a scheme of reconstruction. The newly issued shares or securities in the first company are treated under subsection (2) as forming part of the existing holding of shares or securities in the second company. Since the shares or securities are issued for no consideration there is no enlargement of the holding as defined in section 1163(2).

*Section 1165: **Other interpretation***

3314. This section sets out the meaning of company, shares and scheme of reconstruction in this Chapter. It is based on section 842(4) of ICTA.

3315. Under *subsection (1)* "company" has the meaning given by section 1121, based on section 832(1) of ICTA, and references to company in this Chapter are read in accordance with section 99 of TCGA. In section 842(4) of ICTA the definition of company in section 288 of TCGA is applied in addition to section 99 of that Act. The only difference is that section 1121 omits a local authority and alocal authority association from the definition of company and this can have no relevance to an investment trust.

*Chapter 5: **Other Corporation Tax Acts provisions***

*Section 1166: **Scotland***

3316. This section provides interpretative rules in relation to Scotland. It is based on sections 24, 488, 780 and 832 of ICTA, paragraph 30(1) of Schedule 12 to FA 1997 and section 1320(1) of CTA 2009. The corresponding provision for income tax is in section 1008 of ITA.

*Section 1167: **Sources of income within the charge to corporation tax or income tax***

3317. This section is based on section 832(1) of ICTA. The corresponding provision for the Income Tax Acts is in section 1009 of ITA.

*Section 1168: **Payment of dividends***

3318. This section provides when dividends are treated as paid. It is based on section 834(3) of ICTA and regulation 15(4) of the Authorised Investment Funds (Tax) Regulations 2006 (SI 2006/964).

3319. The section does not rewrite the words making an exception by reference to provisions in Chapter 3 of Part 12 of ICTA that deal differently with dividends treated as paid under that Chapter. Following earlier amendments of that Chapter, there are now no such provisions nor any such dividends.

3320. However, *subsection (2)* recognises that other provisions may make such an exception to the general rule. Regulation 15(4) of the Authorised Investment Funds (Tax) Regulations 2006 (SI2006/964) provides a different definition of "distribution date" for a distribution period of an authorised investment fund. That regulation is therefore included as an origin for this subsection.

*Section 1169: **Settlements and trustees***

3321. This sectionprovides interpretative rules in relation to settlements and trustees for the purposes of the Corporation Tax Acts by reference to Chapter 2 of Part 9 of ITA. It is based on section 832(2A) of ICTA.

*Section 1170: **Territorial sea of the United Kingdom***

3322. This section takes the territorial sea of the United Kingdom into account in the meaning of "United Kingdom" for the purposes of the Corporation Tax Acts. It is based on section 830(1) of ICTA.The corresponding provision for income tax is in section 1013 of ITA.

*Section 1171: **Orders and regulations***

3323. This section sets out the rules for making orders and regulations. It is based on section 828 of ICTA. The corresponding provision for income tax is in section 1014 of ITA.

3324. *Subsection (2)* identifies "excluded powers". These are the powers that have their own rules. Paragraphs (a) to (h) deal with powers in other Acts, in which sections corresponding to this section provide rules.

3325. Paragraph (g)(i) deals with the power to designate a market, so that it is treated in the same way as a recognised stock exchange. This exclusion rewrites the mention of section 578B(9ZA) of ICTA in section 828(2) of ICTA.

3326. Paragraph (g)(ii) deals with the power to specify an investment transaction for the purposes of the rules for permanent establishments. This exclusion rewrites the mention of paragraph 3(3) of Schedule 26 to FA 2003 in section 828(2) of ICTA.

3327. *Subsection (5)* sets out three exceptions to the rule in *subsection (4)* that a statutory instrument is subject to the negative resolution procedure.

3328. Paragraph (a) deals with the power in section 73A of FA 2004 to designate an international organisation so that the construction industry scheme does not apply to it. See *Change 64* in Annex 1.

3329. Paragraph (b)(i) deals with the power to designate an international organisation as a bank. This exception rewrites the mention of section 840A(1)(d) of ICTA in section 828(4) of ICTA.

3330. Paragraph (b)(ii) deals with the new power in section 1180(2) to make transitional or savings provision.

Section 1172: Apportionment to different periods

3331. This section sets out how apportionments to different periods are to be made. It is based on section 834(4) of ICTA.

Section 1173: Miscellaneous charges

3332. This section sets out a table of the provisions relevant to any reference in the Corporation Tax Acts to the provisions to which this section applies. It is based on section 834A of ICTA. The equivalent provision is made for income tax in section 1016 of ITA.

3333. The provisions in the table are all types of income or other amounts chargeable under the charge to corporation tax on income that were charged in predecessor legislation under Case VI of Schedule D in section 18 of ICTA.

3334. The reference in Part 3 of the table to regulation 18(4) of the Offshore Funds (Tax) Regulations 2009 (SI 2009/3001) derives from the substitution made by regulation 126(5) of those Regulations in section 834A of ICTA for the former reference there to section 761 of ICTA.

3335. For reference to this table, see in particular section 91 (losses from miscellaneous transactions).

Part 25: Definitions for purposes of Act and final provisions

Overview

3336. This Part contains definitions for the purposes of the Act and provisions that introduce the Schedules, give powers to remedy errors and omissions and provide for the extent, commencement and short title of the Act when enacted.

Section 1174: Abbreviated references to Acts

3337. This section provides details of abbreviations used in this Act.

Section 1175: Claims and elections

3338. This section provides that a claim or election must be made in writing. It is based on paragraphs 57 to 59 of Schedule 18 to FA 1998. The corresponding provision for income tax is in section 1020 of ITA.

Section 1176: Meaning of "connected" persons and "control"

3339. This section applies the meaning of "connected" and "control" in sections 1122 and 1124 to the provisions of this Act unless otherwise indicated in respect of a particular provision. It is based on numerous provisions that invoke the meaning of those terms in, respectively, sections 839 and 840 of ICTA (rewritten in those sections).The corresponding provision for income tax is in section 1021 of ITA.

3340. In the source legislation for sections 511 to 513 (approved charitable investments and loans) the meaning of "control" is not defined. It has been brought within the application of section 1124. See *Change 40* in Annex 1.

Section 1177: Minor and consequential amendments

3341. This section introduces Schedule 1.

Section 1178: Power to make consequential provision

3342. This section provides a power for the Treasury to make by order consequential amendments additional to those contained in Schedule 1. It is new.

3343. The power is in substance the same as that in section 1323 of CTA 2009. As with that power, it will not be exercised without the agreement of the Tax Law Rewrite Project's Consultative and Steering Committees to the proposed modifications.

3344. *Subsection (2)* provides that the power may not be used after 31 March 2013. It is sensible to enable additional consequential amendments to be made in this way only over a limited period, and it would in any case become progressively more difficult to do so accurately as subsequent Finance Bills are enacted. The date of 31 March 2013 takes account of this while giving a reasonable amount of time for missed consequential amendments to come to light.

3345. *Subsection (4)* provides that the power may be used to make provision having retrospective effect. Whether that would be appropriate would need to be considered on a case-by-case basis.As the power can be used only to make provision in consequence of this Act, any retrospective effect is limited to provision having effect from the date the Actcomes into force.

Section 1179: Power to undo changes

3346. This section provides a power for the Treasury to undo changes in the law made by the Act for the purpose of restoring the effect of the law to what it was immediately before 1 April 2010. It is new. A corresponding provision is in section 1324 of CTA 2009.

3347. The powerwill not be exercised without the agreement of the Tax Law Rewrite Project's Consultative and Steering Committees to the proposed modifications. It will make it possible for any errors made in rewriting the source legislation, or in making consequential amendments, to be corrected without recourse to a Finance Bill.

3348. *Subsection (2)* provides that the power may not be exercised after 31 March 2013. As with section 1324 of CTA 2009, it is considered sensible to time-limit the power in this way, especially as successive Finance Acts may make it progressively more difficult to make such amendments. The time limit will provide a reasonable period for errors to come to light.

3349. *Subsection (4)*provides that the power may be used to make provision having retrospective effect. Whether that would be appropriate would need to be considered on a case-by-case basis.

Section 1180: Transitional provisions and savings

3350. This section introduces Schedule 2 and provides for the Treasury to make transitional or savings provisions additional to those contained within the Schedule. It is new. A corresponding provision is in section 1325 of CTA 2009.

3351. The powerwill not be exercised without the agreement of the Tax Law Rewrite Project's Consultative and Steering Committees.

3352. *Subsection (3)* provides that the power may be used to make provision having retrospective effect.

Section 1181: Repeals and revocations

3353. This section introduces Schedule 3.

Section 1182: Index of defined expressions

3354. This section introduces Schedule 4.

Section 1183: Extent

3355. This section provides for the Act to form part of the law of each part of the United Kingdom.

Section 1184: Commencement

3356. This section provides for the commencement of the Act.

3357. This Act deals for the most part only with corporation tax. However, it does amend legislation relating to income tax and capital gains tax, mostly consequentially. Separate provision is made about commencement in relation to those amendments.

Section 1185: Short title

3358. This section specifies the short title for the Act.

Schedule 1: Minor and consequential amendments

Overview

3359. This Schedule makes minor and consequential amendments.

3360. The commentary on this Schedule makes specific points about certain of the amendments made.

Part 1: Income and Corporation Taxes Act 1988

Section 342: Tax on company in liquidation

3361. Section 342(9) of ICTA applies to an assessment made by virtue of section 8(4) of that Act. It should have been repealed when sections 206(1) and 213 of, and Schedule 23 to, FA 1993 repealed section 8(4) of ICTA. Section 8(4) dealt with a situation where rates of tax were uncertain. Section 342(9) is obsolete and is repealed without replacement.

Section 343: Company reconstructions without a change of ownership

3362. Section 343(11) of ICTA predates Corporation Tax Self Assessment and is now redundant. It is repealed without replacement.

3363. Section 343(12) of ICTA is a saving for the amendments made to the predecessor of section 343(9) and (10) of that Act by FA 1986. It is now spent, and is repealed without replacement.

Section 505: Charitable companies: general

3364. Section 505(1AA) defines "relevant foreign distribution" for section 505(1)(c)(iib). Subsection (1)(c) was repealed by paragraph 4(3) of Schedule 14 to FA 2009 leaving the definition otiose. The repeal of section 505(1AA) was overlooked by FA 2009 and that is now being corrected.

Section 511: The Electricity Council and Boards, the Northern Ireland Electricity Service and the Gas Council

3365. The section deals with the Electricity Council and Boards, the Northern Ireland Electricity Service and the Gas Council. None of these bodies now exists. The only part of the section that has not so far been repealed is subsection (7). This deals with the application of the Corporation Tax Acts to the Gas Council. It is obsolete and is repealed without replacement.

Section 513: British Airways Board and National Freight Corporation

3366. The section ensures continuity of tax treatment for the successor company of the British Airways Board and the successor company of the National Freight Organisation. The section is obsolete and is repealed without replacement.

Section 767B: Change of company ownership: supplementary

3367. Section 767B(1) and (3) of ICTA refer to section 86 of TMA (interest on overdue tax) in so far as it has effect in relation to accounting periods ending on or before 30 September 1993. These references are spent and are repealed without replacement.

Section 768A: Change in ownership: disallowance of carry back of trading losses

3368. Section 768A(3) of ICTA is the commencement provision for that section. It is spent and is repealed without replacement.

Section 768B: Change in ownership of company with investment business: deductions generally

3369. Under paragraph 6(b) of Schedule 28A to ICTA, the amounts to be apportioned between notional accounting periods in section 768B(4)(c) of ICTA include excess business charges.

3370. Paragraph 7(1)(aa) of Schedule 28A to ICTA states how the apportionment of excess business charges is to be made.

3371. Section 768B(7) and (9)(b) of ICTA states how the apportioned charges are to be treated for the purposes of sections 75 and 338 of that Act.

3372. Paragraphs 13(1)(c) and 16(1)(aa) of Schedule 28A to ICTA are the provisions corresponding to paragraphs 6(b) and 7(1)(aa) of that Schedule which apply in a case which comes within section 768C, rather than section 768B, of that Act.

3373. The "charges" in section 768B(7) and (9)(b) of ICTA and paragraphs 6(b), 7(1)(aa), 13(1)(c) and 16(1)(aa) of Schedule 28A to that Act are charges on income. The scope of corporation tax relief for "charges on income" has been progressively cut down, and nowadays only charitable donations can rank as charges: see section 338A of ICTA, which is rewritten in Part 6 of this Act.

3374. To come within paragraph 6(b) or paragraph 13(1)(c) of Schedule 28A to ICTA, a payment must meet three conditions.

- It must be a charitable donation within section 338A(2)(b) or (c) of that Act.
- It must be wholly and exclusively for the purposes of the company's business.
- It must not be deductible in computing profits or any description of profits for the purposes of corporation tax (for example, as an expense of management within Part 16 of CTA 2009). See section 338A(3) of ICTA.

3375. It is not possible for a payment to meet all three of those conditions. Section 768B(7) and (9)(b) of ICTA and paragraphs 6(b), 7(1)(aa), 13(1)(c) and 16(1)(aa) of Schedule 28A to that Act are therefore obsolete, and are repealed without replacement.

Section 774: Transactions between dealing company and associated company

3376. Section 774 of ICTA is not rewritten, as it is obsolete. This Schedule consequentially amends it, because its repeal is outside the scope of this Act. HMRC will refer section 774 of ICTA to the Law Commission for inclusion in a future Statute Law (Repeals) Bill.

Section 776: Transactions in land: taxation of capital gains

3377. Like section 772 of ITA, section 833 does not rewrite the second limb of the definition of "land" in section 776(13)(a) of ICTA. That limb is repealed without replacement.

3378. In Schedule 1 to the Interpretation Act 1978 land is defined as including "buildings and other structures, land covered with water, and any estate, interest, easement, servitude or right in or over land". Although the Interpretation Act 1978 was largely a consolidation, the definition of land was new and only applies from the commencement of that Act.

3379. The origin of section 776(13)(a) of ICTA is section 32(12)(a) of FA 1969. This definition therefore predates the definition of land in Schedule 1 to the Interpretation Act 1978.

3380. The definition of "land" in force in 1969 was that contained in the Interpretation Act 1889. In section 3 of that Act land was defined as including "messuages, tenements, and hereditaments, houses and buildings of any tenure". This section was derived from section 4 of Lord Brougham's Act of 1850. The definition was never appropriate for Scotland, where messuages and hereditaments were unknown to the law.

3381. There is nothing in the definition of "land" in the Interpretation Act 1978 which is not also within the definition of "land" in section 776(13)(a) of ICTA.

3382. The Interpretation Act 1978 refers to "buildings and other structures". Section 776(13)(a) of ICTA merely refers to "buildings". But this cannot be read as excluding "structures", because what is a building is a question of degree and circumstance and case law makes it clear that virtually any kind of structure is capable of being a building.

3383. Adopting the Interpretation Act definition of "land" for the purposes of this Chapter would only be a change in the law if a "structure" (a) was not, a matter of normal English usage, "land", (b) was not a "building" (and was therefore not brought within "land" by the second limb of section 776(13)(a) of ICTA), and (c) was nevertheless brought within "land" by the provision in the Interpretation Act that "land" includes buildings and other structures. There is no reason to believe that there are such "structures".

3384. The Interpretation Act 1978 refers to "land covered with water"; section 776(13)(a) of ICTA does not. But there is no doubt that for legal purposes land includes every species of ground as well as waters and marshes. The term "land covered with water" has been used in legislation to distinguish, for rating purposes, land covered by artificial bodies of water such as reservoirs, filter beds belonging to water companies, canals, dry docks etc; no such distinction would be appropriate in the context of section 776 of ICTA, and therefore none is made.

3385. Finally, section 776(13)(a) of ICTA refers to "any estate or interest in land or buildings", whereas the Interpretation Act 1978 is more specific, referring to "any estate, interest, *easement, servitude* or *right in or over land*" (emphasis added). Nonetheless, the section 776(13)(a) definition of land includes the rights italicised above. It is couched in generic terms and does not need to mention specific interests in land, including those particular to Scots law.

3386. It is therefore a matter of historical accident that section 776 of ICTA includes its own non-exhaustive definition of "land", rather than using the standard non-exhaustive definition in the Interpretation Act 1978. This Act therefore omits the second limb of section 776(13)(a) of ICTA as redundant.

3387. This Act does not rewrite the first limb of section 776(13)(a) of ICTA as a Chapter-wide definition. Instead, references to "the land" are expanded to "all or part of the land" where appropriate.

3388. See also the commentary on the amendments made by this Schedule to paragraph 21A of Schedule 15 to FA 2000 and paragraph 11A of Schedule 5 to ITEPA.

Section 777: Provisions supplementary to section 776

3389. Section 777(4) of ICTA provides (to summarise) that documents are not conclusive evidence of persons' intentions. It is repealed without replacement, because it merely declares what the courts would hold anyway.

Schedule 23A: Manufactured dividends and interest

3390. Paragraph 7A(9) of Schedule 23A to ICTA is repealed without replacement. Following paragraph 5 of Schedule 13 to FA 2007 and the repeal of section 737A of ICTA, it is not possible for a deemed manufactured payment to give rise to "relevant tax relief" within the meaning of paragraph 7A(10) of Schedule 23A to ICTA. So it is not necessary to extend the disallowance of relief in paragraph 7A(2) to deemed manufactured payments.

3391. Paragraph 8(3)(a) of Schedule 23A to ICTA is repealed without replacement, as it is unnecessary. See *Change 51* in Annex 1.

Schedule 28A: Change in ownership of company with investment business: deductions

3392. Paragraphs 6(b), 7(1)(aa), 13(1)(c) and 16(1)(aa) of Schedule 28A to ICTA are repealed without replacement, on the ground that they are obsolete. See the commentary on the repeal by this Schedule of section 768B(7) and (9)(b) of ICTA.

3393. Paragraph 11(4) of Schedule 28A to ICTA defines "post-change accounting period" for the purposes of that paragraph. This expression no longer appears in that paragraph, therefore paragraph 11(4) of that Schedule is now otiose. It is repealed without replacement.

Part 2: Other enactments

Inheritance Tax Act 1984

Section 23: Gifts to charities

3394. This amendment extends the relief given by section 23 (gifts to charity) to gifts to a registered club. See the commentary on Chapter 9 of Part 13. It is based on paragraph 9(2) of Schedule 18 to FA 2002.

Finance Act 1989

Section 102: Surrender of company tax refund etc within group

3395. Section 102(3)(c) of FA 1989 refers to the payment of the tax credit comprised in franked investment income. This reference is obsolete, and section 102(3)(c) of FA 1989 is repealed without replacement.

Schedule 12: Close companies: consequential provisions

3396. The provisions mentioned in paragraph 1(a) of Schedule 12 to FA 1989 are rewritten in the Act. Paragraph 1(a) of that Schedule is rewritten with paragraphs 3 and 4 of that Schedule in sections 31, 465 and 1102 (companies with small profits, close companies and company distributions: powers to obtain information). Paragraph 1(c) and (d) of that Schedule are rewritten with paragraphs 3 and 4 of that Schedule in sections 401B and 421A of ITTOIA, which are inserted by this Schedule. Paragraph 1(b) of Schedule 12 to FA 1989 is spent and is not rewritten. Paragraph 1 of Schedule 12 to FA 1989 is therefore repealed.

Taxation of Chargeable Gains Act 1992

Section 190: Tax recoverable from another group company or controlling director

3397. The definition of "director" in section 190(13) of TCGA refers to section 168(8) of ICTA, which has been rewritten and repealed. Accordingly, the amendment to that subsection refers not only to section 452, which is based on section 417(5) of ICTA, but also to section 67(1) and (2) of ITEPA, which are based on section 168(8) of ICTA.

Section 217D: Industrial and provident societies and co-operatives

3398. Section 217D of TCGA rewrites and relocates the provisions in section 486(8), (9) and (12) of ICTA which are about corporation tax on chargeable gains.

Sections 256, 256A, 256B, 256C, 256D: Charities and gifts of non-business assets etc

3399. The separation between income tax and corporation tax also results in a separation of the legislation giving relief from tax for charities. Bodies constituted as charitable trusts are within the charge to income tax and capital gains tax while those constituted as companies or other forms of body corporate are within the charge to corporation tax.

3400. ITA amended section 256 of TCGA and inserted sections 256A and 256B to make specific provision for charitable trusts. This Act completes the process by making specific provision for charitable companies by amendment to section 256 and by the insertion of sections 256C and 256D. See the commentary on section 493.

Section 257: Gifts to charities etc

3401. This amendment extends the relief given by section 257 of TCGA to gifts to a registered club. See commentary on Chapter 9 of Part 13. It is based on paragraph 9(3) of Schedule 18 to FA 2002.

Charities Act 1993

Section 10: Disclosure of information to Commission

3402. Section 10(2) of the Charities Act 1993 allows institutions, undertakings or bodies listed in paragraphs (a) to (e) to disclose Revenue and Customs information to the Charity Commission.

3403. The exclusions in new subsection (2A) of section 10 of the Charities Act 1993 are necessary because Part 11 also rewrites claims under sections 507 and 508 of ICTA which, although exempting income under section 505(1) of ICTA, are not claims for exemption made under that section. See *Change 36* in Annex 1.

Section 25A: Meaning of "Scottish recognised body" and "Northern Ireland charity"

3404. For these amendments see *Changes 32, 35, 36*and*37* in Annex 1.

Finance Act 2000

Schedule 15: The corporate venturing scheme

3405. Schedule 15 applies only in relation to shares issued on or after 1 April 2000 but before 1 April 2010 (see section 63(4) of FA 2000). For that reason, Schedule 15 is not being rewritten.

Paragraph 21A

3406. In paragraph 21A of Schedule 15 to FA 2000, this Schedule omits the reference to the second limb of section 776(13)(a) of ICTA, for the reason given in the commentary on this Schedule in relation to that provision.

3407. For the definition of "property deriving its value from land" in paragraph 21A of Schedule 15 to FA 2000, this Schedule substitutes a suitable reference to section 833 of this Act, which, like that paragraph, is a corporation tax provision.

Paragraph 46(2)

3408. Part 6 of Schedule 15 provides for the withdrawal or reduction of investment relief on the disposal of "relevant shares" (as defined in paragraph 2). For the purposes of that Part, paragraph 46(2) lists four types of disposal including:

"(a) by way of a bargain made at arm's length for full consideration.

3409. One of the requirements for relief to be available under Part 7 of Schedule 15 on the disposal of shares to which investment relief is attributable is set out in paragraph 67(3):

"(3) The second requirement is that the disposal on which the loss is incurred must be a disposal of the kind described in paragraph (a), (b), (c) or (d) of paragraph 46(2).

3410. *Change 11* in Annex 1 omits the words "for full consideration" from section 244(4)(a) rewritingparagraph 29(4)(a) of Schedule 16 to FA 2002. Section 68(2)(a) also omits those words when rewriting section 575(1)(a) of ICTA for the purposes of share loss relief in this Act.

3411. Paragraph 46(2)(a) of Schedule 15 to FA 2000 is the only other place in the Tax Acts where those words qualify the words "bargain made at arm's length". *Change 11*, therefore, also omits them from paragraph 46(2)(a) for the purposes of both Part 6 and Part 7 of Schedule 15.

Capital Allowances Act 2001

Section 63: Cases in which disposal value is nil

3412. This amendment provides that section 63(2) of CAA, which provides that the disposal value of plant and machinery disposed of by way of gift to a charity or certain other bodies is nil, also applies to a gift to a registered club. See the commentary on Chapter 9 of Part 13. It is based on paragraph 9(3) of Schedule 18 to FA 2002.

Section 99: The monetary limit

3413. The monetary limit for the purpose of expenditure by a company on long-life assets depends on the number of associated companies the company has. The changes in the rules for companies with small profits apply also to this rule. See *Change 3*in Annex 1.

Section 253: Companies with investment business

3414. The amendment to section 253(7) of CAA amends an error in the source legislation: the reference to section 768C(11) of ICTA should be to section 768C(5) of that Act. These provisions are rewritten in sections 682(13) and 699(3) of the Act.Since the provision being amended is merely a subjection, this correction does not change the law.

Schedule A1: First-year tax credits

3415. `For the amendments to Schedule A1 see *Changes 32, 35, 36*and*37* in Annex 1.

Finance Act 2002

Schedules 34 and 35: Stamp duty: withdrawal of group relief and withdrawal of relief for company acquisitions: supplementary provisions

3416. The definitions of "director" in paragraph 8(4) of Schedule 34 to FA 2002 and paragraph 9(4) of Schedule 35 to that Act both refer to section 168(8) of ICTA, which has been rewritten and repealed. Accordingly, the amendments to those sub-paragraphs refer not only to section 452, which is based on section 417(5) of ICTA, but also to section 67(1) and (2) of ITEPA, which are based on section 168(8) of ICTA.

Income Tax (Earnings and Pensions) Act 2003

Section 68: Meaning of "material interest" in a company

3417. This provision amends section 68(2) and (3) of ITEPA for the sake of consistency with section 457. See the commentary on that section. This amendment is a drafting clarification, and does not change the law.

Schedule 2: Approved share incentive plans

3418. This Schedule amends paragraph 80 of Schedule 2 to ITEPA in line with the rewrite of section 234A of ICTA in the Act. See *Change 58* in Annex 1.

Schedule 5: Enterprise management incentives

3419. In paragraph 11A of Schedule 5 to ITEPA, this Schedule omits the reference to the second limb of section 776(13)(a) of ICTA, forthe reasons given in the commentary on this Schedule in relation to that provision, and substitutes a suitable reference to section 188(3) of ITA. Paragraph 11A of Schedule 5 to ITEPA and section 188 of ITA are very similar provisions.

Companies (Audit, Investigations and Community Enterprise) Act 2004

Section 54: Becoming a charity or a Scottish charity: requirements

3420. This amendment replaces a reference to section 505(1) of ICTA with a reference to the sections of this Act which rewrite that section. See *Changes 32, 35, 36 and 37* in Annex 1.

Income Tax (Trading and Other Income) Act 2005

Section 148D: Lessor under long funding operating lease: periodic deduction

3421. This amendment substitutes for section 148D new sections 148D to 148DB in the same terms as sections 363 to 365 of this Act. Those sections of this Act are based on section 502E of ICTA which corresponds, for corporation tax purposes, to section 148D of ITTOIA.

Section 148E: long funding operating lease: lessor's additional expenditure

3422. This amendment substitutes for section 148E new sections 148E to 148EB in the same terms as sections 366 to 368 of this Act. Those sections of this Act are based on section 502F of ICTA which corresponds, for corporation tax purposes, to section 148E of ITTOIA.

Section 148F: Lessor under long funding operating lease: termination of lease

3423. This amendment substitutes a revised section 148F in the same terms as section 369 of this Act. That section of this Act is based on section 502G of ICTA which corresponds, for corporation tax purposes, to section 148F of ITTOIA.

Chapter 3 of Part 4: Dividends etc. from UK resident companies and tax credits etc. in respect of certain distributions

3424. These provisions insert a number of sections and make other amendments in this Chapter (and inserts paragraph 78A in Schedule 2) to achieve the separation of the income tax effect of sections 249 and 252 of ICTA and related provisions from the equivalent corporation tax effect rewritten in this Act.

Section 415: Charge to tax under Chapter 6

3425. This provision replaces the reference to section 419 of ICTA with a reference to section 455 for the sake of consistency with section 460.

Finance Act 2005

Section 84: Taxation of securitisation companies

3426. Subsection (7) is not rewritten. That subsection set out conditions relating to the first regulations to be made under the section. The first regulations have been made (SI 2006/3296) and the subsection no longer has any application.

Income Tax Act 2007

Section 151: Losses on disposal of shares: interpretation of Chapter

3427. This amendment provides a stand alone definition of "investment company" in place of the definition by cross–reference to and modification of the definition in section 130 of ICTA. References to savings banks and banks for savings are omitted. The amended definition is the same as that in section 90(1) of this Act. See *Change 21*in Annex 1.

Sections 346, 348(7), 356, 361, 363, 365, 368, 369 and 373: Community investment tax relief

3428. These provisions amend sections 346, 348(7), 356, 361, 363, 365, 368, 369 and 373 of ITA to conform those provisions to the corresponding provisions of this Act (see the commentary on sections 227, 229, 238, 244, 246, 248, 251, 252 and 260).

Sections 340 and 341: Application and criteria for accreditation and terms and conditions of accreditation

3429. Section 219(1)(a) of this Act provides that accreditation under the powers in Chapter 2 of Part 7 of ITA has effect for the purposes of Part 7 of this Act. The new subsections introduced by these amendments complete the picture by clarifying in ITA that the powers in Chapter 2 of Part 7 of that Act can be exercised for corporation tax purposes as well as income tax purposes. They make explicit something that is already implicit.

Section 355: Securities or shares: no claim after disposal or excessive receipts of value

3430. This minor textual amendment corrects a typographical error in the description of section 364(1) of that Act.

Section 364: Value received by investor during 6 year period: securities or shares

3431. This minor textual amendment removes words from section 364(1)(d) of ITA which are unnecessary and have, accordingly, not been included in the corresponding section 247(1)(d) of this Act.

Chapter 6 of Part 13: Avoidance involving leases of plant and machinery

3432. These amendments amend sections 809ZA and 809ZC and replace section 809ZB with new sections 809ZE and 809ZF. The effect of these amendments is to conform the structure of Chapter 6 of Part 13 of ITA with that of Chapter 2 of Part 20 of this Act. That Chapter of this Act is based on sections 785B to 785E of ICTA which correspond for corporation tax purposes to sections 809ZA to 809ZD of ITA.

Section 991: Meaning of "bank"

3433. This provision amends the definition of "bank" to bring the income tax and corporation tax rewrite of the source legislation into line. See *Change 65* in Annex 1.

Section 999: Meaning of "local authority"

3434. This provision amends the definition of "local authority", in relation to Northern Ireland, to bring the income tax and corporation tax rewrite of the source legislation into line. See *Change 60* in Annex 1.

Section 1000: Meaning of "local authority association"

3435. This provision amends the definition of "local authority association" to bring the income tax and corporation tax rewrite of the source legislation into line.

Schedule 2 Part 6: Transitionals and savings: losses on disposal of shares

3436. New paragraph 57A inserted in Schedule 2 to ITA clarifies the application of the transitional provisions in Part 6 of that Schedule (losses on disposal of shares) in cases where bonus shares have been issued. It ensures that the provisions in the form that they apply to the original shares also apply in the same form to the corresponding bonus shares whenever issued. Part 5 of Schedule 2 to this Act (losses on disposals of shares) contains a paragraph in the same terms. See *Change 20* in Annex 1.

Finance Act 2008

Schedule 19: Reduction of basic rate of income tax: transitional relief for gift aid charities

3437. This Schedule to FA 2008 provides additional relief for gift aid donations. Paragraph 1(3)(a) of Schedule 19 refers to section 505(1)(c)(ii) of ICTA as the section under which a charitable company claims exemption for the donation. Before amendment by CTA 2009 section 505(1)(c)(ii) referred to tax under Case III of Schedule D. CTA 2009 amended section 505(1)(c)(ii) to refer to those parts of CTA 2009 which replaced Schedule D Case III. Paragraph 1(3)(a) of Schedule 19 was not amended, however, leaving that statutory reference to refer only to non-trading profits on loan relationships (section 299 of CTA 2009). The reference in Schedule 19 should instead have referred to section 505(1)(c)(iizb), exemption from tax under Part 7 of CTA (annual payments), since gift aid payments are treated as annual payments under section 25 of FA 2002. This amendment substitutes for the implied reference to section 505(1)(c)(iizb) a reference to a claim for exemption by virtue of section 472 or 475 of this Act.

3438. It is not considered that this changes the law since the current reference to section 505(1)(c)(ii) does not make proper sense and Parliament cannot have intended to change the effect of Schedule 19. Accordingly paragraph 1(3)(a) must be interpreted to refer to section 505(1)(c)(iizb).

Charities Act (Northern Ireland) 2008

Section 45: Meaning of "Scottish recognised body" and "England and Wales charity" in sections 43 and 44

3439. For these amendments see *Changes 32, 35, 36*and *37* in Annex 1.

Company Tax Act 2009

Section 221A: Sums to which sections 217 to 221 do not apply

3440. Section 774G(7) of ICTA provides, to summarise, that if section 774A or 774C of that Act applies then sections 277 to 281 of ITTOIA and sections 217 to 221 of CTA 2009 (lease premiums) do not. In consequence of the rewrite of sections 774A to 774G of ICTA for corporation tax purposes in this Act, section 774G(7) of ICTA is rewritten for corporation tax purposes as new section 221A of CTA 2009.

Section 520: Provision not at arm's length: non-deductibility of relevant return

3441. The reference to any deduction against total profits in subsection (2)(b) is amended to refer to any deduction from total profits. This is for consistency with the terminology used in the Act to describe the way in which effect is given to reliefs which operate against total profits. See Step 2 of section 4(2).

Section 1219: Expenses of management of a company's investment business

3442. See the commentary on section 4 for an explanation of this amendment.

Schedule 2: Transitionals and savings etc

Part 1: General provisions

3443. These paragraphs ensure continuity of the law, despite the fact that this Act repeals and rewrites provisions.

3444. Paragraph 2 makes clear that the proposition about the continuity of the law in paragraph 1 does not apply to changes in the law made by this Act.

3445. The paragraphs in this Part stand instead of section 17(2) of the Interpretation Act 1978 and provide a comprehensive set of transitional arrangements.

Part 3: Currency

3446. A number of changes were made to the currency provisions in Schedule 18 to FA 2009. They took effect for accounting periods beginning on or after 29 December 2007. This Part of the Schedule ensures that the old rules continue to apply where a loss is carried back to an accounting period that commenced before 29 December 2007.

3447. The Schedule also enables a company to elect that the new rules only take effect for accounting periods beginning on or after the date of Royal Assent to FA 2009.

Part 5: Losses on disposal of shares

Disposals of new shares

3448. See the commentary on section 74 and *Change 19* in Annex 1.

Relief after an exchange of shares for shares in another company

3449. See the commentary on section 87 and *Change 19* in Annex 1.

Interpretation of Chapter

3450. This paragraph preserves the application of the definition of "investment company" in the source legislation in relation to shares issued before 1 April 2010. See *Change 21* in Annex 1.

Application in relation to corresponding bonus shares

3451. This paragraph clarifies the application of the transitional provisions in this Part in cases where bonus shares have been issued. It ensures that the provisions in the form that they apply to the original shares also apply in the same form to the corresponding bonus shares whenever issued. See *Change 20* in Annex 1.

Part 11: Close companies

3452. The saving for certain exceptions to the charge under section 455 (close companies: charge to tax in case of loan to participator) is based on section 420(2) of ICTA. It includes a minor change to bring the law into line with practice. See the commentary on section 456 and *Change 30* in Annex 1.

Part 12: Charitable companies etc

Transactions in deposits

3453. The exemption under section 56(3)(c) of ICTA in relation to transactions in deposits is preserved to take account of any relevant matters still in existence that pre-date the loan relationships legislation of FA 1996. See the commentary to section 486.

Exemption for investment income and exemption for certain miscellaneous income

3454. These provisions reflect changes made FA 2009 to the taxation of distributions. Dividends of non-United Kingdom resident companies paid before 1 July 2009 were chargeable to tax but not dividends of United Kingdom resident companies.

Transactions with substantial donors and non-charitable expenditure

3455. The treatment of non-charitable expenditure was amended and the rules in relation to substantial donors were introduced in FA 2006. This Part of the Schedule preserves the previous treatment where relevant (see in particular the commentary on sections 496 and 516).

3456. Section 508, which rewrites section 506B(9) of ICTA, incorporates a prospective amendment to that subsection made by paragraph 15 of Schedule 9 to the Housing and Regeneration Act 2008. Under this saving provision section 508 reflects unamended section 506B(9) until the Order bringing in the amendment has been made and paragraph 15 comes into force.

Part 14: Co-operative housing associations and self-build societies

Concurrent exercise of functions

3457. Sections 644 and 653 provide a clear separation of powers between the Secretary of State and the Welsh Ministers for bodies in England and Wales. However, where the body is a "cross-border body", that is a body which operates both in England and Wales, these provisions preserve the concurrent exercise of functions by the Secretary of State and the Welsh Ministers. See article2(c) of SI 1999/672 in relation to concurrent exercise, and paragraph 3(2) of Schedule 3 to the Government of Wales Act 1998 for the definition of "cross-border body".

Delegation of functions to the Regulator of Social Housing

3458. This provision concerns the delegation of functions to the Regulator of Social Housing. Paragraphs 13 and 14 of Schedule 9 to the Housing and Regeneration Act 2008 amend sections 488(7A) and 489(5A) of ICTA respectively from a day to be appointed. Until that day is appointed, the provision in this Schedule preserves the existing arrangements. See also, in Schedule 1 to this Act, the amendments of the Transfer of Housing Corporation Functions (Modification and Transitional Provisions) Order 2008 (SI 2008/2839), which enable this provision to operate as if the substituted references to the Housing Corporation were references to the Regulator of Social Housing, in accordance with that Order.

Part 15: Transactions in securities

Transactions in securities: general

3459. This paragraph makes transitional provision for transactions in securities. It concerns corporation tax cases straddling 1 April 2010.

3460. *Sub-paragraph (1)* lays down the general rule that Part 15 supersedes Chapter 1 of Part 17 of ICTA. Most of the differences between that Chapter and Part 15 of this Act are verbal and not substantive. See the commentary on that Part. The only change in the law made in that Part is the replacement of references to "the Board" with references to officers of Revenue and Customs. See Change5 in Annex 1 and the commentary on section 740.

3461. *Sub-paragraph (2)* ensures that the six-year time limit for making assessments is not disturbed.

3462. *Sub-paragraph (3)* requires preliminary notifications commencing counteraction to be given under section 743 of this Act (and not under section 703(9) of ICTA) after 31 March 2010. Once HMRC have started counteraction under the new law, everything falls to be done under the new law.

3463. *Sub-paragraph (4)* provides that, if preliminary notification has been given under section 703(9) of ICTA before 1 April 2010, the old law (including, for example, the appeal provisions) continues to apply after 31 March 2010.

3464. Paragraph 129 of Schedule 2 to ITA also makes transitional provision for transactions in securities. It concerns income tax cases straddling 6 April 2007. The drafting of that paragraph was criticised by the First-Tier Tribunal in Grogan v Commissioners for HMRC.[8] HMRC do not agree with the First Tier-Tribunal's view of that paragraph. But, in this paragraph, the opportunity has been taken to forestall future disputes over the validity of counteraction notices by making different transitional provision for corporation tax cases.

Part 16: Factoring of income etc

Application of section 771 (finance arrangements: exceptions)

3465. Section 771 is based on section 774E of ICTA.

3466. *Sub-paragraph (1)* of this paragraph is a saving for the second sentence of section 774E(1) of ICTA, which was repealed by paragraph 9(3)(b) of Schedule 25 to FA 2009. This saving applies in relation to transfers before 22 April 2009 in accounting periods which begin before that date and end on or after 1 April 2010.

---

8 SC/3184/2008.

3467. Section 774E(4)(b) of ICTA originally read as follows:

"(4) Section 774B or 774D does not apply so far as the structured finance arrangement is an arrangement in relation to which –

(b) paragraph 15 of Schedule 9 to the Finance Act 1996 (repo transactions and stock-lending) applies, or …

3468. Paragraph 9 of Schedule 14 to FA 2007 substituted a new section 774E(4)(b) reading as follows:

"(b) Schedule 13 to the Finance Act 2007 (sale and repurchase of securities) applies, …

3469. In that substituted version, CTA 2009 inserted before "applies" the words "or Chapter 10 of Part 6 of CTA 2009 (repos)."

3470. The amendment made by paragraph 9 of Schedule 14 to FA 2007 applied with effect in relation to an arrangement that comes into force on or after 1 October 2007: see article 3 of the Finance Act 2007 (Schedules 13 and 14) Order 2007 (SI 2007/2483).

3471. Furthermore, because of article 5 of that instrument, the pre-FA 2007 version of paragraph 15 of Schedule 9 to FA 1996 is still in force in relation to arrangements which would have been within Schedule 13 to FA 2007 but for having come into force before 1 October 2007.

3472. Section 774E(4)(b) of ICTA, as amended by FA 2007 and CTA 2009, is rewritten to section 771(5)(b) and new section 809BZN(5)(b) of ITA (which is inserted by Schedule 5 to TIOPA). *Sub-paragraph (2)* of this paragraph accordingly makes transitional provision for arrangements which came into force before 1 October 2007. See also paragraph 78 of Schedule 2 to CTA 2009 for modifications with which paragraph 15 of Schedule 9 to FA 1996 (as it stood before the substitution made by paragraph 18 of Schedule 14 to FA 2007) has effect.

Application of section 779 (income-transfer under loan or credit transaction)

3473. This paragraph is a saving for the words in section 786 of ICTA omitted by paragraph 9(1)(d) of Schedule 25 to FA 2009. This saving applies in relation to transfers before 22 April 2009 in accounting periods which begin before that date and end on or after 1 April 2010.

Part 17: Manufactured payments and repos

Manufactured dividends and manufactured overseas dividends: distributions paid before 1 July 2009

3474. This is a saving for provisions repealed by paragraphs 11 and 12 of Schedule 14 to FA 2009. These savings applyin relation to distributions paid before 1July 2009 in accounting periods which begin before that date and end on or after 1 April 2010.

Manufactured overseas dividends: overseas dividends paid before 22 April 2009

3475. The paragraph headed "Manufactured overseas dividends: overseas dividends paid before 22 April 2009" is a saving for provisions repealed by paragraph 1 of Schedule 29 to FA 2009. This saving applies in relation to overseas dividends paid before 22 April 2009 in accounting periods which begin before that date and end on or after 1 April 2010.

Part 21: Transfers of trade without a change in ownership

3476. These savings preserve the effect of the closing sentences of section 343(2) and (4) of ICTA.

Part 22: Use of different accounting practices within a group

3477. It is possible – although in practice very unlikely – that there could be companies with periods of account which (a) began before 1 January 2005 but (b) have not ended before the entry into force of this Act. Accordingly, the Schedule contains a saving for section 51(6)(a) of FA 2004.

Part 23: Company distributions

3478. The paragraphs in this Part primarily rewrite date-related rules in the source legislation for Part 23 of the Act or the commencement rules for amendments of that source legislation.

Exempt distributions

3479. This paragraph switches off paragraph 8(1) of this Schedule (which preserves the effect of a transitional or savings provision repealed by this Act) in respect of the repeal by this Act of the Corporation Tax (Implementation of the Mergers Directive) Regulations 2009 (SI 2009/2797), which amended section 213(4) of ICTA. It does so to allow the rule in section 1081(1) to apply to the whole of the first accounting period of a company to which this Act applies (that is, the first accounting period to end on or after 1 April 2010) rather than only to the part of that accounting period that follows the effective date of those regulations (distributions made on or after 11 November 2009). See *Change 66* in Annex 1.

Schedule 3: Repeals and revocations

3480. This Schedule contains repeals and revocations of enactments, including some spent enactments.

3481. The repeals and revocations in Part 2 of this Schedule have effect only for the purposes of corporation tax (and in one case also PRT).

Schedule 4: Index of defined expressions

3482. This Schedule provides an index of defined expressions used in this Act. Nearly all of the definitions appear in this Act, but a few are contained in other Acts.

COMMENCEMENT

3483. The substantive provisions of this Act come into force on 1 April 2010. Section 1184 provides for it to have effect:

- for corporation tax purposes, for accounting periods ending on or after that day, and
- for income tax and capital gains tax purposes, for the tax year 2010-11 and subsequent tax years.

HANSARD REFERENCES

3484. The following table sets out the dates and Hansard references for each stage of this Act's passage through Parliament.

Stage	*Date*	*Hansard or other Parliamentary reference*
House of Commons		
Introduction	***19 November 2009***	***Vol 501 Col 141***
Second Reading Committee	***15 December 2009***	

These notes refer to the Corporation Tax Act 2010 (c.4) which received Royal Assent on 3 March 2010

Stage	***Date***	***Hansard or other Parliamentary reference***
Second Reading (formal)	*5 January 2010*	*Vol 503 Col 137*
Joint Committee on Tax Law Rewrite Bills		
First Report of Session 2009–2010	*11 January 2010*	*HL 31 2009-2010*
		HC 232 2009-2010
House of Commons		
Third Reading	*4 February 2010*	*Vol 505 Cols 491 to 499*
House of Lords		
Introduction	*4 February 2010*	*Vol 717Col381*
Second and third readings	*2 March 2010*	*Vol 717 Cols 1409 to 1414*
Royal Assent	*3 March 2010*	*HL Vol 717 Col 1443*
		HC Vol 506 Col 965

ANNEX 1: MINOR CHANGES IN THE LAW

CHANGE 1: SMALL PROFITS RATE AND MARGINAL RELIEF: DROP THE NEED FOR A CLAIM:SECTIONS 18, 19, 20 AND 21

This change removes the requirement that a company should make a claim for small profits rate or marginal relief.

Section 13(1) of ICTA provides that a company "may claim" that its basic profits are charged at the small companies' rate. And section 13(2) makes the same provision for marginal small companies' relief. The general approach of this Act is not to require a claim if the relief can be shown in a return.

In practice a claim for small companies' relief is usually made in a return, by putting an "X" in a box. In accordance with SP1/91, HMRC accept that such an entry is a valid claim.

The provisions that govern claims are not the same as the provisions that govern returns. But in practice dropping the need for a claim has only the following two consequences, both of which relate to the time available for "claiming" the relief.

First, the absolute time limit for making a claim is replaced by a time limit that may vary according to the particular circumstances. That may be because the return is issued late or because the taxpayer makes a late return. Accordingly, HMRC are no longer able to refuse a claim because it is late by reference to an absolute time limit: returns time limits and sanctions apply and they depend on the date the return is issued and made.

Second, mistake relief claims under paragraph 51 of Schedule 18 to FA 1998 are possible if too much tax is paid as a result of omitting to include the relief in the tax return. Claims under paragraph 51 of Schedule 18 to FA 1998 must be made within six years of the end of the accounting period to which the return relates.

This change is in taxpayers' favour in principle and may benefit some taxpayers in practice. But the numbers affected and the practical effects are likely to be small.

CHANGE 2: SMALL PROFITS RATE AND MARGINAL RELIEF: IGNORE "PASSIVE COMPANIES": SECTIONS 25 AND 26

This change enacts SP5/94 which excludes some non-holding companies from those treated as "associated companies".

Although the HMRC practice in this area is presented formally as a statement of practice it contains an element of concession. So its enactment is a change in the law.

The statement of practice applies only if the company does not carry on a trade (see section 26(1)(a)). And it applies only to a "holding company". So it must have at least one 51% subsidiary (see section 26(1)(b)). Those conditions are straightforward.

The statement of practice includes three detailed conditions (and a definition of 51% subsidiary). Section 26 sets out six conditions for a company to be a "passive company" in an accounting period.

The first condition (corresponding to the first detailed condition in SP5/94) is that the company has no assets in addition to shares in its subsidiaries. Subsection (5) of the section relaxes this condition for assets representing a dividend received.

The second condition (corresponding to part of the third detailed condition in SP5/94) is that the company has no income other than dividends from its subsidiaries.

The third condition (corresponding to part of the third detailed condition in SP5/94) is that any dividends received by the company are distributed in full. The section expresses this condition in more detail than the statement of practice because a company cannot distribute a dividend that it receives: the dividend received is part of its profits, out of which it may pay a dividend of its own. So subsection (4) of the section sets out a "redistribution condition" which compares the dividends received with dividends paid.

The fourth condition (corresponding to part of the third detailed condition in SP5/94) is that the company has no chargeable gains.

The fifth condition (corresponding to part of the second detailed condition in SP5/94) is that the company is not entitled to a deduction for management expenses. A company may incur minor administrative expenses. But the benefit of the treatment in the section is incompatible with a deduction for management expenses.

The sixth condition (corresponding to part of the second detailed condition in SP5/94) is that the company is not entitled to a deduction for qualifying charitable donations.

This change is in taxpayers' favour in principle. But it is expected to have no practical effect as it is in line with generally accepted practice.

CHANGE 3: SMALL PROFITS RATE AND MARGINAL RELIEF: RELAXATIONS IN THE TEST FOR BEING AN ASSOCIATED COMPANY: SECTIONS 25 AND 28 TO 30 AND SCHEDULE 1(SECTION 99 OF CAA)

This change enacts parts of ESC C9.

Under section 13(4) of ICTA two companies are associated, for the purpose of small companies' relief, if one has control of the other, or if both are under the control of the same person. "Control" is construed in accordance with section 416 of ICTA (see now section 450 of this Act).

ESC C9 has four main parts, set out in paragraphs 2, 3, 4 and 5 of the concession.

Paragraph 2: Fixed-rate preference shares

Under section 416(2) of ICTA a company controls another if it possesses the greater part of its share capital. Share capital includes preference shares.

So a lending company providing finance to a borrowing company by way of preference shares may technically control the borrowing company with the result that the two companies are associated. Furthermore, all borrowing companies controlled in this way by the lender are associated with each other.

By concession, some holdings of fixed-rate preference shares are ignored for the purpose of determining control for the purposes of small companies' relief. The concession applies if the holding of fixed-rate preference shares is the only reason for two companies to be treated as associated.

Section 28 enacts this part of the concession.

Paragraph 3: Loan creditors

Under section 416(2) of ICTA a company controls another if it possesses such rights as would entitle it to the greater part of the assets of the other company. A loan creditor may have such rights.

So a loan creditormay technically control the borrowing company with the result that the two companies are associated. Furthermore, all borrowing companies controlled in this way by the lender are associated with each other.

By concession loans made between companies that are otherwise completely unconnected are ignored if the loan creditor is not a close company or is a "bona fide commercial loan creditor". And there is a similar concession if unconnected companies are controlled by a common loan creditor.

Section 29 enacts this part of the concession.

Paragraph 4: Trustees

Under section 416(1) of ICTA a company is associated with another if one controls the other or both are under common control. ICTA does not specifically exclude control which is established by rights and powers held on trust. By concession, such rights and powers are ignored.

Section 474(1) of ITA (which applies also for corporation tax purposes – see section 1169 of this Act) substitutes a notional person for the trustees. That notional person is not a company and so cannot be an associated company. It follows that ESC C9 is not needed to prevent a trustee company and a company which it controls from being treated as associated. Similarly, if section 474(1) of ITA treats the trustees of two settlements as separate notional persons, the concession is not needed to prevent two companies controlled by different settlementsfrom being treated as associated.

The concession applies only if the rights and powers in two companies are held by the trustees of a single settlement. Section 30 enacts this part of the concession.

Paragraph 5: Relatives

Section 417(3) and (4) of ICTA (see now section 448 of this Act) defines "associate" to include a relative. By concession, in some circumstances, HMRC restrict the definition of "relative" to a husband, wife or minor child. This part of the concession depends on there being "no substantial interdependence" between the companies concerned. This test forms part of the review of the associated companies rules, announced by the Chancellor in his Autumn 2007 Statement on Tax Simplification Reviews. For the moment this Change does not legislate paragraph 5 of the concession.

Capital allowances

It is not clear from the words of the concession whether or not it applies also for the purpose of section 99 of CAA (monetary limit for long-life assets). In practice the concession is applied for the purpose of section 99 of CAA. Schedule 1 to the Act amends the capital allowances rule so that the treatment in sections 28 to 30 applies also to the monetary limit for long-life assets.

This change is in taxpayers' favour in principle. But it is expected to have no practical effect as it is in line with generally accepted practice.

CHANGE 4: TRADING INCOME: OMISSION OF REFERENCES TO A COMPANY CARRYING ON A PROFESSION OR A VOCATION: SECTIONS 36, 188, 452, 456, 673, 837, 851, 860, 864, 880, 883, 886, 939, 957, 1071 AND 1119

This change omits references to a profession and to a vocation where the source legislation refers to the carrying on by a company of a trade, profession or vocation.

The change is reflected in numerous sections in Part 3 of CTA2009 (trading income). It is included in the origins of the main provisions affected in CTA 2009, where it is acknowledged as Change 2. It is carried through into sections 36, 188, 452, 456, 673, 837, 851, 860, 864, 880, 883, 886, 939957 and 1071 of this Act. It is also carried through into paragraph (b) of the definition of "period of account" in section 1119 of this Act.

There are strong grounds for believing that for the purposes of the charge to corporation tax there are no activities that should be taken to constitute the carrying on of a profession or vocation by a corporate body or unincorporated association. There was a full discussion of the issues involved in Change 2 in Annex 1 to the commentary on CTA 2009.

It is theoretically possible that the application of trading income rules to activities that a company could argue is a profession or a vocation could lead to a change in the measure of taxable profits.

This change is in principle adverse to some taxpayers and favourable to others. But it is expected to have no practical effect as it is in line with generally accepted practice.

CHANGE 5: REFERENCES TO "OFFICER OF REVENUE AND CUSTOMS" AND "HER MAJESTY'S REVENUE AND CUSTOMS": SECTIONS 37, 199, 472 TO 478, 480, 481, 484 TO 488, 495, 504, 507, 510, 511, 514, 525, 527, 533, 540, 545, 546, 561, 565, 571 TO 578, 582, 586, 587, 592, 658, 670, 671, 710, 713, 740, 743 TO 746 AND 977

This change replaces references to the "Board of Inland Revenue" in the source legislation with references to "an officer of Revenue and Customs" or "Her Majesty's Revenue and Customs".

It brings the income and corporation tax codes back into line.

References in the source legislation to the "Commissioners of Inland Revenue (however expressed)" are treated by section 50(1) of CRCA as references to "the Commissioners for Her Majesty's Revenue and Customs". The rest of this note accordingly refers to the Commissioners for HMRC ("the Commissioners") rather than to the Board of Inland Revenue.

The provisions affected by this change authorise or require things to be done by or in relation to an officer of Revenue and Customs rather than by or in relation to the Commissioners. This reflects the way in which Her Majesty's Revenue and Customs is organised and operates in practice. Section 13 of CRCA allows nearly all functions conferred on the Commissioners to be exercised by any officer. All of the functions affected by this change, which are in the main concerned with administrative processes, are in fact exercised by officers of the Commissioners, and the Commissioners themselves are not personally involved in their exercise.

Where the source legislation provides for a claim or election to be made to the Commissioners, this Act does not expressly state to whom such a claim or election is to be made. Where a notice to deliver a corporation tax return has been issued, paragraphs 57 and 58 of Schedule 18 to FA 1998 require the claim to be made in the return or by amendment of the return if possible. A return must be made to the officer who issued it. A notice amending a return must be made to an officer. Similarly, where the claim is made outside a return or amendment, paragraph 2(1) of Schedule 1A to TMA requires the claim to be made to an officer.

This change has no implications for the amount of tax due, who pays it or when. It affects (in principle and in practice) only administrative matters.

CHANGE 6: INTERPRETATION: REFERENCES TO SCOTTISH AND NORTHERN IRELAND LEGISLATION: SECTIONS 44, 64, 67, 486, 488, 511 AND 1119

This change is about the extent to which references to "Act" are to be interpreted as including references to Scottish and Northern Irish primary legislation.

"Northern Ireland legislation" is defined in section 24(5) of the Interpretation Act 1978 (the 1978 Act) and the definition applies generally by virtue of section 5 and Schedule 1 to the 1978 Act. It is the term commonly used in legislation when referring to Northern Irish primary legislation. The definition of "Northern Ireland legislation" has seven limbs, (a) to (g).

Section 832(1) of ICTA defines "Act" to include Acts of the Parliament of Northern Ireland and a Measure of the Northern Ireland Assembly. So it expressly covers limbs (b) and (d) of the definition of "Northern Ireland legislation" in the 1978 Act. As a consequence of various deeming provisions contained in Schedule 12 to the Northern Ireland Act 1998, it also covers limbs (c), (e) and (f) of the definition of "Northern Ireland legislation". Only limbs (a) and (g) of the definition of "Northern Ireland legislation" are not covered.

To simplify the definition of "Act" the current wording in section 832(1) of ICTA is replaced in section 1119 with an unqualified reference to "Northern Ireland legislation". The change in the law is that limbs (a) and (g) of the definition of "Northern Ireland legislation" are now covered, although the change is formal rather than substantial as the provisions mentioned in those limbs are not relevant to the Corporation tax Acts.

"Act" on its own does not include Acts of the Scottish Parliament (see the definition of "Act" in Schedule 1 to the 1978 Act). But it is appropriate that references to "Act" in sections 44, 64,

67, 486, 488 and 511 should include references to Acts of the Scottish Parliament. In each of these cases the extension of the meaning of "Act" can only be advantageous to taxpayers.

This change is in taxpayers' favour in principle and may benefit some in practice. But the numbers affected and the amounts involved are likely to be small.

CHANGE 7: INDUSTRIAL AND PROVIDENT SOCIETIES: ENACTMENT OF ESC C5: SECTION 47

This change gives statutory effect to ESC C5.

ESC C5 stated that:

"TA 1988 s 393(8) enables a company with a trading loss brought forward under TA 1988 s 393(1) to set off the loss not only against the trading income of the accounting period but also against any interest or dividends on investments which would have been taken into account as trading income but for the fact that they are charged to tax under other provisions.

In the case of a registered industrial and provident society carrying on a trade, the following items of income may be regarded as trading income for the purposes of s 393(8)--

(a) interest brought into the computation of corporation tax profits as income underSchedule D Case III;

(b) annual interest received under deduction of tax;

(c) amounts assessable under Schedule D Case V.

Section 47 gives effect to this concession with a number of necessary modifications.

The reference to interest in (a) has been replaced with a reference to amounts that are chargeable under section 299 of CTA 2009 (charge to tax on non-trading profits from loan relationships) and the reference to amounts assessable under Case V in (c) has been replaced with a reference to amounts arising from possessions out of the United Kingdom. The reference to annual interest received under deduction of tax has not been rewritten as any such income would now be caught within the reference to amounts chargeable under section 299 of CTA 2009.

This change is in taxpayers' favour in principle. But it is expected to have no practical effect as it is in line with generally accepted practice.

CHANGE 8: TRADING LOSSES: RESTRICTIONS: CONTRIBUTION TO THE FIRM IN PLACE OF CONTRIBUTION TO THE TRADE: SECTIONS 56, 57, 58, 59, AND 60

This change provides for certain restrictions on the use of trade losses, incurred by companies acting as limited partners or as members of limited liability partnerships (LLPs), to operate by reference to the company's contribution to the firm (rather than contribution to the trade, as in the source legislation). It also deals with a number of consequential matters and clarifies a number of points about what is included in a company's contribution.

Contribution to the firm

For companies that are members of LLPs, the source legislation restricted loss relief against total profits by reference to the company's *contribution to the limited liability partnership* (see section 118ZC(2) and (3) of ICTA).

By contrast, for companies that are limited partners (that are not also members of LLPs), the source legislation restricted loss relief against total profits by reference to the company's *contribution to the trade* (see section 118(3) of ICTA).

But partnership law is more likely to look at capital contributed to the partnership (referred to in the relevant sections of the Act as the firm), rather than to capital contributed to a trade that the partnership carries on. For instance, a company might become a limited partner in a partnership formed under the Limited Partnership Act 1907 (LPA). Under section 4(2) of the LPA the company, at the time of entering into the partnership, contributes a sum or sums as capital (or property valued at a stated amount). The LPA does not prevent further amounts being contributed at a later date. But the intention of the LPA is that the contribution is to the firm, not the trade. The firm uses the capital contributed to fund its various activities – be that one trade or more than one trade and any investments etc that the firm might hold. And the company has limited liability for the debts and obligations of the firm, rather than just for the debts and obligations of any trade that the firm happens to carry on.

The Act reflects this by providing that total profit or group relief restrictions on trade losses operate in relation to a company's "contribution to the firm" rather than "contribution to the trade". This is, in principle, taxpayer-favourable as it may allow total profit relief or group relief to be obtained by reference to a larger amount than would otherwise be the case.

Firm carries on more than one trade

Some consequential changes have been made to cater for the possibility that a firm might carry on more than one trade.

If a firm carries on only one trade, the restriction of trade loss relief against total profit or group relief by reference to the contribution to the firm means that the company can get such relief for losses up to the amount at risk, and no more. But if the firm carries on more than one trade, restricting total profit or group relief for trade losses in each trade by reference to the contribution to the firm might result in the company getting such relief for more than the amount at risk. Clearly the source legislation does not allow this in the case of limited partners (who are not also members of LLPs) as it restricts relief for trade losses against total profits by reference to the amount of capital contributed to each trade.

So in the case of limited partners (who are not also members of LLPs) the Act restricts the total profit relief available in respect of losses from all trades carried on by the firm to the amount that the company has at risk.

As noted earlier, for LLPs a member's contribution is already in terms of the contribution to the LLP. But the source legislation does not explicitly deal with the possibility that an LLP might carry on more than one trade. Accordingly, to ensure that a consistent policy is applied throughout the sections (that is, the relief available is restricted to the amount at risk), the restriction mentioned in the preceding paragraph has been explicitly applied in relation to members of LLPs as well. This is in principle taxpayer-adverse in the case of members of LLPs.

Contribution to an LLP

The source legislation provides that the contribution to an LLP is the greater of the amount which the company has contributed to it as capital (so far as it is not recoverable) and the amount of the company's liability on a winding up (see section 118ZC(2) of ICTA).

But the total amount the company has at risk in an LLP is, in principle, the sum of what has been contributed as capital to the LLP and the additional amount that the company could be called on to meet in a winding up of the LLP.

The Act provides that a company's contribution to an LLP takes account of the total amount at risk, namely any amounts contributed as capital to the LLP (see section 60(2)) and any further amounts for which the company is liable on a winding up (see section 60(7)).

Profits or losses in accordance with generally accepted accounting practice

The Act provides explicitly, where the source legislation did not, instances where a reference to profits or losses means amounts calculated in accordance with generally accepted accounting practice. See sections 57(9) and 60(4).

Capitalised profits

The Act also explicitly provides that capitalised undrawn profits are included in an individual's contribution. See sections 57(3) and 60(3).

Contributions to a firm — trading profits not drawn

The Act also provides that a company's share of trading profits, taken into account in determining the company's contribution to the firm, is calculated by looking at periods where such profits were made, and ignoring trading losses in other periods. The source legislation did not contain an equivalent provision. The effect is broadly to determine a company's share of undrawn trading profits as the amount that the company would have received if such profits had been distributed fully on a period by period basis. See section 57(8).

This change is adverse in principle and in practice to some taxpayers and favourable to others. But the numbers affected and the amounts involved are likely to be small.

CHANGE 9: TRADING LOSSES: RESTRICTIONS: WITHDRAWAL OF CAPITAL IGNORED WHERE AMOUNTS CHARGED TO TAX AS PROFITS OF A TRADE: SECTIONS 57 AND 60

This change amends the way in which the trading losses of limited partners or members of limited liability partnerships are restricted.

One of the elements in the restriction of such a trading loss is the net amount contributed to the firm (the full amount contributed less any capital withdrawn) by the limited partner or the member of the limited liability partnership. It is,however, possible that amounts of capital withdrawn may be regarded for tax purposes as profits. In these circumstances it is inequitable to restrict loss relief by reference to those amounts. This change corrects this potential inequity.

This change is in taxpayers' favour in principle and may benefit some in practice. But the numbers affected and the amounts involved are likely to be small.

CHANGE 10: TRADING LOSSES: RESTRICTIONS: RESTRICTIONS NOT TO APPLY WHERE AN OVERSEAS PROPERTY BUSINESS CARRIED ON IN THE EXERCISE OF FUNCTIONS CONFERRED BY OR UNDER THE LAW OF A TERRITORY OUTSIDE THE UNITED KINGDOM: SECTION 67

This change brings the position of an overseas property business that is carried on in the exercise of functions conferred by or under the law of a territory outside the United Kingdom in line with the treatment of an overseas property business that is carried on in the exercise of functions conferred by or under an Act of the United Kingdom government or the Scottish Parliament.

If an overseas property business is not carried on on a commercial basis then relief for losses can only be obtained if the business is carried on in the exercise of functions conferred by or under specific legislation. In these limited circumstances it is considered inequitable that relief may only be obtained if the legislation in question is United Kingdom legislation. The change extends the scope of the relief to functions conferred by or under the law of a territory outside the United Kingdom.

This change is in taxpayers' favour in principle and may benefit some in practice. But the numbers affected and the amounts involved are likely to be small.

CHANGE 11: SHARE LOSS RELIEF, COMMUNITY INVESTMENT TAX RELIEF AND THE CORPORATE VENTURING SCHEME: OMIT THE WORDS "FOR FULL CONSIDERATION": SECTIONS 68 AND 244 AND SCHEDULE 1(PARAGRAPH 46(2)(A) OF SCHEDULE 15 TO FA 2000)

This change deletes the words "for full consideration" which qualify "by way of a bargain made at arm's length". It removes words which are not in practice applied to impose any additional requirement.

There are three places in the Tax Acts where the words "by way of a bargain made at arm's length" are qualified by the words "for full consideration". These are:

- section 575(1)(a) of ICTA (relief for losses on unquoted shares in trading companies);
- paragraph 29(4)(a) of Schedule 16 to FA 2002 (community investment tax relief); and
- paragraph 46(2)(a) of Schedule 15 to FA 2000 (the corporate venturing scheme).

Paragraph 46(2)(a) of Schedule 15 to FA 2000 is also applied for the purposes of paragraph 67 of that Schedule by paragraph 67(3).

All these provisions apply for corporation tax purposes only. Prior to ITA, section 575(1)(a) and paragraph 29(4)(a) of Schedule 16 to FA 2002 also applied for income tax purposes.

Section 575(1)(a) of ICTA and paragraph 67 of Schedule 15 to FA 2000 are concerned with the circumstances in which an allowable loss incurred on a disposal of shares may be claimed as a relief in calculating taxable income. The phrase "for full consideration" has not caused practical difficulty in relation to the application of either of those provisions.

Case law (Berry v Warnett (1982), 55 TC 92 HL[9] and Bullivant Holdings Limited v CIR (1998), 71 TC 22 ChD[10]) confirms that a bargain may be made at arm's length if a full and fair price is paid. Whether the price is full and fair is to be determined by reference to the circumstances of the disposal and it is clear that the price paid may be full and fair notwithstanding that it is substantially below open market value.

If the words "for full consideration" mean no more than that a full and fair price is paid in the circumstances of the disposal, the words are otiose. If they have independent meaning, this may require that the price paid is not less than market value, if market value is greater than the amount which is a full and fair price in the circumstances of the disposal. But in practice no such requirement is imposed.

Accordingly the words "for full consideration" have been omitted from section 131(3)(a) of ITA rewriting section 575(1)(a) of ICTA for income tax purposes. See Change 20 in Annex 1 to the explanatory notesonITA.

This Act similarly omits those words from section 68(2)(a) of this Act rewriting section 575(1)(a) of ICTA for corporation tax purposes and amends Schedule 15 to FA 2000 so that the words do not apply for the purposes of paragraph 67 of that Schedule (see below).

Paragraph 29 of Schedule 16 to FA 2002 and paragraph 46 of Schedule 15 to FA 2000 are concerned with the withdrawal or reduction of tax relief previously obtained.

These paragraphs contrast with the only other provisions in the Tax Acts dealing with the withdrawal or reduction of investment reliefs, namely:

- section 299(1)(a) and (b) of ICTA and section 209(2) and (3) of ITA (withdrawal or reduction of EIS relief); and
- section 266(2)and (3) of ITA (withdrawal or reduction of VCT relief).

In those provisions, the words "by way of a bargain made at arm's length" appear without any qualification.

In practice, the provisions for the withdrawal or reduction of CITR are operated on the same basis as the similar provisions relating to EIS relief and VCT relief - see paragraph 7020 of HMRC's Community Investment Tax Relief Manual (CITM7020).

---

9 [1982] STC 396
10 [1998] STC 905

The words "for full consideration" have accordingly been omitted from section 361(4)(a) in Part 7 of ITA rewriting Schedule 16 to FA 2002 for income tax purposes. See Change 20 in Annex 1 to the explanatory notesonITA.

This Act similarly omits those words from:

- section 244 rewriting paragraph 29(4)(a) of Schedule 16 to FA 2002 for corporation tax purposes and
- paragraph 46(2)(a) of Schedule 15 to FA 2000 (see Schedule 1).

The effect of this change is to conform provisions in each of the venture capital schemes dealing with the same issues, by removing from some of them words which are either otiose or apply a test which in practice is not required to be met.

This change is in taxpayers' favour in principle. But it is expected to have no practical effect as it is in line with generally accepted practice.

CHANGE 12: SHARE LOSS RELIEF: CORRESPONDING BONUS SHARES: SECTIONS 73 AND 90

This change legislates the practice that corresponding bonus shares are qualifying shares for share loss relief.

The change in section 73(3) is equivalent to that made in section 135(4) of ITA and brings the provisions for share loss relief for investment companies back into line with the provisions for share loss relief for individuals. See Change 23 in Annex 1 to the explanatory notes on ITA.

When shares are issued by way of bonus they are not issued for consideration. Bonus shares do not, therefore, meet the requirements of section 573(6) of ICTA (rewritten as section 73(2)) that the company has subscribed for the shares in consideration of money or money's worth.

In practice, where ordinary shares in the same company, of the same class and carrying the same rights as shares for which the company has subscribed are issued by way of bonus, claims for relief on the disposal of the shares issued by way of bonus are accepted.

Accordingly, section 73(3) has been included to provide that, where a company which has subscribed in consideration of money or money's worth for shares in a qualifying trading company is issued with bonus shares in that company which are of the same class and carry the same rights (corresponding bonus shares), the company is treated as having also subscribed for the corresponding bonus shares in consideration of money or money's worth.

This means that the corresponding bonus shares are shares which have been subscribed for by the company for the purposes of section 68(1).

Section 73(4) has been added to make clear that the corresponding bonus shares are treated as subscribed for at the time the original shares were subscribed forin actual consideration of money or money's worth. This is principally for the purposes of section 69(4)(a), which has no equivalent in Chapter 6 of Part 4 of ITA.

The definitions of bonus shares and corresponding bonus shares are in section 90(1) and (2).

The effect of this change is to put on a statutory basis an existing practice which is favourable to taxpayers.

This change is in taxpayers' favour in principle. But it is expected to have no practical effect as it is in line with generally accepted practice.

CHANGE 13: SHARE LOSS RELIEF: RESTRICTIONS ON THE AMOUNT OF SHARE LOSS RELIEF: SECTION 75

This change refines and extends the provision in section 576(1) of ICTA which restricts the amount of share loss relief available in a case where qualifying shares forming part of a holding are disposed of.

This change is the same as that made in section 147 of ITA for the purposes of relief against income tax. See Change 26 in Annex 1 to the explanatory notes on ITA.

Section 576(1) of ICTA provides that, if a company disposes of qualifying shares forming part of a holding, the amount of relief must not exceed the sums which would be allowed as deductions in computing the allowable loss if the shares had not been part of the holding.

For the purposes of corporation tax on chargeable gains, where shares are pooled in a section 104 holding (see section 104 of TCGA) or a 1982 holding (see section 109 of TCGA), the total consideration given for all the shares in the pool is averaged across the shares. This means that, when there is a part disposal of shares out of the holding, a proportion of this consideration is deducted in computing the chargeable gain pro-rata to the number of shares disposed of over the total number of shares in the pool. This may result in an allowable loss on the disposal of such shares being greater than it would have been if the shares had not been pooled.

This provision is designed to limit the share loss relief available in such cases to no more than what would have been the amount allowable as a deduction in calculating the loss if the shares had not been pooled. Ignoring incidental costs of acquisition and disposal, this equates in most cases to the amount subscribed for the shares. It is a general rule, but is of special relevance to the case where some of the shares in the pool are not qualifying shares.

In connection with the changes in section 76 described in *Change 16* in Annex 1, section 75 refines the circumstances in which the provision applies as follows:

- where the qualifying shares disposed of form part of a section 104 holding or a 1982 holding at the time of the disposal or formed part of such a holding at any earlier time (*subsections (1)* and *(2)*);
- where both qualifying shares and shares that are not capable of being qualifying shares are acquired or disposed of on the same day and are treated by virtue of section 105(1)(a) of TCGA for the purposes of corporation tax on chargeable gains as acquired or disposed of by a single transaction (*subsections (3)* and *(4)*); and
- where the qualifying shares in a company are treated for the purposes of corporation tax on chargeable gains by virtue of section 127 of TCGA as the same asset as other shares in the same company that are not capable of being qualifying shares or as debentures of the same company (*subsections (5)* and *(6)*).

The section has the following effects:

- Subsections (1) and (2) rewrite the provision in section 576(1) with two changes.
- The first change is that subsection (2) only applies to shares which are pooled in a section 104 holding or a 1982 holding. It requires the allowable deductions for the qualifying shares to be re-calculated as if the qualifying shares did not form part of the section 104 holding or the 1982 holding. But it does not affect the calculation of the allowable deductions in any other way. For example, if there has been an issue of corresponding bonus shares in respect of original qualifying shares, the re-calculated allowable deductions are apportioned in the usual way across the original shares and the corresponding bonus shares.
- The second change is that subsection (2) expressly applies if the company disposes of all the shares in the section 104 holding or the 1982 holding and at some time those shares and other shares which have been disposed of earlier formed part of the same holding (see subsection (1)(b)(ii)). This deals with the effect on the allowable cost of the shares in the

pool where the other shares were acquired at a different price from that of the shares now being disposed of. It is a clarification of the scope of the provision in section 576(1) of ICTA.

- Subsections (3) to (6) are new. They are limited to mixed holdings (see the commentary on section 76 and *Change 14*) and deal with the residual situations where the cost of shares which are not within a section 104 holding or a 1982 holding is also subject to averaging.
- Subsections (3) and (4) deal with the circumstances where the cost of qualifying shares and shares which are not capable of being qualifying shares acquired on the same day are subject to averaging.
- Subsections (5) and (6) ensure that the limit is calculated separately in relation to the qualifying shares in the case of a reorganisation, such as a rights issue, involving qualifying shares and shares which are not capable of being qualifying shares or debentures. In those circumstances, the allowable deductions by reference to which the limit is to be calculated in accordance with this subsection are likely to differ from the cost of acquisition of the qualifying shares calculated in accordance with section 129 of TCGA.

Subsection (8) explains what is meant by "shares that are not capable of being qualifying shares" for the purposes not only of this section but also section 76. See *Change 14* for a detailed explanation of why a mixed holding has been defined in terms of a holding which includes such shares. *Subsection (9)* extends this meaning for the purposes only of subsection (5) to cover re-organisations involving the issue of shares of a different class.

The effect of this change is mainly clarificatory. In particular the reference in section 75(1)(b)(ii) to the shares having formed part of such a holding that is a section 104 holding or a 1982 holding at an earlier time prevents the taxpayer claiming an amount of relief greater than the actual cost of the qualifying shares disposed of by advancing an argument that the restriction on the amount of share loss relief does not apply on the disposal of the whole of a holding.

This change is adverse to some taxpayers in principle and in practice. But the numbers affected and the amounts involved are likely to be small.

CHANGE 14: SHARE LOSS RELIEF: MEANING OF A MIXED HOLDING: SECTION 76

This change substitutes for the meaning of a mixed holding in section 576(1) of ICTA a new definition of a mixed holding.

This change is the same as that made in section 148(1) of ITA for the purposes of relief against income tax. See Change 27 in Annex 1 to the explanatory notes on ITA.

Section 576(1) of ICTA contains a rule for identifying shares disposed of by a person out of a holding which comprises:

"(a) shares for which he has subscribed ("qualifying shares"); and
(b) shares which he has acquired otherwise than by subscription.

This distinction has remained unchanged since the introduction of this provision by section 37 of FA 1980. At that time and at the time of its consolidation in 1988 as section 576(1) of ICTA, the wording was adequate to distinguish between shares which would qualify for share loss relief and those which would not.

Following the changes to the definition of qualifying trading company made by FA 1998 and FA 2001, the fact that this is the distinction made by section 576(1) of ICTA has become less evident.

At the time of a disposal of shares from a holding, those or other shares in the holding may be known to be incapable of ever being qualifying shares, even though they were subscribed for. This can be because:

- the company failed to meet either the gross assets requirement or the unquoted status requirement at the time of issue of the shares; or

- the company has failed to meet the condition that it has carried on its business wholly or mainly in the United Kingdom in relation to the shares. If the failure in relation to those shares was only during a period that ended more than 12 months before other shares in the holding were issued, it does not cause the other shares to be incapable of being qualifying shares.

Section 76(1), accordingly, provides that a mixed holding is one which, at the time of the disposal in question, includes shares that are not capable of being qualifying shares and "other shares", that is shares which at that time may or may not qualify for relief on their disposal.

Shares that are not capable of being qualifying shares are defined in section 75(8) as not only shares acquired otherwise than by subscription, but also shares in relation to which the gross assets requirement or the unquoted status requirement or the requirement as to the carrying on of business wholly or mainly in the United Kingdom has not been met.

The effect in principle of this change depends on whether the rule as amended results in different shares being identified as disposed of by the taxpayer from those identified under the rule in the source legislation. Identification of different shares may in principle result in the amount of share loss relief available on the disposal in question being less, more or the same and may also affect the relief available on a subsequent disposal. But in practice mixed holdings are treated as including all holdings of shares in a company some of which qualify for share loss relief and some of which do not qualify (see paragraph 47010 of HMRC's Venture Capital Schemes Manual).

This change is in principle adverse to some taxpayers and favourable to others. But it is expected to have no practical effect as it is in line with generally accepted practice.

CHANGE 15: SHARE LOSS RELIEF: IDENTIFICATION OF WHICH SHARES ARE DISPOSED OF: SECTION 76

This change legislates the practice that, if the identification rule in section 576(1) of ICTA identifies that some but not all of the qualifying shares in the mixed holding are disposed of, the rule is also applied to determine which of those shares are disposed of.

This change is the same as that made in section 148(2) of ITA for the purposes of relief against income tax. See Change 28 in Annex 1 to the explanatory notes on ITA.

It is stated explicitly in section 76(2)(b) that the rule as amended by *Change 14*so applies.

The effect in principle of this change depends on whether the rule as amended results in different shares being identified as disposed of by the taxpayer from those identified under the rule in the source legislation. Identification of different shares may in principle result in the amount of share loss relief available on the disposal in question being less, more or the same and may also affect the relief available on a subsequent disposal. But in practice the qualifying shares disposed of and the proportion of the loss attributable to those shares is determined on a just and reasonable basis. This normally gives the same result as the rewritten legislation (see paragraph 47150 of HMRC's Venture Capital Schemes Manual).

This change is in principle adverse to some taxpayers and favourable to others. But it is expected to have no practical effect as it is in line with generally accepted practice.

CHANGE 16: SHARE LOSS RELIEF: IDENTIFICATION OF SHARES DISPOSED OF OUT OF A MIXED HOLDING: SECTION 76

This change expands and clarifies the rules for identifying the shares disposed of, in cases where the company disposes of some only of the shares in a mixed holding. As to what constitutes a mixed holding, see *Change 14*.

Section 576(1) of ICTA sets out a general rule that, where shares are disposed of out of a mixed holding, the shares disposed of are to be identified on a last in first out (LIFO) basis.

This rule is modified by section 576(1C) of ICTA in the case of a mixed holding which includes shares to which investment relief within the meaning given by Schedule 15 to FA 2000 (corporate venturing scheme) is attributable.

Shares forming a section 104 holding or a 1982 holding are regarded for the purposes of corporation tax on chargeable gains as indistinguishable parts of a single asset. Thus, the consideration given for the shares in the holding is spread evenly across the shares and there is no need for the purposes of corporation tax on chargeable gains to identify the specific shares disposed of.

The LIFO identification rule is, however, necessary for the purposes of section 573 of ICTA to identify whether, on the disposal of some only of the shares out of such a holding consisting partly of shares that are not capable of being qualifying shares, the shares disposed of are qualifying shares.

Shares of the same class held by the company in the same capacity normally constitute a section 104 holding or a 1982 holding (see sections 104 and 109 of TCGA). Section 107 of TCGA, however, provides special rules for identifying shares where there are acquisitions and disposals within a ten day period. Where some but not all of the shares acquired within a ten day period are disposed of within that period, section 107 of TCGA identifies the shares disposed of on a first in first out (FIFO) basis.

Section 105 of TCGA contains rules in relation to shares acquired on the same day. In practice, if some but not all of the shares of the same class acquired on the same day are shares that are not capable of being qualifying shares and if some only of the shares acquired on that day are disposed of, the question whether and to what extent the shares disposed of are qualifying shares is determined for the purposes of section 573 of ICTA on a just and reasonable basis; normally pro rata to the number of shares acquired on that day.

In rewriting the rule in section 576(1) of ICTA, the approach taken in section 76 is to ensure that the identification rules for share loss relief are wholly consistent with the identification rules for corporation tax on chargeable gains, so that:

- so far as the rules in sections 105 and 107 of TCGA serve conclusively to identify whether and to what extent the shares disposed of out of a mixed holding are qualifying shares, those rules are explicitly applied (see subsections (3)(a)(i) and (4));
- so far as shares acquired on different days are included in a section 104 holding, the LIFO rule in section 576(1) of ICTA is applied separately to the shares in the section 104 holding (see subsections (3)(a)(ii) and (5)); and
- so far as shares acquired on different days are included in a 1982 holding, the LIFO rule in section 576(1) of ICTA is applied separately to the shares in the 1982 holding (see subsections (3)(a)(ii) and (5)).

In a case where the mixed holding includes shares to which investment relief is attributable, subsections (3)(a), (4) and (5) are displaced by subsections (3)(b) and (6).

In some cases those rules do not conclusively determine whether and to what extent the shares disposed of are qualifying shares. They may, for example, identify that some only of shares of the same class acquired on the same day are disposed of. In that case it is necessary to determine whether any of the shares disposed of are shares that are not capable of being qualifying shares. Subsection (7) legislates existing practice by providing an explicit rule that the determination is to be made on a just and reasonable basis.

This change only has any effect on taxpayers in the rare circumstances of the disposal at a loss of qualifying shares being some only of a number of shares acquired at separate times not earlier than nine days before the date of the disposal. The change applies a FIFO rule rather than a LIFO rule. The effect may be adverse or favourable depending on whether the shares identified as disposed of are or are not qualifying shares and, if qualifying shares were subscribed for at different times, the respective amounts subscribed for the qualifying shares. In all other circumstances, it has no effect for taxpayers.

This change is in principle and in practiceadverse to some taxpayers and favourable to others. But the numbers affected and the amounts involved are likely to be small.

CHANGE 17: SHARE LOSS RELIEF: SHARES TO WHICH SECTION 127 OF TCGA APPLIES: SECTION 77

This change makes explicit the time at which, among others, corresponding bonus shares are treated as issued for the purposes of section 76. It is, in part, consequential on the inclusion of section 73(3) (see *Change 12*) which treats corresponding bonus shares as subscribed for by the company.

This change is the same as that made in section 149(2) of ITA for the purposes of relief against income tax. See Change 31 in Annex 1 to the explanatory notes on ITA.

The time at which such shares are treated as issued to or acquired by the company claiming relief needs to be ascertained for a number of purposes. See section 89 and *Change 20.*

The time at which corresponding bonus shares are treated as issued to or acquired by the company claiming relief also needs to be ascertained for the purpose of determining which shares are disposed of in accordance with the identification rules in section 576(1) and (1C) of ICTA, rewritten in section 76.

Section 77(1) has been included for this purpose. A different approach from that in section 89(2) has been adopted. Section 76 applies where the holding includes shares to which investment relief within the meaning given by Schedule 15 to FA 2000 (corporate venturing scheme)is attributable. In cases where it so applies, section 76 applies the rules in paragraph 93 of Schedule 15 to FA 2000. For consistency, section 77(1) follows the wording in paragraph 93(7) of that Schedule.

Section 77(1) and paragraph 93(7) of Schedule 15 to FA 2000 do not apply only to issues of corresponding bonus shares. They also apply to allotments of shares for payment, for example by way of rights, which meet the requirements of section 126(2)(a) of TCGA and to which section 127 of that Act applies.

This ensures that, if investment relief is not attributable to the shares in the existing holding or the new shares, new shares issued by way of rights within section 126(2)(a) of TCGA are treated for the purposes of section 76 as acquired at the same time as the shares in the existing holding.

But if investment relief is attributable to the shares in the existing holding or to new shares allotted for payment, section 77(1) does not apply to the allotment. This is because paragraph 81 of Schedule 15 to FA 2000 provides that, if there is such an allotment for payment and investment relief is attributable either to the shares in the existing holding or to the allotted shares, section 127 of that Act does not apply.

In addition to making the necessary provision consequent on the explicit treatment of corresponding bonus shares as being subscribed for, this change has the effect, for the purposes of section 76, of treating rights issue shares as issued earlier than the date on which they are actually issued, except as described in the preceding paragraph.

If the rights issue shares form part of a mixed holding and some only of the shares in the mixed holding are disposed of, the effect of this change is to prevent the taxpayer from claiming a greater amount of relief or from obtaining relief earlier than would be the case under generally accepted practice (see paragraphs 47400 and 48350 of HMRC's Venture Capital Schemes Manual), by advancing an argument that the rights issue shares are to be identified as being among the shares disposed of by reference to the actual date of their issue.

This change is adverse to some taxpayers in principle. But it is expected to have no practical effect as it is in line with generally accepted practice.

CHANGE 18: SHARE LOSS RELIEF: NOMINEES AND BARE TRUSTEES: SECTION 77

This change makes clear that, if shares of the same class are held as to some directly by the company and as to the others by a nominee or bare trustee for it, all the shares are included in a single holding of the company for the purposes of section 76.

This change is the same as that made in section 149(3) of ITA for the purposes of relief against income tax. See Change 32 in Annex 1 to the explanatory notes on ITA.

A company which has subscribed for shares may subsequently wish to transfer the shares into the name of a nominee or bare trustee. On a disposal of the shares on behalf of the company by the nominee or bare trustee, the allowable loss for the purposes of corporation tax on chargeable gains and the entitlement to relief under section 573 of ICTA is that of the company not that of the nominee or bare trustee.

The effect of this change is to prevent the taxpayer from claiming a greater amount of relief or obtaining relief earlier than has hitherto been the case in practice, by advancing an argument that, where a company has beneficial holdings of shares one of which is held directly and the other of which is held through a nominee or bare trustee, the provisions of section 76 should be applied separately.

This change is adverse to some taxpayers in principle. But it is expected to have no practical effect as it is in line with generally accepted practice.

CHANGE 19: SHARE LOSS RELIEF: RESOLUTION OF CONFLICTING PROVISIONS: SECTIONS 74 AND 87 AND SCHEDULE 2 (DISPOSALS OF NEW SHARES, AND RELIEF AFTER AN EXCHANGE OF SHARES FOR SHARES IN ANOTHER COMPANY)

This change makes clear that the provisions of section 74 do not apply to an exchange of shares to which section 87 applies. It resolves an apparent conflict between section 304A of ICTA, rewritten by ITA as sections 576J and 576K of ICTA, and section 575(2) of ICTA, rewritten in section 74, which arises from the way in which section 575(2) of that Act achieves its purpose.

This change is the same as that made in sections 136(2) and 145(3) of ITA for the purposes of relief against income tax. See Change 24 in Annex 1 to the explanatory notes on ITA.

Section 575(2) of ICTA is an anti-avoidance provision. Its purpose is to prevent a person from obtaining share loss relief in respect of shares that are not capable of being qualifying shares in a company ("Oldco") by swapping them for shares in another company ("Newco") that are capable of being qualifying shares, except to the extent that the person gives additional consideration for the shares in Newco. For example, the shares in Oldco may not be capable of being qualifying shares because they were purchased from another shareholder. This provision has existed since the introduction of share loss relief in 1980.

Section 304A of ICTA was first applied for the purposes of share loss relief as part of the changes to the meaning of "qualifying trading company" made by FA 1998. It deals with the continuity of the requirements to be met by Newco following an exchange of qualifying shares in Oldco for qualifying shares in Newco without change of ownership.

Section 575(2) of ICTA applies to the issue of ordinary shares ("new shares") by Newco in an exchange or scheme of reconstruction within section 135 or 136 of TCGA relating to shares ("old shares") in Oldco. The new shares are in these circumstances "issued in consideration of … money's worth", that is the transfer or cancellation of the old shares. Accordingly, if Newco is a qualifying trading company in relation to the disposal of the new shares, the new shares disposed of are qualifying shares (see section 573(6) of ICTA rewritten in section 73(2)). This is the case whether or not the old shares are capable of being qualifying shares.

Section 575(2)(a) of ICTA operates to prevent share loss relief being obtained on the disposal of the new shares where the old shares were not themselves capable of being qualifying shares by requiring the following assumptions to be made:

- first, that section 127 of TCGA does not apply to the exchange or scheme of reconstruction, so that there is a disposal of the old shares for the purposes of corporation tax on chargeable gains; and
- second, that on that assumed disposal an allowable loss would have been incurred for those purposes.

Section 575(2)(a) of ICTA then requires that share loss relief would have been obtainable on the assumed disposal on the basis that it was a disposal by way of a bargain made at arm's length. This is a consequence of the express reference in section 575(2)(a) of ICTA to the allowable loss being incurred "in disposing of [the old shares] as mentioned in subsection (1)(a) above". Section 575(1) of ICTA sets out the categories of disposal in respect of which a claim for share loss relief may be made, including in paragraph (a) a disposal "by way of a bargain made at arm's length for full consideration". This requirement is rewritten in section 68(2)(a). See the commentary on section 68 and *Change 11* in Annex 1.

Unless, on the assumptions described, share loss relief would have been obtained on the assumed disposal of the old shares, share loss relief may not be obtained on the disposal of the new shares, except to that extent that any "new consideration" has been given for the new shares (see section 575(2)(b) of ICTA rewritten in section 74(4) and (5)).

Section 304A of ICTA is one of the provisions applied by section 576(4A) of that Act with modifications for the purposes of defining a qualifying trading company by reference to the requirements of section 293 of ICTA. Section 304A of ICTA has been rewritten by ITA with the required modifications, in sections 145 and 146 of ITA for the purposes of relief against income tax and in sections 576J and 576K of ICTA for the purposes of relief against income subject to corporation tax. See the commentary on sections 145 and 146 of, and Schedule 1 to, ITA in the explanatory notes on that Act.

Section 304A of ICTA relates to an exchange of securities within section 135 of TCGA affecting old shares which are qualifying shares. The type of exchange to which section 304A of ICTA applies is one which involves no change of ultimate ownership. It typically occurs when a new holding company is placed above a previously loss making company as one of the steps in obviating difficulties arising under company law in relation to distributable profits.

The effect of section 304A of ICTA as modified and applied by section 576(4A) of that Act is that, if the exchange meets the requirements of section 304A(1) of ICTA, the new shares are capable of being qualifying shares and the requirements for Newco to be a qualifying trading company are to be applied as if Oldco and Newco were one and the same company. In particular, the unquoted status requirement in section 293(1A) of ICTA (rewritten in section 143 of ITA and section 576H of ICTA) and the gross assets requirement in section 293(6A) of ICTA (rewritten in section 142 of ITA and section 576G of ICTA) are to be met only at the time of issue of the old shares by Oldco.

But if the assumptions required by section 575(2)(a) of ICTA are to be applied to an exchange falling within section 304A(1) of that Act, the requirement that the assumed disposal arises by way of a bargain made at arm's length is unlikely to be capable of being met. This would prevent a claim for share loss relief on the disposal of the shares in Newco and render nugatory the application of section 304A of ICTA for the purposes of share loss relief.

Change 24 in Annex 1 to the explanatory notes on ITA resolves that apparent conflict, for the purposes of relief against income tax, by providing in section 145(3)(a) of ITA that nothing in section 136(2) of that Act applies to an exchange falling within section 145(1) and cross–referring to that provision in section 136(2) of that Act.

But it was not within the scope of ITA, an income tax rewrite Act, to make the equivalent changes in sections 575(2) and 576J of ICTA for the purposes of relief under section 573 of that

Act against income subject to corporation tax. It is within the scope of a corporation tax rewrite Act to make them and this change accordingly does so.

The effect of this change is to ensure that, in relation to shares in Newco issued on or after 1 April 2010, the legislation no longer contains an apparent conflict between provisions. The conflict is apparent in the sense that it arises in principle but has no effect in practice.

This change is in taxpayers' favour in principle. But it is expected to have no practical effect as it is in line with generally accepted practice.

CHANGE 20: SHARE LOSS RELIEF: TIME OF ISSUE OF CORRESPONDING BONUS SHARES: SECTION 89, SCHEDULE 1 (PARAGRAPH 57A OF SCHEDULE 2 TO ITA) AND SCHEDULE 2 (APPLICATION OF PART 5 OF SCHEDULE 2 IN RELATION TO CORRESPONDING BONUS SHARES)

This change inserts an explicit provision in section 89 determining the time at which corresponding bonus shares are treated as issued to a company. It is consequential on the inclusion of section 73(3) which treats corresponding bonus shares as subscribed for by the company (see *Change 12*).

This change is the same as that made in section 150(3) of ITA for the purposes of relief against income tax. See Change 34 in Annex 1 to the explanatory notes on ITA.

The time at which such shares are treated as issued to the company claiming relief needs to be ascertained for the purposes of determining:

- the beginning of the period during which the qualifying trading company must carry on its business wholly or mainly in the United Kingdom (section 78(5)(a));
- the times at which the gross assets requirement is to be met (section 84(1)(a) and (2)(a));
- the time at which the unquoted status requirement is to be met (section 85(1)); and
- if section 87 applies, the time at which the new shares are to be treated as having been issued for the purposes of section 88(2)(b).

A provision corresponding to section 89(2) has been included in Part 5 of Schedule 2 with appropriate adaptation where the matter in question is whether, in relation to the application of transitional provisions,corresponding bonus shares are treated as having been issued before, rather than on, a particular date. A consequential amendment has been made by Schedule 1 adding in Part 6 of Schedule 2 to ITA a provision mirroring that in Part 5 of Schedule 2 to this Act.

This change is a necessary direct consequence of the inclusion, to the advantage of taxpayers, of the explicit treatment of corresponding bonus shares as being subscribed for.

This change is in taxpayers' favour in principle. But it is expected to have no practical effect as it is in line with generally accepted practice.

CHANGE 21: SHARE LOSS RELIEF: INVESTMENT COMPANY: OMISSION OF REFERENCE TO SAVINGS BANK AND BANK FOR SAVINGS: SECTION 90, SCHEDULE 1 (SECTION 151 OF ITA) AND PART 5 OF SCHEDULE 2 (INTERPRETATION OF CHAPTER 5 OF PART 4)

This change results in certain savings banks and banks for savings no longer falling within the definition of "investment company" for the purposes of share loss relief in Chapter 5 of Part 4 of this Act and Chapter 6 of Part 4 of ITA.

Section 576L(1) of ICTA and section 151(1) of ITA apply the definition of investment company in section 130 of ICTA, with modification, for the purposes of share loss relief under section 573 of ICTA and Chapter 6 of Part 4 of ITA.

The definition of "investment company" in section 130 of ICTA, which applies for the purposes of Part 4 of ICTA, is as follows:

> ""investment company", means any company whose business consists wholly or mainly in the making of investments and the principal part of whose income is derived therefrom, but includes any savings bank or other bank for savings except any which, for the purposes of the Trustee Savings Bank Act1985 is a successor or a further successor to a trustee savings bank

The principal use of the term in Part 4 of ICTA was for the purposes of section 75 of ICTA (expenses of management: investment companies). FA 2004 repealed that section in relation to accounting periods beginning on or after 1 April 2004 and replaced it with the current provisions in sections 75 to 75B of ICTA (rewritten in Part 16 of CTA 2009). The current provisions apply to "companies with investment business" as defined in section 130 of ICTA (rewritten in section 1218(1) of CTA 2009) That definition was inserted in section 130 of ICTA by FA 2004 and is as follows:

> ""company with investment business" means any company whose business consists wholly or partly in the making of investments.

The notes on clauses to the Finance Bill 2004 state in relation to that definition that:

"the reference to savings banks has now been removed on the grounds that it is obsolete.

The definition of "investment company" was retained in section 130 of ICTA for the reasons given in the notes on clauses to Finance Bill 2004:

"**26** The current definition of an "investment company" has not been repealed. The definition of an "investment company" will remain relevant for the purposes of:

- section 573 ICTA (where it helps identify the companies entitled to relief against income in respect of losses on unquoted shares in trading companies); and
- the transitional rules in Clause 43.

This change replaces the cross-reference to and modification of the definition of "investment company" in section 576L(1) of ICTA and section 151(1) of ITA by a stand alone definition in section 90(1) of this Act and section 151(1) of ITA in the following terms:

> ""investment company" means a company—
>
> (a) whose business consists wholly or mainly in the making of investments, and
>
> (b) which derives the principal part of its income from the making of investments,
>
> but does not include the holding company of a trading group.

This wording omits reference to "any savings bank or other bank for savings except any which, for the purposes of the Trustee Savings Bank Act 1985 is a successor or a further successor to a trustee savings bank". The omission applies, for corporation tax purposes, only in relation to the disposal on or after 1 April 2010 of shares issued on or after that date and, for income tax purposes, only in relation to the disposal on or after 6 April 2010 of shares issued on or after that date. See Part 5 of Schedule 2 (interpretation of Chapter) which preserves the effect of the source legislation in relation to shares issued before the relevant date. The omission has two effects.

First, no such savings bank or bank for savings is eligible for share loss relief under section 68 of this Act on such a disposal as it no longer meets the requirement that the investor is an investment company.

This is potentially adverse to taxpayers in principle and in practice, but no such bank is known to carry on business in the United Kingdom which includes the making of investments in shares in companies capable of being qualifying trading companies.

Second, the requirements in section 78(2)(b) and (3)(b) of this Act and section 134(2)(b) and (3)(b) of ITA, that to be a qualifying trading company the company must not be an investment company at the times mentioned, can be met by a company that is such a savings bank or bank for savings in relation to a disposal to which the new definition applies.

This is potentially favourable to taxpayers in principle but has no effect in practice, as it is also a requirement of section 78(2)(b) and (3)(b) of this Act and section 134(2)(b) and (3)(b) of ITA that the company is not at those times a trading company (as defined in section 90(1) of this Act and section 151(1) of ITA). Such a bank is a trading company within that definition, notwithstanding that it may be a mutual trader and the profits of its trade are not within the charge to tax on trade profits.

This change has an effect which is adverse to some taxpayers in principle and in practice. But the numbers affected and the amounts involved are likely to be small. It also has an effect which is in taxpayers' favour in principle but whichis not expected in practice to alter the position for taxpayers.

CHANGE 22: SHARE LOSS RELIEF: TIME OF DISPOSAL: SECTION 90

This change makes explicit the accounting period in which the disposal is to be treated as occurring for the purpose of share loss relief.

The availability of share loss relief is dependent upon an allowable loss being incurred for the purposes of corporation tax on chargeable gains and this can only be incurred on a disposal within the meaning given in TCGA.

The provisions of TCGA which determine when a disposal occurs, including in particular section 28 of that Act, do not apply to Chapter 5A of Part 13 of ICTA. But in practice "the accounting period in which the loss was incurred" referred to in section 573(2) of ICTA is taken to be the accounting period in which the disposal is made or treated as made for the purposes of corporation tax on chargeable gains in accordance with TCGA.

Section 90(7) contains explicit provision to this effect.This change is similar to that made in section 151(8) of ITA for the purposes of relief against income tax. SeeChange 35 in Annex 1 to the explanatory notes on ITA.

Although this change in principle affects the timing of relief and could be favourable to some taxpayers and adverse to others, it is entirely in line with generally accepted practice and so has no practical effect.

CHANGE 23: RECALCULATION OF EEA AMOUNT: SECTION 113

This change clarifies how the EEA amount is recalculated in a case where the EEA amount arises in a period that is longer than a year.

In accordance with paragraph 11 of Schedule 18A to ICTA the EEA amount must be recalculated in accordance with the "applicable UK tax rules". Those rules include (paragraph 14 of the Schedule) any necessary splitting of the loss period in which the EEA amount arises to produce assumed accounting periods.

The amount that is available for surrender is limited to the amount given by the recalculation.

The recalculation necessarily involves apportionment of the EEA amount to the assumed accounting periods. But there is no rule to say how the comparison of the original and recalculated amount should be done: the original amount is for the whole loss period; the recalculated amount is for the assumed accounting periods.

Example

An EEA company has a loss of £12,000 for the period 1 January 2010 to 30 June 2011. None of the loss qualifies otherwise for relief from corporation tax (section 402(1)(b) of ICTA). All of the loss meets the conditions in section 403F(2) of ICTA.

Assumed accounting period	*EEA amount*	*Capital allowances(+)/ balancing charges(-)*	*Recalculated amount*
1.1.10 to 31.12.10	*8000*	*-2000*	*6000*
1.1.11 to 30.6.11	*4000*	*+3000*	*7000*

In this (unlikely) case, neither recalculated amount exceeds the EEA amount of £12,000. So it is apparently possible to argue that the amount available for surrender is £13,000. This result is illogical given that the EEA amount is only £12,000, but it is not explicitly excluded by Schedule 18A to ICTA. Section 113(3) removes the possibility of this illogical result by making it clear that the maximum amount available for surrender in relation to all the assumed accounting periods comprised in the EEA period cannot be more than the qualifying part of the EEA amount.

This change is adverse to some taxpayers in principle. But it is expected to have no practical effect as it is in line with generally accepted practice.

CHANGE 24: MULTIPLE CLAIMS FOR GROUP RELIEF: SECTION 141

This change clarifies the position if more than one claim is made for a company's loss etc.

Section 403A of ICTA limits a group relief claim to the smaller of:

- the "unused part of the surrenderable amount"; and
- the "unrelieved part of the claimant company's total profits".

Any claim for group relief reduces the surrendering company's unused part of the surrenderable amount and the unrelieved part of the claimant company's total profits. In general, earlier claims limit the amounts of later claims. So, in dealing with multiple claims, it is necessary to know in what order to deal with the claims.

Before Self Assessment for companies it was possible to say when a claim became final. Usually, that would be because the inspector had made an assessment giving effect to the relief and the appeal period had expired. So section 403A(6) of ICTA identifies the previously claimed group relief as that which has been the subject of claims that have become final.

Under Self Assessment it is not generally possible to know whether an enquiry will be made (paragraph 24 of Schedule 18 to FA 1998), so extending the time limit for withdrawing claims (paragraph 74(1)(b) of the Schedule). To overcome this practical difficulty there is a practice, set out in paragraph 80220 of the HMRC Company Taxation Manual, of simply dealing with claims in the order in which they are made (whether or not they are final).

This Act enacts the practice.

In most cases the total amount of relief is not affected by this change. But, in principle, the relief may be given to one company instead of another.

This change is in principle adverse to some taxpayers and favourable to others. But it is expected to have no practical effect as it is in line with generally accepted practice.

CHANGE 25: GROUP RELIEF: RESTRICTION OF SURRENDER BY COMPANY OWNED BY CONSORTIUM: SECTION 148

This change relaxes the restriction that is made when group relief is surrendered by a company that is owned by a consortium and is also a member of a group.

The policy is that the total relief surrendered outside the group should not exceed the net loss (if any) of the group as a whole. So the losses etc of the surrendering company are treated for this purpose as reduced by any group relief claims that could be made by other companies in the group.

Example 1

A company (C) owned by a consortium has a trading loss of £10,000 for its accounting period of 12 months ended 31 December 2009 available for surrender to the members (M1, M2 etc) of the consortium. C's subsidiary (S) has profits of £2000 for its accounting period of 12 months ended 31 December 2009.	

Under section 405(2) of ICTA, S is assumed to make a group relief claim to cover its profits. S's corresponding accounting period (see section 413(2A) of ICTA) is the 12 months ended 31 December 2009. So the assumed claim is for £2000 and (because no other companies are involved) that is the amount of the "potential group relief". So C's "loss or other amount" available for surrender to M1, M2 etc is reduced under section 405(1) of ICTA to £8000, the net loss of the group as a whole.

Example 2

The facts are the same as in Example 1 except that S's accounting date is 30 September. The effect of section 413(2A) of ICTA is that, in relation to C's accounting period ended 31 December 2009, S's corresponding accounting period is the whole of the 12 months ended 30 September 2009.

The effect of section 405(2) of ICTA is that S is assumed to make a claim for group relief equal to the total of its profits of its entire accounting period ended 30 September 2009 (that is, its corresponding accounting period). Section 405 of ICTA does not provide for an apportionment of S's profits, even though S could actually claim relief against no more than £1500, its profits attributable to the "overlapping period" (see section 403A of ICTA). So the £2000 restriction stands.

In section 148(5) the "maximum amount of group relief that could be given" on a claim by S may require an apportionment of S's total profits. This makes no difference in Example 1. But in Example 2 C's loss available for surrender is treated as reduced to £8500, instead of £8000.

This change is in taxpayers' favour in principle and may benefit some in practice. But the numbers affected and the amounts involved are likely to be small.

CHANGE 26: GROUP RELIEF: EQUITY HOLDER'S SHARE OF PROFITS OR ASSETS REFERABLE TO UK TRADE: SECTION 181

This change simplifies the calculation of the percentage of profits or assets to which an equity holder is entitled in cases involving non-UK resident companies.

The basic rule for all companies is that the percentage of profits to which an equity holder is entitled is calculated by reference to a company's total profits (paragraph 2 of Schedule 18 to ICTA, rewritten in section 165). If the company has no profits it would be impossible to say what the percentage is. So, in cases where the company has no profits, the calculation is made by reference to £100 total profits.

There is a similar basic rule in paragraph 3 of Schedule 18 to ICTA, rewritten in section 166, for assets to which an equity holder is entitled in a winding up.

Paragraph 5F of Schedule 18 to ICTA deals with non-UK resident companies in which an equity holder's entitlements may be related to a company's "UK trade". Sub-paragraph (7) caters for the possibility that the profits or assets referable to the UK trade are less than £100. The calculation is done on the assumption that the profits or assets referable to the UK trade are £100.

In accordance with the assumption in paragraph 5F(7)(c) of Schedule 18 to ICTA, the total profits or assets (adjusted if necessary in accordance with paragraph 2 or 3 of the Schedule) cannot be less than £100. Section 181 rewrites paragraph 5F(7) of Schedule 18 so that, if the profits or assets referable to the UK trade are between nil and £100, the actual amount is used in the calculation.

The change affects only Assumptions 2 and 3. Assumption 4 (rewriting paragraph 5F(7)(c) of Schedule 18 to ICTA) retains the reference to £100.

In cases where the non-UK resident company's profits or assets referable to its UK trade are more than zero but less than £100 this change may alter the percentage calculated (particularly if those profits or assets are small). But it is unlikely to result in a change to the conclusion about the extent of an equity holder's stake in a company.

This change is in principle and in practice adverse to some taxpayers and favourable to others. But the numbers affected and the amounts involved are likely to be small.

CHANGE 27: CHARITABLE DONATIONS RELIEF: GIFTS AND BENEFITS LINKED TO PERIODS OF LESS THAN 12 MONTHS: PRIORITY BETWEEN METHODS OF CALCULATING ANNUALISED AMOUNTS OF GIFTS AND BENEFITS: SECTION 198

This change clarifies the operation of the rules about annualising the amounts of gifts and benefits in the various different sets of circumstances which can arise, by providing a priority rule to cater for certain cases where more than one of the statutory rules could apply in relation to a given set of circumstances.

If a company makes a donation of money to a charity, and receives a benefit in consequence of doing so, that benefit may affect whether the donation is "qualifying" (section 191). And that in turn affects whether the company obtains tax relief for the donation under section 190 as a qualifying charitable donation.

The source legislation (section 339(3DB) to (3DD) of ICTA) contains rules to counter tax advantages from fragmentation of the time periods attaching to donations or to consequent benefits. In particular, section 339(3DD) of ICTA (rewritten in section 198) lays down the method of annualising either the gift, or both the gift and the benefit, in different circumstances. Those circumstances are set out in section 339(3DB) and (3DC) of ICTA, rewritten in section 198 of this Act as conditions A to D.

But the source legislation does not set out what is to happen if the circumstances fall within one of Conditions C and D and within one of Conditions A and B, which in theory can occur.

This change provides a priority rule to cater for such cases, which is located in Step 2 of section 198(8). It provides that, in such a case, the rule relating to Conditions C and D takes priority.

This change is in principle adverse to some taxpayers and favourable to others. But it is expected to have no practical effect as it is in line with generally accepted practice.

CHANGE 28: COMMUNITY INVESTMENT TAX RELIEF: PERMIT DEDUCTION OF EXPENSES INCURRED BY DIRECTOR, EMPLOYEE OR ASSOCIATE: SECTION 250

This change permits consideration given by a director or employee of an investor or by an associate of such a director or employee for a benefit or facility provided by the CDFI to be deducted in calculating value received.

Paragraph 35 of Schedule 16 to FA 2002, rewritten in section 249, provides for the circumstances in which the investor receives value from the CDFI for the purposes of determining whether any CITR falls to be reduced or withdrawn.

One of those circumstances (paragraph 35(1)(d)) is the provision by the CDFI of a benefit or facility for:

"(i) the investor or any associates of the investor, or

(ii) directors or employees of the investor or any of their associates.

Associate is defined in paragraph 50 of Schedule 16 to FA 2002, rewritten in section 268.

Paragraph 36(d) of Schedule 16 to FA 2002 determines the amount of the value received in a case falling within paragraph 35(1)(d) as:

"(i) the cost to the CDFI of providing the benefit or facility, less

(ii) any consideration given for it by the investor or any associate of the investor.

But paragraph 36 does not permit the deduction of any consideration:

- "in a case where the benefit or facility is provided to a director or employee, given by the director or employee or by any associate of the director or employee, or
- in a case where the benefit or facility is provided to an associate of a director or employee, given by the associate or by the director or employee.

As the consideration is most likely to be given by the recipient of the benefit or facility, this may put the investor in a worse position if the benefit or facility is provided to a director or employee or an associate of a director or employee than if the benefit or facility is provided to the investor itself or an associate of the investor.

In rewriting paragraph 36(d) of Schedule 16 to FA 2002 in section 250 this omission has been rectified.

This change is in taxpayers' favour in principle and may benefit some in practice. But the numbers affected and the amounts involved are likely to be small.

CHANGE 29: OIL TAXATION: DEDUCTION FOR EXCESS OF NOMINATED PROCEEDS: SECTION 283

This change clarifies the meaning of section 493(1A)(b) of ICTA.

For income tax and corporation tax purposes a separate "ring fence trade" is deemed to exist by virtue of section 16 of ITTOIA (for income tax) or section 492(1) of ICTA (rewritten in section 279 for corporation tax). The activities making up the ring fence trade are set out in section 16(2) of ITTOIA and section 492(1)(a) to (c) of ICTA (rewritten in section 274 for corporation tax).

Section 493 of ICTA contains rules which ensure that the correct value of oil or gas is brought into account in computing the profits of the ring fence trade. Section 493(1A) of ICTA deals with what is termed "an excess of nominated proceeds". This is a concept that is part of the Petroleum Revenue Tax (PRT) regime. It allows a company to "nominate" a crude oil sales contract (within the crude oil forward market) as being a contract through which crude oil will actually be delivered, rather than only being a financial (or "paper") transaction. The "excess" may arise if crude oil is delivered through a contract that has not been so nominated, and HMRC's value exceeds the actual contract price of the oil (the excess is calculated by multiplying the volume delivered by the price/value difference).

Where this is the case, the same "excess" is also treated as a deduction by virtue of section 493(1A)(b) of ICTA. But the wording of section 493(1A)(b) is unclear in referring to "any trade to which section 492(1) [of ICTA] does not apply". It is not clear whether this refers to the activities listed in section 492(1)(a) to (c), or to the deemed "separate trade" referred to in the full-out words of section 492(1), or to both. The use of the word "any" in "any trade" suggests a wide application. The explanatory notes published with the legislation that introduced this provision (section 151 of FA 2006) state that the intention is to give a deduction in computing profits of the non-ring fence trade, whereas the wording of section 493(1A)(b) might suggest that it only applies in the case of a separate trade that is deemed to exist by section 492(1).

Section 283 therefore clarifies the legislation by expanding the reference to refer to both the concept of the deemed separate trade, and the activities listed in section 492(1) of ICTA, thereby making it clear that the deduction can be given against the profits of any non-ring fence trade, not solely a deemed trade created by section 279.

This change is in principle adverse to some taxpayers and favourable to others. But it is expected to have no practical effect as it is in line with generally accepted practice.

CHANGE 30: CLOSE COMPANIES: CHARGE TO TAX ON LOANS AND ADVANCES TO PARTICIPATORS: EXCEPTION FOR SMALL AMOUNTS: SECTION 456 AND SCHEDULE 2

This change brings into line with practice the statutory exception, for small amounts, from the charge to tax on loans and advances made to participators in close companies. It does so by extending the exception to include not only loans but also advances.

Section 419 of ICTA imposes a charge to tax when a close company (otherwise than in the ordinary course of a business carried on by it which includes the lending of money) makes any loan or advances any money to an individual who is a participator in the company or to an associate of a participator in the company.

Section 420(2) of ICTA makes an exception to this charge when the amounts are small. So far as relevant, it provides:

"Section 419(1) shall not apply to a loan made to a director or employee of a close company, or of an associated company of the close company, if –

(a) neither the amount of the loan, nor that amount when taken together with any other outstanding loans which –

(i) were made by the close company or any of its associated companies to the borrower; and

(ii) if made before 31st March 1971, were made for the purpose of purchasing a dwelling which was or was to be the borrower's only or main residence;

exceeds £15,000 and the outstanding loans falling within sub-paragraph (ii) above do not together exceed £10,000; … and

(c) the borrower does not have a material interest in the close company or in any associated company of the close company;

but if the borrower acquires such a material interest at a time when the whole or part of any such loan made after 30'h March 1971 remains outstanding the close company shall be regarded as making to him at that time a loan of an amount equal to the sum outstanding.

Section 420(2) of ICTA makes no reference to advances. But it would be anomalous to exclude advances from section 420(2) of ICTA, because an advance to a participator in a close company would then be subject to the charge under section 419 of ICTA in circumstances in which, if the participator had received the money by way of loan, section 420(2) of ICTA would have sheltered it from tax.

In practice, therefore, HMRC apply section 420(2) of ICTA to loans and advances alike.

Section 456 and the saving for close companies in Part 11 of Schedule 2, which are based on section 420(2) of ICTA, bring the law into line with practice.

This change is in taxpayers' favour in principle. But it is expected to have no practical effect as it is in line with generally accepted practice.

CHANGE 31: CHARITABLE COMPANIES: GIFTS TO ELIGIBLE BODIES UNDER SA DONATE: CLAIMS: SECTION 475

Under this change an eligible body is not required to claim exemption from tax if it receives a qualifying gift as a result of a direction under section 429(2) of ITA (the "SA Donate" scheme).

Section 25(10) of FA 1990 treats a gift, which is both a qualifying donation for gift aid under Chapter 2 of Part 8 of ITA and paid to a charitable company, as the receipt, under deduction of income tax, of an annual payment of an amount equal to the grossed up amount of the gift. "Charitable company" is defined in section 25(12)(a) of FA 1990 to include not only companies established for charitable purposes but also bodies within section 507 of ICTA.

Section 505(1)(c)(iizb) of ICTA exempts annual payments and therefore qualifying donations received by a charitable company so far as they are applied for charitable purposes. Section 505 contains a general requirement for a claim for all the exemptions mentioned in the section. However section 83(4) of FA 2004 overrides this in one particular respect. It treats a charitable company as having made a claim to any exemption to which it is entitled under section 505(1)(c)(iizb) of ICTA in respect of qualifying donations which are received as a result of a direction under SA Donate by virtue of section 429(2) of ITA. (SA Donate allows an individual to give repayments of tax due under self-assessment to a charity of choice.)

Section 507 of ICTA gives eligible bodies, on receipt of a claim, the same exemption as charitable companies which apply the whole of their income to charitable purposes. But section 83(4) of FA 2004 does not include eligible bodies within its definition of charitable companies, leaving such bodies with the need to claim for relief on qualifying donations received as a result of a direction under section 429(2) ITA.

This change gives eligible bodies exemption if qualifying donations are received as a result of a direction under section 429(2) ITA without the need to make a claim, thus putting them on the same footing as charitable companies.

This change is reflected in the sections as follows.

Section 472 rewrites the exemptions for qualifying donations paid to charitable companies in section 505(1) of ICTA and section 25(10) and (12) of FA 1990. Subsection (5) rewrites section 83(4) of FA 2004 which exempts charities receiving qualifying donations under SA donate from the need to make a claim. Section 475 is the equivalent for eligible bodies of section 472, and subsection (7) exempts these bodies from making claims if qualifying donations are received under SA Donate, in the same way as section 472(5) does for charitable companies.

This change has no implications for the amount of tax paid, who pays it or when. It affects (in principle but not in practice) only administrative matters.

CHANGE 32: CHARITABLE COMPANIES: EXEMPTION FOR POST-CESSATION RECEIPTS OF CERTAIN TRADES: SECTIONS 478, 479, 485, 490, 491, 492 AND SCHEDULE 1

This change introduces an exemption from corporation tax, in the case of charitable companies, for the post-cessation receipts of trades whose profits would be exempt if the trade had not ceased.

In contrast with the equivalent income tax rules in ITA, adjustment income is subsumed within trading profits and, therefore, unlike the position for income tax, is already covered by the charitable exemptions.

Post-cessation receipts are taxed under Chapter 15 of Part 3 of CTA 2009. There is no exemption for post-cessation receipts in the source legislation for charitable companies, other than the exemption in section 46 of FA 2000 (rewritten in sections 480 to 482) which applies only if the receipts are below a certain level. But HMRC practice is to treat post-cessation receipts as exempt from corporation tax if they arise from a trade that benefited from the exemption in section 505(1)(e) of ICTA (rewritten as section 478).

If a trade is treated as two separate trades in accordance with section 479(2) and (3) any post-cessation receipts are apportioned to the two parts (and this could mean completely apportioned to just one part if relating only to that part) and an exemption is then available for the receipts apportioned to the charitable part.

This change is in taxpayers' favour in principle. But it is expected to have no practical effect as it is in line with generally accepted practice.

CHANGE 33: REQUIRING AN APPORTIONMENT TO BE JUST AND REASONABLE: SECTIONS 479, 599, 875, 880, 952, 956 AND 994

This change requires certain apportionments that are not required by the source legislation to bemade on a just and reasonable basis to be made on such a basis.

In some cases where there is an apportionment under legislation rewritten in this Act, theapportionment is required by the source legislation to be made on a just and reasonable basis.In other cases, it is required to be made only on a just basis or only on a reasonable basis, orthere are no requirements. In new tax legislation it is now the practice to require anapportionment to be just and reasonable. For example, before it was repealed by ITEPA,section 140B(4) of ICTA (inserted by FA 1998) required a just and reasonable apportionmentto be made of any consideration given partly in respect of one thing and partly in respect ofanother. There is no reason why an apportionment should not be on a just and reasonablebasis. And it is desirable that all apportionments should be made on the same basis.

On the other hand, section 784(4) of ICTA provides that "the amount to be deducted ... shall be such proportion of the capital expenditure which is still unallowed as is reasonable" (rather than such proportion as is just and reasonable).

If an apportionment under legislation rewritten in this Act is not required tobe made on a just and reasonable basis, the rewritten provision requires the apportionment tobe made on a just and reasonable basis. The changes are as follows.

- Sections 505(1B) and 784(4) of ICTA and section 120(6) of FA 2006 require apportionments (or a "proportion") to be reasonable. Sections 479, 875(5)(a) and 599 respectively require those things to be just as well as reasonable.
- Sections 343(9), 343ZA(7), 518(9) and 783(8) of ICTA require apportionments to be just. Sections 952, 956, 994 and 880 respectively require apportionments to be reasonable as well as just.

The same change has been made in previous rewrite Acts to provide a uniform expression of the basis on which apportionments are to be made.

This change makes minor amendments to a number of existing rules, but is expected tohave no practical effect as it is in line with generally accepted practice.

CHANGE 34: CHARITABLE COMPANIES: LIMIT ON EXEMPTION FOR PROFITS ETC OF SMALL-SCALE TRADES AND CERTAIN MISCELLANEOUS INCOME: SECTIONS 480, 481 AND 482

This change rewrites the limit on the level of a charitable company's income for the purposes of the exemption for profits etc of small-scale trades in section 480 and certain miscellaneous income in section 481 by reference to the charitable company's incoming resources rather than in terms of its gross income. It also removes the requirement that the exemption for profits etc of a small-scale trade can apply only if the trade is carried on wholly or partly in the United Kingdom.

Section 46 of FA 2000 provides for an exemption from corporation tax for certain profits or other income or gains of a charitable company which are chargeable to corporation tax. The exemption applies in respect of a trade or to miscellaneous charges included in section 843A of ICTA.

ITA collects together a list of miscellaneous income charges in section 1016. This forms the list of those charges to which exemption under section 527 of ITA applies for income tax. The same approach is taken for corporation tax. Schedule 1 to CTA 2009 inserts a list as section 834A of ICTA, which is rewritten in this Act in section 1173.

Section 46(3) of FA 2000 provides that one of the requirements for the exemption to apply is that the charitable company's "gross income" must not exceed the "requisite limit". The "requisite limit" is defined in section 46(4) of that Act and depends on the charitable company's incoming resources for the chargeable period.

Section 482 sets out the condition about the level of the trading and miscellaneous income that has to be met if the exemptions in sections 480 and 481 are to apply.

The condition operates by reference to the incoming resources associated with the trading activity and miscellaneous transactions whose profits are not exempt under other provisions. Tax law brings into account receipts that would not normally feature as incoming resources for accounting purposes – for example balancing charges under the capital allowances rules. The new definition ensures that all potentially taxable receipts are brought within its compass.

The source legislation aimed to bring in turnover for trading activity and gross receipts for miscellaneous transactions within section 843A of ICTA. But these terms are not used in charity accounting. "Incoming resources" is familiar to those involved in preparing or working with charity accounts. And since charity accounting does not allow offset between income and expenditure in determining disclosure (in contrast with the disclosure in the accounts of commercial organisations), it is relatively easy to check the limits.

It is not clear in section 46 of FA 2000 whether "gross income" includes incoming resources from an activity which gives rise to a loss, in cases where a profit would be taxable. But incoming resources from an activity are included irrespective of whether there is a profit or a loss.

This change aligns the rewritten legislation with the way it is considered section 46 of FA 2000 is operated in practice.

This change is in taxpayers' favour in principle. But it is expected to have no practical effect as it is in line with generally accepted practice.

CHANGE 35: CHARITABLE COMPANIES: EXEMPTION FOR PROFITS FROM FUND-RAISING EVENTS: SECTIONS 483, 490, 491, 492 AND SCHEDULE 1

This change gives statutory effect to ESC C4 (trading activities for charitable purposes).

The concession provides an exemption for the profits of various fund-raising activities which amount to a trade, but which are only undertaken to raise money for charity. The concession does not apply in circumstances where an attempt is made to use it for tax avoidance. To reflect this, the new statutory exemption is subject to the restrictions in section 492.

The fund-raising event has to be of a kind that falls within the exemption from VAT under Group 12 of Schedule 9 to the Value Added Tax Act 1994. This Schedule provides an exemption from VAT for the supply by a charity of goods and services in connection with an event that is organised primarily to raise money for itself or other charities. The Schedule defines "event" and places certain limits on the number of events that a charity can hold in the same location in any given year.

Section 483, in line with the extra-statutory concession, is linked to the VAT legislation to provide consistency in tax treatment.

This exemption is also extended to the bodies listed in section 490 and to scientific research associations (see section 491).

This change is in taxpayers' favour in principle. But it is expected to have no practical effect as it is in line with generally accepted practice.

CHANGE 36: CHARITABLE COMPANIES: EXEMPTION FOR INCOME FROM INTELLECTUAL PROPERTY ETC: SECTIONS 488, 490, 491 AND SCHEDULE 1

This change provides an exemption from corporation tax for certain income from intangible assets, whether or not the income is annual in nature.

Schedule 29 to FA 2002 introduced a comprehensive regime for corporation tax for income and gains arising from intangible fixed assets, rewritten as Part 8 of CTA 2009. Those rules apply in general only to certain assets (principally, but not exclusively, those created or acquired on or after 1 April 2002). But all income from royalties and certain telecommunication rights falls within the regime – see sections 896 and 897 of CTA 2009. These are all covered by the existing exemption in section 505(1)(c)(iic) of ICTA, rewritten as section 488(3)(a).

Assets that do not fall within the rules of Part 8 of CTA 2009 are referred to in that Act as "pre FA 2002 assets". Any chargeable gains arising from those assets is exempt in the hands of a charitable company under section 256 of TCGA, provided the necessary conditions are met. But any income from those assets that does not fall within Part 8 of CTA 2009 is only exempt if it falls to be treated as an annual payment and is thus exempt under section 505(1)(c)(iizb) of ICTA.

In practice HMRC allow an exemption for income from pre-FA 2002 intangible assets, whether or not it is annual in nature. This change is in line with that practice, and mirrors the change made for income tax in section 536 of ITA. The rewritten legislation adopts the concept of a non-trading gain on an intangible fixed asset, and is written in terms that assume that the income in question would be such a gain, even though the assets fall outside Part 8 of CTA 2009.

Note that this extension only applies in the case of what would be a non-trading gain if Part 8 of CTA 2009 were to apply. If a gain arises in respect of a pre-FA 2002 asset in the course of a non-charitable trade the exemption in this section does not apply.

This change also affects the exemptions available to the bodies listed in section 490 and to scientific research associations under section 491 and is relevant to a number of entries in Schedule 1.

This change is in taxpayers' favour in principle. But it is expected to have no practical effect as it is in line with generally accepted practice.

CHANGE 37: CHARITABLE COMPANIES: EXEMPTION FOR INCOME FROM ESTATES IN ADMINISTRATION: SECTIONS 489, 490, 491, 492 AND SCHEDULE 1

This change provides an exemption to charitable companies which are liable to corporation tax on estate income charged under Chapter 3 of Part 10 of CTA 2009, to the extent that the income is applied to the purposes of the charitable company.

Estate income is income from property held by the personal representatives or administrators of the estate of a deceased person on behalf of the beneficiaries of the estate.

There is a long-standing HMRC practice of treating United Kingdom estate income received by charities as exempt, and of allowing repayment claims in such cases. This change puts this on an explicit statutory basis.

This exemption is also extended to the bodies listed in section 490 and to scientific research associations (see section 491) and is relevant to a number of entries in Schedule 1.

This change is in taxpayers' favour in principle. But it is expected to have no practical effect as it is in line with generally accepted practice.

CHANGE 38: CHARITABLE COMPANIES: MEANING OF NON-CHARITABLE EXPENDITURE: SECTIONS 496 TO 498

This change clarifies the meaning of "non-charitable expenditure".

Section 506(1) of ICTA defines "charitable expenditure" as:

"(subject to subsections (3) to (5) below) expenditure which is exclusively for charitable purposes.

Section 506(3) to (5) of ICTA treats certain payments, investments or loans as amounts of non-charitable expenditure.

Section 505(4) of ICTA restricts a charitable company's tax exemption by reference to non-charitable expenditure. "Non-charitable expenditure" is not defined but, by implication, it is expenditure which is not charitable expenditure.

Sections 496, 497 and 498 set out the definition of "non-charitable expenditure" in some detail, to reflect practice and HMRC guidance.

Section 496(1)(a) to (d), supported by section 497, provides in relation to trades, property businesses and miscellaneous transactions, that it is *losses* which may count as non-charitable expenditure, rather than those expenses which are required to be taken into account in calculating the profits or losses concerned.

Section 496(1)(a) to (d) also ensures that such losses do not count as non-charitable expenditure if corresponding profits would have been exempt under the provisions about small-scale trades, fund-raising events, lotteries or property income in sections 480, 483, 484 and 485. And section 496(1)(a)(i) makes it clear that losses made in a charitable trade do not count as non-charitable expenditure.

Section 498 supports section 496(1)(d), making it clear that expenditure (which is not itself defined in the source legislation) includes capital expenditure, but not the making of investments or loans or the repayment of loans made to the charitable company. Section 496(1)(g) and (h) then make specific provision about investments or loans that are not approved charitable investments or loans, reflecting section 506(4) of ICTA.

This change is in principle adverse to some taxpayers and favourable to others. But it is expected to have no practical effect as it is in line with generally accepted practice.

CHANGE 39: CHARITABLE COMPANIES: ACCOUNTING PERIOD IN WHICH CERTAIN EXPENDITURE TREATED AS INCURRED: SECTION 499

This change makes it explicit that the time when expenditure is treated as incurred depends on UK GAAP.

Section 506(2) of ICTA provides that, for the purposes of section 505 of ICTA:

"where expenditure which is not actually incurred in a particular accounting period properly falls to be charged against the income of that accounting period as being referable to commitments (whether or not of a contractual nature) which the charitable company has entered into before or during that period, it shall be treated as incurred in that period.

Section 506(2) of ICTA was first enacted in FA 1986 and advanced the time that certain expenditure is recognised, on the basis that charitable companies may have some flexibility in this regard. As a result of subsequent developments in accounting practice, the legislation now implicitly mirrors UK GAAP.

Section 499 is based on section 506(2) of ICTA, and makes the reference to UK GAAP explicit.

Section 499 is drafted in terms of the position if UK GAAP had applied, because there is no legal or other obligation requiring all charitable companies to prepare their accounts in accordance with UK GAAP. In particular "Accounting and Reporting for Charities: Statement of Recommended Practice (revised 2005)", which imposes a requirement to account in accordance with UK GAAP on charitable companies (with certain exceptions), is not mandatory in Scotland and Northern Ireland. Neither does it apply to charitable companies which are able to prepare accounts on a "receipts and payments" basis rather than an "accruals" basis. This could, for example, apply to unincorporated associations whose turnover and assets do not exceed the statutory limits.

This approach ensures parity of treatment as between charitable companies operating in different parts of the United Kingdom or adopting different bases of accounting.

This change is in principle adverse to some taxpayers and favourable to others. But it is expected to have no practical effect as it is in line with generally accepted practice.

CHANGE 40: CHARITABLE COMPANIES: APPROVED CHARITABLE INVESTMENTS: SECTIONS 511, 512, 513 AND 1176

This change modernises the list of investments qualifying as approved charitable investments for the purposes of the rules restricting exemptions.

Although the list is based on Part 1 of Schedule 20 to ICTA (qualifying investments), it does not replicate the approach taken in that Part.

Part 1 of Schedule 20 to ICTA defines qualifying investments by specifying certain investments itself, and also by referring to investments falling within Part 1, Part 2 (apart from paragraph 13) or Part 3 of Schedule 1 to the Trustee Investment Act 1961 (TIA 1961).

For trust law purposes TIA 1961 has been largely superseded by the Trustee Act 2000 (TA 2000). TA 2000 increased significantly the range of investments trustees can invest in, and it would be a significant change in the law to allow any investment in accordance with TA 2000 to be treated as an approved charitable investment. But it would be unhelpful to continue to refer for tax purposes to a Schedule to an Act (TIA 1961) that trustees no longer need to refer to for investment purposes.

So the detail of investments covered by Schedule 1 to TIA 1961 is incorporated in sections 511 and 512 in an updated form.

This has been done by referring to the types of investment that a charitable company can hold on "an approved basis". So investment in, for example, fixed or variable interest securities issued by any of Her Majesty's Government, the government of any overseas territory within the Commonwealth and the government of any state within (broadly) the European Union (EU) is reduced to securities issued by the government of any state in the EU and of any other state. This is wider, and so (strictly) is a taxpayer-favourable change. And rather than list the large number of individual entities in whose securities a charitable company can hold an approved investment, reference is made to the international entities listed in the directive on the taxation of interest payments. Again, this is a taxpayer-favourable change.

This approach tends to broaden the scope of possible investments, but in a way that is in keeping with HMRC practice in relation to claims that an individual investment should be regarded as qualifying, as set out in paragraph 9(1) of Schedule 20 to ICTA.

When it comes to the ability to hold an approved investment in the securities of (broadly) a non-listed company, the anti-avoidance provisions in Part 4 of Schedule 1 to TIA 1961 have been largely repeated.

A more detailed analysis of where the approved investments in the source legislation appear in the rewritten sections 511 and 512 is as follows:

Schedule 20 to ICTA	*Section 511*	*Section 512*
Paragraph 2	See details below relating to investments listed in TIA 1961	
Paragraph 3	Types 2 and 4	
Paragraph 3A	Types 3 and 4	
Paragraph 4	Type 5	
Paragraph 5 (note: the Unlisted Securities Market no longer exists)	Type 1	Subsection (1)(h)
Paragraph 6	Type 8	

Schedule 20 to ICTA	*Section 511*	*Section 512*
Paragraph 6A	Type 1	Subsection (1)(g)
Paragraph 7	Type 9	
Paragraph 7A	Type 11	
Paragraph 8	Type 11	
Paragraph 9	Type 12	

Part 1 of Schedule 1 to TIA 1961:	*Section 511*	*Section 512*
Paragraph 1: Savings Certificates	Type 6	
Paragraph 1: Other	Type 1	Subsection (1)(a)
Paragraph 2 (note: only deposits in the National Savings Bank are still relevant)	Type 10(a)	

Part 2 of Schedule 1 to TIA 1961	*Section 511*	*Section 512*
Paragraph 1: Treasury Bills and Tax Reserve Certificates	Type 6	
Paragraph 1: Northern Ireland Treasury Bills	Type 7	
Paragraph 1: Other	Type 1	Subsection (1)(a)
Paragraph 2 (but principal must be guaranteed as well as interest)	Type 1	Subsection (1)(a)
Paragraph 3 (but assumes nationalised industries are not an issue in the United Kingdom and are not likely to be an issue elsewhere)	Type 1	Subsection (1)(b)
Paragraph 4 (and extended to securities issued outside the United Kingdom)	Type 1	Subsection (1)(b)
Paragraph 4A (and extended to securities issued outside the United Kingdom and drops requirement about parameters for setting the interest rate)	Type 1	Subsection (1)(b)
Paragraph 5 (and extended to securities issued outside the United Kingdom)	Type 1	Subsection (1)(c) and (d)
Paragraph 5A (and extended to securities issued outside the United Kingdom and drops requirement about parameters for setting the interest rate)	Type 1	Subsection (1)(c) and (d)
Paragraph 5B	Type 1	Subsection (1)(b) and (c)
Paragraph 6	Type 1	Subsection (1)(h)
Paragraph 7	Type 1	Subsection (1)(h)
Paragraph 9 (but some loans and deposits are not covered as this is considered unnecessary)	Type 1	Subsection (1)(b)

Part 2 of Schedule 1 to TIA 1961	***Section 511***	***Section 512***
Paragraph 9A (but drops requirement about parameters for setting the interest rate)	Type 1	Subsection (1)(b)
Paragraph 10A	Type 8	
Paragraph 12	Type 10(b)	
Paragraph 13	Formerly excluded by paragraph 2 of Schedule 20 to ICTA – now excluded by reference under Type 5	
Paragraph 14	Type 5	
Paragraph 15	Type 6	
Paragraph 16	Type 1	Subsection (1)(b)
Paragraph 17 (but principal must be guaranteed as well as interest)	Type 1	Subsection (1)(b)
Paragraph 18 (but assumes nationalised industries are not an issue in the United Kingdom and are not likely to be an issue elsewhere)	Type 1	Subsection (1)(b)
Paragraph 19	Type 1	Subsection (1)(b)
Paragraph 20	Type 1	Subsection (1)(c) and (d)
Paragraph 21	Type 1	Subsection (1)(i)
Paragraph 22 (but some loans and deposits are not covered as this is considered unnecessary)	Type 1	Subsection (1)(b)
Paragraph 23 (and extended to similar societies outside the EU)	Type 10(c)	
Paragraph 24	Formerly excluded by paragraph 2 of Schedule 20 to ICTA – now excluded by reference under Type 5	

Part 3 of Schedule 1 to TIA 1961	***Section 511***	***Section 512***
Paragraph 1 (and extended to securities issued outside the United Kingdom)	Type 1	Subsection (1)(i)
Paragraph 2	Type 1	Subsection (1)(e)
Paragraph 2A	Type 1	Subsection (1)(g)
Paragraph 3	Type 8	
Paragraph 4 (and extended to securities issued outside the EU and to securities of non-EU incorporated companies)	Type 1	Subsection (1)(i)

Part 3 of Schedule 1 to TIA 1961	***Section 511***	***Section 512***
Paragraph 5 (and extended to similar societies outside the EU)	Type 1	Subsection (1)(f)
Paragraph 6	Type 8	

Part 4 of Schedule 1 to TIA 1961	***Section 513***
Paragraph 1	Not covered – this is taxpayer-favourable
Paragraph 2	Covered by Conditions A and B
Paragraph 2A	Covered by Conditions A and B
Paragraph 3	Covered by Condition C

Paragraph 3(b) of Part 4 of Schedule 1 to TIA 1961 excludes from approved investments shares or debentures which have not paid dividends in each of the preceding five years but deems dividends to have been paid by a company where one of the reasons for its formation is to acquire the control of another company or companies. This exception to the dividend rule is rewritten in section 513(8). "Control" in these circumstances is not defined by TIA. In practice the definition in section 840 of ICTA (rewritten in section 1124) applies and this is now made statute. Section 1124 therefore applies for the purposes of section 513(8) as a result of section 1176(2).

This change is in principle adverse to some taxpayers and favourable to others. But it is expected to have no practical effect as it is in line with generally accepted practice.

CHANGE 41: NON-UK COMPANIES: SECTIONS 520, 535, 536, 541, 579 AND 581

This change clarifies the basis on which non-UK companies which are members of a group UK REIT are charged to tax.

A non-UK resident company is chargeable to (corporation) tax on its chargeable gains only if they accrue on the disposal of assets in the United Kingdom that are used in a trade carried on through a permanent establishment in the United Kingdom (section 10B of TCGA). This is consistent with the limitation on the charge to corporation tax set by sections 5 and 19 of CTA 2009. Such assets cannot be "involved in property rental business".

Section 124(3) of FA 2006 provides that:

"Corporation tax shall be charged in respect of gains accruing to C (residual) at a rate determined without reference to section 13 of ICTA (small companies rate).

Paragraph 32(3) of Schedule 17 to FA 2006 provides that (in the case of a non-UK company):

"The property rental business of the company in the United Kingdom shall be treated as if it were (subject to the application of this Part) chargeable to corporation tax.

It is implausible that these rules override section 10B of TCGA. So this Act makes clear that the rules about the taxation of chargeable gains do not apply to non-UK resident companies.

But there is an important distinction between companies not resident in the United Kingdom (to which section 10B of TCGA applies) and non-UK companies (to which some sections in Part 12 of this Act apply). The distinction concerns dual resident companies. These are companies resident in the United Kingdom and resident in another territory (see section 521(1)).

Dual resident companies are not affected by the rule in section 520(3) because their world-wide profits are within the charge to corporation tax. It follows that they do not meet the condition in section 520(2)(b). But they are within the rules about chargeable gains and assets of UK REITs (see sections 535 to 537 and 579 to 581).

The change removes any possibility that a charge to tax on the chargeable gains of a non-UK resident company is imposed by Part 4 of FA 2006.

This change is in taxpayers' favour in principle and may benefit some in practice. But the numbers affected and the amounts involved are likely to be small.

CHANGE 42: UK REITS: CONDITIONS AS TO PROPERTY RENTAL BUSINESS: EXCLUSION OF NON-MEMBER'S INTEREST: SECTION 529

This change excludes from a group's property rental business the percentage of that business held by a non-member of the group.

For the purposes of the tests in section 529 the property rental businesses of members of a group are treated as a single business. The tests are:

- whether the business involves at least three properties; and
- whether a single property represents more than 40% of the value of all the properties in the business.

The number of properties involved (the first test) is not affected by this Change.

A company in the group may have a minority shareholder. In accordance with section 533(3) that shareholder's interests in the company are excluded from the financial statements required by that section. The effect of this Change on the second test is illustrated by the following examples.

Example 1

Company A (the principal company of the group) has a property worth £40. Company B (wholly owned subsidiary of A) has a property worth £20. Company C (75% subsidiary of A) has a property worth £40. The remaining 25% interest in C is held by a non-member of the group.

If 100% of the value of C's property is taken into account, the 40% test is passed (40 is not more than 40%x(40+20+40)). If only 75% of the value of C's property is taken into account, the 40% test is failed (40 is more than40%x(40+20+30)).

Example 2

Company A (the principal company of the group) has a property worth £25. Company B (wholly owned subsidiary of A) has a property worth £30. Company C(75% subsidiary of A) has a property worth £45. The remaining 25% interest in C is held by a non-member of the group.

If 100% of the value of C's property is taken into account, the 40% test is failed (45 is more than 40%x(25+30+45)). If only 75% of the value of C's property is taken into account, the 40% test is passed (33.75 (75%x45) is not more than40%x(25+30+33.75)).

It is easier in general to pass the 40% test if the interest in the subsidiary's property is restricted to the extent of the parent's holding. And applying the test in that way follows the economic reality of the relationship.

This change is in principle and in practice adverse to some taxpayers and favourable to others. But the numbers affected and the amounts involved are likely to be small.

CHANGE 43: ENACTMENT OF REGULATIONS: SECTIONS 551 TO 554, 561 TO 568, 573 TO 577,AND 584 TO 598

This change relates to the enactment and revocation of:

- SI 2006/2864: the Real Estate Investment Trusts (Breach of Conditions) Regulations 2006 (except regulation 11);
- SI 2006/2866: the Real Estate Investment Trusts (Joint Ventures) Regulations 2006;

- SI 2007/3425: the Real Estate Investment Trusts (Joint Venture Groups) Regulations 2007; and
- SI 2007/3540: the Real Estate Investment Trusts (Breach of Conditions) (Amendment) Regulations 2007

These regulations were made by the Treasury under sections 114 to 116 and 138 of FA 2006 and sections 973 and 974 of ITA.

The regulation-making powers are not rewritten to the extent that regulations made under them are enacted in this Act. The omission or restriction of the various regulation-making powers means that it is no longer possible to amend by secondary legislation the provisions enacted in this Act.

But some regulation-making powers are retained.

- Section 543(8) (based on section 115(3B) of FA 2006) is a power to specify the criteria to be applied by HMRC in deciding whether a charge under section 543 should be waived.
- Section 554 (based on section 114 of FA 2006) contains powers to provide that a charge does not arise or is reduced if the company takes certain action and for the collection of information.
- Section 600 (based on section 136A of FA 2006) is a power to treat persons as members of a group UK REIT.

This change has no implications for the amount of tax due, who pays it or when. It affects (in principle and in practice) only administrative matters.

CHANGE 44: UK REITS: NOTIONAL AMOUNT CHARGED FOLLOWING BREACH OF CONDITION: EXCLUSION OF NON-MEMBER'S INTEREST: SECTION 567

This change excludes from the total market value of a group's assets the value of the percentage of those assets held by a non-member of the group.

If there is a breach of Condition 2 in section 108(3) of FA 2006 (balance of business: assets involved in tax-exempt business) a charge to tax is imposed by regulation 7A of SI 2006/2864 (inserted by regulation 5 of SI 2007/3540). The amount of the charge is based on the market value of the assets involved in the UK property rental business of G (property rental business).

Some of those assets may be held by a company in which a non-member of the group has an interest. In that case, the non-member's percentage of the assets may be excluded from the financial statements prepared under paragraph 31 of Schedule 17 to FA 2006 (see, in particular, sub-paragraph (5)).

Section 567 of this Act rewrites the rule in regulation 7A of SI 2206/2864. It includes, in subsection (4)(c) of the section, a rule excluding a non-member's share in the assets of the group. The exclusion is on the same basis as that for the purposes of financial statements (see section 533(3)).

This change reduces the amount that may be charged to tax on the occasion of a breach of the balance of business (assets) condition.

This change is in taxpayers' favour in principle and may benefit some in practice. But the numbers affected and the amounts involved are likely to be small.

CHANGE 45: CORPORATE BENEFICIARIES UNDER TRUSTS: TREATMENT OF TRUSTEES' EXPENSES: SECTION 611

This change makes explicit some of the rules about the way expenses, incurred by trustees in connection with income to which a corporate beneficiary is entitled, reduce the amount of the beneficiary's income for tax purposes.

Section 611 applies sections 500 and 503 ITA to a corporate beneficiary. These sections are concerned with the treatment of trustees' expenses in a case where a beneficiary, liable to income tax, is entitled to trust income as it arises. This is where the beneficiary has an interest in possession (IIP).

Section 689A(2) ICTA, which was repealed by ITA, made reference to the effect on a beneficiary with an IIP where the trustees have incurred expenses. But section 689B was the only provision in ICTA that provided details of the tax treatment of trustees' expenses in relation to IIP income (as well as other income from trusts, for example discretionary payments).

This part of section 689B is rewritten in section 503(2) and (3) of ITA. Other rules introduced by sections 500 and 503 of ITA are based on established practice and case law – see *Change 91* in Annex 1 to the explanatory notes accompanying ITA.

There are few, if any, examples of a trust in which there are corporate beneficiaries with an IIP and so this change is very unlikely to have any effect for corporation tax purposes.

This change is in principle adverse to some taxpayers and favourable to others. But it is likely to have no practical effect as it is in line with generally accepted practice.

CHANGE 46: CO-OPERATIVE HOUSING ASSOCIATIONS AND SELF-BUILD SOCIETIES: CHANGE FROM TAX YEAR TO ACCOUNTING PERIOD: SECTIONS 642, 647, 648, 651, 655 AND 656.

This change amends the references to year of assessment in relation to co-operative housing associations (section 488 of ICTA) and self-build societies (section 489 of ICTA).

These bodies are all within the charge to corporation tax. However, in the source legislation, their claims to exemption in respect of rents receivable from tenants are in terms of tax years. This is because there is also a potential impact on the tenant's income tax liability - for example, the tenant might have been entitled to deduct the rent payable as an expense for tax purposes.

In addition, earlier versions of the legislation transferred entitlement to relief for interest payable from the association/society to the tenant under the relief for mortgage interest provisions until that relief was abolished. It therefore made sense to operate by reference to tax years.

In contrast, the exemption from corporation tax on chargeable gains in respect of disposals of property by these bodies to their members has always been by reference to an accounting period.

As the link to mortgage interest relief has now gone the rationale for retaining the tax year as the basis of the claim and relief is significantly reduced and this change therefore standardises the claim and relief on the basis of an accounting period.

There is no need for a transitional provision as these bodies can claim for part of a tax year or accounting period so no there be no gaps in eligibility for exemption.

This change is in principle and in practice adverse to some taxpayers and favourable to others. But the numbers affected and the amounts involved are likely to be small.

CHANGE 47: CO-OPERATIVE HOUSING ASSOCIATIONS AND SELF-BUILD SOCIETIES: DEPARTMENT FOR SOCIAL DEVELOPMENT FOR NORTHERN IRELAND: SECTIONS 644, 645, 649, 653 AND 657.

This change replaces references to "the Head of the Department of the Environment for Northern Ireland", "the Head of the Department for Social Development for Northern Ireland" and "the Department of the Environment for Northern Ireland" with "the Department for Social Development".

Article 6(e) and Part 5 of Schedule 4 of the Departments (Transfer and Assignment of Functions) Order (Northern Ireland) 1999 (SI 1999/481) transferred housing functions under the Housing (Northern Ireland) Orders 1981 to 1992 from the Department of the Environment to the Department for Social Development (DSD). In view of the transfers of functions and the responsibility of the DSD for other matters relating to housing, it is appropriate for the functions under sections 488 and 489 of ICTA relating to Northern Ireland to be exercisable by the DSD. This change therefore replaces the references in sections 488(6)(b) and (8) and 489(12) of ICTA to "the Department of the Environment for Northern Ireland" with the "Department for Social Development".

Article 5 of the Scotland Act 1988 (Transfer of Functions to the Scottish Ministers etc) Order 2004 substituted the reference to "the Head of the Department for Social Development for Northern Ireland" in section 488(6)(iii) of ICTA. It is unclear whether there was sufficient power under this Order to make that substitution. Subsections (5) and (6) of section 645 make it clear that the functions concerned are exercisable by the DSD as regards Northern Ireland.

By virtue of paragraph 11(2) of Schedule 12 to the Northern Ireland Act 1998, references in section 488 of ICTA to the Head of a Department are to a Minister. In sections 644, 645 and 649 functions are expressed to be conferred on the Northern Ireland department concerned, rather than on the Minister in charge of the department, in line with modern practice.

This change has no implications for the amount of tax due, who pays it or when. It affects (in principle and in practice) only administrative matters.

CHANGE 48: RECEIPT OF CLUB BENEFITS BY MEMBERS: ARM'S LENGTH AGREEMENTS FOR EMPLOYMENT OR FOR GOODS OR SERVICES: SECTION 660

This change removes certain formalities which apply where a club member supplies goods or services to the club or is employed by the club and the club wishes to satisfy the requirements for tax exemptions.

In order to qualify as an amateur sports club paragraph 3(1) of Schedule 18 to FA 2002 requires that only the ordinary benefits of a community amateur sports club can be provided to members and guests. Those benefits are set out in paragraph 3(3) of Schedule 18. A club's powers are thus restricted to the actions which allow them to provide those benefits to their members. Paragraph 3(4) of Schedule 18 however makes provision for clubs to enter into agreements to pay for goods or services or to pay remuneration to a member and to continue to satisfy the requirements for exemption. The main rule is that where there are such agreements with members then they must be at arm's length.

Paragraph 3(4) also imposes the condition that the terms of such agreements with the member should be approved by the club's governing body without the member concerned being present. In practice HMRC do not enforce this rule, being only concerned that the agreement is at arm's length. This change omits these formalities in the rewritten section. This means that the only requirement is that the agreement should be at arm's length. This does not, of course, exclude the necessity for evidence demonstrating that the agreement is at arm's length.

This change is in taxpayers' favour in principle. But it is expected to have no practical effect as it is in line with generally accepted practice.

CHANGE 49: CHANGES IN COMPANY OWNERSHIP: COMPANY WITH INVESTMENT BUSINESS: RESTRICTION ON RELIEF FOR NON-TRADING LOSS ON INTANGIBLE FIXED ASSETS: SECTIONS 681 AND 698

This change clarifies the restriction imposed by section 768E of ICTA, when there is a change in the ownership of a company with investment business, on relief for a non-trading loss on intangible fixed assets.

If there is a change in the ownership of a company with investment business, and the relevant conditions are met, section 768E of ICTA has effect to prevent relief being given for a non-trading loss on intangible fixed assets incurred before the change of ownership against profits arising after that change.

In particular, section 768E(5) of ICTA provides that a loss made in any accounting period beginning before the change of ownership may not be set off against profits under section 753(3) of CTA 2009.

But an unrelieved non-trading loss on intangible fixed assets is not, as such, set against profits. Section 753(3) of CTA 2009, so far as relevant, says:

"To the extent that the loss is not set off … it is carried forward to the next accounting period of the company and treated as if it were a non-trading debit of that period

Section 768E(5) of ICTA blurs the distinction between:

- calculating the company's non-trading gain or loss under section 751 of CTA 2009; and
- setting a non-trading loss against profits under section 753(1) of that Act.

Section 768E(5) uses wording derived from paragraph 35(1) of Schedule 29 to FA2002, which has been rewritten as section 753(1) of CTA 2009; it does not reflect section 753(3) of that Act.

The purpose of section 768E of ICTA is set out in section 768E(1) of that Act. It is therefore considered that the courts would adopt a rectifying construction of section 768E(5) of that Act in order to restrict relief which would otherwise be given under section 753(3) of CTA 2009.

Accordingly, sections 681(3) and 698(4) (which are based on section 768E(5)(a) and (b) respectively of ICTA) reflect the wording of section 753(3) of CTA 2009. This has different effects in the context of sections 681(3) and 698(4). In a case within section 681(3), profits arising after the change in ownership cannot be sheltered at all. In a case within section 698(4), the extent to which profits arising after the change in ownership can be sheltered is restricted. This reflects the differing wording of section 768E(5)(a) and (b) of ICTA: "profits" and "so much of those profits".

This is a change in the law, in that it prevents taxpayers arguing for an alternative interpretation.

This change is adverse to some taxpayers in principle. But it is expected to have no practical effect as it is in line with generally accepted practice.

CHANGE 50: CHANGES IN COMPANY OWNERSHIP: COMPANY WITH INVESTMENT BUSINESS: ASSET TRANSFERRED WITHIN GROUP: RESTRICTION ON RELIEFS FOR NON-TRADING LOSS ON INTANGIBLE FIXED ASSETS AND PROPERTY LOSSES: SECTIONS 698, 700 AND 701

This change clarifies the restrictions imposed by sections 768D and 768E of ICTA on relief for, respectively, property losses and non-trading losses on intangible fixed assets when there is a change in the ownership of a company with investment business and an asset is transferred within the corporate group of which that company is a member.

If there is a change in the ownership of a company with investment business, and section 768C of ICTA (deductions: asset transferred within group) applies, sections 768D and 768E of ICTA have effect to prevent relief being given for, respectively, property losses and non-trading losses on intangible fixed assets incurred before the change of ownership against profits arising after that change.

Sections 768D(6)(b) and 768E(5)(b) of ICTA quantify this restriction by reference to the amount of profits which "represents the relevant gain within the meaning of [section 768C of that Act]", but they do not expressly define this technical expression.

But sections 768D(6)(b) and 768E(5)(b) of ICTA only apply in cases in which section 768C of that Act applies, and it would be anomalous if the words under review had a different meaning in sections 768D(6)(b) and 768E(5)(b) of ICTA from the meaning which they have in section 768C(8) of that Act. Sections 768D(6)(b) and 768E(5)(b) of ICTA therefore refer to section 768C(8) of that Act by implication. Since section 768C(8) of ICTA only applies if section 768C(6) of that Act applies, sections 768D(6)(b) and 768E(5)(b) of that Act also refer to section 768C(6) of that Act by implication and so are similarly restricted by that provision.

Section 698 of this Act (restriction on relief for non-trading loss on intangible fixed assets) is based on section 768E of ICTA, and sections 700 and 701 of this Act (disallowance of UK property business losses and disallowance of overseas property business losses) are based on section 768D of ICTA. Sections 698(2), 700(2) and 701(2) of this Act mirror the restriction in section 768C(6) of that Act. They therefore expressly restrict the application of sections 698, 700 and 701 of the Act.

This limitation is a change in the law, since it prevents HMRC arguing that any of these restrictions has a wider scope.

This change is in taxpayers' favour in principle. But it is expected to have no practical effect as it is in line with generally accepted practice.

CHANGE 51: MANUFACTURED PAYMENTS AND REPOS: DEFINITION OF "MANUFACTURED INTEREST": SECTION 801 AND SCHEDULE 1

This change:

- adopts the definition of "manufactured interest" used in the loan relationships regime in rewriting the unallowable purpose test for manufactured payments; and
- abolishes the power to apply, with modifications, prescribed provisions of TMA to manufactured interest.

Section 539 of CTA 2009 (relationships treated as loan relationships etc: manufactured interest etc) defines "manufactured interest" in relation to a manufactured interest relationship. A company has a manufactured interest relationship if (a) an amount is payable by or on behalf of a company or to a company under arrangements relating to the transfer of an asset representing a loan relationship and (b) this amount either (i) is representative of interest under the loan relationship or (ii) falls to be treated as representative of such interest when it is paid. Such an amount is "manufactured interest".

"Loan relationship" is defined in section 302 of CTA 2009. Also, Part 6 of that Act treats certain other matters as loan relationships.

Paragraph 1(1) of Schedule 23A to ICTA defines "manufactured interest" as:

"an amount –

(a) which is representative of a periodical payment of interest on United Kingdom securities [as defined in paragraph 1(1) of that Schedule], and

(b) which, under a contract or other arrangements for the transfer of the securities, one of the parties is required to pay to the other

These two definitions are similar but not the same.

"Manufactured interest" as defined in CTA 2009, unlike "manufactured interest" as defined in ICTA, does not necessarily relate to United Kingdom securities. Paragraph 4(1) of Schedule 23A to ICTA however, provides:

"This paragraph applies in any case where, under a contract or other arrangements for the transfer of overseas securities, one of the parties (the "overseas dividend manufacturer") is required to pay to the other ("the recipient") an amount representative of an overseas dividend on the overseas securities; and in this Schedule the "manufactured overseas dividend" means any payment which the overseas dividend manufacturer makes in discharge of that requirement

Paragraph 1(1) of Schedule 23A to ICTA gives "overseas securities" a wide definition, and any manufactured interest as defined in CTA 2009 which does not relate to United Kingdom securities is a MOD. (The converse does not hold; a MOD relating to foreign shares is not manufactured interest within either definition.)

Broadly speaking, therefore, manufactured interest as defined in CTA 2009 is either manufactured interest as defined in ICTA or else a MOD.

There are two technical differences between the two definitions of "manufactured interest".

First, "United Kingdom securities" is defined using the expression "securities", which is non-exhaustively defined in paragraph 1(1) of Schedule 23A to ICTA as including any loan stock or similar security. It is logically possible for an instrument to rank as a "United Kingdom security" as defined in paragraph 1(1) without being a loan relationship as defined in CTA 2009. In this respect, the ICTA definition is wider than the CTA 2009 definition.

Second, "manufactured interest" as defined in CTA 2009, unlike "manufactured interest" as defined in ICTA, is not necessarily representative of a periodical payment. In this respect, the CTA 2009 definition is wider than the ICTA definition.

"Manufactured interest" is defined in these two different ways for historical reasons. Schedule 23A to ICTA (manufactured dividends and interest) was inserted by FA 1991; in that Schedule, "manufactured interest" was chiefly used in provisions relating to income tax which have since been rewritten in ITA. By contrast, CTA 2009 uses "manufactured interest" in the corporation tax provisions relating to loan relationships, which are based on FA 1996. The income tax provisions of Schedule 23A to ICTA were rewritten in Chapter 2 of Part 11 and Chapter 9 of Part 15 of ITA and repealed.

"Manufactured interest", as defined in paragraph 1(1) of Schedule 23A to ICTA, is used in:

- the definition of "manufactured payment" in paragraph 7A(10) of that Schedule (manufactured payments under arrangements having an unallowable purpose); and
- the power given by paragraph 8(3)(a) of that Schedule to apply, with modifications, prescribed provisions of TMA to manufactured interest.

The opportunity has been taken to simplify and harmonise the corporation tax legislation by adopting the CTA 2009 definition of "manufactured interest" in rewriting paragraph 7A(10) of Schedule 23A in section 801 of this Act.

In principle, adopting the CTA 2009 definition of "manufactured interest" in section 801 of this Act changes the scope of the unallowable purpose test for manufactured payments, because it narrows the definition of "manufactured interest" in one respect and broadens the definition in another respect. In principle, the former change to the definition is favourable to some taxpayers and the latter change is adverse to some taxpayers.

But, in the context of this provision, the technical differences between the two definitions of "manufactured interest" do not amount to any difference in practice.

As paragraph 8(3)(a) of Schedule 23A to ICTA has been superseded by Corporation Tax Self Assessment, Schedule 1 repeals it as unnecessary. The Treasury has not exercised its power to make regulations for corporation tax purposes under paragraph 8(3)(a). Abolishing this power therefore has no practical effect.

This change is in principle adverse to some taxpayers and favourable to others. But it is expected to have no practical effect as it is in line with generally accepted practice.

CHANGE 52: TRANSACTIONS IN LAND: COMPANY CHARGEABLE: PROVIDER OF OPPORTUNITY TO REALISE A GAIN: SECTION 821

This change omits words from section 776(8) of ICTA indicating that where a gain on a transaction of land that is charged under that section is derived from an opportunity of realising a gain provided by another person and as a result that person is liable for the tax, it does not matter whether or not the opportunity was put at the disposal of the person to whom the gain actually accrues.

Section 776 of ICTA charges gains of a capital nature relating to the land to corporation tax where the gains are made by persons connected with land or the development of land and the statutory conditions are met.

In certain circumstances, companies which are liable to pay corporation tax in the United Kingdom may enter into transactions in land as a result of which value, or an opportunity of realising a gain, is provided to another person (who may not be so liable). In such cases, section 776(8) of ICTA lays down that the provider of the value or, as the case may be, the opportunity is the company chargeable to corporation tax under section 776.

Section 776(8), so far as relevant, reads: "If all or any part of the gain accruing to any person is derived from value, or an opportunity of realising a gain, provided directly or indirectly by some other person..., whether or not put at the disposal of the first–mentioned person ...".

In Yuill v Wilson (1980), 52 TC 674[11] on page 706, Goff LJ criticised the drafting of what is now section 776(8):

"I find it very difficult to appreciate what [the words "whether or not put at the disposal of the first-mentioned person" in what is now section 776(8)] were intended to cover. In the case of *value* I can well see that a gain may be derived by one person from value provided by another, whether directly or indirectly, without that value being put at the disposal of the first-mentioned person; for example, if A pays money to B as consideration for the grant of an option to C. As at present advised, however, I find it very difficult to see how one can gain from an *opportunity* provided by another without that opportunity being put at the disposal of the first-mentioned person. (emphasis added)

As it is considered that no sensible meaning can be given to the words "whether or not put at the disposal of the first-mentioned person" so far as they relate to the earlier words "an opportunity of realising a gain", in rewriting the passage under review section 821 (transactions in land: company chargeable) refers only to the value provided by another person and not the opportunity of realising a gain.

If this view were incorrect, then the restriction of the scope of section 821 might in some circumstances exclude taxpayers from liability under the "transactions in land" Part.

This change is in taxpayers' favour in principle. But it is expected to have no practical effect as it is in line with generally accepted practice.

CHANGE 53: TRANSACTIONS IN LAND: CLEARANCE PROCEDURE: SECTION 831

This change gives the Commissioners for HMRC responsibility for granting or denying clearance concerning transactions in land.

Section 776 of ICTA is a complex anti-avoidance provision concerning transactions in land. Section 776(11) lays down a statutory clearance procedure. It provides that the taxpayer company is to provide particulars of the transaction to "the inspector to whom it makes its return of income".

This could cause theoretical difficulties if the taxpayer:

- is not legally obliged to file a self-assessment return;
- does not file a self-assessment return; and
- wishes to obtain clearance under section 776(11) of ICTA.

In practice, if the taxpayer makes a clearance application to the HMRC office dealing with that taxpayer's affairs, that HMRC office processes the application.

---

11 [1980] STC 460.

Section 831, which is based on section 776(11) of ICTA, gives the responsibility for clearances concerning transactions in land to the Commissioners for HMRC, rather than the officer to whom the taxpayer makes a return of income. This is consistent with section 707 of ICTA (transactions in securities: clearance procedure), which is rewritten in section 749 of this Act.

This change in the law, in practice, has no effect on the administration of the clearance procedure for transactions in land.

This change has no implications for the amount of tax paid, who pays it or when. It affects (in principle but not in practice) only administrative matters.

CHANGE 54: TRANSACTIONS IN LAND: POWER TO OBTAIN INFORMATION: "REASONABLY REQUIRES": SECTION 832

This change expressly restricts the particulars that an officer of Revenue and Customs may require to be provided, under section 778(1) of ICTA, to those particulars which the officer may reasonably require.

Section 778(1) of ICTA enables the Board or an inspector to require a person to give them such particulars "as the Board or the inspector think necessary" for the purposes of section 776 of that Act (transactions in land).

In section 832, the opportunity has been taken to modernise this language and expressly impose the criterion of reasonableness. This is consistent with the way in which HMRC exercise the power in practice.

This change has no implications for the amount of tax paid, who pays it or when. It affects (in principle but not in practice) only administrative matters.

CHANGE 55: SALE AND LEASE-BACK ETC: RESTRICTION OF EXCESSIVE LEASE RENTALS: RELATIONSHIP WITH ACCOUNTING PRACTICE: SECTIONS 838 AND 865

This change puts on a statutory basis HMRC's published practice on the interaction between section 779 of ICTA (sale and lease-back: limitation on tax reliefs) and the accounting treatment for finance lease rentals.

The Inland Revenue set out in Statement of Practice 3/91 (SP3/91) its view on the timing of deductions for rentals payable by lessees under finance leases. It also published an article supplementing SP3/91 in the *Tax Bulletin*,February 1995 (TB15). The material in SP3/91 and TB15 is substantially reproduced in paragraphs 61105 to 61185 of HMRC's Business Income Manual (BIM61105 to 61185).

Generally speaking, the effect of SP3/91 is that tax relief is given for finance lease rentals in the period in which they are charged in calculating the lessee's accounting profit or loss. If a lessee makes a payment under a lease, and the economic benefit of the payment extends over several periods of account, then (broadly speaking) the accounting treatment is to charge the payment as expenditure in the periods of account to which the payment in economic substance relates. Thus under SP3/91 tax relief is not necessarily given in the period in which the finance lease rental payment is made; tax relief may be deferred to later periods.

Section 779 of ICTA is an anti-avoidance provision restricting tax relief for excessive rentals paid under sales and lease-backs of land. If it applies to a payment, tax relief for that payment is deferred (and may in certain circumstances be denied altogether). Section 782 of ICTA (leased assets: special cases) is a similar provision applying to transactions involving assets other than land. Sections 779 and 782 of ICTA apply for the purposes of both income tax and corporation tax.

HMRC's practice, as published in TB15 and BIM 61105, is to apply SP3/91 before making any adjustments under section 779 of ICTA (see BIM 61105). Depending on the facts, this may mean that there is no need for any adjustments to be made under section 779 of ICTA.

FA 1998 introduced specific legislation which (broadly speaking) is to the same effect as SP3/91, but goes further. Section 42 of FA 1998 has been rewritten for the purposes of income tax and corporation tax in, respectively, section 25 of ITTOIAand section 46 of CTA 2009 (use of generally accepted accounting practice in calculating trade profits). Section 272 of ITTOIA and section 210 of CTA 2009 apply, respectively, section 25 of ITTOIA and section 46 of CTA 2009 in calculating profits of a property business.

Under section 25 of ITTOIA and section 46 of CTA 2009, trade profits are calculated in accordance with GAAP, subject to adjustments required or authorised by law. These provisions operate by reference to receipts and expenses to be brought into account, not by reference to payments made. But sections 779 and 782 of ICTA do not acknowledge GAAP. And they assume that tax relief is given for payments made rather than expenses brought into account. So there is a conflict. The Act resolves this in this way.

First, it acknowledges that a calculation for tax purposes is made in accordance with GAAP.

Second, it provides that, if deductions for tax purposes are allowed for (eg) the rental payments under a lease, the first step is to calculate:

(a) the total expenses to date brought into account, in accordance with GAAP, in respect of the payments; less

(b) the total deductions allowed in previous periods for the payments.

Third, it then provides for the rules currently contained in section 779 or 782 of ICTA to be applied to the figure given by that calculation, so that the deduction allowed for the period is that figure as reduced by those rules (but is the unreduced figure if those rules do not require a reduction to be made).

Resolving the conflict in this way – rather than making the adjustments required by sections 779 and 782 of ICTA first and then applying GAAP to give relief for lease rental expenditure – could, in principle, affect the periods in which relief is given. This could be favourable to the taxpayer, adverse to the taxpayer or favourable to the taxpayer in some respects and adverse to the taxpayer in other respects. The extent to which it would be favourable or adverse would depend on the facts and, in particular, on the rental profile of the lease under review.

This change is in principle adverse to some taxpayers and favourable to others. But it is expected to have no practical effect as it is in line with generally accepted practice.

CHANGE 56: SALE AND LEASE-BACK ETC: EXCLUSION OF SERVICE CHARGES ETC TO BE ON JUST AND REASONABLE BASIS: SECTION 843

This change requires that, in calculating the amount of a payment for which tax relief is restricted under section 779 of ICTA, a just and reasonable amount must be excluded from the rent or other payment in respect of services or the use of relevant assets or rates usually borne by the tenant.

Section 779 of ICTA is an anti-avoidance provision which restricts tax relief for excessive payments of rent (and similar charges) in respect of land. Section 779(6)(d) provides that:

- in calculating the amount subject to restriction it is necessary to exclude so much of any payment as is in respect of services or the use of assets or rates usually borne by the tenant; and
- in determining the amount to be so excluded provisions in any lease or agreement fixing the payments or parts of payments which are in respect of services or the use of services may be overridden.

But section 779 of ICTA does not indicate either what considerations would justify such an override or what criterion should be used instead. In 1964, when this anti-avoidance provision was first introduced, it was natural to envisage that the decision to override the lease or agreement would be taken by the Inland Revenue. But that does not sit easily with Self Assessment.

Section 843 therefore replaces the overriding provision of section 779(6)(d) of ICTA with a requirement to exclude so much of the payment as is just and reasonable.

This change has no implications for the amount of tax paid, who pays it, or when. It affects (in principle but not in practice) only administrative matters.

CHANGE 57: COMPANY DISTRIBUTIONS: PREMIUM PAID ON REDEMPTION OF SHARE CAPITAL: SECTION 1024

This change narrows the scope of the stipulation in section 211(7) of ICTA that premiums paid on redemption of share capital are not treated as repayments of share capital.

Section 211(7) of ICTA is not limited in its application and therefore potentially applies across the entirety of ICTA. It appears however to have no practical application beyond Chapter 2 of Part 6 of ICTA, which sets out what is to be treated as a distribution.

This change therefore makes it explicit that this particular stipulation applies only to the question of what is to be treated as a distribution.

This change is in principle adverse to some taxpayers and favourable to others. But it is expected to have no practical effect as it is in line with generally accepted practice.

CHANGE 58: COMPANY DISTRIBUTIONS: DUTY TO PROVIDE A TAX CERTIFICATE: INTEREST THAT IS NOT A QUALIFYING DISTRIBUTION: SECTIONS 1104 AND 1106 AND SCHEDULE 1

This change makes clear that section 234A of ICTA applies to a payment of interest only where interest is treated as a distribution, in whole or in part, and not to all payments of interest made by a company.

The origins of section 234A of ICTA lie in section 33 of FA 1924. The provision was introduced specifically to deal with what were known as "tax free dividends", that is dividends paid by a company to its shareholders where the income tax had already been settled. It was felt that the shareholder should be given more detailed information about the amounts involved and the tax deducted. The provision was largely unchanged through the Income Tax Act 1952 (section 199) and the Income and Corporation Taxes Act 1970 (section 242).

It was amended by paragraph 19 of Schedule 24 to FA 1972 when the imputation system was introduced and the distinction between a qualifying and non-qualifying distribution was introduced. The amendment, which was described as consequential, made separate provision for the two different categories of distribution, and amended the requirements in relation to a qualifying distribution to refer to the tax credit attaching to such a distribution.

This became section 234 of ICTA, with the key provisions being in subsections (3) and (4). Section 32 of F(No 2)A 1992 introduced section 234A of ICTA to deal with payments made directly into a bank account. Section 234(3) and (4) of ICTA were repealed and restated in section 234A of ICTA, along with further provisions to cover direct payment into an account held by the recipient or a nominee.

Section 234A of ICTA applies where "dividend or interest is distributed" by a company – subsection (1) – and this wording has been unchanged from the introduction of the provision in 1924. It may be inferred from this that the section only applies to distributions and not to ordinary payments of interest made by a company. This is reinforced by the penalty provision in section 234A(9) of ICTA (which refers to "distribution"), and by the commencement provision for section 32 of F(No.2)A 1992, which introduced section 234A of ICTA (the new provision was applied to "distributions begun after the day on which this Act is passed").

But section 234A(6) of ICTA refers to "interest which is not a qualifying distribution or part of a qualifying distribution". The definition of a qualifying distribution is in section 14 of ICTA, and that definition covers the vast majority of distributions, with the exception of certain types of bonus issue of shares or securities. It is very difficult to see how a payment of interest could therefore fit within the scope of a distribution that is not a qualifying distribution. Section 234A(6) of ICTA could therefore be read as applying to all payments of interest made by a company, including banks, and not just those that are treated as distributions.

If that were true, however, it would overlap with section 975 of ITA, which is the provision under which banks, building societies and other payers of interest deliver tax deduction certificates, and would impose a penalty for failure to comply, whereas none is stipulated in the case of section 975 of ITA.

The origins of section 975 of ITA lie in section 50 of FA 1963. The Royal Commission on the Taxation of Profits and Income (the Radcliffe Committee)reported in 1955 in the following terms:

> "though the law requires that a company's dividend warrants shall be accompanied by statements giving particulars of the tax deductions made,...there is no statutory obligation on a person who deducts tax from any interest ... to furnish a similar certificate" (Cmd 9474).

The Commission clearly reported on the basis that section 199 of the Income Tax Act 1952, the precursor of section 234A(6)of ICTA, did not apply to all payments of interest and that a new provision would therefore be desirable.

Published guidance and commentaries do not comment explicitly, but the prevailing practice is that certificates for the deduction of income tax from interest payments are delivered under section 975 of ITA.

This change treats section 234A(6) of ICTA as otiose; it appears to have no effect if confined to distributions, and there is evidence from the history of the provision that it was not intended to apply to all payments of interest made by companies.

The change therefore removes any argument that section 234A of ICTA could apply to all payments of interest made by a company, including banks, and could therefore lead to a penalty for failure to comply, as opposed to section 975 of ITA which is enforceable by the recipient of the payment and where no penalty is set down in the tax legislation.

The change also affects the consequential amendment in Schedule 1 of paragraph 80 of Schedule 2 to ITEPA which replaces a reference to section 234A of ICTA with the appropriate rewritten provisions of this Act.

This change has no effect on any liability to tax. Itis in principle favourable to some taxpayers, by removing a requirement on them, and adverse to thosetaxpayers who might have received certificates but do not now do so. But it is expected to have no practical effect as it is in line with generally accepted practice.

CHANGE 59: INTERPRETATION: DEFINITION OF "PERSONAL REPRESENTATIVES" FOR THE PURPOSES OF THE CORPORATION TAX ACTS: SECTION 1119

This change applies the defined term "personal representatives" for the purposes of the Corporation Tax Acts.

It brings the income tax and corporation tax codes back into line.

The application of the defined term to the Income Tax Acts is described in Change 150 in Annex 1 to the explanatory notes on ITA. This note draws substantially on the contents of that note.

With the exception of sections 229 and 701 of ICTA, wherever the term "personal representatives" is used in the Corporation Tax Acts, other than in CTA 2009 and Part 4 of FA 2004, the term is undefined. Places where it is so used include the following provisions on which this Act is based:

- Section 254(12) of ICTA (interpretation of Part 6 of ICTA) (see section 1117);

- section 417(3) of ICTA (meaning of "associate" for the purposes of Part 11 of that Act (close companies)) (see section 448);
- section 777(7) of ICTA (provisions supplementary to sections 775 and 776 of that Act (transactions in land)) (see section 825);
- section 784(2) of ICTA (leased assets subject to hire-purchase agreements) (see section 875 but note the rewrite does not use the term "personal representatives")
- paragraph 50(1) of Schedule 16 to FA 2002 (meaning of "associate" for the purposes of that Schedule) (see section 268).

Section 229(1) of ICTA (interpretative provisions for sections 219 to 228 of ICTA) defines "personal representatives" as "persons responsible for administering the estate of a deceased person". Section 701(4) of ICTA (rewritten in section 968 of CTA 2009) had a more detailed definition that had some similarities with the definition of "personal representatives" formerly in section 111(3) of FA 1989, which is the basis of the definition in section 989 of ITA (see Change 150 in Annex 1 to the explanatory notes on that Act). The definition in section 701(4) of ICTA provided that:

> ""Personal representatives" means, in relation to the estate of a deceased person, his personal representatives as defined in relation to England and Wales by section 55 of the Administration of Estates Act 1925 and persons having in relation to the deceased under the law of another country any functions corresponding to the functions for administration purposes under the law of England and Walesof personal representatives as so defined.

Section 55(1)(xi) of the Administration of Estates Act 1925 provides that:

> ""personal representative" means the executor, original or by representation, or administrator for the time being of a deceased person, and as regards any liability for the payment of death duties includes any person who takes possession of or intermeddles with the property of a deceased person without the authority of the personal representatives or the court, and "executor" includes a person deemed to be appointed executor as respects settled land.

The definition in section 55 of the Administration of Estates Act 1925 refers to executors as well as administrators. Under English law, executors are generally appointed by the will. Administrators are appointed by the court where no one is appointed as executor by the will or where the deceased dies without leaving a valid will.

English law recognises three other categories of executor. The first is executor according to the tenor, who on the terms of the will is appointed to perform the essential duties of an executor where the deceased person has failed to nominate a person to be his executor. The second is executor de son tort, who is a person who takes upon himself the position of executor or intermeddles with the goods of the deceased person without having been appointed executor or administrator. The third is special executor, the term given to a person who is a trustee of settled land at the time of the death.

The position is similar for Northern Ireland.

For the purposes of Scottish law, an executor is appointed either expressly or impliedly by the deceased, in which case he is known as an executor nominate, or by the court, in which case he is known as an executor dative. So the term "executor" under Scottish law is broadly equivalent to an "executor or administrator" under English law. Scottish law also recognises judicial factors and executor-creditors who may be appointed by the court to administer the deceased's estate or part of it. Although a judicial factor could not be described as an executor, such a factor might be regarded as an "administrator".

So, whether in relation to England and Wales or any other part of the United Kingdom, a deceased person's personal representatives within the meaning of section 701(4) of ICTA are the persons responsible for administering the person's estate.

Accordingly, the first limb of the definition in section 1119, that personal representatives are:

> "in the United Kingdom, persons responsible for administering the estate of the deceased,

catches the same persons in relation to each part of the United Kingdom as did section 701(4) of ICTA, but does so more directly and succinctly (and broadly matches the definition in section 229(1) of ICTA).

It follows from this that the application of the first limb of the definition in section 1119 in relation to the provisions in the Corporation Tax Acts which use the expression "personal representatives" without definition, including those rewritten in this Act, reflects the ordinary meaning of that term in each part of the United Kingdom.

The second limb of the definition in section 1119 is in similar terms to the equivalent part of section 701(4) of ICTA. It provides that personal representatives are:

> "in a territory outside the United Kingdom, those persons having functions under its law equivalent to those of administering the estate of the deceased

Section 701(4) of ICTA was rewritten in section 968 of CTA 2009, for the purposes of Chapter 3 of Part 10 of that Act (beneficiaries' income from estates in administration) in terms matching those in section 989 of ITA. The definition in section 1119 matches section 968 of CTA 2009 but applies for the purposes of the Corporation Tax Acts (whether in CTA 2009, this Act or elsewhere). As a result, section 968 of CTA 2009 is repealed by this Act.

That leaves the question of whether there is any change involved in applying the second limb to provisions in the Corporation Tax Acts which use the expressions "personal representatives" without definition, as those provisions apply to countries and territories outside the United Kingdom.

The terms "executor" and "administrator" are not terms of art in relation to countries and territories outside the United Kingdom. But it seems likely that a court would hold that references to "personal representatives" in tax legislation would, in the absence of a definition, cover the people that most closely resemble executors or administrators in the United Kingdom. In view of what is said above, that means the people who have functions corresponding to those of personal representatives in the United Kingdom, that is, functions equivalent to those of administering the estate of the deceased.

References to "personal representatives" without definition in the Corporation Tax Acts, including in those provisions on which this Act is based, can be read as references to anyone with responsibility for administering a deceased person's estate, including those with equivalent responsibilities in other jurisdictions. These provisions can be divided into two categories.

In the first category are provisions which confirm that, on an individual's death, rights and liabilities which are or would otherwise have been conferred on the individual are conferred on the individual's personal representatives.

In this context it is clear that the references to "personal representatives" are to whoever in fact has the role of administering the property of the deceased person. These provisions are intended to confirm that such persons have the same ability and responsibility to deal with the deceased individual's tax affairs as the individual would have had if the individual were still alive, and are subject to the same tax liabilities.

Provisions in this category rewritten in this Act include section 777(7) of ICTA. Such provisions which are not being rewritten include paragraph 62 of Schedule 18 to FA 1998 which provides that personal representatives may vary or revoke a claim, election, application or notice to the extent the deceased could do so if alive.

The second category covers those provisions which apply only because a person has died, so that his or her property is being administered by his or her personal representatives.

In this category of cases, the fact that someone has died creates a gap in the law (or at least a doubt as to what the law is) or requires some special arrangement to be made. The provisions in question fill the gap or satisfy the requirement. So it is consistent with the aim of these provisions for them to be interpreted as applying in all cases in which a person has died and his or her property is being administered by others.

Provisions in this category rewritten in this Act include:

- section 220(3) of ICTA which provides that the residence and ordinary domicile of personal representatives are the same as those of the deceased in relation to the conditions for disapplication of the company distribution rules to a purchase of the company's own shares; and
- the meaning of "associate" given by section 417(3) of ICTA and paragraph 50(1) of Schedule 16 to FA 2002, which provide that a person who has an interest in shares or obligations forming part of a deceased's estate is an associate of the personal representatives of the deceased.

Provisions in this category which are not being rewritten include section 76(5)(d) of ICTA, which provides that a deceased person's personal representatives count for the purposes of determining amounts relevant to the expenses of insurance companies as would have been the case had the deceased been alive.

As a consequence of the inclusion of this definition in section 1119, the definition to the same effect in section 968 of CTA 2009 is, as mentioned above, no longer necessary and is repealed by Schedule 3 to this Act. Section 229(1) of ICTA is also repealed.

This change has no implications for the amount of tax paid, who pays it or when. It affects (in principle but not in practice) only administrative matters.

CHANGE 60: CORPORATION TAX ACTS DEFINITIONS: MEANING OF "LOCAL AUTHORITY" IN RELATION TO NORTHERN IRELAND: CLAIMS: SECTION 1130 AND SCHEDULE 1

This change defines "local authority", in relation to Northern Ireland, explicitly in terms of relevant district councils rather than by reference to authorities with power to raise a rate.

Section 842A of ICTA defines "local authority" in the Corporation Tax Acts in relation to each of England and Wales, Scotland and Northern Ireland as "an authority of a description specified" in a list of institutions relevant to each of those parts of the United Kingdom.

In relation to Northern Ireland, section 842A(4) of ICTA specifies:

(a) an authority having power to make or determine a rate;

(b) an authority having power to issue a precept, requisition or other demand for the payment of money to be raised out of a rate.

Section 842A(5) of ICTA defines "rate" for the purposes of that section as "a rate the proceeds of which are applicable for public local purposes and which is leviable by reference to the value of land or other property".

The Office of the Legislative Counsel in Northern Irelandhas advised that this definition of "local authority" in relation to Northern Ireland is now inappropriate. Section 842A of ICTA refers to an authority with power to make or determine "a rate". But there are two different kinds of "rate" in Northern Ireland: adistrict rate which is set by district councils and a regional rate which is set by the Departmentof Finance and Personnel, which are levied as one rate by the Department of Financeand Personnel. Section 842A of ICTA could therefore be construed as defining as a "localauthority" an entity which is part of central government in Northern Ireland. This is not the intended effect of this provision and would produce a result out of step with the equivalent provisions for the meaning of "local authority" in England and Wales and Scotland.

In addition, the Office of the Legislative Counsel in Northern Ireland has advised that the wording ofsection 842A(4)(b) of ICTA is inapt for the local rating system in Northern Ireland as there is no analogue in that jurisdiction for the term "precept" and the term "requisition" is not used.

The definition in section 842A(4) of ICTA has therefore been rewritten so that it captures only district councils constituted under section 1 of the Local Government Act (Northern Ireland) 1972 and does not extend to theDepartment of Finance and Personnel.On this basis there is no need to replicate section 842A(4)(b) of ICTA as no other relevant authorities fall within that limb.

An amendment in Schedule 1 to the Act makes a corresponding change to section 999(3) of ITA.

This change affects the scope of provisions referring to local authorities in relation to Northern Ireland. It makes explicit the bodies to which the term refers but does not in practice change the scope of the definition. The change affects in principle the taxation of such bodies (for example, see section 984 (exemption for local authorities etc in the United Kingdom)) and of companies holding securities issued by such bodies (for example, see section 806 (meaning of "UK securities" in Part 17 (manufactured payments and repos))). While in principle it cuts down the potential scope of the definition, it has no such effect in practice.

This change is adverse to some taxpayers in principle. But it is expected to have no practical effect as it is in line with generally accepted practice.

CHANGE 61: NON–UK RESIDENT COMPANIES: TRANSACTIONS THROUGH BROKERS: SECTION 1145

This change removes a difference between:

- the wording of one of the conditions which determines whether or not, in relation to transactions carried out by a non–UK resident company (otherwise than as a trustee) through a broker in the United Kingdom, the broker is the permanent establishment of the non–UK resident company and
- the wording of the parallel condition which determines whether,in relation to transactions carried out by any other non–UK resident through such a broker, the broker is the UK representativeofthe non–UK resident.

Prior to the enactment of section 148 of, and Schedule 26 to, FA 2003, sections 126 and 127 of FA 1995 applied to determine who was the UK representative of a non–UK resident (including a non–UK resident company) in respect of income or chargeable gains arising through a branch or agency in the United Kingdom. Section 127 of FA 1995 provides that certain branches or agents are not UK representatives in relation to income or chargeable gains arising from a transaction carried out through them, including, in particular, brokers who meet certain conditions in relation to the transaction.

Following the enactment of section 148 of, and Schedule 26 to, FA 2003, the provisions of FA 1995 only apply in relation to non–UK residents who are not companies and to non–UK resident companies in the capacity of trustee. The FA 2003 provisions determine whether or not a person is the permanent establishment of a company in another territory and, in the case of a permanent establishment in the United Kingdom, provide for the permanent establishment to be the UK representative of the non–UK resident company in relation to income or chargeable gains arising through the permanent establishment.

Under Schedule 23 to FA 1995, a branch or agency which is a UK representative is responsible for assessment and payment of the income tax and capital gains tax chargeable on the income and chargeable gains of the non–UK resident arising through the branch or agency. Under section 150 of FA 2003, a permanent establishment in the United Kingdom is responsible for assessment and payment of corporation tax on income or chargeable gains attributable to the permanent establishment.

Section 148(3) of FA 2003 provides that a company is not regarded as having a permanent establishment in a territory by reason of its carrying on business there through an agent of independent status acting in the ordinary course of the agent's business. Schedule 26 to FA 2003 supplements that provision by, among other things, setting out the conditions under which transactions carried out through a broker in the United Kingdom are treated as carried out through an agent of independent status.

Paragraph 2 of Schedule 26 to FA 2003 provides for conditions that apply in determining whether a broker is a permanent establishment in respect of transactions carried out by a non-UK resident company through the broker in the United Kingdom. Under the FA 2003 legislation it was intended that these conditions would be the same as those that apply when determining, under section 127(2) of FA 1995, whether a broker is the UK representative of any other non-UK resident in relation to transactions carried out by that non-UK resident through the broker.

Section 127(2)(d) of FA 1995 contains the words "(apart from this paragraph)". But those words are not included in the parallel condition in paragraph 2(2)(d) of Schedule 26 to FA 2003. No change was intended and that provision is in practice operated in the same way as section 127(2)(d) of FA 1995.

The effect of the additional words in section 127(2)(d) of FA 1995 is that the question whether the broker is to be regarded as the UK representative of the non–UK resident in relation to the income (or other amounts) in question is to be determined without reference to the condition in that paragraph. They are considered necessary to avoid the impasse that would otherwise arise in operating the condition in accordance with the following analysis:

- A transaction falls within section 127(2)(d) of FA 1995 only if there is no income or other amount chargeable to tax for the same tax year in relation to which the broker is the non–UK resident's UK representative.
- If there is any other income or amounts deriving from another transaction carried out by the broker for the non–UK resident, section 127(1)(b) and (2) apply to determine whether the broker is the non–UK resident's UK representative in relation to it.
- For the broker not to be the non–UK resident's UK representative, the second transaction must fall within section 127(2).
- But absent the words "(apart from this paragraph)", in applying the condition in section 127(2)(d) to the second transaction, the question whether the condition is met depends on whether it is met in relation to the first transaction.

This change removes the potential for such an impasse in the provisions for determining whether a broker in the United Kingdom is the permanent establishment of a non–UK resident company in relation to transactions carried out by the non–UK resident company through the broker. It does so by adding words equivalent to "(apart from this paragraph)" in section 1145(6).

This change is in taxpayers' favour in principle. But it is expected to have no practical effect as it is in line with generally accepted practice.

CHANGE 62: MEANING OF PERMANENT ESTABLISHMENT: SUBSTITUTION OF REFERENCE TO INCOME FOR REFERENCE TO CHARGEABLE PROFITS IN PARAGRAPH 4(3) OF SCHEDULE 26 TO FA 2003: SECTION 1148

This change substitutes a reference to a non–UK resident company's income in section 1148(3) for the reference to its chargeable profits in paragraph 4(3) of Schedule 26 to FA 2003.

This change is identical to the change made in rewriting paragraph 4(3) of Schedule 26 to FA 2003 in section 821(3) of ITA in relation to the limit on liability to income tax of non–UK resident companies under section 815 of that Act. See Change 121 in Annex 1 to the explanatory notes on ITA.

Paragraph 3 of Schedule 26 to FA 2003 sets out conditions relating to investment transactions carried out by a non–UK resident company (other than a company in the capacity of a trustee) through an investment manager in the United Kingdom.If the conditions in paragraph 3(2) are met, the investment manager is not a permanent establishment of the non–UK resident company in relation to the investment transactions. The non–UK resident company's profit on those transactions are chargeable not to corporation tax but to income tax and then only to the extent provided by section 815 of ITA.

Paragraph 4 of Schedule 26 to FA 2003 sets out the requirements of "the 20% rule" referred to in paragraph 3(2)(d) of that Schedule. This rule relates to the percentage of "relevant excluded income" in which the investment manager and connected persons may have a beneficial interest. It is equivalent to section 127(5) of FA 1995 which prior to FA 2003 applied to all non–UK residents but which since the enactment of section 148 of, and Schedule 26 to, FA 2003 only applies where the non–UK resident is not a company (other than a company in the capacity of a trustee).

The basis on which the legislation in FA 2003 was prepared was that it was not to affect the law under FA 1995, except so far as required to adopt the concept of permanent establishment in place of branch or agency in relation to non–UK resident companies (other than companies in the capacity of trustees).

It is clear from the reference in the definition of "relevant excluded income" in section 127(5) of FA 1995 to "such of the profits and gains of the non–resident...as...for the purposes of Chapter 1 of Part 14 of the ITA(limits on liability to income tax of non–UK residents) would fall (apart from the requirements of section 819 of that Act) to be treated as disregarded income (see section 813 of that Act)" that the defined term in FA 1995 is limited to income and does not include gains. This is reflected in section 821(2) of ITA.

The reference to "the aggregate of such of the chargeable profits of the company" in paragraph 4(3) of Schedule 26 to FA 2003 is, therefore, in practice read as referring to income only.

Accordingly, section 1148(3) refers to "the total of the non–UK resident company's income for the accounting periods" which derives from the relevant investment transactions.

This change is in taxpayers' favour in principle. But it is expected to have no practical effect as it is in line with generally accepted practice.

CHANGE 63: INVESTMENT TRUSTS: DISPOSAL OF SHARES OR SECURITIES FROM A HOLDING: SECTION 1162

This change puts into legislation a well-known and established concession relating to the 15% holding limit condition.

Under section 842(1) of ICTA, the Commissioners of HMRC may approve a company as an investment trust only if it is shown to their satisfaction that the company meets certain conditions. One of these conditions is that no holding in a company (other than an investment trust or a company that would qualify as an investment trust if its shares were included in the official UK list) represents more than 15% of the investing company's investments ("the 15% holding limit condition").

Section 842(2), read with subsection (3)(b) of that section, provides for some exceptions. One of these is that if a holding in a company met the 15% holding limit condition when it was acquired or when it was last added to, it is treated as continuing to meet the condition until further shares or securities are acquired in that company.

In addition, where there is a disposal of shares or securities from a holding that exceeded the 15% holding limit and immediately after the disposal the holding represents 15% or less of the investing company's investments, HMRC treats the holding as continuing to represent 15% or less by value of the investing company's investments in later accounting periods until the holding is next enlarged.

This is set out in the HMRC Company Tax Manual as follows:

"If a company has a holding which, at 6 April 1965 or at the date of acquisition, exceeded the percentage limits, it may dispose of part of the holding to bring the reduced holding within the 15 per cent limit. So long as no addition is made to the holding, approval should not be withdrawn for any subsequent accounting period solely because the reduced holding has appreciated relative to the other investments so that it exceeds 15 per cent of the company's investments.

In section 1162(4) and (5) this concession is worded:

"(4) Subsection (5) applies if-

(a) a company disposes of shares or securities from a holding it has in a company,

(b) immediately before the disposal the holding represents more than 15% by value of the investing company's investments, and

(c) immediately after the disposal the holding represents 15% or less by value of the investing company's investments.

(5) For the purpose of determining whether the investing company meets condition E in accounting periods later than that in which the disposal was made, the holding is treated (if it does not already fall to be so treated under subsection (3)) as continuing to represent 15% or less by value of the investing company's investments until the holding is next enlarged.

This change is in taxpayers' favour in principle. But it is expected to have no practical effect as it is in line with current practice.

CHANGE 64: PROCEDURE FOR MAKING ORDERS AND REGULATIONS: SECTION 1171

This change concerns the procedure for making regulations in connection with the construction industry scheme in Chapter 3 of Part 3 of FA 2004. In accordance with section 73A of FA 2004 the Treasury may by order designate an international organisation to be exempt from the obligation, as a contractor, to deduct tax from payments to sub-contractors.

There are three main parliamentary procedures for making orders, depending on the degree of scrutiny thought appropriate.

- No scrutiny: Sometimes Parliament may decide that it does not need any control over the exercise of a power.
- Negative resolution procedure: The order can become law without adebate or vote inParliament. It can beopposed and may be rejected but not amended.
- Affirmative resolution procedure: The order is subject to affirmativeresolution. It cannotcome into effect until bothHouses have approved adraft statutory instrument in a vote.

Most tax regulations are made under the negative resolution procedure. That is the general rule in:

- section 828 of ICTA;
- section 570B of CAA;
- section 717 of ITEPA;
- section 873 of ITTOIA; and
- section 1014 of ITA.

But there are exceptions in each Act for regulations that are routinely administrative, for which no Parliamentary scrutiny is considered necessary.

The power to designate an international organisation for the purpose of the construction industry scheme was in section 582A(1) of ICTA (applied by subsection (6) of that section). That power was excepted from the negative resolution procedure in section 828(3) of ICTA by subsection (4) of that section. So the power fell within the "no scrutiny" procedure.

ITA rewrote most of the rules about international organisations in section 979 of ITA. But that section does not apply to the construction industry scheme. Instead, ITA inserted section 73A of FA 2004. That section is an exception to the general rule in section 1014(4) of ITA that orders or regulations are to be made under the negative resolution procedure (see subsection (5)(a) of that section). So the power iswithin the "no scrutiny" procedure.

The difficulty is that the ITA rules apply only to powers "under the Income Tax Acts". The deduction under section 61 of FA 2004 is "a sum equal to the relevant percentage of ... the payment". On the face of it, that sum is neither income tax nor corporation tax, although it may be treated as either by section 62(2) or (3)(c) of FA 2004.

It is possible that, to the extent that section 61 of FA 2004 is part of the Corporation Tax Acts, there is no exception to the general rule in section 828(3) of ICTA that a power such as that in section 73A of FA 2004 is to be exercised by an instrument subject to the negative resolution procedure.

This change excludes the order-making power under section 73A of FA 2004 from the negative resolution procedure required under subsection (4) of section 1171. The effect of the change is to restore the position to what it was before ITA and bring the income tax and corporation tax rules back into line.

This change has no implications for the amount of tax due, who pays it or when. It affects (in principle and in practice) only administrative matters.

CHANGE 65: CORPORATION TAX ACTS DEFINITIONS: AMENDMENT OF SECTION 991 OF ITA: SCHEDULE 1

This change corrects an error in section 991 of ITA and brings the definition of "bank" in the Income Tax Acts and Corporation Tax Acts into line.

Section 840A of ICTA defines "bank" for the purposes of any provision of the Corporation Tax Acts that applies this definition. Prior to the amendment of this section by paragraph 226 of Schedule 1 to ITA, the section applied for both the Income Tax Acts and the Corporation Tax Acts.

Among the categories of body which make up the defined term in section 840A of ICTA is "a relevant international organisation which is designated as a bank for the purposes of that provision by an order made by the Treasury". The "provision" referred to is the provision that applies the definition of "bank" in this section. An order made under this power may therefore affect some but not all of the provisions that apply the definition. While the only order made to date using this power (the European Investment Bank (Designated International Organisation) Order 1996 (SI 1996/1179), repealed by Schedule 3 to ITA) applied for the purposes of all such provisions, there may be circumstances in which it would be desirable to restrict the scope of the designation under such an order.

Section 991 of ITA expresses the power to designate an international organisation as a bank "for the purposes of this section", that is, for the purposes of section 991 of ITA, rather than for the purposes of the provisions that apply the definition. It therefore omits the option to designate an international organisation as a bank for the purposes of some but not all provisions.

Section 1120 rewrites section 840A of ICTA but includes that option in its expression of the power as it applies to the Corporation Tax Acts (see subsection (5)). Schedule 1 to the Act therefore amends section 991 of ITA to restore the option in the income tax definition and to keep the income tax and corporation tax codes in line.

This change has the potential to limit when an international organisation is treated as a bank for the purposes of some provisions of the Income Tax Acts. Whether that leads to an increase or decrease of tax (or whether there is any effect) depends on the affected provision and the circumstances of the affected taxpayer.

This change is in principle adverse to some taxpayers and favourable to others. But it is expected to have no practical effect as it is in line with generally accepted practice.

CHANGE 66: COMPANY DISTRIBUTIONS: DEMERGERS: SCHEDULE 2

This change disapplies paragraph 8(1) of Schedule 2 in respect of the repeal by this Act of regulations that amend the source legislation for section 1081(1). As a result, section 1081(1) applies to the whole of the first accounting period of a company to which this Act has effect.

Section 213 of ICTA provides that certain distributions made in the course of a demerger are excluded from references to "distribution" in the Corporation Tax Acts (see the definition of that term in section 832(1) of ICTA). The Corporation Tax (Implementation of the Mergers Directive) Regulations 2009 (SI 2009/2797) amended section 213(4) of ICTA, substituting the words "resident in a memberState" for the words "UK resident" in setting out a condition applying to companies relevant to the demerger. The regulations ensure that the United Kingdom is, in respect of distributions in a demerger, fully compliant with its obligations under Directive 90/434/EEC of the European Council on cross-border mergers etc of limited liability companies.The effect of the amendment is to increase the number of cases in which distributions in the course of a demerger are exempt distributions (and are therefore taken out of the charge to income tax or corporation tax on income). Section 1081(1) rewrites section 213(4) of ICTA as so amended, and accordingly provides that one condition for exemption under the provisions about exempt distributions is that "each relevant company must be resident in a member State at the time of the distribution".

The regulations came into force on 11 November 2009 and have effect in relation to distributions falling within section 213(3) of ICTA made on or after that date. The Act repeals the regulations in full. Paragraph 8(1) of Schedule 2 preserves the remaining force of a transitional or saving provision associated with a provision rewritten by the Act notwithstanding the repeal by the Act of that transitional or saving provision. Without the change made by this paragraph, the application of the amendment made by the regulations for distributions made on or after 11 November 2009 would continue to have effect for some companies in respect of the first accounting period to which this Act applies.

The Act comes into force on 1 April 2010 and has effect for corporation tax purposes for accounting periods ending on or after that day. It therefore applies to accounting periods beginning as early as 2 April 2009. Because of the change made by this paragraph, the law as restated in section 1081(1) applies to any distribution made in that first accounting period. There is therefore no question of having to apply different rules (that is, those in this Act and those as they existed in ICTA before the regulations had effect) to the same accounting period. This change ensures, having regard to the need for a statement of compatibility under section 19 of the Human Rights Act 1998, that the law to be enacted in the Act is also compliant with the United Kingdom's obligations under Directive 90/434/EEC of the European Council on cross-border mergers etc of limited liability companies.

The change may further increase the number of cases in which distributions in the course of a demerger are exempt distributions. That reduces the incidence of the charge to income tax or corporation tax on income for those who benefit from the change.

This change is in taxpayers' favour in principle and may benefit some in practice. But the numbers affected and the amounts involved are likely to be small.

ANNEX 2: EXTRA-STATUTORY CONCESSIONS, CASE LAW, AND LIST OF REDUNDANT MATERIAL NOT REWRITTEN

This Annex is in three parts:

- Table 1: a list of ESCs and Statements of Practice that are rewritten in this Act;
- Table 2: a list of Changes which involve enacting case law principles; and
- Table 3: a list of provisions that are redundant in whole or in part and are omitted by this Act.

TABLE 1

The following ESCs and Statement of Practice are rewritten in this Act.

ESC etc	*Description*	*See Annex 1*
ESC C4	Charitable companies: trading activities	Change 35
ESC C5	Industrial and provident societies: relaxation of section 393(8) of ICTA.	Change 7
ESC C9	(Paragraphs 2 to 4 only) Small profits relief: associated companies	Change 3
SP 5/94	Small profits relief: associated companies	Change 2

TABLE 2

The following table sets out a change in the law which involves giving statutory effect to principles derived, wholly or mainly, from case law.

Topic	*Change number*	*Section*
Agricultural societies – reference to livestock breeding changed to breeding any kind of animal	n/a	989

TABLE 3

The omission of provisions which are redundant in whole or in part is an integral part of the rewrite process.In some cases provisions have become redundant with the passage of time; in others they have become unnecessary as a result of the approach taken to the rewriting of related provisions.

For ease of reference, those omissions worthy of specific explanation are listed in the table below. The table also sets out where those explanations can be found.

Redundant provision	*Topic*	*See commentary on section etc*
ICTA s.234A(6)	Company distributions	1104 and Change 58
ICTA s.249(3)	Company distributions	1049
ICTA s.342(9)	Companies in liquidation	Schedule 1: section 342 of ICTA
ICTA s.343(11)	Transfers of trade without a change of ownership	Schedule 1: section 343 of ICTA
ICTA s.343(12)	Transfers of trade without a change of ownership	Schedule 1: section 343 of ICTA

Redundant provision	***Topic***	***See commentary on section etc***
ICTA s.393(9)	Excess charges	45
ICTA s.393A(2D)	Ring fence losses	37
ICTA s.393A(7) to (8)	Excess charges	37
ICTA s.403ZD(3)(b)	Non-commercial property losses	102
ICTA s.403D(2)(a)	Non-chargeable profits	108 and 140
ICTA s.403D(11)	EEA and other relief	107
ICTA s.492(5)	Oil taxation	306
ICTA s.505(1)(aa)(part)	Charitable companies	485
ICTA s.505(1)(e)(part)	Charitable companies	479
ICTA s.505(1AA)	Charitable companies	Schedule 1: section 505 of ICTA
ICTA s.511	Continuity of tax treatment	Schedule 1: section 511 of ICTA
ICTA s.513	Continuity of tax treatment	Schedule 1: section 513 of ICTA
ICTA s.573(4)	Share loss relief	71
ICTA s.575(1)(a)	Share loss relief: "for full consideration"	68
ICTA s.576(1D)(b)	Share loss relief	76
ICTA s.704 A(a) to (c)	Transactions in securities	735
ICTA s.768A(3)	Change in company ownership	Schedule 1: section 768A of ICTA
ICTA s.768B(7)	Change in company ownership	Schedule 1: section 768B of ICTA
ICTA s.768B(9)(b)	Change in company ownership	Schedule 1: section 768B of ICTA
ICTA s.776(13)(a) (part)	Definition of "land"	833
ICTA s.777(4)	Transactions in land	Schedule 3
ICTA s.832(1) (part)	Definition of "the Board", "collector", "farm land", "inspector", "market garden land" and "qualifying policy"	1119
ICTA s.832(2) (part)	Definition of "company"	1121
ICTA s.832(3) (part)	Construction of "tax"	1119
ICTA s.834(3) (part)	Interpretation: reference to Chapter 3 of Part 12 of ICTA	1168
ICTA Sch.20 para.9(2)	Meaning of "loan"	511
ICTA Sch.23A para.7(1) (part)	Manufactured payments and repos	796 and 797
ICTA Sch.23A para.7A(9)	Manufactured payments and repos	Schedule 1: Schedule 23A to ICTA

Redundant provision	***Topic***	***See commentary on section etc***
ICTA Sch.23A para.8(3)(a)	Manufactured payments and repos	801
ICTA Sch.28A para.5(3) (part)	Change in company ownership	691
ICTA Sch.28A para.6(b)	Change in company ownership	Schedule 1: section 768B of ICTA
ICTA Sch.28A para.7(1)(aa)	Change in company ownership	Schedule 1: section 768B of ICTA
ICTA Sch.28A para.11(4)	Change in company ownership	Schedule 1: Schedule 28A to ICTA
ICTA Sch.28A para.13(1)(c)	Change in company ownership	Schedule 1: section 768B of ICTA
ICTA Sch.28A para.16(1)(aa)	Change in company ownership	Schedule 1: section 768B of ICTA
FA 1989 s.102(3)(c)	Surrender of tax refund within group	Schedule 1: section 102 of FA 1989
FA 1989 s.102(4A) (part)	Surrender of tax refund within group	965
FA 1989 Sch.12 para.1(1)(b)	Close companies	Schedule 1: Schedule 12 to FA 1989
FA 1997 Sch.12 para.11(14)	Extended definition of Capital Allowances Act	919
FA 2000 Sch.15 para.46(2)(a)	Corporate venturing scheme: "for full consideration"	Schedule 1: paragraph 46(2) of Schedule 15 to FA 2000
FA 2002 Sch.16 para.4(2)	Community investment tax relief	219
FA 2002 Sch.16 para.29(4)(a)	Community investment tax relief: "for full consideration"	244
FA 2002 Sch.18 para.9(1)	Community amateur sports clubs	Overview of Chapter 9 of Part 13
FA 2002 Sch.18 para.3(4)(part)	Community amateur sports clubs	660
FA 2006 s.103(3)	Definition of REIT	523 and 524
FA 2006 s.121(2)(a),(b)	Distributions by UK REITs	548

GRANGIS - UK PUBLISHING 2022.

www.ingramcontent.com/pod-product-compliance
Lightning Source LLC
LaVergne TN
LVHW060210210926
848481LV00008B/2683
9798885590471